The Victoria History of the Counties of England

EDITED BY WILLIAM PAGE, F.S.A.

KU-361-614

A HISTORY OF
HAMPSHIRE
AND THE
ISLE OF WIGHT
INDEX

INDEX TO THE
VICTORIA HISTORY
OF
HAMPSHIRE
AND THE
ISLE OF WIGHT

PUBLISHED FOR
THE UNIVERSITY OF LONDON
INSTITUTE OF HISTORICAL RESEARCH
REPRINTED FROM THE ORIGINAL EDITION OF 1914
BY
DAWSONS OF PALL MALL
FOLKESTONE & LONDON
1973

Issued by
Archibald Constable and Company Limited
in 1914

Reprinted for the University of London
Institute of Historical Research
by
Dawsons of Pall Mall
Cannon House
Folkestone, Kent, England
1973

ISBN: 0 7129 0596 0

HAMPSHIRE COUNTY LIBRARY

R 942.27

C000126803

7579345

0712905960 LH

Originally printed in Great Britain by
W. H. Smith & Son, London
Reprinted in Belgium by Jos Adam, Brussels

CONTENTS OF INDEX VOLUME

THE VICTORIA HISTORY OF THE COUNTIES OF ENGLAND

The publication of the volumes which form the History of Hampshire and the Isle of Wight is due to the financial support afforded by the Right Hon. the Viscount Hambleden, the Right Hon. the Viscount Alverstone, G.C.M.G., the Right Hon. the Lord Ashcombe, Mr. O. E. D'Avigdor Goldsmid, D.L., Mr. Somerset A. Beaumont, D.L., and the late Mr. Frank McClean, F.R.A.S., of whose public spirit and generosity it is here desired to make special recognition.

INDEX

TO THE

DOMESDAY OF HAMPSHIRE

AND

SURVEY OF WINCHESTER

PERSONAL NAMES[1]

Adelina the jester, i, 454*a*, 457*b*
Æilmer, i, 464*a*
Ælfec, i, 464*a*
Ælfer, i, 463*b*
Ælfeth, i, 460*a*
Ælfric the Englishman. *See* Alvric
Ælfstan a beadle, i, 535
Ælfwig, abbot of Winchester New Minster, i, 417
Ælfwine a beadle, i, 535
Ælfwine a moneyer, i, 536
Ælmer, i, 521*b*
Ælnod', i, 461*a*, 521*b*
Ælwacre, i, 491*a*
Ælwi, i, 505*a*
Æthelsige, abbot of Ramsey, i, 435
Æthewold a reeve, i, 535
Agemund or Aghemund, i, 428, 466*a*, 480*a*, 496*b*, 506*a*, 506*b*, 508*a*, 513*b*, 515*a*
Ailardessone a moneyer, i, 536
Airaf, i, 469*b*
Aisil a beadle, i, 536
Aiulf the chamberlain, i, 425, 516*b*. *See also* Humfrey
Alan [of Britanny], Count, i, 476*a*
Albert of Lotharingia. *See* Lotharingia
Albold' the cook, i, 451*a*
Albus. *See* White
Aldrectus. *See* Eldred, Odo's brother
Aldret, i, 480*a*
Aldwin, i, 485*a*
Alestan 'de Boscumbe.' *See* Boscumbe
Alfred, i, 399, 400
Algar, i, 485*b*, 494*b*, 512*b*, 516*b*, 521*b*

Alisius, William, i, 498*a*
Almar, i, 458*a*. *See also* Elmar, Elmer
Almer, i, 509*a*
Alnod, i, 459*a*, 465*a*, 481*b*, 488*a*, 495*b*, 500*a*, 511*b*, 523*a*. *See also* Elnod
Alnod Cild, i, 486*a*
Alnod the priest, i, 476*a*
Alric, i, 455*b*, 457*a*, 461*a*, 482*b*, 505*a*, 506*a*, 508*a*, 525*a*
Alsi, i, 417, 429, 470*a*, 471*a*, 487*a*, 502*b*, 518*b*, 525*a*. *See also* Berchenistre
Alsi, abbot. *See* Ramsey, abbot of
Alsi son of Brixi, i, 443, 469*b*, 505*a*, 506*a*, 524*b*
Alsi the priest, i, 476*a*, 485*a*
Altei, i, 479*b*
Alviet, i, 486*a*
Alvred, i, 479*b*, 511*a*
Alvred the priest, i, 430, 502*a*
Alvric, i, 477*b*, 479*b*, 483*b*, 492*b*, 493*a*, 497*a*, 498*a*, 500*b*, 503*b*, 505*a*, 512*a*, 513*a*, 513*b*, 514*b*, 515*a*, 516*a*, 522*b*, 524*a*, 524*b*, 525*b*, 526*a*
Alvric Petit (parvus), i, 509*b*, 514*b*
Alvric the physician, i, 514*a*
Alvric the priest, i, 465*a*, 465*b*
Alward, i, 471*a*, 478*a*, 482*b*, 492*b*, 495*a*, 498*a*, 504*a*
Alwi, i, 489*a*, 495*b*, 499*a*, 506*b*, 509*a*
Alwi son of Saulf, i, 506*a*
Alwi son of Turber or Torber, i, 505*b*, 507*a*
Alwin, i, 460*a*, 465*b*, 472*b*, 479*a*, 481*a*, 482*a*, 485*b*, 487*b*, 499*b*, 501*a*, 501*b*, 506*b*, 509*b*. *See also* Elwin

Alwin Ret (Aluret ?), i, 437, 505*b*
'Alwinus,' i, 439*a*, 439*b*
Alwold, i, 457*a*, 513*a*, 516*a*
Andeli, Richer de, i, 516*b*. *See also* Richer
Andrac, i, 500*a*
Andrebod a moneyer, i, 534, 536
Angot, i, 476*b*. *See also* Ansgot
Anschil the priest, i, 516*b*
Anschitil, i, 479*b*, 482*b*, 522*b*
Anschitil son of Osmund, i, 503*a*, 516*b*
Ansfrid, i, 499*a*
Ansgot, i, 463*b*. *See also* Angot
Anslevile, William de, i, 477*b*
Arundel, Roger, i, 418
Aubigny, William d', i, 535
Aubrey the chamberlain, i, 425, 503*b*, 534
Audoenus 'Naparius,' i, 536
Auti, i, 486*a*, 505*a*
Azor, i, 482*b*, 484*b*, 523*a*, 523*b*

Basset, Ralph, i, 527, 529
Bayeux, Odo, bishop of, i, 422, 423, 486*a*, 510*a*, 526*b*
Belet, William, i, 438, 499*a*
Berchenistre, Alsi, i, 506*b*, 509*a*
Bernard, i, 512*b*
Bernard the chamberlain, i, 425, 429, 514*a*
Bernard chancellor of the queen, i, 528
Bertram, William, i, 491*b*, 534
Beteslau, Ulveva, i, 429, 472*a*
Bienfaite, Richard de. *See* Tonebrige
Blacheman, i, 502*a*, 523*a*, 523*b*
Bloiet, Ralf, i, 405, 492*a*
Blois, Henry, bishop of, i, 527

[1] Including those of Religious Houses holding lands.

Boda, i, 484*a*, 486*a*, 497*a*
Bolla or Bolle, i, 459*a*, 488*a*, 513*b*, 514*a*, 515*a*, 519*b*, 520*b*, 521*a*, 526*a*
Bolne, i, 507*a*
Borghill, i, 471*a*
Boscumbe, Alestan de, i, 410, 455*a*, 492*a*
Boulogne, count of. *See* Eustace
Boulogne, countess of, 429
Braiose, William de, i, 492*a*
Bretevile, Gislebert de, i, 473*a*, 495*a*, 516*b*
Bricsmar, i, 486*b*, 503*a*
Brichtwine a beadle, i, 536
Brictric, i, 457*a*, 460*a*, 494*a*, 499*b*
Brictuin, i, 520*b*
Brithmar the goldsmith, i, 537
Brixi, i, 514*b*. *See also* Alsi
Bruning, i, 519*b*, 525*b*
Bundi or Bondi, i, 496*a*, 496*b*, 500*b*, 501*b*, 525*b*

Carisbrooke Castle, chapel of St. Nicholas in, i, 519*a*
Carisbrooke Priory, i, 407, 409
Carle, i, 421, 493*b*
Cava the reeve, i, 468*b*
Cepe, Ulvric, i, 459*b*
Cerisy, abbey of, i, 423
Chening, i, 495*a*
Chenna, i, 510*a*
Cheping, i, 421, 428, 434, 454*a*, 459*a*, 463*b*, 489*a*, 489*b*, 490*a*, 490*b*, 491*a*, 504*b*, 510*b*, 514*a*, 516*b*, 518*a*, 534
Chernet, Hugh de, i, *note* 479*a*
Chernet, William de, i, 440, 441, 478*b*, 479*a*, 485*b*
Chertsey, the abbey of, i, 416, 422, 472*b*
Chester, Hugh, earl of, i, 478*b*
Chetel, i, 477*b*, 478*b*, 492*a*, 513*a*, 516*a*, 516*b*, 518*a*, 519*a*, 519*b*, 520*b*
Chipping an Englishman, i, 533, 534
Cild, Alnod, i, 486*a*
Clare, Richard de. *See* Tonebrige
Codolf, i, 488*b*
Cola, Cole, i, 410, 505*b*
Cola the huntsman, i, 425, 507*a*, 509*b*
Cole of Basinge, i, 505*b*
Coleman, i, 492*a*
Colgrin, i, 511*a*
Coolf, i, 512*b*, 517*a*
Cormeilles, the abbey of, i, 406, 407, 419, 501*a*; abbot of, i, 400, 516*b*
Cormeilles (Cormelies), Gozelin de, i, 420, 501*a*
Coutances, Geoffrey, bishop of, i, 427, 516*b*

Craon, Guy de, i, 438, 496*a*
Crispin, Milo, i, 508*b*
Croc, Rainold, i, 516*b*. *See also* Rainold
Croc, Croch the huntsman, i, 427, 430, 501*a*
Curci, Courcy, Richard de, i, 533

Dapifer. *See* Eudo
Denewulf, bishop. *See* Winchester, bishop of
Doda, i, 455*b*
Donnus, i, 518*b*
Douenold, i, 523*b*
Durand, i, 459*b*, 463*a*, 492*b*, 511*a*, 512*a*, *note* 511*b*
Durand the barber, i, 430, 502*a*

Eadgyth, Queen. *See* Eddid
Eadwine, an English thegn, i, 429
Ealdred, archbishop, i, 420
Eddeva, i, 458*b*, 507*b*
Eddid, Queen, i, 413, 420, 424, 435, 450*b*, 451*a*, 453*b*, 459*a*, 470*b*, 471*b*, 473*a*, 473*b*, 479*b*, 504*b*, 506*b*, 532
Eddulf, i, 506*b*
Edith, Queen. *See* Eddid
Edmund, i, 506*a*, 509*b*, 516*b*
Edmund son of Payn, i, 429, 509*b*
Ednod, i, 464*b*, 497*a*, 505*b*, 515*a*, 523*a*, 523*b*
Edric, i, 421, 434, 455*b*, 463*b*, 472*a*, 472*b*, 484*a*, 487*b*, 491*a*, 493*b*, 498*b*, 512*a*, 514*a*, 524*a*, 524*b*
Edward, i, 459*b*, 478*b*, 491*b*, 494*b*, 495*b*, 502*b*
Edward, King, i, 402, 404, 414, 425, 436, 462*a*, 466*b*, 470*b*, 521*a*, 525*b*
Edward the sheriff (of Wiltshire). *See* Sarisberie
Edwi, i, 505*b*, 511*a*, 525*a*
Edwin, i, 479*b*, 504*b*
Edwin the huntsman, i, 425, 508*b*
Edwin the priest, i, 505*a*
Elded (wife of Oswold), i, 460*a*
Eldred, i, 460*b*, 476*b*
Eldred or Ældred, Odo's brother, i, 427, 437, 470*a*, 499*b*, 509*a*, 537
Elfelm, i, 509*a*
Elmar, i, 486*a*, 509*b*
Elmer, i, 476*b*, 522*a*
Elnod, i, 513*b*, 526*a*
Elric, i, 459*b*
Elric, the sons of, i, 516*b*
Elsi, i, 473*a*, 495*b*
Elsi, abbot. *See* Ramsey, abbot of
Elveva, i, 502*a*
Elwin, i, 490*b*
Ely, the abbey of, i, 462*a*

Emma [mother of Edward the Confessor], Queen, i, 532
Emma [widow of Cnut], Queen, i, 416, 435, 473*a*
Erlenc, i, 482*b*
Ernulf, i, 504*b*
Estan, i, 508*b*, 521*a*
Esturmi. *See* Sturmi
Eu, Ow, William de, 405, 410, 491*b*, 499*b*, 512*b*
Eudes. *See* Eudo, Odo
Eudo [Dapifer] son of Hubert [de Ryes], i, 443, 491*a*
Eustace [of Boulogne], Count, i, 477*a*
Evreux, the count of, i, 516*b*
Exeter, Osbern, bishop of, i, 469*a*
Ezi, i, 414, 481*b*, 489*b*, 503*a*
Ezi the sheriff, i, 439, 472*a*, 497*b*

Fadrelin or Faderlin, i, 438, 481*b*, 487*a*, 499*a*, 534
Fécamp, William de, i, 464*b*
Fiscanno. *See* Fécamp
Fitz Osbern. *See* William
Flambard, Flammard, Flamme or Flanbart, Rannulf, i, 415, 426, 502*a*, 512*b*, 533 *note*
Forist, William, i, 522*b*
Forst, Alwin, i, 519*a*
Fulchered, i, 471*a*
Fulchi, i, 504*a*
Fulcoin or Fulcuin, i, 511*a*, 511*b*
Fulcold, i, 492*b*
Fulghel, i, 516*b*

Geford a reeve, i, 535
Geoffrey, i, 460*a*, 461*a*, 461*b*, 462*a*, 465*a*, 484*b*, 486*a*, 493*b*, 523*a*, 523*b*, 524*a*
Geoffrey, bishop. *See* Coutances, bishop of
Geoffrey the chamberlain, i, 425, 427, 430, 456*a*, 502*b*
Gerin, i, 516*b*, 525*b*
German, i, 442, 465*b*, 480*b*
Gervase, brother to Hugh of the Isle, i, 426
Gherui, i, 455*b*
Gifard, Osbern, i, 516*b*
Gifard, Walter, i, 506*a*
Gilbert, i, 461*a*
Gilbert 'Taleator,' i, 536
Giraud', i, 464*a*
Gisulf the king's scribe, i, 536
Glastonbury, the abbey of, i, 416, 473*a*; abbot of, i, 424, 473*a*
Gloucester, the abbey of, i, 416, 472*a*
Glowecestre, Durand de, i, 425, 443, 493*b*, 516*b*. *See also* Milo and Walter
Godesa, i, 525*a*
Godeswale, Edwin, i, 528
Godfrey a reeve, i, 535
Godfrey 'Taleator,' i, 536

Goding, i, 483*a*

Godman, i, 458*a*, 498*a*

Godric, i, 476*b*, 484*a*, 497*a*, 500*b*, 505*a*, 508*a*, 512*a*, 513*b*, 515*a*, 519*b*, 520*a*, 520*b*, 522*b*, 524*b*, 525*a*, 525*b*

Godric the priest, i, 524*b*

Godwin, i, 421, 447, 457*a*, 458*b*, 459*b*, 462*a*, 462*b*, 464*a*, 480*b*, 481*b*, 482*b*, 485*b*, 494*a*, 494*b*, 500*a*, 503*a*, 504*b*, 510*a*, 511*a*, 516*b*

Godwin 'chen,' i, 536 *note*

Godwin the priest, i, 469*a*, 486*b*

Godwine, earl, i, 410, 451*b*, 452*a*, 458*b*, 476*b*, 477*a*, 478*a*, 478*b*, 483*a*, 488*a*, 488*b*, 502*a*, 504*a*, 521*a*, 526*b*

Godwine the falconer, i, 509*a*

Godwine a reeve, i, 535

Godwine 'Socche,' 'Ceoca,' i, 536

Golleve, i, 507*b*

Gozelin, i, 408, 426, 444, 481*a*, 496*b*

Gozelin son of Azor, i, 517*b*, 523*a*

Grentemaisnil, Hugh de, i, 516*b*

Grestain, the abbey of, i, 473*b*

Grimbald the physician, i, 536

Gueda, Countess, i, 452*b*, 458*b*

Guert, i, 492*b*

Gytha. *See* Gueda

Hacon, i, 452*b*

Hadewsa, wife to Hugh the sheriff, i, 424

Harold, Earl, i, 403, 414, 427, 450*a*, 451*b*, 452*a*, 453*a*, 456*a*, 458*a*, 458*b*, 477*a*, 477*b*, 478*b*, 483*a*, 488*b*, 490*b*, 491*a*

Heldered or Heldred, i, 480*b*, 482*b*, 488*a*

Henry I, i, 529

Henry son of Ruald, i, 534

Henry the treasurer, i, 426, 430, 500*a*

Herbert, i, 484*b*, 497*b*, 498*a*

Herbert the chamberlain, i, 422, 425, 430, 431, 470*a*, 483*a*, 499*b*, 527, 529, 534; daughter of, 431

Herbert the forester, i, 455*a*

Herbert son of Remi, i, 499*b*

Herbrand, i, 500*b*, 524*b*

Hercus, i, 462*a*

Herding, i, 470*b*

Hereford, Walter, bishop of, i, 419, 469*a*

Hereford, Miles 'de Gloucester,' earl of, i, 425

Hereford, Roger earl of, i, 407, 410, 413, 453*b*, 454*a*, 517*b*

Hereford, William Fitz Osbern, earl of, i, 406, 407, 408, 409, 410, 420, 425, 454*a*, 462*b*, 478*a*, 505*a*, 505*b*, 520*a*

Herlebald, i, 480*b*

Herould or Herold, i, 457*a*

Herpul, i, 518*b*

Hesdin, Hesdinc, or Hesding, Arnulf, Ernulf' de, i, 421, 472*a*, 487*b*

Holengar, i, 512*a*

Hugh, i, 429, 460*b*, 486*b*, 487*a*, 488*b*, 493*b*, 495*b*, 499*a*, 509*b*

Hugh 'cementarius,' i, 464*a*

Hugh, earl of Chester. *See* Chester

Hugh 'of the Isle,' i, 426

Hugh the sheriff, i, 424, 491*a*

Hugh son of Baldri, Baldric, i, 419, 438, 444, 496*a*

Hugh son of Osmund, i, 502*b*, 513*a*

Hugh with the beard (Barbatus), i, 502*b*

Humfrey, i, 517*b*, 520*a*, 520*b*, 521*a*, 525*a*

Humfrey (Aiulf's brother), i, 516*b*

Humfrey the chamberlain, i, 425, 430, 500*b*

Hunger, i, 431, 474*b*, 504*b*

Hunta, i, 514*b*

Hyde Abbey. *See* Winchester

Ilgeramnus, i, 491*a*

Imma. *See* Emma.

Ingulf, Ingulphus, i, 400, 488*a*

Innocent, Pope, i, 435

Jumièges, the abbey of, i, 419, 435, 444, 473*a*

Juran, i, 519*b*

Justan, i, 465*b*

Justin, i, 512*b*

Ketel, i, 471*b*

Lanch, i, 451*a*

Lang, i, 456*b*

'Lardarius,' 'Lardinarius,' i, 536

Latinarius, Hugh, i, 510*a*

Lefsi, i, 465*b*, 483*a*

Leman, i, 451*b*, 452*a*

Leoflæd Ecregeles, i, 536 *note*

Leuing or Leving, i, 466*b*, 511*b*, 516*a*, 522*b*

Leuuin' the forester, i, 450*b*

Leving. *See* Leuing

Lewin, i, 462*b*, 465*a*, 465*b*, 476*b*, 504*a*, 508*b*

Limesey, Ralf, Radulphus de, i, 406, 410, 455*a*

Lincoln, William de Roumare, earl of, 425

Linxi, i, 501*a*

Liof, i, 524*a*

Lire or Lyre, la vieille Lyre, Eure, St. Mary of L'ore, the abbey of, i, 406, 407, 409, 410, 419, 420, 421, 454*a*, 517*b*, 519*a*

Lire or Lyre, the abbot of, i, 409, 516*b*; monks of, i, 517*b*

Livol, i, 523*b*

Lotharingia, Albert of, i, 424

Luuing, a beadle, i, 536

Maci, Hugh, i, 478*b*

Mainard, i, 497*a*

Mal. *See* Malf

Maldoit, Mauduit, Robert, i, 533, 534

Maldoit, Malduit, Malduith, William, i, 424, 429, 432, 435, 436, 488*a*, 492*a*, 533

Malf or Mal, Godric, the sons of, i, 508*a*, 515*b*, *note* 441

Malger. *See* Mauger

Manno, i, 463*b*, 497*a*

Marescal, Geoffrey, i, 430, 431, 500*b*, 501*b*

Marlborough. *See* Merleberge

Marmoutier, abbey of, 426

Mathild, Matilda [wife of William I], Queen, i, 427, 437, 451*a*, 499*b*

Mauduit. *See* Maldoit

Mauger or Malger, i, 461*b*, 464*b*, 518*b*

Merleberge, Alvred de, i, 421, 493*b*

Meruen, i, 483*a*

Miles, Milo the porter, i, 431, 503*a*

Milo the constable, Miles 'de Gloucester,' i, 425

Milton, the abbey of, i, 416, 473*b*

Montgomery. *See* Shrewsbury, Roger, earl of

Mont St. Michel, the abbey of, i, 419, 444, 469*a*

Mortain, Robert, Count of, i, 408, 416, 435, 457*a*, 476*b*, 516*b*

Mortemer, Ralf de, i, 416, 420, 421, 428, 434, 435, 464*a*, 466*a*, 484*a*, 489*a*, 512*b*, 516*b*, 534

Nigel, i, 511*a*, 511*b*, 512*a*, 520*b*, 521*b*, 522*b*, 523*b*

Nigel the physician, i, 421, 430, 501*b*, 516*b*

Norman, i, 480*b*, 499*b*, 503*a*

Ocsen, i, 497*b*

Oda or Odo, i, 457*a*, 457*b*, 482*a*, 499*a*. *See also* Wincestre

Odeman, i, 458*a*

Odo, Bishop. *See* Bayeux

Odo the steward, i, 470*a*

Oidelard, i, 490*a*, 490*b*, 512*b*

Oirant, i, 524*b*
Oismelin, i, 492*a*
Olward, i, 481*a*. *See also* Ulward
Ordwold, i, 416, 432, 494*b*
Orenet, William, i, 509*b*
Osbern, i, 459*b*, 463*b*, 464*a*
Osbern, bishop. *See* Exeter, bishop of
Osbern the falconer, i, 503*b*
Osbert son of Thiard, i, 533
Osgot, i, 522*a*, 523*a*
Osmund, i, 477*b*, 505*b*
Osulf, i, 487*a*
Ow, William de. *See* Eu

Pagen, i, 513*b*, 514*b*
Pancevolt or Pancevold, Bernard, i, 421, 423, 494*a*, 513*b*, 516*b*
Papald', i, 495*a*
Perci, Alan de, i, 438
Perci, Percy William de, i, 438, 487*b*
Peret, i, 514*b*
Pevrel, i, 521*b*, 522*a*
Pevrel, William, i, 463*a*
Phitelet, i, 479*a*
Picot, i, 440, 445, 455*b*, 479*a*, 507*b*
Pîtres, Pisteo, Roger de, i, 425, 497*b*
Poitou, Roger of, i, 457*a*
Pont de l'Arche, William de, i, 527, 529, 535
Port, Adelis de, i, 534
Port, Emma de, i, 438, 534
Port, Henry de, i, 423, 425, 534
Port, Porth, Hubert de, i, 424, 487*a*
Port, Porth, Hugh de, i, 405, 408, 414, 418, 419, 421, 422, 423, 424, 427, 428, 429, 434, 436, 437, 438, 439*a*, 439*b*, 441, 444, 445, 454*a*, 454*b*, 463*a*, 466*a*, 468*b*, 469*b*, 470*a*, 471*a*, 471*b*, 472*b*, 478*b*–487*b*, 495*b*, 497*b*, 499*b*, 509*b*, 512*b*, 516*b*, 534, *note* 485*a*
Port, John de, i, 438, 534
Port, Orence de, i, 424
Pugnant or Puingiant, Richard, i, 495*a*, 516*b*

Radfred the priest, i, 451*a*
Rainald, i, 463*a*, 493*b*, 520*b*
Rainald the baker, i, 520*a*
Rainold son of Croc or Croch, i, 426, 501*a*, 517*b*. *See also* Croc
Ralf, i, 462*a*, 484*b*, 485*a*, 485*b*, 493*b*, 495*a*, 496*b*, 497*a*
Ralf the priest, i, 461*a*
Ralf the son of Seifrid, i, 443, 464*b*, 466*a*
Ramsey, Æthelsige, Elsi the abbot of, i, 435, 473*a*, *note* 467*a*

Rannulf, i, 463*a*, 488*a*
Ravelin, i, 508*b*
Ricardus Arch'uns, 430
Richard, i, 429, 504*b*, 522*a*
Richard a reeve, i, 535
Richard 'Tailator,' i, 536
Richer, i, 462*a*, 462*b*, 465*a*. *See also* Andeli
Richer the clerk, i, 420, 421, 467*a*
Ricoardus, i, 492*a*
Ridel, Geoffrey, i, 527, 529
Rivers (Redvers, Redivers), Baldwin de, i, 407, 535
Rivers (Redvers, Redivers), Richard de, i, 407
Robert, i, 459*b*, 461*a*, 485*b*, 489*a*, 496*b*, 512*b*, 518*b*, 519*b*
Robert the clerk, i, 461*a*
Robert, dapifer of Hugh de Port, 418, 427
Robert son of Gerold, i, 424, 488*a*, 489*a*
Robert son of Hamon, i, 535
Robert son of Murdac, i, 503*b*
Robert 'Taleator,' i, 536
Roger, i, 437, 497*a*, 522*a*, 523*a*
Roger brother to Hugh 'of the Isle,' i, 426
Roger son of Gerold, i, 425, 444, 534
Roger, Earl. *See* Hereford, and Shrewsbury, earls of
Romsey, the abbey of, i, 416, 474*b*; abbess of, i, 474*b*
Roumare, Gerold de, i, 425
Roumare, William de, Earl of Lincoln, i, 425
Ruald, i, 471*a*
Ruald son of Faderlin, i, 534

St. Denis, abbey of, i, 408
St. Ethelreda, monks of, i, 416
St. John, Robert de, i, 438
St. John, Thomas de, i, 535
St. Ouen, monks from, i, 420
St. Peter and St. Swithin, the church of. *See* Winchester
St. Quintin, Herbert de, i, 535
St. Quintin, Hugh de, i, 422, 485*a*, 510*a*, 512*b*, 514*a*, 514*b*, 535
St. Victor-en-Caux, the church of, i, 489*b*
Saintes, the bishop of, i, 509*b*
Salide, i, 511*a*
Salisbury, bishop of, 424
Saolt, i, 516*a*
Sarisberie [Salisbury], Edward de, i, 473*b*, 487*b*, 512*b*
Sariz, i, 506*b*
Saul, i, 514*b*
Saulf or Saolf, i, 476*b*, 481*b*, 509*b*, 511*b*, 513*b*, 514*b*
Saulf's wife, i, 513*b*

Sauord, i, 458*a*
Sawin, i, 458*a*, 465*a*, 466*b*, 507*b*, 509*b*, 513*b*, 514*b*, 523*b*
Saxi, i, 453*b*, 501*a*, 501*b*
Sberne, i, 504*b*
Sceva, i, 506*a*
Seward the huntsman, i, 426, 470*a*
Sexi, i, 498*b*, *note* 495*b*
Sheriffs. *See* Edward, Ezi, Hugh
Shrewsbury, Roger [de Montgomery], Earl of, i, 405, 410, 420, 477*a*, 500*a*, 510*b*, 526*b*, *notes* 418, 485*a*
Simon son of Hugh the sheriff, i, 424
Sired, i, 478*a*, 483*a*
Siric the chamberlain, i, 429, 505*b*
Siward, i, 505*a*, 510*a*
Soartin, i, 521*b*, 525*a*
Spirites, Spirtes, i, 421, 501*b*
Stenesnoc, i, 483*b*
Stephen, King, i, *note* 477*a*
Sterre, i, 483*b*
Stigand, Archbishop [of Canterbury], i, 413, 416, 420, 452*a*, 462*a*, 462*b*, 467*a*, 474*a*
Stilla, Alwin, i, 460*b*
Stirman, Stephen, i, 516*b*
Sturmi, Geoffrey, i, 432
Sturmi, Sturmid, Richard, i, 416, 432, 464*a*, 494*b*
Suarting, i, 511*a*
Suein, i, 502*b*

Tedgar, i, 451*a*
Tetbald', i, 451*a*
Tezelin, i, 483*a*
Theobald, Archbishop, i, 435
Thierri, the king's cook, i, 536
Thol, i, 491*b*. *See also* Tol
Thomas, Archbishop [of York], i, 420, 468*b*
Ticheb[orne], Walter de, i 536
Todeni, Ralf de, i, 516*b*
Tofig an Englishman, i, 410
Tol the Dane, i, 491*b*. *See also* Thol
Tonebrige (*alias* de Clare), Richard de, i, 451*a*
Tosti, i, 491*b*
Tostig, Earl, i, 427, 454*b*, 458*a*, 496*b*, 510*a*, 517*a*, 524*b*, *note* 408
Tostill, i, 516*b*
Toui or Tovi, i, 462*b*, 483*b*, 487*a*, 488*a*, 488*b*, 489*a*, 501*a*, 520*b*, 521*a*, 525*b*
Travers, i, 520*a*
Troarn, the abbey of, i, 420, 478*a*
Tunbi, i, 478*a*
Tunbridge. *See* Tonebrige
Turald, i, 477*b*, 524*a*
Turbert the huntsman, i, 426, 513*b*
Turchil, i, 520*a*
Turgis, i, 524*a*

Turi, i, 502a

Turstin, i, 460a, 465b

Turstin the chamberlain, i, 425, 480b, 494b, 516b

Turstin the engineer, i, 516b

Turstin 'parvus,' i, 464a

Turstin Rufus, i, 464a

Turstin son of Rolf, (Fitz Rou), i, 423, 494a

Twynham [Christchurch], the canons of, i, 416, 426, 476a

Ulflet, i, 458a

Ulgar, i, 515b

Ulmar, i, 455b

Ulnod, i, 458a, 458b, 481a, 500b, 522a, 523b, 524b, 525b, 526a

Ulsi, i, 525b

Ulstan, i, 488b, 497b

'Ulstanus Episcopus,' i, 443

Ultain', i, 461a

Ulveva (Wulfgifu), i, 429, 479a, 493a, 505b, 506b, 514a

Ulveve, i, 451a, 456a

Ulviet, i, 507a, 509b, 513b, 520a

Ulviet (Wulfgeast) the huntsman, i, 425, 507b, 517b, 518a

Ulvret, i, 502a

Ulvric, i, 480b, 481a, 506a, 507b, 515a, 518b

Ulvric (Wulfric) the huntsman, i, 426, 509a

Ulward, i, 450b, 465b, 476b, 481a, 492b, 512a, 525a. See also Olward

Ulwi, i, 511b

Ulwin, i, 499b

Unlof, i, 521b

Vaux, Oliver de, i, note 438

Vaux, Petronilla de, i, 438

Venoix, Geoffrey de. See Marescal

Venoix (Wenoye), John de (John le Venor), i, 430

Venoix (Venouz, Venuiz, Venuz), Robert de, i, 430, 431

Visdelupo, Humfrey, i, 508b

Vitalis the priest, i, 456b

Wachelin, bishop of Winchester, i, 452b, 453a, 459a–68a, 510b, 518b

Waleran, i, 490b, 506b

Waleran the huntsman, i, 424, 426, 428, 444, 470a, 496b, 514a

Walter, i, 459b, 463a, 463b, 478a, 480a, 481b, 482a, 505b

Walter, bishop of Hereford. See Hereford, bishop of

Walter son of Other, i, 425, 472b, 497b

Walter (de Gloucester) son of Roger de Pistes, i, 422, 425, 497b

Warene, William de, i, 492a

Warine, a reeve, i, 535

Wenesi, i, 484b, 492a

Westminster, the abbey of, i, 416, 424, 472b

Wherwell, the abbey of, i, 416, 475a ; abbess of, i, 516b

Whitby, St. Hilda's Abbey, i, 438

White, Ulward, i, 473a (Yorks.)

Wibert the clerk, i, 462b

Wigot of Lincoln, i, 535

Wigot of Wallingford, i, 441, 508b

Wikings, i, 403

Willac. See Wislac

'Willelmus,' i, 439a, 439b

William I, i, 406, 407, 416, 419, 421, 423, 424, 427, 428, 435, 437, 450a–459a, 470b, 471b, 472a, 496a, 499a, 499b, 504b, 517a–518b

William II, i, 446

William, i, 462a, 463b, 465a, 465b, 485a, 511a, 522a, 523b, 525a

William the archer ('Arcuarius'), i, 430, 499a

William Fitz Osbern, earl of Hereford. See Hereford, earl of

William de Hoctona, i, 535

William son of Azor, i, 408, 426, 444, 517b, 521a

William son of Baderon, i, 425, 498b

William son of Estur, Stur, i, 408, 414, 426, 427, 498b, 516b, 517b, 518a, 519a

William son of Manne, i, 438, 498a

William son of Odo, i, 535

William son of Osbert, i, 535

William 'Tailatori,' i, 531

Wiltune [Wilton], the abbey of, i, 405, 416, 519a

Wincestre, Oda, Ode or Odo de, i, 418, 427, 477b, 502b, 504a, 504b, 509a, 513a, 516b. See also Oda, Eldred

Winchester, bishops of, 407, 417, 419, 422, 424, 425, 428, 431, 441, 489a, 494b, 504b, note 477a ; Denewulf bishop of, 403 ; Wachelin bishop of, 414, 452b, 453a, 459a–468a, 510b, 518b ; William Giffard, bishop of, i, 527, 529

Winchester, New Minster (St. Peter of Winchester) afterwards Hyde Abbey, 403, 416, 418, 419, 422, 424, 426, 428, 429, 436, 443, 444, 469a–472a, note 466b, abbots of, 469b, 470a, 470b, 471a, 471b, 522a ; Ælfwig, abbot of, 417

Winchester, Old Minster (St. Peter and St. Swithin, church of), 404, 408, 416, 419, 422, 442, 443, 473a, 489b, 507a ; monks of, 416, 435, 436, 463b–468b, 473a, 507a

Winchester, St. Mary, abbey of, 416, 473b, 474a, 496a ; abbess of, 473b, 496a ; nuns of, 419, 436, 496a

Windesores, Odin de, i, 431, 465b

Wislac or Willac, i, 486b, 512b, 514a, 515a, 525b, 526a

Wistrinc, i, 503b

Wit, Alwin, i, 508a

Wodecote, Henry de, i, note 481b

Worcester, bishop and monastery of, i, 443

W(u)lfric, i, 460a

Wulfward, i, 435, 440

York, archbishop of, i, 444

PLACE NAMES

Abaginge, i, 525a

Abbot's Anne. See Anne

Abbotstone [Abedestune], i, 422, 463a

Abedestone. See Adgestone

Abedric. See Awbridge

Abla. See Marable

Aburthoun, i, note 418

Acangre. See Oakhanger

Achelie, Aclei. See Oakley

Adelingeham. See Ellingham

Adgestone [Abedestone], i, 458a

Adrintone. See Arreton

Afton [Affetune], i, 517a

Alalei, i, 524b

Allington [Ellatune], i, 498a

Alresford [Alresforde], i, 420, 459b

Alton [Aultone], i, 419, 436, 470b, note 450. See also Anstey, Willhall

Alton Hundred. See Neteham

Alverstoke [Alwarestoch], i, 404, 442, 466b

Alverstone [Alvrestone], i, 521a

Alvington [Alwinestune], i, 406, 518b

Alwarestoch. *See* Alverstoke
Alwinestune. *See* Alvington
Alwinetune, i, 512*b*
Ambledune. *See* Hambleden
Amesbury (Wilts.) [Ambresberie], i, 408, 455*a*
Amport [Anne], i, 434, 484*a*. *See also* Cholderton and Sarson
Andover [Andovere, Andevere], i, 402, 419–20, 456*a*, *note* 418
Andover Hundred [Andovere, Andovre], i, 453*b*, 456*a*, 472*a*, 473*b*, 477*b*, 484*a*, 488*b*, 491*a*, 493*a*, 495*a*, 496*b*, 498*b*, 501*a*, 503*b*, 506*b*
Andret, i, 476*a*
Anne, i, 420, 491*a*. *See also* Amport, Monxton, Thruxton
Anne, Abbot's [Anna], i, 472*a*. *See also* Anne, Little
Anne, Little [Anna], i, 475*b*
Anne Savage, i, *notes* 484*b*, 491*a*
Anstey [Hanstige], i, 450*b*
Aoltone. *See* Upton Grey
Apleford [Apledeforde], i, 519*b*, 525*a*, 526*a*
Aplestede, i, 483*a*
Arnewood [Ernemude], i, 510*a*
Arreton [Adrintone], i, 403, 409, 457*b*, *note* 521*a*. *See also* Briddlesford, Hale, Merston, Periton, Standen, Sullens, Week
Ashe [Esse], i, 491*a*
Ashey Down, i, *note* 457
Ashhurst, i, *note* 513*b*
Ashley in Milton [Esselei, Esselie], i, 511*b*, 515*b*
Atehalle. *See* Hale
Atherfield [Avrefel], i, 518*a*
Aultone. *See* Alton
Avere. *See* Avon
Avington [Avintune], i, 464*b*
Aviston [Avicestone], i, 522*b*, 524*b*
Avon [Avere], i, 477*b*, 484*b*, *note* 485*a*
Avrefel. *See* Atherfield
Awbridge [Abedric], i, 480*b*, 494*a*

Baddesley, North [Bedeslei], i, 490*a*
Baddesley, (South) [Bedeslei], i, 511*a*
Badingborm, i, *note* 418
Badminstone [Bermintune, Burmintune], i, 511*b*, 512*a*
Bailocheslei. *See* Bashley
Bamborough Castle (Northants), i, 431
Bangbourn [Bedingeborne], i, 457*b*
Barnsley in Brading [Benverdeslei, Benveslei], i, 458*b*, 522*a*
Barnsley (Glouc.) [Bernesleis], i, 443

Bartley (?) [Berchelei], i, 504*b*
Bartley Heath in Odiham, i, *note* 504*b*
Barton, i, 422, *note* 463*b*
Barton Stacey [Bertune], i, 401–2, 452*b*, 489*b*, 497*b*. *See also* Bransbury, Drayton
Barton Stacey Hundred [Bertune], i, 452*b*, 467*a*, 488*b*, 489*b*, 494*a*, 497*b*, 498*a*, 500*b*, 504*a*
Bashley in Milton [Bailocheslei], i, 476*a*
Basing [Basinges], i, 476*a*
Basingstoke [Basingestoches], i, 401–3, 419, 421, 456*a*, *b*, 469*a*
Basingstoke Hundred [Basingestoch, Basingestochs, Basingestoc], i, 402, 456*a*, 469*a*, 471*b*, 479*a*, 487*a*, 493*b*, 502*b*, 509*a*
Battramsley [Betramelei], i, 514*b*, *note* 446
Beaulieu. *See* Hartford Farm, Otterwood
Beceslei. *See* Beckley
Beckley in Christchurch [Bichelei], i, 512*a*
Beckley in Milton, i, *note* 512*a*
Beckley in Ringwood (?) [Beceslei], i, 513*a*
Bedcot [Bedecote], i, 455*b*
Beddelie. *See* Clare Park
Bedeslei. *See* Baddesley
Bedhampton [Betametone, Bedhamtone], i, 403, 418, 422, 434, 471*a*
Bedingeborne. *See* Bangbourn
Bekendenere, i, *note* 418
Beneclege, Beneclei, Benedlei. *See* Bentley
Benestede. *See* Binstead
Bentley [Benedlei], i, 463*b*
Bentley in Mottisfont [Beneclege, Beneclei, Benetlege], i, 430, 499*a*, 505*b*
Bentley Wood, i, *note* 499*a*
Benverdeslei, Benveslei. *See* Barnsley
Berarding. *See* Brading
Berchelei. *See* Bartley
Bermesplet. *See* Bermondspitt
Bermintune, Burmintune. *See* Badminstone
Bermondspitt Hundred [Bermesplet], i, 477*b*, 482*b*, 486*a*, 490*b*, 493*a*, 500*b*, 503*b*, 504*b*, 505*b*. *See also* Odingetone
Bernesleis. *See* Barnsley
Berntone, i, *note* 418
Bertune. *See* Barton Stacey
Beslow (Salop) [Beteslawe], i, 429
Bessete. *See* Bradshott
Betestre. *See* Bistern
Betramelei. *See* Battramsley

Bibury (Glouc.), i, 443–4
Bichelei. *See* Beckley
Bickton [Bichetone, Byketone], i, 478*b*, *note* 418
Bieforde, i, 459*b*
Bighton [Bighetone], i, 471*a*, *note* 478*b*
Bile, i, 513*a*
Binstead [Benstede], i, 422, 466*a*, 486*a*, *note* 450
Binstead (I.W.) [Benestede], i, 520*b*
Birmingham in Sway, i, *note* 511*b*
Bishop's Sutton. *See* Sutton
Bishops Waltham. *See* Waltham
Bishopstoke [Stoches], i, 460*b*
Bistern with Crow [Betestre, Crone, i, 515*b*, 516*a*
Biteslesiet, Bitlesgete. *See* Buddlesgate
Blackpan [Bochepone], i, 522*a*
Blandford, Long (Dors.), i, *note* 508*b*
Blandford St. Mary (Dors.), i, *note* 508*b*
Blendworth, i, *notes* 410, 478*a*
Boarhunt [Borehunte, Borhunte], i, 427, 434, 468*a*, 477*a*, 483*a*
Bocheland. *See* Buckland
Bochepone. *See* Blackpan
Bocolt. *See* Buckholt
Boldre [Bovre], i, 514*b*. *See also* Baddesley, Battramsley, Pilley, Sway, Walhampton
Boldrebridge, i, *note* 514*a*
Boldreford [Bovreford], i, 514*a*
Bolende. *See* Bullington
Bonchurch [Bonecerce], i, 521*a*
Bordwood in Brading [Bordourde], i, 521*b*
Borgate. *See* Burgate
Bortel, i, 476*a*
Boseberg. *See* Bosmere
Bosham [Boseham], i, 469*a*
Bosmere Hundred [Boseberg], i, 451*b*, 468*a*, 473*a*, 478*a*, 483*a*
Bossington [Bosintone], i, 488*b*
Botley [Botelie], i, 490*a*
Bountisborough Hundred [Mantesberge], i, 462*b*, 463*a*, 474*a*, *b*, 491*a*, 496*a*
Bourne, West, i, 526*b*
Bovecombe. *See* Bowcombe
Bovecome, Bouecombe Hundred, i, 517*a*, 518*b*, 519*a*, 525*b*
Boviete. *See* Boyatt
Bovre. *See* Boldre
Bovre, Bovere Hundred. *See* New Forest
Bovreford. *See* Boldreford
Bowcombe in Carisbrooke [Bouecombe], i, 408–9, 421, 434, 517*b*
Boyatt in Otterbourne [Boviete], i, 500*b*
Bradewatre *See* Broadwater

Brading [Berarding], i, 521b. See also Adgestone, Alverstone, Aviston, Barnsley, Blackpan, Bordwood, Cheverton, Hardley, Kerne, Nunwell, Rowborough, Wolverton

Bradley [Bradelie], i, 461a

Bradshott in Selbourn [Bessete], i, 492b

Bramdean [Brondene, Biondene], i, 431, 503a, 504a

Bramley [Brumelai], i, 479b

Bramshaw. See Fritham

Bramshill, Great, in Eversley [Bromeselle], i, 495b

Bramshill, Little, in Eversley [Bromeselle], i, 483b

Bramshott [Brenbresete], i, 435, 487b. See also Chiltley, Lidshott

Braniston [Brandestone], i, 521b

Bransbury in Barton Stacey [Brandesberee], i, 467a

Breamore [Brumore], i, 443, 455b. See also Chardford, Outwich, Rockshore

Breilesforde. See Briddlesford

Brenbresete. See Bramshott

Breston Hundred, i, 494b

Brestone. See Broughton

Briddlesford in North Arreton [Breilesforde], i, 521b

Brighton, i, 442

Brixton. See Chilton, Lymerston

Broadwater (Sussex) [Bradewatre], i, 508b

Broad Windsor (Dors.), i, 431

Broc. See Brook

Broceste. See Brockenhurst

Brochelie. See Brookley

Brochematune. See Brockhampton

Brocheseve, i, 501b

Brockenhurst [Broceste], i, 412, 516a, notes 446, 514a. See also Brookley

Brockham Farm, i, note 501b

Brockhampton [Brochematune], i, 468a, b, 483a

Brocton Hundred. See Thorngate

Bromeselle. See Bramshill

Brondene, Biondene. See Bramdean

Brook [Broc], i, 517a

Brookley [Brochelie], i, 515a, note 446

Broton Hundred. See Thorngate

Broughton [Brestone], i, 401-2, 420, 443, 453a, 455b, 468b See also Bentley Wood, Pittleworth

Brown Candover. See Candover

Brownwich in Titchfield [Burnewic], i, 417, 463b

Brumelai. See Bramley

Brumore. See Breamore

Buckholt [Bocolt], i, 513b

Buckland [Bocheland], i, 482b

Buddlesgate, i, note 463b

Buddlesgate Hundred. [Bitelesiete], i, 460b, 464a, 489a, 494b

Bullington [Bolende], i, 475b

Burbage (Wilts.) [Burbach], i, 432

Burgate in Fordingbridge [Borgate], i, 403, 455b, 507b

Burghclere, i, note 465. See also Clere

Buriton. See Sunworth

Burley, i, note 510b

Burnewic. See Brownwich

Byketone. See Bickton

Calbourn. See Swainston, Watchingwell, Westover

Cambridge, i, 528

Campessete. See Kempshott

Candover [Candevre], i, 428, 431, 505a, note 503

Candover, Brown [Candevre], i, 6, 442, 443, 505a

Candover, Chilton [Candevre], i, 462b

Candover, Preston [Candevr], i, 420, 477b, 482b, 490b, 493a, 504b

Canterbury, i, 531

Canterton in Minstead [Cantortun], i, 405, 510a

Cantune. See Compton

Carisbrooke. See Alvington, Bowcombe, Chillerton, Pann, Rowbury, Shide

Carisbrooke Priory, i, 407, 409

Catherington, i, notes 410, 478a

Cauborne. See Swainston, Westover

Cauborne Hundred, i, 518b

Cela. See Chale

Celatune. See Chilton

Celeorde. See Chilworth

Celertune. See Chillerton

Celtone. See Chawton

Celvecrote, i, 524b

Ceptune. See Chalton

Ceptune Hundred. See Finchdean

Cerdeford, Cerdifort. See Chardford

Cerewartone. See Cholderton

Cevredone. See Cheverton

Chaddleworth (Berks), i, 418

Chale [Cela], i, 519a, 525b. See also Gotten, Walpan

Chalton [Ceptune], i, 478a, 478b, note 410

Chardford [Cerdeford, Cerdifort], i, 436-7, 439, 443, 445, 478b, 479a, 485b, 488a, 495b, 507a

Chawton [Celtone], i, 404, 427, 482a

Chelmestune. See Kilmiston

Chementune. See Kimpton

Chenep. See Knapp

Chenistone. See Knighton

Chenol. See Knowle

Chepstow Castle, i, 410

Cheverton in Brading [Cevredone], i, 520a

Chilbolton [Cilbodentune], i, 416, 464a, 494b

Chilcomb [Ciltecumbe], i, 428, 434, 440, 442, 463b

Chillerton [Celertune], i, 523a, 523b

Chiltley in Bramshott [Ciltelei], i, 451a

Chilton in Brixton [Celatune], i, 522b, 524a

Chilworth [Celeorde], i, 494b

Chineham i, 428, 480a, note 466a

Chingescamp. See Kings-camp

Chingestune. See Kingston

Chippenham (Wilts.), i, note 507b

Chochepon, i, 458b

Cholderton [Cerewartone], i, 484b, 495a, 498b, 503b

Christchurch, i, 416, 426, 535, note 513a, 535. See also Twinham, Hinton, Hubborn, Hurn, Beckley, Knapp, Stanpit, Winkton

Christchurch Hundred. [Egheiete], i, 454b, 473b, 476a, 486b, 513b. See also Sirlei

Church Oakley. See Oakley

Chuteley Hundred [Cillei] i, 468a, 470b, 482a, 486a, 488a, 491b, 496a, 497b

Cicemtone Hundred, i, note 402

Cilbodentune. See Chilbolton

Cildeest. See Yaldhurst

Cillei. See Chuteley

Ciltecumbe. See Chilcomb

Ciltelei. See Chiltley

Clanfield, i, notes 410, 478a

Clanville [Clavesfelle], i, 484b

Clare Park [Beddelie], i, 465b

Clatford [Cladford], i, 410, 453b

Clatinges, i, 439, 441, 479b, 485b

Clavesfelle. See Clanville

Clere, i, 465a, 481b, 498b, 508b. See also Kingsclere

Clere Hundred. See Kingsclere

Clerewoodcote, i, note 481b

Cliddesden [Cleresden], i, 493b, note 502b

Cliff (?) [Sclive], i, 510b

Cocherlei, i, 515a, note 446

Colbury. See Ashhurst

Colchester, i, 414

Colemore [Colemere], i, 500b

Combe [Cumbe], i, 487b

Combe (?) Isle of Wight [Seutecome], i, 522*b*

Compton [Cuntune], i, 428, 437, 499*a*, note 463*b*

Compton [Cantune], i, 517*a*

Copnor in Portsea [Copenore], i, 488*a*

Corhampton [Quedementune], i, 481*a*. See also Lomer

Corondel. See Crondal

Cosham [Coseham, Cosseham], i, 434, 451*b*, 486*a*, 503*a*

Cove in Yateley [Coue], i, 442, 465*b*

Cowesfield (Wilts.) [Cuvlestone, Cuvelesfeld], i, 432

Cranbourne [Cranburn, Gramborne], i, 470*a*, note 418

Crawecumbe (Somers.), i, 416

Crawley [Crawelie], i, 460*b*

Crofton in Titchfield [Croftune], i, 440, 476*a, b*. See also Stubbington

Crondal [Crundele], i, 404, 442, 465*b*

Crondal Hundred [Corondel], i, 465*b*.

Crux Easton. See Easton

Cuntune. See Compton

Cuvlestone, Cuvvelesfeld. See Cowesfield

Dean [Dena, Dene] in Thorngate Hundred, i, 453*b*, 468*b*, 497*a*, 497*b*

Dean, East [Dene], i, 420, 497*a*

Dean, West, i, 420

Deane in Chuteley Hundred [Dene], i, 491*b*, notes 488*a*, 491*b*, 497*b*

Denebrige. See Dunbridge

Depedene. See Dibden

Dibden, i, note 513*b*

Dodintune. See Totton

Dogmersfield [Ormeresfelt], i, 502*b*, note 504*b*

Down, the [Done, Ladone], i, 457*a*, 457*b*

Draycot (Wilts.) [Draicote], i, 430–1

Drayton in Barton Stacey [Draitone], i, 470*a*, note 418

Drayton juxta Brickton, i, note 408

Drocheneford Hundred, i, 466*a*

Drodintone, i, 525*a*

Droxford [Drocheneford], i, 435, 466*a*

Dummer [Dummere], i, 482*b*, 504*b*

Dunbridge [Denebrige], i, 495*a*

Dungewood in Shorwell [Duniorde], i, 518*a*

Dunham Massey (Cheshire), i, note 478*b*

Durley in Eling [Durle, Derleie], i, 509*b*

Durns Town [Durands Town], i, note 511*b*

East Dean. See Dean

East Hoe. See Hoe

East Meon. See Meon

East Popham. See Popham

East Wellow. See Wellow

East Worldham. See Worldham

Eastley in South Stoneham [Estleie], i, 500*a*

Easton [Estune], i, 460*a*

Easton, Crux [Estune], i, 426, 501*a*

Eastrop [Estrope], i, 493*b*

Ebintune, Edintune. See Ovington

Eccleswelle. See Itchingswell

Edefele, Efedel Hundred. See Odiham

Edlinges. See Eling

Effelle. See Yately

Efford in Milford [Einforde], i, 516*a*

Egheiete Hundred. See Christchurch

Egrafel, i, 520*a*

Einforde. See Efford

Eisseburne. See Hurstbourne Priors

Eling [Edlinges], i, 401–2, 408, 423, 434, 454*a*, note 446. See also Durley, Hanger, Marchwood, Netley, Ower, Tatchbury, Testwood, Totton

Ellatune. See Allington

Ellingham [Adelingeham], i, 507*a*. See also Rockford

Ellisfield [Esewelle], i, 486*a*

Elvetham [Elveteham], i, 422, 472*b*

Embley in East Wellow [Emelei], i, 494*b*

Empshott [Hibesete], i, 430, 510*b*

Enham, Knight's [Etham], i, 429, 506*b*

Ermud. See Yarmouth

Ernemude. See Arnewood

Eschetune, i, 495*b*

Eseldecome. See Shalcombe

Esewelle. See Ellisfield

Esse. See Ashe

Esseborne. See Hurstbourne Tarrant

Esseborne, Esseburne Hundred. See Pastrow

Esseham. See Lasham

Esselei, Esselie. See Ashley

Esselei Hundred. See Sutton, Bishop's

Essessentune. See Exton

Essuete. See Sheat

Estede, i, note 418

Estmeone. See Meon, East

Etha, Insula de, i, note 418

Etham. See Enham

Etharin, i, 458*b*

Eversley [Evreslei], i, 472*b*. See also Bramshill

Evingare Hundred, i, 464*b*

Evreland, Evrelant. See Yaverland

Ewhurst [Werste], i, 481*b*

Ewshott, i, note 465*b*. See also Itchell

Exbury. See Gatewood

Exeter, i, 431–2

Exton [Essessentune], i, 414, 466*b*

Eyeworth near Fritham [Jvare], i, 455*a*

Faccombe [Facumbe], i, 447, 456*b*

Falegia, Falelie. See Fawley

Falemere Hundred, i, 463*b*

Fareham [Fernham], i, 403–4, 414, 440, 462*a*

Fareham Hundred [Ferneham], i, 462*a*

Farleigh Wallop [Ferlege], i, 503*b*, note 502*b*

Farley, i, 429

Farley Chamberlain [Ferlege], i, i, 499*b*

Farnborough [Ferneberga], i, 431, 465*b*

Farringdon [Ferendone], i, 469*a*

Fawley [Falegia, Falelie], i, 467*b*, 510*b*. See also Badminstone, Hardley, Langley, Stanswood, Stone

Fawley Hundred [Falelei], i, 459*b*, 464*b*

Ferlege. See Farleigh and Farley

Ferlei. See Quarley

Ferneberga. See Farnborough

Ferneham. See Fareham

Fernhill in Milton [Fernehelle], i, 512*a*

Fiddlesworth, i, 418

Fifield [Fifhide], i, 429, 493*a*

Finchdean Hundred [Ceptune], i, 451*a*, 452*a*, 478*a*

Finley [Finlei], i, 502*a*

Flexland, la, i, 430

Fordingbridge [Forde], i, 489*a*. See also Bedcot, Burgate, Goreley, Midgham

Fordingbridge Hundred [Fordingbrige], i, 455*a*, 478*b*, 485*a*, 488*a*, 489*a*, 496*b*, 503*b*, 507*a*, 510*a*

Forest. See New Forest

Foxcot [Fulsescote], i, 496*b*

Fratton in Portsea [Frodintone], i, 492*a*, note 418

Freefolk [Frigefolc], i, 443, 464*b*, note 419

Freshwater(King's) [Frescewatre], i, 409, 517*a*. *See also* Afton, Compton, Wilmingham

Freshwater (Prior's), i, 523*a*

Frigefolc. *See* Freefolk

Fritham in Bramshaw [Truham, Trucham], i, 446–7, 510*b*, 511*a*, 512*b*, 514*b*

Frodintone. *See* Fratton

Froyle [Froli], i, 474*a*

Fullerton in Wherwell [Fugelerestune], i, 469*b*

Fulsescote. *See* Foxcot

Funtley [Funtelei], i, 476*b*, 489*a*, 502*a*

Gadetune. *See* Gotten

Gatcombe [Gatecome], i, 519*b* *See also* Chillerton, Sheat

Gatewood in Exbury (?) [Gatingeorde], i, 513*b*

Gerlei (in Chuteley Hundred), i, 488*a*, 491*b*, 497*b*. *See also* Goreley

Godalming (Surr.), i, 426

Godesmanescamp. *See* Godshill

Godshill in Fordingbridge [Godesmanescamp], i, 515*a*

Godshill (I.W.), i, 409. *See also* Apleford, Lesland, Rowde, Scottesbrook, Stenbury

Goodworth [Godorde], i, 475*b*

Goodworth Hatford. *See* Goodworth

Goreley [Gerlei], i, 503*b*

Gotten [Gadetune,], i, 519*b*

Grafton. *See* Penton

Greatham in Neteham Hundred [Greteham], i, 450*b*

Greatnam in Lyndhurst or Brockenhurst [Greteham], i, 514*a*, *note* 446

Grinstead East (Wilts.), i, *note* 428

Hale in Arreton [Atehalle], i, 520*b*

Haliborne. *See* Holybourn

Halingei, Helinghei, Helingey. *See* Hayling Island

Hallege. *See* Headley

Hamstead [Hamestede], i, 522*b*, 524*a*

Hambledon [Ambledune, Hamledune], i, 438, 478*b*, 487*b*

Hanger in Eling [Hangre], i, 508*a*

Hannington [Hanitune], i, 467*b*, 508*b*

Hanstige. *See* Anstey

Hantone, Hantune, Hantonia. *See* Southampton

Harbridge [Herdebrige], i, 429, 514*a*

Hardley in Brading [Hardelie], i, 520*a*

Hardley in Fawley [Hardelie], i, 513*b*

Hariforde. *See* Hartford

Hartford farm (?) [Hariforde], i, 513*a*

Hartley Mauditt [Harlege, Herlege], i, 404, 424, 432, 435, 488*a*, 492*b*

Hartley Westpall [Harlei or Herlei], i, 503*b*, 505*a*

Haseley [Haselie], i, 458*b*

Hastings, i, 417, 437

Hatang, i, 431, *note* 503*b*

Hatch Warren [Heche], i, 502*b*

Havant [Havehunt], i, 468*b*

Hayling i, 416, 419

Hayling Island [Halingei, Helinghei, Helingey], i, 420, 435, 444, 451*b*, 468*a*, 473*a*, *note* 478*a*

Headley [Hallege], i, 477*a*

Headbourn Worthy. *See* Worthy

Heceford, i, 526*a*

Heche. *See* Hatch Warren

Heckfield. *See* Mattingley

Hefedele Hundred. *See* Odiham

Heldelie, i, 518*a*

Hemreswel Hundred, i, 525*b*

Henert. *See* Herriard

Hentune. *See* Hinton

Herdebrige. *See* Harbridge

Herdel. *See* Hordle

Herne. *See* Hurn

Herriard [Henert], i, 482*b*

Hibesete. *See* Empshott

Highclere. *See* Clere

Highcliff, i, *note* 510*b*. *See also* Cliff

Hinchelesey [Hincelveslei, Hincelveslai], i, 515*a*, *note* 446

Hinton (Admiral) [Hentune], i, 511*b*, 512*a*, *note*

Hinton Ampner [Hentune], i, 467*b*

Hoburne. *See* Hubborn

Hoddington [Odingetone], i, 468*a*

Hoe, East [Hou], i, 481*a*

Holdenhurst [Holeest, Holehest], i, 415, 423, 454*b*, 476*a*, *note* 408

Holdshott Hundred [Holesete], i, 472*b*, 483*b*, 490*b*, 492*a*, 495*b*, 496*a*, 503*b*, 505*a*

Holstune, Houstun. *See* Houghton

Holybourn [Haliborne], i, 450*b*, *note* 501*b*

Hook in Titchfield [Houch], i, 480*b*

Hordle [Herdel], i, 512*b*. *See also* Arnewood

Hore. *See* Ower

Horringford [Ovingefort], i, 525*a*

Horton, i, *note* 509*b*

Hoteleston. *See* Nettleston

Hotlop, i, 506*b*

Hou. *See* Hoe

Houch. *See* Hook

Houghton [Holstune, Houstun], i, 434, 435, 462*b*, 480*b*, 494*b*, 503*a*

Houghton North [Holstune], i, 477*b*

Hound [Hune], i, 481*a*. *See also* Netley

Hubborn in Christchurch [Hoburne], i, 513*b*

Huncheford, i, 525*b*

Hune. *See* Hound

Huntingdon, i, 528

Hurn in Christchurch [Herne], i, 486*b*

Hurstbourne Priors [Eisseburne], i, 465*a*

Hurstbourne Tarrant [Esseborne], i, 401–2, 414, 420, 456*b*

Hyde Abbey, i, 416, 424

Ibsley [Tibeslei], i, 485*b*. *See also* Goreley

Icene. *See* Itchen Abbess

Idsworth, i, *note* 478*a*

Iford in Christchurch, i, *notes* 477*b*, 484*b*, 485*a*

Iping (Sussex), i, *note* 427

Irtlingborough (Northants), i, *note* 466*a*

Itchell (now Ewshott in Crondall) [Ticelle], i, 442, 465*b*

Itchen Abbess [Icene], i, 419, 436–7, 496*a*

Itchen Stoke [Stoche], i, 474*b*

Itchingswell [Eccleswelle], i, 467*b*

Ivory Lodge, i, *note* 455*a*

Jvare. *See* Eyeworth

Kempshott [Campessete], i, 480*a*

Kerne in Brading [Lacherne], i, 458*a*

Kilmiston [Chelmestune], i, 459*b*, 460*b*

Kimpton [Chementune], i, 484*b*. *See also* Littleton, Shoddesden

Kingsclere [Clere], i, 401–2, 414, 419, 456*b*, 471*b*, 534, *note* 487*a*. *See also* Tidgrove

Kingsclere Hundred [Clere], i, 467*b*, 474*b*, 481*b*, 490*a*, 498*b*, 502*a*, 508*a*, 534

Kingsley, i, *note* 450*a*

King's-camp [Chingescamp], i, 462*a*

King's Sombourn. *See* Sombourn

Kingston [Chingestune], i, 518*a*

Knapp in Christchurch [Chenep], i, 486*b*, *note* 481*b*

Knighton [Chenistone], i, 457*a*, 525*b*

Knight's Enham. *See* Enham

Knowle nr. Kingsclere [Chenol], i, 481*b*, 490*a*, note 487*a*

Knowle (Somers.) [Chenolle], i, note 481*b*

Kyngesmille, i, *note* 418

Lacherne. *See* Kerne

Ladone. *See* Down, the

Lammere. *See* Lomer

Lamore, i, 522*a*

Langley in Fawley [Langelie], i, 509*b*, 510*a*

Langstone Harbour, i, 403

Larode in West Tisted [La Rode, Larode], i, 499*b*

Lasham [Esseham], i, 452*b*

Latelie. *See* Netley

Laverstoke [Lavrochestoche], i, 419, 429, 472*a*

Leckford [Lechtford], i, 469*b*

Leckford Abbess [Lecford], i, 474*a*

Lenimcode, i, 525*b*

Lentune. *See* Lymington

Lepene. *See* Pann

Lesborne, i, 498*a*

Lesland *or* Lisland in Godshill [Litesland, Liscelande], i, 458*a*, 521*b*

Lesteorde. *See* Testwood

Lestred. *See* Testwood

Letley. *See* Netley

Levegarestun, i, 521*a*

Levintun. *See* Lymerston

Lickpit in Basing [Lichepet], i, 471*b*

Lidshott in Bramshott [Lidessete], i, 482*a*

Limerston. *See* Lymerston

Lincoln, i, 431, 528, 530

Linhest. *See* Lyndhurst

Linkenholt [Linchehou], i, 472*a*

Lis. *See* Lyss

Lisland in Godshill [Liscelande], i, 458*a*

Litchfield [Liveselle, Ludeshelve, Ledeshelve, Lydeshelve], i, 422, 481*b*, note 471*b*

Litesland. *See* Lesland

Littleton in Kimpton [Liteltone], i, 484*b*, note 463*b*

Liveselle. *See* Litchfield

Lockerley [Locherlega, Locherlei, Locherslei], i, 420, 468*b*, 483*b*, 506*a*, 506*b*, note 509*a*

Lomer in Corhampton [Lammere], i, 436, 471*a*, note 418

Longford (Wilts.), i, note 507*b*

Longparish. *See* Middleton

Longstock [Stoches], i, 474*a*

London, i, 432, 530, 532, 536

Luccomb [Lovecombe], i, 458*a*

Lyewood Farm, i, *note* 499*b*

Lygeput, i, *note* 418

Lymerston in Brixton [Levintun], i, 518*a*, 526*a*

Lymington [Lentune], i, 511*b*, note 514*a*

Lyndhurst [Linhest], i, 403, 408, 455*a*, note 514*a*. *See also* Greatham

Lyss [Lis], i, 473*b*

Mainsborough Hundred [Maneberge, Manesberg, Manesbrige], i, 462*b*, 469*a*, 487*a*, 489*b*, 494*b*

Malmesbury (Wilts.), i, 402

Mansbridge Hundred [Manebrige], i, 467*a*, 471*b*, 481*a*, 495*a*, 498*a*, 500*a*, 500*b*, 501*a*.

Mantesberge Hundred. *See* Bountisborough

Mapledurham [Malpedresham], i, 414, 429, 451*a*

Mapledurwell [Mapledrewelle], i, 424, 487*a*

Mapleham, i, 515*a*

Marable (?) [Abla], i, 459*a*

Marchwood in Eling [Merceode], i, 509*b*

Mattingley in Heckfield [Matingelege], i. 505*a*

Melebroc. *See* Milbrook

Melevsford, i, 524*b*

Melleford. *See* Milford

Meon [Mene], i, 410, 417, 462*b*

Meon, East [Estmeone, Mene, Menes], i, 416, 452*a*, 461*b*, notes 415, 418. *See also* Westbury

Meon, East, Hundred [Mene], i, 452*a*, 461*b*

Meonstoke [Menestoche], i, 403, 452*a*

Meonstoke Hundred [Menestoch, Menestoc], i, 451*b*, 461*b*, 466*b*, 471*a*, 473*b*, 478*b*, 481*a*, 487*b*, 500*a*

Meon, West [Menes, Westmeone], i, 414, 420, 461*b*, note 418. *See also* Wesbury

Merceode. *See* Marchwood

Mersley Down, i, *note* 457*a*

Merston [Merestone], i, 520*b*

Messley in Newchurch (?) [Messetone], i, 521*a*

Meton, i, *note* 418

Miceldevre. *See* Mitcheldever

Michaelmarsh. *See* Awbridge

Middleton [Middeltune], i, 475*b*

Midgham in Fordingbridge [Mingeham], i, 507*a*, 507*b*

Milbrook [Melebroc], i, 442, 467*b*. *See also* Shirley

Milford [Melleford], i, 412, 515*b*, 516*a*, note 446. *See also* Efford, Yaldhurst

Milton [Mildeltune], i, 509*b*. *See also* Ashley, Bashley, Fernhill, Ossemley, and Wootton

Mindeslei. *See* Minley

Mingeham. *See* Midgham

Minley in Yateley [Mindeslei], i, 505*a*

Minstead [Mintestede], i, 515*b*. *See also* Canterton

Mitcheldever [Miceldevre], i, 418, 422, 428, 440, 469*b*

Mitcheldever Hundred [Miceldevre], i, 469*b*

Modrestan. *See* Mottiston

Monks Sherbourne. *See* Sherbourne

Monxton (?) [Anne], i, 456*a*

Morden (Camb.), i, *note* 477*a*

Morden, East (Dors.), i, *note* 509*a*

Morestead, i, *note* 463*b*

Mottisfont [Mortesfunde, Mortelhunte], i, 420, 468*b*, 506*b*. *See also* Bentley, Dunbridge

Mottiston [Modrestan], i, 522*b*

Mulcetone, i, 506*a*

Nateley [Nataleie], i, 479*b*

Neatham [Neteham], i, 401–2, 450*a*, note 450*b*

Neeton. *See* Niton

Neteham. *See* Neatham

Neteham Hundred, i, 447, 450*a*, 469*a*, 470*b*, 474*a*, 477*a*, 482*a*, 485*b*, 486*a*, 487*b*, 490*b*, 492*a*, 492*b*, 494*a*, 497*b*, 498*a*, 499*b*, 501*b*, 504*b*, 510*a*

Nether Wallop. *See* Wallop

Netley in Eling [Nutlei], i, 513*b*, 515*a*, note 446

Netley in Hound [Latelie], i, 495*a*

Nettleston [Hoteleston], i, 459*a*

Nettleston in St. Helens [Hotelestone], i, 525*a*

Neutibrige. *See* Nytimber

Newchurch, i, 409. *See also* Messley

New Forest, the, i, 411–13, 424, 426–7, 445–6, 454*b*, 510*b*, 535, note 423, 535

New Forest Hundred [Bovere, Bovre], i, 446, 455*a*, 475*a*, 476*a*, 510*b*, 514*a*

Newton Stacey [Niwetone, Nywetonem], i, 438, 498*a*, note 418

Newton Valence [Neventone], i, 494*a*

Newtown River (I. of W.) i, 434

Niton [Neeton], i, 409, 459*a*

Noclei. *See* Nutley

Nonoelle. *See* Nunwell

Norman Court, i, *note* 462*a*

Northam, i, 414, 503*a*

Northampton, i, *note* 534

North Houghton. *See* Houghton

Norton farm in Selbourn [Nortone], i, 485b, 490b

Norton farm in Wonston [Nortune], i, 504a

Notesselinge. *See* Nursling

Nunwell in Brading [Nonoelle], i, 458a

Nursling [Notesselinge], i, 464a

Nutley [Nuttlie, Noclei], i, 430, 500b. *See also* Netley

Nytimber [Neutibrige], i. 478a, 526b

Nywetonem, i, *note* 418. *See also* Newton

Oakhanger in Selbourne [Acangre], i, 436, 504b

Oakley [Achelie], i, 510b, 514a

Oakley, Church [Aclei], i, 482a, 488a, 496a, notes 491b, 497b

Oakley, North, i, *note* 481b

Odecote. *See* Woodcote

Odetone, Odetune. *See* Wootton

Odiham i, 403, 415, 420, 450a, 504b, note. *See also* Bartley

Odiham Hundred, i, 450a, 452b, 472b, 493a, 502b, 504b. *See also* Odingetone Hundred

Odingetone. *See* Hoddington

Odingetone *or* Odingeton Hundred [now in Odiham and Bermondspitt], i, 468a, 482a, 493b, 496a

Olvestune. *See* Woolston

Optune. *See* Upton

Opwarneford, i, *note* 418. *See also* Warnford

Ordie. *See* Worthy

Orham, i, 520a

Ormeresfelt. *See* Dogmersfield

Ossemley in Milton [Oselei], i, 511a

Otoiche. *See* Outwich

Otterbourne [Otreburne], i, 434, 489a. *See also* Boyatt

Otterwood in Beaulieu [Otreorde], i, 513b

Outwich in Breamore [Otoiche], i, 496b

Overton [Overtune], i, 461a, 472a. *See also* Polhampton

Overton Hundred [Overetune, Overetun], i, 461a, 472a, 491a, 491b

Over Wallop. *See* Wallop

Ovingefort. *See* Horringford

Ovington [Ebintune, Edintune], i, 462b, 474a

Ower in Eling [Hore], i, 473a

Owslebury in Twyford, i, 460a

Oxelei, i, 515a

Pacombe, i, *note* 456b

Pann in Carisbrooke [Lepene], i, 524b

Pastrow Hundred [Esseborne, Esseburne], i, 453b, 472a, 481b, 487b, 501a

Pauncefooteshill in Romsey, i, 423

Penton Grafton [Penitone], i, 420, 473b. *See also* Clanville

Penton Mewsey [Penitone], i, 477b

Periton in Arreton [Prestetone], i, 520b

Pilley [Pisteslei, Pisteslai, Pistelei], i, 446–7, 512b, 514a, 515a

Pittleworth in Broughton [Puteleorde, Puteorde], i, 468b, 500b

Polhampton in Overton [Polemetune], i, 534, 466a, 491b, note 419, 534

Popham, i, *note* 418

Popham, East [Popeham], i, 470a

Porchester [Porcestre, Portcestre], i, 402, 432, 451b, 492b

Portsdown Hundred [Portesdon], i, 451b, 468a, 471a, 477a, 482b, 486a, 488a, 492a, 492b, 503a

Portsea [Porteseye], i, *note* 418. *See also* Copnor, Fratton

Portsmouth, i, notes 482b, 483b

Portsmouth Harbour, i, 403

Preston Candover. *See* Candover

Prestetone. *See* Perriton

Puddletrenthide (Dors.), i, 418

Puteleorde, Puteorde. *See* Pittleworth

Quarley [Ferlei], i, 456a

Quedementune. *See* Corhampton

Redbridge [Rodbrige], i, 487a

Redbridge Hundred [Rodbridge, Rodbrige], i, 441, 454a, 467b, 473a, 475a, 487a, 503a, 508a, 509b, 510a, 510h, 513a

Rincvede. *See* Ringwood

Ringwood [Rincvede], i, 454b, notes 408, 415. *See also* Beckley, Bisterne, Sandford

Ringwood Hundred [Rincvede], i, 454b, 514a

Ripley in Sopley [Riple], i, 486b, 507b, note 485a

Rockbourn [Rocheborne], i, 402, 414, 436, 443, 455b, 507a, 507b. *See also* Rockstead

Rockford [Rocheford], i, 485a

Rockshore in Breamore (?) [Rochesire], i, 485a

Rockstead Farm [Rocksyth], i, note 485a

Rocksyth. *See* Rockstead

Rodbridge. *See* Redbridge

Rode. *See* Rowde

Rodeberge. *See* Rowborough

Rodedic Hundred, i, 446–7, 509b, 510a, 512b, 515a

Romsey [Romesy], i, 423, 474b

Ropley, i, *note* 499b

Rowborough in Brading [Rodeberge], i, 522a

Rowbury in Carisbrooke, i, *note* 522a

Rowde in Godshill [Rode], i, 523a

Roweste, i, 513b

Rowner [Ruenore], i, 492a

St. Faith, i, *note* 463b

St. Helens *or* Sullens [Selins], i, 521b. *See also* Nettleston

St. Mary Bourne. *See* Swampton

Salisbury (Old Sarum), i, 420, note 462a, 472b

Saltern Wood, i, 434

Sande. *See* Sandown

Sandford, i, 403, 415, 457b, note 513a

Sandown [Sande], i, 458b

Sanhest, i, 514b, note 446

Sarson in Amport [Soresdene], i, 497a

Satewelle, i, *note* 418

Savernac, Forest, i, 432

Scaldeford. *See* Scottlesbrook

Sceptone, Sceptune. *See* Shipton

Sclive. *See* Cliff

Scottlesbrook in Godshill (?) [Scaldeford], i, 458a, 522a, 523a

Seacombe (Glouc.), i, *note* 533

Selborne [Selesburne, Selesborne], i, 451a, note 498a. *See also* Bradshott, Norton, Oakhanger

Selbourne Hundred. *See* Neteham

Seldeflet. *See* Shalfleet, i, 524a

Seldene. *See* Shaldern

Selesburne. *See* Selborne

Selins. *See* St. Helens or Sullens (?)

Sencliz. *See* Shanklin

Seneorde. *See* Sunworth

Seutecome. *See* Combe or Sharcombe

Shalcombe nr. Brook [Eseldecome], i, 519a

Shaldern [Seldene], i, 493a

Shalfleet [Seldeflet], i, 524a

Shallows, The, i, *note* 514a

Shanklin [Sencliz], i, 523b

Sharcombe in Shorwell (?) [Seutecome], i, 522b

Sheat in Gatcomb [Essuete, Soete], i, 524b, 525b

Sherbourn, Monks [Sireborne,] i, 486a. *See also* Chineham

Sherbourne St. John [Sireburne], i, 429, 444, 479*a*

Sherfield English [Sirefelle], i, 484*a*

Shide in Carisbrooke [Sida Side], i, 518*a*, 523*a*, 523*b*

Shilvington, i, *note* 508*b*

Shipton Bellenger [Sceptone, Sceptune], i, 488*b*, 493*b*. *See also* Snoddington

Shirley in Millbrook [Sirelei], i, 489*b*

Shoddesden in Kimpton [Sotesdene], i, 506*b*

Shorwell [Sorewelle], i, 518*a*, 523*b*, *notes* 409, 519*a*. *See also* Atherfield, Cheverton, Dungewood, Sharcombe, Woolverton

Shurley Hundred [Sirlei] i, 477*b*, 484*b*, 486*b*, 496*b*, 498*b*, 507*b*

Sida, Side. *See* Shide.

Sidmonton [Sidemanestone], i, 474*b*

Sigeonsworth in Titchfield [Sugion], i, 480*a*

Silchester [Silcestre], i, 410, 490*b*, 492*a*

Sireborne, Sireburne. *See* Sherbourne

Sirefelle. *See* Sherfield

Sirelei. *See* Shirley, Shurley

Slacham, i, 410, 455*a*

Snoddington in Shipton Bellenger [Snodintone], i, 483*b*

Soberton [Sudbertune], i, 405, 451*b*, 452*a*, 459*b*, 500*a*. *See also* East Hoe

Soete. *See* Sheat

Soflet, i, 459*a*

Sombourne, King's [Sumburne], i, 403, 435, 457*a*, 491*b*, 497*a*

Sombourne, Little [Sumburne], i, 494*a*

Sopley [Sopelie], i, 498*b*, *note* 485*a*. *See also* Ripley

Sorewelle. *See* Shorwell

Sotesdene. *See* Shoddesden

Sotwelle (Berks), i, *note* 419

Southampton [Hantone, Hantune], i, 409, 410, 420–1, 425, 427–8, 432, 446, 467*a*, 489*b*, 494*b*, 516*b*, 528, *note* 536

Southwick, i, *note* 483*a*

Sparsholt, i, *note* 463*b*

Standen in Arreton [Standone], i, 521*a*

Staneberie. *See* Stenbury

Stanes. *See* Stone

Staneude. *See* Stanswood

Staneham, Stanham. *See* Stoneham.

Stanpit in Christchurch [Stanpeta], i, 486*b*

Stanton St. John (Oxford), i, *note* 535

Stanswood in Fawley [Staneude], i, 454*a*

Stenbury in Godshill [Staneberie], i, 459*a*

Steventon [Stivetune], i, 509*a*

Stoche. *See* Itchen Stoke, Stockbridge (?)

Stoches. *See* Stoke, Bishopstoke, Longstock

Stockbridge (?) [Stoche], i, 502*b*

Stoke [Stoches], i, 461*a*

Stoke Charity [Stoches], i, 461*b*

Stone in Fawley [Stanes], i, 442, 509*b*

Stoneham, North [Staneham], i, 471*b*

Stoneham, South [Stanham], i, 420, 467*a*. *See also* Allington, Eastley

Stratfield [Stradfelle], i, 495*b*, 505*a*

Stratfield Mortimer [Stradfelle], i, 491*a*

Stratfield Turgis [Stradfelle], i, 483*b*

Stratfieldsaye [Stradfelle], i, 496*a*

Stratton, East, i, *note* 470*a*

Stratton, West [Stratune, Weststrattonam], i, 470*a*, *note* 418

Stubbington in Crofton [Stubitone], i, 480*b*

Sualefelle. *See* Swallowfield

Suantune. *See* Swampton

Sudberie, i, 505*b*

Sudbertune. *See* Soberton

Sudhamptunam. *See* Southampton

Sueia, Suei. *See* Sway

Sugion. *See* Sigeonsworth

Sullens (?) [Selins], i, 521*b*

Sumburne. *See* Sombourne

Sunworth in Buriton [Seneorde], i, 410, 478*a*

Sutelesberg Hundred (Wilts.), i, *note* 402

Suthingewerthe, i, *note* 418

Sutton, Bishop's [Sudtone], i, 477*a*

Sutton, Bishop's, Hundred [Esselei], i, 463*a*, 477*a*, 503*a*, 504*a*

Sutton, Long [Sudtune], i, 465*b*

Sutton Scotney, in Wonston [Sudtune], i, 488*b*, 504*a*

Sutton Walrond (Dors.), i, 424

Swainston in Calbourn [Cauborne], i, 518*b*

Swallowfield [Sualefelle, Soanesfelt, Solafel], i, 495*b*

Swampton in St. Mary Bourne [Suantune], i, 434, 436, 490*a*

Swarraton [Swarewetonam], i, 418, *notes* 418, 470*a*

Sway in Boldre [Sueia, Suei], i, 445, 475*a*, 511*a*, 516*b*. *See also* Birmingham

Tadley, i, *note* 461*a*

Tatchbury in Eling [Taceberie, Teocreberie], i, 439, 472*a*, 513*b*

Tedorde. *See* Tidworth

Testwood in Eling [Lestred, Lesteorde, i, 487*a*(?), 510*b*

Tewkesbury, i, 404

Thedden Grange, i, *note* 450*a*

Thorley [Torlei], i, 524*b*

Thorngate Hundred [Brocton, Broctone], i, 452*b*, 462*a*, 468*b*, 483*b*, 488*b*, 493*b*, 495*a*, 497*a*, 497*b*, 499*a*, 500*b*, 505*b*

Thoroughham. *See* Fritham

Thruxton (?) [Anne], i, 501*a*

Thuinam, Tuinam. *See* Twynham

Tibeslei. *See* Ibsley

Ticefelle. *See* Titchfield

Ticelle. *See* Itchell

Tiderlege, Tederleg. *See* Tytherley

Tidgrove in King's Clere [Titegrave], i, 487*a*

Tidworth, South [Tedorde, Todeorde], i, 488*b*, 501*a*

Timsbury [Timbreberie], i, 474*a*

Tisted, West [Tistede], i, 463*a*. *See also* Larode

Titchfield [Ticefelle], i, 403, 456*b*. *See also* Brownwich, Crofton, Hook, Sigeonsworth

Titchfield Hundred [Ticefelle, Ticefel], i, 456*b*, 462*b*, 463*b*, 476*a*, 480*a*, 489*a*, 490*a*, 492*a*, 502*a*

Titegrave. *See* Tidgrove

Tochiton. *See* Tufton

Todeorde. *See* Tidworth

Torlei. *See* Thorley

Totton in Eling [Totintone, Dodintune], i, 475*a*(?), 508*a*

Treyford (Sussex), i, *note* 418

Truham, Trucham. *See* Fritham

Truham Hundred, i, 446

Tufton [Tochiton], i, 475*a*

Tunworth [Tuneworde], i, 479*b*

Twyford [Tuiforde], i, 460*a*. *See also* Owslebury

Twynham [Thuinam, Tuinam], i, 403, 421, 454*b*, 476*a*

Twynham (Christchurch), i, 414

Tytherley [Tiderlege, Tiderlei, Tederleg], i, 437, 468*b*, 495*a*, 497*a*, 505*b*, 506*a*

Tytherley, East, i, 420

Tytherley, West, i, 420

Udemanecote. *See* Woodmancote

Ulvredestune, Ulvretune. *See* Woolverton

Ulwarcumbe, i, 519*b*
Ulwartone. *See* Wolverton
Upton in Hurstbourne Tarrant [Optune], i, 453*b*
Upton Grey [Aoltone], i, 482*a*. *See also* Hoddington
Utefel, i, 516*a*

Valpenne. *See* Walpan
Velokedone, i, *note* 418
Verilham, i, 430
Vernham Dean, i, *note* 453*b*

Walde. *See* Wield
Walhampton [Wolnetune], i, 511*b*
Wallop [Wallope], i, 402, 420, 453*b*, 484*a*, 506*a*, note 441
Wallop, Nether [Wallope], i, 453*a*
Wallop, Over [Wallope], i, 452*b*
Walpan in Chale [Valpenne], i, 518*a*
Waltham, Bishops, i, 460*b*
Waltham, Bishops, Hundred, i, 460*b*
Warblington [Warblitetone], i, 526*a*, 526*b*. *See also* Nytimber
Wardham. *See* Worldham
Warnborough [Wergeborne, Warneburn], i, 438, 496*a*
Warnborough, South, i, *note* 482*b*
Warnford [Warneford], i, 471*a*, 481*a*. *See* Opwarneford
Warochesselle. *See* Wroxall
Watchingwell in Calbourne [Watingewelle], i, 519*a*
Week in Arreton [Wica], i, 403, 414, 457*b*, *note* 463*b*
Welford Hundred, i, 475*a*
Welige. *See* Wellow
Wellow [Welige], i, 517*a*
Wellow, East [Weleue], i, 428, 506*a*. *See also* Embley
Wellow, West (Wilts.), i, 506*b*
Wenechetone, Weristetone, Witestone. *See* Winston
Wenesistune. *See* Wonston
Weregraves, i, *note* 418
Wergeborne. *See* Warnborough
Werildeham. *See* Worldham
Weringetone. *See* Winkton
Werste. *See* Ewhurst
Westbury in East and West Meon [Wesberie], i, 481*a*
Westmeone. *See* Meon, West
Weston, i, *note* 482*b*

Weston Patrick [Westone], i, 493*b*
Westover in Calbourn [Cauborne], i, 519*b*
Weststrattonam. *See* Stratton, West
Weyhill, i, *notes* 473*b*, 484*b*
Wheatley, i, *note* 450*a*
Wherwell [Wherewellam], i, 419, *note* 418. *See also* Fullerton
Whippingham [Wipingham, Witingeham], i, 409, 459*a*, 520*a*, 525*a*
Whitchurch [Witcerce], i, 443, 464*b*. *See also* Witnal
Whitcomb [Witecome], i, 519*b*
Whitfield [Witesfel], i, 520*b*
Whitwell. *See* Whitcomb
Wica. *See* Week
Wickham [Wicheham], i, 480*a*
Widley. *See* Cosham
Wield [Walde], i, 463*a*
Wigarestun, i, 514*b*
Wight, Isle of [With, Wit], i, 403, 405, 407-9, 414-16, 420, 425-7, 433-4, 441, 445-6, 454*a*-5*b*, 457*a*-9*a*, 476*a*, 510*b*, 517*a*-26*b*, 535, *note* 422, 507*b*
Wildehel. *See* Willhall
Willhall [Wildehet], i, 497*b*
Wilmingham in Freshwater [Wilmingeham], i, 517*b*
Wimborne (Dors.), i, 427, *notes* 479*a*, 507*b*, 509*a*
Wimeringes. *See* Wymering
Winchester[Wincestre, Wintonia], i, 399, 400, 408, 410, 413, 415, 419, 421, 426-32, 436, 444, 453*a*, 453*b*, 456*a*, 457*a*, 461*b*, 468*b*, 472*b*, 474*b*, 475*b*, 477*b*, 481*a*, 489*b*, 494*b*, 496*a*, 503*b*, 504*a*, 505*a*, 515*b*, 527-37, *note* 438 ; Guild Hall, i, 531 ; streets, i, 530, 535, 537
Winchfield [Winesflet], i, 472*b*, *notes* 480*a*, 504*b*
Windenaie. *See* Witnal
Winesflet. *See* Winchfield
Winesflot. *See* Winslade
Winhall Farm, i, *note* 450*a*
Winkton in Christchurch [Weringetone], i, 496*b*
Winnal, i, *note* 463*b*
Winslade [Winesflot], i, 480*a*. *See also* Kempshott
Winston [Wenechetone, Weristetone, Witestone], i, 459*a*, 522*a*, 523*b*

Wintonia. *See* Winchester
Witcerce. *See* Whitchurch
Witesfel. *See* Whitfield
Witingeham. *See* Whippingham
Witnal in Whitchurch [Windenaie], i, 464*b*
Wodecote. *See* Clerewoodcote
Wolnetune. *See* Walhampton
Wolverton [Ulvretune], i, 502*a*
Wolverton in Brading [Ulwartone], i, 458*b*. *See also* Woolverton
Wonston [Wenesistune], i, 467*a*. *See also* Cranbourne, Norton, Sutton Scotney
Woodcote [Odecote], i, 431, 438, 499*a*, 534, *note* 481*b*
Woodcott in Bramdean, i, *note* 503*a*
Woodmancote [Udemancote,] i, 443, 469*b*
Woolbeeding (Sussex), i, *note* 427
Woolston in St. Mary extra [Olvestune], i, 501*a*
Woolverton in Shorwell or Brading [Ulvredestune], i, 524*a*. *See also* Wolverton
Wootton (I.W.) [Odetone], i, 459*a*
Wootton in Milton [Odetune], i, 515*a*
Wootton St. Lawrence [Odetone], i, 468*a*, 486*a*
Worcester, i, *note* 534
Worldham(?) [Wardham], i, 510*a*
Worldham, East [Estwerldham, Werildeham], i, 430, 501*b*
Worsley, i, *note* 409
Worthy [Ordie], i, 466*b*, 489*b*, 494*b*
Worthy, Abbot's [Ordie], i, 470*a*
Worthy, Headbourne [Ordie], i, 428, 434, 436, 489*b*
Worthy, King's [Ordie], i, 452*b*
Wortinge [Wortinges], i, 470*b*
Wrefordi, i, *note* 418
Wroxall [Warochesselle], i, 458*b*
Wymering [Wimeringes], i, 402, 451*b*. *See also* Cosham

Yaldhurst in Milford [Cildeest], i, 514*b*
Yar, i, 434
Yarmouth [Ermud], i, 525*b*
Yateley(?) [Effelle], i, 483*b*. *See also* Cove, Minley
Yaverland [Everelant, Evreland], i, 403, 457*b*, 521*b*
York, i, 432

GENERAL INDEX

NOTE.—The Domesday Introduction and Translation are indexed separately. The articles on Geology, Palaeontology, Botany and Zoology being usually in the form of lists are not indexed. The following less obvious abbreviations are used :—adv., advowson ; b., brother ; cast., castle ; chant., chantry ; chap., chapel ; coll., college ; ct., court ; ctss., countess ; d., daughter ; dchss., duchess ; dk., duke ; D. and C., Dean and Chapter ; f., father ; hund., hundred ; ind., industries ; man., manor ; mchnss., marchioness ; m., mother ; mon., monastery ; pop., population ; sch., school ; sis., sister ; sts., streets ; vsct., viscountess ; w., wife.

Aas, Felicia, ii, 132 ; Hen., ii, 317 ; Will., ii, 278
Abadam, see Ap Adam
Abaginge, see Bagwich
Abarowe, see Beere and Burgh
Abban, John, v, 146
Abbas, Sir Geoff., v, 169
Abbas Aunt, see Abbotts Ann
Abbess Grange (Leckford), iv, 446, 447
Abbess Lodging (Romsey), iv, 453
Abbess Roding (Essex), iv, 370
Abbess Wood (Romsey), iv, 452
Abbey Mill (Romsey), iv, 455
Abbies Bridge (Winchester), v, 31
Abbodeston, see Abbotstone
Abbot, fam., see Abbott
Abbots Ann, see Abbotts Ann
Abbot's Barton (Winchester), v, 1 ; man., ii, 114 ; v, 20 ; mill, v, 36, 49
Abbot's Barton Farm (Winchester), v, 20
Abbot's Copse (Priors Dean), iv, 436
Abbot's Mill (Kingsclere), iv, 250
Abbotstone, iv, 122, 188, 192-5
Abbotstone Down, v, 545
Abbots Worthy (Kings Worthy), iii, 245, 389 ; iv, 415, 430, 432
Abbots Worthy House (Kings Worthy), iv, 430
Abbott (Abbot), Edw., iii, 318 ; Geo., archbp., ii, 115, 322 ; iv, 36, 41 ; Hen., iv, 497 ; Maurice, iv, 367 ; Thos., iv, 628 ; Will., iii, 447 ; W., iii, 271
Abbotts Ann, ii, 16 ; iv, 333, 334-6, 400 ; man., ii, 121 ; iv, 334, 353, 413 ; pop., vi, 438 ; Rom. rem., i, 300, 343 ; sch., ii, 395 ; iv, 336
Abbott's Common (Romsey), iv, 452
Abbott's Wood (Romsey), iv, 452, 468
Abedestone, see Adgestone
Abel, John, ii, 218
Abergavenny, Geo. Nevill, Ld., iv, 151, 441 ; Hen. Nevill, Ld., iv, 441
Aberval, Walt. de, iv, 82
Abie, ii, 376
Abingdon, Willoughby Bertie, earl of, iv, 69
Abingdon, de, John, ii, 160 ; Pet., ii, 209 ; iv, 620
Abingdon Abbey, ii, 7 ; iv, 288, 607 n
Abinger, Ld., v, 134
Abington, —, v, 554
Ablingeton, ii, 163
Abraham, v, 33

Abraham's (Hartley Wintney), iv, 79, 80
Abshot, man., ii, 186
Acangre, see Oakhanger
Acanthopterygii, i, 197
Accleghe, see Oakley, North
Acclei (Damerham), iv, 587 n
Ace, see Azo
Achaden, Thos., bp. of, ii, 193
Achangre, see Oakhanger
Achard, iv, 7 n
Achard, Rob., iv, 243
Acheson, Martha, iv, 363
Achonry, Sim., bp. of, ii, 37, 180, 232
A'Court, Eliz., v, 288 ; Will., v, 224 ; see also Court
A'Court Holmes, Will. H. A., v, 140, 160, 230, 288 ; see also Holmes-A'Court
Acres, Joan de, iii, 247
Acridiodea, i, 110
Acton (de), Alban, iv, 71 ; Edw., iv, 71, 205 ; Isabel, iv, 604 ; Jas., iv, 139 ; Joan, v, 118, 604 ; (Sir) John, iv, 226, 276, 604 ; v, 118 ; Jos., iv, 71 ; Mich., iv, 276
Aculeata, i, 114
Adam, of Northampton, v, 45 ; abbot of Titchfield, ii, 182, 186
Adam, ap., see Ap Adam
Adames Dene (Longparish), iv, 406
Adams, Edm., v, 484 ; H., v, 391, 398 ; Jem, v, 548 ; John, ii, 81 ; Sarah, iv, 614 ; Theoph., v, 215 ; Rev. Will., v, 155, 156 ; —, ii, 453
Adamson, Rich., v, 520
Adbury Park (Burghclere), iv, 277
Adderton, see Arreton
Addesley (Lyndhurst), iv, 631
Addington, Hen., ii, 354
Addison, Mrs., iv, 295
Adelard, prior, ii, 160, 163
Adeline, the jester, iv, 360
Adelingham, see Ellingham
Adeliza, queen, v, 48 n
Adgestone, man. (Brading), v, 160
Adgeton, v, 140
Adhelm, v, 477
Adherton, see Arreton
Ad Lapidem, i, 380 ; iii, 478 n
Admodesham, John de, v, 481 n
Admundesthorp, Will., v, 305
Adnitt, Jesse, v, 127
Adrintone, see Arreton
Adstoke, see Stoke (St. Mary Bourne)
Advent Tyrrells, see Northavon
Ady, Eliz., ii, 511
Ædmundestorp, see Edmundsthorp Benham

Ælfeah [Ælfheah], iii, 76 ; iv, 6
Ælfgyfu, see Emma, queen
Ælfheres Stapol (Fyfield), iv, 366
Ælflaed (Athelfleda, Elfleda, Ethelfled), ii, 6, 126, 132 ; iv, 460, 587, 592
Ælfric (Ælfrige, Alfric), iii, 309 ; iv, 617 ; abbot, ii, 121 ; iv, 251 ; ealdorman, v, 296 ; seal of, i, 397
Ælfsige, bp. of Winchester, iv, 6, 277, 334
Ælfswith, iv, 251
Ælfweard (Elfward), ii, 116 ; iv, 366
Ælfwine, iii, 76 ; iv, 251
Ælmer, see Athelmar
Ælnod, see Æthelnod
Ælsinus, Psalter of, ii, 240
Ælwacre, iv, 198
Ælwi (Alwi), iv, 22, 35, 501, 506 ; the priest, iv, 564, 568
Aese, John de, iii, 104
Æsemeresworth, see Ashmansworth
Ætheldryth, iv, 213
Æthelingadene, ii, 474
Æthelnod (Ælnod, Alnod, Alnoth, Ethelnod), iv, 123, 232, 295, 560, 620 ; v, 158, 173 ; abbot, ii, 121 ; the priest, v, 98
Æthelnod Cild, iv, 231
Æthelric, iv, 239
Æthelwold, see Ethelwold
Afford, ch., ii, 188
Afford, water of, see Ashford Water
Afton, v, 210
Afton, man. (Freshwater), v, 242
Afton (de), (Sir) Rich., v, 213, 242 ; Will., v, 242
Afton Down (Freshwater), v, 240
Afton House (Freshwater), v, 535
Agar, Edw. L., v, 116 ; Hen. J., iv, 564 ; Sidney J., iv, 580, 602, 604, 606 ; Welbore E., iv, 606
Agates, v, 453
Agemund, iv, 374, 535, 536, 549, 555, 598
Aghneld, Nich., v, 421
Agilbert, ii, 2
Agneil, see Aygnel
Agnes, abbess of Nunnaminster, ii, 126 ; v, 475, 476
Agriculture, v, 493-511
Aguillun, Isa., ii, 506 ; Mab., iv, 492 n ; Marg., ii, 506 ; iii, 137 ; v, 91 ; Maud, iv, 492 n ; Rob., ii, 506 ; iii, 137 ; v, 91 ; Will., ii, 506 ; iii, 137 ; iv, 492 n
Aidstone, see Adgestone
Ailesbury, earl of, ii, 349 ; mqss. of, v, 532

Ailesbury [Aylesbury], Sir Thos., v, 378
Ailward [Alward], iii, 249, 269 ; v, 23
Ailward, Aileward fam., see Aylward
Airaf, iv, 184
Aire, Bald. de, iv, 129 ; see also Ayres
Airye, Ad., iv, 226
Aisheley, farm (Dorset), ii, 149
Aisshe, man., ii, 159
Aistulf, king, i, 391
Aitard, Geoff., v, 181
Aitken, Jas., v, 393
Aiulf, iv, 542
Akyr (Eversley), iv, 33
Alalei, v, 164
Alan, iv, 314 ; v, 49 ; prior, ii, 222, 223
Albany, dk. of, v, 201
Albemarle, Isabel, ctss. of, ii, 154, 230 ; iii, 171 ; iv, 553, 597, 598, 640, 641, 643, 645 ; v, 81, 91, 94, 96, 140, 141, 168, 181, 183, 184, 187, 213, 222, 224, 226, 230, 231, 234, 242 n, 256, 257, 259, 260, 273, 274, 275, 279, 284, 287, 312 n ; Philippa, dchss. of, v, 222 n ; dks. of : Edw., v, 222 ; Geo., iii, 178 ; iv, 346 ; v, 382 ; earls of : v, 220 ; Bald. de Betun, iv, 213 ; Thos. de Fortibus, iv, 213 ; Will. de Fortibus, iii, 166, 171 ; iv, 213 ; v, 91
Albemarle [Aumarle], de, Agnes, v, 96 ; Eliz., v, 160 ; Geoff, v, 96, 160 ; Iseult, v, 160 ; Reg., v, 95 ; Will., v, 95, 96, 160, 192, 238 ; fam., iv, 597
Alberoni, card., v, 388
Albert, iv, 531 n ; king of I. of W., i, 391 ; of Tisa, ii, 193 ; prince consort, v, 199, 200
Albery, Thos., iii, 58
Albigneye, see Daubeney
Albin, J., v, 461
Albini, see Daubeney
Alchorne [Alcorn, Alcorne], Alex., v, 160, 280 ; Grace, v, 160 ; —, v, 471 ; fam., v, 147
Aldbourn, man., ii, 168
Alder, Rev. Gilb., iv, 174 ; Rev. Herb., iv, 174 ; St. John, iii, 144 ; Mrs., iv, 174
Alderbury (Plaitford), iv, 542
Aldermaston (Berks.), ii, 227
Aldermoresmede (Timsbury), iv, 486
Aldershot, ii, 102 ; iv, 1, 2-5, 6 ; v, 433, 450, 546 ; adv., iv, 4 ; camp., iv, 2 ; char., iv, 4 ; ch., iv, 3 ; fishing, v, 467 n ; hosps., iv, 2, 5 ; man., iv, 2, 3 ; Nonconf., iv, 4 ; peat, v, 454 ; pop., v, 443 ; pottery manuf., v, 491 ; Rom. Cath., iv, 4 ; schs., ii, 395 ; soldiers' institute, iv, 2 ; Wellington's statue, iv, 2
Aldershot beagles, v, 542
Aldershot Lodge, (Aldershot), iv, 2
Aldershot Park (Aldershot), iv, 2
Aldersnapp, iii, 78
Alderson, Thos., iv, 437
Alderton (Wilts.), iv, 514
Alderton, Joan, iv, 94 ; Rich., iv, 94
Aldgate Nunnery, v, 171
Aldington, ii, 160, 163
Aldington, Hen. of, v, 44
Aldred, archbp. of York, iv, 506
Aldret, iv, 179
Aldridge, Ellen, iv, 548 ; Geo., v, 98 ; Matth., v, 98 ; Will., iv, 548
Aldridge Hill, ii, 451

Aldrigemore (Timsbury), iv, 486
Aldwark (Yorks), iv, 34
Aldwin, iv, 584
Aldworth, Rich., ii, 377 ; iv, 140
Ale-conner (ale-taster), v, 473
Alen, fam., see Allen
Alestan, iv, 52
Alexander, Edith, iv, 394 ; Will., iv, 393, 394
Aleyn, fam., see Allen
Alfgar, iv, 587
Alfinton, see Alvington
Alfnoth, abbot, ii, 121
Alfred, king, ii, 5, 116, 122, 252 ; iv, 183, 288, 587 ; v, 295 ; statue, v, 5
Alfred, iii, 424 ; iv, 288 ; the butcher, v, 86
Alfric, see Ælfric
Alfsig, the goldsmith, v, 220
Algae, i, 79-80
Algar, iv, 579, 619
Algar, Rich., iv, 226
Algiers, bombardment of, v, 401
Alhmund, bp. of Winchester, iv, 27
Alice, abbess of Nunnaminster, ii, 126 ; abbess of Wilton, v, 229 ; prioress of Wintney, ii, 149
Alice Holt Forest, ii, 431, 432, 434, 440, 441, 442, 453, 462, 483, 490, 498, 515, 518, 519 ; iv, 7, 27 ; Rom. rem., i, 306
Alice la Burgeise, v. Hen. Butcher, v, 46
Aliners, Thos., v, 164
Alington, Ld., v, 547, 548, 553
Alington, Julius, iv, 167
Alis [Aliz], Emma, ii, 221 ; Rog., ii, 221 ; iii, 485 ; v, 304 n ; Thos., iii, 485 ; Will., ii, 160 ; iii, 485
Alison, Rev. Meyrick O., iv, 384
Alisotescroft (Eversley), iv, 33
Alissislond (Bramley), iv, 141
Aliz, fam., see Alis
Alkin, Eliz. [Parliament Joan], v, 382
Allbrook (Otterbourne, iii, 440
Allbrook farm (Otterbourne), iii, 443
All Cannings (Wilts.), ii, 122 ; man., ii, 55, 125
Allcroft, Walt., iv, 319
Allder, Thos., iv, 140
Allectus, v, 359
Allen, riv., iv, 586, 590, 592
Allen [Alen, Aleyn, Allin], Chas., v, 144, 145, 184, 188 ; Dan., v, 487 ; Ed., v, 391 ; Edw., iv, 471 n ; Fran., iii, 286 ; Joan, v, 275 ; J., v, 391 ; J. R., ii, 236 ; Launce. B., iv, 622 n ; Mary B., iv, 622 n ; Rich., ii, 212 ; iv, 20 ; v, 273, 486 ; Rob., iv, 28 ; v, 570 ; Sarah, iv, 28 ; Capt. Thos., iii, 184 ; Thos., iv, 20, 383 ; v, 487 ; Thos. W., iv, 286 ; Will., ii, 375 ; iii, 207 ; W. B., v, 537
Allenford, iv, 592
Alley, Sir John, iv, 185 n
All Hallon field (W. Tytherley), iv, 524
Allingham, Will., iv, 639
Allington, iii, 481 ; man., iii, 485 ; Rom. coins, i, 343
All Souls' College (Oxf.), ii, 262, 292, 319 ; iv, 383
Allwardis (Heckfield), iv, 45
Almar [Almer], iv, 438 ; v, 173 n
Alneto, de, John, iii, 448 ; Steph., iii, 448 ; Thos ; iii, 448
Alnod, Alnoth, see Æthelnod
Alnwick (Northumb.), ii, 183
Alphege [Elphage], archbp. of Canterbury, ii, 6, 7, 8 ; v, 51
Alpher, Rich., iv, 598

Alre, riv., iii, 41, 304, 349
Alreham, Will. of, v, 109
Alresford [New Alresford], ii, 21, 23, 62, 71, 73, 96, 101, 102 ; iii, 37, 302, 346, 348-54 ; v, 39, 306, 311, 324, 328 n, 331, 343, 423, 430, 434, 513, 544 ; adv., iii, 353 ; char., iii, 353 ; ch., iii, 352 ; fair, v, 417, 435 ; ind., v, 454, 455 n, 482 ; man., v, 418 ; mills, v, 49 n, 478, 479 ; pop., v, 437 ; Rom. rem., i, 324 ; schs., ii, 387, 391, 395, 401, 402
Alresford, Old, i, 306, 346 ; iii, 302, 304, 349 ; adv., iii, 306 ; char., iii, 306 ; ch., iii, 306 ; man., iii, 304 ; pop., v, 447 ; Rom. rem., i, 306
Alresford (de), Nich., ii, 181 ; Thos., iii, 56
Alric, iv, 47, 202, 525, 618 ; v, 191
Alsi [Elsi], iii, 142 ; iv, 22, 35, 47, 146, 186, 549 ; v, 126, 172, 212, 218 ; abbot, iv, 419 ; the priest, v, 126
Alt, Tympany, ii, 113
Alta, John, ii, 120
Altei, iv, 115
Altham, Jas., iii, 387, 388 ; v, 265
Alton, ii, 21, 30, 62, 63, 71, 96, 101, 102, 121, 251, 471, 473-83, 485, 486, 487, 488, 492, 510, 515 ; v, 324, 409, 416, 418, 423, 428, 430, 431, 434, 450 ; char., ii, 482, 483 ; ch., ii, 117, 118, 514, 517 ; fairs, v, 417, 435 ; house of industry, v, 488 ; ind., v, 453, 461, 474, 482, 484, 488, 490 ; man., ii, 114, 474 ; v, 2 n ; mill, v, 490 ; pop, v, 437 ; Rom. rem., i, 294, 306 ; schs., ii, 367, 387, 482 ; iv, 13 n
Alton, Little, man. (Wilts.), ii, 114
Alton, hund., ii, 471-523 ; iii, 3 n ; iv, 67 ; v, 328 n, 331, 336
Alton, riv., see Wey
Alton, pass of, ii, 473 ; v, 39
Alton [Aulton], de, John, ii, 30 ; iv, 7 ; Nich., iii, 412 ; Walt., ii, 190, 191 ; Will., ii, 115, 190, 258
Alton Eastbrook, ii, 471, 473, 474, 480 ; man., ii, 121
Alton Priors (Wilts.), ii, 474
Alton Westbrook, ii, 471, 473, 474, 477, 480, 493, 509, 513 ; fair, ii, 477
Alum Bay, v, 240, 453
Alum Chine (Bournemouth), v, 134
Alum Green (Minstead), iv, 635 ; v, 442 n
Alum trade, v, 453
Alured [Alvred], iv, 174, 211 ; the priest, iv, 248, 270 ; the reeve, iv, 588
Alver, riv., iii, 218
Alverstoke, ii, 108 ; iii, 140, 202-8, 245 ; v, 331, 356, 419, 431 ; char., iii, 207 ; ch., ii, 63, 68 ; iii, 206 ; deanery, ii, 101, 102 ; man., ii, 20, 109 ; iii, 203 ; pop., v, 441 ; sch., ii, 395
Alverstone (Brading), v, 291 ; brick and tile works, v, 466 ; man., v, 160, 163 ; sch., v, 157
Alverstone, Ld., v, 157, 160, 180, 195
Alviet, iv, 240
Alvington (Carisbrooke), v, 222, 227, 228, 229, 270
Alvred, see Alured
Alvric, iv, 8, 42, 57, 63, 141, 625 ; v, 81 n, 116, 117, 120, 213, 248, 274, 288 ; the priest, iv, 281, 301
Alwara, iii, 203
Alward, see Ailward
Alwele, Edw., v, 49

Alwi, *see* Ælwi
Alwin [Alwine, Alwyn, Aylwin], ii, 492, 518; iii, 246; iv, 15, 109, 225, 377 *n*, 391, 393, 443, 553; v, 46, 124; abbot, ii, 117, 121; bp., ii, 8, 9, 216; iii, 65, 384, 428; v, 55, 56, 298
Alwin Forst, v, 274
Alwrico, v, 100 *n*
Alwyn, Thos., ii, 284, 366
Alyar, iv, 542
Alyffes Water (Upper Clatford), iv, 360
Alymor, Agnes, ii, 125
Alynton, Rob., ii, 41, 42; Sir Rog. de, iv, 211
Ambersham, North and South, iii, 63, 77-78; v, 437 *n*
Amberwood (Fordingbridge), iv, 568; Rom. rem., i, 326
Ambledune, *see* Hambledon
Ambley (Hurstbourne Tarrant), iv, 321
Ambresbury, iv, 631
Ambrose, Adml. John, iv, 279; John, iv, 279
Ameredith, Hercules, iv, 317
Amersham (Bucks.), iv, 215 *n*
Amery farm (Alton), ii, 474
Amesbury (Wilts.), ii, 25, 202, 420; iv, 85, 115; v, 228; ind., v, 453
Amesbury Priory (Wilts.), iv, 514, 525, 526, 527, 533, 554, 555
Amfrey, Hen., v, 112; Nig., v, 112; Rob., v, 112; Will., v, 112
Amherst, Will., v, 192 *n*; Lt.-gen., v, 190 *n*
Amice, abbess, ii, 132
Amisius, iv, 45 *n*
Ammys, Rich., v, 172
Amondsham, Gid., iii, 483
Ampfield, iii, 401, 417, 421; v, 528; sch., ii, 395
Amphineura, i, 103
Amphyllis, abbess of Godstow, iv, 256
Amport, ii, 16, 63; iv, 333, 337-44, 359, 362 *n*, 385; adv., iv, 344; char., iv, 344; ch., iv, 343; mans., iv, 337-9; mills, iv, 339; Nonconf., iv, 344; pop., v, 438; sch., ii, 395; iv, 344
Amport House, iv, 337
Ampthill, Ld., v, 198 *n*
Anabaptists, ii, 79
Anacanthini, i, 199
Anastasius, prior, ii, 141
Andely, *see* Daundely
Anderdon, Jas. P., v, 100
Anderson, Const., iv, 9; Edm., iii, 312; Jos., iv, 448, 450; v, 540; Sam., iv, 9
Anderson-Pelham, Major Cecil H., v, 174, 194, 202; Evelyn C., v, 174, 194, 202
Anderton, Rob., ii, 80, 81
Andevere, Laur., v, 39
Andover, ii, 21, 26, 62, 63, 71, 79, 96, 101, 102, 168, 219, 251; iv, 320, 333, 342, 345-58, 361, 362, 363, 367, 373, 377, 383, 396, 397, 406, 450, 528; v, 296, 303, 311, 318, 409, 423, 428, 430, 431, 434, 450; adv., iv, 355; chant., iv, 355; chap., iv, 355; char., iv, 356-58; ch., ii, 219, 220; iv, 354, 355; coins, i, 343; fair, iv, 346; v, 435; hosps., iv, 345, 356; v, 418; ind., v, 351, 427, 454, 455, 474, 476, 482, 484, 489; mans., iv, 351-54; mkts. and fairs, iv, 350, 351; mills, iv, 351; Nonconf., iv, 356; racing, v, 543; Rom. rem., i, 294,

Andover (*cont.*)
304, 320-2, 331, 343; iv, 346; sch., ii, 395; iv, 357
Andover, hund., iv, 333; v, 331
Andover Canal, v, 452, 454
Andover Down Farm (Andover), i, 302
Andover harriers, v, 537
Andover Priory, ii, 41, 106, 219-21, 289; iv, 355
Andredsweald, i, 377, 380, 384, 392, 394; ii, 11, 412; v, 295
Andrew, abbot of Quarr, ii, 139; the merchant, v, 479; prior of Carisbrooke, ii, 231; reeve, iv, 211
Andrew, John, ii, 157, 158; Thos., iv, 212 *n*, 213, 217; Will. de, ii, 109, 115
Andrewes [Andrews], Const., iv, 208, 283; Dummer, iii, 484; Eliz., iv, 283; John, iv, 14; Kath., iii, 269; iv, 208, 283; Launc., bp., ii, 87, 480; iii, 84, 297; v, 154; Phil., v, 177, 231; Rich., iv, 208, 283; Thos., ii, 387, 515; iv, 159; Ursula, iv, 208, 283; W. G., ii, 197
Androsmede (Timsbury), iv, 486
Andwell, ii, 222; iv, 113 *n*, 149, 150, 156, 176, 177, 178; ind., v, 455; man., ii, 225; iv, 176, 177; mills, iv, 151, 176, 178; pop., v, 439
Andwell Priory, ii, 41, 106, 223-25, 288; iv, 150, 151, 153, 176, 177-8; brother Rob. of, ii, 222
Andyke (Barton Stacey), iv, 417
Anesia (de), Rich., iv, 510; Rob., iv, 510
Angell, John, iii, 241
Angers, Will., bp. of, ii, 146
Angles, i, 375, 376, 377; ii, 413
Anglesey, earls of:—Arth. Annesley, iv, 16; Chris. Villiers, v, 228; John Annesley, iv, 16; Rich. Annesley, iv, 16
Angling, v, 560, 568
Anglo-Saxon remains, i, 373; inscriptions, ii, 234
Anglote, Rob., iv, 315
Angot, iii, 225
Angot, Hugh, iv, 338
Anjou, Geoff., count of, v, 291, 306
Anmore, man. (Hambledon), iii, 90, 98, 239
Ann, Little (Abbott's Ann), ii, 132, 137; iv, 279, 333, 334, 335-6, 400, 402, 411 *n*
Ann [Anne], de, Hen., iv, 339, 344, 385 *n*; John, iv, 340, 342, 359, 366; Mich., iv, 367; v, 39; Phil., iv, 340, 359; Sybil, iv, 342; Thos., ii, 20; iv, 340, 342, 366, 367; *see also* Cholderton
Anna, Will., v, 173
Anna Bek, de Becco, de Bec-Man, *see* Monxton
Annadown, Hen., bp. of, ii, 129; Thos., bp. of, ii, 37
Anna Savage, *see* Sarson
Anna Valley, iv, 334
Anne, queen, iv, 193; v, 12, 88; statue, v, 8
Anne (of Bohemia) queen, ii, 43; iv, 89
Anne (Boleyn) queen, iv, 161
Anne (of Cleves), queen, iii, 375, 376, 456; iv, 259, 261, 265, 348, 428, 553, 584, 598, 618; v, 228 *n*, 277
Anne (of Denmark), queen, iv, 516 *n*
Anne, fam., *see* Ann
Annebault, Claude d', v, 327, 374

Annecy, Rich. de, ii, 521, 522
Annesley, Arth., iv, 16; Fran., iv, 509; Jas., iv, 16; John, iv, 16; Rich., iv, 16; Thos., ii, 167
Annetts, John, iv, 339 *n*
Anniler, de, Hilary, iv, 498 *n*, 501; Rob., iv, 498 *n*, 501
Ann Savage, *see* Sarson
Anschitel, iii, 168, 372, 414; iv, 149, 153
Anselm, archbp., ii, 10, 11, 216
Ansfrid, iv, 331
Anslevile, Will. de, v, 129
Anson, Ld. Geo., v, 389, 392, 393
Anstey (Alton), ii, 187, 471, 473, 477, 478; v, 413
Antelope cricket ground (Southampton), v, 574
Anthmanys (Sherborne St. John), iv, 158
Anthozoa, i, 96
Anton, riv., i, 331; iv, 359, 377, 381, 411; v, 560, 562
Anton, East (Smannell), iv, 345, 346, 357, 358 *n*
Antone, *see* Southampton
Antrim, ctss. of, iv, 36; Randal MacDonnell, earl of, iv, 36
Antrobus, Sir Edm., v, 532; Thos., iii, 118, 120, 318
Ants, i, 114
Antt, Bridg. F., iv, 476; Geo., iv, 476; Jane L., iv, 476
Anvers, of, Reg., v, 45; Thos., v, 45
Ap Adam [Abadam, Badeham, de Pageham], Eliz., iv, 536, 589; John, iv, 536, 537, 589; Thos., iv, 537, 589; *see also* Pagham
Apelderford, *see* Appleford
Aplegarth, *see* Applegarth
Apless (Hambledon), iii, 239
Apodes, i, 202
Apola, John de, ii, 134
Appelman, Nich., v, 481
Apperly, — [Nimrod], iv, 167 *n*; v, 515, 516
Appleby, John, v, 127
Apple Farm (North Sandown), v, 166
Appleford, man. (Godshill), ii, 180; v, 161, 171-2, 175; chap., v, 177
Appleford, North (Godshill), v, 172 *n*
Appleford [Apelderford], de, Steph., iv, 338; Will., iii, 84, 101; iv, 338
Applegarth [Aplegarth], Helen, iii, 58; Humph., iii, 58; John, iii, 22; Will., iii, 58
Appleshaw, ii, 137, 163; iv, 333, 337, 340, 341, 344, 358-9, 368, pop., v, 438; Rom. rem., i, 295; sch., ii, 395
Applestead, ii, 164
Appleton [Eppelton], Alice, iv, 474; John, iv, 474; v, 486
Appley (St. Helens), v, 166, 192, 268
Appley Towers (St. Helens), v, 190
Appuldercombe, man. (Godshill), ii, 231, 232; iv, 271; v, 161, 171, 183, 202, 237, 247 *n*, 535
Appuldercombe Priory, ii, 41, 106, 231-2
Ap-Rice, John, ii, 136, 151
Apsanger (Kingsclere), iv, 250
Apse, man. (Newchurch), ii, 152, 154, 159; v, 172, 180, 184
Apse Heath (Newchurch), v, 177
Apsley, Sir Edw., v, 471
Apsley Farm (Hurstbourne Priors), iv, 288
Apulderfield (Kent), iv, 358 *n*
Apulgate, Isold, ii, 125

Aquila, *see* Laigle
Arachnida, i, 165
Arborfield (Berks.), iv, 180
Arbuthnot, Edm., iv, 292, 294;
    Eliz., iv, 292; —, Lady, iv, 292
Archdeacon [Arcedeacon], Cath.,
    v. 280; Chaloner, v, 280, 282
Archer, Andr., Ld., iv, 578; Thos.,
    Ld., iv, 578
Archer, Andr., iv, 578; Anne, iv,
    578; Eliz., iv, 563, 578, 579;
    Eliz. A., iv, 578; Fred., v, 544,
    549; Hen., iv, 561, 562, 578;
    Maria, iv, 578; Rich. le, iv, 506;
    v, 305; Sarah, iv, 578; Thos. (le),
    ii, 187, 188; iv, 561, 563, 578
Archer Lodge (Sherfield-upon-Lod-
    don), iv, 103
Arderne, Will., iv, 94
Ardfert, John, bp. of, ii, 223; iv,
    179
Areton, Will., ii, 388
Argentein [Argenton], de, John, v,
    155, 228; Peverel, v, 230; Will.,
    v, 230
Aria, Lewis, iii, 201
Arle, riv., *see* Meon
Armada, Spanish, v, 377
Armagh, Mich. Boyle, archbp. of,
    iv, 54
Armorer, Thos., iii, 512
Armsworth (Old Alresford), iii,
    304; v, 515
Armsworth House (Old Alresford),
    iv, 304
Army, Hants. regiments, v, 357
Arnald, *see* Arnold
Arnewood (Lymington), iv, 646;
    v, 81, 82, 89 n, 111, 114
Arnewood [Arnewode, Arnwood],
    Edw., v, 120; Ernemude, v,
    113; Jas., v, 114; Sim., of, v,
    114; Thos., ii, 163
Arney [Ernys], Alice, v, 200;
    Christine, iv, 224, 579; Joan, iv,
    224, 579; John, iv, 579, 617; v,
    200; Kath., iv, 579; Nich., v,
    200; fam., iv, 573
Arneys (Fordingbridge), iv, 573
Arniss farm (Fordingbridge), iv,
    573
Arnold, iv, 367
Arnold [Arnald], Chas., ii, 511;
    Edm., iv, 352; Fran., iv, 20;
    Grey, iv, 476; John, v, 49; Marg.,
    iv, 476; Matth., ii, 348; Thos.,
    ii, 354, 355; v, 198; Will., v, 254
Arnwood, *see* Arnewood
Arreton, ii, 25, 69, 180, 391; v, 138,
    139-51, 276; adv., ii, 21; v, 150;
    char., v, 150; ch., ii, 230, 231;
    v, 148; man., ii, 137, 138, 139;
    v, 140; Nonconf., v, 150; pop.,
    v, 448; schs., ii, 406, 408; v, 151
Arreton Down, i, 316, 386
Arreton Manor House (Arreton), v,
    141
Arreton Shute, v, 140
Arrow Croft (Chawton), ii, 498
Arsic, John, v, 241; Marg., v, 241
Arsk, Joan de, v, 281
Arthingshoote, *see* Hardingshute
Arthur, prince of Wales, iv, 72,
    656; v, 176, 321
Arthur, Eliz., iv, 373; Hen., iv,
    373; John, iii, 288
Arthur's Hame (Romsey), iv, 457 n
Artone, Alice, ii, 129
Arundel, constitutions of, ii, 45
Arundel [Arundell], ctsses. of:—
    Alesia [Alice], iii, 149; iv, 150;
    Marg., iv, 545; earls of, ii, 513;
    iv, 637; v, 364, 366, 367; Edm.,
    iv, 151; v, 173; Hen., ii, 476;
    iii, 130, 131; iv, 572, 627, 632 n;

Arundel (*cont.*)
    Hugh, iii, 95; Rich., ii, 475;
    iii, 158; iv, 388; v, 313; Thos.,
    ii, 519; iv, 545; Will., ii, 476,
    519; iii, 83 n, 95, 411, 507; iv,
    468, 540, 545, 632
Arundell of Wardour, Ladies:
    Anne, v, 93; Kath., iii, 78; Lds.,
    v, 87, 467; Hen., iv, 608, 617;
    v, 93, 120; Jas., iv, 23; Thos.,
    v, 86, 92, 93
Arundel [Arundell] (of, de), Ad.
    ii, 139; Anne, iii, 135, 419;
    Cath., iv, 531; Edm., ii, 207, 208;
    Eliz., Lady, iv, 531 n; Geoff., iv,
    47, 225; Hugh, ii, 495; iii, 383;
    iv, 150, 152, 156; Jas. E., iv,
    23; Sir John, iii, 496, 507; iv,
    531; v, 366; John, ii, 519; iii,
    419; v, 314, 522; Marg., ii, 519;
    Rob., iii, 383; iv, 225; Rog., iv,
    225, 226; Sir Rich., iii, 498;
    Thos., archbp., ii, 44, 45, 46,
    171, 174; Thos., ii, 497; iii, 83;
    v, 99 n; Will., ii, 497; iii, 95,
    135, 383; iv, 156; fam., iv, 608
Arvald, king of Wight, i, 380
Ascelina, ii, 221
Aschebourne, T., ii, 290
Asclepiodotus, v, 359
Asebrugges (Longparish), iv, 408
Ash [Asshe, Fraxino] (de), Hen.,
    iii, 445; John, ii, 161; iii, 392,
    396; Pet., iii, 396; Will., v, 148
Ashburnham, Jane, iv, 393; John,
    v, 347; Will., iv, 393
Ashburton, Louisa Baring, Lady,
    iv, 511, 542, 558 n; Lds., iv,
    184, 187, 191, 196; v, 557, 558;
    Alex. Baring, iii, 395, 398; iv,
    186, 193, 541, 658; v, 248;
    Fran. D. Baring, iii, 395; iv, 183,
    186, 193, 195, 196; Fran. D. E.
    Baring, iv, 193; Will. Baring,
    iii, 395; iv, 541
Ashby, Sir —, v, 386
Ashcliff (Bonchurch), v, 155
Ashcombe (Wilts.), iv, 23
Ashdown Copse (S. Tidworth), iv,
    391
Ashe, iv, 197, 198-202, 206, 216;
    adv., iv, 201; ch., iv, 198, 201;
    man., ii, 376; iv, 139, 198-200;
    pop., v, 442; sch., ii, 395
Ashe House (Ashe), iv, 198
Asheley, *see* Ashley
Ashe Park (Ashe), iv, 198, 200; v,
    560
Ashe Warren House (Ashe), iv,
    198, 200 n
Ashey, iv, 400 n; v, 138 n, 179,
    180; man., ii, 137; v, 181
Ashey Down, v, 177
Ashfield (Romsey), iv, 452
Ashford, iii, 78; man., iii, 79; water-
    cress, v, 455
Ashford Hill, iv, 250, 252, 266, 267
Ashfordhill Farm (Kingsclere), iv,
    261
Ashford Water (Fordingbridge), iv,
    568
Ashingdon (Ess.), iv, 304
Ashlake, brickmaking, v, 466
Ashlett, iii, 292
Ashley, ii, 73, 172; iii, 401; iv, 438,
    439, 440-2; v, 81, 82, 114, 124;
    man., v, 419, 440, 474, 477, 481;
    pop., v, 447; Rom. rem., i, 313,
    326; iv, 440; sch., ii, 395, 401
Ashley, North (Ringwood), iv, 603,
    605, 606, 609, 610; v, 82, 133
Ashley, Lady Dorothy, v, 97; Lady
    Eliz., v, 97 n; Ant., Ld., ii, 338;
    iii, 261; iv, 358, 454 n, 583, 589,
    594

Ashley [Asheley], Agnes de, ii, 126;
    Ant., iv, 591; Ant. E., iii, 437;
    iv, 454; Edm., iii, 459; Eliz., iv,
    537; Gabriel, iv, 537; Hen., iii,
    459; Isabel, iii, 459; Joan, iv,
    537; John, ii, 28; Kath., iv, 537;
    Rich., iv, 537; Rob., iii, 459; iv,
    148; Thos., ii, 205; Thomasine,
    ii, 130; Tom, v, 532; Tristram,
    iv, 537; Wilf. W., iv, 454, 457,
    459; fam., iv, 537
Ashley Arnewood, man., v, 114, 115
Ashley Commons, v, 124
Ashley Heath (Ringwood), iv, 606
Ashley House (Ashley), iv, 440
Ashley Walk, iv, 559, 568, 573, 623
Ashley Warren Down (Kingsclere),
    iv, 254
Ashley Warren Farm (Kingsclere),
    iv, 254
Ashley Wood, iv, 440, 454
Ashmansworth, iv, 273, 274-5;
    Nonconf., iv, 274; pop., v, 442;
    sch., ii, 395; iv, 274
Ashstead (Calbourne), v, 218 n
Ashton, iii, 275
Ashton [Assheton], Chris., v, 329;
    Geo., iii, 12; John, ii, 41, 42;
    iv, 351; Rich., v, 77; Sir Rob.,
    iii, 156, 158; Steph., v, 27, 28;
    Thos., v, 77, 80; Will., iv, 3
Ashurst (Eling), iv, 546
Ashurst, Eliz., iv, 54; Hen., iv, 54;
    Mrs., iv, 553
Ashwood (Ashe), iv, 198
Aske, John, iii, 17; Rob., iii, 18
Askerswell (Dors.), iv, 604
Aspale (de), Mirabel, iv, 455;
    Thos., iv, 455
Assebrigge (Carisbrooke), v, 222
Asserio [Asser], de, Bertrand, ii,
    195, 197; Gerald, ii, 195; Rigaud,
    bp. of Winchester, ii, 16, 28, 190,
    191, 192, 193, 195; iv, 399; v,
    76, 277
Asshe, *see* Ash
Asshefield (Romsey), iv, 452
Assheford, Thos., ii, 179, 180
Assheton, *see* Ashton
Assigny, Marcus de, ii, 380, 385
Associated Portland Cement Manu-
    facturers (Newport), v, 455
Asthorp, Sir Will., iv, 551
Astineton, John de, v, 112
Astley, Sir Jacob, v, 341
Aston, East and West (Long-
    parish), iv, 348 n, 403, 406, 407,
    408
Aston, Lady Jane, iv, 154, 204
Aston [Eston], Hen. de, iii, 23;
    Rob. de, v, 194; Walt., ii, 121
Astor, Waldorf, v, 553
Asturdinge (Freshwater), v, 240
Astwick, Alice, iii, 358; John, iii,
    358
Atehalle, man., *see* Hale
Atfield, Will., iv, 266
Athelfleda, *see* Ælflaed
Athelmar [Ælmer, Elmar], iii, 444;
    iv, 240; v, 206
Athelstan, king, ii, 6; iii, 403,
    479; iv, 174, 251; v, 90
Athelwalch, v, 294
Athelwold, *see* Ethelwold
Athelyngton, Will. de, iv, 605
Atherfield (Shorwell), v, 209, 210,
    238, 242, 278, 279; brickmaking,
    v, 465; man., v, 281
Atherfield farm (Shorwell), v, 211
Atherfield Green (Shorwell), v, 211
Atherley, Arth., v, 155, 173, 175,
    182, 229, 230; Arth. H. H., v,
    164; Geo., iii, 298; Hen. F., iv,
    539; Lt.-Col., v, 164; fam., v,
    172

Atherton, *see* Arreton

Athlone, Chas. Wilmot, vsct. of, iv, 196

Atkins [Attkins], John, v, 208; John S., iv, 554; Marg., iv, 107; Martha, iv, 363; Mary, iv, 303; Rich., iv, 169, 363; Thos., iv, 107; Will., iii, 422

Atkinson, John, iv, 503; Will., ii, 200, 212

Atmore, fam., arms, iii, 358

Atrebates, i, 262; v, 293

Atril, *see* Attril

Attechurch, Ralph, v, 39

Attehurst, *see* Hurst

Attelode, Agnes, v, 227

Attenalre, Alice, v, 262; Barth., v, 262

Attenborough, R. P., iv, 484

Attenesse, Alice, iv, 457 *n*

Attenho (King's Somborne), iv, 470

Atterigg, Thos., iv, 165 *n*

Attkins, *see* Atkins

Attoyes, Gerald de, iv, 319

Attril [Atril], John, iv, 614; —, v, 188

Attwood, John, iv, 330; fam., iv, 485

Aubeoyle, John, ii, 212

Aubertin, fam., iii, 343

Aubigny, de, *see* Daubeney

Aubrey, iv, 594; the chamberlain, iv, 42

Aubrey, Anne, iv, 85; Arabella, iv, 85; Eliz., iv, 85; Harcourt, iv, 85; Herb., iv, 85; Judith, iv, 85; Rich., ii, 185, 186; *see also* Awbery

Aubyn, Alice, iv, 474; Phil., iv, 474

Aucheston, *see* Adgestone

Audeby, Nich. de, iii, 291

Audley [Audeley, Audeli], Anne Tuchet, Lady, iv, 473 *n*, 657; Marg. Tuchet, Lady, iv, 552; Lds., ii, 144; iv, 644; Geo. Tuchet, iv, 370, 371; Hen. Tuchet, iv, 473 *n*; Jas. Tuchet, iv, 354, 552; John Tuchet, iv, 473 *n*, 541 *n*, 657

Audley [Audeley, Audlye] (de), Eliz., iv, 59 *n*, 594; Hen., ii, 519, 521; iii, 296; iv, 301; Hugh, ii, 479; iii, 247; iv, 576; Joan, iii, 194; John, iii, 109; iv, 342, 354, 552; Julia, iii, 214, 241; Marg., iii, 247; iv, 361, 458, 576; Rich., iv, 59 *n*, 302 *n*, 541, 594; Rob., iii, 194; Sir Thos., ii, 185; Walt., ii, 187; iii, 400; Will., iii, 214, 241

Audley's Wood (Cliddesden), iv, 145

Audoenus, ii, 160

Audret, ii, 152

Augustine, abbot, ii, 139

Augustinis, de, Agnes, iv, 413; Augustine, iii, 39; iv, 413, 432, 447

Aula, de, John, iv, 69; Juliana, iv, 20; Kath., v, 206; Maud, iv, 69; Ralph, iv, 69; Rog., v, 163, 206; Thos., v, 141, 142, 164, 181 *n*, 193, 206; Will., iv, 69; fam., v, 174, 181, 203, 208; *see also* Hall

Aulton, *see* Alton

Aulus Plautius, v, 293

Aumarle, *see* Albemarle

Aumary, count of Evreux, iii, 86

Aunfrey, Rog., v, 44

Aunstell, Rich., ii, 113

Auntediche, *see* Andyke

Aureval, de, Mabel, ii, 496

Auriel, Edm., iii, 30; Edw., iii, 30

Aurifaber, *see* Goldsmith

Austeburne, *see* Osborne

Austen, Edw., ii, 497; iv, 172; Rev. Geo., iv, 171, 172; Jane, ii, 496, 500; iv, 171, 172 *n*, 198; John, iv, 172 *n*; Col., v, 567

Austin, Hub. J., iv, 430; Lionel, v, 486

Austin canons, religious houses of, ii, 56, 104, 152-81

Austin friars, ii, 15, 57, 192; v, 23; priory of (Lond.), iv, 108

Auverstone, *see* Alverstone

Aux, chevalier d', v, 328

Auyten, Will., ii, 182, 186

Auythestone, *see* Adgestone

Avan, Thos., iv, 555

Avene et Tibesleia, Rich. de, iv, 579

Avenel, Hawise, v, 114; Nich., v, 114; Will., v, 114

Averayesmead, ii, 515

Avery, Rich., iv, 266; Will., v, 93, 96, 108, 132

Avice [Hadewis(e), Havisia], abbess of Nunnaminster, ii, 126; abbess of Romsey, ii, 132, 160; prioress of Wintney, ii, 149, 151

Avicestone, *see* Adgestone

Avington [Yabyndon], ii, 108; iii, 302, 306-8, 312; v, 356; man., ii, 61, 114; iii, 307; pop., v, 448; sch., ii, 395

Avington Lake (Alresford), v, 564

Avington Park (Carisbrooke), v, 227

Avon, hamlet, ii, 145, 159; iv, 561; v, 81, 82, 127, 128

Avon, riv., iv, 560, 563, 567, 570, 579, 594, 596, 604, 606; v, 115, 409, 434, 466, 559, 560, 563, 564

Avon, de (of), Joan, v, 130 *n*; John, v, 130 *n*; Maud, iv, 620; Rich., iv, 620

Avon Castle (Ringwood), iv, 607

Avon Chamberlain, *see* Southavon

Avon Hills (Sopley), v, 128

Avonmead (Christchurch), v, 95 *n*

Avon Tyrrell, *see* Northavon

Avranches, Will., bp. of, iii, 230

Awbery, John, iv, 65; *see also* Aubrey

Awbridge (Michelmersh), iii, 401, 424, 425; iv, 506; ch., iii, 426; man., iv, 438, 439

Awdley, fam., *see* Audley

Awerlond, *see* Yaverland

Ayer, Rich., v, 325

Aygnel [Agneil], John, iv, 528, 573; Laur., iv, 550, 573; Maud, iv, 528, 550

Aylesbury, *see* Ailesbury

Ayleswardes (Mattingley), iv, 49

Ayliff [Aylyffe], Brian, iv, 248; Dorothy, iv, 248, 258, 261; Eliz., iv, 259; John, iv, 239, 248; Mary, iv, 266 *n*; Pet., iv, 266 *n*; Rich., iv, 248, 257, 258, 259, 261; Rob., iv, 248; Thos., iv, 257, 258; fam., iv, 207, 239

Ayliffe's manor (Andover), iv, 354; mill, iv, 351

Ayling, John, v, 349; Louisa, iii, 216

Aylmer (de), Joshua, iv, 610; Will., iv, 361, 604

Aylward [Aileward], Agnes, v, 243; Sim., v, 243; Thos., iii, 126

Aylwin, *see* Alwin

Aymer [Aylmer], bp., v, 50 *n*, 55, 168, 218

Aymo, prior, ii, 216

Aynellsland (Odiham), iv, 88

Aynes, Lewis, iv, 548

Aynsley (Dorset), ii, 146, 147

Ayoll, Jacob, v, 114 *n*

Ayreminn, Rich. de, ii, 128

Ayres, Hen., v, 486; Jas., v, 461; *see also* Aire

Ayshlatchmore (Brockenhurst), iv, 626

Azo [Ace], iii, 505, 512; dyer, v, 479

Azor, iv, 373, 396; v, 142 *n*, 145, 147, 155, 158, 160-63, 165, 167, 173, 181, 183, 195, 200, 206, 212, 213, 231, 234, 241, 242, 251, 272, 274, 280

Baber, John, iv, 54; John D., iv, 54 *n*; Mary, iv, 54

Babington, John, iii, 205

Bachamton, Hamo de, iv, 560, 561

Bache, la (Hordle), v, 111

Bachelor, *see* Batchelor

Bachiere, Will. le, v, 45

Back, John, iv, 2

Backhouse, Eliz., ii, 516; Flower (Flora), iii, 12; Jas., v, 489 *n*; (Sir) John, ii, 516; Sam., ii, 516; Will., iii, 12

Bacon [Bacoun, Bacun], Anne, iv, 548; (Sir) Fran., iv, 121; v, 94; Greg., ii, 367; Hen., ii, 110; John, iv, 548; Nich., iv, 192 *n*; Peyton, iv, 121; Capt. Philemon, v, 381; Rich., iv, 548; v, 98, 114; Sim., ii, 165, 218; iv, 252; Will., iii, 498, 499

Baconneau, Nich., iii, 72

Bacoun, Bacun, *see* Bacon

Badcock, Guy, v, 76

Badd, Emmanuel, iii, 214; iv, 325; v, 190; (Sir) Thos., iii, 214; iv, 325

Baddeby (de), Edith, iv, 588; Maud, iv, 588; Will., iv, 588

Badderley [Baddeley] (de), John, ii, 220; Rich., iv, 315

Baddesden, John, ii, 284

Baddesley, North, ii, 99, 105, 160; iii, 462, 463-5; iv, 189, 438, 488, 508; pop., v, 445; schs., ii, 401

Baddesley, South (Boldre), iv, 616, 619, 622, 623, 625 *n*; v, 280

Baddesley, Geoff. de, iv, 616, 625

Baddesley Preceptory, ii, 187; iii, 463; iv, 190; v, 212

Baddingebourne, *see* Bathingbourne

Badeham, *see* Ap Adam

Baderon, iv, 245 *n*, 278, 339

Badgecroft, Agnes, ii, 61

Badger, Rich., iii, 324; Will., ii, 310, 311

Badley [Badele, Beddelie], man. (Crondall), iv, 1, 8-9

Badley (St. Mary Bourne), iv, 295

Badley Pound Farm, *see* Barley Pound Farm

Badnam Creek, i, 310, 343

Baehildestocc (Fyfield), iv, 366

Baerhael (Farley Chamberlayne), iv, 444 *n*

Bagehott, *see* Bagot

Bagger, Rob., v, 473

Baggesley, *see* Bashley

Bagley, Hen., iv, 291

Bagot (Bagehott), Chas., iv, 576 *n*; Egerton A., iii, 45

Bagster, fam., iv, 213

Bagwich, man. (Godshill), v, 172

Bahuchet, Sir Nich. de, v, 363

Baigent, Fran. J., ii, 369; John, ii, 521; W. H., iii, 487

Bailey [Bayley], Fran., iv, 516; F., v, 541; Hinton, iii, 448; John, v, 191, 231, 518; Nath., iv, 192; Rich., v, 538, 539; Thos., ii, 366; —, iv, 22

Bailey Hall Farm (Hannington), iv, 229
Baillyf, see Bayliff
Bainbridge, Geo., iv, 110, 501, 516; Rog., iv, 516; Thos., iv, 516; Will., iv, 110
Baines, Hen. R., iv, 448; Martha A. E., iv, 448; see also Baynes
Baird, Douglas, v, 554
Baizeley Copse (Micheldever), v, 558
Baker [Pestour, Pistar, Pistor], Agatha, iv, 476; Edm., iv, 477, 491; Eliz., ii, 482; iii, 79; iv, 271; Emma, iii, 422; Frances, ii, 510; Geo., iv, 628; Sir Hen., iv, 632; Rev. Hen. C., iv, 391; Rev. Hen. de F., iv, 391; Jane, iv, 522; Joan, iv, 477, 491; v, 163, 220; (Sir) John, ii, 158, 279, 290, 365; iii, 70, 72, 79; iv, 172, 271, 420, 436, 477; v, 484; Josiah, v, 172; Margery, iv, 477; Mary, iii, 432, 526; Nich., iv, 477, 491; Ralph, iv, 473n, 476; Rebecca, iii, 415; iv, 296 n; (Sir) Rich., iii, 72, 79; Rob., iii, 415; iv, 296 n, 476, 477, 491; Thos., iv, 409; v, 163, 220, 484 n; Tristram, iv, 470, 477; Ursula, iv, 420; Walt., iv, 477; Will., ii, 301; iii, 79, 415; iv, 367, 477, 491, 492; Mrs., ii, 482; —, iv, 211, 397
Baker's Farm (Priors Dean), iv, 436
Baker's Hates (Eversley), iv, 33
Baker's Lane (Eversley), iv, 33
Bakewell, John S., iii, 379; Mary E., iii, 379
Bal, see Ball
Balbe, Jacob, v, 458
Baldeham (Romsey), iv, 459
Baldet [Baudet], Christine, iv, 548; Elias, iv, 548, 550, 552 n; Ellen, iv, 548; John, iv, 548; Phil., iv, 548; Rob., iv, 548; Steph., iv, 548; Ursula, iv, 548
Baldham (Romsey), iv, 455
Baldock, Rob. (de), ii, 31; iv, 82
Baldred, iv, 388
Baldri, iv, 57, 191, 225, 227
Baldwin, count, v, 298, 469; earl, v, 224, 291
Baldwin [Baldwyn], Agnes, iii, 107; Mary, iv, 613; Maud, iv, 573; Rich., iii, 107; Thos., iv, 573, 605; Will., iv, 380
Balet, Will., ii, 254
Balfour, Jabez, v, 157
Balksbury Camp (Andover), iv, 346
Ball (Bal, Balle), John (le), iii, 96; v, 47; Nath., ii, 382; Rich., iii, 109; Rob., iv, 424; Will., iv, 424
Ballard, Frances, iv, 441; Millicent, iv, 441; Rob., iv, 441
Balloxley, see Bashley
Balon, Dru de, v, 86 n
Baltimore, Anne, Lady, v, 93; Cecil, Ld., v, 93
Balweys, Will., ii, 205, 206
Bame, Christina, v, 482
Bamford, Thos. H. B., v, 186
Bamfylde, Sir Rich., ii, 347
Bampfield, Eliz., iv, 604; Lewis, iv, 604
Banastre, see Bannister
Banbury, Gilb., ii, 512; iii, 124; Joan, ii, 512
Bancroft, Rich., ii, 320, 340
Band, Edw., iv, 286
Bandet, Rog., ii, 127
Banester, see Bannister
Banetts (Brockenhurst), iv, 626
Bangor, bp. of, v, 368; Thos. Skirvington bp. of, v, 324

Banister, fam., see Bannister
Banister Park (Southampton), iii, 430; v, 575
Banister's Court, man. (Millbrook), iii, 430
Bank of England notes, manuf. of, v, 489, 490
Banks, (Sir) Jacob, v, 94, 95; Mary, v, 94
Bannebury, see Banbury
Bannister [Banastre, Banester, Banister], Edith, ii, 131; (Sir) Edw., ii, 86; iii, 106, 107, 430; v, 147, 162; Hen., v, 269; Isabel, iii, 106; Mary, iii, 106; Nich., iii, 106; v, 367, 368; Rich., iv, 26; Will., iv, 33; fam., v, 148, 182
Bantry Bay, battle of, v, 386
Banystreet-in-Whitnapp (Romsey), iv, 452
Baptists, iii, 139, 200, 207, 215, 232, 296, 299, 534; iv, 4, 14, 18, 26, 41, 62, 98, 108, 139, 266, 277, 299, 304, 356, 371, 409, 468, 486, 497, 502, 510, 534, 536, 558, 591, 613, 623, 629, 633, 649; v, 109, 115, 124, 127, 136, 177, 186, 189, 245, 264, 271, 277, 291
Barantyne [Barentyn], Eliz., iii, 398; iv, 522; Fran., iii, 398; John, iii, 398; iv, 522; (Sir) Will., iii, 358, 398; iv, 522
Barbache, ii, 172
Barber, see Barbour
Barbflete [Barbeflet, Barbesfluit, Barnflete], (de) Alice, iii, 429; Lucy, iv, 473; Maud, iii, 429; Nich., ii, 193; iii, 429, 520; iv, 459; Parnel, iv, 459; Rich., iii, 429, 459
Barbot, John, iii, 214; Rob., iii, 187
Barbour [Barber, Barbur], (le) Sir Dav., iii, 53; Isabel, iv, 459; John, iii, 513; v, 239; Pet., iv, 459; Will., iv, 127, 484
Barcley, Alex., v, 18
Bardesley, Thos., iv, 382
Bardolf [Bardolph], Hugh, ii, 506; iii, 137; Isabel, ii, 506; iii, 137; John, ii, 506; iii, 137; Ralph, ii, 154; v, 112; Rob., ii, 166; iii, 158; Thos., ii, 506; iii, 137; Will., ii, 506
Bardolfeston (Puddle), ii, 131
Barefleet, Matth. de, v, 466 n
Barell, John, iii, 255
Bare Mill (Whitchurch), v, 489
Barentyn, Barentyne, see Barantyne
Baret, see Barret
Barfield (Lymington), iv, 639
Barford, Will., iv, 576
Bargates (Christchurch), v, 83, 109
Barham, Chas. Middleton, Ld., v, 400
Barham, Jos. F., iv, 484
Baril, Bercher, iii, 513
Baring [Barringe], Ad., iv, 589; Alex., see Ashburnham, Ld.; Chas. T., iv, 430; Fran., see Ashburnham, Ld.; (Sir) Fran. T., iv, 430, 521; Fred. A., iv, 183; Rev. F., iv, 511; Sir Godf., v, 269; Hen., iv, 563, 565, 606; Louisa, see Ashburnham, Lady; P. C., v, 284; (Sir) Thos., iii, 391; iv, 521; v, 134, 519, 521; T. C., v, 251, 253; Will., see Ashburnham, Ld.; Will. H, iv, 521; W. H., iv, 497
Barker, Rev. Alf. G., iv, 104, 106, 108; Fran., iv, 250 n, 355, 356; Geo., iv, 108; Geo. W., iv, 108;

Barker (cont.)
Col. Jas., v, 140; Jane, iii, 435; John, iii, 435; Mary, iv, 26; Nych., ii, 57; Dr. —, iii, 93, 109
Barker-Hahlo, Herman, iv, 631
Barker-Mill, Sir John, iii, 435, 437, 499; v, 528; Mrs. Vaudrey, iii, 435; iv, 473, 450, 480, 485, 503, 507, 510, 552, 558; —, iii, 435; iv, 499; see also Mill
Barkesdale, John, iii, 87
Barkham, see Burkham
Barkley, see Berkeley
Barksdale (Bramley), iv, 141
Barkworth, John B., iii, 244
Barley [Barley Pound], man., see Badley
Barley, Anne, iv, 248; Dorothy, iv, 248; Eliz., iv, 247; Hen., iv, 247, 248; Rich., iv, 248; Will., iv, 248
Barley Mow (Winchfield), iv, 109
Barley Mow Farm, Old (Winchfield), iv, 109
Barley Pound Farm (Crondall), i, 305; v, 5
Barlie Bridge (Hartley Mauditt), ii, 508
Barlow, Andr., iii, 432; Grace, iv, 502; John, ii, 478; Matth., iv, 502; Sary, iv, 502
Barming (Kent), iv, 259 n
Barnabe, Johanne, ii, 125
Barnaby, Gab., iv, 272; Mrs., v, 79
Barnack [Barnacke], John, v, 16; Ralph, ii, 365
Barnard, Eliz., iii, 215; Hen., v, 527, 540; Nich., iv, 622 n, 623; —, Canon, ii, 356; see also Bernard
Barne Place (Liss), iv, 84
Barnerdesligh, man. (Brading), ii, 159; v, 161
Barnes, Alb. W. S., iii, 94; Edw., iv, 363, 380, 388
Barnes Grange (Breamore), iv, 598
Barnet hill (Priors Dean), iv, 436
Barnethorpe, ii, 126
Barnett, F., v, 245; Rev. Leigh B., iv, 198; Will., bp., ii, 51
Barnflete, see Barbflete
Barn Green, tithing (Hambledon), iii, 238, 240
Barn's farm (Breamore), iv, 598
Barnsfield Wood (Ringwood), iv, 606
Barnsley, man. (Brading), v, 161
Baron, fam., see Barron
Barons' war, v, 310
Baroper, see Beaurepaire
Barre, Eliz., iv, 102; Hawise atte, iv, 569; John, iv, 102; (Sir) Thos., iv, 102, 103, 569
Barrefield, see Turfields
Barrett, Anne, iv, 271; Arth., iv, 271; Chas., iv, 271; Christine, iv, 271 n; Edw., iv, 352, 353; Eliz., iv, 271, 279, 352; Geo., iv, 271, 279, 352; v, 552; G., v, 551; John, iv, 271; v, 264; Philippa, iv, 271; Rob., iv, 271; Maj., iv, 139; v, 517
Barrett of Newburgh, Edw., Ld., iv, 60, 257 n, 258, 271, 279, 352
Barringe, see Baring
Barrington, Sir Fitz. W., v, 219, 220; Sir Fran., v, 219; Sir John, v, 178; Louisa E., v, 219; Sir Thos., v, 219; Winifred, v, 219
Barron [Baron, Barun], Chas., iv, 2; Geoff., v, 45; Geo., iv, 555; Isabel, v, 45; John, iii, 294; iv, 178; Julia, iii, 294
Barrowe, Geo., iv, 92; Marg., iv, 92; Rob., iv, 92

Barrow Hill (Eling), iv, 546
Bart, Jean, v, 385
Bartelmelo, *see* Bartholomew
Barter, John, iv, 568; Rob. S., ii, 366; v, 576; —, v, 16
Bartholomew [Bartelmelo, Bartylmew], Anne, iv, 568, 569; Chas., iv, 558; John, v, 85 *n*, 119, 120; Rich., ii, 139, 146; iv, 569; Thos., iv, 568, 569; Will., iv, 569
Bartlemy & Turpin, v, 465
Bartlett, Edw., iii, 279; iv, 520 *n*; Joan, iii, 279; iv, 520; John, iv, 469; v, 78; Jos., v, 453; Rich., iv, 82
Bartlett's Down (Faccombe), iv, 314
Bartley, riv., iv, 546, 556, 635
Bartley, Geo., iv, 557
Bartley Heath (Odiham), iv, 66 *n*, 87, 88, 94
Bartley Lodge (Eling), iv, 546
Bartley Regis, iv, 615, 632
Bartmestone, *see* Brykmerston
Bartolettes (Faccombe), iv, 314
Barton (I. of W.), v, 197; ch., ii, 289; man., v, 198, 199
Barton (Milton), v, 99 *n*, 124, 125
Barton (S. Stoneham), iii, 481; man., iii, 486
Barton (Winchester), *see* Abbot's Barton
Barton (de), Frank, v, 171, 173; John, iv, 532; J., iv, 140; Rich., iii, 381; iv, 532; Rob., v, 181, 201; Thos., ii, 173, 175; iv, 532; Victor, v, 575; Will. H., v, 171; Maj., v, 537
Barton Croft (King's Worthy), iv, 430
Barton Farm (Milton), v, 99 *n*
Barton Oratory (Whippingham), ii, 104, 180-1; v, 163, 174, 198
Barton Peverel, man. (S. Stoneham), iii, 486
Barton Stacey, ii, 173; iii, 401; iv, 402, 415, 416, 417-22, 430, 477; v, 308, 324, 328 *n*, 331; adv., iv, 422; char., iv, 422; ch., iv, 417, 420-2; Church Farm, iv, 417; fair, iv, 417; v, 417; man., iv, 407 *n*, 417-19; v, 242; Nonconf., iv, 422; pop., v, 438; riots, v, 433; schs., ii, 395; tumuli, iv, 417
Barton Stacey, hund., iv, 415
Barton Stacey Belt, iv, 402, 417
Barton Wood (I. of W.), i, 347
Bartue, Emma, ii, 125
Bartylmew, *see* Bartholomew
Barun, fam., *see* Barron
Barun v. Will. le Espicer, v, 45
Barwell, Rich., iii, 136
Barwicke, John, iv, 594; Will., v, 461
Barwis, Jane, v, 189
Baseley, Alice, iv, 293
Baseville, Nich. de, v, 272
Bashley (Milford), v, 81, 89 *n*, 116, 124, 126; mill, v, 126
Bashley Common, v, 124
Basilmede (Romsey), iv, 452
Basing, ii, 33, 101, 176, 209, 371; iv, 113, 114, 115-27, 128, 129, 147, 167, 231, 337, 338, 579; v, 295, 343; adv., iv, 126; chalk quarries, v, 454; chap., iv, 127; char., iv, 127; ch., iv, 113 *n*, 123-6, 138; farm sch., v, 511; ind., v, 455; mans., iv, 115, 526; mills, iv, 115, 121; Nonconf., iv, 115; pop., v, 439; schs., ii, 395
Basing, Ld., iii, 384; v, 556; Geo. L. Sclater-Booth, Ld., iv, 121

Basing [Basyng], (de), Hamo, iii, 400; Hugh, ii, 111, 115; Joan, iii, 251; iv, 121; (Sir) John, iii, 251; iv, 121; v, 311, 484; Ralph, ii, 128, 135, 188; iv, 121; Will., prior, ii, 110, 115, 177, 179, 188, 190, 198, 199, 200; v, 55
Basingbourne (Crookham), iv, 5
Basing Byfleet, man. (Basing), iv, 113 *n*, 121
Basing House (Basing), ii, 315, 379; iv, 116, 117-20, 122, 124, 126, 161, 250, 335, 433; v, 340, 347
Basingstoke, ii, 21, 23, 26, 62, 63, 71, 96, 101, 102, 176, 208, 209, 210, 214, 215, 251, 369, 370, 371, 372, 376, 377, 378, 379, 380, 381, 384, 385; iv, 113, 114, 121 *n*, 122, 126, 127-40; 148, 167, 172, 178, 251, 266, 321, 346, 411; v, 311, 318, 324, 328 *n*, 331, 380, 414 *n*, 425, 426, 427, 428, 430, 431, 434, 544, 576; adv., ii, 21; iv, 138; battle, iv, 129 *n*; chap. and gild of the Holy Ghost, ii, 214-15; iv, 128, 137, 138, 164; char., iv, 139, 200, 206; chs., iv, 126, 135-8, 509; courts, iv, 131; ind., iv, 133; v, 455, 456, 459, 461, 473, 474, 484; Liten, the, iv, 128; mans., ii, 224; iv, 32, 46, 134-5; v, 419; mkts. and fairs, iv, 127, 129, 133; v, 409, 416, 495; mills, iv, 128, 129, 134; Mote Hall, iv, 127, 128; pop., v, 450; racing, v, 543; Rom. Cath., iv, 138; Rom. rems., i, 305, 343; St. John's Hosp., ii, 105, 208-11; iv, 146; v, 418; schs., ii, 368, 387, 395; iv, 128, 139, 140
Basingstoke, hund., iv, 113-81
Basingstoke canal, iv, 2, 15, 72, 76, 87, 90, 109, 115, 117, 128, 147, 149, 176; v, 431
Basingstoke Grammar School, ii, 368-85, 387
Basingstoke Merton, *see* Taulkes
Basket-making, v, 455
Baskett [Basket], Anne, v, 280; Barbara, v, 280; Edw., v, 192; Jane, v, 192; John, iv, 67, 91; v, 145, 172, 180, 192, 198; Rich., v, 145, 160, 172, 180, 184, 280; Thos., v, 180, 192
Baskerville [Baskervyle], Agnes, iv, 605; Ralph de, iv, 592, 594; Thos., iv, 633
Basset [Bassett], Agnes, iii, 486; iv, 255; Alan, ii, 223; iv, 77, 150, 152, 156; Alina, iv, 150; Dionisia, iv, 61, 62; Ela, iii, 378; iv, 178; Eliz., iii, 313; Fulk, iv, 150; Gilb. (de), iv, 77, 150; Isabel, iv, 77; Joan, iii, 310; Juliane, iv, 255; (Sir) Phil., iii, 378; iv, 100 *n*, 150, 152, 178, 569; Ralph, v, 21; Rich., iii, 313; iv, 255; Rob., iv, 501; Thos., iv, 255, 329; T., ii, 301; Walt., iv, 501; (Sir) Will., iv, 62, 255; —, iii, 479; fam., v, 460
Basset's Mill (Lockerley), iv, 501
Bassingbourn, de, Isabel, iv, 417; Warin, iv, 417
Bastard's Virgate (Kingsclere), iv, 255
Basyng, *see* Basing
Bat [Batte], Alan, ii, 30; Marg., v, 29; Will., v, 456
Batchelor [Bachelor, Bachelure], Ingram, iv, 266 *n*; John, iv, 222; Rich., v, 479 *n*; Will., iv, 222, 299

Batecombe (Christchurch), v, 97 *n*
Batell, Thos., iii, 269
Bates, Sir Ed., iv, 232, 240, 244; Sir Ed. P., iv, 232; Syd. E., iv, 232, 240
Batesford, John de, iv, 248
Bath (Somers.), ch., iv, 72; infirmary, iv, 613; priory, v, 117, 120
Bath [Bathe, Bathonia], Geoff. de, iii, 89; iv, 93; Isaac, ii, 389; Thos., v, 473
Bathampton, Phil. of, v, 86
Bath and Wells, bps. of, ii, 24, 89, 95, 169, 294, 339; iv, 551, 584, 586 *n*, 589; Bubwith, iv, 562; Burnell, ii, 169; iv, 73, 377; Button, iv, 72, 73; Drokensford, ii, 24; iii, 204, 255, 262, 285; iv, 42, 63, 72, 199, 394; v, 118, 242; Fitz Jocelin, iv, 72, 73, 74; Giffard, *see* York, archbp. of; Godfrey, iv, 72; Harewell, iv, 74; Jocelin, iv, 72, 73, 626; Will. Knyght, ii, 294; Roger, iv, 73 *n*
Bathe, *see* Bath
Bathingbourne, man. (Godshill), v, 172
Bathonia, *see* Bath
Baths, Roman, i, 298, 308, 310, 311, 316, 359
Bathwick (Somers.), ii, 137
Bathurst, Edw., iv, 94; Sir Fred., v, 574; Gen. Hen., iii, 445; John, iv, 8; Mary, iii, 445
Batmanson, Johan, iv, 194; John, iv, 194
Batrachians, i, 206
Batramsley, *see* Battramsley
Bats, i, 239
Batson, Anne, v, 130; Edw. B., v, 130; Stanlake, v, 130; —, v, 555
Batte, *see* Bat
Batten, Anne, iv, 580; Ant., iv, 580, 611; Fran., iv, 611; Hannah, iii, 318, 345; Jas., iii, 318; iv, 611; John, iv, 611; v, 199; Maj. John M., v, 199; Judith, iv, 611; Will., iv, 580, 611; *see also* Battin
Battenberg, princess Hen. of, v, 198, 201, 224, 226
Battery House, Sandown, v, 157 *n*
Battin, Jas. M., iv, 70; *see also* Batten
Battle Abbey (Suss.), ii, 108, 477
Battlesworth, Thos., iii, 240
Battramsley (Boldre), iv, 615, 617-18; bailiwick, ii, 427; v, 455
Battramsley House (Boldre), iv, 616, 618
Batt's (Hartley Wintney), iv, 79
Batt's brook, iv, 84
Baudet, *see* Baldet
Baughurst, ii, 93; iv, 170, 221, 234, 238, 239, 249, 273, 275-7, 415, 435; pop., v, 442; sch., ii, 396; iv, 275, 277
Bauldoxfee (Eling), iv, 548 *n*
Baulkwill, Rev. Will. R. K., v, 229
Baureper, *see* Beaurepaire
Bave, Dr. Chas., iv, 637; Eleanor, iv, 637
Bavelingham, Maud [Mabel] de, iv, 254; Thos. de, iv, 254
Baverstock, Thos., iii, 481
Bawdewin, Marg., ii, 124
Bax, Col. Will. I., iv, 240
Baxendale, Jos. W., ii, 470; iii, 420; N., iii, 488; Mrs., v, 530; —, v, 529, 530
Baybridge, iii, 302, 332, 334
Bayes, Sophia, iv, 78, 80, 91

Bayeux, Odo, bp. of, ii, 484 ; iv, 549, 623 ; v, 97, 224 n, 300
Bayeux, Bevis de, iv, 512 n
Bayford [Byford], Amelia C., iv, 571 ; Joan, iv, 510, 571 ; Will., iv, 510 n, 571
Bayley, see Bailey
Bayliff [Baillyf], John, v, 231 ; Rich., iii, 498
Baylnclislegh, see Bashley
Baylyes landes (Stratfield Turgis), iv, 63
Baynard, Agnes, iv, 54 ; Edm., iv, 53, 54 ; Edw., iv, 64 ; Eleanor, iv, 53 ; Geo., iv, 132 ; Jane, iv, 49 ; John, iv, 54 ; Joyce, iv, 53, 54 ; Laur., iv, 54 n ; Phil., iv, 53, 54 ; Rob., iv, 49, 53, 54 ; Thos., iv, 54 n
Baynes, Rev. Don, iv, 391 ; Lucy, v, 180 n ; John, v, 180 n ; see also Baines
Bayntun, Andr., iv, 296 ; Sir Ed., iv, 185, 295, 296 ; Fran., iv, 185 ; Hen., iv, 185 ; Isabel, iv, 185, 296 ; Joan, iv, 185 ; (Sir) John, iv, 185, 296 n ; Nich., iv, 185 ; Rob., iv, 185 ; fam., iv, 295
Beach, Amb., iii, 461 ; Henrietta M., iv, 224 ; Mich., iv, 202 ; Will., iv, 226 ; v, 521 ; Maj. Will. A. H., iv, 205, 207, 220, 221, 224, 227, 228, 435 ; Will. H., iv, 207 ; Will. W. B., iv, 201, 206, 207, 220 ; v, 522
Beacon Hill (Burghclere), iv, 277, 285 ; Rom. rem., i, 344
Beaconshaw, see Beconshaw
Beadon, Rev. —, ii, 465
Beagles, v, 542
Beale, see Bele
Beales (Hartley Wintney), iv, 79, 80
Bean Lands (Odiham), iv, 98
Beaper (Brading), v, 163
Beard, Ben., iii, 88
Beare (Godshill), v, 203 n
Beareridge Coppice (Hurstbourne Tarrant), iv, 319, 321
Bearroc forest, i, 392 ; ii, 412
Bear's Green (Hartley Wintney), iv, 79
Beatrice, abbess, ii, 126
Beauchamp, man. (Niton), v, 188
Beauchamp (de), Agnes, iv, 542 ; Anne, iii, 410 ; iv, 151, 441 ; Aundrina, v, 188, 237 ; Eleanor, iv, 542 ; Giles, v, 241 n, 242 ; Guy, iii, 520 ; Hen., iv, 151, 441 ; Hugh, v, 188, 237 ; Ida, iv, 577 ; Idonea, v, 188, 274 ; Idoneus, v, 237 n ; Isabel, ii, 509 ; iv, 151, 388, 441 ; Joan, v, 188, 237 ; (Sir) John, iv, 92, 193, 392 n, 545, 577, 627, 631, 633 ; v, 188, 237 n, 241 n ; Oliver, iii, 223, 225, 229 ; Pet., iv, 542 ; Rich., iii, 226, 229 ; iv, 151, 185, 441, 540 ; Thos., ii, 138 ; iv, 392 n, 627 ; Walt., iv, 571 n ; Will., ii, 509, 415 ; iv, 151, 540, 571 n ; v, 188, 237 ; fam., iii, 411, 486 ; iv, 366 ; arms, iii, 520
Beauchamps Court (Niton), v, 188
Beauclerk, Ladies :—Charlotte, iv, 109 n ; Marg., iv, 110 ; Lds. :— Amelius, iv, 110 ; Rev. Fred., iv, 111 ; Geo., iv, 110, 111
Beauclerk, Hen., ii, 117 ; Fred. E., iv, 111
Beaucoup, count, v, 549
Beaufitz, Will., ii, 216
Beaufo, see Beaufoy
Beaufort, dks. of, iii, 106 ; v, 355, 521, 528, 554, 573 ; Hen. Somerset, iii, 105

Beaufort, Edm., v, 223, 320 ; Hen., v, 223 ; see also Winchester, bp. of ; John, ii, 475, iii, 143 ; iv, 130, 347, 540 ; Marg., ii, 475, 476 ; iii, 143, 411 ; iv, 130, 348 ; v, 92
Beaufoy [Beaufo] (de), Ellen, iii, 435 ; John, iii, 435 ; John H., iii, 384 ; Olimpyas, iii, 435 ; Rich., iii, 435
Beaulieu, ii, 71, 73 ; iv, 609, 650-5 ; v, 391, 462 ; ch., iv, 652 ; fair, iv, 652 ; v, 435 ; ind., v, 466 ; man., ii, 464, 469 ; iv, 650-2 ; v, 125, 464, 518 ; mills, iv, 652 ; v, 564 ; pop., v, 446 ; Rom. rem., i, 344 ; iv, 650 ; sch., ii, 396
Beaulieu riv., i, 6, 244 ; iii, 290 ; iv, 546, 616, 630, 650, 652 ; v, 387, 468, 560, 564
Beaulieu, Isabel Hussey-Montagu, ctss. of, iv, 651 ; Edw. Hussey-Montagu, earl of, iv, 651
Beaulieu Abbey, ii, 11, 13, 58, 59, 61, 104, 140-6, 436 ; iii, 258, 294 ; iv, 330, 331, 491, 552, 571, 572, 616, 640, 650, 652-4 ; v, 186, 320, 321 ; cloth-making, v, 481 ; wool trade, v, 476
Beaulieu Heath, iv, 626
Beaumont, Will., vsct., ii, 478
Beaumont [Beaumond] (de), Capt. A. P., iv, 546, 549 ; Sir Hen., ii, 478 ; John, ii, 478 ; iii, 149 ; John H., iv, 637 ; Lauretta, iii, 103 ; Rich., ii, 222, 223, 224, 225 ; Rob., iii, 103 ; Thos. W., v, 154
Beauple, Sir Rob., v, 364
Beaurepaire (Brading), see Beaper
Beaurepaire (Sherborne St. John), ii, 474, 512 ; iv, 58, 106, 142, 143, 144, 160, 162, 165-7, 169, 172 n, 202, 289, 435 ; mill, iv, 159, 167
Beaurepaire House (Sherborne St. John), iv, 158, 167
Beausarvice, Eliz., iv, 134 ; Joan, iv, 134 ; John, iv, 134 ; Will., iv, 134
Beausevall, Rich. de, iv, 343
Beauworth, iii, 302, 311, 313 ; pop., v, 447 ; sch., ii, 396
Beaver, Chas., v, 521 ; Will., ii, 158 ; Col., v, 513 n
Beche (atte, de la), Edm., iv, 353 ; Nich., ii, 227 ; v, 284 ; Ralph, iv, 570
Bec Hellouin Abbey (France), iv, 342, 343, 380, 381, 385, 386
Bechesfonte, Christine, iv, 474 ; Rob., iv, 474
Bechinstoke, man. (Wilts.), ii, 114
Becke [Beck], Ambrosia, iv, 303 ; Hen. iv, 488 ; John, prior, ii, 223 ; Rich., ii, 212 ; iv, 303 ; Will., iii, 361
Beckenshaw, see Beconshaw
Beckering, John de, iii, 361
Becket [Beckett, Beket], Agnes, iii, 525 ; Alice, iii, 429 ; iv, 340, 341, 362, 392, 522 n ; Joan, iv, 392 ; John, ii, 502 ; iii, 47, 48, 53 ; Margery, ii, 502 ; iv, 166, 172, 203 ; Nich., iii, 525 ; Nigel, iii, 47 ; Oliver, ii, 502 ; iv, 166, 172, 203 ; Rich., iii, 47, 429 ; iv, 302, 340, 341, 392 ; Thos., ii, 12, 13, 19, 153, 160, 482 ; v, 360, 418 ; Val., iii, 47 ; Will., iii, 47
Beckett's Down (Brown Candover), iv, 183 n
Beckford, Fran. L., v, 280 ; Harriet, v, 271 ; Joan, v, 280 ; Susannah, ii, 507
Beckheath (Beaulieu), iv, 650
Becking (agric. term), v, 500

Beckington, Rev. Thos., ii, 279, 286 ; v, 17
Beckley (Christchurch), v, 81, 84 ; estate, v, 101
Beckley, Jas., iii, 422
Becklond (Bentley), iv, 27
Becksettle Farm (Colemore), iv, 423
Beconshaw [Beaconshaw, Beckenshaw, Beconsawe, Bekynshale], Alice, ii, 97 ; iv, 563, 564, 565, 566 ; v, 119 ; Anne, iv, 279 ; Benj., iv, 279 ; Eliz., iv, 563 ; John, iv, 279 ; Pet., iv, 279, 281 ; Rich., iv, 189, 258, 279, 554 ; v, 119 ; Walt., iv, 258 ; Sir White, ii, 97 ; iv, 563 ; Will., iv, 134, 189, 554, 563, 565 ; fam., iv, 580
Bedbury Mead (Bedhampton), iii, 142
Beddeshethe (Abbotts Ann), iv, 334 n
Bedecotes (Fordingbridge hund.), iv, 559
Bedell [Bedel, Bedyl], John, v, 16, 329 ; J., ii, 279, 290 ; Rog. le, iv, 498 ; Dr., ii, 303
Bedeman, Lawr., ii, 41, 42
Bedenham (Alverstoke), iii, 203, 209
Bedesdene (Abbotts Ann), iv, 334 n
Bedford, Isabel, ctss. of, iv, 198 ; v, 184, 222, 241 n ; Gert. Russell, dchss. of, iii, 391 ; dks. of, iv, 34, 380, 562, 626, 632 ; v, 198 n, 368 ; Fran. Russell, iii, 391 ; Geo. Nevill, v, 118 ; John of Lancaster, iv, 343, 380, 385 ; John Russell, iii, 391, 398 ; v, 144 ; Wriothesley Russell, iii, 391 ; Ingram de Couci, earl of, v, 158 n, 222
Bedforde, Thos., iv, 538 n
Bedham, Steph., v, 460 ; Thos., v, 460
Bedhampton, ii, 25, 96, 117 ; iii, 140, 142-4 ; v, 328 n ; bridge, ii, 47 ; chalk pits, v, 454 ; pop., v, 441 ; salt making, v, 469 ; sch., ii, 396
Bedingfield, Ant., iv, 121 ; Marg., iv, 121
Bedlecombe, Mark, v, 98 ; Martin, v, 98
Bedminster, prebend of (Salisbury), ii, 347
Bed-ticking manuf., v, 488
Bedyl, fam., see Bedell
Bedylls (Priors Dean), iv, 436
Beecher, Sir Will., v, 335
Beech Hill, iv, 57 ; man., iv, 60, 62, 104
Beech Hill House, iv, 57
Beech House (Christchurch), v, 84
Beechwood (Eling), iv, 546
Bee-keeping, iv, 455
Beel, see Bele
Beenham Court (Kingsclere), iv, 249, 250, 260, 266
Beere [Bere] (atte, de la), Ad., iv, 244, 579, 629 ; Barnabas, v, 292 ; Hugh, iii, 393 ; Joan, v, 237 ; John, iv, 224, 226, 227, 579 ; Kath., iv, 224, 579 ; Nich., ii, 486 ; v, 237 ; Rich., ii, 486, 489, 512 ; iii, 254, 255, 323 ; iv, 328 ; Sybil, iv, 224, 579 ; Thos., ii, 229, 486, 512 ; iv, 224, 579 ; Will., iii, 398 ; v, 48
Bees, i, 114
Beeston, Anne, iii, 196 ; v, 73 ; Geo. St. L., iii, 196 ; Hen., ii, 338, 366 ; v, 73 ; Thos., iii, 196
Beetles, i, 121, 123
Beeton & Burmester, iv, 287

Beggar's Clump (Ashe), iv, 198
Beglystok (Abbotts Ann), iv, 334 n
Béhuchet, admiral, v, 312
Behunger Coppice, see Buggenore
Beket, see Becket
Bekingham, Agnes, iv, 58, 60 ; Will., iv, 58
Bekton [Beketon] Farm (Hordle), v, 111
Bekynshale, see Beconshaw
Bekynton, see Beckington
Bel, see Bele
Belamy, Belanney, fam., see Bellamy
Belanney, man. (Southwick), iii, 163
Beldham, Will., v, 574
Bele [Beale, Beel, Bel], Jacob del, iv, 45 ; Jas., v, 33 ; Joan, iii, 89, 90 ; Pet., iv, 436 ; Capt. Rich., iv, 437 n ; Maj. Rich., iv, 437 ; Rich. le, iii, 89, 90 ; iv, 436 ; Thos., v, 130 n ; Walt. v, 130 n ; Will., iv, 436 ; see also Bell
Beles (Hartley Wintney), iv, 79, 80
Belesme, Rob. of, see Shrewsbury, earl of
Belet, Will., iv, 331, 332
Beletoun the Jew, iv, 338
Beleys (Priors Dean), iv, 436
Belfore, Sir Will, v, 342
Belgæ, i, 262, 285, 385
Belhouse, man. (Essex), iv, 271
Belknap, Joan, iv, 382 n ; Sir Rob., iv, 382 n
Bell, Rob., v, 140 n, 264 ; Laur., iii, 422 ; Walt., v, 529 ; —, v, 198 n ; see also Bele
Bellamy [Belamy, Belanney, Bello Alneto, Belmy, Belny] (de), Bald. iii, 163 ; Jane, iii, 139 ; John, ii, 125 ; iv, 261 ; J., v, 535 ; Rob., iii, 146 ; Will., iii, 146, 163
Bell Croft (St. Helens), v, 193
Belleau, — de, iii, 536
Bellewe [Bellowe], Hen., iv, 609 n ; John, iv, 453, 549, 595
Bell Hill (Carisbrooke), v, 229 n
Bellingham, (Sir) Edw., iv, 441, 482 ; v, 328
Bello Alneto, see Bellamy
Bells (Bramley), iv, 142
Belmayne, John, iv, 110
Belmont (Bedhampton), iii, 142
Belmy, Belny, fam., see Bellamy
Belus, Will., iv, 608
Belverge, Rich., v, 285
Bembridge, v, 138 n, 157, 161, 206 ; fort, v, 351 ; quarries, v, 462 ; sch., ii, 407
Bembridge Down, v, 157
Bembridge Farm (Brading), v, 162
Benbridge, Thos., ii, 72
Benbury, Thos., iv, 528
Bencraft, Russell, v, 575
Bendeng [Bending] (de), Ad., iv, 75, 84, 93, 254 ; Alda, iv, 79, 110, 111 ; Alice, iv, 254 ; Juliana, iv, 79 ; Maud, iv, 84 ; Maurice, iv, 110 ; Pet., iv, 110, 111, 112 n ; Steph., iv, 75, 79, 110, 112 n, 527 ; Walt., iv, 75, 84 ; Will., iv, 75, 84, 92, 93
Bene, la (Monk Sherborne), iv, 231
Benedict, v, 223 ; bp. of Cardica, iv, 202 ; the Jew, iv, 340
Benedictines, ii, 104, 108-37
Benestede, see Binstead and Binsted
Benet, Benett, see Bennett
Benetfield (Basingstoke), iv, 129
Benettyshey (Christchurch), v, 85
Benewardle (Godshill), v, 174
Beneyt, see Bennett
Benfield, de, Isabel, iv, 165 n ; Rich., iv, 165

Benger, Anne, iv, 457 ; John, iii, 324 ; iv, 457, 457 n ; Kath., iv, 457 ; Rich., iii, 324 ; iv, 457
Benham (de), Agnes, iv, 260 ; Alice, iv, 260 ; Eleanor, iv, 260 ; Joan, iv, 260 ; John, iv, 253, 260 ; Marg., iv, 260 ; Phil., iv, 260 ; Rich., iv, 260 ; Will., iv, 260
Benley (Evingar hund.), iv, 273 n
Bennett (Benet, Benett, Beneyt, Bennet, Benyt), Agnes, iii, 164, 204 ; Edith, iv, 354 ; Eliz., v, 95 n ; Geo., ii, 385 ; Hugh, iii, 146 ; Sir Humph., iv, 103 ; v, 261, 353 ; Joan, iv, 634 ; John, ii, 317 ; iv, 75 n, 294, 354, 407 ; (Sir) Levinus, v, 148, 199, 261 ; Margery, iv, 407 ; Rich., iii, 164 ; v, 282, 484 ; Rich. H. A., v, 280, 284 ; Rob., ii, 197 ; Thos., iii, 487 ; iv, 201, 472 ; v, 261 ; Will., iii, 178 ; Will. B. P., v, 95 n ; —, v, 538 ; fam., v, 283
Benny, Chas. W., iv, 433
Benskin, Mrs., iv, 655
Bensted, Benstede (Alton), see Binsted
Bensted [Bensteade, Benstede] (de), Edm., ii, 485 ; Edw., ii, 485 ; Imania, iii, 146 ; (Sir) John, ii, 485 ; Phil., iii, 146 ; Thos., ii, 182, 186 ; Will., ii, 485
Benstrow (Longstock), iv, 449, 449 n
Bentinck, Ld. Geo., v, 555
Bentinck, Eliz., iii, 466 ; iv, 450 ; Hen., see Portland, dk. of ; Walt. T. E., ii, 501 ; Will., iii, 466 ; —, iv, 592 ; fam., arms, iii, 279
Bentley, iii, 101, 173, 483, 501 ; iii, 217 ; iv, 27-30 ; v, 331, 357 ; pop., v, 443 ; sch., ii, 396
Bentley, Gt. and Little, mans. (Mottisfont), iv, 506-7
Bentley, John, ii, 40 ; iv, 218
Bentworth, ii, 145, 483 ; iii, 356 ; iv, 66, 67, 68-71, 81, 86 ; pop., v, 439 ; sch., ii, 396
Bentworth [Little Bentworth], man. (Bramley), iv, 142, 143
Bentworth (de), Maud, iv, 69, 143 ; Rev. Rich., bp., iv, 68 ; Will., iv, 143
Bentworth Hall [Bentworth Juxta Alton], man. (Bentworth), iv, 68, 69
Bentworth Lodge (Bentworth), iv, 68
Benyon, Hannah, iv, 434 ; Jas. H., iv, 56, 57, 434 ; Mary, iv, 433 ; Rich., iv, 433, 434 ; —, iv, 434, 435
Benyt, see Bennett
Beorhtnathes stone (Calbourne), v, 220 n
Beorn, Rich., dk. of, v, 56
Beornhelm, abbot of Newminster, ii, 121
Beornstan [Brinstan], bp. of Winchester, ii, 6, 201
Beortric, king, iv, 288
Berard, John, prior of Breamore, ii, 172
Berchelei (Odiham), iv, 66, 94
Berchenistre, Alsi, iv, 171, 377, 378 ; Sariz, iv, 377, 378
Berd, see Bird
Berdmore, Rev. Scrope, iv, 634, 638
Bere, forest of, i, 379, 384 ; ii, 189, 191, 432, 434, 441, 442, 462 ; iii, 94, 142, 144, 148, 158, 161 ; iv, 440, 469, 470 ; v, 370, 383
Bere, hill (Andover), Rom. rem., i, 304, 344
Bere, man. (Soberton), iii, 264

Bere, fam., see Beere
Berebrygge (Winchester), mill, v, 479 n
Bereford (de), Sir Bald., iv, 540 ; Denis, iv, 605 ; John, iv, 605 ; Ralph, ii, 218 ; iii, 69 ; Will., iv, 198
Berelay (Niton), v, 203 ; brick manuf., v, 466
Bereleigh, man. (East Meon), iii, 71
Beremead (Christchurch), v, 86
Bere Mill (Freefolk), iv, 282
Bereminton (Christchurch), v, 89 n
Berenger, Alice, iv, 512 ; Anastasia, iv, 512 ; Emma, iv, 512 ; Geo., iv, 354 ; (Sir) Ingram [Ingelram], iii, 485 ; iv, 340, 512, 513, 514 ; Isabel, iv, 354 ; Joan, iv, 512 ; John, iii, 485 ; iv, 512 ; Nich., iii, 8 n, 485 ; iv, 512
Beresford, Ld. Marcus, v, 550, 551
Beresford, Col. Chas. E. de la P., iv, 655
Bereuton, Bereweton, see Broughton
Berewe, see Burgh
Berewyk, Berewick, see Berwick
Berfords, man. (Southampton), ii, 163
Berghe, see Burgh
Berghes, les (Gatcombe), v, 246
Berghton, see Broughton
Beriberi (Calbourne), v, 218
Berill, Will., iv, 455
Bering, Walt., iv, 146
Beriton, see Buriton
Berkeley, iv, 99
Berkeley [Barkley, Berkele, Berkley], Alice, iv, 580 ; Christine, ii, 486, 503, 516 ; iv, 28 ; (Sir) Edw., ii, 486, 503, 504, 516 ; iii, 515 ; iv, 28, 502, 580, 612, 621 ; Eliz. (de), ii, 128 ; iii, 291 ; iv, 520, 543, 580, 612, 636 ; Grantley, v, 569 ; (Sir) John (de), ii, 76 ; iii, 291 ; iv, 520, 543, 543 n, 580, 609, 636 ; v, 96, 99, 114, 128, 129, 130, 132, 317 ; Kath., iv, 99, 636 ; v, 114 ; Laura, ii, 486, 503, 516 ; Maud, iv, 580 ; (Sir) Maur., ii, 480, 482 ; iv, 99, 148, 347, 520 n, 524 n, 537, 580, 609, 636 ; v, 104, 109, 114 ; Rich., v, 484 ; Thos., v, 537, 580 ; (Sir) Will., ii, 67 ; iii, 397 ; iv, 99, 580, 608, 636 ; v, 96, 104, 109, 113, 129, 151, 223 n, 326 n ; —, v, 347
Berkham, see Burkham
Berkhamstead Grammar School, (Herts.), ii, 208
Berkley (Eling), iv, 548, 555
Berkshire, Dan, v, 517 ; —, v, 518
Berman, John, ii, 134
Bermondspit, hund., iii, 355
Bernand, Will., ii, 227, 229
Bernard, the chamberlain, iv, 604
Bernard, Joan, v, 213 ; John, ii, 287, 366 ; Sim., v, 213 ; Thos., iii, 240 ; v, 130 ; fam., iv, 76 ; see also Barnard
Bernard Marsh (Newtown), v, 268
Bernardsley, man. (Dorset), ii, 156
Bernardsmead (Christchurch), v, 86
Berncrofte, La (Sherborne St. John) iv, 158
Berne, Pet. at, ii, 178, 179
Berners, Joan Bourchier, Lady, iv, 361 ; Lds., v, 555 ; John Bourchier, iv, 361
Berners, Will., ii, 56, 124, 138, 151, 159
Bernevall, (de) Aubrey, iv, 329 ; Bern., iii, 106 ; Cecily, iv, 329, 330 ; Gilb., iv, 329, 330 ; Hen.,

Bernevall (*cont.*)
  iv, 321, 324, 329, 330; Reg., iv, 329; Rog., iii, 293; iv, 324, 329, 330
Bernsfield Heath, v, 85
Bernwin, ii, 3
Berrewe, *see* Burgh
Berrfoteslane (Calbourne), v, 218
Berry, Sir Benj., iii, 184; John, iv, 8 n; Rev. Will. F., iv, 658
Berrydown (N. Waltham), iv, 221
Berrydown Court (Overton), iv, 210, 211
Berryfroyle (Froyle), ii, 501
Berry Grove Farm (Liss), iv, 85 n
Berryhill (Heckfield), iv, 45
Berthon, Rev. Edw. L., iv, 453, 466; v, 459
Berthon Boat Co., v, 459
Berthon Priors, man., ii, 114
Bertie, Thos., v, 111
Berton (atte, de, de la), Jas., iv, 225, 443; John, iii, 445; iv, 226, 443; Mary, iv, 443; Matilda, iii, 403; Nich., iv, 225, 443; Rich., iii, 379; Rob., iii, 403; Rog., iv, 226, 443 n; Will., iv, 443
Bertonesdowne (Barton Stacey), iv, 417
Bertram, Capt. Collingwood, v, 535; Rob., iv, 213, 558; Will., iv, 213
Berupery, *see* Beaurepaire
Berwe, *see* Burgh
Berwick, Rich. Noel-Hill, Ld., iv, 335; Will. Noel-Hill, Ld., iv, 335
Berwick [Berewick, Berewyk, Berwik] (de), John, ii, 521; iii, 148, 149, 150; iv, 146, 147, 418; Will., ii, 198
Besemerale (Weyhill) *see* Clanville
Besilles, Margery, iv, 105; Sir Pet., iv, 105
Best [Beste], Hen., iii, 19, 83, 101, 125, 395; v, 117, 123; John, ii, 113; (Rev.) Thos., iv, 335; Capt. Thos. G., iv, 335, 336, 359, 361; Will. de, iv, 276
Betestre, *see* Bisterne
Bethell, Rich., ii, 121; iv, 186 n, 428; v, 5, 283; Will., iv, 428; Zach., iv, 428
Bethin, Ant., v, 473
Bethune, *see* Betun
Betsworth, fam., *see* Bettesworth
Bettell, Rich., v, 32 n
Bettesthorn [Bettesthorne] (de), Agnes, iv, 520, 636; Eliz., iv, 520, 543, 609, 636; v, 114; Helen, iv, 520, 610; Joan, iv, 520, 636; John de, iii, 291; iv, 543, 635, 636, 638; v, 305; Marg., iv, 520, 610, 636, 638; v, 114; Reg., iv, 635; v, 114; Rich., iv, 520, 610, 636; Rog., iv, 636 n; v, 114; Walt., iv, 636; Will., iv, 636 n; v, 114
Bettesthorne (Ringwood), *see* Bisterne
Bettesworth, Augusta, v, 180; Bridg., iv, 424; Ellen, iv, 424; Jos., v, 180; Sir Pet., iv, 424; Rob., iii, 115; Thos., iii, 89 n, 244; iv, 424; —, v, 12; fam., v, 181
Bettre, John le, iv, 551 n
Betts [Bettys], Jas., iv, 550, 554; John, ii, 215
Bettsworth, fam., *see* Bettesworth
Betun (Bethune, Betune), Agnes, ii, 173; Bald. de, iv, 213, 360
Beverey, Rob., ii, 159
Beverley, Anne, iii, 204; (Sir) Geo., iv, 169; Marg., iv, 169; Rob. (de), iii, 290; iv, 543; Thos., iii, 204

Bevyll, John, v, 87
Bew (Abbotts Ann), iv, 334 n
Bewchamp, *see* Beauchamp
Bewcombe, *see* Bowcombe
Bewmonds (Winchester), v, 3 n, 11
Bewroper, *see* Beaurepaire
Beyff, Ant., v, 148
Bible Christians, ii, 495; iii, 55, 301, 309, 340; iv, 14, 30; v, 150, 169, 245, 268, 291
Bibury Club, v, 543, 544
Bicanhyrst (Brown Candover), iv, 183 n
Bica's Wood (Calbourne), v, 218 n
Bichetone, Bicton, *see* Bickton
Bickhurst fields (Brown Candover), iv, 183 n
Bickley, Hen., iii, 193, 196; Thos., iii, 150
Bicknell, Rob., iv, 93
Bickton (Fordingbridge), iv, 567; man., ii, 119, 121; iv, 560, 568-9; mill, iv, 569
Bidborowe grange (Newchurch), v, 181
Bidon, Will., iv, 111
Bieda, v, 293
Bienlegh, *see* Binley
Bifleet, *see* Byfleet
Bigbury, man. (Newchurch), v, 181
Bigg, Dorothy, iv, 232; Hen., ii, 366; Lovelace, iv, 232; Mary, iv, 232; Rich., iv, 537; Walt., iv, 243; Will., iv, 232
Biggs, Sir John, iii, 112; Will., v, 514, 520
Bigg-Wither, Harris, iv, 232, 244; (Rev.) Lovelace, iv, 232, 240, 244; Rev. Reg. F., iii, 454; iv, 244
Bighton, ii, 63, 117; iii, 37, 38-40; iv, 223; man., iii, 38; pop., v, 437; sch., ii, 396
Bighton Wood House (Bighton), iii, 38
Bignell (New Forest), ii, 446
Bignell Field (Odiham), iv, 89
Bigod, le, Alina, iv, 150; Hugh, iv, 52, 474; John, iv, 474; Maud, iv, 52, 474; Rob., iv, 453; Rog., iv, 52, 150, 399, 474
Bikston, *see* Bickton
Bilcroft (Faccombe), iv, 314
Bilgrove copses (Knights Enham), iv, 377
Billingham (Shorwell), v, 278, 279, 282
Billinghurst farm (Binsted), ii, 486
Bilson, Leo, iii, 89, 112; Susanna, iii, 112; (Sir) Thos., ii, 83, 85, 314, 315, 316, 319, 366; iii, 89, 90, 300; iv, 201, 317; v, 154
Bilson-Legge, Hen., ii, 477; fam., iii, 322
Bindon, vsctss., v, 333
Bindon [Byndon, Bynedone], (de) Edith, iv, 610; Joan, iii, 415; iv, 481, 520, 610; Thos., iii, 415, 526; iv, 481, 520, 610; v, 312
Bindsworth (Hartley Mauditt), ii, 508
Bineheie (Lasham), iv, 81
Bingham [Byngham], Eleanor, iv, 330, 588; Geo., v, 95 n; Joan, iv, 330, 583; Jos., ii, 97, 98; iv, 430; Mary, iv, 330, 583, 588; Rich., v, 112, 120; Col., v, 352
Binley (St. Mary Bourne), iv, 288, 295; Rom. rem., i, 304
Binstead (I. of W.), v, 138, 151-5, 219; pop., v, 448; Quarr abbey, *see* that title; quarries, v, 151, 462; sch., ii, 407
Binstead Hill, *see* Bentworth Lodge

Binsted (Alton), ii, 137, 241, 249, 471, 480, 483-90, 511, 514, 515, 517, 518, 521; char., ii, 490; ch., ii, 488; mans., ii, 484; pop., v, 437; Rom. rem., i, 305; sch., ii, 396, 490
Binsted, John, iii, 251
Binsted Popham, man. (Binsted), ii, 484, 485
Binsted St. Clare, man. (Binsted), ii, 485
Binsted Wyck (Binsted), ii, 483
Birch [Burch], Fran. H., iv, 9 n; Lt.-Col. Geo. F., iv, 9; Jane, iv, 613; J. W. B., iv, 422
Birchenwood (Bramshaw), iv, 625
Birchmore (Arreton), v, 140
Birchwood (Sherfield English), iv, 510
Bird [Berd, Bierd, Birde, Burd, Byrde], Alfwin [Alwine], v, 22, 476 n; Ant., v, 28; Eliz., iii, 536; iv, 450, 513; Jas., ii, 83; John, v, 99 n, 484; Owen, iii, 204; Rich., iv, 450, 513; Rob., v, 368; Will., ii, 516
Birds, i, 208
Birinus, St., bp., ii, 1, 2, 3; v, 50, 55
Birmingham (Boldre), iv, 619
Biron, duc de, iv, 161
Biset, *see* Bisset
Bisham Priory (Berks.), iv, 261, 265, 277, 612
Bishop, Chas., iv, 258; Geo., v, 80; John, iii, 536; Jordan le, v, 45; Louisa F. K., iii, 50; Rich., iii, 379, 381; Rob., iv, 642; Will., iii, 12, 379; iv, 408; —, v, 514
Bishop Morley's College for Matrons (Winchester), iv, 79
Bishopp's Ashley (Ecchinswell), iv, 250
Bishopp's Greene (Ecchinswell), iv, 250
Bishops' Acre (Bonchurch), v, 155
Bishop's Down (Bishop's Waltham), iii, 276
Bishop's Inclosure (Tadley), iv, 219
Bishop's Sutton, iii, 41-5; v, 308, 324, 328 n, 331, 514; adv., ii, 21; iii, 45; cloth trade, v, 478; man., ii, 23, 37; iii, 42; mill, v, 478; pop., v, 438; sch., ii, 396
Bishop's Sutton, hund., iii, 37
Bishopstoke, ii, 91; iii, 302, 308-10; v, 308, 563; ch., ii, 212; iii, 310; man., ii, 37; iii, 309; mill, v, 451; pop., v, 448; Rom. rem., i, 344; sch., ii, 396
Bishops Waltham, i, 379; ii, 8, 12, 23, 29, 36, 37, 39, 48, 88, 101, 102; iii, 274, 275, 276-82; v, 323, 324, 328 n, 331, 346, 426; adv., iii, 281; ch., iii, 279; ind., v, 466, 478, 491; man., iii, 277; v, 418; mills, v, 49 n, 478; pk., iii, 278; pop., v, 440; Rom. rem., i, 309, 324; sch., ii, 396
Bishop's Waltham, hund., iii, 274
Bishop's Wood Farm (Tadley), iv, 219
Bishop's Wood Stream (Tadley), iv, 219
Bishton, *see* Bickton
Bisset [Biset, Bissett], Ela, iv, 569 n; Emma, iv, 588; Geo. M., iv, 588; Hen., iv, 582; Isabel, iv, 569 n, 582; Iseuld, iv, 582; John, iii, 487; iv, 569, 584, 588; Manser, ii, 169; iv, 560, 569, 582, 586; Marg., iv, 582, 588; Margery, iv, 569, 582; Maurice G., v, 142, 185 n; Will., iv, 582
Bisshopesclere, *see* Burghclere

Bisshophey (King's Somborne), iv, 470

Bisson, Arnoul, v, 491

Bisterne (Ringwood), ii, 62; iv, 550, 603, 606, 609, 612, 614, 635 n, 636 n; chap., iv, 612; chant., iv, 612

Bisterne Close (Burley), iv, 603, 613

Bitfanger Copp (Woodcott), iv, 331, 332

Bithewood, Thos., v, 483

Bitterne (South Stoneham), ii, 23, 66, 161; iii, 482; v, 297; ind., v, 455 n, 465, 466; man., iii, 484; Rom. rem., i, 322, 330-39

Bizo, John, iv, 139

Blacheman, v, 231

Blachford, Anne, iv, 571; Barrington P., v, 200; Eliz., v, 200; Isabella, v, 200; John, v, 228; Rob., iv, 571, 573; v, 200; Rob. P., v, 146, 200

Black, Alice, iii, 390; Audoenus, iii, 390

Blackburne, John, iii, 373; iv, 204

Black death, see Plague

Blackden Bryle [Blackden Raggs] (Hurstbourne Tarrant), iv, 320, 321

Blackdown [Blekedon] (Beaulieu), iv, 650, 651

Blacke Lake, le (Crondall), iv, 6

Blackforde (W. Wellow), iv, 535

Blackgang (Chale), v, 235

Black-Hawkins, E. B., iv, 295

Blackheathfield (Farnham), iv, 1, 2

Black Hedge (Yattley), iv, 21

Blackhouse (Hartley Wintney), iv, 51

Blacklake (Basing), iv, 115

Blackland, John de, v, 182 n

Blacklands [Blackland] (Arreton), v, 140, 142

Blackmoor (Selborne), ii, 176, 177, 452; iii, 3, 4, 5, 16; brick manuf., v, 466; man., iii, 10; Rom. rem., i, 306, 340, 342, 344

Blackmore (Broughton), iv, 493

Blackmores landes (Stratfield Turgis), iv, 63

Blackpan, man. (Brading), v, 162, 170 n, 192 n

Blackpan, Phil. de, v, 147, 174; Thos., v, 144 n

Blackstoke (Christchurch), v, 94

Blackwater (Arreton), iv, 21; v, 140, 145; prehist. rem., i, 258

Blackwater, riv., iv, 2, 15, 20, 32, 39, 94, 99, 409, 535, 540, 542, 546

Blackway(e), Thos., iv, 250 n, 356

Blagden, T., v, 461

Blagdon Hill Wood (Martin), iv, 592

Blagge, Mary, iv, 472; Thos., iv, 472

Blagrave, Ant., iv, 536; Dan., iv, 435; Jane, iv, 536; Sir John, iv, 536; Jos., iv, 220; Magdalen, iv, 536; Col., iv, 533

Blake, Eliz., v, 140; E. S., v, 142; Fred., v, 142, 542; Jas., v, 140; Joan, iv, 356; John, iii, 16; iv, 357; v, 29, 41, 127, 248, 467, 479 n, 536; Nich., iv, 358 n, 363, 507; Pet., iv, 335, 353, 357, 507; Rich., iv, 353, 356, 357, 407; adml. Rob., v, 381, 382; Rob., iii, 96; Sarah, iv, 335, 353, 507; Scott, v, 140; S. T., v, 542; Thos., v, 536; Will., iii, 322, 323, 453; iv, 353, 357; v, 107

Blakedon [Blakedown], (de), Alice, iv, 617; John, iii, 46, 50; iv, 617; Nich., iii, 46, 50

Blakedounesdiche (South Damerham), iv, 588

Blakedyche, le, (Romsey), iv, 459

Blakemore, see Blackmoor

Blakerede (Crondall), iv, 6

Blakewatere (Pamber), iv, 433

Blaklethacre (Andover), iv, 346

Blanc, Edm., v, 553; see also Le Blanc

Blanchampy (Romsey), iv, 452

Blanchard, Pontius, iv, 319

Blandford (Dors.), ii, 126, 159

Blankpage [Blankpayn], Thos., ii, 182, 186

Blashford (Ellingham), iv, 563, 604

Blatch, Jas., iv, 126, 137, 178

Blattodea, i, 110

Bleadon, man. (Somers.), ii, 114

Bleakdown, man. (Godshill), v, 170, 174, 184

Blekedon (Beaulieu), see Blackdown

Blendworth [Blednewyth, Blenelworth, Bleneworth], iii, 82, 84; pop., v, 444; Rom. rem., i, 310; sch., ii, 396

Blessington, Will. Stewart, earl of, iv, 54; Murrough Boyle, vsct., iv, 54

Blewbury, John de, ii, 288

Blewmantell, John, iv, 528

Blisford (Hyde), iv, 568

Bliss, G., iii, 412

Blisset's Farm (Kingsclere), iv, 267

Blissmore Hall, see Clanville

Blissmore Hall Acre (Weyhill), iv, 396, 397, 398

Blois, Hen. de, see Winchester, bp. of

Blome, Will., iii, 106

Blond, see Blount

Blondeville, Randolph de, iii, 103

Blonewrth, see Blendworth

Blood, Col., iv, 21

Bloswood Lane (Whitchurch), iv, 300

Blount [Blond, Blund, Blunt], (la, le), Annora, iv, 367; Chas., iv, 631, 632; (Sir) Edw., ii, 509; iv, 597, 645; Edw. W., iv, 180; Elias, iv, 338 n; Joan, iv, 219; v, 45, 99 n; John, iv, 407 n; Jordan, v, 479 n; Mary, iv, 447; Mountjoy, v, 256; Thos., iv, 110; v, 45; Walt., iv, 219, 528, 597; Will., ii, 486, 503; iv, 28, 367

Blountysmere (Colemore), iv, 423

Bloxham, John of, ii, 267

Blucke, Matth., v, 98

Bluet, Eleanor, iv, 53; John, ii, 128; iv, 53; Marg., iv, 53; Parnel, iv, 302; Ralph, iv, 52, 53

Blund, see Blount

Blundell, Sir Geo., v, 335; Rich., iii, 381; Will., iv, 589; Lt., v, 261 n

Blunden [Blundene], Andr., iv, 82; John, iv, 137; Rich., iv, 82; Will., iv, 82, 83, 140; Mrs., iv, 128

Blunt, see Blount

Bluntesdon, Hen. de, ii, 203, 205

Blyette, Ann, iv, 51

Blynman, Hugh, iv, 624

Blyth, Sir Arth., v, 134

Boarhunt, ii, 108; iii, 144-7; A.-S. rem., i, 378; ch., iii, 146; v, 463; mans., ii, 168; iii, 145; v, 469; pop., v, 441; schs., ii, 396

Boarhunt [Borhunt, Borhunte, Burhunt] (de), Gilb., iii, 146; Hen., iii, 99, 145, 146; Herb., iii, 145;

Boarhunt (cont.) iv, 259; (Sir) John, iii, 98, 239, 363; iv, 172, 202, 259; Marg., iii, 145; iv, 259; Mary, iii, 363; iv, 172, 202, 259; Maud, iii, 97; Rich., iii, 165; iii, 97 n, 145; Thos., iii, 97, 145, 406; iv, 259; Walt., iii, 159; Will., iii, 146; v, 305

Boarhunt Herbelyn, man. (Boarhunt), iii, 145, 146

Boar Mead (Stratfield Turgis), iv, 63

Boat manufacture, v, 459

Boats Copse (Vernham Deans), iv, 329 n, 330

Boccambe Down (Ashmansworth), iv, 274

Bochere, see Butcher

Bockelodgings (Beaulieu), iv, 654

Bockhampton, man. (Christchurch), v, 99

Bockhampton, Middle, (Bransgore), v, 108 n

Bockhampton, North, (Bransgore), v, 108 n

Bockhampton, South, (Burton), v, 108 n

Bockhampton, Hamon of, v, 99 n; John de, v, 128

Bocking, John B., iii, 11; Ralph, iii, 11

Bocland [Bockland, Boclonde, Bokeland, Bokland] (de), Amice, iv, 45, 46, 156; Edw., iv, 45, 156; Geo., v, 250; Jane, v, 183 n, 250; John, iv, 494, 628; Mabel, v, 183 n; Marg., iv, 628; Lt.-Gen. Maur., v, 177, 183, 185, 187; Maud, iii, 107, 168; Nich., iv, 628; Nigel, v, 89 n; Ralph, iv, 493, 494, 628; Rob., ii, 146; (Sir) Thos., iv, 494, 628; Walt., ii, 174; Will., iii, 107; fam., iv, 621; see also Buckland

Bocombe, see Bowcombe

Boda, iv, 498, 521, 532

Boddicott, Edm., iv, 94; Mary, iv, 94; Rich., iv, 9, 94; Sarah, iv, 9, 94

Bodenewell, John, iv, 296 n

Bodenham, Anastasia, iii, 489; iv, 512, 513 n; Rich., iii, 485; iv, 513; Rob., iii, 485; iv, 512, 513 n; Steph., iii, 485; iv, 512, 513 n

Bodham, Thos.. iv, 33 n

Bodley, Jane, iv, 166; Sir John, iv, 166

Body, John, ii, 78

Bodyers (Christchurch), v, 85

Boeles, see Bowles

Boghurst, man., ii, 114

Bogmoor' Hill, iv, 183 n, 189

Bohun [Boun] (de), Engler, v, 143; Hen., ii, 207; iv, 493; Humph., see Hereford, earl of; Joan, ii, 207; iii, 255, 324, 441; iv, 328, 493; v, 247; (Sir) John, iii, 386, 387, 388, 441; iv, 374; v, 247, 273 n; Joscelin, iv, 58, 97; Marg., ii, 192; iii, 374; Oliver, ii, 192; iii, 374; iv, 65, 148; Will., iv, 130; fam., iv, 369, 428

Bohunt Farm (Bramshott), ii, 491; v, 437 n

Bois, see Boys

Bokeland, Bokland, see Bocland

Bokerly ditch (Martin), iv, 592

Boket, Will., iv, 610

Bold [Boolde], Arth., ii, 492; Hen. le, iii, 123, 192, 193; Jas., iii, 125; John, ii, 492; iii, 193, 240; Rob., iii, 125, 192, 204; Sybil, ii, 137; Will., iii, 192, 193

Boldre, ii, 62, 159, 419, 420 ; iv,
615, 616-23, 629, 643, 648 ; v,
81, 82 ; adv., ii, 21 ; iv, 622 ;
chant., iv, 622 ; char., iv, 623 ;
ch., iv, 621, 622 ; mans., iv, 616 ;
mills, iv, 618, 620 ; Nonconf., iv,
623 ; pop., v, 442 ; sch., ii, 396
Boldre, East, iv, 616, 649
Boldre, hund., iv, 615
Boldre, riv., *see* Lymington
Boldreford bridge, iv, 616
Boldrewood (New Forest), ii, 454,
465 ; v, 572
Bole, Le (Bentworth), iv, 68
Bole, Isabel, v, 119 ; John, v, 119,
124 ; Rich., v, 319 ; Will., v,
119 ; *see also* Boles and Bowles
Bolende, Bolendon, *see* Bullington
Bolenore, *see* Bouldnor
Boles, Col., v, 342 ; *see also* Bole
and Bowles
Bolingehill Farm (Buriton), iii, 90
Bolle [Bolla, Bolne], iv, 227, 500,
563, 628 ; v, 146, 172 *n*, 198
Bolney, Barth, ii, 317 ; Eliz., iv,
447 ; Geo., iv, 449 *n* ; John, ii, 318
Bolour, *see* Buller
Bolre, *see* Boldre
Bolshams [Boltesham] man. (Kingsclere), iv, 258
Bolt, John, v, 285, 459 ; Rich., v,
482 ; Will., v, 482 ; *see also* Boult
Boltishams Farm (Kingsclere), iv,
266 *n*
Bolton, Lavinia, dchss. of, iv, 192 ;
dks. of, iv, 107, 108, 109, 120,
158, 181, 192, 193, 611 ; v, 572 ;
Chas. Powlett, iv, 46, 115, 116,
117, 122, 123, 127, 139, 191 *n*, 192,
193, 250, 251, 409, 433 *n*, 545,
632 ; v, 224 ; Harry Powlett, ii,
382 ; iv, 46, 117, 191 *n*, 251,
339, 409 ; v, 224 ; Jean, Lady,
iv, 46, 117, 191 *n*, 251 ; Lds.,
iv, 108, 117, 127, 130, 149,
179, 181, 232, 255, 348, 525 ; v,
140 ; Thos. Orde-Powlett, iv,
46, 117, 122, 191, 251 ; v, 224 ;
225, 251 ; Will. Orde-Powlett, iv,
46, 157 ; Will. H. Orde-Powlett,
iv, 249 ; Will. P. Orde-Powlett,
iv, 122, 191, 193 ; Will. T. Orde-
Powlett, iv, 251
Bolton, Alex., iv, 397 ; Sir Fran., v,
134 ; fam., iv, 181
Bolton's Bench (Lyndhurst), iv,
631
Bolyndene, *see* Bullington
Bolynier, Will., v, 98
Bometa, *see* Boyatt
Bompas, Chas. C., iv, 496 ; Hen.
M., iv, 493, 496
Bonchurch, v, 138, 155-6, 206, 231,
327 ; ind., v, 462 ; pop., v, 448 ;
Rom. Cath., v, 155 ; Rom. rem.,
i, 347 ; sch., ii, 407
Bond, Ant., v, 72, 185 ; Denis, iii,
484 ; iv, 619, 620 ; Sir Hen., v,
343 ; John, iv, 619, 647 ; v, 73,
114 ; John W. G., iv, 620 ;
Leonora S., iv, 619 ; Mary, iv,
619, 647 ; Nath., iv, 620 ; v, 114,
115 ; Nich., iii, 212 ; Rob., v,
96 ; Will., v, 96
Bondi, *see* Bundi
Bone, Dav., iii, 250 ; Mary, iii, 250
Bonecerce, Bonechirche, *see* Bon-
church
Bonehetone (de), Agnes, iii, 39 ;
John, iii, 39
Bonell, Will., iii, 425
Bonet, Nigel, iii, 95 ; Will., iii, 95
Boneta, *see* Boyatt
Bonevyle, *see* Bonville
Bonewood, iii, 217

Bonham, Alice, iii, 78, 259, 261 ;
iv, 367 ; Hen., iii, 87 ; Maur. de,
iv, 577 ; Thos., iii, 71, 78 ; Walt.,
iii, 259, 261, 262 ; iv, 93, 367 ;
—, v, 538 *n* ; fam., v, 155, 172,
173, 231
Bonham-Carter, Geo. L., iii, 87,
113 ; John, ii, 393 ; iii, 87, 204 ;
v, 229 ; *see also* Carter
Bonhayt [Bonheit], Alice, iii, 533 ;
Rob., iii, 533 ; Rog., iii, 512
Boniface, quarryman, v, 462 ; St.,
ii, 4
Boniface, —, v, 538
Bonner, Thos., iii, 184
Bonsergaunte, John, iii, 205
Bonville [Bonevyle], Eliz., ii, 496 ;
Florence, ii, 496 ; Hen., ii, 119,
122 ; Joan, ii, 496 ; iv, 116 ;
John, ii, 496 ; iv, 116 ; Sir Will.
de, iv, 338 *n*
Bonyer, Mary, iii, 29 ; Rob., iii, 29 ;
Sir Will., iii, 29
Bonyng [Bonynges], (de), Hen. iii,
106, 110 ; Isabel, iii, 106 ; Sim.,
ii, 512 ; iv, 8 ; Sybil, ii, 512 ;
iv, 8
Boolde, *see* Bold
Boorden, *see* Bordene
Boore, *see* Boldre
Boorhunt, *see* Boarhunt
Booth, C., v, 575 ; Col. Blakeney,
v, 279
Boothby, Fanny, v, 126 ; Susannah,
iii, 394 ; Will., v, 126
Borard, *see* Borrard
Borde, Phil., iv, 345
Bordean (East Meon), iii, 65
Borden Camp (Headley), iii, 52, 53
Bordene [Borden], Joan, v, 192,
212 *n* ; Rich. de, iii, 396
Boreman, Capt., v, 350
Borer, Will., v, 521
Borhunt, Borhunte, *see* Boarhunt
Bormede (Stratfield Turgis), iv, 63,
64
Borough Cleere, Boroughclere, *see*
Burghclere
Borough Court, man. (Odiham), iv,
93
Boroughe, Edw., iv, 212
Borowclere, *see* Burghclere
Borrard [Borard], Geoff. (de), iii,
150 ; iv, 28 ; v, 195 *n* ; John, ii,
158, 160
Borrell, Thos., ii, 185
Bortel, Bortel Bashley, *see* Bostell
Borthwood, man. (Brading), v,
162
Borthwood Farm (Newchurch), v,
184
Bosanquet, Hen., iv, 396
Boscawen, Gen. Edw., v, 390
Boscher, Boschiri, *see* Bourchier
Bosco, *see* Boys
Boscombe (Bournemouth), v, 134,
135
Boscombe Chine (Bournemouth),
v, 134
Bosden, Edw., iii, 486
Boset, Janin, v, 269
Bosington, Bosintone, *see* Bossing-
ton
Bosley Farm (Christchurch), v, 98
Bosmere, hund., iii, 128
Bosse, Hen., v, 109
Bossewell, *see* Boswell
Bossington, iv, 489, 491-3 ; mans.,
iv, 491 ; pop., v, 446 ; Rom.
rem., i, 344
Bossington (de), Joan, iv, 507 ;
Nich., iv, 506
Bossington House (Bossington), iv,
491
Bosson, Rich., iii, 97

Bostell (Christchurch), ii, 152 ; v,
81, 98
Bostock, Rich., iii, 43 ; Sam., iii,
445, 447
Bosuton, *see* Bossington
Bosvile, Rob., ii, 315
Boswell [Bossewell], Edw., iv, 320 ;
John, iv, 264 ; —, iv, 294, 321
Bosynton, *see* Bossington
Botany Bay Mill (Whippingham),
v, 197
Boteler, Botellier, *see* Butler
Botelie, *see* Botley
Botereaux, *see* Botreaux
Boterel, Hamon, iv, 319
Botes, man., *see* Vernham, West
Botes, de, Eleanor, iv, 330 ; Geoff.,
iv, 330 ; Gilb., iv, 329, 330 ;
John, v, 39
Botiler, Botiller, *see* Butler
Botisdone (Vernhams Dean), iv, 329
Botkyn, Fran., iii, 178
Botley, ii, 97, 137, 213, 310, 317 ;
iii, 276, 462, 465-7 ; man., iii,
466 ; pop., v, 446 ; Rom. rem.,
i, 344 ; sch., ii, 396 ; strawberry
trade, v, 455
Botley, (de), (the) Brian, iii, 466 ; John,
iii, 466 ; Thos., iii, 466, 467
Botley and South Hants Farmers'
Club, v, 505
Botreaux, Will., Ld., ii, 486, 487 ;
iii, 262 ; v, 118
Botreaux [Botereaux, Botreux],
(de), Aubrey [Aubree], iv, 521,
522, 524 ; v, 97 ; Eliz., iii, 204 ;
iv, 551, 564 *n* ; Isabel, iv, 564 ;
Marg., ii, 486 ; iii, 204 ; iv, 564 ;
v, 119 ; (Sir) Will., iii, 204 ; iv,
521, 551, 552, 564
Bottele, *see* Botley
Bottom Down (Whitchurch), iv, 300
Bottom Meade (Wootton St. Laur-
ence), iv, 239
Botwell, man. (Wilts.), ii, 114
Botysplace, man., *see* Vernham,
West
Boucher, Jas. G., iii, 288 ; *see also*
Bourchier
Bough, le, (Kingsley), ii, 515
Boughton, Marg., iii, 269 ; iv, 159 ;
Thos., iv, 159
Boulder Wood (Plaitford), iv, 542
Bouldnor (Shalfleet), v, 272 ; man.,
v, 275
Boulogne, Eustace, count of, iii,
42 ; v, 298
Boulsbury (Damerham), iv, 587 *n*
Boulsbury Wood (Damerham), iv,
589 *n*
Boult, Sim., iv, 232 ; *see also* Bolt
Boultbee, Charlotte A., iv, 634 ;
Maj. C., iv, 633 ; Vice-Adm.
Fred. M., iv, 634 ; Thos. P., v,
134
Boulter, Edm., iv, 336, 401, 402,
406, 409, 412, 414
Boun, *see* Bohun
Bountisborough, hund., ii, 420 ; iv,
188
Bourchenyer, John, ii, 273
Bourchier [Boscher, Boschiri, Bou-
chier, Bowcher], Agnes, v, 126 ;
Eleanor, iv, 473 ; v, 162 ; Eliz.,
iv, 531 ; Fulke, iv, 531 ; Joan, iv,
361 ; John, iv, 361 ; v, 179 ;
Rob., v, 126 ; Thos., ii, 273 ;
Walt., v, 179 ; (Sir) Will., iv,
473 ; v, 89 *n*, 126, 162 ; —, v,
325 ; *see also* Boucher
Bourdigny, Rich. de, ii, 227, 228
Bourges, archbp. of, v, 317
Bourghclere, *see* Burghclere
Bourhunt Herberd, *see* Boarhunt
Bourke, Lady Honora, iv, 433

Bourley, fam., *see* Burley
Bourley Bottom (Crondall), iv, 5
Bourley Hill (Crondall), iv, 6
Bourman, Edw., v, 482
Bourne, riv., i, 394 ; iv, 287, 288,
  295, 391, 512 ; v, 134, 562
Bourne [Burne] (de), Ann S., iv,
  549, 558 ; Maud, ii, 125 ; Rich.,
  ii, 213, 214 ; iii, 324, 421 ; iv, 255,
  256 ; v, 273 *n*, 277 ; Will. S., v,
  87 ; Mrs., iv, 549 ; —, v, 382
Bournemouth, ii, 386 ; v, 83, 133-7,
  331, 433 ; adv., v, 136 ; chs., v,
  135 ; man., v, 135 ; Nonconf., v,
  136 ; Rom. Cath., v, 136 ; schs.,
  ii, 388, 396
Bouverie, Rev. Arundell, iv, 523 ;
  Sir Chris., iii, 270 ; Eliz., iii,
  270 ; Freeman, iii, 270 ; John, iii,
  71, 270
Bouverie-Campbell-Wyndham, Car-
  oline M., iii, 246, 248, 253
Bovecombe, Bovecome, *see* Bow-
  combe
Boveney, man. (Bucks.), iv, 64 *n*
Bovenhurst (Crondall), iv, 6
Boviet, *see* Boyatt
Bovill, B., v, 522 ; Will. de, iii, 362
Bow, brook, iv, 103, 140, 158
Bowbridge House, iv, 106 *n*
Bowcher, *see* Bourchier
Bowcombe (Carisbrooke), v, 210,
  221, 241, 260, 269, 270, 409 ;
  man., v, 200, 213, 228, 234, 282 ;
  wool trade, v, 476
Bowcombe, hund., v, 138, 209
Bowcombe Down, Rom. rem., i,
  348
Bowden-Smith, Fred. H., iv, 626
Bowell, —, v, 576
Bowen, Anne, iii, 398 ; iv, 256,
  487 ; John, iii, 398 ; iv, 256 ;
  Louisa, iv, 487 ; Matth., iii, 398 ;
  iv, 256, 487 ; Will., v, 95 *n* ;
  Capt., v, 400
Bower, Hen., iv, 621 ; Col., v, 527
Bowerman [Bowreman], Alice, v,
  200 ; Barbara, iv, 605 ; Joan, v,
  144, 160, 200, 216, 217 ; Marg.,
  iv, 604 ; Nich., v, 160, 162 *n*,
  200, 216, 217 ; Rich., v, 200 ;
  Thos., v, 200, 216 ; Will., iv, 604,
  605 ; v, 216, 217 ; fam., v, 215 *n*
Bowers (Odiham), iv, 92
Bowes, Thos., v, 320
Bowey, Thos., v, 373
Bowker, Fred., v, 70
Bowland, John, iii, 421
Bowles [Boeles], (de), Alice, iv, 58 ;
  Cath., iv, 616 ; Eliz., v, 187 ;
  Ellis, iv, 58, 62 ; John, v, 80 ;
  Will., v, 187, 264 ; Gen., v, 137 ;
  —, v, 543 ; *see also* Bole and
  Boles
Bowling, Capt., v, 549
Bowman, Will., v, 285
Bowmeade (Rotherwick), iv, 99
Bownamesditche (Froyle), ii, 501
Boworth, man. (Dors.), iv, 587
Bowreman, *see* Bowerman
Bowsum, Geo., ii, 256
Bowyer, Chas., v, 517 ; Christine,
  iv, 570
Bowyer's Common (Steep), iii, 78
Box (Wilts.), v, 462
Boxall, John, ii, 308, 366
Boxe, John, iv, 107
Boxgrove Priory (Suss.), ii, 119 ;
  iii, 271
Boyatt man. (Otterbourne), iii, 401,
  402, 442-3
Boyce, Rev. W. A., iv, 265 *n*
Boyd, Mary, v, 78 ; W. S., iv, 365
Boyland, de, Alice, iv, 605 ; John
  iv, 605

Boyle, Eleanor, iv, 54 ; Eliz., iv,
  54 *n* ; Honora F., iv, 54 ; Mary,
  Lady, iv, 54 ; Mich., *see* Armagh,
  archbp. of ; Murrough, iv, 54 ;
  Peter, iv, 435
Boyne, —, iv, 351
Boynton, John, v, 264
Boys [Bois, Bosco], (de, du, le),
  Giles, v, 305 ; Hen., v, 201 ;
  Hugh, iii, 505 ; Joan, iv, 176 ;
  (Sir) John, iv, 176, 347, 443 ; v,
  201 ; (Sir) Nich. iv, 102 ; v,
  223 ; Pet., iv, 77 *n* ; Thos., ii,
  214 ; iii, 434 ; *see also* Wood
Brabason, Ad. de, v, 143 ; Margery
  de, v, 143
Brabon, Thos., iv, 22
Braceborough, man., ii, 126
Brackley, Rich., ii, 378, 379
Bracourt, *see* Borough Court
Bradanleag, *see* Bradley
Bradburne, —, v, 573
Bradbury, Johanna, ii, 296
Braddene, Joan de, v, 187
Bradebrigg (Romsey), iv, 452, 454
Bradefeld (Christchurch), v, 85
Bradelegh, Bradelie, *see* Bradley
Braden, Ant. de, iv, 278, 279 ;
  Isabel de, iv, 278
Bradenham (Froyle), ii, 501
Bradeston [Bradestan, Bradones-
  ton], (de), Agnes, iv, 34 *n* ; Eliz.,
  iv, 34 ; Ella, iv, 34 ; Isabel, iv,
  33 ; Rog., iv, 589 ; Thos., iv, 7,
  33, 34
Bradeway, *see* Bradway
Bradfield, Jas., iv, 252
Bradford (Wilts.), ii, 122, 223
Bradford, Ld., v, 551
Bradford, Sam., v, 471
Bradford farm (Wimborne), iv, 613,
  614
Brading, ii, 26, 62, 69, 100, 170,
  171, 172 ; v, 138, 140, 156-70,
  190, 195, 206, 208, 267, 374, 426 ;
  advs., ii, 21, 22 ; v, 168 ; char.,
  v, 169 ; chs., v, 167 ; mans., v,
  159, 164 ; mkts. and fairs, v, 158,
  159 ; Nonconf., v, 169 ; pop., v,
  448 ; Rom. rem., i, 313 ; sch.,
  ii, 407
Brading, Joan, v, 191 ; Marg., v,
  169 ; Thos., v, 169, 191
Bradley [Bradlega], iii, 356 ; iv,
  197, 202-5 ; lazar house, ii, 169 ;
  man., iv, 202 ; pop., v, 439
Bradley, man. (Whitchurch), iv, 302
Bradley, Edw., iii, 241 ; Fred., iii,
  216 ; Hen., iv, 202 ; Jack, v,
  528 ; Rev. John, bp., iii, 529 ;
  —, iii, 334
Bradley Hill, iv, 302
Bradley Wood (Bradley), iv, 202
Bradley Wood (Whitchurch), iv,
  302
Bradoneston, *see* Bradeston
Bradsell, —, iii, 535
Bradshaw, Aug. H., iv, 81 ; John,
  ii, 181 ; iv, 253 ; Sally H., iv, 365
Bradshott (Selborne), ii, 471 ; iii,
  7, 10 ; ind., v, 466
Bradway [Bradeway], Agnes, iv,
  520, 636 ; Hen., iv, 481, 520 ;
  John, iv, 481, 520, 636 ; Kath.,
  iv, 481
Brady, Matth., iii, 169
Braiboeuf, *see* Brayboef
Brailsford, Edw., iv, 628
Brainford, Gen., v, 342
Brainsbury (Barton Stacy), ii, 108
Braishfield [Braisfelde] (Michel-
  mersh), iii, 425 ; ch., iii, 426
Braishfield (de), Emma, iv, 468,
  476 ; John, iii, 425 ; Maud, iii,
  425 ; Nich., iv, 468, 476

Braithwaite [Braithwait], Rev.
  Thos., iv, 379 ; Thos., ii, 344,
  366 ; Messrs., v, 396
Brake, Hen. J. E., iv, 22 ; Hen. W.,
  iv, 15, 22
Brambelshute, *see* Bramshott
Brambleham (Froyle), ii, 501
Bramble Hill (New Forest), ii, 446
Bramblehill walk (Bramshaw), iv,
  623
Brambles, i, 69
Brambridge (Owslebury), iii, 334 ;
  mill, v, 451
Brambridge, Gilb. de, v, 451
Brambridge House (Twyford), iii,
  334, 339
Bramdean, ii, 177 ; iii, 37, 45-50,
  245 ; v, 544 ; pop., v, 440 ; Rom.
  rem., i, 307 ; v, 465 *n* ; sch., ii,
  396
Bramdean [Bramden, Bromdene]
  (de), Hen., iii, 46, 47 ; Hugh,
  46, 50 ; Rich., prior, ii, 166, 168 ;
  Steph., iv, 49
Bramley, ii, 21, 137, 226 ; iv, 60,
  113, 114, 140-5, 158, 165 ; ch.,
  iv, 143, 167 ; man., iv, 141 ;
  mills, iv, 141 ; pop., v, 439 ;
  Rom. rem., iv, 140 ; sch., ii, 396
  iv, 141
Bramley, Thos., ii, 119, 122 ; v,
  484 ; *see also* Bromley
Bramley Frith Wood, iv, 141
Bramsbury, *see* Bransbury
Bramschote, *see* Bramshott
Bramsell, Bramshall, *see* Bramshill
Bramshaw, iv, 537, 544, 615, 623-6 ;
  v, 81 ; mans., iv, 623 ; pop., v,
  446 ; sch., ii, 396, 397
Bramshaw, East, iv, 623
Bramshill (Eversley), ii, 150, 222 ;
  iv, 35, 41, 66, 114 ; v, 533 ;
  chap., iv, 35, 41 ; mill, iv, 40 ;
  Moore Place Farm, iv, 40 ;
  Northlonde, iv, 39 ; pop., v, 443,
  444
Bramshill, Great, man. (Eversley),
  iv, 35, 39
Bramshill, Little, man. (Eversley),
  iv, 35
Bramshill, Hen. de, iv, 35, 114 *n*
Bramshill House (Eversley), iv, 33,
  37-9
Bramshill Park, iv, 33, 35, 48
Bramshott [Bramshote], ii, 93, 471,
  491-6 ; iii, 82 ; v, 420, 421, 430,
  464 ; ch., ii, 494 ; ind., v, 457,
  459, 490 ; mans., ii, 492 ; pop.,
  v, 444 ; sch., ii, 397, 495, 496
Bramshott [Brambelshute, Bramschote, Brembelshute, Brembilsite, Bremesete, Bremlessete,
  Bremsholt], Bald., iii, 169 ; Eliz.,
  ii, 492 ; v, 142, 146, 147, 247 ;
  Geo., v, 142, 146, 147 ; John,
  ii, 492 ; iii, 169 ; v, 247, 273 ;
  Kath., ii, 492 ; v, 247 ; Laur. de,
  iv, 477 ; Marg., ii, 492 ; Will.,
  ii, 492 ; iii, 169, 362 ; v, 142, 146,
  231, 247 ; fam., iv, 162
Bramshott Grange (Bramshott), ii,
  491
Bramshott Moor, v, 454 *n*
Bramshott Place (Bramshott), ii,
  491, 492
Bramston, Augusta, iv, 226 ; Edm.,
  iv, 201, 207, 226 ; Henrietta M.,
  iv, 201, 207, 226 *n* ; Rev. John,
  ii, 115 ; v, 74 ; Wither, iv, 201,
  207, 220, 226, 228 ; Mrs., iv, 228
Branches Wood (Melchet Pk.), iv,
  540
Brand, Barbarina, iv, 22 ; Thos.,
  iv, 22
Branden, *see* Bramdean

Brander, Chas., v, 95 ; Rev. Gust., v, 84, 95 ; Gust., v, 85, 94, 95, 110 ; John, v, 94, 95
Brandesberee, Brandesbiri, see Bransbury
Brandon, dks. of, iii, 45
Brandon, Eliz., iv, 531 ; J., iv, 5 ; Sir Thos., iv, 531
Brandun, see Bramdean
Branewyk, Hen. de, ii, 181, 186
Brangwayne, Thos., v, 482
Branksome Park (Bournemouth), v, 134
Bransbury [Bransebury] (Barton Stacey), iii, 401 ; iv, 415, 416, 417 ; man., ii, 114 ; iv, 419
Bransbury Common, iv, 417 ; v, 560
Bransgore, v, 108, 128 ; ch., v, 107, 108 ; sch., ii, 397
Branston (Newchurch), v, 181
Branthwaite [Branthwayte], Rich., iii, 353 ; iv, 608 ; Thos., iv, 608
Braose [Breuse], de, Agnes, iv, 282 ; Eve, iv, 360 ; Maud, iv, 360 ; Pet., iv, 282 ; Will., iii, 386 ; fam., arms, iii, 386
Brarholme, John, ii, 125
Brasenose College (Oxf.), v, 253
Brasier, Rich., ii, 223
Brasses, ii, 481, 482, 489, 495 ; iii, 29, 34, 44, 119, 126, 151, 287, 296, 322, 338, 359, 380, 405, 412, 421 ; v, 65, 73, 149, 176 n
Brassey, Bithiah, iv, 412 ; Nath., iv, 412
Bratley (New Forest), ii, 446
Braunche, Nich., iv, 85
Braundesburie, see Bransbury
Bray [Braye], de, Alice, iv, 352 ; Sir Edw., ii, 149 ; iii, 105 ; Hen., iii, 459 ; Joan, iii, 105 ; Kath., iv, 283 ; Nich., iv, 352 ; Ralph, iv, 484 ; Sir Reg., iii, 105, 124 ; iv, 283 ; v, 187, 219, 220, 223
Brayboef [Braiboeuf, Brayboeuf], de, Hen., iv, 39, 122, 148, 184, 337, 338, 360 ; v, 241 ; Hugh, iii, 9, 459 ; iv, 39, 148, 341 ; Joan, iv, 39 ; John, iv, 341 ; Rob., iii, 458 ; iv, 341 ; Will., iii, 9, 459 ; iv, 122, 123, 148, 196, 341, 358, 360 ; v, 243 ; fam., iv, 35 n, 195, 359, 420 ; v, 210
Braybrooke, Gerard, v, 238 ; Joan, v, 238
Braye, see Bray
Brayesfeld, Brayfeld, see Braishfield
Breach Farm (Bighton), iii, 38
Breach Farm (Sherfield), iv, 104
Breamore, ii, 23, 145, 169, 172, 238, 239, 240 ; iv, 313, 559, 563, 571, 572, 596-602, 606 ; v, 564 ; ch., ii, 234, 237 ; iv, 598-601 ; man., ii, 172 ; iv, 596 ; mills, iv, 598 ; pop., v, 444 ; sch., ii, 397
Breamore [Brommore, Bromore] (de, of), Agnes, ii, 171 ; iv, 598 ; Anne, iv, 433 ; Clemencia, iv, 572 ; Gena (Geva), ii, 171 ; iv, 571, 598 ; Joan, iv, 571 ; John, ii, 171 ; iv, 510 n, 571, 572, 598 ; Marg., iv, 571 ; Nich., iv, 126 ; Rob., ii, 174, 175 ; v, 126 ; Roycia, iv, 572 ; Walt., iv, 572
Breamore Bulborn, man. (Breamore), iv, 597
Breamore Courtenay, man. (Breamore), iv, 596, 598
Breamore Priory, ii, 27, 49, 56, 61, 104, 168-72 ; iv, 540, 553, 561, 562, 579, 584, 595, 598, 616, 618, 645 ; v, 112, 130, 167 n, 168

Breauté, Fulke [Fawkes], de, iv, 82 ; v, 91 n, 466, 469
Breche (Ewhurst), iv, 247, 248
Breche, le (Heckfield), iv, 45, 46
Breche, la (Sherfield), iv, 104
Breche, la (Wolverton), iv, 270
Brechin, — Forbes, bp. of, iv, 41
Bree, Ven. Will., iv, 633
Breitt, Sir Peircy, v, 391
Brembelshute, Brembeshete, Brembilsite, see Bramshott
Bremelshawe, see Bramshaw
Bremerton, man., ii, 163
Bremesete, Bremlessete, see Bramshott
Bremmer, see Breamore
Bremmessage, Bremsaghe, see Bramshaw
Bremshott, Bremshote, Brenbresete, see Bramshott
Brendemore (Eversley), iv, 33
Brendon, see Bramdean
Brengrave (Abbotts Ann), iv, 334 n
Brenningfaud, Alan de, iv, 100 n
Brent, Anne, iv, 456 n, 495, 578 ; Clarice, iv, 577 ; Eliz., iv, 456 ; Ida, iv, 577 ; Joan, iv, 577 ; John, iv, 456, 577 ; Maud, iv, 456 ; Rich., iv, 456, 495 ; Rob., iv, 573 n, 577 ; Will., iv, 456, 578
Brentingham (Calbourne), v, 218
Brerding, see Brading
Breston, Brestone, see Broughton
Brestowe, see Bristow
Bret, see Brett
Bretecombe (Gatcombe), v, 246
Bretevile [Breteuil], de, Gislebert [Gilbert], iv, 35, 57, 339, 438, 457 n, 501, 507, 517, 551 ; Will., v, 301
Brethren's Foundation (Winchester), v, 78
Breton, John, iv, 612 ; Matilda [Maud], iii, 396 ; v, 96 ; Rich., v, 96 ; Rog., v, 96
Brett [Bret, Britt] (de) Christine, ii, 485 ; Eliz., iv, 456 ; Gilb., iii, 228 ; Humph., iii, 96 ; Jas., v, 126 ; John, ii, 37 ; iii, 101, 228 ; Rob., ii, 485 ; Capt., v, 339 ; Maj., v, 126
Brettell, Rich., iii, 136
Breuse, see Braose
Brewer [Brewere], C., v, 554 ; John H., iv, 528 ; J. H., v, 532 ; Rachel, iv, 625 ; Will., iii, 483 ; iv, 533 ; see also Briwere
Brewerton, John, iii, 291 ; iv, 636 ; Kath., iii, 291 ; iv, 636 ; Werburg, iv, 636
Brewes, see Brus
Brewning, see Bruning
Breyanesheth (Rowborough), v, 230
Brexton, Will., v, 29
Brian, see Bryan
Brianzon, de, Eleanor, iv, 53 ; Will., iv, 53
Briccheston, see Brighstone
Brice [Bryce], Eliz., iv, 327 ; John, iv, 528 ; Capt. Rob, iv, 254 ; Will., iii, 19 ; v, 32, 532 ; —, ii, 130
Brickenden, Rebecca, iv, 327 ; Rich., iv, 327 ; Will. J., iv, 327
Brickhill Coppice (Bradley), iv, 202
Brickhurst fields (Brown Candover), iv, 183 n
Brick-kiln Wood (Freefolk), iv, 284
Brickmaking, v, 268, 272, 428, 465-6
Bricknell, Rich., iii, 447 ; Susan, iv, 98

Brickville, see Brikeville
Briclesworth, Will. de, iv, 16
Brictuin, v, 145
Bridcombe, Ralph, ii, 340
Briddlesford, man. (Arreton), v, 141 ; chap., ii, 62
Briddlesford, Will. de, v, 142
Brideport, see Bridport
Bridewells, v, 429
Bridge Court [Bridge], man. (Godshill), v, 173, 175
Bridgeman, Sir Orlando, iii, 261, iv, 358
Bridgemary (Alverstoke), iii, 202
Bridges [Brigge, Brygges] (atte, de, de la), Ant., iv, 487 n ; Geo., v, 8 ; Joan, ii, 132 ; John, v, 173, 175, 184 ; Capt. John S., iv, 5 ; Juliane, v, 173 ; Pet., iv, 338 n, 340, 341, 342, 355, 362, 378 ; Ralph, iii, 150 ; Capt., v, 545 ; Col., iv, 139 ; —, iv, 3 ; see also Brydges
Bridges, repair of, v, 429
Bridgewater, dk. of, v, 533
Bridmore (Charford), i, 393
Bridport, Ld., v, 396, 397
Bridport, John de, iii, 62
Brienni (Carisbrooke), v, 222
Brigae, iii, 323 ; iv, 493
Brigge, see Bridges and Brydges
Brigham, Constance, iii, 150
Brighstone [Brixton], v, 209, 211-15, 219, 248, 278, 279, 281, 411, 411 n ; mans., ii, 114 ; v, 211, 411, 420 ; pop., v, 448 ; prehist. rem., i, 260 ; Rom. rem., ii, 318, 348 ; sch., ii, 407
Brighstone Grange (Brighstone), v, 211
Bright [Bryght], Benj. H., iii, 457 ; Hen., iii, 457 ; John, iv, 522 ; Nich., ii, 158 ; Rich., iv, 427 ; Rog., v, 472 n ; Walt., ii, 91
Brightestone, see Brighstone
Brightmerston (de), Agnes, iv, 392 ; Geo., iv, 392 ; Isabel, iv, 392 ; Joan, iv, 392 ; Steph., iv, 392
Brightwell, see Brittwell
Brightwold, abbot, ii, 121
Brigstocke, Capt. Thos. R., v, 180 ; Will. P., v, 181 ; Miss, v, 179 ; fam., v, 186
Brihtelm, bp., iv, 193
Brikeville [Brickville, Brikevile, Brykevile] (de), John, iv, 506 ; Ph., iv, 362 n ; Rich., iv, 506 ; Thos., iii, 414 ; iv, 506 ; v, 305 ; Will., iv, 506
Brimmore, Brimor, see Breamore
Brinckman, C. E. W., v, 558, 558 n
Brindley, —, iv, 287
Brinesford (South Damerham), iv, 587 n
Brinkebon, John, iii, 124
Brinkhale, John, iii, 414 ; iv, 457 ; Thos., iii, 414
Brinknoll, ii, 163
Brinnage, Rob., iii, 358
Brinsham Stile (Faccombe), iv, 314
Brinstan, see Beornstan
Briscoe, Geo., iv, 491, 492, 493, 515 ; John, iv, 476
Brisei, v, 284
Bristelden, see Bursledon
Bristol, iv, 351 ; v, 377, 379 ; glassworks, iv, 453
Bristol, John, iv, 43
Bristow [Brestowe], John, iv, 140 ; Kath., iii, 393 ; Rob., iii, 393 ; iv, 511 ; Will., iv, 479
Britell, Walt., prior, ii, 225
Britford (Wilts.), i, 393 ; iv, 527 n, 624 ; priory, iv, 626

Brithmere [Brithmar], abbot, ii, 121 ; the goldsmith, v, 459
Brithnoth, prior, ii, 114
Brithwold, bp. of Winchester, ii, 114
Brito, iii, 106
Britt, see Brett
Brittany, Alan, count of, iii, 226, 228 ; John, count of, iii, 228 ; dk. of, v, 366
Brittwell [Brightwell], Edw., v, 176 ; Ralph de, iv, 481 n
Briwere [Briwer], Beatrice, ii, 172 ; Galiena, iv, 474 ; Joan, ii, 154 ; iv, 440, 449, 471, 476, 481 ; John, ii, 172 ; iv, 482 ; v, 223 ; Rich., iv, 474 ; Will., ii, 140, 172 ; iii, 196, 424, 492, 498, 505 ; iv, 108, 174 n, 314, 440, 442, 449, 451, 469, 470 n, 471, 473, 474, 477, 480, 481, 482, 483, 484, 486, 487, 503, 504 ; v, 11 ; see also Brewer
Brixden, see Brighstone
Brixenden, see Bursledon
Brixhill (Yateley), iv, 21
Brixi, iv, 22, 47, 186, 525 ; v, 120
Brixton, Brizteston, see Brighstone
Broad [Broade, Brode], Barbara, v, 280, 281 ; Dan., v, 160 ; Grace, v, 146 n, 160, 280 ; John, v, 204 ; Mary, ii, 388 ; Rich., v, 280, 281 ; Will., v, 146 n
Broad-bayes manuf., v, 487
Broad Ell (Longparish), iv, 406
Broadfields (Merston), v, 146, 268
Broadford Mead (Stratfield Turgis), iv, 63
Broad Halfpenny Down (Hambledon), v, 574
Broadhanger (Froxfield), iii, 76
Broadlands (Romsey), iv, 452, 453, 454, 460, 469 ; fishery, v, 562
Broc, see Brook
Broca Pightle (Hartley Wespall), iv, 44
Brocas, Agnes, iv, 58, 202 ; Anne, ii, 502 ; iii, 53, 213 ; iv, 166, 169, 203, 283, 617 n ; Barbara, iv, 203 ; (Sir) Bern., ii, 166, 222, 502, 512 ; iii, 10, 52, 145, 146, 212, 213, 363, 449 ; iv, 89, 144, 160, 165, 166, 167, 169, 172, 202, 203, 231 n, 259, 289, 290, 373, 434, 435, 443 ; Bern. A., iv, 167 ; Edith, ii, 502 ; iii, 9 ; iv, 166, 168, 169, 203 ; Eliz., iv, 203, 617 n ; Isabel, Lady, iv, 167 n ; Jane, iv, 166, 167 ; Joan (Lady), ii, 512 ; iv, 166, 167, 202, 617 ; (Sir) John, ii, 502 ; iii, 213, 486 ; iv, 121, 146, 166, 167, 169, 203, 283 ; Kath., ii, 166 ; iii, 212 ; iv, 259 ; Marg. (Lady), iv, 121, 167 n, 169, 203 ; Margery, iv, 617 n ; Mary (Lady), ii, 166 ; iii, 145, 146, 263, 449 ; iv, 144, 169, 170, 172, 202, 259 ; Menandus, ii, 227 ; Oliver, iv, 167, 435 ; (Sir) Pexall, iii, 53, 213, 229 ; iv, 143, 166, 172, 203, 204 ; Philippa, iv, 160 ; Raulin, iv, 169 ; Rob., iv, 166, 167 ; Thos., iii, 53, 213, 363 ; iv, 143, 144, 166, 167, 169, 172, 204 ; Will., ii, 215, 502 ; iii, 52, 213 ; iv, 54, 58, 60, 121, 160, 166, 167, 169, 170, 202, 203, 231, 290, 434, 435 ; fam., iv, 106
Brocas Copse (Steventon), iv, 171
Brocas Head, see Broxhead
Broceste, see Brockenhurst
Brocham, see Burkham
Brochelie, man., see Brookley
Brochemtune, see Brockhampton
Brochesene, see Broxhead
Brock, Brocke, see Brook

Brockenhurst, ii, 159 ; iv, 615, 622, 626-9, 648 ; v, 308 ; brick manuf., v, 466 ; mans., ii, 464 ; iv, 626 ; pop., v, 442 ; schs., ii, 397
Brockesheved, see Broxhead
Brockett, Edm., iv, 166 ; John, ii, 379
Brockhampton (Havant), ii, 108 ; iii, 123, 128, 141 ; iv, 396 n
Brockhill (Hurstbourne Tarrant), iv, 321
Brockhurst (Alverstone), iii, 202 ; char., iii, 208
Brockley [Brocklea] (de), Sir Alf., v, 290 ; Alvric, iv, 626 ; Bald., v, 290 ; Rich., v, 290
Brocknes, Brocknest, see Brockenhurst
Broclea, man., see Brookley
Brocliford (South Damerham), iv, 587
Brode, fam., see Broad
Brode Croft (Andover), iv, 346
Brodehalewyk (Pamber), iv, 433
Brodesmede (King's Somborne), iv, 474
Brodheye, Geoff., v, 274 ; Wymarc, v, 274
Brodie, C. G., v, 140 ; Mrs., v, 204
Brok, Broke, see Brook
Brokaker (Sherborne St. John), iv, 158
Brokehouse, ii, 147
Brokehurst, see Brockenhurst
Brokenberry Gore Common (Niton), v, 187
Brokenst, see Brockenhurst
Brokeslade (Penton Mewsey), iv, 381
Brokforlong (Laverstoke), iv, 208
Brokhampton, see Brockhampton
Brokholee (Barton Stacey), iv, 417
Brokhurst, Juliana, iv, 258 ; Rog., iv, 258 ; Will., iv, 258
Brokhurste (South Damerham), iv, 587 n
Brokkesheld, see Broxhead
Brokle, man., see Brookley
Bromdene, see Bramdean
Brome, man. (Itchen Stoke), iv, 194
Brome, Thos. atte, iv, 293
Bromefelde Farm (Christchurch), v, 85
Bromehouse (Itchen Stoke), iv, 194
Bromelega, see Bramley
Bromeselle, Bromeshull, see Bramshill
Bromfield, Hen., iv, 618 ; v, 200 ; John, v, 229 ; John T., iv, 618 ; Will. A., iv, 616 ; v, 187 n ; fam., v, 230
Bromflete, Edw., v, 200, 238 ; Joan, v, 200, 238 ; Thos., ii, 479 ; iv, 224 n
Bromforlang (Arreton), v, 142 n
Bromhaies (Beaulieu), iv, 650
Bromholm Priory (Norf.), ii, 209
Bromle, Bromlegh, Bromleye, par., see Bramley
Bromley [Bromle] (de), Cath., iv, 477 ; John, v, 483 ; Rich., iii, 23 ; Rog., iii, 353 ; Will., iv, 477 ; see also Bramley
Bromley Hill, see Bramshill
Brommore, Bromore, see Breamore
Brompton, John of, ii, 418
Bromshott Bridge (Yateley), iv, 21
Bromwich, man. (Titchfield), iii, 209, 217, 225
Bromwich, John, iii, 225 ; Lucas, iii, 225 ; Thos., iii, 225
Bromyard, Rob. de, ii, 190, 191
Bromyshill, see Bramshill
Brondene, see Bramdean

Brook (Bramshaw), iv, 623, 637
Brook (I. of W.), v, 209, 210, 212, 215-17, 275 ; chap., v, 291 ; man., v, 215 ; pop., v, 448 ; schs., ii, 407
Brook (King's Somborne), iv, 470
Brook Cottages (Shorwell), iv, 249
Brooke [Brook], Ladies :—Anne, iv, 562, 586, 601 ; Eliz., iv, 562 n ; Lds., ii, 346 ; Fran. Greville, iv, 562, 597 ; Fulke Greville, iv, 562 ; Rob. Greville, iv, 562
Brooke [Broc, Brock, Brocke, Broke] (atte, de, de la), Alice, iv, 254 ; Barbara, iv, 302 ; Beatrice, iv, 254 ; Damietta, iv, 254 ; Dorothea, iv, 303 ; Edith, iv, 100 ; Eleanor, iv, 254 ; Eliz., ii, 129, 130, 131, 132 ; iv, 303 ; Geo., iii, 97 ; v, 334 ; Gunilda, iv, 93 ; Hen., prior, ii, 113, 115 ; Col. Howard, v, 535 ; John, iv, 100 ; v, 216 ; Maud [Mabel], iv, 254 ; M. S., iv, 357 ; Nich., iv, 100 ; Ranulf, iv, 254 ; Rich., iv, 299, 303 ; Rob., iv, 303 ; Thos., iv, 303 ; v, 484 ; Will., ii, 513 ; iii, 419 ; iv, 541, 598 ; see also Brooks
Brooke-Hitching, Sir Thos., v, 193
Brooke House (Hawley), iv, 21
Brooker, Amb., iv, 317 ; Thos., v, 75
Brook Green, v, 215, 245, 272
Brookhampton, ii, 159
Brook Heath (Minstead), iv, 638
Brookheath (Rockbourne), i, 344
Brooklands (Lyndhurst), iv, 631
Brookley, man. (Brockenhurst), iv, 615, 627, 628
Brookley, fam., see Brockley
Brooks, Geo., v, 522 ; see also Brooke
Broombridge (Itchen Stoke), iv, 194 n
Broome (Fleet), iv, 5
Broomchille (Hartley Wespall), iv, 42
Broom manuf., v, 459
Broomy (Ellingham), iv, 563
Broomy Lodge (Ellingham), iv, 559, 563
Broomy New Inclosure Cottage (Ellingham), iv, 563
Brotherton, Thos. of, iv, 52
Brougham, Ld., ii, 383 ; iv, 430, 622 n
Broughton, ii, 163, 262 ; iv, 489, 493-7, 506, 515, 523 ; v, 426, 431 ; ch., iv, 492, 496, 497, 509 ; man., iv, 82, 493, 494, 498, 525 ; pop., v, 446 ; Rom. rem., i, 312, 322, 323, 344 ; iv, 493 ; schs., ii, 397
Broughton, hund., ii, 421 ; iv, 489
Broughton (de), Christina, iv, 122 ; Jas., iv, 494 ; Maria, iv, 365 ; Rich., iv, 494 ; Rob., iv, 456 n ; Sim., iv, 494 ; (Sir) Thos., iv, 335 ; 456 n
Broughton Castle (Oxon.), ii, 317
Broughton-Delves, Sir Brian, iv, 509 ; Lady, iv, 509
Broughton Down (Broughton), iv, 519
Broughton House (Broughton), iv, 493, 496
Brouke, see Brook
Brounker, Thos., iii, 169
Brous, see Brus
Brown Candover, ii, 116, 117, 344 ; iii, 42 ; iv, 182, 183-4, 186, 187, 189 ; man., ii, 121 ; iv, 183 ; pop., v, 448 ; sch., ii, 397 ; iv, 183
Brown, Dyer and Edmonds, v, 7

Browne [Brown], Anne, iv, 370, 370 n; (Sir) Ant., ii, 513, 514, 516; iii, 115, 195, 328, 442; iv, 34, 196, 200; Cath., iv, 370; Chas., v, 168 n; Christian, iv, 370; Dav., iv, 427; Edw. H., bp., ii, 100; iv, 158; Eliz., iv, 69, 271; v, 250; Eliz. G., iv, 427; Ethelreda, iv, 370; Fran., ii, 513; (Sir) Geo., iv, 271, 272, 370 n; v, 250; Harold, ii, 100; iv, 158; Sir Hen., iv, 172; Sir Humph., iv, 370; Lady Jane, iv, 271; John, ii, 385; iv, 69, 370; John S., iii, 171; Jos., iv, 145; Leonard, v, 200; Lucy, Lady, iv, 34; Mabel, Lady, iv, 278; Marg., v, 119; Mary, iv, 121, 370; Nich., v, 277; Robarde, ii, 57; Rev. Thos., ii, 374; iv, 267; (Sir) Thos., ii, 79; iv, 278, 370, 613, 633, 638, 649; v, 109, 136; Will., iii, 263; iv, 631, 632 n; v, 119, 120; (Sir) Wistan [Weston], iv, 121, 370; Col., v, 342; Dr., ii, 54; Major, v, 573; Maj.-Gen., iii, 342; v, 343; —, iii, 136; v, 576; see also Brune

Browne's Voyde Place (Sopley), v, 128

Browning [Brownyng], Ant., iii, 137; Hen., v, 47; John, abbot, ii, 144, 146; Thos., ii, 297, 298, 301; —, iv, 497; see also Bruning

Browning Hill (Baughurst), iv, 275

Brownjohn [Brownejohn], Emily, iv, 530, 534; Emma, iv, 534; John, iv, 281, 530, 534; Mary, iv, 281; Sarah, iv, 534

Broxhead [Broxhed], man. (Headley), ii, 471; iii, 52-3

Broxhead Common, iii, 52

Broxholme, John, iv, 549, 595

Bruant, Oudinus, ii, 218

Bruce, And., iv, 249; Lt.-Col. Courtenay W., iv, 21, 549; Dav., see David, king of Scots; Capt., v, 335; see also Brus

Bruddecombe, Sir Rob. of, iv, 407

Brudenell [Brudinell, Brutenell], Agnes, iv, 656; v, 273; Alice, iv, 656; v, 273; Edm., iv, 656; v, 220 n, 273; Geo., see Montagu, dk. of; Mary, see Montagu, dchss. of; Thos., v, 114; fam., v, 161

Bruen, see Brune

Bruge [Bruges] (de, le), Ad., iii, 435; iv, 552; And., ii, 150; Edm., iii, 435; iv, 552; Sir Giles, iv, 190; Walt., iii, 435; iv, 549, 552

Brumelai, Brummeleghe, see Bramley

Brummel's acre, la, (Breamore), iv, 598

Brumora, Brumore, see Breamore

Brundon, see Bramdean

Brune [Bruen, Brun, Brunne, Bruyn] (de, le), Chas., iii, 219; Constance, iii, 260; Eliz., iii, 218; Geo., v, 114; (Sir) Harry [Hen.], iii, 218, 219, 515; iv, 568; v, 242, 275; Hugh, ii, 18; (Sir) Ingram, iii, 218; v, 100; Isolda, iii, 218, 228; v, 100 n; (Sir) John, iii, 219; iv, 419, 568; v, 242; Kath., iv, 419; Marg., iii, 204, 256; Mary, v, 114; (Sir) Maur., iii, 204, 218, 226, 239, 256, 260; iv, 568, 643; v, 98, 100; Nich., iii, 219; Phil., iii, 219; Rich., v, 284; Thos., iii, 219; iv, 84, 419, 473, 568, 610; (Sir)

Brune (cont.)
Will., iii, 218, 219, 226; iv, 253 n, 568, 572; fam., iv, 184; see also Browne

Brunecandevere, see Brown Candover

Brunewych, see Bromwich

Bruning, v, 237, 248

Bruning [Brewning], Ant., ii, 84; iii, 48, 167, 240, 378; Chas., iii, 48; Christina, iii, 167, 240; Edw., iii, 70; Eleanor, iii, 167, 240; Eliz., iii, 48; Ellen, iii, 70; Fran., iii, 167, 240; iv, 296 n; Rich., ii, 84; iii, 48, 70, 167, 240, 334; iv, 296 n; Will., iii, 240; see also Browning

Brunkardoure, see Brown Candover

Brunne, see Brune

Brus [Brous], Agnes, iii, 260, 445; Ingram, iv, 474; Joan, iv, 474; John, iv, 475; Nich., iii, 260, 445; Pet. de, iii, 10; Rob., iv, 382 n, 475; Walt., iv, 382 n; see also Bruce

Brutenell, see Brudenell

Bruton, Alice, iii, 88; John, iii, 228; Rich., iii, 88, 228; Will., iii, 226

Bruton Abbey (Somers.), iii, 131

Brutons (Christchurch), v, 96

Bruyn, see Brune

Bryan [Brian], Eliz., v, 216 n, 251; Nich., v, 251; Pet., v, 216 n, 251; Phil., ii, 278; Will., iii, 184

Bryce, see Brice

Brydges [Brigge, Brygges], Anne, iii, 308; Ant., iv, 166, 203, 611; Barbara, iii, 213; iv, 166, 203; Geo., iii, 307, 308; iv, 62; Geo. R., iv, 190; Hea., iv, 536, 611; Humph., iii, 358, 370; Jas., iii, 39, 40, 307, 318; iv, 536; Jane, iv, 62; Margery, iv, 611; Sir Rich., iv, 611; see also Bridges

Bryers, Pet., v, 168 n

Brygandine, —, v, 371, 373

Brygges, see Bridges and Brydges

Bryght, see Bright

Brygwyn, earl, iii, 269

Brykemerston (Eling), iv, 548

Brykevile, see Brikeville

Brykoresland, ii, 182

Brymbelshawe, see Bramshaw

Brythons, i, 261

Bubbe, Alice, iv, 573; Rog., iv, 573

Bub's Cross (Winchester), v, 20

Bubwith, Nich., v, 562

Buccleuch, Eliz. Scott, dchss. of, iv, 652; Hen. Scott, dk. of, iv, 652; Walt. F. Montagu-Douglas-Scott, dk. of, iv, 652

Buccomb, see Bowcombe

Buchannan, Chas., ii, 97

Buck [Bukke], John, iii, 312; v, 177

Bucket [Buckett], John, iv, 485; Rev. Matth., iv, 527, 530; Will., iii, 294

Bucketts Down (St. Mary Bourne), iv, 295

Buckfield (Sherfield-upon-Loddon), iv, 103

Buckholt (West Tytherley), iv, 489, 519; glass manuf., v, 491; pop., v, 446; Rom. rem., i, 344

Buckholt Forest, ii, 435; iv, 507; v, 491

Buckholt Forest, East Bailey of (West Tytherley), iv, 495, 523

Buckholt Forest, West Bailey of (West Tytherley), iv, 523

Buckholt Hill, iv, 490

Buckingham, Maud [Anne], ctss. of, iii, 113; Anna Eliz., dchss. of, iii, 307, 308; iv, 536; dks. of, iv,

Buckingham (cont.)
381, 636; v, 178, 241, 349; Edw. Stafford, iii, 116; iv, 361; Geo. Villiers, v, 98, 335, 378, 379; Hen. Stafford, iii, 116; iv, 361, 576; Humph. Stafford, iii, 113; iv, 370; Rich. Temple, iii, 39, 307; iv, 536

Buckingham [Bukyngham], John de, ii, 39, 267; iv, 627

Buckingham and Chandos, Rich. P., duke of, iv, 191

Buckinghamshire, earl of, ii, 486

Buckland (Lymington), iv, 646

Buckland (Portsmouth), iii, 140, 141, 194

Buckland (de), Clarice, iv, 526; Hugh, iv, 526; Joan, iv, 646; (Sir) John, iv, 526, 646; v, 114; Marg., iv, 526; v, 114 n; Maud, Lady, iv, 526; Nigel, iv, 646; v, 114; Ralph, iv, 526; Rob., iv, 526, 646; (Sir) Thos., iv, 526, 646; Walt., iv, 253 n; Will., iv, 526, 646; v, 114; see also Bocland

Buckland Hill (Lymington), iv, 639

Buckler, John, v, 218; Will., iv, 617

Bucklers Hard (Beaulieu), iv, 650; v, 387, 397, 398, 403, 458; oyster beds, v, 469

Buckley, Wilfrid, iii, 376

Bucknill [Bucknall, Bucknel], Sir John C., v, 134; J., v, 391, 398; Ralph, iii, 87; —, iv, 45 n

Bucks and Bolts (Faccombe), iv, 314

Bucksgate, see Bukesgate

Budbergh, Herman de, iii, 106

Budbridge, man., (Arreton), v, 140, 142

Budbridge, Hen. de, v, 142; Rob., v, 142

Budd, Fran., v, 540; F., iv, 139; Rich., v, 77; Will., v, 73; —, v, 574

Budden, Dan., v, 142; Thos., v, 142

Buddle (Niton), v, 188

Buddlesgate, hund., iii, 401; iv, 400, 415, 438, 439, 489, 492, 544; v, 324, 331

Budell Whatle, see Wheatley (Binsted)

Budmoremead (Christchurch), v, 97 n

Bugby, John, iii, 101

Buggenore(s) (Godsfield), iv, 185, 189

Buggenoresthorn (Swarraton), iv, 189, 195 n

Bugs, i, 160

Buhurche, Phil. de, v, 479 n

Bukbridge, Will., iv, 102

Bukesgate [Bucksgate] (de), Ad., iv, 507, 520; Eugenia, iv, 507; Helen, iv, 520, 524 n, 610; Hugh, iv, 610; Isabel, iv, 520, 524; Joan, iv, 520, 610; Kath., iv, 520, 610; Rich., iv, 520, 524, 610

Bukke, see Buck

Bukyngham, see Buckingham

Bulandun, see Bullington

Bulborn, see Breamore Bulborn

Buldoxley, ii, 159

Bule, see Bull

Bulehus, Thos. de, iii, 512

Bulesdon, see Bullesdon

Bulford, Sim., v, 483

Bulgy, Rich., iii, 258

Bulhall (Winchester), v, 6

Bulkeley [Bulkley], Anne, iv, 570, 573; Barth., iv, 646; Cath. E., iv, 577; Chas., iv, 561, 562, 570, 620; Christian, iv, 570 n; Sir Dewy, iv, 570; Eleanor, iv, 561,

Bulkeley (*cont.*)
562 ; Eliz., iv, 562, 569 ; Hen., iv, 573 ; Jas. C., iv, 570 ; Joan, iv, 573 ; John, iv, 562, 570, 572 ; Kath., iv, 570 *n* ; Marg., iv, 570 ; Mary, iv, 549 ; v, 114 ; Rob., iv, 570, 573 ; Thos., iv, 570, 646 ; (Sir) Will., iii, 295 ; iv, 549, 560, 570, 573 ; v, 114

Bull [Bule], Ad., v, 49 ; Dav., v, 168 ; Eliz., v, 243, 280, 284 ; Hen. le, ii, 198 ; v, 150 ; Jane, v, 243 ; John, v, 220, 243 ; Rich., v, 220, 243, 280 ; Thirza, iv, 331 ; —, v, 220 ; fam., v, 283

Bullaker, Mrs., ii, 76, 78

Buller, Alex., v, 237 ; Eliz., v, 237 ; John, v, 188, 237

Bullesdens [Bullesdons], man. (Bramley), iv, 142

Bullesdon [Bulesdon], John, iv, 142 ; Lucy, iv, 142 ; Thos. (de), iv, 142, 492 ; Will., iv, 142

Bullington, ii, 132 ; iv, 400, 402-3, man., ii, 137 ; iv, 402, 411 *n*, 412 *n* ; pop., v, 439 ; Rom. rem., i, 344

Bullington, of, Alex., iv, 402 ; Annora, iv, 402 ; Geoff., iv, 402 ; Rob., iv, 402 ; Thos., iv, 402

Bullock [Bulloc, Bullocke], Hugh, iv, 539 ; Margery, iv, 36 ; Rob., iv, 35 ; Sidney L., iv, 243 ; Will., iv, 93 ; fam., iv, 92 *n*

Bullocks, man. (Odiham), iv, 92

Bullocks Farm (Odiham), iv, 92

Bull Ring (Brading), v, 156

Bull's Bushes Copse (Church Oakley), iv, 223

Bull's Bushes Farm (Church Oakley), iv, 223

Bull's Down Copse (Bramley), iv, 143

Bull's Down Farm (Bramley), iv, 143

Bulscroft (Monk Sherborne), iv, 231

Bulsden, Bulsdens, *see* Bullesdens

Bulslade Diche (Eling), iv, 547

Bunbury, Joan, ii, 151

Bundi [Bondi], iv, 57, 225 ; v, 183 *n*

Bunny (Hordle), v, 111

Bunny, Rich., iv, 324

Bunster, Hugh de, v, 128

Burbage (Wilts.), ii, 161, 163 ; prebendary of, iv, 323

Burbage [Burbache], Rob., iv, 481, 527 *n*, 533 ; Will., v, 170 *n*

Burbank, Thos., iv, 468

Burch, *see* Birch

Burchenwood House (Bramshaw), iv, 625

Burchettes, le, (Sherborne St. John), iv, 158

Burci, Serlo de, iv, 592

Burcleare, Burcler, *see* Burghclere

Burcot, of, Ad., iii, 400 ; John, iii, 400 ; Nich., iii, 400

Burcot's Farm (East Stratton), ii, 116 ; iii, 400

Burcum, *see* Burkham

Burd, *see* Bird

Burdett [Burdet, Burditt], John, iv, 522 ; Marg., iv, 522 ; Mary Anne, iv, 522 ; Rich., ii, 510 ; Sir Rob., ii, 346 ; Thos., ii, 510

Burdon, J., v, 461

Bure (Christchurch), v, 82, 94, 109

Bure, brook, v, 84

Bure Homage (Highcliff), v, 84

Burells (cloth), v, 479, 480

Buren Place (Christchurch), v, 85

Burford, John, v, 48

Burgate, Nether, man. (Fordingbridge), iv, 560, 567, 569, 573, 576 ; mills, iv, 570

Burgate, Over, man. (Fordingbridge, ii, 143, 145 ; iv, 560, 570, 571

Burgate, Hugh de, iv, 570

Burgate House (Fordingbridge), iv, 568

Burgate Stuckton (Fordingbridge), iv, 567

Burge, Hub., ii, 365, 366

Burgess [Burgeise, Burges, Burgeys] (la, le), Alice, v, 46 ; John, ii, 128, 149 ; iv, 23 ; Rob., iii, 145 ; Thos., bp., ii, 354 ; iv, 23, 88 ; Walt., ii, 171 ; Walt. de la Brigge, v, 163 ; Will., iii, 22 ; Will. R., iv, 23

Burgh [Abarowe, Berewe, Berghe] (atte, de, de la), Andrea, iv, 561 ; Anne, iv, 561 ; Ant., iv, 73, 561 ; Aveline, iv, 81 ; Christine, ii, 510, 561 ; Edm., iv, 9 *n* ; Edw., iv, 560, 561 ; Eleanor, iv, 561, 562 ; Eliz., iv, 561, 561 *n*, 610 ; Erasmus, iv, 561 ; Geo., iv, 73 ; Hen., iv, 9 *n* ; Hub., *see* Kent, earl of ; Isabel, ii, 510 ; iv, 561 ; John, ii, 510 ; iv, 73, 193, 198, 561, 562 ; John T., iii, 270 ; v, 523, 536, 537 ; Margery, iv, 6 *n*, 9 *n*, 92 ; Maur., iv, 561 ; Nich., iv, 6 *n*, 9 *n* ; Rich., iv, 81 ; Rob., iv, 9, 73, 92 ; v, 119 ; Thos., iii, 204 ; Walt., ii, 510 ; iv, 130, 561, 562 ; (Sir) Will., iv, 6 *n*, 561 ; fam., arms, iii, 270 ; *see also* Clanricarde, earls of

Burgham, Agnes, v, 142 ; John, v, 142 ; Will., v, 142

Burghclere, ii, 195 ; iv, 249, 250, 273, 277-81, 285, 286, 293, 294 ; v, 462 ; ch., ii, 248 ; iv, 279 ; ind., v, 466 ; man., iv, 277 ; v, 419, 420, 421 ; pop., v, 442 ; Rom. Brit. rem., i, 344 ; sch., ii, 397

Burghersh (de), Barth., iv, 159 ; Hen., iv, 116 ; (Sir) John, ii, 519, 521 ; iii, 370 ; iv, 395 ; Marg., ii, 519 ; Matilda [Maud], ii, 519, 521 ; iv, 395

Burghforlang (Longstock), iv, 449

Burghley, Rob. Cecil, Ld., *see* Salisbury, earl of ; Will. Cecil, Ld., ii, 315, 316, 375

Burghton, *see* Broughton

Burghunt, *see* Boarhunt

Burgoyne [Burguynon] (de), Charlotte, Lady, iv, 579 ; Hugh, iv, 519 ; Sir John, iv, 579 ; v, 179 ; Maud, iv, 519

Burhunt, *see* Boarhunt

Burials and burial urns, v, 84, 85, 98, 127 ; Jutish, i, 387 ; Neolithic, i, 259, 260 ; Roman, i, 289, 290, 291, 304, 305, 317, 334 ; Teutonic, i, 387

Buriton, ii, 76, 411 ; iii, 82, 85-93, 116 ; lime burning, v, 454 ; pop., v, 444 ; sch., ii, 397

Burke, Ulick, iii, 49, 53

Burket, Will., v, 520

Burkham (Bentworth), iv, 68 ; man., ii, 470 ; iv, 70

Burksete (Lasham), iv, 81

Burley (Ringwood), iv, 427, 464 ; iv, 603, 607, 613, 615, 632 ; mans., ii, 464 ; iv, 611 ; quarries, v, 463 ; sch., ii, 397

Burley [Bourley, Burlee] (de), Agatha, iii, 71 ; Alice, iv, 611 ; Amice, iv, 569 ; Barnaby, v, 289, 339, 347 ; Beatrice de, iv, 569 ;

Burley (*cont.*)
Eliz., v, 142 *n* ; Ernald, v, 39 ; Geo., iv, 330 ; John, iii, 71 ; iv, 609, 611 ; v, 142, 289 ; Margery, iv, 611 ; Rich., iv, 569, 611 ; Sir Sim., iv, 110 *n*, 569 ; Will., ii, 78

Burley Batten, man. (Ringwood), iv, 611

Burley Beacon (Ringwood), iv, 609

Burley Mills, man. (Ringwood), iv, 611

Burne, fam., *see* Bourne

Burnell [Burnel], Edw., iv, 377 ; John, iv, 591 ; Maud, iv, 377, 379 ; Phil., iv, 379 *n* ; Rob., *see* Bath and Wells, bp. of ; Thos., iv, 379

Burne Place (Christchurch), v, 85

Burnewick, *see* Bromwich

Burnstow (Abbotts Ann), iv, 334 *n*

Burrant Harbard, *see* Boarhunt

Burrant's farm (Hazeley), iv, 51

Burraper, *see* Beaurepaire

Burrard, Anne, iv, 628, 647, 649 ; Betty, iv, 647 ; Eliz., iv, 647 ; Geo., iv, 620, 649 ; (Sir) Harry, iv, 620, 628 ; John, iv, 628, 641, 647 ; Mary, iv, 647 ; Paul, iv, 628, 647 ; Sarah, iv, 647 ; Will., iv, 617, 620, 642

Burrell, Rich., iv, 203 ; R. A., iii, 279

Burridge Feild (Whitchurch), iv, 300

Burrough, Sir Jas., iv, 336 ; John, iv, 336 ; Thos., iv, 336

Burroughs, Sam., iv, 253 ; Sarah, iv, 253 ; *see also* Burrows

Burrow Island (Portsmouth), pop., v, 450

Burrows, E. H., ii, 491 ; Montagu, ii, 294 ; *see also* Burroughs

Burry, *see* Bury

Bursey, Anne, v, 125 ; Frances E., v, 125 ; John, v, 125 ; Will., v, 125

Bursledon, iii, 274, 275, 283-4 ; v, 369, 370, 397 ; pop., v, 446 ; schs., ii, 397 ; ship-building, v, 387, 391, 398

Burstelade, la (Wherwell), iv, 411

Burstlesden, *see* Bursledon

Burstowe, Osbert de, iv, 15

Burt, Will., ii, 325, 338, 366

Burtmere [Burgsmere] Pond (Faccombe), iv, 314

Burton (Brockenhurst), iv, 634

Burton (Christchurch), ii, 152 ; v, 82, 83, 85, 95 *n*, 99 *n*, 108 ; ch., v, 107

Burton (Whippingham), *see* Barton

Burton, Agnes, v, 119 ; Alice, iii, 396 ; Dick, v, 524, 531 ; Jas., v, 205, 231 ; John, ii, 337, 345, 346, 347, 366 ; iii, 313 ; Rich., iii, 396 ; v, 119 ; Rob. de, iv, 160 ; Walt., v, 143 ; Will., v, 77 ; Col. Will. H., iv, 616

Burton Hall, Christchurch, v, 84

Burton Meadow (Christchurch), v, 109

Burton Monastery (Staffs.), ii, 108

Burwell (Hambledon), iii, 241, 245

Bury, man., ii, 168

Bury [Burry, Burye] (de), Agnes, iv, 392 ; Hen., iv, 392 ; Herb., iv, 552 ; Rob., iv, 206, 369 ; Thos., iii, 346

Bury Court (Bentley), iv, 27

Burydonfield (Froyle), ii, 501

Burye, *see* Bury

Buryemede (Romsey), iv, 452

Bury Farm (Eling), iv, 553

Bury Hill (Upper Clatford), iv, 359, 360

Bury House (Eling), iv, 553

Burylond, *see* Newton Bury
Bury St. Edmunds (Suff.), abbey, ii, 108
Buryton, *see* Buriton
Busemerhale, *see* Clanville
Bush, Chas., iv, 70 ; John M., iv, 18 ; Ralf, v, 99 ; Rev. T. H., v, 107
Bushell, Capt. Browne, v, 339
Bussuse, Thos. de, iii, 511, 512 n
Bust, Anna, iv, 502 ; Grace, iv, 502 ; Wm. D., iv, 220
Bustard, Ant., iv, 92
Bustard Manor Farm (Martin), iv, 592
Bustehorne, Rich. de, ii, 156
But, *see* Butt
Butbancke (Faccombe), iv, 317
Butcher [Bochere], Cath., iv, 358, 476 ; John, ii, 257 ; iv, 476 ; Phil. le, iv, 293 ; Ruth, iv, 476
Bute, John Stuart, earl of, v, 84, 85 ; Ld., ii, 349
Butelesheite (South Damerham), iv, 586, 587
Butlege (E. Worldham), ii, 518
Butler [Boteler, Botellier, Botiller, Botiler, Pincerna] (de, le), Alice, iii, 374 ; Anne, ii, 493 ; Chas., ii, 385 ; iv, 239 ; Edm., v, 96 ; (Sir) Edw., iv, 622 n ; v, 128, 529 ; Fred. J., iii, 18 ; Geo., v, 516 ; Hen., ii, 358 ; Herb., iii, 395 ; Isa., iv, 500 ; Jas., ii, 493 ; iii, 18 ; v, 319 ; Joan, iii, 124, 131, 166 ; iv, 500 ; v, 128 ; John, ii, 207, 479, 486, 491, 493 ; iii, 18, 19, 124, 131, 166, 167, 168 ; iv, 500, 501, 607 ; v, 29, 32, 464 ; Marg., iii, 167 ; Margery, iv, 500 ; Phil., iii, 396 ; Rich., ii, 166 ; iii, 535 ; Rob. C., ii, 492 ; Sophia, ii, 492 ; Thos., ii, 389, 492 ; iii, 18, 19 ; v, 215, 523, 537 ; Will., iii, 374 ; iv, 624 n ; W. N., iv, 19 ; Capt., v, 356 ; Mrs., iii, 17
Butler's Barn (Lockerley), iv, 500
Butler's Wood (Lockerley), iv, 500
Butlesgate [Buttlesgate], Will. de, iv, 587, 589
Butman, Rob., ii, 376
Butsash (Fawley), iii, 275 ; iv, 615
Butser Hill, i, 384 ; iii, 85 n, 111
Butt [But] (de), Sir Chas. P., v, 134 ; John, ii, 30 ; Nich., iv, 605 ; Phil. de, iv, 605
Butt Close (Whitchurch), iv, 300
Butter Croft (Long Sutton), iv, 18
Butterflies, i, 4, 130
Butter Wood (Greywell), iv, 76
Butterworth [Butworth] (de), Alf., iv, 345 ; Will., iii, 345 ; iv, 135
Buttesthorne (de), Eliz., iv, 580 n ; Goda, iv, 388 ; John, iv, 388, 580 n
Buttlesgate, *see* Butlesgate
Button, Sir Amb., iv, 647 ; Anne, iv, 628 ; Cecily, iv, 628 ; Edw., iv, 647 ; Hen., iv, 647 ; John, iv, 619, 628, 647 ; v, 115 ; Mary, iv, 647 ; Will., iv, 609, 647 ; bp., iv, 72, 73
Buttons Copse (Priors Dean), iv, 436
Buttons Lane (Priors Dean), iv, 436
Butts, man., ii, 290
Butts Green (Lockerley), iv, 500
Butvillens, Will., iii, 241
Butworth, *see* Butterworth
Buxhill, Alan de, iv, 540
Buyiton, *see* Buriton
Buzun, Marg., v, 241 ; Will., v, 241
By, Ad. le, v, 479 n
Byams House (Eling), iv, 547
Byckton Romsey, *see* Bickton

Bycroft (Romsey), iv, 452
Bydeborough, ii, 139
Byencroft (Bentley), iv, 27
Byfield, Adoniram, iii, 318 : Rich., iii, 16
Byfleet [Bifleet, Byflet, Byflete], Alice, iii, 395 ; iv, 19, 121 ; John, iii, 396 ; iv, 19, 121 ; Mary, iv, 121 ; Rich. de, iv, 604 ; Rob., iii, 396 ; iv, 19, 121 ; Thos., iii, 395, 396 ; iv, 19, 121
Byfleet Manor Farm (Basing), iv, 115
Byford, *see* Bayford
Bygbrooke, Rob., ii, 258
Byggesplace (Faccombe), iv, 314
Bykelynche (Odiham), iv, 88
Byketon (Fordingbridge), *see* Bickton
Byketon, John, v, 482 ; Will., de, ii, 182, 186
Bylands (Stratfield Turgis), iv, 63
Byle, le (Burghclere), iv, 277
Byles, Thos., ii, 91
Byndloss, John, v, 471
Byndon, Bynedone, *see* Bindon
Byng, Sir Geo., iii, 178 ; v, 388 ; John, iii, 178 ; v, 390, 392
Byngham, *see* Bingham
Byrcher, Agnes, ii, 124
Byrde, *see* Bird
Byrhtelm, iv, 27
Byris, Roland, iv, 378
Byrnric, iv, 213
Byron, Adm. John, v, 394, 399
Byrt, Will., ii, 193
Byrte, Maud, prioress, ii, 135
Bysouthwood [Bysouchwood], iv, 625 n
Bysse, Sir John, iv, 388
Byturle, John, iv, 407 n, 418
Byvedon, de, Joan, iii, 415 ; iv, 481 ; Thos., iii, 415 ; iv, 481
Bywes (Carisbrooke), v, 222

Cadbury (Mottisfont), iv, 507
Cadbury Farm (Mottisfont), iv, 507
Cadeham, Rob. de, iv, 318
Cadiz, expedition to, v, 388
Cadland [Cadlands] (Fawley), v, 210, 362 ; man., ii, 181, 184, 186 ; iii, 293 ; iv, 228 n
Cadnam (Eling), iv, 489, 544, 555
Cadnam, riv., iv, 546
Cadnam Common, iv, 546
Cadogan, earl, v, 224, 225
Cadurcy, *see* Chaworth
Caedwalla [Ceadwalla, Cedwalla], i, 380 ; ii, 3 ; iv, 27 ; v, 294
Caer Gwent, *see* Winchester
Caerleon-on-Usk, i, 319
Caer Peris, i, 330
Caer Segont, i, 272, 273
Caerwent [Keyrewent], de, Ithel, iv, 604 ; Nich., iv, 13
Cæsar, Sir Julius, iii, 178
Cage, Lewis, iii, 20 ; Rob., iii, 20 ; Will., iii, 20
Cailly, Thos. de, iii, 373
Cain, —, v, 520
Caines, fam., *see* Keynes
Caines Court, man. (Niton), v, 188
Cairns, earl, v, 134
Cakebreddi (Greywell), iv, 76
Calaway, Sir John, v, 326 n
Calbourne, ii, 4 ; v, 209, 210, 211, 214, 217-21, 247, 266, 267, 268, 272 ; adv., v, 221 ; chap., v, 221 ; char., v, 221 ; ch., v, 220, 221 ; man., v, 212, 219 ; mkts. and fairs, v, 218 ; mills, v, 220 ; Nonconf., v, 221 ; pit dwellings, i, 260 ; pop., v, 449 ; Rom. rem., i, 348 ; sch., ii, 407

Calbourne, hund., v, 209, 210
Calcott (Leckford), iv, 446
Calder, Sir R., v, 399, 400
Caldwell, Capt. F. E., iv, 74
Caleshale, Will. de, v, 182
Caleto, John de, ii, 231
Calland, John, iv, 71
Calleva Atrebatum, *see* Silchester
Calley, *see* Cawley
Callipoli, *see* Gallipoli
Calmady, Adml., v, 514
Calmoor (Netley Marsh), iv, 546
Calne (de), Bald., iv, 407 n, 420 ; Euphemia, iv, 420 ; (Sir) Herb., iii, 52 ; iv, 420 ; Marjory, iv, 420
Calshot Castle [Calshot] (Fawley), iii, 292 ; v, 289, 331, 349 n, 362, 373 ; pop., v, 446
Calshot Point, v, 325
Calston [Calstone] (de), Joan, iv, 521 ; Laur., iv, 521 ; v, 228 ; Rog., iv, 377, 379 ; Thos., iv, 521, 588 ; v, 228
Calthorpe, Barbara, Lady, iv, 75 ; Lds., iv, 5, 74 ; Aug. C. Gough-Calthorpe, iv, 76 ; Hen. Gough-Calthorpe, iv, 75 ; Somerset J. Gough-Calthorpe, iv, 76 ; v, 190
Calthorpe [Calthorp], Cath., iv, 75 n ; Eliz., Lady, iv, 521 ; Frances, iv, 75 n ; Sir Hen., iv, 75, 76 ; Priscilla, iv, 70 ; Reynolds, iv, 75, 76 ; Sir Will., iv, 521
Calthrop, man. (Berks.), ii, 290
Calva, de, Beatrice, iv, 512, 514 ; Ruald, iv, 512, 514
Calveley, Sir Hugh, v, 366
Calvert, Sir Geo., iv, 92 ; —, v, 521
Cambridge, Anne, ctss. of, iv, 347 ; Rich., earl of, ii, 204, 205, 475 ; iii, 153 ; iv, 427 ; v, 318
Cambridge, Thos. of, iv, 403, 410
Cambridge Hospital (Aldershot), iv, 2
Camburnecroftys (Cliddesden), iv, 145
Camel man. (Somers.), iv, 198, 392
Camelford, Thos. Pitt, Ld., iv, 335
Camel Regis, *see* Camel
Cameron, Gen. Sir Will. G., v, 84 ; Mrs., iv, 626 n
Camerton, man. (Somers.), iv, 551
Cammel, Chas., iii, 91
Camois Court, (Suss.), iv, 413
Camoys [Camois] (de), Eleanor, iv, 39, 82 ; Eliz., iii, 68 ; iv, 39, 82, 148, 547 ; (Sir) Hugh, iii, 68, 148, 158, 459 ; iv, 39, 82, 547, 548, 555 ; Isabel, ii, 132 ; (Lady) Joan, iii, 374 ; iv, 39 ; John, iii, 60 ; iv, 82, 547, 548 n ; Marg., iv, 82, 547, 548 n ; Margery, ii, 129 ; Ralph, ii, 207, 493 ; iii, 60, 62, 68, 239, 241 ; iv, 82, 547 ; Rob., iv, 82 ; Thos., iv, 82, 548 n ; fam., iv, 123 ; arms, iii, 239, 374
Campania [Campeny], de, John, v, 98, 99, 108 ; Margery, iii, 68, 69 ; Pet., iii, 68 ; Will., iii, 68
Campbell, Col. Alex., v, 248 ; Caroline F., iii, 248 ; Jane, v, 248 ; John, iii, 248 ; John H., iii, 248 ; Miss, iv, 139
Campden [Campeden], John de, ii, 196, 197, 198, 267 ; v, 61, 65
Campeny, *see* Campania
Campessete, *see* Kempshott
Campion, Abra., iii, 27 ; iv, 646 ; Hen., iii, 27 ; iv, 646 ; Rich., iii, 27
Cams, man. (Fareham), iii, 214
Camsbishop (Fareham), iii, 209
Camvil, Frances, iv, 112
Canaan (Liss), iv, 85 n

Canada (W. Wellow), iv, 539
Cancelot, Will., ii. 229, 230
Candefer, Candeura, Candever, par., *see* Brown Candover, Chilton Candover, and Preston Candover
Candever (Hartley Mauditt), *see* Candovers
Candever, fam., *see* Candover
Candevre, par., *see* Brown Candover, Chilton Candover, and Preston Candover
Candevre Abbatis, *see* Brown Candover
Candieura, *see* Preston Candover
Candle manuf., v, 460, 461
Candover, par., *see* Brown Candover, Chilton Candover, and Preston Candover
Candover, riv., iv, 195; v, 562
Candover [Candever], de, Christine, iii, 396; Rich., iii, 396; Rog., ii, 182, 186
Candover House (Brown Candover), iv, 183
Candovers, farm (Hartley Mauditt), ii, 508
Candovers, man. (Hartley Mauditt), ii, 510
Candovre, *see* Preston Candover
Canefield (Lockerley), iv, 500
Caneford, Rich. de, ii, 174, 175
Cane meadow (Heckfield), iv, 45, 47
Canevacier, Will. le, v, 34
Canford, man. (Dors.), ii, 172
Canham's Lodge, *see* Cannon's Lodge
Caningmersshe (Damerham), iv, 586
Canne [Cans] (de), Herb., iv, 359; John, v, 112; Ralph, ii, 110
Canning, Geo., v, 265; Sim., ii, 121
Cannon [Canoun, Chanon], Denys, ii, 41, 221; John, v, 461; Kempton, v, 554, 555; Mornington, v, 552, 554, 555; Rich., iv, 112; Thos., iv, 525; v, 542, 548, 553, 554
Cannon Bridge (Stratfieldsaye), iv, 57
Cannon Court (Kingsclere), iv, 250
Cannon Heath Down (Kingsclere), iv, 250; v, 547
Cannon Heath Farm (Kingsclere), iv, 250
Cannon Park (Kingsclere), iv, 250
Cannons, —, v, 537
Cannon's Lodge (Kingsclere), iv, 120, 250
Canoun, *see* Cannon
Cans, *see* Canne
Cansangers, *see* Chauntsingers
Cantel, Rob., iv, 500
Canterbury (Kent), ii, 8
Canterbury, archbps. of, ii, 320, 340; iii, 42; iv, 41, 284; v, 247, 263, 303; Geo. Abbot, ii, 115, 322; iv, 36, 41; Alphege [Elphege], ii, 6, 7, 8; v, 51; Anselm, ii, 10, 11, 216; Thos. Arundel, ii, 44, 45, 46, 171, 174; Baldwin, v, 291; Thos. Becket, ii, 12, 13, 19, 153, 160, 482; v, 360, 418; Hen. Chicheley, ii, 262, 292; iv, 88; Will. de Corbeuil, v, 302; Thos. Cranmer, ii, 52; Will. Howley, ii, 359; iii, 42; iv, 254, 264 *n*, 345; Sim. Islip, ii, 36; Steph. Langton, iv, 88; v, 308, 309; Will. Laud, ii, 88, 89, 95, 323, 500; iv, 36; v, 248; John Morton, ii, 48; iv, 225, 336; John Peckham, ii, 164, 165, 173; Plegmund, ii, 5; Reg. Pole, ii, 58, 72, 159, 162, 373; Walt. Reynolds, ii, 150; Stigand, ii, 9;

Canterbury (*cont.*)
iii, 65, 444; iv, 419; v, 51; John Stafford, ii, 286; John Stratford, ii, 16, 28, 29, 30, 102, 111, 118, 155, 161, 170, 195, 229; iii, 261, 461; iv, 42, 146, 153, 176 *n*, 302, 325, 493; v, 215, 235; Theobald, ii, 216; iii, 130; iv, 373; Hub. Walter, iv, 58; v, 307; Will. Warham, ii, 52, 294; iii, 71; iv, 165, 225, 227, 228, 229, 239, 249, 258; v, 18; Rob. Winchelsey, ii, 23
Canterton (Minstead), iv, 615, 635; man., iv, 559, 624, 637, 638; v, 568
Canterton (Preston Candover), iii, 376
Canterton (de), Alice, iv, 508, 548, 637; And., iv, 637; John, iv, 508, 548, 637; Nich., iv, 637; Ralph, iv, 637; Thos., ii, 84; Will., iv, 548, 637
Canteshangra, *see* Chauntsingers
Canute, *see* Cnut
Capell, Arth., Ld., iv, 431
Capell [Capel, Capella] (de), Ad., ii, 214; Barth., iii, 444; Edw., iv, 431; Eliz., iv, 125, 126; Sir Giles, iv, 431; (Sir) Hen., iii, 441; iv, 431; (Sir) Will., iv, 431
Capelyn [Caplen, Capleyn], John, iii, 483, 503, 508, 527; iv, 413
Capon, Hen., iv, 302; John, bp. of Salisbury, ii, 388; Will., ii, 387, 388; iii, 525
Capron, Ant., iii, 78; fam., iii, 300
Carbonel, Sibel, ii, 25, 132; *see also* Carvanell
Cardeville [Cardenville, Cardevile, Cardville] (de), Alice, iv, 577; Eugenia, iv, 332; Joan, iv, 577; (Sir) Rich., iv, 255, 269, 332, 519, 520, 524, 577; v, 305; Sanchea, iv, 255; (Sir) Will., iv, 494, 520, 577, 582; fam., iv, 573; *see also* Careville
Cardeyf, Hen., ii, 209
Cardica, Benedict, bp. of, iv, 202
Cardon, Rob., v, 473
Cardonell [Cardonnell], Ad., iii, 143, 293, 294; Mary, iii, 143, 293, 294; Pet., iii, 293; —, v, 489
Cardville, *see* Cardeville
Cardwell, Edw., vsct., ii, 358
Carelieu, Geoff. de, iv, 319
Careville (de), Joan, iv, 302; Parnel, iv, 301; Ralph, iv, 301; Rob., iv, 302; *see also* Cardeville
Carew, Alice, Lady, iv, 420; Dan., iv, 338 *n*; Dorothy, v, 112, 120; Sir Edm., iv, 338; Eliz., iv, 338; (Sir) Geo., v, 112, 120, 374; Hen., ii, 82; v, 112, 120; Joan, iv, 338; John, iv, 338, 343; Leonard, iv, 338; Marg., iv, 338; Sir Matth., iv, 420; Mercy, iv, 419; Nich., iv, 338, 419; (Sir) Thos., iv, 338, 338 *n*; v, 111, 112, 120, 123, 200
Carey [Carie, Cary, Carye], Sir Geo., ii, 81; iv, 626; v, 224, 225, 226, 227, 240, 287 *n*, 331, 332, 378; John, iv, 626; Rich., iv, 370; Rob., v, 377; Sergt.-Maj., v, 340
Carey's Sconce (I. of W.), v, 289, 351
Carhampton, hund., ii, 169
Carie, *see* Carey
Caries Sconce, *see* Carey's Sconce
Carique, Will., iv, 95
Carisbrooke, ii, 69; iv, 40 *n*; v, 204, 209, 210, 216, 221-35, 241, 242, 243, 246, 248, 253, 259, 262, 270,

Carisbrooke (*cont.*)
271, 275, 293, 347, 418; adv., ii, 21, 138, 139; v, 234; chant., v, 234; chap., v, 234; char., v, 235; ch., ii, 230; v, 232; man., v, 222, 230; mills, v, 230; Nonconf., v, 235; pop., v, 449; Rom. Brit. rem., i, 316, 348; schs., ii, 407
Carisbrooke, hon. [ldshp.] of, iv, 553; v, 141, 146, 187, 195, 199, 201 *n*, 204, 206, 222
Carisbrooke Castle, iv, 508 *n*; v, 90, 210, 215, 219, 222-7, 228, 246, 248, 251, 254, 261, 273, 279, 288, 300, 312, 339, 350, 351, 378, 462; chap., v, 234; iron quarrels, v, 464
Carisbrooke Park, *see* Parkhurst Forest
Carisbrooke Priory, ii, 41, 106, 230-1; iv, 365; v, 164, 171, 176, 189, 229, 234, 239, 256 *n*, 284
Caritate (de), Godf., iii, 444; Hen., iii, 448; John, iii, 444
Carle, iv, 147, 512
Carleton, Anne H., *see* Dorchester, Lady; Arthur H., *see* Dorchester, Ld.; Charlotte, *see* Dorchester, Lady; Capt. Dudley, v, 543; Dudley W., *see* Dorchester, Ld; Frances L., iv, 155; Guy, *see* Dorchester, Ld.; Henrietta A., *see* Dorchester, Lady; Maria L., iv, 155
Carlisle, bps. of, iv, 86; Thos. Merks, ii, 37, 44, 45; Hugh Percy, v, 186
Carlisle, Eliz., ctss. of, iii, 159, 234, 235; earls of, Chas., iii, 234; Edw., iii, 159, 234; Will., iii, 159
Carlow, hon. of, iv, 52
Carlton (Somers.), iv, 62
Carlyle, Thos., iii, 395
Carlyon, Col. Tredenham F., iv, 15
Carmelian, Pet., ii, 119
Carmelites, ii, 15, 57, 105, 193
Carnac, Col. John, iv, 611
Carnarvon, Henrietta, ctss. of, iv, 281; earls of, iv, 274, 281, 285, 286, 313, 332; v, 557; Geo. E. S. M. Herbert, iv, 253, 278, 279, 294; Hen. G. Herbert, iv, 253, 294; Hen. H. M. Herbert, iv, 281; Hen. J. G. Herbert, iv, 253, 294
Carnegie, fam., arms, iii, 330
Carnivora, i, 242
Carnver, Joan, iv, 420; Rich., iv, 420
Carpenter, Grace, iv, 634; Thos., iii, 180, 194, 310; fam., arms, iii, 234
Carpenter-Garnier, John, iii, 234, 235; v, 558 *n*, 559
Carr, Thos., v, 126
Carrill, *see* Caryll
Carter, Alice, iv, 144; Dorothy, v, 229, 230; Edw., v, 155, 181, 183, 184; Geo., v, 531, 532; Harriet, v, 155; Hen., ii, 443; (Sir) John, ii, 210, 215; iii, 180, 204; v, 229; John M., v, 489 *n*; Jos., iv, 71, 107, 170, 238, 403; Rich., iv, 144; R., v, 391; Sarah, iv, 613; Susannah, iii, 204; Capt. Will., v, 388; Miss, iv, 606; fam., v, 172, 231; *see also* Bonham-Carter
Carter, Sons, & Lewis, v, 489 *n*
Carteret, Ld., iv, 71
Carteret, Anna, iii, 69; Bridg., iii, 69; Edw., iii, 69; iv, 413; Isabella, iii, 69; Rob., iv, 186
Carter's Common (Romsey), iv, 452

Carvanell, Pet., iv, 271, 352; Sanchia, iv, 279, 352; see also Carbonel

Carver, —, v, 544

Carvyle, Cecily de, v, 191; Hen. de, v, 191

Carvyles (Ecchinswell), iv, 250

Cary, Carye, see Carey

Caryll [Carrill], Eliz., ii, 507; John, ii, 493; iv, 353; Marg., iii, 97; Margery, ii, 508; Mary, iii, 97; Phil., iii, 97; (Sir) Rich., ii, 507, 516; iii, 145; fam., arms. ii, 507

Carys (Brockenhurst), iv, 626

Cascades, the (Hurstbourne Priors), iv, 287

Casewell, John, iii, 99, 344

Casford, John, v, 173

Cason, Edw., iv, 77

Cass, Agnes, iii, 441; Rich., iii, 441

Castanier, Anne, iii, 536

Castell, John, iv, 569; Will., iv, 628

Castle, Eliz., iv, 620; Joan, iv, 620; John, iv, 620; Will., iv, 620

Castlefield (Andover), Rom. Brit. rem., i, 302, 344

Castlehold (Carisbrooke), v, 234, 235, 259

Castle-land (Chawton), ii, 498

Castlemaine, vsct., see Tylney, earl

Castle Malwood (Minstead), iv, 635

Castleman, Hen., v, 100

Castle Ralph, Will. de, ii, 503

Caston, Eliz., iv, 140

Caswall, Jane, iv, 23 n; Rev. Rob. C., iv, 23

Catchet Wolcorner (King's Somborne), iv, 470

Catelyn, see Catlin

Cater, Rich., iii, 168

Catescroft [Catesmede] (Timsbury), iv, 486

Catherine, see Katherine

Catherington, ii, 73; iii, 64, 82, 94-101; adv., iii, 101; char., iii, 101; ch., iii, 100; mans., iii, 94; pop., v, 444; sch., ii, 397

Catisfield (Fareham), iii, 209; char., iii, 215

Catlees (Froyle), ii, 504

Catlin [Catelyn], Mary, iv, 169; Phil., iv, 169; Rob., iv, 303

Catrington, see Catherington

Catteley, Rich., ii, 504

Cattle, v, 501, 503, 504, 506, 510; prices, v, 493, 494, 495, 496, 497

Cattyk, John, ii, 111

Caty, John de, iv, 92

Caudata, i, 207

Caulfield, Reg. M., iii, 76

Caunterbury, Alice, iv, 382 n; Edw., iv, 382 n; Thos., iv, 382 n

Causeway Acre (Christchurch), v, 109

Causingrey (Basing), iv, 115

Causway (Baughurst), iv, 275

Cauz, Geoff. de, iv, 68; John de, ii, 114

Cave, Adrian, iii, 120; Chas., iii, 120; Chas. J. P., iii, 91; Laur., iii, 120; Laur. T., iii, 91; Lucy, iii, 120

Cave-dwellers, i, 255

Cavelichill (King's Somborne), iv, 470

Cavendish (de), Alice, iv, 392; Julia, iv, 340, 341, 342, 362, 392; Phil., iii, 69; Rich., iv, 341, 342, 362, 392; Will. H., iv, 450

Cawden and Cadworth, hund. (Wilts.), iv, 544 n, 594

Caweburn, Cawelbourne, Cawelburna, see Calbourne

Cawley [Calley], Ralph, iv, 353; Will., v, 78

Cawode, Jas., iv, 64

Caynefeilds (Lockerley), iv, 500

Caynes Court, see Caines Court

Cazalet, Rev. W. G., iv, 71

Cazenove, Walt. de P., v, 574

Ceadwalla, see Caedwalla

Cealwin, king of Wessex, v, 295

Cecil, Ld. Arth., iv, 616

Cecil, Sir Rob., see Salisbury, earl of; Will., ii, 315, 316, 375

Cecily, d. of Baldred, iv, 388; princess, v, 147; prioress of Wintney, ii, 149, 151

Ceddas, v, 27

Cedwalla, see Caedwalla

Celature, see Chilton

Celeworda, see Chilworth

Celvecrote, v, 160 n

Cement manuf., v, 454-5

Centipedes, i, 163

Centurion's Chapel (Wolverton), v, 169 n

Centurion's Copse (I. of W.)., Rom. Brit. rem., i, 316, 348

Cenwalh [Cenwalch, Kinewald], i, 391; ii, 2, 108; iii, 304, 348

Ceoseldene, ii, 116

Cephalopoda, i, 105

Cerdeford, see Charford

Cerdic, i, 1, 382, 385; ii, 1; v, 222, 293, 294

Cerdicesford, see Charford

Cerdiceslea, v, 293

Cerdicesora, see Charmouth

Cerdic's Ford, see Charford

Cerewarton, see Cholderton

Cerne, John, ii, 113

Cerne Abbey (Dors.), v, 320 n

Cetacea, i, 250

Chabannes, —, de, v, 202

Chabeneys, Will. de, v, 241

Chaby Watercourse (Romsey), iv, 455

Chacombe, Rich., de, ii, 161, 163

Chaddenwick, man. (Wilts.), iv, 199

Chaddesle, Rich. de, i v, 202

Chaddleworth (Berks.), ii, 146

Chadgrove (Longstock), iv, 449

Chadreton, John, iii, 192; v, 326

Chadwell estate (Winchester), v, 78

Chadwick, Jas., ii, 384, 385; Pet., v, 473

Chaffin [Chafin, Chaffyne], Amphyllis, ii, 477; iii, 414; iv, 22; Bamfield, ii, 477; Geo., ii, 477, 516; Mary, iii, 169; Thos., ii, 477; iii, 414; iv, 22; Will., iii, 169; v, 85 n; —, v, 142 n; fam., arms, ii, 516

Chalcombe (de), Cecily, iv, 440, 474; John, iv, 440, 474; v, 125, 126; Thos., v, 125, 126

Chalcraft, Will., ii, 495

Chalcroft (Brading), v, 160 n

Chaldecote, Val de, iii, 485

Chalden, par., see Shalden

Chalden Common (Niton), v, 187

Chaldon (Faccombe), iv, 317

Chale, iv, 610; v, 188, 209, 210, 220, 235-40, 249, 264, 281; adv., v, 239; chap., v, 239; char., v, 239, 240; ch., v, 238, 239; grange, ii, 230; man., v, 170 n, 236, 237; mills, v, 238; Nonconf., v, 239; pop., v, 449; sch., ii, 407

Chale Bay, v, 468

Chale Common, v, 236

Chalecroft, see Chalcroft

Chale Farm (Chale), v, 236

Chalfhunte, Rich. de, ii, 127

Chalfversh (Petersfield), iii, 117

Chalfversh, fam., see Chalvers

Chalghton, see Chalton

Chalgrave, man. (Freefolk), iv, 208, 283, 285

Chalgrave [Chelegrave], Rich. of, iv, 283; Will. of, ii, 203; iv, 283, 284

Chalk (Wilts.), v, 291

Chalkcroft Lane (Penton Mewsey), iv, 381

Chalk industry, v, 454

Chalkton, see Chalton

Challdown, see Chaldon

Challeton, see Chalton

Challoner [Chaloner], Rob., iv, 523; Sir Thos., v, 330; Will., ii, 198

Chally (King's Somborne), iv, 470

Chaloner, see Challoner

Chalons, cloth, v, 478, 479, 480, 482

Chalton [Chalughton], iii, 82, 102-10; adv., iii, 109; char., iii, 110; ch., iii, 107; man., iii, 84, 103; pop., v, 444; sch., ii, 397

Chalton wood, iii, 158

Chalvemede (Odiham), iv, 88

Chalvers [Chalfversh] (de), Hen., iii, 117; Sigar, iii, 117; Warren, iii, 117

Chamberlayne [Chamberlain, Chamberlayn, Chamberleyn] (the), Alice, ii, 129; iii, 298; Andr., iv, 265, 267; Beatrice, iv, 392; Charlotte, iv, 455; Christine, iv, 340, 341, 342, 362, 392; Geoff., iv, 443; Herb., iii, 123, 260; Humph., iv, 492; John, ii, 450; iv, 200, 266, 340, 341, 362, 392, 429, 522; Julia, iv, 392; Marg., iii, 429; iv, 340, 341, 342, 362, 392, 522; Margery, iv, 200; Ralph, iii, 298; Rich., iv, 443; Rob., iv, 443; v, 200; Tankerville, ii, 470; iii, 298, 420, 463, 464, 472, 477, 486, 487; iv, 487, 488, 502, 508; v, 230, 559; Thos., iii, 464; iv, 455; v, 230, 329, 574, 575; T., v, 558 n; T. W., iii, 297; Will., ii, 351; iii, 96, 193, 297, 477; iv, 340, 341, 342, 362, 392, 450, 454, 455, 487, 548 n; —, iv, 443; v, 274, 517, 538, 546; fam., arms, iii, 420; v, 230

Chamberlaynes hold (Longparish), iv, 407

Chambers, Alice, iv, 224, 225; F., v, 113; Rich., iv, 224, 225

Chameleygh, man., ii, 159

Champayne, John de, iv, 121

Champernoun, Joan, iv, 326

Champflour [Champfloure, Champfleur, Champflower, Chawnflower], John, ii, 367, 480; v, 125; fam., ii, 482

Champion [Champyon], Hugh, v, 91 n; Pet., v, 484; —, v, 527

Champneys, Agnes, ii, 316; John, v, 172; Marg., v, 172

Chanceaus [Chancels] (de), Aimery, iv, 141, 142; Andr., iv, 319; Cecily, iv, 141 n; Geon, iv, 319; Pet., iv, 319; Thos., iv, 141 n, 142 n

Chancumbe (de), Amice, iii, 250; Thos., iii, 250

Chandler [Chaundler] (le), Ad., iii, 483; Geo., iv, 357; John, ii, 49, 171, 172; Rich., ii, 285; iii, 214; Thos., ii, 197, 285, 287, 290, 292, 294, 314, 365; v, 17; Walt., iii, 228, 283

Chandlers Ford (North Stoneham), iii, 479; brickmaking, v, 465; sch., ii, 397

Chandos, dks. of, iv, 537; Hen. Brydges, iv, 536; Jas. Brydges, iii, 39, 40, 307, 318; iv, 536; Jane Brydges, Lady, iv, 62; Geo. Brydges, Ld., iv, 62
Chanon, see Cannon
Chantries, ii, 62, 65, 66, 480, 500; iii, 335, 338, 377, 394, 398, 525, 526; iv, 123, 152, 238, 355, 435, 468, 612, 622, 649; v, 16, 17, 109, 123, 169, 177, 203, 206, 217, 234, 252, 263
Chantry House (Godshill), v, 170
Chanyn, Margery, ii, 478; Rich., ii, 478
Chapel Copse (Fyfield), iv, 368
Chapeleyn, see Chaplin
Chapel field (Ellingham), see Chappell field
Chapel Field (Preston Candover), Rom. Brit. rem., i, 306
Chapelhaye (Breamore), iv, 596
Chapellayne, see Chaplin
Chapgate (Whitchurch), iv, 299
Chaplin [Chapeleyn, Chapellayne], Ernest, v, 539; Horace, v, 539; Joan, iv, 571; Thos., iv, 571; Walt., ii, 135; —, v, 539
Chapman, Agnes, iv, 96; Alice, iv, 570; John, ii, 78; iv, 570; v, 484; Thos., iv, 96
Chapmansford (St. Mary Bourne), iv, 296; mill, iv, 289
Chapmansford Farm (St. Mary Bourne), iv, 296
Chapman's Hall (Winchester), v, 2, 476 n, 477
Chappell (Highclere), iv, 285
Chappell Field (Ellingham), iv, 563, 567
Charcoal burning ind., v, 457
Charford, ii, 172, 229; iv, 559, 560-3, 564, 571, 577, 578, 597, 601; v, 124, 293; adv., iv, 562; battle, i, 381, 393; iv, 560 n; chap., iv, 562; man., iv, 457 n, 560; pop., v, 445
Chark, man. (Titchfield), ii, 139, 181; iii, 217, 225
Charlcot (Whitchurch), ii, 114; iv, 299
Charles I, iv, 143 n, 172, 299, 300, 651; v, 111, 254 n, 344, 347, 568
Charles II, iii, 239; iv, 275; v, 257, 268
Charlton [Charleton] (Andover), ii, 146, 148; iv, 345, 346, 354, 381; ch., iv, 355; man., iv, 353; Nonconf., iv, 356
Charlton, fam., see Cherleton
Charlton Heath, iv, 320
Charlwood (Ropley), ii, 181; iii, 55
Charmouth (Dors.), battle, ii, 4; v, 293
Charrington, Spencer, iv, 109, 111
Charte, John, v, 44
Charter Alley (Wootton St. Laurence), iv, 239
Charterhouse (Somers.), i, 324
Charteris, —, v, 562
Chartford, see Charford
Chartham (Kent), A.S. rem., i, 388
Chase, Christine, ii, 507; John, ii, 90; iv, 44, 436; Thos., ii, 507; iv, 436; Will., ii, 507; Capt., ii, 92
Chatelain, Jean B. F. E. de, iv, 634
Chatfield, John, iii, 98, 99; Will., iii, 98
Chatham (Kent), dockyard, v, 383, 386, 387
Chatham, Will., earl of, v, 93
Chatter Alley (Dogmersfield), iv, 72
Chatter Alley Green (Dogmersfield), iv, 72
Chatteris, Will., iv, 292

Chattis Hill (Broughton), v, 554
Chaucer, Alice, ii, 519, 521; Maud [Matilda], ii, 519, 521; iv, 395; (Sir) Thos., ii, 519, 521; iv, 382, 395; fam., arms, ii, 519
Chaucourt (King's Somborne), iv, 470
Chaueton, Chaulghton, Chaulton, see Chalton
Chauncy, Isaac, iv, 345
Chaundler, see Chandler
Chaunterel, Ralph, ii, 109
Chauntsingers, man. (Alton), ii, 479
Chauton, see Chalton
Chavecroft, see Chalcroft
Chawcrofts (Rotherwick), iv, 99
Chawner, Edw., iii, 27; Hen., iii, 27
Chawnflower, see Champflour
Chaworth [Cadurcy], (de), Agnes [Gundred], iv, 471; Eliz., iv, 431; Geoff., iii, 259; Isabel, ii, 509; iv, 471; John, iv, 431; Marg., iv, 431; Maud, ii, 173, 509; iv, 471, 504, 538; Pain, iii, 254; iv, 252, 471, 538; (Sir) Pat., ii, 173, 509, 511; iv, 108, 469, 470, 471, 473 n, 476, 480 n, 485, 504, 533, 537, 538; Sir Will., iv, 431; fam., arms, ii, 509
Chawton, ii, 471, 474, 492, 496-501, 514; iv, 116; v, 77; char., ii, 501; man., ii, 496; v, 419; pop., v, 437; sch., ii, 397, 501
Chawton House (Chawton), ii, 496, 497, 498, 499
Chawton Park (Chawton), ii, 496; brick manuf., iv, 465 n
Cheeke, fam., see Cheke
Cheeks Farm [Cheakes] (Bentley), iv, 27
Cheesehill, Pet. of, ii, 284
Cheilostomata, i, 97
Cheiroptera, i, 239
Cheke [Cheeke, Chicke], Dav., v, 252; Dorothy, v, 117; Edw., v, 119, 146, 163, 251, 253; Eliz., v, 253; Hen., v, 117; Joan, v, 163, 220; John, v, 119, 163, 164 n, 220, 252; Rich., v, 253; Rob., v, 252; Thos., v, 146, 220, 251 n, 252
Chekebull, Isabel de, ii, 193
Chekenhull, see Chikvell
Chelbaltone, see Chilbolton
Cheledwelle, v, 413
Chelegrave, see Chalgrave
Cheleton, see Chilton
Chelewarton, see Cholderton
Cheleworth, see Chilworth
Chellingwood, see Chillingwood
Chelmestune, see Kilmeston
Chelsea, man., iv, 495
Chelworth (Wilts.), ii, 169
Chelyngwod, see Chillingwood
Chementune, see Kimpton
Chenduit, Maud, iv, 547; Ralph, iv, 547
Chenelmestune, see Kilmeston
Chenictehalla (Winchester), v, 1
Chening, iv, 501, 517
Chenistone, see Knighton
Chenna, iv, 637
Chenol, see Knowl
Cheping, iii, 372; iv, 52, 419; v, 174, 198, 231, 296
Chepmanessela, see Chapman's Hall
Chequer Green (Stratfieldsaye), iv, 57
Cherdeford, see Charford
Chere, Rog., v, 476
Cherford, see Charford
Cheriton, i, 344; iii, 42, 302, 311-14; v, 39, 342, 517; adv., iii, 313; battle, iii, 311; iv, 161; char., iii, 314; ch., iii, 313; man., iii,

Cheriton (cont.)
312; v, 419, 420, 421; pop., v, 447; Rom. coins, i, 344; sch., ii, 397; truffle ind., v, 455
Cheriton, Nich. de, ii, 168
Cheriton Wood, iii, 311; v, 342
Cherlecole (de), Isabel, ii, 176; Rog., ii, 176; iii, 10
Cherleton [Charlton], Edw., Ld., ii, 475; iv, 347, 348, 427, 430
Cherleton [Charlton] (de), Benedicta, iii, 226; Elias, iii, 226; Joan, ii, 475; iv, 347; Joyce, ii, 475; iv, 347, 348
Cherlwood (Breamore), iv, 598
Chernbyne, Will., ii, 203, 205
Chernet [Orenet] (de), Geoff., iv, 561; Hugh, iv, 561; Iseult, iv, 561; John, iv, 561; v, 124; Will., iv, 424 n, 559, 561; v, 124
Chernocke exhibition (Winchester College), v, 78
Chertese, John, ii, 178
Chertsey, Rob., v, 40
Chertsey Abbey (Surr.), ii, 108; iv, 74, 75, 109, 110, 265
Cherytone, see Cheriton
Cheselburgh, John, ii, 138, 139
Cheselden [Cheseldene, Chusylden] (de), John, v, 479 n; Walt. ii, 147, 149; Will., ii, 120
Chessam, Rich., ii, 57, 190, 191
Chessell, man. (Shalfleet), v, 220, 272, 273
Chessell Down, A.-S. rem., i, 386
Chester, earls of, v, 162, 265, 267, 290; Edw., iv, 184, 219, 222; Hugh, iv, 568; Randolph de Blondeville, iii, 103
Chesterland (Liss), iv, 84
Chetel [Chetle], iii, 196; iv, 568; v, 129, 159, 200, 237
Chetwynd, vscts.:—John, iv, 413, 619, 621; Walt., iv, 413; Hester, vsctss., iv, 413, 619, 621
Cheverdon (de), Alda, iv, 110; Joan, iv, 111; John, iv, 110, 111
Cheverton, see Chewton
Chewe, Thos., v, 113
Chewton [South Chewton] (Milton), v, 82, 94, 126 n, 419; ch., ii, 219; fishery, v, 95 n; man., ii, 159; v, 126; mill, v, 95
Chewton Bunney (Milton), v, 124, 134
Cheyney [Cheyne, Cheyny] (de), Eliz., Lady, iv, 370; (Sir) Fran., iii, 135, 436; iv, 636; Sir Hugh, iv, 609; Joan, iv, 616; John, iv, 185, 324; Ralph, iv, 616; Rich., v, 191; (Sir) Rob., iv, 325 n, 435; Rog., iv, 368; (Sir) Thos., ii, 115, 339, 340, 366; iii, 405; iv, 324, 325, 370; v, 191; Werburg, Lady, iv, 636
Cheyney [Cheyne] court, v, 38, 47, 48
Cheyney Court (Winchester), v, 12
Cheyney Court (Wootton St. Lawrence), iv, 240
Cheyny, see Cheyney
Chichdells, Little (Bentworth), iv, 68
Chicheley, Hen., archbp. of Canterbury, ii, 262, 292; iv, 88
Chicherel, Will., v, 92
Chichester (Suss.), v, 359; cathedral, v, 462, 463; oyster dredging, v, 468; Rom. rds., i, 321, 322; sch., ii, 300
Chichester, bps. of, ii, 19; Andrewes, see Winchester, bps. of; Duppa, see Winchester, bps. of; Luffa, v, 462; Manningham, ii, 337; iii, 427; Moleynes, ii, 287; v, 319, 369;

Chichester (cont.)
Nevill, ii, 17; iv, 323; le Poor, see Durham, bps. of; Praty, iv, 102; Sherborne, ii, 294; Shuttleworth, ii, 359
Chichester, Thorne, dean of, v, 336
Chichester, Will., dk. of, iv, 342; earl of, iv, 591; Ld. Spencer, iv, 244
Chichester, Anne, v, 180 n; Sir Bruce, v, 522; (Sir) John, v, 180; Pet. de, ii, 146
Chicke, see Cheke
Chickenhall, Chickville, see Chikvill
Chidden (Hambledon), i, 326; iii, 237, 238, 242
Chidioke, Sir John, v, 104; —, Lady, v, 104
Chikvill [Chekenhull, Chickenhall, Chickville, Chikenhull] (de), Alan, iii, 298; Beatrice, iii, 479; Hugh, iii, 298; v, 173, 199, 305; John, iii, 298, 479, 480; v, 200; Juliane de, v, 173
Chilbaton, John, ii, 203, 205
Chilbolton, ii, 101, 108; iii, 401, 403–5; iv, 400, 414 n, 417; v, 439; adv., iii, 405; char., iii, 405; ch., iii, 404; man., ii, 114; iii, 403; Rom. rem., i, 344; sch., ii, 397
Chilcomb, ii, 108; iii, 302, 314–16; v, 1, 429, 544; adv., iii, 316; ch., iii, 316; lime burning, v, 454; man., ii, 114; iii, 315, 406, 444; iv, 194 n; pop., v, 448
Child [Childe], Rev. Alf., iv, 365; Dorothy, iii, 39; iv, 22, 100; Rich., iii, 39; iv, 22, 100; Rog., iii, 117; Rev. Thos., iv, 365; Will., iv, 65; Mrs., iv, 365
Child Candover, ii, 187
Childer Hall (Bentworth), iv, 68
Childewick (de), Clarice, iv, 524; Geoff., iv, 524
Chilland [Martyr Worthy], iii, 302, 326
Chillerton, v, 204, 210, 221, 235, 246; iron, iv, 464; man., v, 231
Chillham, Mich. de, iii, 362
Chillingwood, man. (Newchurch), v, 164 n, 181
Chillingwood (de), Geoff., v, 181; Rog., v, 181
Chiltecumbe, see Chilcomb
Chiltele (de), John, ii, 493; Will., ii, 493
Chilternedevre, see Chilton Candover
Chiltley [Chiltele] (Bramshott), ii, 471, 491; man., ii, 493
Chilton (Brighstone), v, 211; man., v, 213
Chilton, Thos., v, 483
Chilton Candover, ii, 187; iv, 182, 183, 184-6; adv., iv, 186; Breaches, The, iv, 185; man., iv, 182, 185, 295; pop., v, 448; Rom. Brit. rem., i, 306, 344; iv, 185
Chilton wood (Chilton Candover), iv, 185
Chilwayes (Hurstbourne Tarrant), iv, 321
Chilworth, ii, 99, 161, 162, 421; iii, 462, 468-9; v, 541; adv., ii, 20; iii, 469; brickmaking, v, 465; char., iii, 469; ch., iii, 469; man., iii, 468; pop., v, 447
Chilworth and Stoneham harriers, v, 542
Chineham (Monk Sherborne), iv, 113, 114, 223, 238; man., iv, 232

Chineham [Chinham], de, Barth., iv, 231 n; John, iv, 231; Rich., iv, 231; Rob., iii, 362; Will., iv, 231
Chingescamp, see Kingescamp
Chingestune, see Kingston
Chinnock, Fred. G., iv, 5; W., iv, 605
Chip [Chippe], John, iv, 477; Rob., iii, 295; Will., iii, 294, 295; v, 214
Chippenham, Alice, iv, 516; Walt., iv, 515 n, 516
Chirchfield (E. Wellow), iv, 535
Chirk, ii, 182
Chirlu, Pet. de, ii, 216
Chisbury (Wilts.), ii, 163
Chiselbury (Wilts.), ii, 161
Chisledon (Wilts.), ii, 119
Chisslands (Headbourne Worthy), iv, 430
Chitterne, man. (Wilts.), iv, 320
Chitterne, John, iv, 327
Chitty, Will., iii, 35
Chiuentone, see Chewton
Chiverton (Winchfield), iv, 111
Chiverton's farm (Winchfield), iv, 111
Chobham (Surr.), ii, 483
Cholderton (Amport), iv, 333, 350, 358, 359, 397, 428 n, 522 n; chap., iv, 344; man., iv, 339, 342, 367; mill., iv, 341
Cholderton, East (Amport), iv, 337
Cholderton, de, Odo, iv, 385 n; Thos., iv, 339, 340, 342, 359, 366, 367; see also Ann
Cholderton Hill, iv, 337, 385
Cholderton Lodge (Amport), iv, 337
Cholmondeley [Cholmele, Cholmelegh], Mary, iv, 184; Capt. Reg. Hen., iii, 251; Rob., iii, 187; iv, 473
Chondropterygians, i, 202
Christchurch [Christchurch Twyneham], i, 325; ii, 71, 102, 104, 139, 154, 251; iv, 597, 645, 648; v, 81, 83-110, 133, 164 n, 222, 307, 311, 318, 331, 343, 355, 356, 387, 409, 417, 418, 423, 426, 429 n, 431, 564; advs., v, 108; antiquities, iii, 344; v, 85; chants., v, 109; chap., v, 85, 109; char., v, 109, 110; chs., v, 101; courts, v, 87; fishery, v, 88, 98; houses, v, 84, 95, 97, 98; inds., v, 88, 451, 457, 464, 466, 467, 469, 486, 488; leper hosp., v, 418; mans., ii, 159; v, 90; mkts. and fairs, v, 87, 88; mills. v, 94, 95, 97, 98, 100; Nonconf., v, 83, 93, 109; pop., v, 445; sch., ii, 397; v, 83, 85
Christchurch, hund., v, 81, 324, 331
Christchurch, East, v, 83, 84, 109
Christchurch, Will., ii, 175
Christchurch Bay, v, 464, 559
Christchurch Castle, v, 88-90, 92, 100 n, 303
Christchurch College (Oxf.), ii, 391
Christchurch Foreign, hund., v, 82
Christchurch Foreign, man., v, 91
Christchurch Harbour, see Christchurch Bay
Christchurch Priory, ii, 27, 35, 49, 57, 58, 61, 104, 152-60, 174; iv, 502, 579 n, 619, 620, 622, 639; v, 86, 87, 93, 94, 96, 98, 99, 100, 101, 117, 123, 126, 132, 161, 172, 174, 180, 183, 188, 270, 285, 290, 470; ch., v, 101; grange, v, 84; priors, ii, 57, 160, 170; iv, 540, 620; v, 164 n, 243, 256, 259, 273, 466; sch., ii, 58; v, 83

Christchurch Twyneham, see Christchurch
Christchurch Westover, hund., see Christchurch
Christian, F. H., iii, 286
Christina [Christiane, Christine], abbess of Romsey, ii, 126; prioress of Wintney, ii, 151; sis. of Edgar Atheling, iv, 461
Christmas, Hen., ii, 490; Jas., iv, 63, 108; John, iv, 61; Matt., iv, 61; Nich., iv, 203, 204, 254; Will., iii, 98
Christ's Hospital (Lond.), ii, 392
Christ's Hospital (Winchester), ii, 388; v, 13, 77
Chroncher, Hen., iii, 248
Chubbe, John, ii, 301
Chuderleg, see Tytherley, West
Chulewarton, see Cholderton
Church Donne (Hartley Wespall), iv, 42
Churchehay, John, v, 132
Churcher, Rich., ii, 387, 392; Will., v, 79
Churcher's College (Petersfield), ii, 387, 392; iii, 120
Churchesmede, le (Newtown), iv, 294
Church Hanger (Kingsclere), iv, 265
Churchill, Geo. O., iv, 655; Will., iv, 656
Church Oakley, ii, 226, 241; iv, 206, 223, 224-8, 231; adv., ii, 25; iv, 228; char., iv, 228; ch., iv, 227; coin, i, 346; mans., iv, 224; pop., v, 441
Churchstrete (Romsey), iv, 452
Churmund, Ad., v, 46; Maud, v, 46; Will., v, 46
Churton, see Cheriton
Chusylden, see Cheselden
Chute (Wilts.), iv, 377; prebend. of, iv, 394
Chute [Shute], Anne R., iv, 161; Anth., ii, 382; iii, 464; iv, 161; Chaloner, iv, 161, 164; Chaloner W., iv, 162, 164; Chas. L., iv, 122, 162, 167, 170; Edw., iv, 161; Eliz., iv, 161; Fran., iv, 248; John, iii, 464; iv, 122, 161, 162, 163, 164, 170; Rich., ii, 197; Thos., iv, 161 n, 520; Thos. L., iv, 161; Thos. V., iv, 161; Will., v, 355; Will. J., iv, 161, 165, 168; v, 520, 536; W. L. W., iv, 170; v, 522; Mrs., iv, 168;—, iv, 105; v, 533
Chute forest [Chute and Finkley forest], ii, 435; iv, 315, 319, 320, 353, 368, 383, 393, 401; v, 201
Chuteley, hund., ii, 420; iv, 223-4; v, 324, 331
Chylton Candevour, see Chilton Candover
Chylworth, see Chilworth
Chynepol (Bullington), iv, 402
Chyrchfeld, man. (Berks.), iv, 64 n
Chyrchocle, see Church Oakley
Chyritone, see Cheriton
Chyveton, see Chewton
Cibber, Caius G., v, 18
Cider manufacture, v, 474-5, 495, 502
Cigoinny [Cygony], Engelard de, iv, 88, 90, 319
Ciltecumbe, see Chilcomb
Ciltestere, see Silchester
Cinderheap, Hen. atte, v, 464
Cinque Ports, v, 377
Cinric, see Cynric
Cirencester, Thos. de, iv, 338
Cistercians, ii, 11, 104, 137
Cisus, iv, 27
Cittesthorn, Rich. de, ii, 166

Civil War, v, 337-53, 380
Claggett, Nich., bp. of Exeter, iv, 218
Clamerkin Creek (Newtown), v, 265
Clamptree, Isaac S., ii, 511
Clanfield [Clanefelde, Clanefeud, Clanffield], ii, 73 ; iii, 64, 82, 110-11 ; adv., iii, 111 ; char., iii, 111 ; ch., iii, 111 ; pop., v, 444 ; schs., ii, 397
Clanricarde, ctsses. of :—Frances de Burgh, v, 229 ; Urania A. de Burgh, iii, 270 ; earls of : Hen. de Burgh, iii, 270 ; John T. de Burgh, iii, v, 523, 523 n, 536, 537 ; Rich. de Burgh, v, 229 ; Smith de Burgh, iii, 270 ; Ulick J. de Burgh, iii, 270
Clanveld, man., ii, 168
Clanville (Weyhill), iv, 394 ; man., iv, 396, 397 ; Rom. rem., i, 295, 344 ; iv, 395 ; sch., iv, 399
Clanville (de), Annora, iv, 367 ; Jordan, iv, 367 ; Luke, iv, 367, 368 ; Rob., iv, 367, 368 ; Sybil, iv, 367 ; Walt., iv, 367 ; Will., iv, 367
Clanville Lodge (Weyhill), iv, 394 396
Clapgate (Whitchurch), iv, 299
Clapham, Paul, iii, 327
Clapperiscroft (Vernhams Dean), iv, 329
Clappyngbrede (Calbourne), v, 218
Clarcke's Lane Ende (Aldershot), iv, 3
Clare, Georgiana, ctss. of, v, 186
Clare (de), Aline, iv, 7 n ; Bevis, iv, 568 ; Gilb., iii, 87, 91, 247 ; iv, 361, 381, 491, 576, 604 ; Isabel, iv, 52 ; Marg., iv, 576 ; Rich., ii, 128 ; iii, 87, 91, 247, 455 ; iv, 52, 381 n, 576 ; Rob., iv, 7 n ; Rog., ii, 146 ; Will., iii, 87, 91, 116, 247, 248, 249, 455 ; iv, 491 ; fam., v, 118 ; arms, iii, 87, 247 ; see also Clere
Clarebold, Nich., iv, 598
Claremont (Surr.), v, 566
Clarence, Isabel, dchss. of, iii, 135 ; iv, 608 ; v, 92, 285 ; Marg., dchss. of, ii, 475, 476 ; dks. of :— Edw., v, 92 ; Geo., iii, 411 ; iv, 540, 608 ; v, 92, 124, 219, 285, 320, 370 ; Lionel, ii, 43, 475 ; Thos., ii, 475 ; iv, 130 ; v, 318
Clarendon, forest of, iv, 540
Clarendon, Catherine, ctss. of, iv, 484 ; earls of : Edw., v, 88, 93 ; Geo., iv, 484 ; Hen., iii, 12 ; v, 93, 94
Clare Park (Crondall), iv, 5, 8
Clarges, Sir Thos., v, 87
Clarice, abbess of Nunnaminster, ii, 126 ; prioress of Wintney, ii, 149, 151
Clarke [Clark], Alured, iii, 405 ; Amy, iii, 488 ; Chris., v, 113 ; Edgar C., v, 140 ; Edm., ii, 369 ; iv, 185 ; Frances, iv, 98 ; Geo., iii, 71 ; iv, 345, 367 ; Godf., iv, 3 ; Sir Hen., ii, 378 ; Humph., iv, 471 ; v, 94 ; Jas., v, 143, 216 ; Jane, iv, 192 ; John, ii, 380 ; iii, 451 ; iv, 301 ; v, 145 ; Rich., ii, 482 ; Col. Stephenson, v, 142, 205 ; Susanna, iv, 529 ; Thos. C., v, 140 ; Tom, v, 517 ; (Rev.) Will., ii, 115 ; iv, 613, 614 ; W. D., iv, 529 ; Mrs.—, iii, 134 ; —, archdeacon, iii, 341 ; —, iv, 300 ; v, 335, 527 ; fam., v, 282 ; see also Clerke

Clarke-Jervoise, Sir Hen., iii, 106, 107 ; Jervoise, iii, 101, 106, 107, 109 ; Rev. Sam., iii, 106 ; fam., arms, iii, 106 ; see also Jervoise
Clarkes Land (Hartley Wespall), iv, 42
Clatford, Lower [Nether], see Goodworth Clatford
Clatford, Upper [North], iv, 333, 359-65, 403 ; adv., ii, 230 ; iv, 365 ; char., iv, 365 ; ch., iv, 364 ; mans., iv, 360 ; mills, iv, 362, 363 ; Nonconf., iv, 365 ; pop., v, 438 ; schs., ii, 405
Clatford (de), Alice, iv, 352 ; Ralph, iv, 352 ; Rog., iv, 352 ; Will., v, 96
Clatford Lodge (Upper Clatford), iv, 360
Clatford Priory (Wilts.), iv, 419
Clatinges (Fordingbridge), iv, 424, 559
Clatterford (Carisbrooke), v, 231 ; paper mill, v, 490 ; Rom. rem., i, 317, 348
Claudh Anton, i, 331
Clauer, le, Ralph, iii, 391 ; Walt., iii, 391
Clausentum, i, 322, 324, 330-5
Clavell [Clavill] (de), Amy, v, 212 ; Bridg., v, 212 ; Elyas, v, 481 n ; Felicia, v, 199 ; Hen., v, 198, 199 ; John, v, 199 ; Rog., v, 212 ; Thos., v, 114
Clavells, man. (Whippingham), v, 199
Clavering, Sir John, iii, 437
Claverle, Claverlegh, Claverley, see Cleverly
Claversden, Upper and Little (Aldershot), iv, 4
Clavill, see Clavell
Claybrook, Rev. —, iv, 266 n
Clay industries, v, 453
Claymond, John, ii, 197 ; iv, 218
Claythorne, ii, 376
Clayton, Chas., iv, 9 ; Hen., iv, 17 ; Randal, iv, 283
Cleare, see Burghclere, Highclere, Kingsclere
Cleaveland, man. (Newchurch), v, 182
Cleaveland Shute (Newchurch), v, 182
Clebton, iv, 352
Cledisdon, see Cliddesden
Cleer, fam., see Clere
Clement, Fran., iii, 114 ; John, iii, 70, 80 ; Will., iii, 70 ; v, 85 n, 119, 120
Clements, Isaac, iii, 127
Clempson, Mary, iii, 196
Clene, John, iv, 302 ; Will., iv, 302
Clenefeld(e), see Clanfield and Clanville
Clerc, see Clerke
Clerc, par., see Burghclere, Highclere, Kingsclere
Clere, West (Kingsclere), iv, 251
Clere [Cleer] (de), Emma, iv, 547 ; Hawise, iv, 82 ; John, ii, 168 ; Ralph, iii, 258 ; iv, 82, 83 ; (Sir) Rog., iii, 258 ; iv, 82 ; Will., iv, 197 ; see also Clare
Clere Episcopi, see Burghclere and Highclere
Clere Prenet (Kingsclere), iv, 257
Cleresden, see Cliddesden
Clere Woodcott [Clerewodcott], man. (Kingsclere), ii, 213 ; iv, 255, 332 n ; farms, iv, 256
Clere Woodland, see Kingsclere Woodlands
Clerke [Clerc, Clerk], Alice, iv, 226 ; Anne, iii, 411 ; iv, 226 ; Benj., v,

Clerke (cont.)
93 ; Cecily le, iv, 68 ; Edm., iii, 8, 227, 307, 393, 400, 483 ; iv, 427 ; Geo., iii, 411 ; Godfrey le, ii, 521 ; Hen., iv, 131, 226, 427 ; v, 256 n ; Jas., iii, 467 ; Jarvis, v, 93 ; Joan, iv, 131 ; John, iii, 334 ; v, 181, 482 ; Jos. J., v, 93, 96 ; Marg., iii, 307, 400 ; Myldred, ii, 125 ; Rob., iii, 359, 399 ; Susanna, v, 496 ; (Sir) Thos., ii, 272 ; iii, 307, 411, 419 ; iv, 226, 427, 428 ; Walt., iii, 399 ; Will. (le), iii, 399 ; iv, 68 ; fam., arms, iii, 307 ; see also Clarke
Clerkes (Heckfield), iv, 45
Clerkes House (Romsey), iv, 452, 453
Clerk's Croft (Aldershot), iv, 4
Clerkynlane (Carisbrooke), v, 222
Clerles Rookehey (Longstock), iv, 449
Cleverly [Cleverlys], man. (Corhampton), iii, 249
Cleverly, John, iii, 249 ; Phil., iii, 249 ; Thos., iii, 249 ; Thurstan, iii, 249 ; Will., iii, 249 ; v, 529
Clewer (Berks.), iv, 215, 259 ; sisterhood, iv, 26
Clewer, Sarah, iii, 250 ; John, iii, 250
Cleybrokes (Whippingham), v, 198
Cleydon, Will. de, iii, 107
Cleyhull (Gatcombe), v, 246
Cleyne, Alice, iv, 392 ; Rog., iv, 392
Cliddesden, iv, 113, 114, 115, 145-7 ; adv., iv, 147 ; char., iv, 147 ; ch., iv, 147 ; mans., iv, 145 ; Nonconf., iv, 145 ; pop., v, 439 ; sch., ii, 397 ; iv, 147
Cliddesden (de), Arnulf, iv, 145 ; John, iv, 146 ; Phil., iv, 146 ; Sim., iv, 146 ; Will., iv, 146
Clife, fam., see Clyff
Cliff (Newchurch), v, 182 Rom. coins, i, 348
Cliffe Park, see Sclive
Clifford, Arth. F., iv, 198 ; Sir Rob., v, 321 ; Rog. de, ii, 169, 173 ; iv, 82 ; Sim., iv, 495 ; —, v, 561, 562
Clifton, John, ii, 488
Cline, la (Wherwell), iv, 411
Clingan, John, v, 109
Clinock, Morris, v, 249
Clinton [Clynton] (de), Eva, Lady, ii, 181 ; iii, 171, 293 ; Ld. Will., iii, 171
Clinton, Col. Fred., v, 113 ; Lt.-Col. Hen. R., v, 113, 127 ; Will., iv, 110 ; —, admiral, v, 376
Clobery, Ann, iii, 484 ; iv, 477 ; Cath., iv, 477 ; Sir John, iv, 477 ; v, 55 ; Mary, iv, 477 ; Susanna, iv, 477
Cloete, Brodrick, v, 547, 549
Clokerle, see Lockerley
Cloppyshay (Carisbrooke), v, 222
Clopton, man. (Wilts.), ii, 159
Clopton, Dorothy, iv, 248 ; Thos., iv, 248 ; Sir Walt., iv, 564
Close (Melchet Pk.), iv, 540
Clotely, see Beaurepaire
Cloth industry, iv, 567 ; v, 451, 476-7, 483, 484
Clonne, Rog. de, ii, 196, 197
Clubmen, v, 346
Cluddysdean, see Cliddesden
Clungeon, John, v, 486
Clutterbuck, Rev. R. H., iv, 381, 411 n
Clydesdale, mqss., ii, 347
Clydesden, see Cliddesden

Clyff [Clife], Hen. de, ii, 217; Mich., ii, 290, 365; Will., v, 17
Clynton, fam., see Clinton
Clyve (de la), John, v, 182; Rich., v, 182; Will., v, 182
Clyve, La, Clyvelond, man., see Cleaveland
Cnolle, see Knowl and Knowles
Cnovylleslond (Pamber), iv, 433
Cnut [Canute], king, ii, 8, 116, 240, 396, 414, 417; iv, 419; v, 51, 56, 297
Coakes, —, v, 557
Coats [Coates], Archibald, iv, 458, 536, 537, 539, 540; John, iii, 370; Mary, iii, 370
Cobb, Frances, iii, 121; John, ii, 344, 366; Mich., iv, 196; Rich., iv, 196; (Sir) Thos., ii, 344; iv, 196
Cobbett [Cobbet], Will., iii, 279, 448, 466; Lt.-Col., v, 350
Cobbus [Cobb], the smith, iv, 548; v, 305
Cobham, Lds., v, 335; John Oldcastle, ii, 46; Will. Brooke, iv, 598
Cobham [Cobeham] (de), Alice, iii, 400; (Sir) John, iv, 339, 341, 515; (Sir) Will., iii, 260, 400
Cobland (Christchurch), v, 85
Cobmersh (Timsbury), iv, 486
Cobreth, Christine, ii, 149; Diana, ii, 149; Rog., ii, 149; Thos., ii, 149
Cochrane, Ld., v, 400
Cochrane, Sir Thos., v, 152
Cockaine, Sir Will., ii, 376
Cockburn, Ld., iv, 51
Cockburn [Cockburne], J. B., iv, 204; Rob. D., v, 528; —, v, 171, 517
Cock Close (Romsey), iv, 468
Cocke [Cok], Joan, iii, 196; John, iv, 224; Marg., iv, 224; Will., iii, 196; see also Coke
Cockeleslond (Hartley Wespall), iv, 42, 64
Cockhune, —, v, 398
Cockley Land (Steventon), iv, 171
Cockroaches, i, 110
Cocks, fam., see Cox
Cock's Bridge (Crondall), iv, 6
Cocum (Barton Stacey), iv, 417
Codebare Poyly, see Codibear
Codelesdon (Beaulieu), iv, 650, 651
Codibear [Codibere, Codibyarpoyle] (Newport), v, 262
Codinge, Rich. de, iii, 406
Codolf, iv, 391
Codrington, —, v, 528, 570, 572
Cœlentera, i, 93
Coelwen, ii, 474
Coffin, Ellis, v, 109
Cofurlang (Highclere), iv, 285
Coggersbrugge (Lyndhurst), iv, 631
Coggeshall (Essex), v, 487
Coggeshall, Ralph de, iii, 152
Coggs (Eversley), iv, 33
Cogin, Rich., ii, 158
Cognatus, Gilbertus, v, 18
Coins, Anglo-Saxon, i, 394, 395, 396; iv, 5; British, i, 273, 285; Brythonic, i, 262; of Charlemagne, v, 415; Gaulish, i, 317; v, 293 n; Merovingian, iv, 5; Roman, i, 275, 285, 287, 289, 290, 291, 294, 295, 297, 300, 302, 303, 305, 306, 307, 309, 310, 311, 312, 313, 315, 317, 318, 326, 334, 340, 341, 342, 343, 344, 345, 346, 347, 348, 349, 377, 395, 396; iii, 125, 472; iv, 295; Stuart, iii, 304; Tudor, iii, 304; Winchester mint, v, 3, 25 n, 311 n

Coish, Hen., v, 30
Coitbury (Winchester), v, 25
Cok, see Cocke
Coke, Anastasia, iv, 571; Sir Edw., v, 334, 633; John, iv, 570; Marg., iv, 571; Rich., v, 147; Thos., ii, 443; iv, 555; Will., ii, 387; iv, 571; fam., iv, 573 n; see also Cocke
Cokefield [Cokefeld], Benedict [Bennet] de, iv, 361, 604
Cokepole, see Puckpool
Coker, Alice, iii, 435; Walt., iii, 435; Will., iv, 573
Cokerel, see Cokrell
Cokeshull (Lasham), iv, 81
Cokespyrks (Priors Dean), iv, 436
Cokkescros (Eling), iv, 547
Cokrell [Cokerel], Johanna, v, 107; Rich., iv, 130
Cokysplace (Sherborne St. John), iv, 158
Cola, iii, 355; the huntsman, iv, 553, 563
Colborne, Sir John, iv, 631
Colbury [Eling], iv, 546, 630; adv., iv, 558; ch., iv, 557; man., ii, 145; iv, 552; man. house, iv, 546, 552; sch., ii, 397
Colby, Chris., iv, 106; Dorothy, iv, 105; Eliz., iv, 105; Thos., iv, 105
Colchester, Thos. de, ii, 197
Coldecot, de, Laur., iv, 535; Mabel, iv, 535
Colden Common, iii, 340
Coldham, Will., iii, 72; iv, 94
Cold Harbour, i, 349
Cold Harbour glassworks (West Tytherley), iv, 519
Cold Harbour Wood, i, 320
Cold Henley, see Cole Henley
Coldrey, ii, 503; iv, 27; man., ii, 503; pop., v, 437
Coldrey (de), Alice, iii, 445; Will., iii, 445
Coldrey House [Coldrey], ii, 503
Coldstone, John, v, 29
Cole, Chas., iv, 85, 86; Eliz., iv, 522; Sir G. L., iv, 44; Jane, iv, 20; John, ii, 17; iii, 427; iv, 85 n, 143, 631; Mabel, iv, 631; Mary, iv, 85, 86; Thos., iv, 85; v, 201, 271; Will., ii, 121; iv, 274 n; Dr., v, 192 n
Colebrooke [Colebrok], Eliz., iii, 68; John, iii, 114; Ralf. de, v, 479 n
Colehayes (Brockenhurst), iv, 626
Cole Henley (Whitchurch), iv, 299, 301, 302, 304; man., iv, 300
Coleman [Colman], Agnes, iv, 39; Hen., iv, 39; John, v, 164; Lancelot, v, 176; Rich., iii, 318; iv, 541; v, 203 n; Susan, iv, 541; Thos., iv, 468; fam., v, 148
Colemans, Gt. (Hartley Wespall), iv, 44
Colemans Moor (Liss), iv, 85 n
Colemede (Romsey), iv, 452, 453
Colemore, iii, 63; iv, 415, 423-5, 436, 437; v, 411 n, 413; adv., iv, 425; ch., iv, 424; Field farm, iv, 423; Hermitage, iv, 423; man., ii, 164, 168; iv, 423, 540; v, 419; pop., v, 444; sch., ii, 397
Colemore, Thos. de, iii, 242
Colemore Farm (Colemore), iv, 424
Colenett, see Colnett
Colengaburna, ii, 116
Colens, see Collins
Coleoptera, i, 121-30
Colepe, le (Carisbrooke), v, 222

Colepeper, Lds., v, 213, 225, 289, 353 n; John, v, 261; Thos., v, 148, 224
Colepeper [Culpepper], Alex., v, 261; Charlotte, v, 213; Cheyney, v, 261; Fran., iv, 383; John, iv, 383; v, 199; Kath., v, 261; Sir Thos., iv, 383
Coleridge, John T., iv, 74; Sam., v, 85
Coles, John, iii, 91; Capt., v, 403
Coleshill (Berks.), ii, 122
Coleville [Colevile, Colville] (de), Agnes, iv, 7 n; Eleanor, iv, 7 n; Ralph, v, 192; Rich., iv, 647, 649; Will., iv, 7, 8, 21 n
Colevillesland (Crondall), iv, 7 n
Colfoxe (Eling), iv, 547
Colgill, Marg., v, 107; Will., v, 87, 107
Colhenlye, see Cole Henley
Colle, see Colles
College Wood (Woodmancott), Rom. rem., i, 306; iv, 186
Colles, lake (St. Mary Bourne), iv, 289, 295
Colles [Colle], Eliz., iv, 562, 606; John, iv, 562, 606; Rich., iv, 137
Collesham (Overton), iv, 211
Collet, John, v, 29
Collett Close (Longparish), iv, 406
Colleve, iv, 570
Collier [Collyer], John, v, 144; —, v, 513 n, 515
Colliers (Christchurch), v, 109
Colliers Wood (Bentworth), iv, 68; v, 457
Collingborne (Wilts.), ii, 121, 137; iv, 294
Collingbourne (Froyle), ii, 501
Collins [Colens, Collyns], Ant., iv, 477; Clara, iii, 248; Dan., v, 231; Harry, v, 473 n; Hen., iii, 248, 249, 287; Mary, iii, 351; Nich., iii, 248; Thos., ii, 353; Will., iii, 248, 253, 320; Miss, iv, 210; fam., arms. iii, 248
Collyer, see Collier
Collyns, see Collins
Colman, see Coleman
Colmannysmore (Liss), iv, 84
Colmer, see Colemore
Colnett [Colenett], Barnebye [Barnabas], v, 142 n, 155, 200; Edw., v, 200; Rich., ii, 315; Will., iii, 392; v, 155, 200
Colney, Eliz., iii, 449; Geo., iii, 449
Cologne, Walt. de, iii, 415
Colpays, Rob., ii, 290
Colpoys, Sir John, v, 397
Colrithe [Colrethe, Colrich(e)], de, Alice, ii, 512; iv, 8; Christine, ii, 503; iv, 28; Eleanor, iii, 242; Rog., ii, 503; iv, 9, 28; Thos., ii, 503, 504; Will., ii, 512; iii, 242; iv, 8
Colshill [Colshull], Isabel, iv, 407; Laur. de, ii, 173
Colson, John, iii, 305; Thos. M., iv, 325
Colte, Anne, ii, 137
Colt Hill (Odiham), iv, 87
Colthurst, Mary A., iv, 567, 580
Coltyng, Will., iii, 241
Columbars [Columbariis, Columbers], de, Avice, iv, 320 n, 353, 377, 393, 394; Gilb., iv, 501, 515 n, 518; Hen., iv, 339, 344; Matth., ii, 142; iv, 339, 340, 353, 377, 456, 494, 498, 501, 508 n, 515, 518, 537; v, 305; Maud, iv, 515; Mich., iv, 320, 353, 377, 393, 503, 515, 518; Nichola, iv, 353, 515 n; Thos., iv, 498, 501, 502, 503, 515

Coluncis, Hugh de, iv, 503 *n*, 507 *n*
Colver House Close (Longstock), iv, 449
Colverle, *see* Culverley
Colville, *see* Coleville
Colwell (Totland), v, 240
Coly [Colye], John, iv, 500 ; Thos., v, 30
Colyngton, Amflesia, iv, 646 ; Thos., iv, 646
Combe (Berks.), ii, 21, 41 ; iv, 380 ; pop., v, 442
Combe [Cumbe] (atte, de), Bald., iv, 392 ; Eva, iv, 598 ; Hen., iv, 637 ; John, ii, 182, 186 ; Matt. iv, 253 ; R., v, 518 ; Walt., iii, 256 ; (Sir) Will., iv, 211, 598
Combe Bissett (Wilts.), ii, 288
Comber, John, v, 243, 274 ; Mary, v, 243
Comberford, Dorothy, ii, 232
Combers (Liss), iv, 84
Combes Hatte (Romsey), iv, 452
Combes Wood (Romsey), iv, 452
Combe Wood (Tunworth), iv, 174
Combley, man. (Arreton), ii, 139 ; v, 142
Combley [Combly] Farm (Arreton), i, 316
Combor, de, Helias, ii, 221 ; Ralph, ii, 221 ; Rob., ii, 220, 221
Comesland (Thruxton), iv, 387
Commius, v, 293
Common Downs (Hurstbourne Tarrant), iv, 321
Common Heath (Hurstbourne Tarrant), iv, 321
Complim, Anne, ii, 95
Compton, ii, 16, 72, 73, 172 ; iii, 401, 406-8 ; iv, 388, 407, 478, 487 ; adv., iii, 408 ; char., iii, 408 ; v, 77 ; ch., iii, 407 ; v, 463 ; mans., ii, 114 ; iii, 406 ; pop., v, 447 ; Rom. coin, i, 344 ; sch., ii, 397
Compton (Berks.), ii, 137
Compton, man. (Freshwater), ii, 139 ; v, 163, 210, 242-3
Compton (King's Somborne), iv, 470 ; man., iv, 104, 438, 475-6
Compton, East, ii, 137
Compton, Hen., Ld., iv, 363, 541, 636, 637 ; v, 114 ; Ld. Spencer D., iv, 511 ; Will., Ld., iv, 363 ; v, 114
Compton, Ad. de, v, 241 *n*, 243 ; Agnes, iv, 15 *n* ; Anne, iv, 636 ; Bridg., iv, 437 ; Chas., iv, 290, 316 ; Eleanor, iii, 291 ; iv, 637 ; Eliz., iv, 423, 437, 637 ; Fran., iv, 635 ; Geo., iv, 316 ; (Sir) Hen., ii, 96, 197 ; iii, 291, 295 ; iv, 531, 541, 543, 637 ; v, 66 ; Hen. C., iv, 580 ; v, 132 ; (Sir) H. F., iv, 555, 638 ; v, 129, 573 ; Hoby, iv, 637 ; Isabel, v, 243 ; Joan, iv, 437 ; (Sir) John, iv, 423, 437, 609, 635, 637 ; v, 40, 129, 146, 243, 572, 573 ; Laur., v, 112 ; Margery, Lady, v, 243 ; Mary, iv, 290, 316 ; Odo, v, 242 ; (Sir) Pet., iv, 363, 531, 541 *n*, 636 ; v, 114 ; Rich., iv, 15 *n*, 97, 423, 543, 636, 637 ; v, 243 ; Rob., v, 242 ; Spencer, iv, 290 ; Thos., iii, 464 ; iv, 339 *n* ; Werburg [Warborough], Lady, iv, 636 ; v, 114 ; (Sir) Will., iv, 531, 541, 636 ; v, 74 ; —, ii, 464 ; fam., iv, 425, 537 ; v, 245, 281 ; arms, iii, 291
Compton Monceux, *see* Compton (King's Somborne)

Compton Wasseling, man. (Compton), iii, 406
Comyn, Eliz., iv, 53
Conaway, *see* Conway
Conder, Mary, v, 193
Condrich, Ad., ii, 198
Conduit, John, iii, 12 ; Jonathan, iii, 420
Conewey, *see* Conway
Coney [Cony], Eliz., iv, 327 ; Frances, iv, 327 ; Geo., iv, 409, 624 ; Hugh, iv, 327 ; Susanna E., iii, 353
Coneygrave, Rob. de, ii, 188
Confold (atte), Edith, iv, 100 ; Isabel, iv, 100 ; Marg., iv, 100 ; Rich., iv, 100
Conford-Holywater (Bramshott), ii, 491 ; sch., ii, 397, 496
Congregationalists, iii, 4, 5, 55, 75, 102, 120, 127, 134, 139, 207, 215, 232, 281, 284, 290, 299, 342, 434, 466 ; iv, 14, 68, 139, 140, 149, 158, 221, 242, 266, 304, 324, 356, 468, 469, 480, 486, 558, 576, 591, 594, 601, 613, 621, 649 ; v, 83, 109, 110, 127, 136, 169, 186, 193, 197, 201, 221, 235, 245, 264, 268, 271
Congreve, Ralph, iv, 43 ; —, iv, 220
Conholt, Lower (Vernhams Dean), iv, 329
Conholt harriers, v, 540
Coningsby, Eliz., v, 194, 207 ; Rich., v, 194, 207
Conisburgh, Rich. of, ii, 475
Conke, John, iv, 500
Connard, Eliz., iv, 36 ; Mary, iv, 80 ; Will., iv, 36, 77, 80
Connell, Eliz., iii, 421
Connere, *see* Colemore
Connop, Hen. C., v, 532
Connyn, Will., ii, 512
Conock, man. (Wilts.), iv, 395
Constable, Barbara, iv, 371 ; Rev. John, iv, 371, 384 ; —, iv, 371
Constable's wall (Winchester), v, 35
Constance, abbess of Wherwell, ii, 137
Constantine, John, iv, 338 *n*
Consuetudinary of Winchester, v, 479
Contarini, Gasparo, v, 323
Conway, Lds., v, 240, 259 ; Edw., iv, 224
Conway [Conaway, Conewey, Conwey], Anne, iii, 48 ; Ann H., iii, 241 ; Eliz., Lady, iv, 597, 645 ; Geo., iii, 242 ; Sir Hugh, ii, 171 ; iv, 597, 645 ; Hugh S., iii, 241 ; Jas., v, 387 ; John, iii, 48 ; Will., iii, 483 ; —, v, 335
Cony, *see* Coney
Conygarth (Romsey), iv, 452
Cooke [Cook], Alice, iv, 393 ; Ann, iv, 373 ; Chris., iii, 354 ; Edm., iv, 470 ; Edw., v, 265 ; Eliz., iv, 373 ; v, 142 *n*, 147 *n* ; Fran., iii, 241 ; Geo., iv, 393 ; Capt. Jas., v, 393 ; Joan, v, 142 *n*, 146, 147, 162, 182 *n* ; John, ii, 136, 148, 197 ; iii, 447 ; iv, 392 *n*, 393, 628 ; v, 142 *n*, 147 *n*, 181 *n* ; Lawr., iii, 71 ; Leonard, ii, 90 ; Marg., v, 142 *n* ; Mary, v, 147, 148 ; Maud, iv, 315 ; Mich., iv, 351 ; Rich., iv, 507 ; iv, 373 ; v, 142, 147, 163 ; Rob., ii, 53 ; iv, 373 ; Russell, v, 231 ; Thos., v, 142, 146, 147, 148, 182 *n* ; Ursula, v, 142 *n* ; Will., iii, 241 ; iv, 315, 345 ; Sir Will. F., iv, 516 ; Col., v, 350 *n*, 523 ; Mrs., iv, 497 ; —, v, 231

Cooks Garden (Hartley Mauditt), ii, 508
Cookson, Jas., iv, 425
Coomb (East Meon), iii, 64, 344
Coombe, man. [West Meon], iii, 344
Coombes (de), Nich., iii, 95 ; Nigel, iii, 95
Cooper [Couper], Sir Alf., v, 124 ; Ant. A., *see* Shaftesbury, earl of ; Edw. E., iv, 211 ; Fred., v, 530 ; Sir Geo., iv, 444 ; v, 530, 557, 558 ; Hannah, iv, 140 ; (Sir) John, iv, 301, 572, 583, 588, 589, 595 ; J., v, 277 ; Thos., bp. of Winchester, ii, 79, 80, 81, 82, 83 ; Will., iv, 339 *n* ; Rev. W. R. A., ii, 505 ; *see also* Cowper
Cooper-Dean, Jas. C., v, 133
Coote, (Sir) Eyre, iv, 569, 573, 582, 584, 586, 587, 590
Cope [Copes], Anne, iii, 241 ; (Sir) Ant., ii, 76 ; iii, 241, 324 ; iv, 33, 37, 41 ; A., iv, 40 ; Sir Denzil, iv, 33, 37, 41 ; Rev. Fran., iv, 92 ; Harriette, Lady, iv, 41 ; Jane, iii, 241 ; (Sir) John, ii, 382 ; iii, 27, 39, 241 ; iv, 32, 34 *n*, 36, 37, 40, 51, 159, 511 ; v, 517, 533, 534 ; Sir John M., iv, 37 ; Margery, iii, 269 ; iv, 159 ; Marianne, iv, 40 ; Sir Monnoux, iv, 37 ; Sir Rich., iv, 37, 40 ; Steph., iii, 135, 143 ; Sir Walt., iv, 427 ; (Sir) Will., iii, 135 ; iv, 40 ; Sir Will. H., iv, 37, 41 ; —, Lady, iv, 33
Coperas, Pet., iii, 179
Copley [Coppeley], Brygget, ii, 125 ; John S., iv, 631 ; Sir Rog., ii, 125
Copner Grounds (Portsea), v, 471
Copnor (Portsmouth), iii, 140, 141, 194 ; man., ii, 182, 186 ; iii, 194 ; salt works, iii, 194 ; v, 471
Coppedehulle (Carisbrooke), v, 222
Coppenthorn (S. Damerham), iv, 587 *n*
Copperas industry, v, 453
Coppidhalle (Kingsclere), iv, 250
Coppidthorne (Calbourne), v, 218
Coppyd bridge (Basingstoke), iv, 129
Coprolite industry, v, 453
Copythorne, iv, 489, 546 ; ch., iv, 557 ; sch., ii, 397
Copythorne Common, iv, 546
Cor [Corr, Cors], John, iv, 151, 284, 299, 323, 336 ; O., iv, 323 ; Rob., iv, 97, 217, 298, 299, 365, 413 ; Will., iv, 97, 217, 414 ; —, iv, 422
Coram, Rog., iii, 420
Corbavia, Pet., bp. of, ii, 16, 29, 123, 213
Corbett [Corbet], John, ii, 87 ; Nich., v, 305 ; Sir Rich., iii, 227, 234 ; Rob., ii, 228 ; Thos., iii, 386 ; (Sir) Uvedale, iii, 153, 234 ; Victoria, iii, 159, 234 ; —, v, 539 ; fam., arms, iii, 386
Cordray [Cordrey], John, iv, 382 *n* ; Rich., v, 172, 173 *n* ; Rob. de, v, 172 ; Thos., iv, 354
Cordry Moores (Whitchurch), iv, 300
Cordwainer, Gilb. le, v, 47, 47 *n*
Cordwainers' trade, v, 456
Corehampton, *see* Corhampton
Corf [Corfe] (of, de), Edw., v, 462 ; Thos., ii, 157, 158 ; Will., ii, 16
Corham, Mabel, iv, 183 ; Rob., iv, 51, 81 ; Rog., iv, 183 ; Will., iv, 183
Corhampton [Corhamtone], i, 378 ; ii, 181, 186, 238, 240 ; iii, 245, 246-54, 319 ; adv., iii, 253 ;

Corhampton (cont.)
char., iii, 253 ; ch., iii, 252 ; man., iii, 246 ; pop., v, 440 ; racing, v, 543 ; Rom. rem., i, 309, 344
Corhampton [Cornhampton] (de), Ad., iii, 246, 248 ; Basile, iii, 246 ; Nich., iii, 247, 248 ; Phil., ii, 149 ; Rich., iii, 247
Cormeilles [Cormailles], de, Agnes, iv, 366, 374 ; Goda, iv, 388 ; Gozelin, iv, 387, 388 ; Hen., iv, 388 ; Hugh, iv, 366, 367, 387, 388 ; Isabel, iv, 388, 413 ; John, iv, 339, 368, 387, 388, 389 ; Rob., ii, 134 ; Rog., iv, 366, 374 ; Thos., iv, 367, 388 ; Will., iv, 388 ; fam., iv, 391
Cormeilles Abbey (France), iv, 391
Cornby, iv, 385
Corne, John, ii, 149
Cornebec, Hamo de, v, 304 n
Corne Downe, Le (Sutton Warbling-ton), iv, 18
Cornehampton, see Corhampton
Cornelea, see Quarley
Cornelius, Thos., iv, 356
Corner, Reg. le, v, 163
Corneweyeshame (Faccombe), iv, 314
Cornford, tool manufacture, v, 457
Cornhampton, Cornhamtone, see Corhampton
Cornhill, Will. of, ii, 253
Cornish, John, iii, 535
Cornwall, earls of : Edm., iii, 356, 457 ; iv, 102, 656 ; Rich., ii, 141, 142, 189 ; iii, 357, 457 ; iv, 102, 656 ; v, 91 n
Cornwallis, Cornelius, iv, 279, 336, 402 ; Eliz., iv, 279, 281 ; Sir Thos., iii, 157, 434 ; Sir Will., v, 113, 117, 396, 399, 400
Cornwallis-West, Col. Will., v, 113, 116, 117, 120
Coroderoy, John, iv, 243
Corondale, see Crondall
Corpus Christi College (Oxf.), ii, 50 ; iii, 334 ; iv, 151, 178, 214, 215, 260, 423
Corr, see Cor
Corrall, Hannah, iv, 259 ; Rob., iv, 259
Corrie [Corry], E. V., v, 562, 563 ; Martha, iv, 219 ; Martin de, iv, 25 ; W. M., v, 562 ; see also Cory
Cors, see Cor
Cortmell, Barnard, v, 474 ; Thos., v, 474
Corton with Ostum St. George (Wilts.), ii, 169, 172
Cory, Eliz., iv, 254 ; Frances, iv, 254 ; Will., iv, 413 ; see also Corrie
Coryton, Fred., v, 519 ; F., ii, 507
Cosham (Carisbrooke), ii, 204, 205 ; v, 230, 234, 270 n
Cosham [Wymering], ii, 181 ; iii, 140, 141, 165 ; v, 297 ; man., iii, 168 ; sch., ii, 397
Cosham [Cossham] (de), John, ii, 157 ; Pet., iii, 164, 168 ; v, 230 n, 305 ; Will., iii, 168, 186 ; v, 305
Coskeville [Oskrewell], (de), Gilb., v, 172, 237 ; Pet., v, 259
Cossam (Newport), v, 263
Cossesson, John, v, 478 n
Cossey, Frances, iv, 62 ; Giles, iv, 62
Cossham, see Cosham
Cossical Copse (Abbotts Ann), iv, 334
Costard, Little (Kimpton), iv, 372
Costards (Meonstoke), iii, 256
Cosyn [Cusyn], Cecily, iv, 564 ; Giles, iv, 315 ; Hugh, iv, 315 ;

Cosyn (cont.)
Jas., prior, ii, 190, 191 ; Joan, iii, 361 ; John, iv, 315, 564 ; Nich., iv, 315 ; Pet., iv, 315 ; Rich., iv, 315 ; Rob., iii, 361 ; Rog., iv, 564 ; Sim., iv, 564 ; Thos., iv, 315 ; Walt., iv, 564 ; Will., iv, 314, 315, 326 n
Cosynstreet (Faccombe), iv, 315
Cotebear, see Codibear
Cotele [Coteel, Coteele, Cotel], Ad., iv, 495 ; Alice, v, 128 ; Ascelina, iv, 495 ; Constance, iv, 495 ; Edith, iv, 551 ; Eleanor, iv, 495 ; Elias [Ellis], iv, 551, 589 ; John, iv, 495 ; Margery de, iv, 551 n ; Mary, v, 187 ; Maud, iv, 495 ; Rich., iv, 551 ; Sir Rob., iv, 551, 589 ; (Sir) Thos., iv, 172, 200, 361 ; v, 179, 180, 181, 184, 187, 244 ; Will., iv, 551 n ; see also Cottle
Cotelesburgh (S. Damerham), iv, 587 n
Cotelestrete (Overton), iv, 211
Cotelshed (S. Damerham), iv, 587 n
Cotenays, Will., iv, 216
Coterel, Coterell, see Cottrell
Cotes (de), Ant., iv, 595 ; John, iv, 320 ; Rhoda, iv, 320 ; Thos., iv, 527 ; Will., iv, 527 ; fam., iv, 296
Cotesburwa (Linkenholt), iv, 324 n
Cotgrave, Eleanor. iii, 213
Cotintone, see Totton
Cotsale, Hyde, v, 207 n
Cotterell, see Cottrell
Cottesmore, Anne, v, 207 ; Hen., v, 194 ; Sir John, v, 207, 243 ; Marg., v, 207 ; Morgan, v, 207 ; Thos., v, 207 ; Sir Will., v, 207
Cottington, Fran. Ld., iv, 252, 253
Cottington, Chas., iv, 253 ; Fran., iv, 253
Cottington Hill (Kingsclere), iv, 229, 249, 252 n, 253
Cottle, E. W., v, 272 ; Rob., iv, 139 ; see also Cotele
Cotton, Benj., v, 242, 535 ; B. T., v, 535 ; Cassandra, iii, 90 ; Chas., v, 242 ; Eliz., iii, 137 ; Fanny, v, 245, 246 ; Fran., ii, 78, 502 ; iv, 166, 203 ; (Sir) Geo., ii, 76, 86, 87 ; iii, 90, 135, 143, 195 ; v, 155 ; Joan, v, 220 ; John, iv, 203 ; John B., iv, 203 ; Sir John H., iv, 391 ; Marg., iii, 53 ; iv, 203 ; Margery, ii, 502 ; iv, 166 ; Rebecca, v, 245 ; (Sir) Rich., ii, 67 ; iii, 135, 137, 139, 143, 144, 195 ; v, 220 ; Capt., iv, 647 ; fam., arms, iii, 136
Cottrell [Coterel, Coterell, Cotterell], Isabelle, iv, 5 ; Joan, ii, 137 ; John, iv, 294 ; Will., v, 195 n
Couchman, Lieut., v, 390
Couci [Coucy], de, Ingram [Ingel-ram], see Bedford, earl of ; Isabel, see Bedford, ctss. of
Coudowne (Barton Stacey), iv, 417
Coudray [Cowdrey, Cowdry] (de), Agnes, (Lady), iv, 170, 417 ; Avelene, abbess of Wherwell, ii, 136, 137 ; Avice, iv, 276, 435 ; Edw., iii, 367 ; Eliz., iv, 418 ; (Sir) Fulk, iii, 367, 368 ; iv, 160, 418 ; Sir Hen., iii, 367 ; Joan, iv, 418 ; John, iv, 418 ; Juliana, Lady, iv, 170 ; Marg., iii, 48 ; Maud, iv, 418 ; Morgan, iv, 276 ; (Sir) Pet., iii, 367 ; iv, 134, 160, 170, 179, 417, 418, 434, 435 ; v, 305 ; Rog., iv, 276, 434 ; (Sir) Thos., iii, 367, 368, 369 ; iv, 160, 170, 418 ; Will., iv, 137, 276, 435

Couffen, John, ii, 187 ; iv, 190
Coufolde, see Cufaud
Coulthard, J. B., iv, 68, 70
Coumb, la (Overton), iv, 211
Countess of Huntingdon's Con-nexion, iv, 139
County Hospital (Winchester), see Royal Hants County Hospital
Couper, see Cooper and Cowper
Courand, —, v, 489
Courci [Curci] (de), Rob., iii, 134, 148, 151 ; Will., iii, 134, 148
Court, The (Long Sutton), iv, 19
Court [Courte], Eleanor, iii, 328 ; Sir Fran., iv, 501, 515, 516 ; Hen., iv, 516 ; Joan, Lady, iv, 516 ; Sim., v, 117 ; Thos., iv, 516 ; see also A'Court
Court Closes (King's Somborne), iv, 470
Court Corner (Pamber), iv, 433
Courtenay [Courtney] (de), (Sir) Edw., iv, 545, 601, 631, 641, 645, 646, 649 ; Eliz., iv, 645 ; Gert., ii, 172 ; iv, 584, 598 ; Hen., ii, 151, 172 ; iv, 427, 553, 584, 597, 645, 646 ; v, 169 ; (Sir) Hugh, iv, 531, 597, 598, 601, 645, 646 ; v, 91 ; Joan, iv, 645 ; Kath., (Lady), iv, 358, 427, 430, 597, 646 ; Marg., iii, 204, 346 ; iv, 531 ; Maud, Lady, iv, 564 ; Muriel, Lady, iv, 531 ; Pet., bp. of Winchester, ii, 48 ; iv, 64 ; v, 56 ; (Sir) Pet., iii, 204, 262, 346 ; iv, 540 ; v, 118, 119 ; (Sir) Thos., iv, 531, 532, 564, 597, 645 ; v, 320 ; (Sir) Will., iv, 358, 427, 597, 646
Courteys, see Curtis
Court Farm [Court House Farm] (Winchfield), iv, 109
Court Hayes, see Court Place
Courthop, Edw., v, 180
Court Land (Milton), v, 126 n
Court Moor (Crookham), iv, 5
Courtney, see Courtenay
Court Place (St. Mary Bourne), iv, 290, 295
Cove (Yateley), iv, 1, 2, 18, 20, 21, 76 ; adv., iv, 26 ; Broomhill farm, iv, 21 ; char., iv, 26 ; ch., iv, 25 ; ind., v, 454, 467 n, 491 ; man., iv, 7, 8, 22 ; pop., v, 443 ; sch., ii, 397
Coventry, Will. Bree, archd. of, iv, 633
Coventry, bps. of, see Lichfield, bps. of
Coventry, earls of, v, 553 ; Geo. W., iv, 570 ; Will., iv, 570
Coventry, Arth., v, 554 ; John, iv, 560, 561, 562, 565, 568, 570, 571 ; v, 94 n ; John B., iv, 570 ; Thos. de, iv, 643 ; Vincent, iv, 324 ; —, ii, 346
Covert, Anne, v, 147 ; Blanch, iv, 497 ; Joan, v, 147 ; John, v, 147 ; Rich., v, 147, 150, 161
Coward, Will., v, 74
Cowbeares (Romsey), iv, 452
Cowdall, Rich., iv, 488
Cow Down (Hurstbourne Tarrant), iv, 321
Cowdown Copse (Goodworth Clat-ford), iv, 403
Cowdrey, Cowdry, fam., see Cou-dray
Cowdrey's Down (Basing), iv, 115
Cowedowne (Wootton St. Law-rence), iv, 239
Cowes [West Cowes], v, 189, 197, 221, 253, 268, 269, 271, 290, 325, 347, 382, 402 ; adv., v, 271 ; char., v, 271 ; ch., v, 271 ; sch., ii, 407 ; shipbuilding, v,

Cowes (cont.)
387, 391; smuggling, v, 401;
trade, v, 197 n, 393
Cowes, East, v, 197, 253, 312, 325;
sch., ii, 398, 407; shipbuilding,
v, 391, 398
Cowes Castle (Cowes), v, 351, 462
Cowfold, see Cufaud
Cowfold Lane (Rotherwick), iv, 99
Cowherds (Southampton), v, 465
Cowkesgrove (Sherborne St. John),
iv, 158
Cowle, Will., iv, 590
Cowleas Meadows (King's Som-
borne), iv, 470
Cowleaze (Andover), Rom.-Brit.
rem., i, 304
Cowper, earl, iv, 454
Cowper [Couper, Cowpar], Edm.,
v, 484; John, iii, 91; Marg., iii,
91; Rich., iii, 91, 93; iv, 289;
v, 164, 181; Spencer, ii, 507;
(Rev.) Thos., ii, 318, 507, 508;
Will. F., see Mount Temple,
Ld.; fam., arms, iii, 437; see
also Cooper
Cowper-Coles, Honora A., iii, 50,
323, 461
Cowperhey (King's Somborne), iv,
470
Cow Plain (Catherington), iii, 94
Cowslad, Thos., iv, 232
Cox [Cocks], Agnes, ii, 124; Eliz.,
iv, 634; John, iii, 427; Rich.,
ii, 297, 298; iv, 387, 651; Rob.,
v, 88, 457; Sarah, iv, 25; Thos.,
iii, 309, 310; Will., v, 517, 521,
527, 539; Dr. —, ii, 302; fam.,
iv, 386
Coxed, John, ii, 366
Cox Leyes, see Foxlease
Coxwell, Gt. and Little, (Berks.),
ii, 140, 141, 143
Coyk, Thos., ii, 182, 186
Coyle, Capt. Roome, v, 385
Coytebury (Winchester), mill, v,
482
Craan, see Crane
Crabbe, Harriet L., iii, 489; John,
iv, 396; Rich., iv, 396 n
Crab Niton, see Niton
Crabracke (Yateley), iv, 21
Crabs Hill, iv, 270
Crabwood, i, 313
Cradill Boxe (Crondall), iv, 6
Cradock, —, ii, 337
Crafts, Edw., iii, 201
Craggs, —, ii, 344
Crambites, i, 144
Crampmoor (Romsey), iv, 452;
sch., ii, 398
Cran, see Crane
Cranborne, man. (Wonston), ii, 116,
117; iii, 389, 402, 458; iv, 39,
341, 358, 420
Cranborne Priory (Dors.), iv, 589;
Rich. de la Rivere, prior of, iv,
589
Cranbury (Hursley), iii, 420
Cranbury House (Hursley), iii, 420
Cranbury Park (Hursley), ii, 470;
iii, 420; v, 558 n, 559
Crane [Craan, Cran] (le), Hugh, iii,
260, 441; iv, 271, 407 n, 418; v,
76; Isabel, iii, 441; iv, 407;
v, 76
Cranecombe (Carisbrooke), v, 222
Cranes Copse (Sherborne St. John),
iv, 167
Cranes Farm (Sherborne St. John),
iv, 167
Cranes Place (Sherborne St. John),
iv, 167
Cranfield, Lionel, v, 181
Cranlegh, Thos., ii, 166

Cranley, Thos. of, ii, 262, 267, 365
Cranlond (Bentley), iv, 27
Cranmer, Thos., archbp., ii, 52
Cranmore (Aldershot), iv, 3
Cranys, see Cranes Place
Craon, de, Alan, iii, 378, 381; Guy,
iii, 378; Maurice, iii, 378;
Muriel, iii, 381
Craule, see Crawley
Craven, Anne, Lady, iv, 100; Lds.,
v, 544; Will., iv, 100
Crawanlea, Crawelie, see Crawley
Crawford, earl of, v, 341
Crawford, John, ii, 185, 186;
Capt., v, 530
Crawley, ii, 73; iii, 401, 408-13;
iv, 379; v, 39; adv., iii, 412;
char., iii, 413; ch., iii, 411;
man., iii, 409; pop., v, 447
Crawley [Crawelie], Alex., iv, 530;
Rich., v, 29
Cray, Alex., iv, 580; Jer., iv, 571,
580; John, iv, 580; Marg., iv,
580; Sarah, iv, 580; Will., iv,
571
Crayford, John, ii, 59, 145
Crecham, see Crookham
Crede, Geo., v, 119; Hen., v, 119
Crediholt, Will., iv, 457 n
Creech, ii, 172
Creedes (Christchurch), v, 85
Creoda, v, 294
Crepestre mill (Winchester), v, 49
Crepse (le), John, iv, 352; Marg.,
iv, 352
Cresselin, iv, 150
Cresswell [Creswell], Alice, iv, 49;
Edw., iv, 40; Isabel, iv, 49;
Jane, iv, 46, 49; John, iv, 46,
49, 91; Mabel, iv, 40 n; Rich., iv,
46, 49; Rob., iv, 40 n, 93; Thos.,
iv, 40, 46, 49; Will., iv, 46, 49
Cresweller [Cressweller], John, v,
199; Mary, iii, 167, 240, 241;
Rich., iii, 62; Will., iii, 167, 240,
241
Creuquer, man. (Farlington), iii,
150
Crewe, Ant., iii, 45; Harrie, v, 30
Cricket, v, 574
Crickets, i, 112
Cricklade, man. (Andover), iv,
353; mill, iv, 351, 353
Cridelestrowe, see Cridlestyle
Cridho (de), Alex., iv, 456, 457;
Rich., iv, 457 n
Cridlestyle, man. (Fordingbridge),
iv, 571, 572; mills, iv, 571
Cridmoor (Godshill), v, 170
Crikelwood, Thos., iii, 533
Crikland, Hugh, ii, 480
Crip Niton, see Niton
Cripps, Hen. L., iv, 198, 200 n
Crischarche de Twenham, see Christ-
church
Crispin, iv, 586
Crispin, Miles, iv, 261
Cristeschirche, see Christchurch
Criswan, iv, 27
Criswick, Thos., iv, 336
Croc, v, 243 n; the huntsman, iv,
391, 393
Croc [Croch] (de), Avice, iv, 353,
393, 394, 533 n; Ellis [Elias], iv,
253, 393; Joan, iv, 394;
Matth., ii, 219; iv, 353 n; Phil.,
ii, 219; iv, 394; Thos., iv, 394;
see also Croke and Crook
Crocker [Krockere], John, v, 96;
Pet. de, iv, 552
Crockerel Hulle, man., see Beaure-
paire
Crockerhill (Fareham), iii, 209
Crockerislond (Liss), iv, 84
Crockford harriers, v, 535, 539

Crockle Hill [Crock-hill, Crockle],
pottery, i, 326, 344
Croft, —, iv, 497
Crofta Dieu (S. Damerham), iv, 586
Crofton (Titchfield), ii, 184; iii,
217, 221; chap., iii, 226; man.,
ii, 182, 186; iii, 226; v, 421;
mill, iii, 226; sch., ii, 398
Crofton, Rich. de, iii, 60, 62
Crofts, Sir John, iv, 412
Croke, Chas., iii, 415; Cuth., v,
484; Sir Dodsworth, iv, 473;
Frances, iv, 283; Sir Geo., iv,
283; (Sir) John, iii, 415; iv, 294,
473, 656; v, 132; Rachel, Lady,
iii, 415; iv, 473, 656; v, 132; see
also Croc and Crook
Crokerestok, see Stoke (St. Mary
Bourne)
Crokham, see Crookham
Crokker (Christchurch), v, 85
Crokydeaysshe (S. Damerham), iv
586
Crompton, Nich., v, 84; Thos., iii,
97
Cromwell, Dorothy, ii, 94; iii, 419;
Hen., iv, 258; Martha, v, 144;
Oliver, protector, iii, 105, 109;
v, 346-7; Oliver, iii, 419, 420;
iv, 258; v, 571; Rich., ii, 94, 337;
iii, 419, 420; iv, 161, 301, 346;
v, 571; Thos., ii, 302, 315; iv,
642; v, 171, 223; Will., v, 144;
fam., arms, iii, 105, 419
Cromwell's Camp, see Oliver Cromwell's Battery
Crondall, ii, 108; iv, 4, 5-14, 27,
28, 32; v, 324, 328 n, 331, 413,
414; adv., ii, 20, 21; iv, 13;
ch., iv, 10; coins, i, 305, 395;
iv, 5; Court Farm, iv, 6;
customary, iv, 6; v, 425;
fisheries, iv, 6, 7; ind., v, 454 n,
491; mans., ii, 114; iv, 3, 6, 15,
21; v, 419, 420; mills, iv, 8;
pop., v, 443; Rom. rem., i, 305,
344; iv, 5; schs., ii, 398
Crondall, hund., iv, 1; v, 423
Crondall, Hen. de, v, 45
Crondall Chase, iv, 6 n
Crook [Crooke], Cecily, iv, 557;
J. C., iv, 180; see also Croc and
Croke
Crooked Billet (Odiham), iv, 87
Crooked Mead (Kingsclere), iv, 250,
267
Crookham, iv, 2, 5, 6, 9, 14; adv.,
iv, 14; char., iv, 5; ch., iv, 13;
sch., ii, 398
Crookham House (Crookham), iv,
5
Crophull, Nich. de, iii, 192
Cropp [Croppe], John, iii, 250;
Leon, iv, 441; Millicent, iv, 441;
Thomasina, iii, 250
Crops, v, 499, 508-9
Crosier, Sir Will., iv, 102
Crosse [Cross], Alice, iv, 226, 573;
Chas., v, 517; Clementia, iv, 573;
John, iv, 573; Will., iv, 226
Crosses, v, 176, 189
Crossley, Crossley D., v, 125
Crosthwaite, —, iv, 399
Croucheman, Christine, iv, 460;
Sim., iv, 460
Crouches (Brading), v, 156
Croude, Will., iv, 477
Croupes, Maud de, iii, 255
Crow (Ringwood), iv, 603, 605, 609
Crowch, Rob., iv, 44
Crowchfeald (Sutton Warblington),
iv, 18
Crowdale, see Crondall
Crowdhill, iii, 309, 333
Crowe, Will., ii, 337

Croweton, Will., iv, 46 n
Crowkes (Heckfield), iv, 45
Crowley, Fred., ii, 482
Crown Farm (Bossington), iv, 491 ; pop., v, 446
Crucheston, John de, iv, 582
Cruft, Will., v, 387
Cruickshank, ——, iii, 298
Crul, Rich., iv, 396
Crumbwell, John de, iv, 81
Crundale, see Crondall
Crustacea, i, 185-96
Crux Easton, ii, 25 ; iv, 308, 311-14, 331, 377, 394, 597 ; v, 242, 425 ; adv., iv, 313 ; ch., iv, 313 ; man., iv, 312 ; park, iv, 313 ; pop., v, 442 ; Rom. rem., i, 344 ; iv, 311 ; sch., ii, 398
Crux Easton, John de, iv, 582
Cruys, Anna, iii, 281
Cryklade, man., see Cricklade
Cryps (Sherborne St. John), iv, 158
Crystals, Anglo-Saxon, i, 388
Ctenophora, i, 95
Ctenostomata, i, 99
Cudunthorn (Abbotts Ann), iv, 334 n
Cufald Wood (Sherborne), iv, 160
Cufaud [Coufolde, Cowfold, Cufaude, Cuffauds, Cuffold], Alex., iv, 122 ; Ellen, iv, 122 ; Fran., iv, 266 n ; Hen., iv, 122 ; John, iv, 122 ; Martha, iv, 122 ; Matth., iv, 122 ; Ralph, iv, 122 ; Rich., iv, 99 ; Rob., iv, 122 ; Sim., iii, 387 ; iv, 122 ; v, 249 ; Thos., iv, 122 ; Will., ii, 78 ; iii, 387 ; iv, 122, 142, 266 n ; Major, iv, 122 n ; fam., iv, 115, 138 ; arms, iv, 122
Cufaude (Lockerley), iv, 500
Cufauds (Basing), iv, 115 ; man., iv, 122
Cufauldsmede, la (Basingstoke), iv, 122
Cuffauds, fam., see Cufaud
Cuffe, Eliz., iv, 54 n ; Fran., iv, 54 n ; Honora F., iv, 54 n ; Mich., iv, 54 n
Cuffell, see Cufauds (Basing)
Cuffnalls (Lyndhurst), iv, 631
Cuffold, see Cufaud
Cuflee (Abbotts Ann), iv, 334 n
Cufoldsaker (Sherborne St. John), iv, 158
Culliford [Cullyford], John, iv, 570 ; Marg., iv, 570 ; Will., v, 114
Cullum, Jane, Lady, iv, 283, 284 ; Sir John, iv, 283
Culm, Rev. Benj., v, 245
Culmeston, Culmestone Gynninges, Culmiston Gymminges, see Kilmeston
Culpepper, see Colepeper
Culver Close (Whitchurch), iv, 300
Culverhayes (Upper Clatford), iv, 360
Culverley (Beaulieu), iv, 650, 651
Cumbe, see Combe
Cumberland, dks. of, v, 394, 546 ; Hen. F., iv, 250
Cumbray, de, Geoff., iii, 98 ; Ralph, iii, 96, 98 ; Will., iii, 98
Cumeton, see Kimpton
Cumpton, see Compton and Kimpton
Cumyngton, Cumynton, see Compton and Kimpton
Cumyns, Rev. R. H., ii, 391
Cundy [Cunde] (de), Aubrey, iv, 329 ; Geoff., iv, 340, 341 ; Gilb., iv, 255, 329, 340 n, 513 n ; Laur., iv, 338 ; Margery, iv, 513 ; Reg., iv, 8
Cuninghame [Cunynghame], Sir Dav., iv, 225 ; Sir Dav. T., iv,

Cuninghame (cont.)
225 ; Maria, Lady, iv, 225 ; see also Cunningham
Cunir, John le, v, 44
Cunliffe, Edw., ii, 375, 385
Cunningham, Alex., iv, 198, 201 ; Col., v, 501 ; see also Cuninghame
Cuntone, see Compton
Cunynghame, see Cuninghame
Cupernham [Cupernam] (Romsey), iv, 452
Cupper, John, iv, 447
Cuppyng, fam., see Kipping
Cuppyngs, man., see Kippings
Curci, see Courci
Curdridge (Bishop's Waltham), iii, 275, 276 ; char., iii, 282 ; sch., ii, 398
Curll [Curle], Edw., iv, 610 ; Eliz., iii, 259 ; Walt., bp. of Winchester, ii, 89, 90 ; iii, 259 ; iv, 254 ; (Sir) Walt., iii, 259, 443 ; Will., iii, 259 ; v, 143 ; fam., arms, iii, 259
Currie, Bertram W., iv, 23 ; Isaac, iv, 23 ; Laura S., iv, 23 ; Laur., iv, 21, 23 ; Raikes, iv, 23 ; Mrs., iv, 253
Curtis [Courteys, Curteis, Curtes, Curteys], Hen., ii, 120 ; Sir Lucius, v, 537 ; Reg., iii, 214 ; Sir Rog., iii, 169 ; v, 400 ; Sarah, Lady, iii, 169 ; Thos., ii, 168 ; iv, 628
Curwen, John, v, 167
Curzon, Ld., iv, 115, 122
Curzon, Eleanor, iv, 348 ; Fran., iv, 348 ; Hen. D., iv, 498, 499 ; John, iv, 348, 521 ; Mary, iv, 521
Curzon-Howe, Lady, v, 84
Curzon Street Farm (Faccombe), iv, 315
Cusand, Will., v, 247 n
Cusaunce (de), Eleanor, iv, 53 ; Sir Pet., iv, 53 ; (Sir) Will., iv, 53
Cushen, Edw., iii, 536
Cusia [Susa], Hen. de, ii, 197
Cust, Lady Eliz., iv, 5
Cusyn, see Cosyn
Cutecombe, Rich. de, iv, 362 n
Cuthred, king of West Saxons, iv, 277, 551
Cuthred [Cutred], iii, 317 ; v, 198
Cutler [Cutiller], Rev. Jas., iii, 288 ; Walt. le, v, 459 ; Will., v, 47
Cutlery industry, v, 459, 460
Cutred, see Cuthred
Cutte (King's Somborne), iv, 470
Cuttelane (Liss), iv, 84
Cutts, John, Ld., v, 224, 225, 226 n, 260, 266, 286, 355
Cwenton field (Steventon), iv, 171
Cyclostomata, i, 99
Cyclostomes, i, 203
Cydyhalefyld (Liss), iv, 84
Cyfrewast, John, ii, 479 ; Sir Rog., ii, 479
Cygony, see Cigoinny
Cynebert, abbot, i, 380
Cynegils [Kynegils], king of Wessex, ii, 1, 2 ; v, 50, 56
Cynric [Cinric], i, 382, 392 ; v, 222, 293, 294
Cynwulf [Cynewulf, Kenulf], king, iii, 418, 504 ; v, 56, 295
Cyrene, John, bp. of, ii, 45

Dabernon [Dabernoun, Dabernoun], Aveline, iv, 81 ; Ingram, iv, 82 ; Isabel, iv, 81 ; John, ii,

Dabernon (cont.)
128, 512 ; iv, 81, 82, 83 ; Rich., iv, 82 ; Walt., iv, 82
Dabridgecourt, Agnes, iv, 58 ; Alice, iv, 59 n ; Barbara, iii, 374 ; Beatrice, iv, 58 ; Dorothy, iv, 59 ; Eliz. (Lady), ii, 475, 476 ; iv, 58, 59 n, 60 ; (Sir) Eustace, ii, 475 ; iii, 95 ; iv, 62, 317 n ; Geo., iv, 59, 61, 65 n ; Hen., iv, 59 ; Sir John, iv, 58 ; Marg., iv, 60, 243 ; Sir Nich., iv, 58 ; Susan, iv, 60 ; (Sir) Thos., iii, 374 ; iv, 58, 59, 60, 61, 62, 65, 243 ; fam., iv, 142 ; arms, iii, 374
Daccombe [Daccumbe] (de), Alice, iv, 541 ; Dorothy, iv, 541 ; (Sir) John, iii, 468 ; iv, 541 ; v, 94, 165 ; Muriel, v, 229 ; Thos., iii, 468, 483 ; v, 229, 230
Dacre, Ladies :—Barbarina Brand, iv, 22 ; Joan Fiennes, iv, 475 ; Lds. :—Greg. Fiennes, iv, 475 ; Rich. Fiennes, iv, 475 ; Thos. Brand, iv, 22 ; Thos. Fiennes, iv, 475
Dacre, G., v, 356
Dagesole (Barton Stacey), iv, 146
Dagge, Hen., v, 95
Dagworth, Eleanor, Lady, v, 128 ; Thos., Ld., v, 128
Dainymore (Heckfield), iv, 45, 46
Dake, John, iii, 136
Dalbier, Col., v, 347
Dale, Agnes, iv, 367, 393 n ; Alice, iv, 393 ; Dorothy, iv, 367 ; Eliz., iii, 326 ; John, iii, 258 ; iv, 367, 392, 393, 394 ; v, 172, 573 ; Val., iv, 367 ; Will., iii, 259, 262, 326, 358 ; iv, 93, 367, 392, 393
Daleron, John, iv, 70
Dalgety, Fred. G., iv, 502, 507, 509, 516 ; Capt. Fred. J., iv, 501, 506, 507, 515, 516, 517
Dallingridge [Dalingrigge], Sir John, iv, 501 ; Kath., Lady, iv, 501 ; Philippa, iv, 501 ; Rich., iii, 124, 126 ; iv, 501 ; Sybil, iii, 124, 126 ; Walt., iv, 501
Dally, see Daly
Dalrymple, Maj. F. B., iv, 546
Dalston, Cath., Lady, iv, 105 ; Sir Geo., iv, 105
Dalton, Rich., v, 483
Daly [Dally], Sir Hen., v, 188, 535 ; John, iv, 143
Dalzell (Lt.-Gen.), Rob., iii, 97
Damerham, Little, man. (S. Damerham), iv, 588, 592
Damerham, South, iv, 559, 581, 582, 583 n, 584, 586-91, 592 ; adv., iv, 591 ; ch., iv, 590 ; mans., iv, 586 ; mills, iv, 590 ; Nonconf., iv, 591 ; pk., iv, 587 ; sch., ii, 398, 405
Dampier, Edw., v, 125
Danby, Hen., earl of, iv, 509
Dancy (Amport), iv, 337
Dandesforde (W. Wellow), iv, 535
Danebury Hill, iv, 198, 483, 525, 526 ; v, 539, 544, 554, 555
Danes, i, 396 ; ii, 4, 5 ; iv, 299 ; v, 295-7, 359
Danes Stream, v, 110, 115, 120
Danett, Gerard, ii, 487 ; John, ii, 487
Daniel, bp. of Winchester, i, 375 ; ii, 2, 3, 4
Daniel [Daniell, Daniels], Edm., iii, 383 ; Sam., v, 277 ; Will., v, 191 n
Daniell (Stratfield Turgis), iv, 63, 65
Danish rem., i, 396-7

Dankyn, Ralf, iv, 367
Danlee (Calbourne), v, 218
Danmore, see Dainymore
Dannell, Nich., ii, 385
Danvers, Ld., iv, 334
Danvers, Agnes, iv, 458, 492; Alice, iv, 64; Geo., ii, 327; John, ii, 327; Nath., ii, 327; Ralph, iv, 64; Rich., iii, 146; Thos., iii, 442; iv, 458, 492; Will., iii, 98, 145, 146; W., ii, 279, 290
Danyelles (Stratfield Turgis), see Daniell
Danyslond (Sherborne St. John), iv, 158
Darby [Derby], A., v, 136; Adm. Geo., v, 395; John N., v, 134; Rob., ii, 286
Darbyshire, John, iii, 285
Darcy, Thos., Ld., iv, 348 n
Darcy, Sir A., ii, 193; Dorothy, Lady, iv, 246, 251; Edith, Lady, iv, 348 n; Sir Geo., iv, 246, 251; Hen., ii, 147; Rich., ii, 284, 366
Darel, Darell, see Darrell
Darling, Sir Chas. J., iv, 626
Darlington, —, vicar of Isleworth, ii, 295
Darly Green (Hawley), iv, 41
Darnell, N., v, 576; Phil. S., iv, 527, 530
Darrell [Darel, Darell, Derrell], Constantine, ii, 516; iii, 168, 193; Joan, ii, 516; Sir Rich., iv, 342, 447, 552, 554; Dr., ii, 200; fam., iv, 588
Dart, J. H., v, 100
Dartmouth (Devon), v, 377, 379
Dartmouth, Frances C. Legge, ctss. of, iv, 232; Will. Legge, earl of, ii, 488; iv, 232; Geo. Legge, Ld., v, 386
Darvalt, Phil., iv, 637
Dashwood, Sir John, v, 538, 538 n
Daubeney, Lds., v, 321; Giles, iv, 35, 64; Hen., iv, 35, 64
Daubeney [Albigneye, Albini, Aubigny, Daubeny, Daubney, Dawbney], Clarice, v, 577; Clement, iv, 80; v, 228; Egidius, iv, 40; Eliz., iv, 428; Ellis, iii, 96, 97, 98; Rev. E., iii, 144; Hen., iv, 577; Hugh, iv, 428; Jas., iv, 428; Julia [Juliana], iii, 96; iv, 577; Oliver, iii, 152; Phil., iii, 151; Ralph, iv, 564; Will., ii, 230; iii, 96; fam., arms, iii, 95
Daubernoun, see Dabernon
Daubyn, John, v, 482
Daundely [Andely], Godf., iv, 185; John, iv, 185, 296; Phil., iv, 185, 296; Richer, iv, 295; Rob., iv, 182, 185; v, 4 n, 39; Rog., iv, 185, 189 n; Walt., iv, 185, 189
Daunfernet, Rob. de, v, 281
Dauntsey, Marg., iv, 510; Phil., iv, 510
D'Aussey, Chas., iii, 536
Dautry, see Dawtrey
Davenant, Cath., iv, 569; Edw., iv, 569; v, 237 n; Eliz., iv, 569; John, bp., iv, 568; John, iv, 569; Rebecca, iv, 569; Thos., v, 237 n; —, v, 496
Davenport, A., v, 535; Capt. S., v, 171
Daventry, de, Joan, v, 199, 200, 228; Sim., v, 199, 200, 228
Daveson, Capt., iii, 483; see also Davidson, Davison
David (Bruce), king of Scots, iv, 89
Davidson, Randall T., ii, 100; see also Daveson and Davison

Davis [Davies], Chas., v, 569, 570; Eliz., iv, 456; Geo., v, 539; John, iv, 442; Thos., iv, 456; v, 184, 187; Mrs., iv, 52
Davison, Will., iii, 178; see also Daveson and Davidson
Davy, Alice, iii, 176; John, iii, 483; Rich., ii, 284
Daw [Dawe], Rich., v, 168; Rob., iii, 310; iv, 94 n
Dawbney, see Daubeney
Dawes, Rev. Rich., iv, 470; Maj., v, 202
Dawkins, Jas., iv, 209
Dawley, Ant., iii, 445; Hen., iii, 445; Walt., iii, 445
Dawson, Matth., v, 549; Will., ii, 297
Dawtrey [Dautry, Dawtry], Blanche, Lady, iv, 520; Christine, Lady, iv, 220; Eliz., iii, 17, 487; iv, 16; (Sir) Fran., ii, 163; iii, 164, 487; iv, 82, 499, 502, 520; v, 146; (Sir) John, iii, 17, 164; iv, 82, 220, 472, 520, 524 n; v, 146, 372; Nich., v, 332; Will., iii, 17; iv, 16; see also Hawtrey
Day, Alf., v, 555; Chas., v, 555; Dan., v, 574; John, iv, 525, 539, 546, 554 n, 555, 556; Sam., v, 539, 545, 555; Thos., iv, 259, 374; Will., v, 555, 556; Mrs., v, 555
Day, Summers & Co., v, 458, 459
Daylandes (E. Wellow), iv, 535
Deacon, Bridg., v, 192; Rich., v, 192; Mrs., v, 518; —, v, 518
Deade, Mrs., v, 504
Deadman's Plack Copse (Longparish), iv, 406
Dealand (Sherfield), iv, 104
Dean, barony of, iv, 521
Dean, East, iv, 489, 498-500, 502, 515, 521, 533 n, 537; adv., iv, 500, 509 n; char., iv, 500; ch., iv, 499; man., iv, 498; pop., v, 446
Dean, West, iv, 424, 489; ch., iv, 524; pop., v, 446; Rom. rem., i, 311, 347
Dean, West, man. (W. Tytherley), iv, 497, 521
Deane, iv, 197, 200, 201, 205-7, 215, 223, 224, 225, 226, 228, 239; adv., iv, 207; char., iv, 207; ch., iv, 207; man., iv, 139, 205-7, 369; pop., v, 442; sch., ii, 398
Deane [Dean, Dene] (de, le), Anne, iv, 210; Capt. Ant., iii, 225; Aveline, iv, 498; A., v, 529, 530; Edw., ii, 168; Eliz., iv, 207; Frances, v, 144; Geoff., iii, 260; Gilb., iii, 370; Hen., archp., ii, 48; Hen., ii, 166; iv, 157; (Sir) Jas., ii, 376; iv, 134, 139, 200, 201, 206, 207; Jane, iv, 283, 284; John, iii, 124; iv, 200, 206; v, 107; Mercy, ii, 78; Nich., v, 144; Rich., ii, 293, 366; iii, 415; iv, 134, 139, 206; v, 17, 382, 383, 484; Rob., iii, 415; Steph., ii, 124, 150; iv, 498 n; Thos., iv, 210, 283, 284, 285; Watson, iv, 207; Will., iii, 415; iv, 157; —, ii, 385
Deane Heath, iv, 205
Deane House (Deane), iv, 205
Deanes (Longparish), iv, 406
Deane Wood, Gt., (Deane), iv, 205
Deangate mill (Winchester), v, 563
Dean Hill, iv, 498
Dean Prior, see Priors Dean
Dean's Piddle (Itchel), iv, 6

Dean's Wood (Hannington), iv, 229
Dear, Jas., iv, 430, 540, 541
Dearing, Dearynge, see Dering
Debarry, Rich., v, 95
Debary, Rev. Pet., iv, 324
Debertine, Alice, iii, 298; Jos., iii, 298
Deboke, Andr., v, 456
Decoy, the (New Forest), v, 560
Decoys, v, 559
Dederyche lande (Stratfield Turgis), iv, 63
Dee, John, iii, 288
Deepdene [Depedene], Agnes, v, 273; Cecily de, iv, 490 n; Thos., v, 273
Deer, i, 5, 246-50; ii, 453
Deerhurst, Ld., ii, 346
Deerhurst, treaty of, v, 297
Deerleap Lane (Eling), iv, 546
Dege, Eliz., iv, 634; John, iv, 634
Deghynghous, le (Winchester), v, 483
Dehany, Phil., iv, 180
Delafaye, Chas., iv, 595
Delamere, John, v, 475; Thos., v, 147; Will., v, 227 n
Delamotte, Mrs., iii, 535
Delbourne, ii, 156
Delgarno, —, v, 282
De la Mare, Agnes, iv, 205, 206; Alice, iv, 191; John, iv, 206; Kath., ii, 129; Margery, iv, 588; v, 230; Maud, iv, 206; Pet., iii, 410; iv, 588; Rob., iv, 205, 206; Thos., iv, 206; Warin, iv, 206; Will., iv, 206; v, 230
De la Warr, Kath., ctss., v, 99; earls, iii, 225; Reg., iii, 225; Thos., iii, 225; Ladies, iv, 406, 414; Anne, iv, 354, 355; Cecily, iv, 407, 412; Lds., ii, 496, 497; iii, 467; iv, 388, 401, 407, 409, 414, 554; John, iv, 335, 336, 412, 414, 512; Reg., iii, 11; v, 99; Rich., iii, 11; v, 99; Rog., ii, 158; Thos., ii, 136; iii, 11, 12; iv, 220, 335, 402, 406, 412, 555; v, 99; Will., iv, 354, 412; v, 99
De la Warr [Warre], Clarice, iv, 512; Eliz., ii, 496; iv, 329; John, iv, 329; Rog., iv, 512; Thos. W., iv, 523; see also Ware
Dell (Kingsclere), iv, 267
Dell fields (Brown Candover), iv, 183 n
Delmé, John, iii, 214; v, 523; Pet., iii, 224; Seymour R., iii, 216, 232, 233; fam., arms, iii, 224
Deltoides, i, 144
Delves, Mary, Lady, iv, 335; Rhoda, Lady, iv, 320; Sir Brian B., iv, 335, 361; Sir Thos., iv, 320
Denbye [Deneby], Hugh, iv, 212; Rich., iv, 407
Dene, la (Longstock), iv, 449
Dene, la (Penton Mewsey), iv, 381
Dene, fam., see Deane
Denebrugge, see Dunbridge
Deneby, see Denbye
Denecourt, man. (Houghton), iii, 415
Dene Maudit, see Deane
Denemede (Stratfieldsaye), iv, 60
Denes (Kingsley), ii, 515
Denewulf [Denewulph], bp. of Winchester, ii, 116; iii, 277, 348; iv, 291; v, 1
Denham (Hartley Mauditt), ii, 508
Denham, John, iv, 456
Denis, see Dennis
Denmead, man. (Hambledon), iii, 237, 240

Denmead, Rich., v, 29
Denmead Molyns [Molens] (Hambledon), ii, 168 ; iii, 241
Dennecourt, see Denecourt
Dennett, Jer., v, 170 ; John, v, 256 ; Louisa, v, 170 ; Marg. A., v, 235
Dennier, Edw., ii, 382
Dennis [Denis, Denys], abbot, ii, 142, 146 ; iv, 650 ; v, 198 ; the clerk, iv, 211, 293 ; prior of Ellingham, ii, 230
Dennis [Denis, Dennys, Denys], Bridg., v, 280 ; Sir Edw., v, 182, 224 n, 280 ; Frances, Lady, v, 280 ; Jonathan, ii, 492 ; Margery, iv, 617 n ; Mich., v, 163, 243, 280 ; Rob., iv, 167 ; Sarah, ii, 492 ; (Sir) Thos., ii, 50 ; iv, 334, 617 ; v, 243, 280 ; Whitehead, ii, 492 ; Will., ii, 383
Denny Lodge (Beaulieu), iv, 650
Dennys, see Dennis
Denpurcuc (Kingsclere), iv, 250
Denton, Will., iv, 196
Denys, see Dennis
De Paravicini, Rev. Fran. B., iv, 371 ; Rev. Fred., iv, 371
Depedene, fam., see Deepdene
Depedene Brow (Dibden), iv, 655
Depenhale, see Dippenhall
Deptford (Kent), v, 370, 372, 375, 376, 383, 386, 387
Derby, Will. de Ferrers, earl of, iv, 77
Derby, fam. name, see Darby
Dereham, Will. de, iii, 412
Derhile, see Doiley
Dering [Dearing, Dearynge, Deryng], Anne, iii, 88 ; Eleanor, iv, 268 ; Hen., iv, 85 ; v, 333 ; Martha, iv, 8 ; Nich., iii, 27, 88 ; iv, 84, 85, 268 ; v, 326 ; Thos., iii, 27, 88 ; Will., iv, 268
Derle, John, prior, ii, 190, 191
Derleie, see Durley, man. (Eling)
Dernford [Derneford] (de), Joan, iv, 216 ; John, ii, 173, 175 ; Walt., iv, 216
Derrell, see Darrell
Dertune, see Durton
Deryng, see Dering
Despenser (le), Eliz., Lady, iv, 440 ; Lds. :—Edw., iv, 440 ; v, 285 ; Hugh, iv, 645 ; Thos., iv, 440
Despenser [Despencer] (le), Ad., iv, 431 ; Aimery, iv, 431 ; Alina, iv, 150 ; Edw., iv, 82, 151, 440 ; Eleanor, iv, 645 ; Eliz., iv, 440, 474 ; Gilb., v, 284 ; (Sir) Hugh, ii, 207, 213 ; iii, 142, 149, 150, 158 ; iv, 82, 89, 150, 151, 156, 379, 418, 440, 471, 474, 481, 512 n, 560 ; v, 274, 284 ; Isabel, iv, 151, 441 ; v, 285 ; Juliana, ii, 128 ; Rich., iv, 151, 441 ; Thos., iv, 151, 474 ; v, 285 ; Thurston, iv, 431 ; fam., iv, 7
Deucumbe (Carisbrooke), v, 222
Devenish [Devenishe, Devenissh, Devenisshe, Devenysh] (de, le), Edith, ii, 506 ; Eliz., ii, 506 ; Hen., v, 482 n ; John, ii, 201, 506 ; iii, 69 ; iv, 481 ; v, 418 ; Maud, ii, 506 ; Nichola [Nichole], ii, 506 ; iii, 69 ; Nich., ii, 506 ; iii, 69, 137, 456 ; v, 4, 313, 494 ; Rich., ii, 201 ; Thos., ii, 506 ; iii, 69, 456 ; v, 39 ; fam., arms, iii, 137
Devercy [Evercy], Pet., v, 146, 148, 161 ; Thos., v, 146, 162 n, 191, 275
Deverell [Deverel], Elias, ii, 156 ; Hen., ii, 148 ; iv, 549 ; John, iii,

Deverell (cont.)
149 ; Will., iii, 149 ; Will. H., iv, 491
Devereux, Amelia C., iv, 571 ; Frances, v, 229 ; Rich., iv, 571 ; Rob., v, 229
De Vesci, John R. W., Ld., iv, 14 ; John, vsct., iv, 54 ; Thos., vsct., iv, 54
Devil's Highway, iv, 51
Devizes (Wilts.), iv, 97
Devon, ctsses. of, ii, 43 ; Amice, iv, 553 ; v, 86, 112, 272, 279 ; Isabel, see Albemarle, ctss. of ; Lucy, v, 86 n ; Mabel, ii, 155 ; v, 88 ; earls of, iv, 457, 508 n, 553, 596 ; v, 241, 246 n, 466, 469 ; Bald. de Redvers, ii, 137, 152, 153, 154, 168, 203, 230 ; iv, 597, 598, 620, 622, 640, 641, 643, 645, 648 ; v, 83, 86, 87, 90, 91, 94, 95, 96, 112, 114, 115, 123, 128, 132, 141, 152, 188, 213, 220, 232, 241, 279, 286, 303 ; Edw. Courtenay, iv, 601, 631, 641 ; Humph. Stafford, v, 160 ; Osgar, iv, 401 ; Rich. de Redvers, ii, 152, 153, 154, 231 ; iv, 620, 622, 645 n ; v, 86, 88, 90, 91, 94, 96, 98, 100, 114, 115, 123, 132, 135, 136, 141, 151, 164 n, 171, 174, 180, 184, 188, 222, 224, 227, 234, 241, 242, 256, 260, 263, 273, 284, 285, 288, 469 ; Thos. Courtenay, iv, 597 ; v, 320 ; Will. Courtenay, iv, 427, 597, 646 ; Will. de Redvers, ii, 137, 154, 203, 230 ; iv, 553, 640, 645 n ; v, 87, 91, 94, 114, 125, 172, 183, 188, 224, 230, 234, 243, 245, 263, 270, 271, 274, 291, 470
Devonshire, shipping statistics, v, 377
Devonshire, Chas. Blount, earl of, iv, 631, 632
Dew, Edw. P., iv, 601
Dewar, A. W., iv, 319, 320, 321 ; Dav., iv, 320, 358, 378, 379 ; D. A., iv, 323 ; D. A. B., iv, 323, 378 ; Geo., iv, 320, 378 ; John, iv, 320
Dewar v. Maitland, iv, 379
Dewdney, see Dudeney
De Winton, Charlotte A., v, 137 ; see also Winton
De Winton-Corry, Miss, iv, 21
Dibden, iv, 544, 547, 557, 655-8 ; adv., iv, 658 ; ch., iv, 657 ; mans., iv, 469, 655 ; pop., v, 446 ; Rom. rem., iv, 655 ; Rom. rd., i, 325, 344 ; sch., ii, 398
Dibden (de, of), Agnes, iv, 656 ; Edm., iv, 656 ; Joan, iv, 656 ; John, v, 109 ; Nich., iv, 656, 658 n ; Osbert, iv, 656 ; Rich., iv, 656 ; Thos., iv, 656
Dibden Hanger, man. (Dibden), iv, 550 n, 656
Dibden Poleyn, man. (Dibden), iv, 656, 657
Dible, J., & Sons, v, 458
Dibsdale, —, v, 7, 8
Dichull, see Itchel
Dickens, Fran., iii, 396 ; F., iv, 121 n ; Rachel, iii, 396
Dickenson [Dickinson], Edw., iv, 15, 16, 72, 73 ; Jas., iv, 73 ; Rog., ii, 83 ; Thos., v, 172
Dicker, J. C., v, 186
Dicker's Farm (Hannington), iv, 229
Dickinson, see Dickenson
Dickman, Walt., iii, 43
Didelard, v, 112
Difford tithing (Fordingbridge hund.), iv, 560

Diford, Nich., ii, 223
Digby, Sir Kenelm, iv, 203, 204 ; Rev. Noel, v, 215
Digerle, Diggerley, see Doiley
Dighere, Hamund le, v, 481
Digweed, Fran., iv, 79 ; John, iv, 250 ; Will. F., iv, 174 ; Will. H. iv, 174, 250, 267 ; fam., iv, 172 n
Dillington, Ant., v, 161, 181, 183 ; Hannah, v, 183 ; Sir John, v, 252 ; Mabel, v, 250 ; Mary, v, 183, 187 ; (Sir) Rob., v, 142, 163, 181, 183, 185, 219, 250, 252 ; Sir Tristram, v, 183, 252 ; Walt., v, 161 ; fam., v, 180
Dillon, Sir John, iv, 54 ; Mary, Lady, iv, 54
Dinan (de), Alan, iv, 607 ; Gervaise, iv, 607 ; Roland, iv, 607
Dineley, see Dyneley
Dingle, Rob., ii, 40 ; iv, 218
Dingley [Dyngley], Amy, ii, 125 ; Eliz., ii, 125 ; v, 282, 283 ; Frances, ii, 125 ; Jas., v, 282 ; Jane, ii, 125 ; (Sir) John, v, 278, 282, 283, 289 ; v, 194, 214 n, 220 ; Lewis, v, 282 ; Marg., v, 282 ; Ralph [Ralf] (de), v, 194, 282 ; Rich., v, 282 ; Rob., v, 113, 184, 198 n, 211, 214 n, 282
Dinno, see Duino
Dinorben Court (Crondall), iv, 5
Dipley Green (Hartley Wintney), iv, 79
Dippenhall [Dipnel] (Crondall), iv, 5, 6, 9, 14
Diptera, i, 154
Dirty Corner (Hustbourne Priors), i, 304 ; iv, 288
Disinhurst, Pet. de, ii, 176, 179
Ditcham (Buriton), iii, 90
Ditcham, Rich. de, iii, 90
Ditchfield, Edw., iv, 470, 471 ; v, 94, 126 n, 229
Dix [Dixe, Dixie], Radigund, iv, 550, 569 ; Thos., iv, 550, 569 ; Wolstan, iv, 225
Dixon, Chas., iii, 103, 110 ; (Rev.) Rich., v, 177, 189, 204 ; Sam., iv, 597 ; Rev. Thos., iv, 397, 398, 399
Dixon & Cardus, seed crushers, v, 455
Dobbes, Will., iv, 94
Dobbins, Rev. Guy, ii, 522 ; Will., iv, 613 n
Dobson, John, ii, 344, 347, 366 ; Rev. Will., iv, 234
Dochmeres feld, see Dogmersfield
Dockenfield, pop., v, 437
Dockes, Great & Little, (Bramley), iv, 141
Dod, —, v, 487
Dodbrook, fishery (Eversley), iv, 34
Dodington [Doddington], Anne, iv, 562, 606 ; Edw., iv, 605 ; Eliz., iv, 562, 606 ; Herb., iv, 562, 606, 610 ; John, ii, 215, 562, 576, 601, 606, 613 ; Kath., iv, 606 n ; Marg., iv, 562 ; (Sir) Will., iv, 562, 571, 572, 595, 597, 598, 601, 605, 606, 610, 630
Dodintune (Eling), iv, 555
Dodner, v, 234
Dodson, Rev. Chris., iv, 384 ; Rev. P. A., iv, 384 ; Rev. Will., iv, 371, 384
Dodsworth, Ant., ii, 87
Doe, Jordan de, iv, 360
Dog and Partridge Inn (Yately), iv, 21, 26
Doget, Alice, v, 275 ; Geoff., v, 275 ; Marg., v, 275 ; Walt., v, 275

Dogmersfield, ii, 99 ; iv, 8, 66, 67, 72-4 ; v, 308 ; adv., iv, 74 ; char., iv, 74 ; ch., iv, 73 ; fair, iv, 73 ; man., iv, 72 ; mills, iv, 72, 73 ; park, iv, 72, 73, 74, 88 ; pop., v, 443

Dogmersfield House (Dogmersfield), iv, 72

Dogra, Nich., iii, 508

Doiley [Doiley Wood] (Hurstbourne Tarrant), iv, 320, 321, 353 n

Doiley Hill (Hurstbourne Tarrant), iv, 319, 320

Doiley Manor (Hurstbourne Tarrant), iv, 319, 320

Dolcoppice, ii, 180

Doleman, fam., v, 198 n

Doles (Hurstbourne Tarrant), iv, 319, 321

Doles Heath, iv, 321

Doles Wood, iv, 320, 321, 345

Dollar, John, iv, 201 n

Dollery, John, iv, 276

Dolmans (Kingsley), ii, 515

Domerham, Ad. de, iv, 586, 587 n

Dominicans, ii, 15, 57, 105, 189 ; v, 5

Dommere, see Dummer

Domus Dei, see God's House

Donalson, Hen. F. S., iv, 399

Donewyco, Pet. de, ii, 154

Doningele (Odiham), iv, 88

Donketon, John de, ii, 110

Donnell, Frances, iv, 441 ; Jas., iv, 441 ; Nich., ii, 385

Donnus, v, 228

Donymeade (Sydmonton), iv, 251, 254

Dorchester (Oxon), ii, 2, 101 ; v, 89 n

Dorchester, Ladies :—Anne H. Carleton, iv, 78 ; Charlotte Carleton, iv, 76, 94, 176, 178 ; Henrietta A. Carleton, iv, 154, 155, 157 ; Lds. :—Arthur H. Carleton, iv, 154 ; Dudley W. Carleton, iv, 78 ; Guy Carleton, iv, 78, 154, 157 ; v, 514 ; Marg., mchnss. of, ii, 475, 476 ; mqsses of :—Evelyn Pierrepont, iv, 494 ; Hen. Pierrepont, iv, 509

Dorchester, John, ii, 160

Dorcrofte (Hartley Wespall), iv, 42

Dore, John, v, 274 ; Thos., v, 274 ; Col., ii, 97

D'Oridant, Chas., iv, 2

Dormer (Rev.) Chas., iii, 106 ; Joan, iii, 435 ; John, iii, 107 ; Mary, iii, 106 ; Rob., iii, 106 ; Thos., iii, 435, 436 ; fam., arms, iii, 106

Dorne, Rob., ii, 445

Dorroll Copse (Ewhurst), iv, 247

Dorset, Anne, ctss. of, iv, 541 ; dk. of, v, 574 ; Thos. Grey, mqss. of, iv, 608

Dorsett, John, ii, 113

Dorsnell [Dorsnelli], Juliane, iv, 104, 475 ; Rob., iv, 104, 475

Dorton (Selborne), mill, iii, 6

Doswell, John, iii, 326

Dotenel, Hen., iv, 590

Dottesley, man., ii, 121

Doubel, Blase, ii, 231

Double Dikes (Christchurch), v, 84

Douenold, v, 183 n

Doughton, man., ii, 121

Doughty, (Sir) Edw., iv, 423 ; v, 517 ; Eliz., iv, 423 ; Frances, iv, 447 ; Geo., iv, 447 ; Geo. B., iv, 447

Doughty-Tichborne, see Tichborne

Douglas, Lady Isabella, v, 516 ; Ld. Chas., ii, 347

Douglas [Douglasse], Eleanor, iv, 166 ; Sir Geo., iv, 166 ; Capt., v, 89

Doune, le (Swarraton), iv, 195

Doune, fam., see Downes

Dounesplatts (King's Somborne), iv, 470

Dounhalf, la (Kimpton), iv, 372

Dounton, see Downton

Dousgunels, Gilb. de, ii, 152, 160 ; v, 101

Dove, John, iv, 499 ; Pet., iv, 324 ; Rob., iv, 523

Dover, Rich. Ingworth, bp. of, ii, 56, 57, 190, 191

Dover [Dovor] (de), Jos., iv, 518 ; Julia, iv, 551 n ; Will., iv, 551 n ; v, 303

Dowce, see Dowse

Dowden, Ann, ii, 478 ; John, ii, 478

Dowell, S., v, 252

Dowles, see Doles

Dowling, Geo. A., iii, 47 ; Rob., iv, 351, 413

Dowman, Dr., ii, 120

Down, Little (Vernhams Dean), iv, 329

Downe, Lower, see Cowedowne

Downe Husband, man., see Hurstbourne Priors, man.

Down End (Arreton), v, 139, 140

Downes [Doune], Geoff., iv, 628 ; Rich., iii, 80 ; Rob. de la, iv, 473 n

Downes Land (Sherfield), iv, 104

Downewood (Bradley), iv, 202

Downewood (King's Somborne), iv, 470

Down Farm (Burghclere), iv, 277

Down Farm (Odiham), iv, 98

Down fields (Brown Candover), iv, 183 n

Down House (Odiham), v, 540

Down Hurstbourne, man., see Hurstbourne Priors, man.

Downing [Downynge], Edw. [Edm.], iv, 97, 365, 620

Downlands (Bramshott), ii, 491, 492

Downlanger (Ashmansworth), iv, 274

Downs, North and South, v, 409

Downshire, mqss. of, v, 543

Downs House (Eling), iv, 546

Downton (Hordle), v, 89 n, 110 ; man., v, 113

Downton (Wilts.), ii, 261, 262, 288, 316

Downton [Dounton], John de, (of) ii, 193 ; v, 114 ; Thos., ii, 172 ; iii, 375

Downynge, see Downing

Dowse [Dowce], Anne, iv, 530 ; Blanch, iv, 497 ; Corn., iv, 218 ; Sir Edm., iv, 497 ; Eliz. (Lady), iv, 174, 494, 495, 527, 624 ; Esther, iv, 529 ; (Sir) Fran., iv, 203, 456, 494, 497 n, 527, 529, 530, 624 ; Gab., iv, 456 ; Geo., iii, 443, 455, 456, 488 ; John, iii, 468 ; iv, 212, 455, 456, 457, 488, 555 ; v, 125 ; Marie, iv, 455 ; Paulet, iv, 488 ; Rich., ii, 76 ; iii, 468 ; iv, 455, 456, 457, 488, 550, 555 ; v, 114 ; Thos., iii, 468, 469 ; iv, 455, 456, 492, 494, 495, 497, 526, 624, 625

Doyle, Diana E. F., iii, 432

D'Oyley [Doyly], Sir John H., v, 120 ; Rob., iv, 43 ; Sarah, iv, 552 ; Thos., iii, 240

Draffehaven (Yarmouth), v, 286

Dragon-flies, i, 112

Draiton mill (Winchester), v, 49

Drake, Constance, iv, 397 ; Sir Fran., v, 377 ; Mary A., v, 213 ;

Drake (cont.)
Thos., v, 78 ; Will., iv, 397 ; W. W., v, 213 ; —, iv, 397, 398 ; v, 534

Drakenorth [Drakenhorde, Drakenworth] (Damerham), iv, 587 n

Drakenorth Coppis (Damerham), iv, 587

Dramford, man. (Devon), iii, 20

Draper, Eliz., iv, 54 ; Gauden, ii, 502 ; John, ii, 49, 57, 58, 158, 159, 160 ; v, 85, 95, 103, 104, 109 ; Marian, ii, 502 ; Mary, Lady, iv, 54 ; Nich., v, 484 ; Sim. le, v, 33 ; (Sir) Thos., iv, 54 ; v, 484 ; Will., ii, 502 ; fam., ii, 505

Drawater, Oliver, iii, 58

Drayton [Drayton Cannes] (Barton Stacey), ii, 117 ; iii, 389 ; iv, 359, 415, 416, 417, 419, 420

Drayton, man. (Farlington), iii, 148, 150

Drayton House (Sherfield-upon-Loddon), iv, 104

Drayton juxta Nunneton, ii, 116

Drayton Park (Barton Stacey), iv, 417

Dregge, John, v, 483

Drepanulae, i, 140

Dreux, Rob., count of, iv, 656

Drewe [Drew], Alice, v, 250 ; Edw., iii, 322 ; Eleanor, v, 249 ; Sir Humph., iii, 322 ; John, v, 250 ; Kath., iii, 322 ; Rich., v, 250 ; Will., iv, 204 ; v, 249, 250

Drewett [Druett], Pet., ii, 258 ; Rich., iv, 229 ; Roland, iv, 229 ; Sibyl, iv, 229 ; Thos., iv, 229 ; Will., iv, 229 ; Maj., v, 345

Drewry, see Drury

Dreyhememers (King's Somborne), iv, 470

Driffed, Thos., iv, 177

Driffelde, Elienora, ii, 41, 224 ; Thos., ii, 41, 224

Drinkwater, Eliz., iv, 8 n ; Rich., iv, 8 n

Drocheneford, see Droxford

Drodintone, Droditone, see Durton

Droegtun, see Drayton

Drogheda, Chas. mqss. of, iv, 522

Drogo, the dyer, v, 477

Drokeneford, Drokensford, Drokinsford, see Droxford

Drope, Edw., iv, 65

Drove, le (King's Somborne), iv, 470

Droxford i, 378 ; ii, 4, 21, 62, 96, 101, 108 ; iii, 274, 275, 284-8 ; v, 528 ; adv., iii, 287 ; char., iii, 287 ; ch., ii, 24 ; iii, 286 ; man., iv, 20, 109 ; iii, 285 ; pop., v, 440 ; schs., ii, 398

Droxford [Drokensford] (de), And., ii, 24 ; Joan, iv, 394 ; (Sir) John, ii, 24 ; iii, 204, 255, 262, 285, 346 ; iv, 41, 42, 63, 72, 199, 213, 226, 265, 313, 394, 597 ; v, 118, 242, 272 n ; Nich., ii, 24 ; Phil., ii, 24 ; iii, 204, 255, 262 ; iv, 199, 394 ; Rich., ii, 24 ; Thos., ii, 24 ; v, 242

Droxford Farm (Droxford), v, 98

Druett, see Drewett

Drumare, Luke de, iv, 129

Drumlanrich, Ld., ii, 346, 347

Drummond, A. C., iii, 293, 295 ; Hen., iii, 395 ; Jas., iii, 437 ; Rob., iii, 293, 294 ; —, v, 572 ; fam., arms, iii, 293

Drury [Drewry], Alice, iii, 358 ; Drew, iv, 620 ; Mary, iii, 150 ; Rob., iii, 358

Dryden, John, v, 201

Dry Knoll (Kings Worthy), iv, 430

Dublin, Hugh Yng, archbp. of, ii, 294
Dublin Farm (Wherwell), iv, 411
Dubosc, Sim., ii, 219
Ducie, Rob., iv, 471 *n*
Duck, Thos., iv, 248
Duckemeade (Kingsclere), iv, 261 *n*
Duckworth, Sir John, v, 399
Dudecompa (Christchurch), v, 85
Dudeney [Dewdney], Barbara, iii, 383 ; Malachy, iii, 309, 310, 383
Dudley, Cecily, Lady, iv, 628 ; Joyce, Lady, iv, 628 ; Edw., Ld., ii, 475, 476 ; iv, 628 ; John, Ld., ii, 475
Dudley, Amb., iii, 12 ; (Sir) Edm., ii, 492 ; iii, 169, 436, 485 ; iv, 353, 580, 628 ; v, 247 ; Eliz., ii, 492 ; iii, 169 ; iv, 580 ; v, 247 ; Sir Hen., v, 329 ; Jane, ii, 167 ; iii, 11 ; (Sir) John, ii, 492 ; iii, 169, 436, 485 ; v, 247 ; Rich., ii, 315 ; iii, 485
Dudmoor (Christchurch), v, 85
Due, John, v, 98 ; Marg., v, 98
Duffield, Edm., iii, 205 ; John, iii, 29
Dugard, Eliz., iii, 196
Dugdale [Dukidale], —, ii, 385
Duino [Dinno], Inguerand de, ii, 41, 227, 228, 229
Duke, Anne, iv, 564 *n* ; John, iv, 342 ; Rob., iv, 564 *n* ; (Rev.) Will., iv, 342
Dukidale, *see* Dugdale
Dulamon, Jacques, iii, 536
Dumare, *see* Dummer
Dumaresq, Miss, iii, 536
Dumbelton, de, John, v, 220 ; Rob., v, 220
Dumbreham, *see* Damerham
Dummer [Dummere], iii, 355, 356, 357-60 ; iv, 179 ; adv., iii, 360 ; char., iii, 360 ; ch., iii, 359 ; mans., iii, 357 ; pop., v, 440 ; schs., ii, 398
Dummer, de, Agnes, v, 113 ; Edm., iii, 484 ; iv, 259 *n*, 619 ; Edw., iii, 481 ; iv, 647 ; v, 114, 252 *n* ; Ellen, iii, 358 ; E., v, 387 ; Geoff., iii, 357, 360 ; Hen., iii, 357 ; (Rev.) John, iii, 357, 358, 360, 489 ; Leonora S., iv, 619 ; Mary, iv, 619 ; Maud, iv, 376 ; Ralph, iii, 357 ; Rich., iii, 310 ; iv, 373 ; Rob., iii, 357, 360 ; v, 113 ; Sybil, iv, 420 ; Thos., iii, 298, 310, 358, 411, 464 ; iv, 420, 455, 488 ; v, 458 ; Thos. L., iii, 420, 477, 486 ; iv, 508 ; Will., iii, 358, 359 ; iv, 373, 376 ; —, v, 230 ; fam., arms, iii, 358
Dummer Andrews Swaythling (Stoneham), v, 447 *n*
Dun, *see* Dunn
Duna (King's Somborne), iv, 470
Dunbar, Chas., iv, 54 ; Capt. Dav., iv, 54 ; Mary, iv, 54
Dunbridge, man. (Mottisfont), iv, 492, 507
Dunbridge, Pet., iv, 508
Dunbridge Farm (Mottisfont), iv, 508
Duncan, Dav., v, 125 ; Rev. John, iii, 382 ; —, iv, 348
Dunce, Will., ii, 521
Dunch [Dunche, Dunches], Dowsabella, iii, 464 ; iv, 453 ; Edm., iv, 54 ; John, iii, 464, 483 ; Sam., iii, 464 ; iv, 453, 468 ; Wharton, iii, 464 ; (Sir) Will., iii, 125 ; iv, 54 ; Maj., iii, 486
Duncombe Close (Christchurch), v, 85

Duncroft Coppice (Faccombe), iv, 314
Duncross Coppes (Abbotts Ann), iv, 334
Dundonald, earl of, v, 392
Dundridge (Chilton Candover), iv, 185
Dune, la (Lasham), iv, 81
Dune, fam., *see* Dunn
Dunewude (Longstock), iv, 449
Dungewood (Shorewell), v, 238
Dunham, Eliz., iv, 431 ; (Sir) John, iv, 431
Dunley (St. Mary Bourne), iv, 295, 299
Dunmore, Alice de, ii, 149, 151
Dunn [Dun, Dune] (de, le), John, iii, 343, 354 ; iv, 392, 393 ; v, 311 ; Rob., iv, 392 ; Sarah, iv, 392 ; Sim., iv, 392 ; (Sir) Will., iv, 392, 393 ; —, v, 554
Dunnebury Hill, *see* Danebury Hill
Dunstan Heath, ii, 450, 451
Dunstaple, Rog. de, v, 476 ; Will. of, v, 44
Dunster (de), Geoff., iv, 278 ; Humph., iv, 278, 279 *n* ; v, 223
Dunwood (East Wellow), iv, 489, 535, 537, 538 *n* ; pop., v, 446
Dunyenston, Hugh de, v, 34
Dupeden, *see* Dibden
Dupehale (Crondall), *see* Dippenhall
Dupehale, Pet. de, iv, 152
Duplessis, Jules, iv, 616
Duppa, Brian, bp., ii, 93
Duquesne, Abr., v, 385
Durand, iv, 616
Durdent [Durdant], Agnes, iv, 353 ; Joan, iv, 353 ; John, iv, 353 ; Nich., iii, 353, 381 *n*, 382, 396 ; Rob., iv, 384
Dureford Abbey (Suss.), iv, 85 ; v, 38 *n*, 39
Durell, Anne, v, 114 ; Thos., v, 114
Dureville, John de, ii, 115
Durford, John, v, 48
Durham, bps. of, ii, 10 ; Chas. T. Baring, iv, 430 ; Ralph Flambard, ii, 10, 117, 121, 152, 160 ; iii, 227 ; iv, 72 ; Rich. le Poor, ii, 226 ; iii, 59 ; iv, 344 ; v, 101, 301 ; Cuth. Tunstall, iv, 165
Durhirde, de la, Alice, iii, 466 ; Thos., iii, 466
Durie, Mrs., iv, 511 *n*
Durley [Durle, Durlye, Dyrle], ii, 116 ; iii, 274, 275, 288-90, 301 ; iv, 538 ; adv., iii, 290 ; char., iii, 290 ; ch., iii, 289 ; ind., v, 457 ; man., iii, 288 ; pop., v, 440
Durley, man. (Eling), iv, 553
Durley Chine (Bournemouth), v, 134
Durley Farm (Eling), iv, 553
Durley Hall Farm (Durley), iii, 300
Durnells (King's Worthy), iv, 430
Durnford [Durneford], John, iv, 646, 649 ; Margery, iv, 646, 649 ; Rich., iii, 403 ; iv, 42
Durngate (Winchester), v, 3, 47
Durngate, Hen. de, v, 33
Durngate Mill (Winchester), v, 49
Durrant, Rev. Reg. N., v, 151 ; Miss, v, 136
Durrington (Wilts.), ii, 289
Durton, man. (Arreton), v, 148
Duslecompa, ii, 152
Dutton, Edw. L., iii, 425 ; Hen., iii, 53, 143, 322 ; Hen. J., ii, 471, 477, 509, 513, 516, 519, 521 ; iii, 12 ; iv, 486 ; Jas. H. L., iii, 425 ; John, ii, 477, 516, 518, 519 ; iii, 12, 53, 322, 425 ; iv, 486 ; John T., ii, 516, 519 ;

Dutton (*cont.*)
iv, 486 ; Mary, iii, 12, 425 ; Ralph, iii, 53, 143 ; Ralph H., iv, 486 ; Rev. Reg., ii, 518 ; fam., arms, ii, 477 ; iii, 53, 425
Duty Corner (Hurstbourne Priors), *see* Dirty Corner
Duxmore (Arreton), v, 140
Dwineford, John de, ii, 175
Dyeing industry, v, 480, 483
Dyer, Ann, iv, 241 ; Edw., iv, 94 *n* ; John, v, 484 ; Steph., iv, 102 ; Sir Thos. R., iii, 331 ; Will., ii, 482 ; iv, 102, 241
Dyes, John, ii, 259
Dygges, John, v, 483
Dyke, Eliz., iv, 268 ; Hen., iv, 268
Dyker, John, iii, 330
Dymer, Will., v, 465
Dymmocke, Sir Edw., iv, 318 ; Frances, iv, 318
Dymperk (Long Sutton), iv, 18
Dyneley [Dineley, Dynelly], de, Alice, v, 173 ; Anne, iv, 271, 279 ; Edw., iv, 224, 271, 279, 352 ; Eliz., iv, 224, 225, 271, 279, 352 ; Fran., iv, 64 ; Marg., iv, 224, 271, 352 ; Philippa, iv, 271 ; Rob., iii, 241 ; iv, 54, 224, 240, 271, 279 ; v, 173 ; Sanchea, iv, 224, 271, 279, 352 ; Thos., iv, 224, 225, 271, 279, 352 ; Will., iv, 258, 271, 279, 352
Dyngeet, Johanna, iv, 25 ; Rob., iv, 25
Dyngley, man. (Church Oakley), *see* Malshanger
Dyngley, fam., *see* Dingley
Dynham (de), Edith, iv, 551 ; (Sir) John, iv, 531 ; Muriel, iv, 531 ; Oliver, iv, 551
Dyrk, John, v, 483
Dyrle, *see* Durley
Dysart, earl of, v, 176 *n* ; Lady, v, 194
Dyson, A., v, 535 ; Rev. Chas., iv, 13, 72 ; Rev. Fran., iv, 391, 394

Eachard, Chris., v, 471
Eachbridge, *see* Eastbridge
Eadred, *see* Edred
Eadgils, riv., v, 218 *n*
Eadwig, *see* Edwy
Eager, *see* Eggar
Ealhswith, queen, ii, 5, 116, 122
Eames, Edw., iii, 407 ; John, v, 219 ; Will., iii, 22, 77, 81
Earle [Earl], Eliz., v, 80 ; Hen., iv, 378 ; Kath., v, 93 *n* ; Thos. H., iv, 378 ; Walt., iii, 518 ; Will. B., iv, 371 ; Lt.-Col. Will. H., iv, 358, 378, 379 ; Mrs., iv, 377, 378 ; —, iii, 346 ; v, 17 ; *see also* Erle
Earlins (Crondall), iv, 6
Earlisman [Earlsman], Jane, v, 163 ; Joan, v, 163 ; John, v, 163, 227
Earlstone, man. (Burghclere), iv, 278, 281
Earlstone, tithing (Burghclere), iv, 245, 273
Earlstone Common (Burghclere), iv, 277
Earlstone Farm (Burghclere), iv, 277
Earnley, Rich., iii, 191
Earth, Jos., ii, 509
Earthworks, i, 262 ; v, 84
Earwigs, i, 109
Easebourne Priory (Suss.), iv, 374
East, Arth., iv, 450 ; A. E., iv, 450 ; Joshua, iv, 427, 447, 448, 450 ; Rob., iii, 184

Eastbridge, man. (Crondall), iv, 5, 9
Eastbrook House (Alton). ii, 474
East Cheap, see Eastbridge
East Cliff (Bournemouth), v, 134, 135
East Cowes Castle (Whippingham), v, 198
East Dean House (East Dean), iv, 498
East Dene (Bonchurch), v, 155
East End (Alresford), v, 514
East End (Baddesley), iv, 616
East End (Tangley), iv, 326
Eastfield (Milton), v, 126
Eastgate (Winchester), v, 3
Eastgate House (Winchester), v, 5
Easthampstead (Berks.), ii, 159
Eastington, ii, 159
Eastleigh, iii, 482 ; man., iii, 486 ; sch., ii, 398
Eastleigh, de, Hugh, iii, 486 ; Nich. de, v, 154 ; Ralph, iii, 486
East Medina Mill (Whippingham), v, 197
East Mill, man., see Cridlestyle
Eastmont, Bridg., v, 212 ; Dorothy. v, 212 ; John, v, 212
East Moor Copse (Maplederwell), ii, 224 ; iv, 149
Eastney (Portsmouth), iii, 129, 141, 195
Eastney, of, Alice, iii, 195 ; Gilb., iii, 195 ; Phil., iii, 195
Easton, ii, 219 ; iii, 302, 312, 317-19 ; v, 77 ; adv., ii, 219 ; iii, 319 ; char., iii, 319 ; ch., iii, 319 ; man., iii, 317 ; pop., v, 448 ; sch., ii, 398
Easton (Freshwater), v, 240
Easton (Longparish), see Aston
Easton Lands (Hartley Wespall), iv, 42, 43 n
Easton Park Wood (Crux Easton), iv, 313
Eastover Copse (Abbotts Ann), iv, 334
East Park (Rockbourne), iv, 584
Eastrop, ii, 26 ; iv, 113, 114, 115, 122, 123, 147-9 ; v, 243 ; adv., ii, 381, 383 ; iv, 149 ; ch., iv, 149 ; man., iv, 147 ; mill, iv, 149 ; pop., v, 439
Eastrop Bridge (Up Nately), iv, 176
Eastrop Farm, iv, 147, 176
Eastwood [Estwod], Thos., v, 381 ; Will., iv, 264
Eaton [Eton, Heaton] (de), Chas., v, 110 ; Pet., iv, 296 ; Rob., iv, 296 ; Will., iii, 178
Ebden, —, ii, 200 ; v, 77
Eblesborne (Wilts.), ii, 169, 172
Ecaudata, i, 206
Ecchinswell, ii, 108, 156 ; iv, 245, 249, 250, 264, 265, 266, 273 ; v, 77 ; man., iv, 253, 254 ; pop., v, 442
Ecclesiastical divisions, ii, 101
Ecclesiastical history, ii, 1
Ech Bridge, see Eastbridge
Echenswelle, see Ecchinswell
Echingham, de, Eva, iv, 268 ; Will., iv, 268
Echinodermata, i, 100
Edboldington, ii, 160
Edburga, abbess, ii, 122, 126
Eddeva, iv, 572 ; v, 161
Eddeworth [Eddesworth], John de, iii, 255 ; Steph. de, ii, 169
Eddulf, iv, 303 n
Ede, E. L., v, 574, 575 ; G. M., v, 574, 575 ; Steph., ii, 290
Edefele, see Hefedele
Edelingdene, ii, 132
Eden, Arth., iv, 448 ; Edw., v, 201 ; Eliz., Lady, iv, 154, 204

Edendon [Edindon, Edington, Edyndon, Edynton, Hedynton] (de, of), (Sir) John, ii, 38, 182, 195, 197, 207, 208 ; iii, 158, 192 ; iv, 373, 459, 616 ; Thos., ii, 208 ; Will., ii, 31, 32, 34, 35, 36, 119, 162, 195, 197, 207, 213 ; iii, 29, 42, 255, 256, 260, 314, 415, 421 ; iv, 7, 58, 63, 69, 147, 148, 179, 181, 373, 374, 388, 392 n, 413, 459, 616 ; v, 11 n, 51, 58, 63, 190, 280 ; fam., arms., v, 58
Ederosy, see Ivychurch
Edes, Rich., v, 256
Edgar, king, ii, 7, 116, 126 ; iii, 78, 307, 309, 323, 333, 340, 348, 413 ; iv, 6, 18, 27, 193, 239, 251, 277, 288, 346, 366, 406, 460, 607 n ; v, 198 n
Edgcumbe, Geo., Ld., v, 187 ; Rich., Ld., iv, 201, 361 ; v, 178, 187, 244 ; see also Mount Edgcumbe
Edgcumbe, Mary, Lady, v, 179, 187 ; Piers, iv, 200 ; v, 179 ; (Sir) Rich., iv, 361 ; v, 173 n, 179, 187 ; Thos., v, 179 ; fam., iv, 201
Edgur, John, iii, 306
Edindon, Edington, fam., see Edendon
Edington, man. (St. Helen's), v, 190
Edington (Wilts.), ii, 126, 131
Edintune, Edyneton, par., see Ovington
Edisbury, Kenrick, iii, 431
Edith, queen (w. of Edw. the Confessor), ii, 132, 474, 506 ; iii, 5, 130 ; iv, 174, 261, 265, 330, 374, 395 ; v, 204
Edith, queen (w. of Hen. I), see Maud
Edith, abbess of Godstow, iv, 257 ; abbess of Nunnaminster, ii, 126 ; d. of Sygar, iv, 501
Edlinges, see Eling
Edlyns, see Grove, (Eversley)
Edmonds [Edmonde, Edmondes, Edmund, Edmunds], Ant., v, 77 ; Barbara, iv, 491 ; Chris., iv, 423 ; Eliz., iv, 491 ; John, ii, 49, 174, 175 ; iv, 491 ; v, 130 ; Rich., iii, 391 ; (Sir) Thos., ii, 174 ; iv, 412, 414, 491, 548
Edmund I, iii, 59 ; iv, 123, 213, 232, 240, 242, 587, 592 ; v, 56
Edmund II (Ironside), ii, 8 ; iv, 243 ; v, 297
Edmund, iv, 211, 495, 542, 619, 623 ; prior of Selborne, ii, 177, 179
Edmundshay (Damerham), iv, 587
Edmundsthorp, de, Alice, iv, 260 ; Hen., iv, 260 ; Isabel, iv, 260 ; Mich., iv, 260 ; Pavia, iv, 260 ; Will., iv, 260
Edmundsthorp [Edmynstrop] Benham, man. (Kingsclere), iv, 252, 260
Ednod, iii, 355 ; iv, 284, 480, 627
Edred [Eadred], king, ii, 122 ; iii, 309 ; iv, 115, 129, 277, 288, 346, 411 n, 413, 446, 447 ; v, 56, 172, 220
Edric, iii, 225 ; iv, 74, 240, 242, 324, 337, 341, 510, 518, 532 ; v, 95, 128, 160, 272, 297
Edryche, Isabel, iv, 537 ; Will., iv, 537
Edulf, the priest, iv, 446, 447
Edward, the Confessor, ii, 8, 417, 421, 492, 493, 512 ; iv, 33, 35, 39, 41, 45, 47, 52, 57, 63, 72, 74, 81, 94, 102, 109, 113, 115, 141,

Edward (cont.)
147, 149, 153, 171, 205, 224, 225, 231, 240, 255, 258, 260, 261, 265, 270, 278, 282, 288, 324, 330, 331, 339, 341, 346, 360, 366, 372, 377 n, 379, 381, 387, 391, 393, 395, 417, 419, 428, 443, 449, 491, 492, 493, 495 n, 499, 500, 501, 502, 506, 512, 513, 515, 519, 521, 522, 535, 536 n, 537, 549, 550, 553, 560, 561, 563, 564, 568, 572, 573, 582, 598, 609, 619, 644, 655 ; v, 140, 141, 143, 146, 147, 148, 174, 187, 206, 228, 231, 246, 298
Edward, the Elder, ii, 5, 6, 116, 122, 126 ; iii, 390, 393 ; iv, 27, 183, 186, 195, 202, 212, 219, 221, 274, 288, 301, 334, 419, 444, 460, 550
Edward, the Martyr, ii, 7
Edward I, ii, 21, 106, 110, 138, 142, 147, 156, 161, 189, 205, 217, 220, 229, 230, 424, 474, 475 ; iii, 42, 176, 413 ; iv, 61, 67, 68, 71, 89, 90, 130, 159, 184, 213, 215, 222, 246, 252, 253, 265, 274, 277, 294, 319, 347, 471, 474, 477, 481 n, 483, 498, 500, 501, 545 ; v, 241 n, 265, 270, 272, 274, 305 n, 306 n, 311, 362
Edward II, ii, 23, 24, 30, 106, 127, 161, 165, 173, 189, 213, 474, 475, 477 ; iii, 153 ; iv, 7, 52, 68, 82, 89, 102, 130, 150, 151, 196, 200, 214, 247, 253, 265, 347, 356, 379, 396, 423, 457, 498, 515, 545, 608, 612, 631, 641 ; v, 219, 222, 265, 284, 362, 417
Edward III, ii, 31, 32, 128, 143, 162, 166, 189, 206, 209, 222, 228, 231, 268, 475, 476, 478 ; iii, 153 ; iv, 33, 34, 45, 58, 110, 150, 175, 176, 200, 208, 214, 227, 231, 247, 251, 318, 334, 369, 427, 440, 475, 481, 506, 516, 524, 536, 543, 545, 627 ; v, 219, 222, 227, 274, 286, 363, 364, 365, 410, 422
Edward IV, ii, 148, 158, 162, 166, 204, 205, 216, 228, 443, 475 ; iii, 65, 227 ; iv, 61, 67, 81, 91, 145, 158, 185, 228, 231, 238, 347, 385, 427, 471 n, 516, 567, 583, 597, 632, 645 ; v, 223, 257, 286, 369, 370, 372
Edward VI, ii, 215, 290, 291, 297, 306, 307, 308, 328, 427 ; iii, 8 ; iv, 36, 72, 138, 200, 278, 320, 347, 348, 396, 454, 460, 484, 506, 552, 584, 597, 608, 623, 638, 646 ; v, 88, 257
Edward VII, v, 12, 200, 405, 544, 548, 550
Edward, pr. of Wales, ii, 475, 476
Edward, iv, 449 ; le draper, v, 481 n
Edward Hillcup (Monk Sherborne), iv, 234
Edwards, Arth. H., iv, 655 ; Cath., iv, 358, 359, 476, 480 ; Edw., iv, 595 ; Eliz., iv, 260 ; Fred. C., iv, 358 ; Hen., iv, 473 ; Jas., iv, 358, 473 ; Jas. C., iv, 358 ; Jeffrey, iv, 5 ; John, iv, 358 ; v, 6 n, 29 ; Mary, iv, 260 ; Montague W., iv, 476 ; Reg. H., iv, 476 ; Rich., iv, 78 ; Thos. H., iv, 476 ; fam., iv, 244
Edwin, iv, 94, 153 ; the huntsman, iv, 260 ; the priest, iii, 372
Edwy [Eadwig, Edwi, Edwig], king, iii, 38, 131, 242, 285, 428, 430 ; iv, 213, 240 ; v, 172
Edwy, iii, 355 ; v, 172
Edwyns (Kingsley), ii, 515
Edyndon, Edynton, see Edendon

Edyneton, see Edington, man. (St. Helens)
Effelle, see Heckfield
Efford (Calbourne), v, 218
Efford, man. (Milford), v, 116
Efford, tithing (Milford), iv, 604 ; v, 81, 82
Efford House (Milford), v, 118
Egbert, king, i, 396 ; ii, 4, 414 ; iii, 285, 348 ; iv, 288, 426 ; v, 56, 218, 275
Egbury (St. Mary Bourne), i, 345 ; iv, 295
Egbury, tithing (Hurstbourne Priors), iv, 273 n, 288, 295
Egbury Castle (St. Mary Bourne), iv, 295
Egerton, Will., iv, 213, 528
Egesford, de, Denise, v, 274 ; Will., v, 274
Eggar [Eager, Egger], John, ii, 387, 482, 521 ; iv, 13 ; Rob., iv, 28 ; R. B., iv, 27 ; Sarah, iv, 28 ; Thos., iv, 27
Eggebury, see Egbury
Egger, see Eggar
Egheiete [Eggieath], hund., v, 81
Eglesfield, Rob. de, ii, 203, 205
Eglinton, Ld., v, 571, 572
Egremont, Jas. E., iv, 589 ; John, iv, 589 ; Mrs., iv, 589
Eilling, see Eling
Eir, see Eyre
Eisseburn, see Hurstbourne Priors
Eissele, see Ashley
Ekeresbury, see Exbury
Elains (Stratfieldsaye), iv, 57
Elcho, Ld., ii, 347
Elcock, Alice, v, 192 ; Bridg., v, 192 ; Mary, v, 192
Elded, w. of Oswald, iii, 333
Eldelond, le, (Sherborne St. John), iv, 158
Eldelonde, la, (Shalfleet), v, 275
Eldon, Lower, Nether, man. (King's Somborne), iv, 478
Eldon, Upper, (King's Somborne), ii, 161, 172 ; iv, 438, 439, 470 ; adv., iv, 480 ; ch., iv, 479, 480 ; man., iv, 477 ; pop., v, 445
Eldon, Ld., ii, 383
Eldred [Heldred], iii, 194 ; iv, 438
Eldred, John, ii, 474 ; v, 95 n, 187 n, 213
Eldrethecumb, v, 198 n
Eldridge, Rich., ii, 515 ; iv, 25, 152 ; Rob., iv, 25 ; Thos., iv, 25 ; Will., iv, 17 ; v, 263
Elea, v, 294
Eleanor of Aquitaine, queen, iv, 270
Eleanor of Castile, queen, iii, 506 ; iv, 540, 545, 607, 631 ; v, 162
Eleanor of Provence, queen, ii, 474 ; iii, 106, 506 ; iv, 89, 130, 213, 319, 347, 645
Eledderstoke, see Stoke Charity
Eleybye, —, ii, 385
Elfelm, iv, 171
Elfleda, see Ælflaed
Elford, Jonathan, v, 125
Elfrida, queen, ii, 132 ; iv, 400, 406, 411 n
Elfthryth, ii, 252
Elfward, see Ælfweard
Elgie, Clara O., iii, 443 ; Edith M. C., iii, 443
Elgifu, see Emma, queen
Elias [Eljas, Elyas], iv, 592 ; v, 47, 49 ; abbot of Quarr, ii, 139 ; the engineer, iv, 252
Elias, Pet., iv, 592
Eling, ii, 20, 21 ; iv, 468, 544, 545, 546-58, 560, 635, 658 ; v, 356, 571 ; adv., iv, 558 ; char., iv, 558 ; chs., iv, 556 ; fairs, iv, 546 ;

Eling (cont.)
mans., iv, 547-55 ; mills, iv, 555, 556 ; Nonconf., iv, 558 ; pop., v, 446 ; Rom. rem., i, 345 ; iv, 546 ; sand pits, v, 453 ; schs., ii, 398 ; iv, 546
Eling, North, iv, 558
Eling (de), Edm., iv, 548 ; John, iv, 548, 560 n ; Maud, iv, 548 ; Rich., iv, 548, 560 ; Rog., iv, 548
Elingforde (S. Damerham), iv, 586
Eliot, Edw., iv, 388 n, 389 ; Edw. J., iv, 389 ; see also Elliot
Elizabeth, queen (w. of Edw. IV), iii, 158, 507 ; iv, 67, 91, 449, 516
Elizabeth, queen (w. of Hen. VII), iv, 348, 427
Elizabeth, queen, ii, 85, 202, 303, 307, 314, 315, 375, 427, 428, 460, 516 ; iii, 19, 58, 65, 67, 84, 97, 136, 153, 176, 247, 388 ; iv, 6, 49, 51, 75, 122, 128, 136, 157, 161, 166, 167, 178, 179, 201, 212, 213, 250 n, 253, 285, 317, 318, 327, 347, 350, 396, 397, 412, 420, 427, 470, 471 n, 472, 483, 484, 486, 488, 506, 509, 523, 527, 539, 568, 587, 597, 598, 601 ; v, 213, 226, 232, 234, 236, 240, 241, 254, 257, 262, 266, 267, 277, 278, 285, 286, 332, 372, 375, 376, 377, 378, 429, 435
Eljas, see Elias
Elkington, Edw., iii, 29
Elkins, Edw., iii, 376
Elkstoke, Will., ii, 212
Ellemeade (Weyhill), iv, 395
Ellenestubb (Basing), iv, 115
Ellingham, ii, 97 ; iv, 559, 560, 563-7, 604, 605, 615, 629 ; v, 119 ; adv., iv, 567 ; char., iv, 567 ; ch., iv, 563, 566 ; mans., iv, 563, 630 ; pop., v, 445 ; sch., ii, 398
Ellingham Priory, ii, 41, 106, 229, 230 ; iv, 564, 565
Elliot [Elliott, Elyot], Alice, iv, 59 n ; Bridg. F., iv, 476 ; Sir Chas., iv, 250 ; Dan., iv, 655 ; Edw., iv, 109 ; Frances, iv, 476 ; Jas., iv, 476 ; Jane, iv, 476 ; John, iii, 387, 388 ; v, 96, 457 ; Marg., v, 135 ; Rich., iv, 59 n ; v, 135 ; Sir Thos., v, 135 ; Will., ii, 208 ; see also Eliot
Ellis, iv, 41, 47
Ellis [Ellys], Anne, iv, 552 ; v, 274 ; Humph., ii, 90 ; Thos., iii, 334 ; iv, 472 ; Welbore, iv, 552 ; v, 274
Ellisfield, ii, 166 ; iii, 355, 356, 360-3 ; iv, 142, 170, 202 ; adv., iii, 363 ; char., iii, 363 ; ch., iii, 363 ; man., iii, 360 ; pop., v, 439
Ellisfield, Thos., iii, 363
Ellson, Anne, iii, 99 ; Will. iii, 99
Ellyett, Rich. D., iii, 432
Ellys, see Ellis
Elmar, see Athelmar
Elmere [Elmore], John, ii, 124, 150, 157, 198, 213
Elmesore (Calbourne), v, 218
Elmestubb, man. (Wilts.), ii, 114
Elm Farm (Pamber), iv, 433
Elm Grove (Kingsclere), iv, 249, 267
Elmham, Stigand, bp. of ; see Canterbury, archbps. of
Elmore, see Elmere
Elphege, archbp. of Canterbury, see Alphege
Elphinston, Adm., v, 393
Elpolesbrygg (Calbourne), v, 218
Elrington, Edw., iii, 90 ; iv, 423
Elsefeld, Elsefeud, see Ellisfield
Elsi, see Alsi
Elson (Alverstoke), iii, 202

Elstead (Surr.), iv, 29
Eltham, John B., iii, 200, 201
Elton, Joanna, iv, 371 ; Pet., ii, 167
Elvetham, ii, 150 ; iv, 2, 66, 67, 74-6, 80, 109, 110 ; adv., iv, 76 ; char., iv, 76 ; ch., iv, 76 ; man., iv, 74 ; pk., iv, 74, 75 ; pop., v, 444 ; sch., ii, 398
Elvetham Bernard (Elvetham), iv, 76
Elvetham House (Elvetham), iv, 74
Elveva, iv, 270
Elvydon (Wilts.), ii, 122
Elwes, Hen. J., iii, 449 ; John M., iv, 491, 492 ; fam., arms, iii, 449
Elwina, abbess of Romsey, ii, 126, 132
Ely (Cambs.), monastery, ii, 108
Ely, bps. of, v, 308, 309 ; John Kirby, iv, 431 ; Will. Longchamp, v, 307 ; John Morton, see Canterbury, archbps. of ; Fran. Turner, ii, 330, 339
Ely, Nich. of, ii, 19 ; iv, 211, 576, 607 ; v, 56, 217, 479
Elyas, see Elias
Elye, Thos., iv, 215, 527
Elyngham, see Rockford
Elyot, see Elliot
Embley, man. (E. Wellow), ii, 421 ; iv, 537
Embley, tithing (E. Wellow), iv, 489
Embley House (E. Wellow), iv, 535
Emborne [Enborne], riv., i, 392, 394 ; iv, 249, 250, 252, 261, 292 ; v, 409
Embris, Hen., iii, 528
Emele, Emelei, see Embley
Emclesworth, Emeleworth, see Emsworth
Emery [Emmery, Emmory], Anne, v, 251 ; Hen., v, 251 ; John, iii, 425 ; v, 456 ; Rob., v, 482
Emery Down (Lyndhurst), iv, 631, 633
Emma [Ælfgyfu, Elgifu], queen, ii, 8, 9, 117, 216 ; iii, 130, 424 ; v, 34 n, 55, 56, 297, 298
Emma, abbess of Godstow, iv, 256, 427 ; the ale-wife, v, 472 ; prioress of Wintney, ii, 149
Emmae Domus (Winchester), v, 302
Emmanuel College (Cambs.), iii, 341
Emmery, see Emery
Emmesworth, see Emsworth
Emmet Hill Cottages (Kingston), v, 249, 279
Emmory, see Emery
Empnesworth, see Emsworth
Empshott, ii, 471 ; iii, 3, 17-19, 26 ; adv., iii, 19 ; ch., iii, 18 ; man., iii, 17 ; pop., v, 438 ; sch., ii, 398
Empson, (Sir) Rich., iii, 436 ; iv, 363
Ems, riv., i, 375, 376, 382
Emsworth, iii, 134 ; 136-7 ; v, 328 n, 409, 431 ; fairs, iii, 136 ; v, 417 ; fisheries, iii, 136 ; v, 468, 469 ; man., iii, 137, 195
Enborne, riv., see Emborne
Endewelle, see Andwell
Endford, man. (Wilts.), ii, 291
Eneford, Rich. de, ii, 110, 111, 115
Englefield, Sir Hen., v, 220 n ; Ismania, ii, 506 ; (Sir) John, ii, 506 ; iii, 69, 456 ; Nichole, ii, 506 ; Phil., ii, 506 ; Rob., ii, 506 ; Rog. de, iii, 260 ; Sir Thos., iv, 608 ; Will., iii, 97
English [Engleys], (l', la), Alice, iv, 510 ; Aline, iv, 510 ; Eliz., iv, 325 ; Gilb., iv, 510 ; Joan, iv, 510 ; John, iv, 325, 510 ; v, 200, 201 n ; Marg., iv, 510 ; Rich., iv, 510 ; fam., iv, 502

Enham, *see* King's Enham and Knight's Enham
Enham Place (Knight's Enham), iv, 377
Enham Raggs (Andover), **iv**, 320
Ennam Militis, *see* Knight's Enham
Enniskillen, John Willoughby, earl of, iv, 522
Entingham, Rog. de, ii, 110
Epillos, i, 263; v, 293
Eppelton, *see* Appleton
Erard, Will., iv, 380
Erchebaud, Walt., iv, 407 *n*
Erchelreston (Burghclere), iv, 277
Erdesope, John de, ii, 222
Ereborrough (Niton), v, 187
Eremuham, Eremuthe, *see* Yarmouth
Erle, John, iii, 168; Maud, iii, 168; T. W., ii, 491; (Sir) Will., ii, 491, 496; iii, 168; fam., arms, ii, 491; *see also* Earle
Erles Milchet, *see* Melchet Park
Erlestona, *see* Earlstone
Erlisford (S. Damerham), iv, 587 *n*
Erlisman, Joan, v, 220; John, v, 219, 220; Rich., v, 219; Thos., ii, 295, 302, 366
Ermud, Ermue, *see* Yarmouth
Erneburga, v, 46
Ernemue, *see* Yarmouth
Ernley [Erneley, Ernlay], Barbara, v, 219; Edm., iv, 507, 555; Fran., iii, 169; (Sir) John, iii, 324; iv, 555; v, 247; Marg., iv, 555; Rich., iii, 169; v, 202, 219, 247; Will., iii, 169; v, 247
Ernys, fam., *see* Arney
Ernys Court, *see* Arneys
Errington, Hen., iv, 335, 361; Mary, iv, 335
Erroll, earl of, v, 569
Erskine, Thos., iii, 178; iv, 33; v, 134
Erthe Pitts (Milton), v, 124
Ervill's Exton, man. (Hambledon), iii, 237, 238, 241
Escheker, Alice del, iv, 561
Eschetune, man., iv, 457 *n*, 561 *n*
Eschotland, *see* Scotland
Escote (de), Edw., iv, 342; Eliz., iv, 520; Giles, iv, 610; Hugh, iv, 519, 520, 524, 610; Joan, iv, 524, 610; Kath., iv, 520, 610; Marg., iv, 520; Walt., iv, 519, 520, 524, 610; Will., iv, 520; *see also* Scot and Scott
Escoutard, Geoff., v, 164
Escudemore, *see* Skidmore
Escures, *see* Scures
Esdaile, Will., iv, 611, 613; Col., iv, 611
Eseldecombe, *see* Shalcombe
Esewelle, *see* Ellisfield
Esher (Surr.), ii, 23, 146
Eskaudfflete, *see* Shalfleet
Esmeresworda, *see* Ashmansworth
Esprai, *see* Sprai
Esse, *see* Ashe
Esseborne, *see* Pastrow
Esseburna Regis, *see* Hurstbourne Tarrant
Essefeld, *see* Ellisfield
Esseham, *see* Lasham
Essele, *see* Ashley
Esselei, hund., *see* Bishop's Sutton
Essentun, Essentune, *see* Exton
Essex, v, 377
Essex, Frances Devereux, ctss. of, v, 229; earls of, ii, 273; iv, 148, 161, 350, 651; v, 79, 229, 344
Essex, Eliz., iv, 35, 64; Thos., iv, 522; (Sir) Will., iv, 35, 64, 522
Esshemaners, *see* Ashe

Esshermeresworth, *see* Ashmansworth
Est Acle (Wootton St. Laurence), iv, 239
Estadderley, *see* Tytherley, East
Estane, iv, 258; v, 155
Estaston, man. (Middleton), ii, 137
Estcourt, Mrs., v, 147
Estden (Bentley), iv, 27
Estdena, *see* Dean, East
Estderlegh, *see* Tytherley, East
Esteney [Estney], John, ii, 486; iii, 445; Julia, iii, 445; Rich., ii, 479
Esteston, *see* Aston
Estfield (Highclere), iv, 285
Estfield, Will., v, 459
Esthamlode (I. of W.), ii, 145
Esthorp, *see* Eastrop
Estistede, *see* Tisted, East
Estlogelonde (Ewhurst), iv, 247, 248
Estmede (Andover), iv, 346
Estmed le Hate, v, 138
Estmene, Estmeone, Estmune, *see* Meon, East
Estney, *see* Esteney
Estok, *see* Stokes
Eston, *see* Aston
Estre, *see* Estur
Estrées, Jean d', v, 385
Estrepaniacho, John de, ii, 223
Estrip, Estrop, *see* Eastrop
Esttystede, *see* Tisted, East
Estur [Estre, Esturs] (de, del), Agnes, v, 202, 219 *n*, 246 *n*; Bald., v, 246; John, v, 145; Maud [Matilda], v, 142, 191, 192, 202, 237, 246; Rog., ii, 152; v, 180; Walt., v, 192; (Sir) Will., iii, 169; v, 181, 191, 192, 202, 219 *n*, 246; fam., v, 194, 248, 281; *see also* Lisle
Esturmy, *see* Sturmy
Estuy, John, iii, 225
Estwatermede (Timsbury), iv, 486
Estwelewe, *see* Wellow, East
Estwod, *see* Eastwood
Etham, *see* Knight's Enham
Ethelard, v, 198
Ethelbald, king, ii, 5; iv, 27
Ethelbert, king, ii, 5; iv, 6
Ethelbriht, iv, 18
Ethelfled, *see* Ælflaed
Ethelgar, abbot of Newminster, ii, 116, 121
Ethelgeard, iii, 59, 242, 320; v, 172
Ethelgiva, abbess of Shaftesbury, iv, 183 *n*, 251
Ethelm, iv, 6
Ethelnod, *see* Æthelnod
Ethelred I, ii, 5; v, 295
Ethelred II, ii, 7, 8, 132; iii, 249, 312, 390, 424; iv, 18, 288, 346, 402, 411; v, 222, 297, 366
Ethelreda, abbess of Nunnaminster, ii, 126
Ethelsig, iii, 131
Ethelwald, king of Sussex, ii, 3
Ethelward [Ethelweard], ii, 116, 252; v, 296
Ethelwold [Athelwold, Æthelwold], bp. of Winchester, ii, 6, 7, 51, 108, 114, 116, 122, 126; iv, 18, 240, 460; v, 6; earl, ii, 132; iv, 406; son of Ethelred I, v, 85
Ethelwulf, king, ii, 4, 252; iv, 278, 288; v, 56
Ethelwulf, earl, *see* Ethelwold
Etheridge, Flower, iv, 614; Jas., iv, 614
Eton, fam., *see* Eaton
Eton College (Bucks.), ii, 216, 230, 265, 285, 306, 307, 361; iv, 61, 90, 231, 386, 419, 567

Etwall, Eliz., iv, 450, 513; Eliz. C., iv, 357; Ralph, iv, 450; Will., iv, 450, 513
Euershott, *see* Ewshott
Eugénie, empress, iv, 15; v, 179
Eugenius III, pope, ii, 219, 221, 224, 225; iv, 103, 198 *n*, 200, 215, 356 *n*
Eukeresbury, *see* Exbury
Euphemia, abbess, ii, 126, 132-3, 137; iv, 402, 412
Eustace, prior of St. Swithuns, ii, 115
Euston, Geo. H., earl of, iii, 242
Evance, Dan., v, 221
Evans, Carbery, iv, 530; Chas., iv, 60; Dorothy, iii, 124; G. P. E., v, 519; Susan, iv, 60; Will., iv, 361; W. H. B., v, 576; Capt., v, 540
Eve, Rich., iv, 5, 16
Evelegh [Eveleigh, Everleigh] (de), Anne, v, 280; John, iv, 93; Will., v, 280; Col., v, 200
Evelyn [Everlyn], Anne, iv, 172; Arth., iv, 374; Eliz., iv, 172, 494, 522; Geo., iii, 98; iv, 172 *n*, 522; (Sir) John, iii, 42, 43; iv, 172, 494, 497, 522; Mynn, iv, 172 *n*; Rich., iv, 172; —, v, 513
Ever, *see* Iford
Everard, Alice, iii, 448; Eliz., ii, 156; iv, 167; John, iii, 448; iv, 520; Lucy, abbess of Romsey, ii, 129, 132; Marg., iv, 167, 520; Sim., v, 172; Will., ii, 156, 308, 309, 366
Evercy, *see* Devercy
Everelant, *see* Yaverland
Everett, Jos., iv, 316; Col., v, 356; fam., iv, 318
Everhanger (Abbotts Ann), iv, 335
Evering, Will., iv, 9
Everingham, Alice de, iii, 255
Everleigh, fam., *see* Evelegh
Everley (Wilts.), ii, 137
Everlond, par., *see* Yaverland
Everlond (Gatcombe), v, 246
Everlyn, *see* Evelyn
Eversley, iv, 31, 32-41, 47; adv., iv, 34, 41; char., iv, 41; ch., iv, 35, 40; fishery, iv, 34; mans., ii, 114; iv, 33-6, 39, 40, 179; mkt. and fairs, iv, 34; mills, iv, 34; Nonconf., iv, 41; pop., v, 443, 444; sch., ii, 398
Eversley, Chas. Shaw-Lefevre, vsct., iv, 46, 47, 430, 611; v, 5, 224
Eversley, de, Gilb., iv, 33, 34, 35; Philippa, iv, 255, 269; Walt., iv, 35, 255, 269
Eversley Cross (Eversley), iv, 32, 33, 41
Eversley Forest, bailiwick of, iv, 34, 35, 122
Everton (Milford), v, 113, 116, 123, 126
Evertsen, Jan, v, 382
Every, Anne, v, 283
Evesham, John de, iii, 95; iv, 317 *n*
Evinely, John de, iv, 333
Evingar, hund., iv, 273; v, 324, 331
Evingdale (Whitchurch), iv, 300
Evreland, *see* Yaverland
Evreslei, *see* Eversley
Evreux, Aumary, count of, iii, 86
Ewart, Alex., v, 65
Ewcline Coleford (Bentley), iv, 27
Ewelme Hospital (Oxon), iv, 395, 396, 399
Ewen, Jane, iii, 347
Ewer (de, le), Philemon, iii, 283, 284; v, 391; Rich., iv, 135; Rob., iii, 68, 135, 137, 148; iv, 7, 89; R., v, 391; Col., v, 350

Ewerelande, Ewerlaund, see Yaverland

Ewhurst, ii, 73 ; iv, 245, 246, 247-9, 257, 258, 272 ; adv., iv, 249 ; chap., iv, 249 ; ch., iv, 248 ; mans., iv, 247 ; pop., v, 442

Ewhurst Farm (Ewhurst), iv, 247

Ewhurst House (Ewhurst), iv, 247

Ewshott (Crondall), iv, 2, 5, 6, 9, 13, 14

Ewyas, de, Rob., iv, 512 ; Sibyl, iv, 512

Exall, Jane, ii, 482

Exbury, i, 260, 325, 345 ; ii, 205 ; iii, 274, 275, 290-1 ; iv, 655 ; adv., iii, 291 ; brick making, v, 466 ; ch., iii, 291 ; man., iii, 290 ; pop., v, 446 ; sch., ii, 398

Excestre, Nich. de, v, 494

Exe, riv., see Beaulieu

Exeter, bps. of, ii, 31 ; iii, 20, 22 ; Nich. Claggett, iv, 218 ; John Grandisson, ii, 268 ; Hugh Oldham, iv, 218, 428 ; Osbern, iii, 20 ; Walt. de Stapleton, ii, 31 ; iii, 22, 415 ; Jas. Turbervil, ii, 309 ; Will. Warelwast, iii, 20

Exeter, earls of, iv, 334, 409 ; Bald., v, 234 ; Gertrude, mchnss. of, ii, 172 ; iv, 584, 598, 618* ; v, 112 ; mqsses. of :—Edw., iv, 644 ; Hen., ii, 151, 172 ; iv, 427, 553, 584, 597, 598, 601, 618,* 646 ; v, 112, 169

Exeter College (Oxf.), v, 208

Exfould (Basing), iv, 115

Exmansford, see Ixnesford

Exmead, iv, 542

Exmouth, Ld., v, 401

Exton, i, 391 ; ii, 68, 108 ; iii, 245, 302, 303, 319-21 ; adv., iii, 321 ; char., iii, 321 ; ch., iii, 321 ; man., ii, 114 ; iii, 320 ; pop., v, 440 ; Rom. rem., i, 345 ; sch., ii, 398

Eyer, see Eyre

Eyeworth (Fordingbridge), i, 326 ; iv, 559, 573

Eyeworth Lodge (Fordingbridge), iv, 568

Eyles, Florentine, ii, 385 ; Jas., iv, 299 ; Jos., v, 523

Eynesham, John, abbot, ii, 119, 122

Eyre [Eir, Eyer, Eyr] (le), Ann, iv, 281 ; Chris., ii, 345, 346, 347 ; iii, 39 ; Dorothy, Lady, iii, 385 ; Eliz., v, 80 ; Geo., iv, 625, 626 ; Geo. E. B., iv, 624, 625, 626 ; Giles, iii, 39 ; Hen., ii, 156, 157, 160 ; iii, 313 ; Jane, v, 183 ; John, iii, 39 ; iv, 29, 107, 414 ; v, 183 ; Jos., iii, 39 ; Phil., iii, 39 ; (Rev.) Rich., iii, 313, 466 ; Rob., iii, 39 ; Thos., ii, 478 ; iv, 614 ; v, 111 ; Walt., v, 29 ; (Rev.) Will., ii, 172, 158, 160 ; iii, 39 ; iv, 107 ; v, 101, 102, 107 ; Rev. W. L. W., iv, 183 n, 195 n

Eyresmede (S. Damerham), iv, 586

Ezi, iv, 550

Faber, Dav., iv, 444 ; Capt. W. V., v, 532

Fabian [Fabyan], Gilb., iv, 435 n ; Isabel, iv, 240 ; John, iv, 240, 435

Fabians, see Tangier Park

Fabyan, see Fabian

Faccombe, iii, 217 ; iv, 308, 314-18 ; v, 305 ; adv., iv, 318 ; ch., iv, 317 ; mans., iv, 314, 326 ; man.

Faccombe (cont.)
house, iv, 314 ; mills, iv, 317 ; pop., v, 442 ; sch., ii, 398 ; iv, 314

Faccombe Court (Faccombe), iv, 314

Faccombe Fifhyde, man., see Faccombe Upstreet

Faccombe Knights, man. (Faccombe), iv, 315, 316

Faccombe Punchardon, man. (Faccombe), iv, 315, 563

Faccombe Sandys, man., see Faccombe Upstreet

Faccombe Sendy, man. (Faccombe), iv, 315, 316

Faccombe Upstreet, man. (Faccombe), iv, 314, 316

Faccombe Wood (Faccombe), iv, 314

Facy [Farsy], Will., v, 142 n, 143, 146

Faderlin, iv, 255, 256, 257, 267, 268, 331, 332

Faire, fam., see Fayre

Faire Crosse House (Stratfieldsaye), iv, 57

Fairele, see Fairlee

Fairelynch Copyce (Hurstbourne Tarrant), iv, 319, 320

Fairfax, Kath. Lady, v, 261 ; Thos., Ld., v, 261

Fairfax, Frances, v, 261 ; Rob., v, 261 ; Thos., v, 261

Fairgrove (Bramshott), ii, 496

Fairlee, man. (Whippingham), v, 199, 263

Fairlee, tithing, v, 138

Fairmeadow (Peniston), ii, 516

Fair Oak Green (Stratfieldsaye), iv, 57 ; sch., ii, 398

Fairs, see Markets and fairs

Fairthorne, man. (Bishop's Waltham), iii, 277, 279 ; Rom. rem., i, 310 ; iii, 277 ; v, 465 n

Fairwise, see Farwill

Fairy Hill (St. Helens), v, 190

Faith, Capt. Thos., iv, 394

Fakcumbe, see Faccombe

Falaise [Faleyse] (de, de la), Alice, iii, 88 ; iv, 568 ; Christine, iv, 572 ; Elias [Ellis], iii, 218 ; iv, 82, 568 n, 572, 576 ; v, 161, 305 ; Pet., iii, 88 ; Ralph, iii, 88 ; iv, 572 ; Will., iii, 218 ; iv, 568, 572, 584 ; v, 100, 305

Falconer [Fauconer, Faukener, Faukoner, Faulkener, Faulknor, Fawconer, Fawkener, Fawkenor, Fawkner] (le, the), Adeline, v, 101 ; Agnes, iii, 124 ; v, 101 ; Alice, iv, 286, 290, 294, 327 ; Dorothy, iv, 261 ; Edw., iv, 261 ; Eleanor, iv, 261, 327 ; Eliz., iv, 290 ; Emma, iii, 195 ; iv, 278, 290 ; Frances, iv, 290 ; Godwine, iv, 171 ; Joan, iii, 392 ; John, iii, 124, 131, 195 ; iv, 261, 264, 267, 279, 290 ; John A. K., iv, 18, 19 ; Kath., ii, 135 ; Margery, iv, 260 ; Nich., iv, 290 ; Pet., iv, 261 ; Ralph, iv, 289, 290 ; (Sir) Rich., ii, 91 ; iii, 124 ; iv, 261, 290, 296, 327 ; Rob., iii, 292 ; iv, 407 ; v, 399 ; Thos., iv, 151, 261 ; Will., ii, 506, 507 ; iii, 124, 131, 136, 137, 195, 371 ; iv, 251, 260, 261, 278, 290, 327, 609 ; v, 273 ; Mrs., iv, 18 ; —, iii, 385 ; fam., iii, 286 ; arms, iii, 69

Falcon Inn (Kingsclere), iv, 249

Falegia, see Fawley

Faleyse, see Falaise

Falkland, Lucius, vsct., v, 256

Falle, Fallele, see Fawley

Fallick, —, v, 177

Falmouth, vsct., v, 553

Familists [Family of Love], ii, 79

Famyell, Rich., v, 485 n

Fane, Anne, v, 130 ; Rev. Edw., v, 130 ; Fred., iv, 563 ; Hen., v, 130

Fanshawe, Sir Hen., iv, 514 n ; John, iv, 258 ; Penelope, iv, 258

Fantosme, Jordan, ii, 253, 254, 255

Faredone, see Faringdon

Fareford, man. (Lincs.), ii, 376

Fareham, i, 321 ; ii, 21, 99, 473 ; iii, 209, 210-16 ; v, 311, 324, 328 n, 331, 409, 423, 433, 434, 450 ; adv., iii, 215 ; char., iii, 215 ; ch., iii, 215 ; ind., v, 465, 482, 488 ; man., iii, 211 ; v, 418, 419, 420, 421 ; pk., iii, 212 ; pop., v, 441 ; schs., ii, 387, 398

Fareham, hund., iii, 209 ; v, 423

Fareham, Sim. de, ii, 213 ; iii, 324, 466

Farenberg, see Farnborough

Farenham, see Vernhams Dean

Faring, Geoff. de, iii, 267

Faringdon, ii, 471, 496 ; iii, 3, 20-22 ; v, 308, 425 ; adv., iii, 22 ; char., iii, 22 ; ch., iii, 21 ; man., iii, 20 ; pop., v, 438 ; sch., ii, 399

Faringdon (Berks.), ii, 140, 143, 145

Faringdon Popham, man. (Faringdon), iii, 21

Farlee, fam , see Farley

Farlega, Farlegh, Farlegh Mortymer, Farle Mortymere, see Farleigh Wallop

Farleigh, man (Whippingham), see Fairlee

Farleigh House (Farleigh Wallop), iii, 364, 365

Farleigh Wallop, ii, 25, 73 ; iii, 355, 356, 364-6 ; iv, 145, 147, 532 ; adv., iii, 365 ; char., iii, 366 ; ch., iii, 365 ; man., iii, 364 ; pop., v, 440

Farley, par., see Farleigh Wallop and Farley Chamberlayne

Farley [Farlee] (de), Hen., iii, 364, 365 ; Will., ii, 195

Farley Chamberlayne, iv, 438, 443-5 ; adv., iv, 445 ; char., iv, 445 ; ch., iv, 445 ; man., iv, 443 ; pop., v, 448

Farley Wallop, see Farleigh Wallop

Farlington, iii, 140, 141, 148-51 ; adv., iii, 151 ; ch., iii, 150 ; man., ii, 168 ; iii, 148 ; pop., v, 441 ; sch., ii, 399

Farlington, Giles, iv, 440 ; Joan, iv, 440, 481 ; John (de), ii, 290, 295, 366 ; iv, 440, 481, 495, 533

Farmer, Chas., iv, 219 ; Thos., iii, 167

Farnall, Marianne F., v, 278

Farnborough, iv, 1, 15-18 ; v, 450 ; adv., iv, 17 ; char., iv, 18 ; Children's Home, iv, 18 ; ch., iv, 15, 16 ; fishing, v, 467 n ; man., iv, 15 ; mills, iv, 16 ; peat, v, 454 ; pop., v, 443 ; Rom. Cath., iv, 15, 18 ; sch., ii, 399 ; iv, 15

Farnborough, de, Amice, iv, 16 ; Hen., iv, 15 ; John, iv, 15, 16 ; Steph., iv, 15, 17

Farnborough harriers, v, 540

Farnborough Hill (Farnborough), iv, 15

Farnborough Park (Farnborough), iv, 15

Farnborough Place (Farnborough), iv, 16

Farndon, see Faringdon

Farnefold, Rob. de, v, 4
Farnelles, see Fernhills Court
Farnham (Surr.), ii, 12, 102 ; iv, 29 ; v, 265
Farnham, Ad., de, prior, ii, 115
Farnhull, fam., see Fernhill
Farquharson, Jas., v, 79
Farr, Anne, iv, 210 ; Will., iv, 210 ; v, 125, 172 ; Will. D., v, 144 n, 173
Farrall's Downe (Upper Clatford), iv, 360
Farrer, Jas., iv, 22 ; Oliver, iv, 22
Farringdon, see Faringdon
Farringford (Freshwater), i, 348 ; v, 241
Farringford, Walt. de, v, 242
Farsy, see Facy
Farthingland (Farnborough), iv, 15
Farwill [Fairwise], Thos., prior, ii, 179, 180
Farylane (Bramley), iv, 141
Fashion, Geo., iv, 548 ; Thos., iii, 295 ; iv, 548 ; West, iii, 295 ; iv, 548
Fashye, Joan, v, 228
Fauconer, see Falconer
Faucumb, see Faccombe
Faukenberge, Walt. de, iv, 75, 84
Faukener, Faukoner, Faulkener, Faulknor, see Falconer
Faulkner's Down Farm (Hurstbourne Priors), iv, 288
Fauntleroy, Brian, iv, 513 ; Hen., iv, 513 ; Isabel, v, 119 ; Tristram, iv, 513 ; v, 119
Faver, see Lefevre
Fawcett, —, ii, 457 ; iv, 519
Fawcon, Marg., ii, 124
Fawconer, Fawkener, Fawkenor, Fawkner, see Falconer
Fawley, ii, 101, 108 ; iii, 274, 275, 292-6 ; iv, 416, 544, 615, 655 ; v, 324, 331, 356 ; adv., iii, 296 ; char., iii, 296 ; ch., iii, 295 ; man., iii, 292 ; pop., v, 446 ; sch., ii, 399
Fawley, hund., iii, 302
Fay, de, Beatrice, iv, 254 ; Philippa, iv, 254 ; Ralph, iv, 254 ; Will., iv, 213
Fay, J. G., & Co., v, 458
Fayre [Faire] Mark le, ii, 201 ; iv, 282 ; v, 482
Fayrebrace [Ferebraz], Edw., v, 149 ; Rich., iii, 441
Fayrle, see Fairlee
Fearon [Feron], Rich., v, 86 ; Will. A., ii, 364, 365, 366 ; v, 17
Fécamp (de), Hugh, iv, 301 ; Rich., iv, 301 ; Will., iv, 301
Fechenham, John, iv, 564 n
Feld, Felda, Felde, fam., see Field
Felde (Fawley), ii, 181
Feldelond, la, (Stratfield Turgis), iv, 64
Feldershey, ii, 207
Fellowes, Edw., iv, 434 ; Hen., v, 521 ; Jas. H., iv, 434 ; Newton, iv, 289 ; v, 521 ; Rich., iv, 434 ; Thos., iii, 366 ; iv, 147 ; Maj., v, 575
Felpottes (W. Wellow), iv, 535
Felton, de, John, iii, 68 ; Rob., iv, 206
Fenn [Fenne], Ad. de la, iv, 255 ; Frances, v, 94 ; Jas., v, 94 ; P., v, 391 ; Rich., v, 94, 95 ; Rob., v, 94
Fenton, Lavinia, iv, 192
Fenwick, Rev. Jas. B., iv, 336 ; John, iii, 136 ; Will., iv, 523 ; —, iii, 136
Ferebraz, see Fayrebrace
Ferendon, see Faringdon

Ferham, see Fareham and Vernhams Dean
Ferlega Camerarii, see Farley Chamberlayne
Ferlei, see Quarley
Ferleye, see Farleigh Wallop
Ferlington, see Farlington
Fermcroft, la, (Beaulieu), iv, 650, 651
Fermor, Arabella, iii, 375 n
Ferneberga, see Farnborough
Ferneham, see Fareham
Ferneley, Edw., iv, 442 n
Fernfurlonge (Kimpton), iv, 372
Fernhill (Arreton), v, 140, 204
Fern Hill (Hawley), iv, 21
Fernhill, man. (Milton), v, 81, 89 n, 125 ; man.-house, v, 124 ; mill, v, 126
Fernhill [Farnhull] (de, of), Joan, v, 99 n ; John, v, 114, 125 ; Rich., v, 89 n, 99, 114, 125 ; Walt., v, 117 n ; Will., v, 114, 117
Fernhill Common (Milton), v, 124
Fernhills Court, man. (Christchurch), v, 100
Fernhurst (Suss.), ironworks, v, 464
Fernyng, Geoff. de, ii, 197
Feron, see Fearon
Ferrand, Sir Pet., iii, 255
Ferrers [Ferrars] (de), Edw., v, 141 n ; Isabel, iv, 77 ; John, v, 117 n ; Maud, iv, 475 ; Rob., iv, 206 ; Thos., v, 313 ; Will., iii, 106 ; iv, 77, 206
Ferrey, Benj., v, 85, 101
Ferringes, Geoff. of, abbot, ii, 121
Ferrour, Rog., iv, 409
Ferryngtes, Pet., iv, 499 ; Thomasine, iv, 499
Ferté, de la, Agnes, iv, 471 ; Gundred, iv, 471 ; Marg., iii, 424 ; Margery, iv, 172 ; iv, 449, 451, 471, 473 n ; Will., iv, 471
Feryngford, Walt. de, iv, 610
Fessant, Hen., iv, 204
Festham [Fescam], Rich., ii, 293, 366
Festing, Rev. G. A., iv, 325 ; Marian L., iv, 325
Fetiplace, Chris., iv, 571 ; Joan, iv, 571
Feversham, Lewis, earl of, iv, 565
Fewings, Jas., ii, 390
Fichet, see Fitchett
Field [Feld, Felda, Felde] (atte, de), Basil, v, 562 ; Constance, iv, 93 n ; Jas., ii, 478 ; John, iv, 93 n, 157, 373 ; Rich., iv, 613 ; v, 177 ; Thos., v, 483
Fielden, Col., v, 453
Fielder [Fylder], Alice, ii, 22, 490 ; Jane, iii, 68 ; John, ii, 125 ; iv, 93 ; Margery, ii, 482 ; Rich., ii, 482 ; Thos., iii, 22
Fielding, John, iv, 169, 354
Fiennes [Fines, Fynes] (de), Anne, iv, 199 ; Constance, iv, 215 ; Edw., iv, 206, 279 ; Eliz., iv, 199, 279 ; Greg., iv, 475 ; Hen., iv, 199, 206 ; Jas., iv, 199 ; Joan, iv, 475 ; (Sir) John, ii, 502 ; iv, 475 ; Marg., iv, 199 ; Maud, Lady, iv, 475 ; Nath., ii, 327 ; (Sir) Rich., ii, 317, 318, 320 ; iv, 199, 200, 206, 207, 212, 215, 225, 226, 227, 279, 475 ; Rob., ii, 502 ; Sir Rog., iv, 475 ; Thos., iv, 475; (Sir) Will., iii, 442 ; iv, 199, 206, 279, 475, 507, 545, 632 ; fam., ii, 262, 317 ; arms, ii, 502
Fiernham, see Vernhams Dean

Fifehead Manor House (Middle Wallop), iv, 525
Fiffyde, par., see Fyfield
Fifhide [Fifhyde, Fyfehide, Fyfhide] (de), Alice, ii, 478 ; Edith, iv, 232 ; Joan, ii, 478 ; Rog., iii, 361, 363 ; iv, 232, 317 ; Will., ii, 478 ; iii, 95, 361, 363 ; iv, 63, 64, 160, 317, 318, 450
Fifhidon, see Fyfield
Fifhydes, man., see Faccombe Upstreet
Fifield, Benj., iv, 458 ; John, iv, 458 ; Kath., iv, 458 ; Silena, iii, 536 ; Walt. de, abbot of Hyde, ii, 118, 121
Figgess, Edgar, iv, 5
Filcis Will (Romsey), iv, 452
Filer, Martin, v, 79
Filey, Joan, iv, 618 ; John, iv, 618 ; Rog., iv, 618 ; fam., iv, 621
Filliol [Filiol, Fillol, Fyloll], Alice, iv, 459, 583 n, 588 ; John, iv, 495 ; Mary, iv, 82 ; Reg., v, 135 ; (Sir) Will., iv, 82, 141 n, 583 n
Finamur, de, Joan, iii, 91 ; Will., iii, 91
Finch [Finche], Ant., iv, 9 ; Rev. Arth. T., iv, 267 ; Miles, v, 97 ; Rev. Rob., iv, 345 ; Will., prior of Breamore, ii, 171, 172
Finchdean (Chalton), iii, 103
Finchdean, hund., iii, 82 ; v, 324, 328 n, 331
Finche, see Finch
Fincton, see Funckton
Fines, see Fiennes
Finian, John, iv, 133
Finkley (Andover), i, 303, 321, 345
Finkley House (Andover), iv, 345
Finkley Park (Andover), iv, 319, 320, 345, 346, 353
Finley (Ewhurst), iv, 248
Finley, de, Godf., iv, 248 ; Maud, iv, 248 ; Rob., iv, 248
Finley's Row (Ewhurst), iv, 248
Fir Croft (Fleet), iv, 5
Fir Grove (Bramshott), ii, 493
Firsteburyesland (Chirk), ii, 182
Firugeden, la, (Monk Sherborne), iv, 231
Fisacres, la, (Gatcombe), v, 246
Fisflete (Timsbury), iv, 486, 487
Fish, John, iv, 508 ; Rose, iv, 508 ; Thos., iv, 353
Fishbourn (Binstead), v, 151
Fishbourne, Nich., iv, 356
Fishbourne Creek, iv, 204
Fisher [Fysher, Fyssher], Augustin, iii, 251 ; Clarice, iii, 71 ; Rev. C. T., v, 290 ; Edw., ii, 482, 483 ; Edwin, ii, 478 ; Eliz., iv, 134 ; Hen., iii, 251 ; John, ii, 53, 483 ; iii, 251, 456 ; iv, 134, 185, 212, 225, 259, 327 ; v, 218, 484, 485 n ; Rev. J. R., iv, 267 ; Margery, iv, 259 ; Payne, iii, 458 ; Rich., iv, 212, 259 ; Rog. S. N., iv, 70 ; Sam., v, 290 ; Will., ii, 483 ; iii, 97, 248, 249, 251, 438, 458 ; iv, 134, 185, 259 ; v, 518, 527, 529 ; —, iv, 70, 183
Fisheries, v, 466-9
Fisherton (Wilts.), i, 254
Fishes, i, 197
Fishhouse (Binstead), v, 151
Fishwicke, Mary, iv, 430 ; Rev. Rob., iv, 430
Fitch, Hen., iv, 253 ; v, 95 n ; Tristram, v, 96
Fitchett [Fichet, Fychet], Eliz., v, 163, 163 n ; Hugh, v, 163 n ; John, v, 163, 163 n, 172 ; Rob., v, 163 n ; Thos., v, 160, 163 ; fam., v, 168, 192

Fitz Adam, Rog., iv, 39, 129 ; Will., iv, 160, 170
Fitz Alan, Alice, ii, 475 ; Hen., *see* Arundel, earl of ; John, iii, 145 ; Rich., *see* Arundel, earl of ; Thos. iv, 632 ; Will., *see* Arundel, earl of ; *see also* Son of Alan
Fitz Aldelin [Fitz Audelin], Juliane, iv, 104, 475 ; Will., iv, 104, 150, 475 ; *see also* Son of Aldelin
Fitz Andrew, Will., iv, 39
Fitz Arard, Steph., iv, 555
Fitz Aucher, Aucher, iv, 568 ; Christine, iv, 568 ; Eliz., iv, 568 ; Hen., iv, 568 ; John, iv, 568 ; Margery, iv, 568 ; Rich., iv, 568
Fitz Audelin, *see* Fitz Aldelin
Fitz Bernard, Eleanor, iv, 254 ; Ralph, iv, 254
Fitz Ellis [Fitz Elys], Christina, v. 130 *n* ; Geoff., iv, 590 ; John, v, 130 *n* ; *see also* Son of Elias
Fitzgarret [Fitzgarrett], Agnes, ii, 503 ; iii, 43 ; Edw., ii, 503 ; iii, 43
Fitz Geoffrey, Warin, iii, 47 ; *see also* Son of Geoffrey
Fitzgerald [Fitz Gerold], Eliz., iii, 375, 387 ; Rob., iv, 594 *n* ; *see also* Son of Gerold
Fitzhamon, Rob., iii, 86 ; *see also* Son of Hamon
Fitzhardinge, Ld., v, 517
Fitz Harris, vsct., *see* Malmesbury, earl of
Fitzhenry, Rob., prior of St. Swithun's, ii, 115 ; *see also* Son of Henry
Fitzherbert, Basil, iv, 69 ; Edw., iii, 486 ; Eliz., iv, 69, 270, 271 ; Marg., iv, 270 ; Matth., iv, 145, 180, 258, 270, 271 ; Pet., iv, 257, 258, 265, 270, 525 ; Reg., iv, 270, 271 ; Thos., iii, 201 ; Will., iv, 524 ; Mrs., iii, 334 ; *see also* Son of Herbert
Fitzherbert-Brockholes, Mary, iv, 69 ; Will., iv, 69
Fitz-Hubert, Sim., v, 142
Fitz Hugh, John, iv, 67, 88, 92, 110, 252
Fitz Jocelin, Reg., *see* Bath and Wells, bp. of
Fitz John, Herb., iv, 270 ; Nich., iii, 483 ; Rich., iv, 81 ; Will., ii, 229 ; iv, 589 ; *see also* Son of John
Fitz Martin, Rich., iv, 590 ; *see also* Son of Martin
Fitz Neal, Rich., v, 307
Fitz Nicholas, Ralph, iv, 160
Fitz Osbern [Fitz Osborne], Rog., v, 222, 241, 299 ; Will., ii, 230 ; iii, 55, 103, 529 ; iv, 42, 360, 365, 547 ; v, 148, 155, 171, 176, 186, 189, 222, 224 *n*, 228, 234, 241, 242, 243, 245, 259, 299
Fitz Osbert, Will., v, 28
Fitz Other, Walt., ii, 479 ; iv, 110, 224, 227
Fitz Pain [Fitz Payn], Edm., iv, 553 ; Rob., iii, 457 ; iv, 588
Fitz Parnel, Marg., iv, 607 ; Rob., iv, 607
Fitzpatrick, Thos., iv, 85
Fitz Peter [Fitz Piers], Alice, iv, 199 ; Geoff., ii, 149 ; iii, 107 ; iv, 79 ; Herb., iii, 142, 261, 366, 367 ; iv, 257, 258, 259, 270, 396, 525, 532 ; Joan, iii, 123, 142 ; iv, 258 *n*, 270 ; John, iii, 142 ; iv, 258 *n* ; Matth., iii, 367 ; (Sir) Reg., iii, 142, 366 ; iv, 145, 146, 180, 199, 252, 257, 258, 270, 272, 305, 525 ; *see also* Son of Peter
Fitz Reginald, John, iv, 270 ; *see also* Son of Reginald

Fitz Robert, Nigel, iii, 47 ; *see also* Son of Robert
Fitz Roger, Emma, iv, 202 ; Rog., iv, 202 ; Will., iii, 212 ; iv, 202 ; *see also* Son of Roger
Fitz Roy, Anne, iii, 69 ; Chas., iii, 69 ; Mrs., iv, 21
Fitz Ruald, Hen., iv, 255, 257, 269, 332
Fitz Stur, *see* Son of Stur
Fitz Thomas, John, iv, 608, 631 ; v, 91 *n*
Fitz Thurstin, Rich., v, 23 *n*
Fitz Ulf, Rob., iv, 550, 635
Fitz Waleran, Will., iv, 351
Fitz Walter, Geoff., iv, 42, 43 ; *see also* Son of Walter
Fitz Warine [Fitzwarren], Eliz., Lady, iv, 531 ; Florence, Lady, ii, 496 ; Lds., ii, 496 ; Fulke Bourchier, iv, 531
Fitz Warren [Fitz Warin], Alan, iii, 46, 50 ; Ivo, v, 316 ; Sir Phil., v, 118
Fitz William, Edm., iii, 435 ; Jane, iv, 143, 278 ; John, ii, 504, 516 ; Lucy, iii, 195 ; iv, 34 ; Mabel, Lady, iv, 196 ; (Sir) Will., ii, 144, 226, 490, 504, 513, 516 ; iii, 18, 90, 105, 117, 135, 359, 442 ; iv, 34, 85, 196, 200, 278 ; v, 325 ; Dr., v, 214 ; *see also* Son of William
Fitz Wygram, Sir Fred. L., iii, 123, 134 ; v, 542 ; Sir F. W., iii, 123
Flambard [Flamme], Ralph [Ranulf, Ranulph], ii, 10, 117, 121, 152, 160 ; iii, 227 ; v, 101, 301
Flanagan, Edm., iv, 654
Flanders, Mary, ctss. of, ii, 126 ; earls of, Matth., ii, 126 ; Theodoric, ii, 127
Flat racing, v, 543
Flaundres, John, iv, 528 ; Rog., iv, 528
Flaxfield [Flaxpool] (Basingstoke), iv, 128
Flaxlande Meade (Eversley), iv, 33
Fleet, iv, 2, 5, 14 ; adv., iv, 14 ; ch., iv, 13 ; Nonconf., iv, 14 ; ponds, iv, 6, 7 ; Rom. Cath., iv, 14 ; sch., ii, 399
Fleet, man. (Dors.), ii, 154, 156, 159
Fleet Farm House (Minley), iv, 21
Fleet Water, riv., iv, 635
Fleetwood, Col. Chas., v, 351 ; Gerard, iii, 54 ; Hen., iii, 29
Fleming [Flemang, Flemyng] (le), Sir Dan., iv, 399 *n* ; Edw., iii, 479 ; iv, 453 ; Sir Fran., ii, 67 ; iv, 453, 454, 455, 554 ; Hawise, v, 162 ; Hen., iv, 146 ; v, 494 ; Hugh, v, 144 *n* ; Jane, iii, 463 ; Joan, Lady, iv, 554 ; John, ii, 203, 205 ; iii, 468, 483, 484, 513 ; iv, 488 ; v, 112 *n*, 144 *n*, 147, 162, 264, 270 *n* ; Kath., iv, 453 ; Phil., v, 254 ; (Sir) Thos., ii, 387, 391 ; iii, 464, 479, 483 ; v, 30, 150, 151, 229, 256, 264 ; Walt., ii, 193 ; iii, 512 ; Sir Will., iv, 454 ; Col., v, 143 ; fam., v, 148 *n* ; arms, iii, 479
Flemmyngysgrove (Cliddesden), iv, 145
Fleshmonger, Will., ii, 271, 294
Fletcher, R. W., iii, 489 ; Will., iii, 294
Flete, le (Crondall), *see* Fleet
Flete, le (Longstock), iv, 449
Flete, de, Joan, iv, 588 *n* ; John, iv, 588 *n*
Fletebridge, Le (Crondall), iv, 6

Flexland, man. (Soberton), iii, 260, 262
Flies, i, 154
Flode, fam., *see* Flood
Flodstock mill (Winchester), v, 49
Flodweye, la (Wherwell), iv, 411
Flood, man. (Binsted), ii, 487 ; iii, 10
Flood, man. (Havant), ii, 488 ; iii, 124
Flood [Flode] (de la), Alice, iii, 60, 62 ; Geoff., iii, 60, 62, 124 ; Nich., ii, 214 ; v, 146 ; —, ii, 97
Flood Place, man. (Binsted), *see* Flood
Flood's Farm (Dogmersfield), iv, 72
Florans [Floryse], Ellen, iii, 533 ; Rob., iii, 533
Flory [Florie] (de), Rich., ii, 223 ; iv, 96
Floryn, Nich., v, 466 *n*
Floryse, *see* Florans
Flower, Walt., v, 536, 539
Floyer, Ann, ii, 485 ; Ant., ii, 485 ; fam., arms, ii, 485
Flushard (Lymington), iv, 639
Fockerby, Thos. de, v, 220 *n*
Fodrington, man., ii, 207
Fogge, Sir Thos., iv, 291
Foillet, *see* Follet
Fold, man. (Fordingbridge), iv, 571, 572
Foley (Bramshott), ii, 491
Foley, Mrs., iv, 568
Foljambe, Eliz., Lady, iv, 105
Folks, Rich., iv, 388
Follet [Foillet, Foliat, Foliot, Folyot, Folyott], Anne A., iii, 216 ; John, ii, 129 ; Rich., ii, 486 ; iii, 290 ; iv, 650 ; Rob., iii, 290 ; v, 305 ; Walt., iii, 290 ; v, 305
Folley, man. (Bramshott), ii, 493
Folquardby [Fulguardby, Fulquardeby], John, ii, 512 ; iv, 8, 9 ; Marg. [Margery], ii, 512 ; iv, 8, 9 ; Thos., v, 277 *n*
Folyot, Folyott, *see* Follet
Fonkehurne, Fonketon, *see* Funckton
Fonsard, John, abbot of Quarr, ii, 139
Fonte, John de, v, 470
Fontelegh-Pageham, man., ii, 182
Fontevrault Abbey (France), iv, 525 ; v, 361 *n*
Fontley, *see* Funtley
Fonts, iii, 14, 29, 55, 62, 74, 84, 126, 139, 144, 147, 170, 219, 231, 235, 243, 253, 266, 280, 287, 291, 296, 313, 316, 319, 322, 327, 329, 335, 338, 359, 365, 369, 377, 380, 393, 398, 405, 417, 431, 439, 450, 452, 460, 471, 480, 532 ; iv, 12, 65, 144, 154, 228, 275, 298, 303, 325, 371, 390, 403, 429, 485, 487, 502, 509, 566, 578, 601, 638 ; v, 58, 74 ; Norman, ii, 241-8 ; Saxon, ii, 238, 239 ; xi. cent., iv, 658 ; xii. cent., ii, 517 ; iii, 19, 22, 24, 40, 92, 160, 257, 272, 284, 289, 330, 331, 347, 352, 423, 467, 469, 488 ; iv, 20, 29, 101, 112, 168, 217, 263, 318, 405, 422, 425, 442, 448, 479, 629 ; xiii. cent., iii, 50, 108, 132, 133, 165, 344, 426, 478 ; iv, 71, 234, 323, 386, 518, 523, 543 ; xiv. cent., ii, 495 ; iii, 80, 151, 465 ; iv, 24, 311, 383, 451, 575 ; xv. cent., ii, 510 ; iii, 57, 119, 198, 232, 385, 412, 527 ; iv, 49, 56, 78, 86, 96, 126, 222, 237, 276, 432, 534, 585, 622 ; xvii. cent., iii, 171 ; iv, 328 ; xviii. cent., iii, 44, 325, 464 ; iv, 61, 445, 500, 593
Fonuner, Hen. de, iv, 89

Footner, —, v, 537
Foquet, fam., v, 200
Foracre (Wherwell), iv, 411
Forbes, Joanna A., iii, 75 ; Mrs., iii, 64 ; —, bp. of Brechin, iv, 41
Forcombe (Steep), iii, 78
Ford (Whitwell), v, 203
Ford [Forde] (de, de la), Ad., iv, 577, 579 ; Agnes, iv, 354 ; Christine, iv, 577 ; Clarice, iv, 577 ; Fred., ii, 486 ; Geoff., iv, 335 ; Jas., iv, 2 ; John, ii, 110 ; iii, 467 ; iv, 335 ; John B., ii, 486 ; Kath., iv, 577 ; Ralph, v, 26 ; Rich., ii, 57 ; iv, 354 ; Will., iii, 114
Forde, par., see Fordingbridge
Fordefieldes (Kingsclere), iv, 250, 261 n
Fordham, Geo., v, 544
Fording (Boldre), iv, 619
Fordingbridge, ii, 21, 37, 62, 63, 69, 71, 96, 101, 171, 172, 229 ; iv, 559, 567-77, 598, 611 ; v, 135 n, 324, 331, 428, 429 n, 563 ; advs., iv, 573 ; bridge, iv, 567 ; chars., iv, 576 ; chs., iv, 573 ; ind., iv, 567 ; mans., iv, 568 ; mkt. and fairs, iv, 567 ; mills, iv, 568 ; Nonconf., iv, 576 ; pop., v, 445 ; Rom. Cath., iv, 576 ; Rom. rem., i, 326, 328 ; iv, 568 ; schs., ii, 399
Fordingbridge, hund., iv, 559
Fordingbridge, Clement de, ii, 211
Ford Mill (Lockerley), iv, 500, 501 n, 517
Foreland (Bembridge), v, 157
Forest, fam., see Forrest
Forest and game laws, ii, 414-19, 421-35
Forest courts, ii, 438
Forester, see Forster
Forestry, ii, 409
Forficularia, i, 109
Forist, see Forrest
Formby, H. C., iv, 512, 513
Forrep Lande, le, (Crondall), iv, 6
Forrest [Forest, Forist], John, ii, 120, 197 ; Thos., ii, 196, 197 ; Will., v, 213 ; Will. C., v, 78
Forstbury, Joan, ii, 173 ; John, ii, 173
Forster [Forester] (de, le), Alice, ii, 129 ; iii, 21 ; Edm., iii, 435 ; Geo., iii, 21 ; (Sir) Humph., iii, 21 ; iv, 252, 256, 532 n, 536 ; H. W., iii, 290, 291 ; v, 575 ; Joan, ii, 209 ; John, iii, 421 ; iv, 535 ; v, 191 n ; Thos., ii, 209 ; (Sir) Will., iii, 21 ; iv, 256, 532, 536 ; see also Foster
Forston (Dors.), v, 108
Fortescue, Sir Adrian, iii, 436 ; iv, 383 ; Anne, Lady, iii, 436 ; iv, 383 ; Frances, Lady, v, 93 n ; Fran., iv, 183 ; John, iii, 105 ; Kath., iv, 208 ; Philippa, iii, 105 ; Thos., iv, 646 ; Will., iv, 208, 646
Forteswell (Carisbrooke), v, 222
Fortibus (de), Avelina, iv, 645 ; Isabel, ii, 154, 230 ; iii, 171 ; iv, 553, 597, 598, 640, 641, 643, 645 ; v, 81, 91, 94, 96, 140, 141, 168, 181, 183, 184, 187, 213, 222, 224, 226, 230, 231, 234, 242 n, 256, 257, 259, 260, 273, 274, 275, 279, 284, 287, 312 n ; Thos., iv, 213 ; Will., iii, 166, 171 ; iv, 213 ; v, 91
Fortin, Denys, iii, 512 ; —, iii, 505
Forton, man. (Longparish), iv, 401, 406, 407
Fortune, Mary, iv, 511
Fortune Hospital (Gosport), v, 393
Foscote, see Foxcott

Foskett Farm (Kingsclere), iv, 266 n
Fossatt meade (Baughurst), iv, 275
Fostebire, Nich., iii, 226
Foster [Fouster], Alice, iv, 488 ; Andrea, iv, 561 ; Andr., iii, 463 ; iv, 453, 455 ; Barrow, iii, 463 ; iv, 453 ; Fran., iv, 380 ; Greg., iv, 488 ; Jas., iv, 9 ; John (le) ii, 131, 164, 193 ; iii, 97, 98, 244, 463 ; iv, 453, 455, 460, 468 n ; Montague, iii, 205, 214 ; Nich., iii, 242 ; Rich., v, 201, 514 ; Sam., iv, 413 ; Thos., iv, 79, 454 ; Will., iv, 41 n ; W. F., ii, 508 ; —, v, 517 ; see also Forster
Foucher, Alice, iv, 617 ; Margery, iv, 617
Founthill, see Funckton
Foure Land Greene (Stratfieldsaye), iv, 57
Fourle, see Fairlee
Fouster, see Foster
Fowell, see Fowle
Fower Landes (Stratfieldsaye), iv, 57
Fowewood cum Forewey, man., ii, 139
Fowle [Fowell], H., v, 532 ; Will., iii, 513 ; iv, 485
Fowler, —, iv, 425
Fowles, see Fold
Fowleston (Botley), ii, 137
Fowncktowne, see Funckton
Fox [Vox] (le), Bohun, ii, 347 ; John, iv, 406 ; v, 481 ; Maud, iv, 406 ; v, 481 ; Rich., ii, 50, 51, 113, 120, 163, 197, 202, 208, 215, 369, 370 ; iii, 42, 187, 333, 334 ; iv, 135, 165, 262, 296, 406, 425, 427, 512 ; v, 24, 51, 76, 322, 481 ; Rob., v, 140 ; (Sir) Steph., iv, 537, 543 ; v, 481 ; W. F., iv, 277 ; Capt., v, 389, 390
Foxbury Hill (Christchurch), v, 85
Foxcombe, see Forcombe
Foxcote (Hannington), iv, 229
Foxcote (de), Ad., iv, 352 ; Edulf, iv, 352 ; Edw., iv, 352, 356 ; Hen., iv, 352 ; Herb., iv, 352 ; Marg., iv, 352 ; Miles, iv, 352 ; Philippa, iv, 352 ; Rob., iv, 352 ; Tho., iv, 352 ; Walt., iv, 352
Foxcott [Foxcote] (Andover), iv, 333, 345, 356 ; adv., iv, 356 ; chap., iv, 355 ; farm, iv, 345 ; man., iv, 351 ; pop., v, 438
Foxcroft, Hen., iii, 343 ; Isaac, iii, 343
Foxdowne (Overton), iv, 211
Foxele, see Foxley
Foxellisdowne (Calbourne), v, 218
Foxenhulle (Kimpton), iv, 372
Foxes, Lower, Upper (Melchet Pk.), iv, 540
Foxholes, John, v, 368
Fox-hunting, v, 513, 571
Foxle, see Foxley
Foxlease (Lyndhurst), iv, 631
Foxley [Foxele, Foxle] (de), Constance, iii, 363 ; iv, 35, 41 ; Eliz., iv, 35 ; (Sir) John, ii, 150 ; iii, 362, 363 ; iv, 35, 41, 42, 47, 545, 627, 631 ; Kath., iv, 35, 64 ; Joan, Lady, iv, 35 ; Margery, iv, 35 ; Maud, Lady, iv, 35 ; Rich., iv, 35 ; Thos., ii, 150, 222 ; iv, 35, 36, 37, 46 n, 63, 64 ; Will., ii, 222, 223
Fox Mills (Romsey), iv, 452, 455
Fox-Strangways, Steph., iv, 537, 543
Foye, —, v, 456
Foyle (Rev.), Edw., iii, 313 ; iv, 376 ; Geo., iv, 376 ; Geo. S., iv,

Foyle (cont.) 373, 376 ; John, iv, 373 ; Mary A., iv, 373
Fozier, Charlotte, iv, 441
Fradin, Fran., iii, 536
Frampton, Jas., iv, 253 n ; Joan, iii, 48 ; iv, 605 ; John, iii, 48 ; iv, 605 ; —, v, 8
Franceys, see Francis
Francheys man. (Priors Dean), see French's
Francis [Franceys], Sir Jas., iv, 423 ; Johanne, ii, 125 ; Rich., iv, 436 ; Rob., iv, 212
Franciscans, ii, 15, 53, 57, 61, 105, 191 ; iv, 4
Francmantel, see Freemantle
Frank, Arth., iv, 568, Eliz., iv, 568 ; Hen., iv, 408 n ; Rich., iv, 568
Frank James Memorial Home (Whippingham), v, 198
Franklin [Frankelyn] (le), Alice, iii, 395 ; Ben., iii, 339 ; Hen., iii, 396 ; Ralph, iv, 152 ; Rich., ii, 202
Frant (Suss.), iv, 214
Frateresmed (Sherborne St. John), iv, 158
Fratton, ii, 226 ; iii, 140, 141, 195 ; fishing, v, 467 ; man., iii, 196 ; v, 412 n, 425
Frauncheville, see Newtown
Fraxino, see Ash
Frazier, Sir Alex., v, 280
Freake, see Freke
Frebody, John, iv, 570 ; Will., iv, 570
Freborne Water (Wolverton), iv, 270
Frederick, Sir Chas. E., iii, 339 ; v, 529 ; fam., arms, iii, 339
Freefolk [Freefolke, Freefolk Sifrewast, Freefolk, South], ii, 108 ; iv, 208, 210, 212, 215, 273, 282-5 ; v, 77 ; adv., iv, 284 ; ch., iv, 283 ; man., ii, 114 ; iv, 284 ; pop., v, 441 ; watercress cultivation, v, 455
Freefolk (de, of), Rich., iv, 406 ; v, 481
Freefolk Priors (Whitchurch), iv, 299, 300
Freefolk Wood (Freefolk), iv, 284 ; v, 514
Frecham, Frances, iii, 251
Freeland, Eliz., ii, 507 ; John, ii, 494, 507 ; iii, 137 ; Nich., ii, 507 ; Rich., ii, 507 ; fam., arms, ii, 507
Freeman, Geo., iii, 270 ; Will., iii, 536 ; iv, 617
Freeman-Heathcote, Sir Thos., iv, 536
Freemantle (Kingsclere), iv, 249, 252-3, 260 ; man., iv, 258
Freemantle (Millbrook), iii, 427, 428, 491
Freemantle [Fremantel] (de), John, iv, 255, 258, 303 ; Selina, iii, 445 ; Sir Will., iii, 445
Freemantle Farm (Kingsclere), iv, 258
Freemantle Park Farm (Kingsclere), iv, 253
Frefolk, see Freefolk
Freind, Thos., v, 460
Freke [Freake], Eliz., iii, 414 ; iv, 22 ; Jane, v, 252 ; John, v, 252 n ; Rob., iv, 589, 594 ; (Sir) Thos., iii, 279, 414 ; iv, 22
Fremantel, see Freemantle
Fremborough, see Farnborough
Fremelesworth (de), Eleanor, iv, 93, 94 ; Joan, iv, 94 ; John, iv, 93, 94 ; Rich., iv, 93, 9 Will., iv, 93

French [Frennsh], Joan, v, 482;
John, iv, 436; Pet. (le) v, 482
Frenchemore Combes (Broughton),
iv, 493
Frenchemore Fulley (Broughton),
iv, 493
French Mill (Godshill), v, 175
Frenchmoor (Broughton), iv, 489,
493, 494
French's man. (Priors Dean), iv,
436
Frendstaple, see Stakes & Stakes
Hill
Frennsh, see French
Frensham (Surr.), iv, 29
Frere (le), Ad., v, 480 n; E. V.,
iv, 174; Geo., iv, 413; Hen. v,
484, 574; John, iii, 461; Rob.,
ii, 255; Tobias, v, 538, 539; Will.,
iv, 520
Freren Court, see Burgate, Over
Freshfield, Edwin, v, 16, 17, 19
Freshwater, ii, 73, 195; v, 209, 217,
240-6, 253 n, 272, 286, 288, 334;
adv., ii, 25; v, 245; char. v,
245, 246; ch., ii, 230, 231; v,
244, 245; man., v, 241; mills,
v, 241, 242; Nonconf., v, 245;
pop., v, 449; Rom. Cath., v, 240,
245; sch., ii, 407; ship-building,
v, 458
Freth, le, (Elvetham), iv, 74
Friars, Black, see Dominicans
Friars, Observant, see Franciscans
Friars, White, see Carmelites
Friars' Conduit (Southampton), v,
486
Fricker, Jack, v, 532
Friends, Society of, ii, 482; iii, 534;
iv, 139, 576; v, 136, 260
Frifhoc, Frigefolc, see Freefolk
Frigidum Mantellum, see Free-
mantle
Frilende, John, ii, 110
Frisadoes (cloth), v, 486, 487
Frith, le, (Wolverton), iv, 270
Frith, Hen., iv, 214; John, iii, 373;
iv, 214; Kath., iii, 373; iv, 214;
Rob., iv, 214; Will., iv, 214
Fritham (Bramshaw), ii, 427, 450;
iv, 615, 616, 623, 625; v, 81
Frithburga, ii, 234, 236, 238; iv,
300, 303
Frith Copp (Woodcott), iv, 331,
332
Frithenwald [Frithwald], iv, 74,
109
Frithstan, bp. of Winchester, ii, 6;
iii, 11; iv, 202, 212, 219, 221
Frithwald, see Frithenwald
Frobreche (Ecchinswell), iv, 250
Frobury, man. (Kingsclere), iv,
254, 257, 271; chap., iv, 265
Frobury Farm (Kingsclere), iv,
255, 266
Frobury Park Copse (Kingsclere),
iv, 255
Froditonia, see Fratton
Froger, abbot of St. Florent, ii, 219
Frogge Meade (Yateley), iv, 21
Frogham (Hyde), iv, 568
Froghemour, ii, 182
Froglane Farm (Pamber), iv, 433
Frogs and toads, i, 206
Frolebyr, Frolleberi, Frollebury,
Frollesbyr, see Frobury
Froman's Farm (King's Somborne),
iv, 477
Frome, John, iv, 443
Fromond, Alice, iii, 445; iv, 476;
John, ii, 199, 290, 301, 305; iii,
300, 445, 485; iv, 60, 477, 657;
v, 17, 126; Maud, ii, 305; iv, 657;
Rich., iii, 445; iv, 476, 485;
Steph., iii, 445; —, iv, 605

Fromond's Court, man. (Sparsholt),
iii, 445; iv, 477, 486 n
Fromunds [Fromonds] (King's Som-
borne), iv, 470, 477
Frost [Froste], Edm., iv, 598;
Juliana, iii, 448; iv, 83, 151, 194;
Walt., iii, 428, 434; Will., iii,
448; iv, 83, 151, 178, 194
Frowbery, see Frobury
Frowd, Rev. Edw., iv, 365
Froxfield, ii, 26; iii, 63, 76-7, 116;
adv., iii, 77; ch., iii, 77; man.,
iii, 76; pop., v, 444; Rom. rem.,
i, 345; sch., ii, 399
Froxfield Green (Froxfield), iii, 76
Froylbery, see Frobury
Froyle, ii, 63, 122, 123, 471, 501-6,
511, 515; v, 243; adv., ii, 505;
ch., ii, 501; cider, v, 474;
coprolite, v, 453; lime burning
ind., v, 454; man., ii, 126, 502; v,
475; pop., v, 437; sch., ii, 399,
506
Froyle, riv., ii, 504
Froyle, Lower, ii, 501, 506
Froyle, North, ii, 501
Froyle, Upper, ii, 501
Froyle House (Froyle), ii, 501
Froyle Place (Froyle), ii, 501
Fry [Frye] (le), C. B., v, 576;
Felicia, iv, 408 n; Hen., iv, 407,
408 n; John, v, 171, 482; Rob.,
ii, 482; Walt., iv, 408; fam., v,
175
Fryer, Bithiah, iv, 412; Capt.
C. G., iii, 326; Delicia, iv, 412;
Dorcas, iv, 412 n; Sir John, iv,
412, 413; Susannah, iv, 412;
Will, ii, 182, 186; Capt., iv, 430
Fryfolk, Fryfolk, South, Fryfolk
Syfrewast, see Freefolk
Frytham, see Fritham
Frytt, Rob., iv, 315
Fuillet, Rich., v, 470
Fulcher, Ralph, iv, 619
Fulchi, iii, 457
Fulcoin [Fulcuin], iv, 619, 620,
644; v, 95, 126
Fulescote, see Foxcott
Fulflood, Hugh de, v, 476
Fulfludd (Weeke), see Fullflood
Fulford (Arreton), v, 140
Fulford, Florence, ii, 496; Sir
Humph., ii, 496; Geo., iv, 649
Fulguardby, see Folquardby
Fulham, Edw., iv, 384
Fulient, Will., ii, 205
Fuller, (Sir) Dowse [Dowce], iv,
261, 455; Frances, iv, 509; John,
iv, 509; Marie, iv, 455; Matth.,
ii, 260; Neston, v, 538; Nich., iv,
455, 637; Pet., v, 160; Rose, iv,
509; Sam. P., iv, 455; Sarah, iv,
637; Thos., iv, 509
Fuller's Bottom (Headley), v, 453
Fuller's earth industry, v, 453
Fullerton, man. (Wherwell), ii, 117,
121; iv, 400, 411, 412, 413, 438
Fullerton, Geo. A., iii, 489; Maj.
Geo. F. D., iv, 104; Sir Jas., v, 94
Fullflood (Weeke), ii, 114; iii, 401
Fulmere, Rob., iv, 45, 156
Fulquardeby, see Folquardby
Funceley, see Funtley
Funckton, man. (Christchurch), v,
98
Funeral chaplets, iv, 336
Fungi, i, 82
Funtley [Funtelei, Funtelegh],
man. (Titchfield), ii, 186; iii, 217,
221, 226; v, 421; iron trade, v,
464
Furgo Hill, i, 345
Furnew [Furneaux], John, ii, 256
Fursey Close, le, (Yateley), iv, 21

Fursiedeneweye (King's Som-
borne), iv, 470
Furze Hill (Ibsley), iv, 579
Furze Hill (S. Tidworth), iv, 391
Furzley (Bramshaw), iv, 623
Futcher, Thos., iii, 241; —, v, 487
Fychet, see Fitchett
Fyfeacres (Faccombe), iv, 315
Fyfehide, Fyfhide, fam., see Fifhide
Fyfhyde, par., see Fyfield
Fyfield, iv, 333, 341, 366-9, 374,
387, 392; adv., iv, 368; char.,
iv, 368; ch., iv, 368; Great
Copse, iv, 366; man., iv, 366,
367; pop., v, 438; Rom. rem.,
i, 294; sch., ii, 399; iv, 369
Fyfield, fam., see Fifhide
Fygeryslane (Carisbrooke), v, 222
Fylder, see Fielder
Fyloll, see Filliol
Fylthier More (Yateley), iv, 21
Fyndone, Will. de, iv, 6 n
Fynemark [Fymarc], Kath., iv
548; Will., ii, 161; iv, 548
Fynes, see Fiennes
Fyshams Acre (Faccombe), iv, 314
Fysher, see Fisher
Fyshill, Alice, ii, 151
Fysshehouse, le (Binstead), v, 151
Fyssher, see Fisher
Fysshe Weres (Broughton), iv, 493
Fystede, Maria, ii, 130

Gabell, Hen. D., ii, 355, 356, 357,
366
Gabriel, John, v, 39, 494
Gaddeshill (Eversley), iv, 32
Gage, Thos., Ld., iv, 578; Henry,
vsct., iii, 69
Gage, Edw., iv, 450, 454; Eliz., iv,
578; Sir Hen., v, 344; (Sir)
John, ii, 478; Rob., ii, 478;
Thos., iv, 562; Will., iii, 178;
W. T., v, 537; Capt., v, 516;
fam., arms, ii, 478
Gailey [Gales] mill (Kingsclere), iv,
250, 257
Gainsborough, Elizabeth Noel, ctss.
of, iv, 450; Edw. Noel, earl of,
iii, 466; iv, 450; Wriothesley
B. Noel, earl of, iv, 450
Gairdner, Rev. Archibald, iv, 286
Galden Common (Freshwater), v,
241
Gale, Edw., iv, 359; John, iv, 98;
Rev. John H., iv, 352; Martha,
iv, 357; Rich., iv, 25; Susan, v,
96; Thos., v, 96; Thos. H., iv,
352
Galerugg, see Garlogs
Galicien [Galliciano], Pet. de, ii,
195, 197, 220; iv, 68, 251
Gallaker, see Gavelacre
Gallan, Will., v, 112
Galley Hill (Selborne), iii, 6
Galley Quay (Southampton), v,
458
Gallipoli, John Yong, bp. of, ii,
294
Gallowe Hill, iv, 3
Gallup [Gallop, Gollop], Eliz., iv,
458; Geo., iii, 499, 535; iv, 458;
H. C., iii, 72; Kath., iv, 458;
Marg., iv, 458; Pet., iii, 499;
Rog., iv, 458
Gallways (Hartley Wintney), iv,
80
Gallycoop (Ashmansworth), iv, 274
Gally Hill (Crookham), iv, 5
Galopyn, Pet., v, 466 n
Galrogge, Galrug, man., see Garlogs
Galrug, Benedict, iv, 528; Juliane,
iv, 528

Gambier, Jas., Ld., v, 400
Gambledown Farm (Lockerley), iv, 502
Gambon, Isabel, iv, 279 ; John, iv, 279
Ganderdown (Dean), iv, 205
Ganderpark (Heckfield), iv, 45
Ganlonde (Carisbrooke), v, 222
Gard (du), Anne, v, 176 ; Eliz., iii, 240 ; Pet., v, 173 ; Rich., v, 151, 169, 170, 176, 177, 184, 187, 193 ; Will., iii, 240
Gardeynclose (Vernhams Dean), iv, 329
Gardiner [Gardner], Jas., iv, 279 ; Jas. W. S., iii, 214 ; Jane, Lady, iii, 213 ; iv, 166 ; Sir John B. W. S., iii, 214 ; Sir John W. S., iii, 214, 215 ; Rich., iii, 381 ; Steph., bp., ii, 52, 53, 63, 64, 65, 70, 71, 291, 301 ; iii, 43 ; iv, 192, 248, 277, 430, 539 ; Thos., iv, 54 ; Sir Will., iii, 213, 214 ; iv, 166, 167 ; fam., iv, 143 ; arms, iii, 214 ; see also Gairdner
Gardinis, de, Isabel, iv, 146 ; Will., iv, 146
Gardino, de, Joan, v, 91 n ; Ralph, v, 191 n ; Rog., v, 91 n
Gardner, see Gardiner
Garland, John, iii, 508
Garlantysbury (Carisbrooke), v, 222
Garlicke (King's Somborne), iv, 470
Garlik, Walt., iv, 216
Garlogs [Garlogge, Garlonge], man. (Nether Wallop), iv, 525, 528, 533
Garnard, Rich., iii, 499
Garnett, —, v, 338
Garnier [Garnyer], Geo., iii, 234, 235 ; iv, 198 ; Thos., ii, 115 ; Will., iii, 234 ; fam., arms, iii, 234
Garnor (Overton), iv, 211
Garnyer, see Garnier
Garrard, Thos., iv, 536 ; Will., iv, 494
Garrat, see Garrett
Garre, le, (Ecchinswell), iv, 250
Garrett [Garrat], Anne, iv, 71 ; Rich., iv, 613 ; Steph., v, 174 ; Will., iii, 124
Garstanmed (Odiham), iv, 88
Garston [Garton, Gastin] (de), John, iii, 286 ; v, 119, 144, 200, 263 ; Rich., v, 118 ; Thos., iv, 206
Garstone (Burghclere), iv, 277
Garston Regis, la, (Heckfield), iv, 45, 47
Garth, Geo., iii, 97, 150 ; Rich., iii, 97, 150, 334 ; Rob., iii, 150 ; T. C., v, 535
Garth hunt, v, 533-5
Garthwaite, Jos., iv, 516
Garton (Christchurch), v, 85
Garton, fam., see Garston
Gascelyn, Isabel, iv, 417 ; Ralph, iv, 417
Gascoigne [Gascoyne], Edw., v, 42, 484
Gascons (Leckford), iv, 466
Gask, John, ii, 512
Gassiott, —, v, 180
Gastin, see Garston
Gaston Copse, iv, 174, 229
Gaston Grange (Bentworth), iv, 68
Gastropoda, i, 104
Gatcliff (Godshill), v, 170 ; quarries, v, 170, 462
Gatcombe, i, 260 ; ii, 97 ; v, 143, 159, 204, 209, 210, 219, 221, 231, 246-9, 281 ; adv., v, 249 ; chant., v, 203 ; char., v, 249 ; ch., v, 248, 249 ; man., v, 145, 202, 246-8 ; mills, v, 248 ; pop., v, 449

Gatcombe, Little, man. (Wymering), iii, 168
Gatcombe, Maud, Lady de ; see Estur, Maud de
Gate [Gates, Gayte], (Sir) Geoff., v, 173, 223 ; Hen., v, 484 ; (Sir) John, iii, 37, 43, 45, 328, 349 ; iv, 296, 608 ; v, 92 ; see also Yate
Gatehouse (Romsey), iv, 452
Gatehouse, Eliz., iv, 361 ; John, iv, 472, 476 ; Ruth, iv, 476 ; Sarah, iv, 476 ; (Sir) Thos., iv, 46, 133, 361, 476, 483, 494, 527
Gater, Caleb, iii, 484, 488 ; John, iii, 313, 479 ; Sarah, iii, 313 ; Will., iii, 484
Gaterygges Place (Romsey), iv, 452
Gates, see Gate
Gatesden, de, (Sir) John, iv, 82, 129, 547 ; Marg., iv, 82, 547
Gatin, Marg., iv, 483 ; Rich., iv, 483
Gatingeorde, iii, 275 ; iv, 544
Gatwicke (Bentworth), iv, 68
Gauden, Sam., ii, 502, 504
Gauefrey, John de, iv, 598
Gaunt, John of, see Lancaster, dk. of
Gauntlett [Gauntlet], Hen., iv, 537 ; John, iv, 537 ; v, 484 ; Rich., v, 484 ; Thos., iv, 537
Gavaire, Nich., ii, 231
Gavelacre [Gavelacre Farm] (Longparish), iv, 406, 407
Gavelacre, Eustace of, iv, 407 ; Maud de, iv, 407
Gaveldune, la, (Linkenholt), iv, 324 n
Gaveston, (de), Sir Arnald, v, 54, 55 ; Marg., v, 159, 183, 222 ; Piers, ii, 23 ; iv, 89 ; v, 159, 162, 183, 222, 284
Gawen, Edith, v, 211 ; John, v, 211
Gayer, Otho, iii, 167, 240
Gaylys mill, see Gailey mill
Gayte, see Gate
Gaze, fam., v, 217
Geale, see Gell
Geberd, see Gerberd
Ged, Will., v, 461
Gefordus, v, 28
Gell [Geale, Gel], Charlotte, v, 78 ; Edm., iv, 211 ; Eliz., ii, 482 ; Joan, iv, 241 ; Thos., ii, 483 ; iv, 241
Genwar, Roland de la, iii, 89
Geoffrey, iv, 146, 171, 218, 289, 372, 607 ; v, 28, 183 n, 231, 232 ; abbot of Newminster, ii, 117 ; abbot of Quarr, ii, 139 ; archbp. of Rouen, iv, 68, 70 ; count of Anjou, v, 291, 306 ; count of Perche, iv, 77 ; the marshal, ii, 518 ; prior of Breamore, ii, 169, 172 ; prior of Ellingham, ii, 229, 230 ; prior of Hamble, ii, 221, 223 ; prior of St. Swithun's, ii, 114 ; prince, v, 26, 306, 360
Geometræ, i, 137
George I., iv, 157, 244, 648 ; v, 290
George II., ii, 431 ; iv, 62, 149 ; v, 286, 389
George III., ii, 99, 351 ; iv, 248, 250, 616, 630, 631, 632 ; v, 393, 569
George IV., iv, 180 ; v, 514
George, prince of Denmark, iv, 345
George, Johan, ii, 57
Gerald [Gerold], iv, 227, 391, 392, 393, 491, 513, 568
Gerard [Girard], archbp. of York, ii, 11 ; prior of St. Denis, ii, 160, 163
Gerard, Rob., iv, 232 ; Will., iv, 392 ; see also Gerrard

Gerberd [Geberd, Gereberd, Gileberd], Alice, iv, 510, 561 ; John, iv, 561 ; Rob., iv, 474, 510 ; Thos., iv, 561 ; Will., iv, 560, 561, 562, 587
Gerdeleigh [Yerlega], de, Alice, iv, 224, 225 ; John, iv, 224, 225 ; Rob., iv, 224 ; Sybil, iv, 224
Gere, Will., v, 173
Gereberd, see Gerberd
Gerin, v, 273
Gerlei, man. (Church Oakley), see Malshanger
Gerlei, man. (Fordingbridge), see Gorley
German, iv, 7, 22
Germayn, Rog., v, 26
Gernon, Hugh, v, 237, 239, 275
Gerold, see Gerald
Gerrard (Christchurch), v, 85
Gerrard, Sir Fran., iv, 412 n ; see also Gerard
Gerrards, man. (Odiham), see Parkers
Gervase, abbot of Quarr, ii, 138, 139 ; prior of Andwell, ii, 225, 226
Gerveise (Calbourne), v, 218
Gervis [Gervais, Gervase, Gervays, Gerveys, Jarvis], Agnes, v, 93 ; Alicie, v, 72 ; And., iii, 40, 56 ; Eliz., v, 93 ; Sir Geo. W. T., v, 93 ; Joan, iv, 467 ; John, ii, 19 ; iv, 211, 240, 293 n ; Lydia, v, 93 ; Rog., ii, 119 ; iii, 39, 56 ; Thos., ii, 166 ; Will., iii, 39, 56 ; v, 72 ; see also Jervis, Jervoise and Tapps-Gervis-Meyrick
Gerway, Isabel, ii, 124
Gery, Rog., iv, 443
Gese, Math., iii, 512
Gewissæ, i, 377, 378 ; ii, 1
Gheast, Edw., iv, 587
Gherni, iv, 596
Gianibelli, v, 225, 226
Gibb, see Gibbs
Gibbings, H. W., v, 140 n
Gibbon, Anne, iii, 204 ; Edw., iii, 87 ; Will., iv, 509
Gibbons, Grinling, iv, 122 ; Capt. John, v, 154 ; Sloane, iii, 536
Gibbs [Gibb], Alice, iv, 317 ; Ant., iii, 443 ; Hen., v, 157 ; Jas., 115 n ; Nich., iv, 317 ; Rob. S., v, 235
Gibson, Edw., iv, 9
Gifford, Ld., v, 517, 534
Gifford [Giffard, Gifforde, Gyffard, Gyfford], Anne (Lady), iv, 9, 516, 518 ; Caleb, iv, 576 ; Eleanor, iv, 7 ; Eliz., iv, 7, 12 ; Geo., iv, 8, 22 ; Godf., iv, 7, 9 ; (Sir) Hen., iii, 225 ; iv, 472, 477, 516, 518, 521, 522, 538 n ; Jane, iv, 9 ; Joan, iv, 8, 9 ; John, ii, 504, 513 ; iv, 6, 7, 8, 9, 12, 518 ; Jos., iv, 605 ; Kath ; iv, 518 ; Mary, iv, 8 ; Osbert, iv, 88 ; Parnel, iv, 9 ; Pet., ii, 513 ; (Sir) Rich., ii, 369 ; iv, 6, 7, 445, 470, 471, 472, 472 n, 516, 518, 522 ; Rob., iv, 8 ; Susan, ii, 504 ; iv, 445 ; Walt., iv, 7, 74, 495 n ; (Sir) Will., ii, 10, 11, 216, 221, 480 ; iii, 206, 470 ; iv, 6, 7, 8, 9, 12, 236, 472, 516, 518, 522 ; v, 239, 326 n
Gignoux, Isaac, iii, 536
Gilbert, abbot of Lire, v, 164
Gilbert [Gilbard, Gylbert] (de), Ad., iv, 521 ; Alicia, iv, 71 ; Arnold, ii, 113 ; Geo., iv, 353, 481 ; v, 161, 162 n, 182, 183, 216 ; Joan, v, 161, 182 n, 183, 207, 216 ; John, iii, 298 ; iv, 353, 407, 481 ; v, 161, 169, 182 n, 183, 200, 207, 216 ; Nich., iv, 407 ; Rich., iv,

Gilbert (cont.)
351; Rob., iv, 481; v, 216; Sibil, v, 231; Thos., iii, 281; v, 216; Vincent H., v, 571, 572, 573; Will., v, 216, 231; Maj., v, 356; fam., v, 181
Gilchrist, Capt. Jas., v, 392
Gildeford, see Guildford
Gilders (Heckfield), iv, 45
Gile, Bindus, ii, 220
Gileberd, see Gerberd
Giles [Gyles], John, iv, 605; Letitia M., v, 235; Thresher, iv, 28; v, 519
Gill, Rev. Dugald C., iv, 221
Gillett [Gillet], H. H., v, 576; Thos., v, 117
Gillicroft (Eversley), iv, 33
Gilling, Will. de, v, 132
Gillingham (Kent), v, 375
Gillingham, Geo., iii, 109
Gillson, Thos., iii, 451
Gilpin, Will., iv, 616, 623; Will. S., iv, 616
Gimises, de, Alice, iii, 149; John, iii, 149, 150 ; Nich., iii, 149
Gimmings, see Gymming
Girard, see Gerard
Girling, Capt. Will., v, 223
Giros, Rob., v, 145
Gisors (de, of), Azo, abbot of Beaulieu, ii, 141, 146; John, iii, 197, 223, 225; v, 304 n; Payn, iii, 223; Will., abbot of Beaulieu, ii, 146
Gladhous (Carisbrooke), v, 222
Glamorgan (de), Alice, v, 146, 251; Amy, v, 146; Anne, v, 251; Denise, v, 251; Eleanor, v, 161; Isabel, v, 162 n, 215; John, v, 146, 162, 162 n, 164, 166, 215, 251; Nichola, v, 161; Nich., v, 146, 147, 161, 162, 215, 216; Pet., v, 215; Phil., v, 165, 166; Ralph, v, 206 n; Rob., v, 161, 162, 163, 166, 167, 212, 215, 275; (Sir) Will., v, 198, 251
Glannvyll, Benedict de, ii, 138
Glascocke, Arth., iv, 77; Edw., iv, 77; Jos., iv, 77
Glasgow, Rob. Wychard, bp. of, iii, 153
Glass, Lady, iv, 32
Glass, ancient, ii, 486, 489, 505; iii, 108, 368, 380, 407, 426, 452; iv, 28, 48, 50, 107, 181, 509, 657; v, 58, 59, 65, 68, 131, 168
Glasse, Geo., iv, 551
Glassedone (Eversley), iv, 33
Glassmaking and pottery, v, 454, 490-1
Glastonbury [Glastonia], of, Alice, iii, 226; Hen., iii, 226; iv, 347
Glastonbury Abbey (Somers.), ii, 108; iv, 551, 588, 589, 592, 594; abbots of, Herlain, iv, 589; John, iv, 590, 591; Michael, iv, 586; Hen. de Solers, iv, 592
Glemsford, de, Beatrice, iv, 340, 341, 342, 362, 392; John, iv, 340, 341, 342, 362, 392
Glidden (Hambledon), iii, 237, 238, 242
Glocester, fam., see Gloucester
Gloucester, i, 268; abbey, see St. Peter's abbey, Gloucester; cathedral, iv, 324, 374, 527
Gloucester, hon. of, iv, 381, 383
Gloucester, bps. of, ii, 98; Will. Warburton, ii, 486
Gloucester, ctsses. of : — Hawise, iii, 113; Marg., iv, 361, 576; Eleanor, dchss. of, v, 223; dks. of, iv, 89, 269, 394; v, 571; Humph., iii, 383; iv, 385, 436, 540, 545, 609,

Gloucester (cont.)
632; v, 223; Rich., iv, 199; v, 370; Thos., ii, 44; Will. H., iv, 632; earls of, iv, 339, 360, 362, 589, 590; Aumary, iii, 116, 117; Gilb., iv, 361, 381, 491, 576, 604; Hugh, iv, 361, 576; Rich., iii, 455; iv, 576; Rob., iii, 86; v, 302, 303, 360; Thos., iv, 440; Will., iii, 86, 113; v, 416
Gloucester [Glocester, Gloucestre, Glowecestre] (de, of), Durand, iv, 108 n, 145; Isabel, ii, 142; John, ii, 146, 149, 165, 168; Lucy, iv, 145; Miles, iv, 145, 422; Rob., iv, 483; Thos., ii, 120; iii, 269; Will., ii, 231
Glover, Hen., iv, 484
Glovers Ditch (Southampton), v, 457
Glove trade, v, 456
Glowcestre, see Gloucester
Glyd, Jas., iii, 30; Mich., iii, 30; Rich., iii, 30
Glyn, Sir Rich., v, 109
Glynn, Rev. Ant. W., v, 191; Edm. J., v, 248, 250; Eliz., v, 248, 250; Eliz. A., v, 250; Frances M., v, 250; Gertrude R., v, 250; Hen. R., v, 191 n; John, v, 191; John H., v, 165, 191; Rich., v, 113; Susannah, v, 191; Will. A., v, 165 n, 190, 191, 193
Gnosham, Thos. de, ii, 17
Goare, see Gore
Goater, Will., v, 546
Goat Lane (Eastrop), iv, 147
Gobard, Cisily, iv, 264
Gobet, John, iv, 598
Gobitz, Hen., v, 109
Gobyun, Jas., iv, 520 n; Margery, iv, 520 n
Goce, iii, 511
Godale, see Goodall
Godard, iv, 58
Godard, Marg., v, 29; see also Goddard
Godbegot House (Winchester), v, 2, 7
Godbiete (Winchester), v, 2, 34
Goddard, Alice, iv, 637; Dan., iv, 624, 625; Dav., iv, 637; Eliz., iv, 625; Hen., iv, 624, 628, 637; Rich., v, 198; Thos., iv, 92, 413, 625, 637, 638; Will., iv, 637; (Rev.) Will. S., ii, 337, 352, 353, 354, 355, 366; iv, 357; Mrs., iv, 266; see also Godard
Goddard Hills (Stratfieldsaye), iv, 57
Godefeld, see Godsfield
Godele (de), Christine, v, 98; Ela, iv, 573; Elias, iv, 573; v, 98
Godesa, v, 191
Godewyn, Godewyne, see Godwin
Godfrey, the baker, v, 86; bp., iv, 72; prior of St. Swithun's, ii, 114
Godfrey, Chas., iv, 487; Eliz., iv, 496; Geo., iv, 496; John, iv, 487, 496; v, 472 n; Rich., iv, 496; Rob., iii, 232; iv, 458 n; Walt., iv, 259, 454, 487, 496
Godfreyes (Hartley Wintney), iv, 79, 80
Godfrey's Farm (Broughton), iv, 496
Goditon [Godyton, Gotton] (de), Alice, iv, 610; Margery, iv, 143; Rob., v, 143, 238; Thos., iv, 610; Walt., v, 235 n; Will., v, 143, 238; fam., v, 237
Godman, v, 173 n; see also Goodman
Godorde, see Goodworth Clatford

Godric, ii, 152, 160; iii, 442; iv, 57, 341; v, 125, 143, 159, 162, 200
Godsfield, ii, 126, 187; iv, 183 n, 188, 189-90; chap., iv, 190; man., ii, 187; iv, 189, 190, 196 pop., v, 447
Godsfield Preceptory, see Baddesley Preceptory
Godshill, ii, 230, 231, 251; v, 138, 139, 170-7, 203, 242; adv., v, 176; chant., v, 177; char., v, 177; ch., v, 175; mans., v, 171; Nonconf., v, 177; pop., v, 448; sch., ii, 367, 387, 394, 407
Godshill, man. (Fordingbridge), iv, 572
Godshill, tithing (Fordingbridge), iv, 559, 568, 615; pop., v, 445
Godshill, North, man. (Godshill), v, 171
Godshill, South, man. (Godshill), v, 171
Godshill, de, Hen., v, 190, 191; Hugh, iv, 570, 571, 579, 629; v, 190; Nich., v, 198; Thos., v, 172
Godshill Coppice [Wood] (Fordingbridge), ii, 443; iv, 568
Godshill Park (Godshill), v, 171
God's House (Portsmouth), ii, 105, 206-8; iii, 191; iv, 81, 493, 494, 525; v, 198, 242, 417; Rob., prior of, iv, 82
God's House (Southampton), ii, 55, 105, 202-5, 228; iii, 386; iv, 145, 158, 228, 231, 547; v, 230, 270, 417, 454, 455, 459, 472, 475; beekeeping, v, 455; wardens, ii, 205
God's House (Yarmouth), v, 217
Godson, Bridg., iv, 112; Eliz., iv, 74; John, iv, 15, 16; Will., iv, 72, 74
Godspur, see Gosport
Godstow Abbey (Oxon.), iv, 255, 256, 257, 260, 270, 296, 332, 427; abbesses of :—Amphyllis, iv, 256; Edith, iv, 257; Emma, iv, 256, 427
Godwin [Godwine], v, 26, 28, 296; earl, ii, 421, 512, 518; iii, 8, 52, 194, 214, 425, 455; iv, 247, 255, 261, 428, 480, 525, 537; v, 100, 126, 155, 161, 171, 183, 297, 298, 299
Godwin [Godewyn, Godewyne], John, ii, 181; iii, 180; Rich., iii, 232; Rob., ii, 158; Thos., iii, 242; v, 78; see also Goodwin
Godwin's Croft (Christchurch), v, 108 n
Godyton, see Goditon
Goff, Lady Adelaide H., iv, 577, 578; Joseph, iv, 577, 578, 579; Mrs., iv, 104
Goidels, i, 260, 261; ii, 234; v, 293 n, 294 n
Golafre, Isabel, Lady, iv, 443; (Sir) John, iii, 506; iii, 69, 456; iv, 382, 443; Nichola [Nichole], ii, 506; iii, 456
Gold [Goolde, Goulde], Ellis, iv, 260; Joan, iii, 294; iv, 260; John, ii, 479; Rich., iii, 294; Will., iii, 96
Goldenhays (Eling), iv, 546
Goldforde, Thos., iii, 88
Goldhorde, la, see Golhord
Goldie, Amelia, v, 280; Thos., v, 280
Golding, Chris., ii, 366
Gold Oak Copse (Pamber), iv, 433
Goldryngs Grove (E. Wellow), iv, 535
Goldsmid, Sir Fran., iv, 516; Sir Isaac L., iv, 506, 516; Sir Julian, iv, 516

Goldsmith [Aurifaber], Alice, iii, 263 ; Hen., iii, 29 ; John, ii, 77 ; iii, 438 ; v, 231 ; Mathias, v, 248 ; Rich., v, 145 *n* ; Will., iii, 263

Goldsmiths' trade, v, 459

Goldston, Joan, iv, 339 ; Rich., iv, 339 ; Thos., iv, 339

Goldstrete, Rich. de, v, 44

Goldwyer [Goldwyre], Edw., iv, 363 ; Mary, v, 95 *n* ; Sarah, iv, 363 ; Will., iv, 619 ; v, 95, 100

Goleigh, man. (Priors Dean), iv, 436

Goleigh Bottom (Priors Dean), iv, 436

Golhord (Amport), iv, 337, 337 *n*, 338, 342, 343

Golhord, de, John, iv, 343 ; Rich., iv, 343

Gollard Copse (Amport), iv, 337, 343

Gollard Farm (Amport), iv, 337, 343

Gollegh, Golley, Golleys, see Goleigh

Gollop, see Gallup

Gollye, see Goleigh

Gomme, Sir Bern. de, iii, 190

Gomshall (Surr.), ii, 146, 148, 149 ; grange, ii, 147

Goncloude, John of, iv, 408

Gonsales, Balthasar, v, 453

Gonshill, Julia, iii, 445 ; Sir Will., iii, 445

Good, see Goodworth Clatford

Goodaker [Goodacker, Goodacre], Hugh, v, 277 ; Rev. Tim., iv, 488, 539

Goodall [Godale, Gondale], Frank, v, 521 ; John, ii, 182 ; Will., iii, 460

Goodbeat, see Godbiete

Goode [Goude], John, v, 481 ; Will., iv, 96 ; fam., iv, 354

Goodenough, Geo. T., v, 163 ; Susannah, v, 163 ; —, v, 220 ; fam., v, 282

Goodfellow, John, v, 313

Goodman [Gudemane], Rob., v, 243 ; Thos., ii, 260

Goodrich, Eliz., iii, 314 ; Rich., v, 132

Goodwin [Goodwyn, Goodwyne], Ant., iv, 622 *n* ; John, iii, 99 ; Thos., iii, 443 ; Mrs., v, 271 ; —, v, 516 ; see also Godwin

Goodworth Clatford, iv, 360, 363, 403-5, 408, 411 ; adv., iv, 405 ; char., iv, 405 ; ch., iv, 404 ; man., ii, 137 ; iv, 403, 411 *n*, 412 ; Nonconf., iv, 405 ; pop., v, 439 ; sch., ii, 399 ; iv, 405

Goodwyn, Goodwyne, see Godwin and Goodwin

Goodyer [Goudyer], Barth., ii, 483 ; Edw., iv, 72 ; Jas., iv, 73 ; John, iii, 121 ; iv, 73 ; Martha, iv, 73 ; Rob., iii, 438

Goodyers Green (Stratfield Turgis), iv, 63

Goolde, see Gold

Gooreley, see Gorley

Goose Green Park (Binsted), ii, 490

Goosehill (King's Somborne), iv, 470

Goosemoor (Broughton), iv, 493

Gordleton (Hordle), v, 111

Gordon, Sir Hen., v, 280 ; Sir Hen. P., v, 280, 284 ; Sir Jas. W. G., v, 237, 280 ; Mary, Lady, v, 280 ; Mary C. J., v, 280

Gordon-Ives, Lt. Cecil M., iv, 70 ; Col. Gordon M., iv, 70

Gore, la, (Milton), see Gore Farm

Gore (South Damerham), iv, 587 *n*

Gore, la, (Upton), iv, 330 *n*

Gore [Goare, Gor] (le), Joan, iv, 499 ; John, v, 98 ; Lucy, v, 98 ; Mary, iv, 529 ; v, 98 ; Nich., iv, 528 ; Rich., iv, 499, 528 ; v, 486 ; Sarah A., iii, 432 ; Thos., iii, 432 ; Will., iv, 528 *n*

Gore Farm (Milton), v, 124

Gorehole (King's Somborne), iv, 470

Gorfen, Alice, iii, 270 ; Marg., iv, 159 ; Will., iii, 269, 270, 271 ; iv, 159

Gorges, Edw., Ld., v, 111, 113, 117, 117 *n*

Gorges (de), Agnes, v, 183 *n* ; Barth., v, 183, 275 ; Eleanor, v, 183, 275 ; Eliz., v, 183 ; Ellen [Elena], v, 172, 182, 231 ; John, ii, 214 ; v, 183, 277 ; (Sir) Ralph, v, 164 *n*, 172, 182, 183, 184, 191, 231, 246, 273, 275, 277 ; Sir Randolf, v, 183 ; (Sir) Theobald, v, 183, 191 ; (Sir) Thos., v, 111, 116, 117, 123, 183 ; fam., v, 181

Goring, Ld., v, 338

Goring, Anne, iv, 268 *n*, 518 ; Constance, iv, 264, 268 ; Eleanor, iv, 268 *n* ; Col. Geo., iii, 189 ; Jane, iv, 268 *n* ; John, iii, 124 ; iv, 268, 518 ; Sybil, iv, 268 *n* ; Will., iv, 268

Gorley, man. (Fordingbridge), ii, 145, 159, 172 ; iv, 572

Gorley, North (Hyde), iv, 568

Gorley, South (Ibsley), iv, 579, 580

Gormanston, Chris. Preston, vsct., iv, 278 ; Kath. Preston, vsctss., iv, 278

Gorrell, Great, Little, (Hartley Wespall), iv, 42

Gorrell Grove (Hartley Wespall), iv, 42

Gort, vsctsses., v, 198 *n* ; Caroline H., v, 202 ; Eliz. M., v, 201

Gosberg, see Gosport

Goselane (Overton), iv, 211

Gosling [Gosselyn], Eliz., iii, 167, 168 ; John, v, 482 ; Phil., v, 520, 523, 536 ; Thos., iii, 167, 168

Gosmer, Sir Rich., iv, 249

Gosport, iii, 173, 202-8 ; v, 350, 356, 365, 379, 382, 383, 384, 388, 400, 409, 429, 430, 431, 434 ; chap., iii, 207 ; char., iii, 207 ; ch., iii, 207 ; Nonconf., iii, 207 ; pop., v, 441 ; printing, v, 461 ; racing, v, 543 ; Rom. Caths., iii, 207 ; schs., ii, 388, 395 ; iii, 208

Gosport and Fareham beagles, v, 542

Gosselyn, see Gosling

Goston, Fran., iv, 514 *n*

Gostwick, Joan, iv, 570 *n* ; John, iv, 570 *n* ; v, 326

Gother [Goter], Andr., iii, 459 ; v, 239 ; Anne, v, 239 ; Thos., v, 231, 285 *n*

Gotten [Gotton] (Chale), v, 237, 238

Gotton, fam., see Goditon

Goudale, see Goodall

Goudbeyete, see Godbiete

Goude, see Goode

Goudge, Rob., iv, 190

Goudyer, see Goodyer

Gough, Barbara, Lady, iv, 75 ; Sir Hen., iv, 75 ; Mary, iv, 205

Gough-Calthorpe, Sir Aug. C., iv, 76 ; Hen., iv, 75 ; Somerset J., iv, 76 ; v, 190

Goulde, see Gold

Goulderech, Will., iv, 365

Gounter, see Gunter

Gourlay, Hen., iv, 180

Gournay, see Gurney

Gower, Jas., v, 517

Gozelin, iii, 68 ; iv, 536 *n*, 598

Grace, Edw., iv, 384 ; v, 72, 75, 80 ; Kath., v, 72 ; Martha, v, 72 ; Rich., iv, 437

Graeme, Chas., v, 516 ; W. T., v, 516 ; —, v, 545

Graffthornes (Faccombe), iv, 314

Grafton, dk. of, v, 531, 555

Grafton, —, iii, 442

Graham, Sir Bellingham, v, 515, 524 ; Mary, iii, 251 ; Rev. M. A. C., v, 79 ; (Sir) Reg., v, 532, 570, 573 ; Rob., iii, 379, 381 ; Thos., iv, 276 ; fam., arms. iii, 379

Grain, prices of, v, 493, 495, 496, 497, 503

Graiwella, see Greywell

Granborough (Christchurch), v, 85, 95 *n*

Grandfathers (Broughton), iv, 496

Grandison, Ld., v, 339, 340

Grandisson, John, bp. of Exeter, ii, 268

Grandmesnil, Hugh de, iv, 380

Grange, the (Aldershot), iv, 2

Grange, the (Farnborough), iv, 15

Grange, the (Hurstbourne Priors), iv, 288

Grange, the, man. (Northington), iii, 394, 395 ; iv, 196

Grange, Harry, v, 532

Grange Lakes (Alresford), v, 564

Grange Park (Swarraton), iv, 195

Granger, iv, 49

Granges, Isabel de, v, 113

Granite Fort (Sandown), v, 157

Grant, Alex., iv, 580 ; Joan, iv, 94 ; John, iv, 94 ; v, 517 ; Nich., v, 474 ; Rich., iv, 565 *n* ; Sarah, iv, 580 ; Will., iv, 565 *n*

Grantham, Thos., iii, 117

Granville, Rob. Carteret, earl, iv, 186

Granville, Capt. Bern., iv, 430

Gras, le, Agnes, iv, 382 ; Dionysia, iv, 627 ; John, iv, 627 ; Mabel, iii, 290, 291 ; Nich., iv, 89 ; Rob., iii, 290, 291 ; Walt., iv, 382

Grasshoppers, i, 110

Grately, i, 320 ; iv, 333, 369-71, 385, 533 *n* ; adv., iv, 371 ; char., iv, 371 ; ch., iv, 370 ; man., iv, 206, 369, 370 ; Nonconf., iv, 371 ; pop., v, 438 ; sch., ii, 399 ; iv, 371

Grately Drove (Grately), iv, 369

Grately Woods (Grately), iv, 369

Graunge Haye (Steventon), iv, 171

Grave, la, (Christchurch), v, 85

Gravelinges Forest (Wilts.), ii, 415

Gravy, John, ii, 158

Gray, see Grey

Grayshott (Headley), ii, 491 ; iii, 51

Greatbridge (Romsey), iv, 452 ; v, 454 *n*

Greatford, man., ii, 126

Greatham, ii, 471, 491, 506 ; iii, 26, 82 ; adv., ii, 508 ; ch., ii, 508 ; mans., ii, 506 ; pop., v, 444 ; sch., ii, 399, 508

Greatham Moor, ii, 506

Great Lodge Park (Binsted), ii, 490

Great Marshall's Farm (Sherfield), iv, 103

Greaves, Edw., iv, 423 ; (Rev.) John, iv, 423 ; Sarah, ii, 483 ; iv, 71

Green [Greene, Grene], Constance, iv, 370, ; Geo., v, 95 *n* ; (Sir) Hen., iv, 206 *n*, 369, 370, 371 ; H. G., v, 563 ; Isabel, iv, 370 ; Jacob, iv, 149 ; John, ii, 212, 293, 366 ; iii, 344, 387 ; iv, 134, 370 ; v, 484 ; Leonard, iv, 406 ;

Green (*cont.*)
Marcellus, iv, 276; Marg., iv, 370; Maud, Lady, iv, 206, 369; Ralph, iv, 206 *n*, 369; Rich., iv, 365; Rob., iv, 277; Susanna, iii, 14; Thos., iii, 144, 167; iv, 423; fam., iv, 366
Greenes, man. (Heckfield), iv, 46
Greenfield [Grenefeld, Grenefield], John, iii, 436; iv, 455, 460; Thos., iv, 460
Greenham's Hill (Aldershot), iv, 2
Greenhouse Farm (Fordingbridge), iv, 568
Greenhurst, Ralph, ii, 256
Greenleyd (Niton), v, 187
Green Park (Itchel), iv, 6
Greenway, Marg., ii, 198
Greenwood, Col., v, 517
Greetanlea, *see* Grately
Gregories Farm (Shalden), iv, 101
Gregory IX, ii, 138, 141, 142, 173, 176
Gregory, John, ii, 158; Marg., iv, 100; Will., iv, 100, 103, 160
Greig, Capt., v, 575; —, v, 393
Greinville, *see* Grenville
Gremne, v, 117
Grene, *see* Green
Grenefeld, Grenefield, *see* Greenfield
Grene Mill Bridge (Yateley), iv, 21
Grenewayscrosse (S. Damerham), iv, 586
Grenfell, Imber & Co., v, 489 *n*
Grenville [Greinville, Grenvyle] (de), Eustace, iii, 116; Joan, iii, 116; Sir John, ii, 519; Marg., ii, 519; Rich. T. N. B. C., iii, 307; Rich. P. T. N. B. C., iv, 191; fam., arms, iii, 308
Grestein Abbey (France), iv, 394, 395, 396, 399
Gretcham (Brockenhurst), iv, 628
Grettelee, *see* Grately
Grettenhamdune (Lyndhurst), iv, 631
Gretton, F., v, 548, 553; J., v, 548
Greville [Greyville], (de), Ad., iv, 495; Anne, iv, 562, 586, 601; Dodington, iv, 601; Fran., iv, 562, 597; Fulk, iv, 562; v, 277; Geoff., iv, 426, 427; Maud, iv, 426; Rob., iv, 562
Grey, Joan, Lady, iv, 238; Ld., iv, 36; v, 335; Reg., Ld., v, 238
Grey [Gray] (de), Cath., iv, 75 *n*; Edw., ii, 475; v, 247; Eliz., iv, 35 *n*, 64, 175; v, 247; (Sir) Hen., ii, 475, 476, 484; iii, 383; iv, 175, 636; Jer., iv, 627, 628; Joan, ii, 475; iii, 375; iv, 347, 348; (Sir) John, ii, 475, 476; iii, 383, 443; iv, 174, 175, 176, 347, 348, 595, 627, 628; Sir Leonard, iv, 35 *n*, 64; Lora, iv, 62; Lucy, iv, 174; Marg. (Lady), iii, 383; iv, 175; Rich., ii, 475, 476; iii, 383; iv, 175; Rob., iv, 225; (Sir) Thos., iii, 153; iv, 36, 608; v, 318; fam., arms, ii, 476; iii, 383
Grey Friars, *see* Franciscans
Greyshank, Ralph, iv, 302
Greyshott, *see* Grayshott
Greyville, *see* Greville
Greywell, iv, 66, 67, 76-9, 87, 97, 178; v, 454; adv., iv, 79; char., iv, 79; ch., iv, 78; fishery, iv, 78; man., iv, 77; mill, iv, 76; Nonconf., iv, 76; pop., v, 443; sch., ii, 399
Greywell Hill beagles, v, 543
Greywell Hill House (Greywell), iv, 76
Griar, John, ii, 91

Grierson, H. K., iii, 484; v, 575
Griffin, Sir Edw., iv, 153, 154; Frances, Lady, iv, 153, 154; John, iii, 250; Rog., v, 113; Will., v, 150
Griffin Inn (Godshill), v, 170
Griffith [Griffithe, Griffiths] (Sir), John, ii, 367; iv, 256; v, 99; Rog., iii, 171; Capt. Thos., v, 526 *n*; Will., ii, 522
Grigg's Green (Bramshott), ii, 491
Grimbald, St., abbot of Newminster, ii, 5, 116, 121
Grimespitte (Carisbrooke), v, 222
Grimsditch (Upton), iv, 330 *n*, 596
Grimstead, man. (Wilts.), iv, 527, 542, 543
Grimstead [Grimsted, Grinstead, Grymstead] (de), Ad., iv, 542; Alice, iv, 527, 542; Andr., iii, 290; v, 542; Eleanor, iii, 290; iv, 542; John, iii, 290; iv, 527, 542, 543, 627; v, 116, 117, 118; Marg., v, 124; Margery, iv, 627; v, 116; Matth., v, 91 *n*; Maud, iv, 627; Pet., iv, 627; Rich., iv, 542; Thos., iv, 627; Walt., iv, 542; Will., iv, 542
Grimston, Will., v, 207, 208 *n*
Grindham, John, iv, 550
Grinstead, *see* Grimstead
Grobham, Geo., iv, 367; John, iv, 447; (Sir) Rich., iv, 447
Grocyn, ii, 294
Grose, Edw., v, 190, 193; (Sir) Nash, v, 190, 193
Grose-Smith, Edw., v, 190; Henley, v, 190
Grotto Copse (Crux Easton), iv, 313
Grouchy, — de, v, 489
Grove, man. (Brading), v, 163
Grove, the, (Eversley), iv, 33
Grove (atte), Ad., iv, 352; Anne, iv, 570; Christiana, iv, 409, 410; Hugh, iv, 562, 570; Joan, iv, 352; John, iv, 352, 409, 570; v, 388; Rob., iv, 570; v, 119; Thos., iv, 23 *n*; Will., iv, 570; —, v, 571
Grovecorris Coppes (Abbotts Ann), iv, 334
Grove Farm (Christchurch), v, 85
Grovemede (Stockbridge), iv, 483
Grove Place (Nursling), iii, 436; iv, 459
Grubbe, Miss, v, 280
Grue, Gerard la, iii, 346
Grunmill, Pet. de, ii, 150
Gryllodea, i, 112
Gryme, John, iii, 507; Rich., iii, 507
Grymstead, *see* Grimstead
Guard, H., ii, 249
Gudemane, *see* Godman and Goodman
Gudeworth, *see* Goodworth Clatford
Gudgeon, —, v, 456
Gueda [Gytha], ctss., iv, 525
Guérin, Maynard, iv, 361
Guidott [Guidotti], Ant., iii, 374; iv, 83; v, 484; Fran., iv, 648; Joan, iv, 648; Patience, iv, 444; Will., iii, 373; iv, 258, 444; (Sir) Will. W., iii, 373; iv, 83, 258
Guildford (Surr.), ii, 137; friary, iv, 265
Guildford [Gildeford] (de), Clementia, ii, 132; Edw., iii, 436; Hen., iii, 253
Guilford, earls of, iv, 14; Fran. North, ii, 99; Fran. North, Ld., ii, 339
Gulston, Dr., ii, 200
Gundeville (de), Hen., v, 99, 100 *n*; Hugh, v, 23 *n*; Rob., v, 99; Will., v, 99
Gundrey, John, v, 96

Gun Hill (Aldershot), iv, 2
Gunildcrofte (Beaulieu), iv, 650, 651
Gunner, E. J., v, 200
Gunter, ii, 159
Gunter [Gounter], Arth., iii, 150; v, 243; (Sir) Geo., iii, 150; v, 243; Jane, v, 243; John, iv, 316; v, 243; Will., iii, 150, 528; Col., v, 469
Gunters (Christchurch), v, 85
Gunville (Carisbrooke), v, 221, 222, 235
Gunwyn, Jas., ii, 167, 168
Gurdon (Selborne), *see* Selborne Makerel
Gurdon [Gurdun] (de), (Sir) Ad., ii, 176, 177, 473, 493, 494, 519; iii, 6, 7, 8, 15, 16, 23, 30, 31, 370; iv, 27; v, 305, 311; Ameria, iii, 6, 7, 30; Constance, ii, 176; iii, 7, 15; Joan, iii, 519; iii, 7, 31
Gurnard (Northwood), v, 268, 351; Rom. rem., i, 317
Gurnard, Rich., iii, 353
Gurnard [Gurnet] Bay, i, 385; v, 268
Gurney [Gournay, Gurnay], Eliz., iv, 536, 589; Hawise, iv, 82; John, iv, 536, 589; Rich., iv, 98; Rob., iv, 492, 536, 589; fam., iv, 537
Gurowski, count D. B., iii, 347
Gussage (Dors.), ii, 203, 204
Guthrum, v, 295
Gutnar Lake (Hayling), v, 469
Guttonspool (Bentley), iv, 27
Guy, the clerk, v, 291; prior of Southwick, ii, 168; iv, 232 *n*
Guy [Guye, Gy], Jas., iii, 372; v, 112; Rob., iv, 548; Will., ii, 205
Guydintill (Brockenhurst), iv, 626
Guyet's Copse (Stratfield Turgis), iv, 63
Guyor, Will., v, 173 *n*
Gwitton, Eliz., iv, 646
Gwyllyn, John, iv, 325
Gwynne [Gwyn, Gwynn], Fran., v, 87; Nell, ii, 95; Nich., prior of Andover, ii, 221; Will., iv, 611
Gy, *see* Guy
Gyan, Thos., ii, 113
Gyffard, Gyfford, *see* Gifford
Gylbert, *see* Gilbert
Gyles, *see* Giles
Gylinges, John, iv, 483; Marg., iv, 483
Gyllporteseys (Calbourne), v, 218
Gymbiles (Faccombe), iv, 314
Gymming [Gimmings, Gymminges] (de), Avice, 273; John, iii, 324; v, 95, 231, 273; Nich., iii, 324
Gylbert, *see* Gilbert
Gysardston (Wilts.), ii, 172
Gytha, *see* Gueda

Haberigge, *see* Harbridge
Haberley, Will., iii, 184
Habin, —, v, 527
Hacche, Hach, *see* Hatch
Hachangre, *see* Oakhanger
Hachard, Thos., iv, 533
Hacheborne, ii, 126
Hachhouse Lane (Ecchinswell), iv, 250
Hacket, *see* Haket
Hackwood [Hackwood Park] (Basing), iv, 115, 122, 179; race-course, v, 543
Hackwood Field (Eastrop), iv, 147, 148
Hackwood House (Basing), iv, 115, 122
Hacle, *see* Oakley

Haddington, man., ii, 114
Haden, Sir Fran. S., iii, 45
Hadewis, Hadewise, see Avice
Hadnall, Anne, iv, 104; Marg., iv,
107; Mary, iv, 107; Steph., iv,
104, 107
Haedde, bp. of Winchester, ii, 2, 101
Hafunt, see Havant
Hagen, Miss, iii, 55; Mrs., iv, 616
Hagenhull (Kingsclere), iv, 250
Haget, see Haket
Hagheman [Haweman], de, Alan,
v, 33, 179; Amice, iv, 33; John,
iv, 33, 34, 41; Nich., iv, 33, 35,
41, 179
Haghyate (Wootton St. Laurence),
iv, 239
Haigh, Eliza, v, 73
Hailinges, see Hayling Island
Haines, see Haynes
Haiward's (Hartley Wintney), iv, 79
Hakepanne, Maud, iv, 537
Haket [Hacket, Haget], Alice, v,
183; Joan, iii, 95; v, 161, 183;
John, v, 142 n, 143, 146, 160, 162,
166 n, 183, 207 n, 216; Julia, iii,
241; Nichola, v, 161, 216; Rob.,
iv, 329; Thos., v, 144, 146 n,
161, 215, 216; Walt., v, 161;
Will., iii, 241
Hakker, John, iv, 349
Hakluyt, Edm., iv, 512; Emma,
iv, 512
Hala, see Hall
Haldershutt, see Aldershot
Haldewey (Faccombe), iv, 314
Haldley, man. (Carisbrooke), v, 200,
231
Hale, ii, 172; iv, 519 n, 559, 560,
561, 562, 563, 573, 577-8, 582,
601; adv., iv, 578; ch., iv, 578;
man., iv, 577; pop., v, 445;
sch., ii, 399
Hale, man. (Arreton), v, 143
Hale, North, man. (Arreton), see
Northale
Hale, fam., see Hall
Halefield (Steventon), iv, 171
Haleford, de la, John, iii, 435;
Marg., iii, 435
Hale Park (Hale), iv, 577
Hales, see Hayles
Hales Monastery, see Hayles Abbey
Halesowen Abbey (Shrops.), ii, 181;
Rich., abbot of, ii, 184
Half-Moon Common (Eling), iv, 546
Halfnakyd, iv, 411
Halinger, see Hayling Island
Halkangre, man., see Oakhanger
Hall (Deane), see Oakley Hall
Hall [Hala, Hale, Halle] (atte, de
la), Annora, v, 143; Edith, v, 143;
Eleanor, Lady, v, 118; Eliz., iv,
49; Frances, iv, 134; Geo., v,
537; Gerald, ii, 478; Hen., ii,
478, 479; v, 143; Hugh, iv,
519 n, 524; v, 304 n; Joan
(Lady), iv, 175; v, 118, 143;
(Sir) John, iii, 485; iv, 49, 134,
139, 175, 206, 212, 473, 512, 570,
604, 656, 657; v, 118, 126, 181;
John C., iv, 458; John M., v,
143; J. C. A., iii, 370, 375;
Kath., iv, 458; Rich., ii, 49, 119,
120, 122, 373; iv, 200; v, 143,
484, 517; Rob., iii, 163; iv, 206;
v, 143; Rob. W., iii, 325; Thos.,
ii, 378; iii, 370, 375, 377; iv,
132, 175, 177 n; v, 143; Will.,
iii, 485; iv, 134, 175, 512; v,
143; —, v, 523, 536
Hallcourt Wood (Shedfield), i, 345
Hallege, see Headley
Halliwell, Rob., iv, 183
Hall Lands (Eversley), iv, 33

Hallowell Close (Hartley Mauditt),
ii, 508
Hall Place (Bentworth), iv, 68
Hall Place (Deane), see Oakley Hall
Hall Place (Yateley), iv, 20
Hall Place Farm (Bentworth), see
Manor Farm
Halson, Chas., v, 140 n
Halstead [Halsted], Sir Laur., ii,
479; Nichola, iii, 192; Rob., iii,
192
Halton, Rev. Lancelot M., iv, 391
Haltreworth (Romsey), iv, 452
Halwarestoke, see Alverstoke
Ham, man. (Baughurst), iv, 276
Ham, man. (Wilts.), ii, 114
Ham, tithing (Baughurst), iv, 275
Hamanfunta, see Havant
Hamberga, Galicanus de, prior of
Ellingham, ii, 230
Hamble, par., see Hamble-le-Rice
Hamble, riv., i, 310, 376, 378, 380,
397; iii, 276, 288, 465; v, 294,
409, 455, 560, 564; oyster beds,
v, 468
Hambledon, i, 379; ii, 21, 38, 362;
iii, 63, 237, 238-44; v, 328 n,
331, 356, 545, 574; adv., iii, 243;
char., iii, 243; chs., iii, 242; fair,
v, 417; man., iii, 239; pop.,
v, 440; sch., ii, 399
Hambledon, hund., iii, 237
Hambledon hunt, v, 517, 523
Hambledon hunt steeplechases, v,
545
Hamble-le-Rice, i, 379; ii, 221, 222,
223; iii, 462, 469-71; v, 189 n,
364, 465; adv., iii, 471; char.,
iii, 471; ch., iii, 470; man., iii,
470; pop., v, 446; sch., ii, 399;
ship-building, v, 391, 458
Hamble Priory, ii, 41, 106, 221-3,
288, 522; iii, 470
Hamborough (Christchurch), v, 85,
95 n
Hamborough, A., v, 173; John, v,
182, 186
Hambridge [Hambrydge, Helm-
bridge], John, v, 142, 142 n;
Ursula, v, 142 n
Hambro, Perceval L., iv, 530
Hambrough, Edm., iv, 30
Hamdown (E. Wellow), iv, 535
Hame (Bentley), iv, 27
Hame [Hamme, Haym] (de), Alina,
iv, 302; John, iv, 302, 456 n;
Rich., iv, 265; Steph., iv, 418,
419
Hamelache (Freshwater), v, 240
Hameldon, see Hamilton
Hamelescroft (Barton Stacey), iv,
417
Hamelton, see Hamilton
Hamelyn, see Hamlyn
Hameseye, Great, Little, (Winch-
field), iv, 109
Ham Farm (Baughurst), iv, 276
Hamilton, dk. of, ii, 340; iv, 525;
v, 543
Hamilton [Hameldon, Hamelton]
(de), Archibald, iv, 562 n; Capt.
Edw., v, 397; Eliz., iv, 562;
Hen., ii, 161, 163; John, ii, 209;
John H., iv, 602; Sibella, v,
156; Will., ii, 146; iii, 334; Rev.
Will. F. T., iv, 18
Hamley, ii, 205
Hamlyn [Hamelyn], Agnes, iv,
605; Egidia, iv, 148; Eliz., iv,
39; John, iv, 605
Hamlyn-Fane, Eveline H., v, 130
Hamme, fam., see Hame
Hamme Albemarle, man., v, 95,
96
Hammen, John, iv, 485

Hammer Iron Pond (Bramshott),
ii, 491
Hammer Vale [Hammer] (Bramshott), ii, 491, 496; ironworks,
ii, 491; v, 464
Hammes, man., v, 95, 96
Hammes, the, (Eversley), iv, 33
Hammond, Agnes, iv, 460; Ann,
ii, 523; Chas. H., iii, 536; Charlotte, ii, 523; Eliz., ii, 523; John,
ii, 304, 523; iii, 436; iv, 460;
v, 563; Marg., ii, 523; Col. Rob.,
v, 224, 347, 350; Will., ii, 523;
see also Hamond
Hammond's Farm (West Worcld-
ham), ii, 522
Hamond [Hamon, Haymond], Sir
Andr. S., iv, 618; Eliz., ii, 485;
Eliz. A., v, 245; Sir Graham E.,
v, 161, 208, 245; Maria, ii, 67;
Rich., iv, 516; Thos., ii, 485;
see also Hammond
Hamond-Graeme, Sir Graham E.
W. G., v, 161, 208
Hampage Wood (Avington), iii, 307
Hampden, Barbara, iv, 13; John,
iv, 395 n
Hampreston (Dors.), ii, 159; iv,
437 n
Hampshire County Cricket Club,
v, 575
Hampshire Cricket Ground Co., v,
575
Hampshire Cross (South Tidworth),
iv, 391
Hampshire Hogs, v, 576
Hampshire Hunt, v, 514, 517, 546
Hampshire Hunt Shire Horse
Society, v, 519
Hampshire regiments, v, 357
Hampshire Rovers, v, 576
Hampstead, Hampstede, man.
(Shalfleet), see Hamstead
Hampstead Marshall, man. (Berks.),
iv, 52, 198, 474
Hampteworth, man., iv, 481 n
Hampton, v, 295
Hampton [Hamton] (de), Anne, iv,
140; Denise, iv, 535; Eliz., iii,
450; iv, 83; Fulk, ii, 114; Geo.,
iii, 455, 458; Joan, iv, 83; John,
ii, 443; iii, 250, 251, 400, 448;
iv, 83, 427, 450; Julia, iv, 83;
Mabel, iv, 535; Phil., iv, 595;
Ralph, iv, 558; Steph., iv, 535;
Thos., iii, 70, 448, 450; iv, 83;
Will., iv, 535, 539, 549; fam.,
arms, iii, 448
Hamstead, man. (Shalfleet), ii, 152;
v, 272, 274; grange, ii, 139
Hamuldon, see Hambledon
Hanbury, Fran., iv, 620; John, iii,
247; Thos., iii, 114, 115, 247,
249; Will., ii, 97; fam., arms,
iii, 247
Hancock, Thos., iii, 184, 530; v,
87; Will., v, 383
Handforte, Will., iv, 325
Handley Coppes (Abbotts Ann), iv,
334
Handlo, de, John, iv, 377, 378,
379; Maud, iv, 377, 379
Hangate (Up Nately), iv, 176
Hanger [Hangre] (Eling), iv, 550
Hanger (Selborne), iii, 4
Hanger, atte, John, iv, 656, 658 n;
Rich., iv, 656
Hangere, le, (Penton Mewsey), iv,
381, 382 n
Hangers Close (Kimpton), iv, 372
Hangleton (de), Joan, iii, 95;
Ralph, iii, 95; Rich., iii, 95, 104
Hangre wood (Stratfieldsaye), iv, 60
Hanitune, see Hannington
Hankford, Sir Will., iii, 163

Hankyn, Rob., v, 48
Hannan, Marg., iv, 562 ; Sir Thos.,
 iv, 562
Hannay, Rev. Jas., iv, 442 ; Will.
 de, iii, 16
Hanneby, Hugh de, v, 223
Hannerford, John, iv, 589
Hanning-Lee, Col. Edw., iii, 39
Hannington, iv, 223, 229-30 ; adv.,
 iv, 230 ; ch., iv, 229 ; man., ii,
 114, 168 ; iv, 229, 420 ; Nonconf.,
 iv, 230 ; pop., v, 441 ; sch., ii, 399
Hannington (Upton Gray), ii, 108
Hannington, Reg., iv, 144
Hannington Lancelevy, man.
 (Kingsclere), iv, 245 n, 257, 258,
 259
Hansard, H. L., iv, 458 ; Jas., iii,
 317
Hanson, Cath., iv, 356 ; John, iv,
 357
Hanstede, Rob. de, v, 246, 247
Hantacheneselе (Winchester), v, 2
Hanton, ii, 114
Hanydon (Wilts.), ii, 137
Hanyton, de, Nich., iii, 328, 329 ;
 iv, 19 ; Will., iv, 167
Haplomi, i, 200
Hapsa, man, see Apse
Harangod [Harengod, Heryngawd]
 (de), Eleanor, iv, 330, 513 ; Mar-
 gery, iv, 450 ; Ralph, iv, 533 n ;
 Steph., iv, 450 ; Thos., iv, 330,
 450, 513 ; (Sir) Will., iv, 450
Harbert, man., ii, 168
Harbert, fam., see Herbert
Harbridge, iv, 361, 601, 603,
 604-6 ; v, 82 ; adv., iv, 606 ;
 char., iv, 606 ; ch., iv, 606 ;
 mans., iv, 630 ; pop., v, 445 ;
 sch., ii, 399
Harcourt, Sim., vsct., ii, 381
Harcourt [Harecourt] (de), Anne,
 iv, 199 ; A. V., v, 190 ; Chris., iv,
 521 ; Eliz., Lady, iv, 635 ; Col.
 Fran. V., v, 193 ; Joan, iv, 521 ;
 John, iv, 360 ; Kath., v, 206 ;
 Kath. J. V., Lady, v, 193 ;
 Miles, iv, 521 ; Rob., iv, 521 ;
 Sim., v, 206 ; Sir Rich., iv, 199 ;
 Walt., iv, 521 ; Will., iii, 152
Hardeleghe, Hardelei (Brading), see
 Hardley
Hardicanute, see Harthacanut
Harding [Hardene] (de), Geo., iii,
 397 ; iv, 196 ; Joan, v, 230 ;
 John, v, 230 ; Rob., ii, 516 ; iv,
 567 ; Walt., ii, 214 ; Will., iv, 53 ;
 Will. W., iii, 399
Hardinge, Fran., iv, 484 ; Rich., ii,
 488 ; Rob., iv, 46 ; Thos., ii, 488
Hardingshute, man. (Brading), v,
 163, 191 n
Hardington (de), John, v, 159, 223
Hardley, man. (Brading), v, 162
Hardley, man. (Fawley), ii, 172 ;
 iii, 275, 294
Hardley, tithing (Bembridge), v,
 138
Hardway (Alverstoke), iii, 202
Hardwell (Berks.), i, 326
Hardwick, Phil., v, 225
Hardwin, Rob., iii, 506
Hardy (le), (Sir) Chas., v, 354, 395 ;
 Rich., v, 198 ; Thos., iv, 398 ;
 Capt., v, 400
Hardyngs Croft (Ashmansworth),
 iv, 274
Hardys, Matth., iv, 647
Hare, Anne, iv, 56 ; Hugh, iv, 278 ;
 Jas., iv, 56
Harebert (Burghclere), iv, 277
Harecourt, see Harcourt
Haredale (Romsey), iv, 452
Haregrove, see Hargreaves

Haremead (Kingsley), ii, 515
Harengod, see Harangod
Harewedon, see Harwedon
Harewell, John, bp. of Bath and
 Wells, iv, 74
Harewood Forest (Wherwell), i,
 322, 392 ; ii, 135, 412 ; iv, 400,
 403, 406, 411
Harford, Anne, ii, 501 ; Heritage,
 iii, 314
Hargreaves [Haregrove, Hargrove],
 Christine, iii, 435 ; Eliz., iv, 580 ;
 John, iv, 580 ; Reg. G., iv, 631 ;
 (Rev.) Thos., iii, 435 ; iv, 384
Hariford [Hariforde], iv, 544, 652
Haringey, see Hayling Island
Haring Woodes, see Longstock
 Harrington
Harland & Wolff, engineers, v, 461
Harley, John, iv, 85 ; Mark, v,
 231 ; (Sir) Rob., iv, 85 n ; v, 342,
 355
Harleys Close (Liss), iv, 84
Harlyngdon, Will., iv, 10
Harmar, Lt.-Col. Chas., iv, 394 ;
 John, ii, 319, 320, 366, 375
Harmondsworth (Midd.), ii, 289,
 290 ; iv, 186
Harmony Hall, see Queenwood
 College
Harmood, Harry, iv, 441 ; Mary, iv,
 441
Harmsworth, Sir Harold, v, 84
Harmwoods (Heckfield), iv, 45
Harnham Hill (Wilts.), i, 383
Harnhill [Harnhull, Harnhulle] (de)
 (Sir), Hen., iii, 444 ; iv, 352, 382,
 392 ; Joan, Lady, iv, 382 ; Sir
 John, iv, 382 ; Marg., iv, 382 ;
 (Sir) Rob., ii, 16 ; iv, 382, 392,
 512 n
Harold I, v, 298
Harold II, iv, 52, 88, 90, 198, 385,
 391, 525, 531 ; v, 143, 163
Harold, Chas., iv, 476 ; Hen., ii,
 135 ; iv, 401 ; Isabel, ii, 135 ; iv,
 401 ; Rich., iv, 349
Harpedene, de, Joan, iv, 520 n ;
 Will., iv, 520 n
Harperstyle (Heckfield), iv, 45
Harpsfield, Nich., ii, 62, 271
Harpur, Walt., v, 145 n ; Will., v,
 145 n
Harrap, Gilb., iv, 27, 28
Harriers, v, 536
Harrington, Sir Jas., v, 345
Harris [Harryes, Harrys], Andr.,
 v, 486 ; Anne, iv, 495 ; C.
 E., iv, 100 ; David, v, 574 ;
 Dorothy, iv, 594 ; Edw., iv,
 495 ; Edw. J., v, 559 n ; (Sir)
 Fran., iv, 495, 496 ; Geo., iv,
 495, 496 ; Hen., ii, 239 ; iv, 173 ;
 Isabel, iv, 495 ; Jas., ii, 349 ;
 iii, 437 ; iv, 20, 656 ; v, 87, 95,
 97, 98, 108 ; Jas. E., iv, 611 ;
 v, 86, 95, 97, 98, 108, 224, 559 ;
 Jenny, iii, 353 ; John, ii, 325, 327,
 328, 366 ; iv, 495, 496, 656 n ; Sir
 J., iv, 101 ; Mich., iv, 77 ; Thos.,
 iii, 131 ; iv, 279 ; Ursula, iv, 495 ;
 Will., ii, 338, 339, 366 ; iv, 75 n ;
 Capt., v, 354 ; —, iv, 172 n, 173 ;
 v, 19, 561 ; fam., iv, 658 ; v, 460
Harrison [Haryson], Anne, iii, 374 ;
 Constance, iv, 425 ; Emma, iv,
 359 ; Geo., iv, 632 ; John, ii, 447 ;
 iii, 374 ; v, 484 ; Sir Rich., iii,
 374 ; Richardson, iii, 379 ; Thos.,
 iv, 425 ; v, 342 ; Will., ii, 197,
 441 ; v, 513 ; Rev. W. D., iii,
 488 ; Maj., v, 351 ; —, ii, 508 ;
 fam., iv, 57
Harrow Field (Overton), iv, 211
Harrow Way, iv, 243 n, 288, 300

Harryes, Harrys, see Harris
Harsnet, Hugh, iv, 647 ; Sarah, iv,
 647
Hart, riv., iv, 74
Hart [Harte], John, iii, 387 ; Thos.,
 iii, 312 ; see also Heart
Harte (Burghclere), iv, 277
Hartford Bridge (Elvetham), iv,
 74, 528 ; v, 428
Hartfordbridge flats, iv, 21
Harthacanut, v, 56, 298
Hartigan, Frank, v, 545, 546
Hartley, Hen. R., ii, 385
Hartley Hanger (Hartley Mauditt),
 ii, 508
Hartley House (Hartley Wespall),
 iv, 42
Hartley Mauditt, ii, 471, 508-11,
 521, 523 ; iv, 102 ; adv., ii, 511 ;
 ch., ii, 510 ; mans., ii, 508 ; pop.,
 v, 437 ; sch., ii, 399, 511
Hartley Park (Hartley Mauditt),
 ii, 508
Hartley Row (Hartley Wintney),
 iv, 79, 428
Hartley University College (Southampton), ii, 385, 386, 390 ; iii,
 492, 535
Hartley Wespall, iv, 31, 42-4, 57,
 63, 64, 65, 99, 104 ; adv., iv, 44 ;
 char., iv, 44 ; ch., iv, 43 ; fisheries,
 iv, 42, 43 ; man., iv, 42 ; mill, iv,
 43 ; pop., v, 440 ; sch., ii, 399
Hartley Wintney, iv, 45, 51, 66, 67,
 76, 79-81, 109, 110, 114 ; adv.,
 iv, 81 ; ch., iv, 79, 80 ; fairs, iv,
 79, 80 ; man., iv, 79 ; v, 418 ;
 pop., v, 444 ; priory, see Wintney
 Priory ; sch., ii, 399 ; iv, 81
Hartley Wood (Hartley Mauditt),
 ii, 510, 511
Hartley Wood Common, iv, 42
Hartlip (Kent), i, 302
Harts (Godshill), v, 170
Hartwedon, Harvedon, see Harwedon
Harvest, Rev. Will., iii, 432
Harvey [Harvy], Agnes, ii, 130 ;
 Alex., v, 229 ; Anne, iii, 101 ;
 Edw. N., iv, 656, 658 ; Hen., v,
 522 ; John, ii, 301 ; v, 171, 227,
 229, 535 ; John G., v, 172, 173,
 535 ; Mary N., v, 264 ; Ralph,
 v, 229 ; Rich., v, 142 ; Thos., v,
 229 ; T. W., v, 528 ; Will., v,
 490 ; Will. H., iv, 502 ; Capt., v,
 522 ; Mrs., v, 157, 197, 205 ; see
 also Hervey
Harward, Rich., v, 65 ; Rob., iii,
 457, 461 ; Walt., iv, 460 ; Will.,
 iv, 474 ; see also Harwood and
 Horwood
Harwedon [Harewedon, Hartwe-
 don, Harvedon], Rob., ii, 207,
 208, 213 ; iii, 324, 456, 457, 466 ;
 iv, 255, 493 ; Will., ii, 207, 208 ;
 iv, 493, 495
Harwell, see Wherwell
Harwich (Essex), v, 375
Harwood, John, iv, 206, 232 ; see
 also Harward and Horwood
Haryson, see Harrison
Hasard, see Hazard
Hasawlt Farm (King's Somborne),
 iv, 470
Hascombe, Will., v, 146 n
Haselber, John, iv, 570
Haseldune (Longstock), iv, 449
Haseley [Haselie], man. (Arreton),
 ii, 138, 139 ; v, 140, 141 n, 143
Haselholt (Hannington), iv, 229
Haselmangrave (Weston Patrick),
 iv, 109
Haselwood [Hasylwood], Will., iv,
 445 ; v, 27 n, 31

Hasker, Dorothy, iv, 143, 180 ; John, iv, 105, 143 ; Mary, iv, 105, 143 ; Thos., iv, 105, 143, 180 ; Mrs., iv, 232

Haskoll, Jas., v, 233

Haslar Bridge (Gosport), v, 400

Haslar Hospital (Gosport), iii, 202 ; v, 393

Hassell, John, iii, 112 ; Rich., iii, 112

Hassock (W. Tytherley), iv, 519

Hastings, mchnss. of, v, 118 ; mqss. of, v, 544, 556

Hastings (de), Anne, v, 127 ; Betty, iv, 647 ; Cath., iv, 110, 608 ; Sir Edw., iv, 624 ; Fran., iv, 608 ; v, 92 ; Geo., iv, 624 ; v, 92, 96 ; Harry, v, 96 ; Hen., iii, 419 ; iv, 608 ; v, 92, 127 ; Hugh, iii, 456 ; Isabel, iii, 456 ; iv, 457, 515 ; v, 228 ; (Sir) John, iii, 11, 23, 26, 227 ; iv, 110 ; v, 88, 486, 487 ; Laur., iii, 11, 17, 23, 26 ; iv, 387 ; Mary, iv, 624 ; Ralph, iv, 647 ; Rob., iv, 121 ; (Sir) Thos., iii, 456 ; v, 219, 405 ; Warren, iv, 542 ; (Sir) Will., ii, 518 ; iv, 460 ; Winifred, v, 219

Haswell, Hugh, iii, 314

Hasylwood, see Haselwood

Hatch (Cliddesden), iv, 113 n, 114, 145 ; adv., iv, 147 ; ch., iv, 147 ; man., iv, 146

Hatch [Hach], Hen. de, iv, 579 ; Will., iii, 240

Hatche (Basingstoke), iv, 129

Hatchet, Rob., iv, 380

Hatchett Pond (New Forest), v, 568

Hatch Warren Farm (Cliddesden), iv, 145

Hatchwoods (Odiham), iv, 87

Hatel, Julian, iv, 495

Hatfield, Isabel, v, 207 ; Steph., v, 207 ; Thos. de, ii, 207, 208

Hatherden (Andover), iv, 346, 352, 353 ; adv., iv, 356 ; ch., iv, 355 ; sch., iv, 357

Hatherden House (Hatherden), iv, 345

Hatherley, Ld., ii, 356

Hathewardcumbe (Carisbrooke), v, 222

Hatmaking, v, 457

Hattingley, de, Gilb., iii, 246 ; Giles, iv, 579 ; Will., iii, 261

Hatton, (Sir) Chris., ii, 318 ; iii, 178 ; iv, 509, 597, 598 ; Jack, iv, 16

Hauckle, Hauekleghe, see Hawkley

Hauford, de, Alice, iv, 64, 65 ; (Sir) Rob., iv, 64

Haughe, Sir Will., iii, 110

Haugton, see Houghton

Haukehurst, see Hawkhurst

Haukes Grove (Hartley Mauditt), ii, 508

Haule Grove (Deane), iv, 205

Haule Heath (Deane), iv, 205

Haule Place (Yateley), see Hall Place

Hausted, Rob. de, iii, 153

Hautclere, see Highclere

Hautoft, de, Maud, v, 45 ; Ralph, v, 45

Hauvill, Walt. de, v, 11.

Havant, i, 321, 378 ; ii, 98, 101, 102, 108 ; iii, 122-7, 142, 302 ; v, 318, 325, 328 n, 331, 356, 409, 426, 427, 434 ; adv., iii, 126 ; char., iii, 127 ; chs., iii, 125 ; inds., v, 474, 482, 484, 490 ; man., ii, 20, 109 ; iii, 123 ; pop., v, 441 ; sch., ii, 399

Havant harriers, v, 541

Havehunt, see Havant

Havenage, Rich. de, iv, 202

Havennes, man., see Northavon

Haven Street, man. (Newchurch), v, 181, 182 n

Havering, (Sir) Rich., iv, 458

Haverkam, Anna, iii, 241 ; Will., iii, 241

Haversham, Nich. de, iv, 542

Haveskle, see Hawkley

Havilland, de, Rev. Chas., iv, 331 ; Mrs., iv, 314

Havington, man., ii, 166

Havisia, see Avice

Havonte, see Havant

Haward, see Hayward

Hawclere, see Highclere

Haweman, see Hagheman

Hawes, Capt., v, 350

Hawke, Edw., Ld., v, 389, 390, 392, 394

Hawker, Edw., iii, 79 ; v, 146 ; Rev. Hen., iii, 81 ; Pet., iv, 402 ; v, 117 ; Pet. J. D., iv, 402 ; Pet. T. R., iv, 406 ; Miss, iii, 79

Hawkhurst (Kingsclere), iv, 250

Hawkin, C. W., ii, 390

Hawkins, Jas., ii, 482 ; Matth., ii, 482 ; Pet., iv, 36 ; (Sir) Rich., v, 97, 113 ; Thos., ii, 513 ; Will. J., ii, 482 ; Dr., iii, 285

Hawkley, iii, 3, 17, 23-4, 26 ; adv., iii, 24 ; ch., iii, 23 ; man., iii, 23 ; iv, 389 ; pop., v, 438 ; sch., ii, 399

Hawkley Hanger, iii, 23

Hawkshaw, Sir John, ii, 493 ; iv, 85 ; John C., ii, 493

Hawles, Agnes, v, 142 ; Harry. v, 149 ; John, iv, 588 ; v, 143 ; Rich., v, 142, 146 ; Rob., v, 143

Hawley, iv, 2, 20, 21, 22 ; adv., iv, 26 ; char., iv, 26 ; ch., iv, 25 ; pop., v, 443 ; sch., ii, 397, 399

Hawley, Dayrell, iv, 605 ; Sir Jos., v, 547

Hawley Common, iv, 21

Hawley Hill Woods (Hawley), iv, 21

Hawley House (Hawley), iv, 21

Hawley Pond (Hawley), iv, 21

Hawnby, ii, 376

Haworth, Capt. Martin, v, 517

Hawstead (Hursley), iii, 421

Hawtrey, Dr., ii, 361 ; see also Dawtrey

Hay, see Hayes

Haycrofte, Will., iii, 96

Haydock [Haydok], Alex., iv, 77 ; Alice, iv, 49 ; Christine, iv, 77 ; Eliz., iv, 96 ; Jas., iv, 99 ; John, iv, 77, 96 ; Marg., iv, 77 ; Thos., iv, 49, 77, 78, 570 n ; v, 327 n ; Will., iv, 77, 99

Hayes [Hay, Hays, Hey] (del, de la), Edw., iv, 200 ; Gerard, iv, 516 ; Sir John, iv, 105, 541 ; Kath., iv, 105 ; Penelope, iii, 99 ; Thos., iii, 99 ; see also Heighes

Haygarth, Emma, v, 213 ; Rev. H. W., v, 213

Hayles [Hales], Edw., iv, 496 ; Rob., ii, 194

Hayles Abbey (Glouc.), ii, 142

Haylie Close, Le [Hayley Copse] (Sutton Warblington), iv, 18

Hayling, North, iii, 129

Hayling, South, iii, 129

Hayling Island, ii, 26, 33, 36, 69, 106, 108, 216, 217, 218, 219, 238, 239 ; iii, 128, 129-34 ; v, 331, 431 ; adv., ii, 20, 21 ; iii, 133 ; char., iii, 134 ; chs., ii, 219 ; iii, 131 ; fisheries, v, 468 ; man., ii, 216 ; iii, 128, 129, 130 ; oyster beds, iii, 129 ; v, 468, 469 ;

Hayling Island (cont.) pop., v, 441 ; racing, v, 543 ; Rom. rem., i, 310, 345 ; v, 465 n ; salt trade, v, 469 ; sch., ii, 399, 405

Hayling Priory (Hayling Island), ii, 41, 216-19 ; iii, 129

Haym, see Hame

Haymond, see Hamond

Haymys, Robarde, ii, 57

Haynes [Haines, Hayne], Joan, iv, 522 ; Steph., iv, 407 n ; Will., v, 228

Hayneswood Coppice (Faccombe), iv, 314

Haynow, Avice, ii, 130

Hays, see Hayes

Hayter, —, v, 147

Haytokesle, ii, 154

Hayward [Haward], Sir Edw., v, 269 ; Hugh, v, 483 ; John, ii, 447, 512 ; Maud, iv, 507 n ; Rich., ii, 197 ; Thos., ii, 512 ; Will., ii, 513 ; iv, 507 n ; see also Heywood

Haywode, Haywood, fam., see Heywood

Haywood (S. Damerham), iv, 587

Hazard [Hasard], John, ii, 124, 301

Hazeley (Heckfield), iv, 45, 47

Hazeley Heath, iv, 35, 45, 47, 48, 79, 114 ; pop., v, 443

Head [Hede], Thos., ii, 48, 49, 50, 113, 114, 120, 129, 135, 151, 158, 162, 167, 171 ; iv, 123

Headbourne Worthy, ii, 4, 98, 108, 238, 239 ; iii, 303 ; iv, 398, 415, 416, 426-30, 480 n ; adv., iv, 430 ; char., iv, 430 ; ch., ii, 275 ; iv, 426, 428 ; mans., iv, 426 ; mill, iv, 256 ; pop., v, 448 ; sch., ii, 399

Headbourne Worthy House (Headbourne Worthy), iv, 426

Head Down (Niton), v, 187

Headley, ii, 93, 471, 491 ; iii, 37, 51-5 ; iv, 267 ; adv., iii, 55 ; char., iii, 55 ; ch., iii, 54 ; man., iii, 52 ; pop., v, 437 ; sch., ii, 399

Headley Common (Headley), iii, 52

Headley Common (Kingsclere), iv, 250, 266

Heald, Rev. C. W., v, 239

Heanfled, abbess of Wherwell, ii, 132, 137

Hearne [Hearn], Jane S., v, 291 ; Rich., iv, 140 ; v, 184 ; Will., v, 205

Hearst, see Hurst

Heart, Rob., iii, 240 ; see also Hart

Heath [Heathe], Allan B., iv, 314, 316 ; John, iii, 111 ; Will. H., iv, 316, 318

Heathcote, Col. Chas. G., iv, 546 ; Frances, Lady, iv, 537 ; Rev. Sam., iv, 537 ; Sir Thos., iii, 420 ; v, 544 ; (Sir) Will., ii, 355 ; iii, 407, 417, 420, 432, 447, 449, 533 ; iv, 413, 492, 537 ; v, 355, 489 ; Sir Will. P., iii, 420 ; fam., arms, iii, 289, 420

Heath Crofts (Bentworth), iv, 68

Heathdown, see Head Down

Heathe, see Heath

Heath End (Tadley), iv, 219, 221

Heather, John, iii, 115

Heatherwold (Burghclere), iv, 277

Heathfield Lodge (Christchurch), v, 84

Heath House (Petersfield), iii, 117, 118

Heath House Farm (Petersfield), iii, 117

Heathley, see Headley

Heathmanstreet Manor Farm (Nether Wallop), iv, 525, 530

Heaton, *see* Eaton
Heaven Hill Hedge (Faccombe), iv, 314
Hebbe, Thos., v, 28
Hebbere, le, Anne, v, 216 *n* ; John, v, 216 *n*
Hecfeld, *see* Heckfield
Heche, *see* Hatch
Heckfield [Hechingfeld], ii, 21 ; iii, 31, 32, 44-51, 65, 81, 114, 156 ; adv., iv, 50 ; ch., iv, 48 ; man., iv, 45 ; mills, iv, 47 ; pop., v, 443 ; Rom. Cath., iv, 51 ; sch., ii, 399
Heckfield Heath, iv, 44, 45
Heckfield Place (Heckfield), iv, 44, 46, 47, 51
Heckley, ii, 204, 205
Hedda, v, 50
Heddenfield (Freshwater), v, 241
Hede, *see* Head
Hedenesbury (Christchurch), v, 85
Hedenesham, v, 228
Hedge End, iii, 466 ; char., iii, 467 ; ch., iii, 466 ; schs., ii, 400 ; iii, 466
Hedger, Eliz., ii, 87
Hedges, Alf., v, 521 ; Tom, v, 518
Hedle, Hedleigh, Hedley, *see* Headley
Hedstokke (S. Damerham), iv, 587 *n*
Hedynton, *see* Edenton
Heenan, —, iv, 15
Hefedele, hund., iv, 66
Hegfeld, Heggefeld, Heghefeld, *see* Heckfield
Heghebrugge (S. Damerham), iv, 587 *n*
Heglingaig, *see* Hayling Island
Heigh [South Heigh] (Binstead), ii, 488
Heigham, *see* Higham
Heighes [Heyes] (de), Agnes, ii, 488 ; Edm., ii, 486, 487 ; iii, 10 ; Edw., ii, 521 ; Eliz., ii, 520 ; Hen., ii, 486, 487, 488, 489, 520, 521 ; iii, 10 ; Joan, ii, 486 ; John, ii, 488 ; iii, 10 ; Laur., iii, 10 ; Martha, Lady, ii, 487, 488 ; iii, 10 ; (Sir) Nich., ii, 486, 487, 488 ; iii, 10 ; Rich., ii, 488, 489 ; iii, 10 ; Sim., ii, 488, 516 ; iii, 10 ; —, ii, 490 ; fam., arms, ii, 487 ; *see also* Hayes
Heighlord, *see* Highlord
Heighton, man., ii, 121
Heilinciga, *see* Hayling Island
Heilman, Bruno, iv, 509
Heir, Nich. le, iv, 53
Hel, abbot of Quarr, ii, 139
Heldelie, *see* Haldley, man. (Carisbrooke)
Heldred, *see* Eldred
Helfelyngs (Bramley), iv, 141
Helgrove, Clement, v, 114
Helhouse, fam., iv, 45
Heling, *see* Hayling Island
Helle (Winchester), v, 6
Helle, Walt. de, v, 35
Hell House Grove (Heckfield), iv, 45
Hellier, *see* Helyar
Hellinglonde (Kimpton), iv, 372
Helmbridge, *see* Hambridge
Helmstan, ii, 4
Helps, Sir Arth., iii, 277 ; v, 491
Helvetham, *see* Elvetham
Helvetham, Isabel, iv, 100 ; John, iv, 100
Helwys, Isabel, iv, 100 ; John, iv, 100
Helyar [Hellier], Eliz., iv, 20 ; v, 107 ; John, iii, 139 ; iv, 20 ; v, 107 ; Thos., iv, 330
Helyon [Helyun] (de, le), Isabel, iii, 485 ; Joan, iv, 519 ; Rob., iii, 485 ; Thos., iii, 485 ; Walt., iii, 485 ; iv, 519, 610

Hemblesworth Giffard, man. (Dors.), iv, 388
Hemele, iv, 274, 288, 300, 301
Hemerford, Thos., ii, 81
Hemibranchii, i, 200
Hemiptera, i, 160
Hempton [Hewton], Rob. de, ii, 168
Hemreswel, hund., v, 209, 210
Henderson, Sir Edm. Y. W., v, 85 ; Rob., iv, 84
Hendley, *see* Henley
Heneage [Henneage], Eliz., iv, 69 ; v, 264 ; Mary, iv, 69, 70 ; Mich., v, 97 ; (Sir) Thos., iv, 584 ; v, 97
Henert, *see* Herriard
Hengham, —, v, 47
Hengistbury Head (Christchurch), v, 83, 84, 134, 135
Henham Wood (Long Sutton), iv, 18
Henley [Hendley], (Sir) Andr., iv, 34, 36, 40, 41 ; Ant., iii, 395, 396 ; iv, 154, 204 ; Barbara, iv, 374 ; Bertie, iv, 154 ; John, iii, 328, 396 ; iv, 71, 374 ; Jos., iii, 396 ; (Sir) Rob., iii, 395, 396 ; iv, 36, 41, 154, 196, 204, 374 ; Walt., ii, 304 ; fam., arms, iii, 395
Henneage, *see* Heneage
Hennessy, Geo., iv, 476, 478 ; Henchersley (Brockenhurst), iv, 626 ; ' George Pop,' v, 537 ; 'Old Pop,' v, 514, 537
Hennezé [Hennezal, Hennezee], de, Louis, v, 491 ; —, v, 491
Henn-Gennys, I, iii, 202
Hennodesferme (Church Oakley), iv, 224
Henry I, ii, 10, 108, 117, 137, 152, 160, 164, 168, 216, 222, 484 ; iv, 68, 72, 74, 75, 88, 97, 109, 176, 208 *n*, 426, 452, 542, 546, 594, 595, 596, 645 ; v, 273, 284, 288, 301, 360
Henry II, ii, 12, 160, 169, 216, 222, 229, 230, 416, 422, 423, ; iii, 42, 65, 130, 152, 158, 173 ; iv, 19, 71, 72, 73, 77, 84, 97, 99, 104, 150, 246, 251, 257, 268, 270, 296, 319, 323, 329, 330, 346, 347, 349, 366, 373, 431, 452, 475, 525, 532, 533, 569, 595, 626, 627, 656 ; v, 213, 270, 291, 303, 360, 415, 416
Henry III, ii, 14, 15, 17, 140, 141, 142, 146, 147, 164, 169, 176, 181, 189, 203, 209, 513 ; iii, 6, 59, 176, 186, 230, 476 ; iv, 7 *n*, 21 *n*, 32, 47, 60, 73, 77, 82, 93, 102, 113, 121, 130, 131, 138, 150, 176 *n*, 184, 196, 206, 211, 213, 246, 251, 253, 256, 257, 259, 260, 265, 270, 315, 319, 323, 329, 333, 335, 343, 346, 347, 353 *n*, 360, 389, 417 *n*, 423, 452, 456, 457, 469, 483, 487, 493, 498, 507, 517, 523, 525, 527, 531, 535, 549, 555, 569, 592, 607, 609, 616, 627, 628, 631, 643, 645 ; v, 241, 308, 310, 361, 362, 415, 416, 417, 418
Henry IV, ii, 168, 206, 210, 221, 231, 291, 509 ; iii, 176 ; iv, 91, 380, 385, 471, 484, 487, 504, ; v, 223, 257, 317
Henry V, ii, 219, 231 ; iii, 113, 130 ; iv, 324, 365, 484 ; v, 229, 232, 257, 266, 267, 317, 367, 368, 369
Henry VI, ii, 168, 230, 286, 288, 482 ; iv, 67, 72, 89, 91, 133, 304, 324, 347, 380, 385, 386, 419, 449, 471 *n*, 567, 573 ; v, 257, 263, 267, 286, 370, 416
Henry VII, ii, 48, 50, 55, 119, 174, 293, 436 ; iii, 174, 186 ; iv, 40, 72, 130, 151 *n*, 164, 169, 199, 348,

Henry VII, (*cont.*)
427, 484, 516, 526, 624, 645 ; v, 216, 257, 279, 321, 370, 372
Henry VIII, ii, 53, 55, 163, 167, 171, 202, 213, 215, 290, 302, 306, 369, 370, 426, 444, 450, 490, 513, 516, 517 ; iii, 109, 117, 143, 153, 227, 376 ; iv, 9, 22, 35, 46, 72, 75, 79, 80, 84 *n*, 85, 93, 108, 138, 161, 183, 186, 196, 208, 229, 243, 254, 255, 317, 324, 332, 334, 374, 411, 412, 419, 423, 427, 432, 433, 446, 447, 451, 452, 468, 476, 487, 488, 493, 495, 502, 512, 525, 527, 535, 552, 587, 591, 597, 632, 646 ; v, 171, 244, 257, 274, 275, 279, 285, 322, 371
Henry, prince, iv, 89
Henry, prince of Wales, v, 94, 95
Henry, iv, 146, 360 ; v, 163 *n* ; abbot of Quarr, ii, 139 ; bp. of Annadown, ii, 129 ; the weaver, v, 480 *n*
Henry, —, iii, 363
Henshaw, Benj., ii, 516 ; Florence, ii, 516
Henslowe, Ralph, iii, 145, 346 ; Thos., iii, 145, 247, 346
Hensting (Owslebury), iii, 332
Henton, *see* Hinton Ampner
Henton (de), John, iv, 418, 419 ; Rob., iii, 99 ; Rose, iii, 97
Hentune, *see* Hinton Ampner
Henville, Rev. C. B., iii, 144 ; Rev. Jas., iii, 170 ; Marg. L., iii, 101, 471
Hepkyn, Hen., iv, 289
Heraclius, patriarch of Jerusalem, v, 306
Herbert, iv, 396, 499 ; v, 181 ; the chamberlain, v, 2, 21 ; the forester, iv, 631
Herbert, Ld. Edw., ii, 337 ; Sidney Ld., v, 137
Herbert [Harbert], Arth., v, 386 ; Auberon, iv, 607 ; Edw., v, 140 *n*, 142, 145 *n*, 150 ; Geo. E. S. M., iv, 253, 278, 279, 294 ; Hen. G., iv, 253, 294 ; Hen. H. M., iv, 281 ; Hen. J. G., iv, 253, 294 ; Phil., iv, 587 *n* ; v, 224 ; Rob., iv, 278 ; Thos., v, 140 *n* ; Sir Walt., iv, 53 ; Will., iv, 587 *n*, 591, 632 ; Miss, iv, 607 ; fam., iv, 274, 313, 332
Herbert Convalescent Home (Bournemouth), v, 137
Herbrand, iii, 442 ; v, 200
Herclega, *see* Hartley Wintney
Herding, ii, 474
Hereald, iii, 229
Hereford, bps. of :—John Butler, ii, 486 ; Geo. I. Huntingford, ii, 350, 357, 366 ; v, 18 ; Ad. Orlton, *see* Winchester, bps. of
Hereford, earls of, iii, 8 ; iv, 7, 148, 339, 340, 369, 428, 456, 480, 481, 532 *n*, 533 *n* ; Humphrey de Bohun, ii, 160, 505 ; iii, 469 ; iv, 147, 428, 480, 527 *n*, 532 ; Miles de Gloucester, iv, 145, 422 ; Rog., iv, 360 ; v, 186, 215 ; Will. Fitz Osbern [Osborne], ii, 230 ; iii, 103, 234, 355, 529 ; iv, 42, 360, 365, 547 ; v, 148, 155, 171, 176, 186, 189, 222, 224 *n*, 228, 234, 241, 242, 243, 245, 259, 299
Hereford, Nich., ii, 41, 42
Herefrith, bp. of Winchester, ii, 4
Herehyrde, *see* Herriard
Heremud, Heremuth, *see* Yarmouth
Herennardus, iv, 255
Hereyard, *see* Herriard
Herford, Walt. de, ii, 154
Herfords (Beaulieu), iv, 654

Heriard, *see* Herriard
Heriet, Ralph, ii, 490, 517
Heringaud, Christine, iv, 431
Herlain, abbot of Glastonbury, iv, 589
Herlege, *see* Hartley Mauditt
Herlei, *see* Hartley Wespall
Herman, John, iii, 184; Will., ii, 293, 366
Hermitage, the (Whitwell), v, 202
Hermit's Tower (Winchester), v, 3, 11
Herne, *see* Hurn
Heron Court (Hurn), iv, 611; v, 96 *n*, 97, 98, 559
Herpul, v, 211, 218
Herrerd, *see* Herriard
Herrevill, Isaac, v, 486
Herriard, iii, 355, 356, 366-9; iv, 66, 81, 170, 396 *n*; adv., ii, 21.; iii, 369; ch., iii, 368; man., iii, 366; iv, 160, 179, 284 *n*; pop., v, 439; sch., ii, 400
Herriard [Heriard, Heryerd] (de), Alex., ii, 115; John, iii, 367; Maud, iii, 368; iv, 160; Nich., iv, 160; Pet., iv, 160; Rich., ii, 149; iii, 367, 368; Rob., iv, 64; Thos., iv, 64
Herriard House (Herriard), iii, 366, 367
Herriard Park, iii, 366; iv, 174, 175; v, 557, 558, 558 *n*
Herrick, Martha, iv, 106; Rob., iv, 106; Sir Will., iv, 106
Herries, John, ii, 172; iv, 296 *n*
Herrin, —, ii, 337
Herring, John, iv, 508; Josephine E., v, 235; Walt., ii, 143, 146; Will., iv, 508
Herryard, *see* Herriard
Hersaunt [Hersant], Dan., v, 486; John, v, 486
Hersent, John, iii, 289
Hertele Candevere, *see* Candovers (Hartley Mauditt)
Hertelegh, *see* Headley
Herteley Winteney, *see* Hartley Wintney
Herteshorne, Alice, iv, 562; Eliz., iv, 562; Will., iv, 562
Hertford, Frances Seymour, ctss. of, iii, 477; earls of, iv, 75 *n*, 84, 456 *n*, 527 *n*, 532 *n*, 570; Edw. Seymour, iii, 477; iv, 75; Will. Seymour, iii, 477
Hertford College (Oxf.), ii, 384; v, 251, 253, 284
Hertham, de, Isabel, iii, 328; Martin, iii, 328
Hertington, Margery, iv, 35
Hertlegh, *see* Hartley Mauditt
Hertle Waspay, Hertligh Vaspal, *see* Hartley Wespall
Herton, Rich. of, ii, 261, 263, 282, 366
Hervart, Phil. d', iii, 536
Hervey, Lord Fran., v, 251
Hervey [Hervy], Rev. Alf. C., iv, 425; Benet, v, 44; Rev. Thos., iv, 425; *see also* Harvey
Hervey-Bathurst, Sir Fred. E. W., iv, 481; Sir Fred. H., iv, 481; Sir Fred. T. A., iv, 481; Louisa, iv, 481
Herward [Herwood], Lawr., iv, 108, 109
Heryngawd, *see* Harangod
Heryngesdene [Heryngesland] (Priors Dean), iv, 436
Heryngeslane (Faccombe), iv, 314
Hesding, Ernulf de, iv, 324
Heselden (Wootton St. Laurence), iv, 239

Heseltine, Chris., v, 573; Godf., v, 573; John P., iv, 620
Hesse, landgrave of, v, 201
Hesseburna Prioris, *see* Hurstbourne Priors
Heterocera, i, 134
Hetesdun (Lasham), iv, 81
Hethe Crofte, le, (Heckfield), iv, 45
Hethefylde, ii, 137
Hethelie, *see* Headley
Hethene Stret, la, Hethenstreet, *see* Haven Street
Hethersetts, Gen., v, 140
Hethhows, le, (Penton Mewsey), iv, 381
Hetlegh, *see* Headley
Hetley, Rich., iii, 248
Heton, Martin, ii, 115
Heuse, *see* Hussey
Heverden, Rich., iii, 240
Heverfield, Cecily, iii, 241; Will., iii, 241
Hevyn (Winchester), v, 6
Hewe, Rob. le, v, 479 *n*
Hewett, Fred., iv, 655; *see also* Huett
Hewlett [Hewlot Hughlot], Abra., iii, 207; Johanna, iv, 25; John, iv, 25; Will, iii, 499
Hewson, Capt. G. F., iii, 331; Mrs., iii, 331
Hewton [Hempton], Rob. de, ii, 168
Hey, *see* Hayes
Heycroft, Will., iii, 68, 144
Heyden [Heydene] (de), Benj., ii, 366; Guy, iii, 37
Heyes, *see* Heighes
Heyland, *see* Hayling Island
Heylin [Heylyn], Pet., iii, 306; —, ii, 90
Heyno [Heyne] (de), Agnes, v, 174; Eliz., v, 174; Grace, v, 174; Guy, v, 174; Joan, v, 169; John, v, 174; Kath., v, 174; Mary, v, 174; Pet., v, 174, 315; Thos., v, 169, 174; Will., v, 174
Heysham, Fred., v, 516; Will., v, 515
Heyterdebury, Phil. de, v, 290
Heytesbury, Lady, v, 244; Marg., Lady, v, 288; Lds. :—Leonard H. A'Court, v, 241; Will. A'Court, v, 224; Will. F. H. A'Court, v, 241, 288; Will. H. A. A'C. Holmes, v, 140, 160, 230, 288
Heythorne, la, (Long Sutton), iv, 18
Heywood (Boldre), iv, 618
Heywood (Weston Patrick), iv, 109
Heywood [Haywode, Haywood] (de), Joan, iii, 250, 251; iv, 373; John, iv, 60; Nich., iv, 60, 373; Osbert, iv, 60; Thomasina, iv, 60; Walt., iv, 250; iv, 60, 475; Col., v, 571; *see also* Hayward
Heywoodland (Stratfieldsaye), iv, 57
Heywood's Farm (Stratfieldsaye), iv, 57, 60
Hiam, Amey, iv, 264; Rob., iv, 264
Hibberd, Jas., iv, 625; John, iv, 625; Will., iv, 625
Hibbis (Farley Chamberlayne), iv, 443
Hibesete, *see* Empshott
Hickley, ii, 203
Hickman, —, v, 518
Hicks [Hickes], Cath., v, 172, 245; Jane, v, 245; John, ii, 97; iii, 199; fam., v, 242
Hickson, Geo., v, 520
Hiddila, priest, ii, 3
Hide, iv, 354
Hide, Arth., iii, 90; Jas., iv, 300; v, 488, 489; Nich., iv, 537; Will., ii, 91; *see also* Hyde

Hideburninga, *see* Headbourne Worthy
Hide Place (Newchurch), v, 184
Higgins, Godf., v, 538; Will., iii, 240; v, 538
Higgons, Bevill, iv, 94; Geo., iii, 387; iv, 94; (Sir) Thos., iii, 387, 388; iv, 94; fam., arms., iii, 387
Higham [Heigham], de, Geo., iv, 266; Joan, iii, 260; Rob., iv, 267
Highbridge (Otterbourne), iii, 440
Highclere, iv, 273, 277, 278, 281, 285-6, 292, 293, 294 *n*, 397; v, 422, 557, 558; adv., iv, 286; char., iv, 286; ch., iv, 285, 286; man., ii, 23, 37, 66; iv, 285; mills, iv, 286; pop., v, 442; sch., ii, 400; iv, 286; wool trade, v, 476
Highclere Castle (Highclere), iv, 285
Highclere Hills, iv, 198
Highclere Street (Highclere), iv, 285
Highcliff, v, 81, 83, 84, 95, 108; ch., iv, 107, 108; sch., ii, 400
Highcliff Castle (Highcliff), v, 84
Highfield, *see* Heckfield
Highfield Park (Heckfield), iv, 44
Highlord [Heighlord], John, iv, 471; v, 94, 229
Highmore, Nath., iv, 568
Highnam Copse (Long Sutton), iv, 18
Hightown (Ringwood), iv, 606, 613
Hilary [Hillary], abbot of Lire, ii, 138; dean of Christchurch, ii, 152, 153, 160
Hildesley, John, v, 87 *n*, 109
Hildon House (E. Tytherley), iv, 515
Hilgrove Copyce (Hurstbourne Tarrant), iv, 319, 320
Hill, man. (Brading), v, 163
Hill [Hyll], Alice, iv, 214; Ann L., iii, 536; A. J. L., v, 575; Chas., iv, 635; Lt.-Col. Chas. F. M., v, 155; Christine, iv, 214; Eleanor, iv, 54; Eliz., ii, 131, 151; iv, 79, 80, 214; v, 280; Hen., iv, 80; Joan, iv, 214; John, iv, 85; Jos., iv, 477; Mary, iv, 335; Mich., iv, 54 *n*; (Rev.) Rich., ii, 151; iv, 79, 80, 81, 335, 516; Rob., ii, 131; iv, 214; Rog., iv, 589; Rosa, v, 155; Thos., ii, 375; iv, 214, 335; Trevor, iv, 54 *n*; V. T., v, 576; Walt., ii, 113; Will., iv, 54 *n*, 335; v, 280; Wills, iv, 54; Woodman, iii, 205; —, ii, 328; fam., v, 156, 173, 182, 195; *see also* Hills
Hillary, *see* Hilary
Hill Brow (Liss), iv, 84, 86
Hill Farm (Newchurch), v, 161, 162 *n*, 184
Hill Head (Titchfield), iii, 222
Hill House (Monk Sherborne), iv, 234
Hillier, Thos., v, 163; *see also* Hillyer
Hillis (Northwood), v, 268
Hill Place (Droxford), v, 524
Hills [Hylles], Thos., iv, 516; v, 527; W. A., v, 144; fam., v, 143; *see also* Hill
Hillsborough, Wills Hill, earl of, iv, 54; Trevor Hill, vsct., iv 54 *n*
Hill Side (Liss), iv, 84
Hillside (Odiham), iv, 67, 88
Hillside House (Worting), iv, 243
Hillstreet (Netley Marsh), iv, 546
Hillyer, Geo. W., iv, 139; *see also* Hillier

Hilman, Thos., iv, 281
Hilmede (Timsbury), iv, 486
Hilsea (Wymering), iii, 141, 165, 166, 168 ; v, 576
Hilsey, John, bp. of Rochester, ii, 54, 190
Hiltingbury (Hursley), iii, 421
Hiltofte, Sim., ii, 179
Hilton, man., ii, 145
Hilton, John, iii, 9 ; *see also* Hylton
Hilwell, Jas., iv, 8 n
Hinchelesey [Hincelveslei, Hinchersley] (Brockenhurst), iv, 626, 628
Hinde, Joan, v, 241
Hindens landes (Stratfield Turgis), iv, 63
Hingsdon, ii, 164
Hinton [Hinton Admiral, Hinton Amerell], v, 82, 83, 84, 108 ; ch., ii, 223 ; v, 107, 108, 109
Hinton, North, man. (Christchurch), v, 96
Hinton (de), Eustace, v, 96 ; Jos., iv, 71 ; Rog., v, 89 n ; Thos., prior of St. Swithun's, ii, 115 ; fam., iv, 502
Hinton Admiral, man. (Christchurch), ii, 159 ; v, 81, 84, 95
Hinton Ampner, ii, 108 ; iii, 302, 321-3 ; adv., iii, 322 ; char., iii, 322 ; ch., ii, 146 ; iii, 322 ; man., ii, 114 ; iii, 321 ; pop., v, 447 ; sch., ii, 400
Hinton Burrant, man. (Catherington), iii, 97
Hinton Daubney, man. (Catherington), iii, 82, 94, 96, 105 ; v, 77, 414 n
Hinton harriers, v, 541
Hinton Markaunt, man. (Catherington), iii, 97
Hinton Park (Hinton Ampner), iii, 321
Hinves, Will., iv, 634
Hinxman, Christian, iv, 356 ; Jacob, iv, 422 ; Jos., iv, 356 ; v, 96
Hipley (Boarhunt), ii, 143 ; iii, 146
Hipley, Basil de, iii, 146
Hippesley, Sir John, iii, 321 ; John W., v, 98 ; Mary, v, 98
Hirsch, Baron, v, 547, 550
Hissaburna, *see* Hurstbourne Priors
Hither Gate (Yarmouth), v, 286
Hoadly, Benj., ii, 98 ; iv, 61, 218 ; John, ii, 197 ; iii, 306 ; iv, 218 ; —, iii, 525 ; v, 79
Hoare [Hore], Anne, iii, 99 ; C. A. R., iii, 469 ; Rev. Edw. T., v, 156 ; Jas., iv, 56 ; John, iii, 99 ; Maur., v, 142 n ; Walt., v, 29, 483
Hobart, Lt.-Col., v, 147
Hobbard, Grace, iv, 502 ; Nich., iv, 502 ; *see also* Hubbard
Hobbes, Thos., iv, 383, 442
Hobbs, Fanny, iii, 204 ; Susanna, iii, 215 ; —, v, 178 n
Hobey, *see* Hoby
Hobluss (Christchurch), v, 98
Hobson, Dan., iv, 606 ; Edw., iv, 606 ; Thos., iv, 618
Hoby [Hobey] Anne, iv, 562, 606 ; Eliz., iv, 456, 578, 637 ; Giles, iii, 419 ; iv, 456, 578 ; Peregrine, iv, 606 n ; Sir Phil., iii, 418, 422 ; (Sir) Thos., iv, 606, 637 ; Will., iii, 418 ; fam., arms, iii, 418
Hochene (Freshwater), v, 240
Hock, iv, 255, 269
Hockley, *see* Oakley
Hodcott (Berks.), iv, 256
Hoddington, man. (Upton Grey), ii, 61, 108 ; iii, 355, 356, 384 ; iv, 121
Hodge, Sir Will., v, 350
Hodges, Will., iv, 8

Hodgson [Hodson], Rev. C. A., iv, 368 ; R. K., iv, 406, 417, 419 ; —, ii, 361 ; v, 30
Hodiam, *see* Odiham
Hodicotte (Berks), *see* Hodcott
Hodmills (Nately Scures), iv, 153
Hodson, *see* Hodgson
Hodyslond (Liss), iv, 84
Hoe, East, man. (Soberton), ii, 166, 168 ; iii, 263 ; iv, 486 n
Hoe, West, tithing, iii, 275
Hoe (de) Lucy, iii, 255, 264 ; Rob., iii, 47, 255, 263, 264 ; Rog., iii, 263, 267 ; Thos., iii, 254 ; Will., iii, 46, 47, 263, 267
Hoel, ap, *see* Powell
Hoese, *see* Hussey
Hofmann, John J., v, 18
Hogmoor, Rom. rem., i, 341, 342
Hohangra, man., *see* Oakhanger
Hoke, man. (Broughton), *see* Oake
Hoke (Lasham), iv, 81
Hoke, fam., *see* Oake
Hokelegh (King's Somborne), iv, 470
Holand, *see* Holland
Holbach, —, v, 243
Holborne Woods (Romsey), iv, 452
Holbury, ii, 143 ; iii, 275 ; iv, 498, 500, 515, 615 ; man., ii, 145 ; iv, 501 ; mill., iv, 500, 517 ; Rom. rem., i, 312, 345 ; iv, 500
Holcombe, Agnes, iv, 84, 419 ; v, 100 ; John, iv, 84, 419 ; v, 100, 146, 231, 275
Holcrofte, Will., iii, 96
Holdenhurst, ii, 152, 154 ; v, 81, 82, 89 n, 109, 133-7 ; adv., v, 136 ; chap., v, 108 ; char., v, 136 ; chs., v, 135 ; man., v, 135 ; pop., v, 445 ; sch., ii, 400
Holdenhurst, hund., v, 81, 91, 133
Holderness, John Ramsey, earl of, v, 180
Holding, Will., iv, 249, 260 n, 267 ; Miss, iv, 267
Holdip, Alice [Alicia], iv, 71, 200 ; Andr., iv, 200, 201, 207 ; Nich., iv, 71 ; Sim., iv, 201, 207
Holdshot, hund., iv, 1, 31-63, 66, 182, 197 ; v, 324, 331
Holdshot, man. (Heckfield), iv, 42, 43, 46 ; chap., iv, 50 ; mills, iv, 46, 47
Holdshot Farm (Heckfield), iv, 47
Holdway [Houldwy], Mary A., iv, 299 ; Rob., iv, 299 ; Sarah, iv, 299 ; Will., iv, 281
Holebroke Hill, iv, 587 n
Holebury, *see* Holbury
Holeest, Holeherst, par., *see* Holdenhurst
Holehurst, Rog. de, v, 89 n, 94 n
Holelane (Eling), iv, 547
Holemore (Sherborne St. John), iv, 158
Hole Mouse, le, (Pamber), iv, 433
Holengar, v, 101
Holewelle, Christine, iv, 508
Holewey, *see* Holloway
Holford, Pet., iv, 222 ; Rob. S., v, 189, 205
Holgate (Binsted), ii, 484
Holgate, Charity, v, 191 ; fam., iv, 366
Holgyle, Will., iii, 333
Holhurst, *see* Holdenhurst
Holland, man. (Berks.), ii, 290
Holland, earl, ii, 440 ; v, 349, 568
Holland [Holand, Holonde] (de, of), Alathea, lady, iv, 442 n ; Edm., ii, 475 ; iv, 130 ; Eleanor, iv, 130, 347, 348, 608 ; Eliz., iv, 130, 347, 348 ; Hugh, v, 324 ; Joan, ii, 475, 476 ; (Sir) John, iii, 120 ; iv, 442 n,

Holland (*cont.*)
543 ; v, 50 ; Marg., ii, 475 ; iv, 130, 347 ; Sir Nath., iii, 420 ; Rob., iii, 83 ; Thos., *see* Kent, earl of ; fam., arms, ii, 476
Hollehurst, *see* Holdenhurst
Holleshote, *see* Holdshot
Hollest, John L., iii, 131
Holliday, Susanna, iii, 333
Hollidays Hill, ii, 451
Hollins, Will., iv, 534 ; v, 78
Hollis, J. S., v, 461
Hollond, Rev. Edm., v, 170
Holloway, man. (Newchurch), v, 182
Holloway, Edith, ii, 130 ; Horatio F. K., iv, 558 ; Rich., ii, 339, 374 ; iv, 40 n ; fam., iv, 527
Holloways (Nether Wallop), *see* Wallop, Middle
Holly Hatch (Ellingham), iv, 563
Hollyngborne, Will., ii, 171, 172
Hollys, *see* Howles
Holm, fam., *see* Holme
Holmage [Holmehegg], Johanna, iii, 525
Holman, F. A., iv, 295
Holme [Holm], Chas., iii, 384 ; (Rev.) Geo., iii, 55 ; v, 249 ; Rich., iv, 327 ; Rog., ii, 122 ; *see also* Holmes
Holmehegg, *see* Holmage
Holmelond (Liss), iv, 84
Holmerslond (Sherborne St. John), iv, 158
Holmes, Leonard, Ld., v, 219, 242, 288 ; Thos., Ld., v, 160, 224, 241, 285, 286, 291
Holmes [Holms], Rev. Benj., v, 245 ; Cath., v, 242 ; Eliz., v, 288 ; (Capt.) Hen., v, 112, 285, 288 ; Jane, iii, 207 ; Sir John, v, 112, 224 n ; Rev. Leonard, v, 288 ; Leonard T. v, 218, 260 ; Mary, v, 288 ; (Sir) Rob., ii, 115 ; iii, 508 ; v, 112, 224, 225, 285, 288 290, 354 n, 381, 384 ; Standley iv, 468 ; Thos., v, 288 ; Adm., v, 390 ; —, iv, 473 ; *see also* Holme and Worsley-Holmes
Holmes-A'Court, Leonard, v, 241 ; Will. F., v, 241, 288 ; *see also* A'Court & A'Court-Holmes
Holme's Mead (Lymington), iv, 639, 642, 643
Holm Hill, ii, 450, 451
Holm Lacy (Herefs.), ii, 131
Holms, *see* Holmes
Holmsley Copse (New Forest), ii, 448
Holmsley Walk (Ringwood), iv, 607
Holnehurst, Holnest, Holnerst, par, *see* Holdenhurst
Holnhurst (Odiham), iv, 97
Holonde, *see* Holland
Holshute, *see* Holdshot
Holt (Nately Scures), iv, 156
Holt (Newnham), iv, 153
Holt [Holte], Anne (Lady), iii, 484 ; iv, 477 ; (Sir) Chas., iii, 484 ; iv, 477 ; Christine, ii, 149, 486, 503, 516 ; iii, 445 ; iv, 9, 28, 194 ; Eliz., ii, 486, 516 ; iv, 28, 194 ; Harold E. S., iv, 15, 16 ; Joan, ii, 488, 516 ; iii, 163 ; iv, 194 ; John, iii, 69 ; Kath., iii, 69 ; Louisa, iv, 367 ; (Sir) Rich., ii, 149, 486, 488, 503, 504, 516 ; iii, 54, 69, 163, 346 ; iv, 9, 28, 194, 641 ; v, 40 ; Walt., iv, 367 ; Will., iv, 611 ; Mrs., iv, 15, 16 ; fam., arms, ii, 488 ; iii, 53
Holte, la, (Holybourne), ii, 512
Holtemede (Kingsclere), iv, 250

INDEX

Holtham, John de, ii, 493

Holtham's Lane (Priors Dean), iv, 436

Holthatche (Kingsclere), iv, 250

Holton, v, 164

Holway (Christchurch), v, 89 n

Holybourne, ii, 63, 471, 480, 501, 511-15; v, 433; man., ii, 512; pop., v, 437; Rom. rem., i, 306, 345; sch., ii, 387, 400, 490, 515

Holybourne Eastbrook, man. (Holybourne), ii, 512, 513

Holybourne Westbrook, man. (Holybourne), ii, 512, 513

Holy Ghost Field (Eastrop), iv, 147, 148

Holy Ghost School, see Basingstoke Grammar School

Holywater Clump, iii, 5 n, 10

Holywell (Bishop's Waltham), v, 558, 558 n, 559

Home, Sir Everard, iv, 90

Home Close (E. Wellow), iv, 535

Homedowne (Whitchurch), iv, 300

Home Grove (Aldershot), iv, 3

Hommed (Kingsley), ii, 515

Hommige, Hen., iv, 604

Hompton Aumarle, see Hinton

Honeys, see Arneys

Honnors (Nether Wallop), see Wallop, Middle

Hony, Miss, iv, 546, 552

Hoo, man., see Hoe, East

Hoo, de, Thos., iii, 159; Will., ii, 110

Hood (le), Al., iii, 225; Joan, iii, 60; Rob., iii, 60

Hook [Hooke] (Newnham), iv, 150, 153, 156, 158; mill, iv, 156; Nonconf., iv, 158

Hook [Hook with Warsash], iii, 220, 222, 233; v, 364; adv., iii, 232; ch., iii, 232; man., iii, 217, 227; iv, 544; salt ind., iii, 221; schs., ii, 400

Hook Common, iv, 153, 156

Hooke (atte), Alice, iv, 99; Ann, iv, 241; Barbara, ii, 492; Eliz., Lady, iv, 241; Sir Hele, iv, 240; Hen., ii, 491, 492, 495; v, 464; Hugh, iv, 99; John, ii, 492, 493, 495; iv, 99; (Sir) Thos., iv, 99, 240, 241, 242; Will., iv, 99; fam., iv, 156; arms., ii, 493

Hooker, Anne, iii, 318; Cornelius, v, 30; Dulcebella, iii, 318; Edw., iii, 318; Mary, iii, 318; Thos., iv, 140; Maj., ii, 92

Hookey, Sam., v, 109

Hook House (Titchfield), iii, 222

Hookmeade (Farnborough), iv, 15

Hook Mortimer, man. (Titchfield), iii, 227

Hookwood, ii, 224

Hoone, John, v, 483

Hooper, Anne, iii, 468; iv, 453; (Sir) Edw., iii, 48, 468; iv, 453; v, 87, 97; Hen., iii, 84; Kath., iv, 453; Rebecca, iv, 569; Rich., iv, 64; (Rev.) Thos., iv, 569; v, 98

Hooppell, Rob. E., v, 134

Hopcoxe (Aldershot), iv, 3

Hope, ii, 154

Hope, H. J., iii, 373; iv, 204; W. H. St. J., iii, 222; Mrs., iii, 373

Hopeyard Pidle (Greywell), iv, 76

Hopgood, Edw., v, 117, 123; Rich., iv, 470

Hop-growing, v, 496, 497, 499, 500, 506, 509

Hopkins [Hopkyn], Christine, ii, 135; John, iii, 418

Hopsonn [Hopson], John, v, 270, 274; (Sir) Thos., iv, 552; v, 155, 244, 270, 274, 285; fam., v, 184

Hopton, Ld., ii, 200; v, 341

Hopton, Eliz., ii, 475, 476; Sir Ralph, iv, 59; Thos., ii, 475

Horder, Agnes le, iii, 502, 526

Horderswood, see Waltham Chase

Hordhulle (Wootton St. Laurence), iv, 239

Hordle [Hordhill], i, 326; iv, 615; v, 81, 82, 89 n, 110-15; adv., v, 115; ch., v, 115, 463; ind., v, 111; mans., v, 112; mill, v, 110, 111, 115; Nonconf., v, 115; pop., v, 442; sch., ii, 400

Hordle Breamore, man. (Hordle), v, 112

Hordle Trenchard, man. (Hordle), v, 112

Hore, (Eling), see Ower

Hore, fam., see Hoare

Horemede (Stockbridge), iv, 483

Horemue, see Yarmouth

Horewood, see Horwood

Horleye, Will. de, ii, 190, 191

Horlock, E., v, 160

Horman, Will., ii, 293, 366

Hormer, man. (Catherington), iii, 99

Horn, see Horne

Hornby, Charlotte, iii, 232; Thos., v, 527; Will., iii, 222, 225; iv, 224 n

Horndean (Catherington), iii, 94; coins, i, 345; racing, v, 543

Horne [Horn], Ad., ii, 320; Eliz., iv, 624; Joan, iv, 624; Mary J., iv, 123; Rich., iv, 624; v, 96, 108; Rob., bp. of Winchester, ii, 73, 74, 75, 76; iii, 351, 528; iv, 357, 429; Will., iii, 54; iv, 211

Horner, Edw., iii, 249; Will., iii, 249

Horniblow, Col. T., iv, 5

Hornley Common, iv, 21

Horringford (Arreton), v, 139, 140; man., v, 143; mill, v, 139, 145 n

Horsebridge (King's Somborne), i, 322; iv, 469; mill, iv, 472

Horsebridge Hill (Northwood), v, 264

Horsedown Common (Odiham), iv, 88

Horseley (Crux Easton), iv, 313

Horseleye, Will. de, ii, 17

Horsenemayn, see Horsman

Horses, v, 501, 503, 510; price of, v, 493, 495, 497

Horsey, Barth., iv, 588; Dorothy, iv, 459, 554 n, 589; (Sir) Edw., iv, 601, 613; v, 224, 228, 260 n, 262, 329; Eleanor, iv, 330, 459, 588; Eliz., v, 237; John, iv, 459, 554, 588; Thos., iv, 330 n, 459, 554, 588, 589; Will., iv, 330, 459, 507, 554 n, 588; fam., iv, 594

Horsey & Sons, v, 461

Horshedd (Romsey), iv, 452

Horsithe, Rich. de, iv, 590

Horsman [Horsenemayn], Piers, v, 48; Rich., v, 6 n

Horstede [Whorstede] (de), John, iii, 224; Marg., iv, 590; Rich., iv, 590; Rob., iv, 590; Sim., iii, 224

Horswell, Anne, iii, 421

Horton, Thos., iv, 240; Will., v, 461 n; see also Houghton

Horton Heath (Bishopstoke), iii, 309

Hortyngeschete, Hortyngshott, Hortyngshute, see Hardingshute

Horway Wood (Christchurch), v, 85

Horwood, Great (Bucks), v, 77

Horwood [Horewood, Horwode] (de), Alice, iv, 214; Christine, iv, 214; Eleanor, iv, 214; Eliz., iv, 214; Hugh, iii, 373; iv, 214; Joan, iv, 214; John, iii, 262, 373; iv, 214; Kath., iv, 214; Rob., ii, 193; Thos., iv, 214; Will. iii, 373, 375, 377; iv, 77, 151, 214, 218; see also Harward & Harwood

Horyngforde, see Horringford

Hosdown, see Hounsdown

Hose, Geoff., ii, 160

Hosebrigg (King's Somborne), iv, 470

Hoskins, Jas., v, 271; John, v, 100

Hospinel, Rominus, iii, 124

Hospitallers, see St. John of Jerusalem, knights of

Hospitals, ancient, v, 417

Hoste, Sir Will., v, 399

Hotelestone, see Nettlestone

Hotlop, iv, 489, 507

Hoton, fam., see Hutton

Hoton Ker, ii, 147

Hotot, see Houtot

Houel, Ad., iii, 68

Houghesplace (Faccombe), iv, 314

Houghton, ii, 163; iii, 401, 413-17; iv, 438, 439, 469; v, 77; adv., iii, 417; char., iii, 417; ch., iii, 416; pop., v, 445; sch., ii, 400

Houghton, riv., iv, 469

Houghton, North, man. (Houghton), iii, 414

Houghton, North, tithing, iii, 402; iv, 439

Houghton [Haugton, Houton], Fred., iv, 538; John, iv, 190; v, 497; Rich., v, 202 n; Thos., A., iv, 190; Will. de, iv, 130; v, 164; see also Horton

Houghton Club, v, 560

Houghton Dencourte, see Denecourt

Houghton Drayton, man. (Houghton), iii, 413; iv, 381

Houghton Edington (Houghton), iii, 415

Houghton Fishing Club, iv, 483; v, 560, 561

Houghton Marshes, iv, 470

Houldwy, see Holdway

Hound [Hound with Netley], ii, 146, 147, 148; iii, 462, 472-8; adv., iii, 478; char., iii, 478; ch., iii, 477; man., ii, 148; iii, 476; pop., v, 446

Hound Green (Mattingley), iv, 45

Houndsdown Hill, Rom. coins, i, 345

Houndsmill (Basingstoke), iv, 135

Houndswell (Southampton), v, 457

Hounsdown (Eling), iv, 546; v, 338

Houscrondle (Longstock), iv, 449

Houton, see Houghton

Houtot [Hotot], And., iii, 328; iv, 219; Isabel, iii, 328; John, iv, 219; Rich., iii, 328; Rob., iv, 219; Will., iv, 219

Houtwyke (Breamore), iv, 598

Hovyngford, see Huffingford

How, tithing, see Hoe, West

How, fam., see Howe

Howard, Ld., v, 376, 377, 378

Howard, Anne, iv, 427; Bern. E., iii, 130; Sir Edw., v, 372, 373; Eliz., iv, 259; Frances, iv, 75; Geo., v, 265 n; John, iv, 361, 624; Phil., iii, 130; Rich., iv, 154; Thos., iii, 130; Will., iv, 259; Mrs., iv, 546; —, v, 556; fam., arms, iii, 131

Howchyn, John, iv, 460

Howe, le, (S. Damerham), iv, 589
Howe, le, (W. Wellow), iv, 535
Howe, Rich., earl, iv, 499 ; v, 392, 395, 396, 397
Howe [How], Edw., v, 169 ; Sir Geo., iv, 562 ; Sir Geo. G., iv, 562 ; Hen., v, 216 ; Sir Jas., iv, 562 ; John, v, 216 ; Sarah, v, 216 ; Will., v, 216
Howett, Sam., v, 381, 382
Howke, Rich. at, iv, 131
Howles [Hollys], Eliz., v, 168 ; Giles, v, 191 ; Hen., v, 143, 162, 181, 183, 191, 192 ; Joan, v, 147 ; John, v, 168 n ; Will., v, 147, 162, 167, 168, 190, 191, 192
Howley, Anne J., iv, 254 ; Will., archbp., ii, 359 ; iii, 42 ; iv, 254, 264 n, 345
How Mill (King's Somborne), iv, 472
Howne, see Hound
Howorth, Rev. John, iv, 509
How Park, see John of Gaunt's Deer Park
Howpitts (Up Nately), iv, 176
Howse, Reg., iv, 572, 627 ; Rob., iv, 572
Howsman, John, iv, 61, 62
Howson, Frances B., iv, 476
Howston, John, iv, 472
Hoy, Mich., v, 202, 236
Hoyes, Janet, iii, 489
Hoyle, Rev. C. E., iv, 2, 4 n
Hoyvill [Hoyville], de, Hugh, iii, 227 ; John, iii, 372 ; Mary, iii, 260 ; iv, 481 ; Phil., iii, 227, 260 ; iv, 199 ; Rich., iii, 227 ; Thos., iii, 260
Hreodbrycg, see Redbridge
Hreutford, v, 294
Huband, Jane, iv, 320 ; (Sir) John, iv, 320 ; Rhoda, iv, 320
Hubbard [Hubberd], John, iv, 476 ; Walt., ii, 490, 517 ; see also Hobbard
Hubborn (Christchurch), ii, 152 ; v, 81, 84, 100
Hubb's Cross (Winchester), see Bub's Cross
Hubert, de Ryes, iv, 198 ; the tapener, v, 479
Huborne, see Hubborn
Huckles Brook, iv, 579
Huddesford, Geo., ii, 362, 363
Huddleston, Eliz., iv, 370 ; Sir Hen., iv, 370 ; Joan, Lady, iv, 521 ; Sir John, iv, 521 ; Marg., Lady, iv, 370
Hudson, Alan, v, 329
Huett [Huet], Chas., iv, 49 ; Ingram, iii, 436 ; John, ii, 281 ; iii, 436 ; see also Hewett
Huffield, John, iii, 167
Huffingford (Arreton), v, 139, 143, 145
Huffingford, (de, of), Walt., v, 145 ; Will., v, 145
Huggins, Will., iv, 355
Hugh, iv, 72, 147, 148, 252, 391, 549, 553, 587, 588 ; v, 97, 130 ; abbot of Beaulieu, iv, 140, 141, 146 ; abbot of Newminster, ii, 117 ; prior of Andwell, ii, 225 ; prior of Carisbrooke, ii, 231 ; prior of St. Swithun's, ii, 115
Hughe Miller's Piddle (Greywell), iv, 76
Hughes, (Sir) Edw., iv, 196 ; v, 399 ; Hen., iv, 196 ; Isabel, v, 145 ; Joan, iv, 196 ; Thos., ii, 355 ; v, 563 ; Rev. Will., v, 248 ; —, v, 145
Hughlot, see Hewlett
Huish, Capt. Mark. v, 179

Hulbert, John, iii, 150 ; J. H., iii, 150
Hull (Yorks), v, 377, 382
Hulle, de, de la, Agnes, iii, 279 ; Alice, iv, 396 ; Randolph, iv, 396 ; Will., iii, 279
Hulles, Will., ii, 188
Hullund, man. (Berks), see Holland
Hulon, Geoff., iv, 610
Hulse, (Sir) Edw., iv, 613 ; v, 571, 575, 597, 602 ; Sir Edw. H. W., iv, 571, 597 ; Hannah, iv, 434
Hulsefelde, see Ellisfield
Hulton [Hwlton], John de, iv, 292 ; Mrs. Preston, iii, 297 ; Rev. P., iii, 297, 299
Hulverstone (Brook), v, 215, 216 n, 217, 253, 272 ; man., v, 275
Hulyn, John, ii, 214
Hulyon, de, Cecily, iii, 255 ; Pet., iii, 255
Humbert, L. M., ii, 197
Humfrideston, see Hulverstone
Humphrey [Humfrey], v, 145, 146, 191, 234 ; abbot of Beaulieu, ii, 146 ; the chamberlain, iv, 424
Humphrey [Humfry], Lawr., dean of Winchester, ii, 115 ; Prudence, iv, 49 ; Rich. F., iv, 414 ; Will., iv, 49
Humphries, Frances, iv, 374 ; Thos., iv, 374 ; Mrs., iv, 257
Huncheford (Arreton), v, 143, 145
Hundeshayward, John, iv, 382 ; Maud, iv, 382
Hundred Menne's Hall (Winchester), v, 66
Hune, see Hound
Hunfredeston, see Hulverstone
Hungate, Eliz., Lady, iv, 105 ; Sir Phil., iv, 105
Hunger, iii, 357
Hungerford (Hyde), i, 262 ; iv, 249, 329, 346, 568
Hungerford, Marg., Lady, ii, 486, 487 ; iii, 204 ; iv, 564, 624 ; v, 119 ; Rob., Ld., ii, 486, 487 ; iv, 564, 624
Hungerford (de), Bridg., v, 205 ; (Sir) Edw., iii, 97 ; iv, 325 ; v, 163 ; Eliz., v, 208 ; Geva, iv, 84 n ; Jane, v, 163 ; Sir John, v, 205 ; Rob., iv, 84 n ; Sir Thos., iii, 416
Hungerford Lane, i, 262 ; iv, 326, 377
Hunlacey, see Holm Lacy
Hunland (Elvetham), iv, 74
Hunnyhill (Carisbrooke), v, 227
Hunsdon, Eliz., Lady, v, 228 ; Geo. Carey, Ld., ii, 81 ; v, 224, 225, 226, 227, 235, 240, 287 n, 331, 332, 378
Hunsdon, Alex., iv, 260 ; Jeremy, iv, 260 ; Mary, iv, 260 ; Pet., iv, 260
Hunspill, Thos., prior of Breamore, ii, 172
Hunstan, de, Godf., v, 215, 216 ; Isabel, v, 146, 215, 216
Hunt [Hunte] (le), Anne, iv, 226 ; Edw., iii, 117 ; v, 391, 398 ; Eliz., iv, 264 ; Felix, iii, 98 ; Fred., iv, 277 ; Geo., iii, 99, 415 ; Hen., iv, 256 ; Hugh, iii, 398 ; Jas. [Jacob], iii, 395, 398 ; iv, 250, 256, 264 ; John, ii, 138, 479 ; iii, 163, 398, 411 ; iv, 200, 226, 256 ; v, 66 ; Juliana, iii, 163 ; Martha, iv, 71 ; Mary, iii, 90 ; Maur., v, 282 ; Nath., iii, 149 ; Nich., iii, 90, 98 ; Rich., iv, 583 ; Rob., ii, 479 ; iv, 69, 70, 71 ; Rog., iv, 200 ; Steph., iv, 281 ; Will., iv, 212, 232, 412 ; Will. A., iv, 426 ; fam., v, 487

Hunter, Dr., ii, 449
Hunting, v, 568-74
Huntingdon, ctss. of, Cath. Hastings, iv, 110, 608 ; v, 92 ; earls of, iv, 151 ; v, 364, 368 ; Fran. Hastings, iv, 608 ; v, 92 ; Geo. Hastings, iv, 624 ; v, 92 ; Hen. Hastings, iv, 608 ; v, 92 ; John Holand, iv, 543 ; Thos. le Blount, iv, 110
Huntingdon, Hen. of, ii, 418, 419
Huntingfield, de, Joan, iv, 282 ; Walt., iv, 282 ; Will., iv, 360
Huntingford, Geo. I., bp. of Hereford, ii, 350, 357, 366 ; v, 18
Hunton (Crawley), iii, 401, 408 ; iv, 379 ; ch., iii, 412 ; man., iii, 409 ; pop., v, 447
Hunton, prior, ii, 259
Hunton Farm, v, 558
Huphusseburn, see Hurstbourne Tarrant
Hupsumburne, see Somborne, Upper
Hurdle manufacture, v, 459
Hurle, Cooke, v, 574
Hurlebat (Christchurch), v, 85
Hurleston, see Earlstone
Hurn, ii, 152 ; v, 81, 82, 83, 84, 133 ; burial mounds, v, 85 ; chap., v, 85, 108 ; man., ii, 159 ; v, 83, 88, 96, 97, 98 ; mill, v, 85, 97 ; sch., ii, 400
Hurn, Phil. de la, v, 97
Hurn Court, see Heron Court
Hursborne, see Hurstbourne
Hursley [Hursele, Hurseleghe], ii, 12, 22, 73, 137, 213, 282, 329 ; iii, 417-22 ; v, 39, 557, 558 ; adv., iii, 421 ; char., iii, 422 ; ch., iii, 421 ; man., ii, 23, 114 ; iii, 418 ; pop., v, 447 ; sch., ii, 400
Hursley hunt, v, 517, 528-30, 546
Hursley Park (Hursley), ii, 470 ; iii, 417 ; iv, 444
Hurst (Harbridge), iv, 604
Hurst, le, (Liss), iv, 84
Hurst [Attehurst, Hearst], Chris., iv, 497 ; John, iii, 428, 434 ; Marg., iv, 497 ; Steph., iv, 419 ; Will., iv, 170
Hurstake (Northwood), v, 268
Hurstbourne, hund., see Pastrow
Hurstbourne, Nether, man. (Hurstbourne Priors), iv, 288
Hurstbourne Fauconers [Hurstbourne Exterius], man. (Hurstbourne Priors), iv, 288, 289, 296
Hurstbourne Hill, iv, 319
Hurstbourne Interius, man., see Hurstbourne, Nether
Hurstbourne Park (Hurstbourne Priors), ii, 465 ; iv, 287, 288, 289, 300
Hurstbourne Priors, ii, 21, 108 ; iv, 273, 275, 287-91, 299 ; v, 77 ; adv., iv, 291 ; char., iv, 291 ; ch., iv, 291 ; Manor Farm, iv, 288, 289 n ; mans., iv, 288 ; mills, iv, 289 ; Nonconf., iv, 291 ; pop., v, 441 ; prehist. rem., i, 259, 262 ; Rom. rem., i, 304, 305 ; iv, 288 ; sch., ii, 400 ; iv, 291
Hurstbourne Tarrant, ii, 63 ; iv, 308, 319-24, 329, 331, 378 ; v, 454 ; adv., iv, 323 ; char., iv, 324 ; ch., iv, 321 ; mans., iv, 319 ; Nonconf., iv, 324 ; pop., v, 438 ; racing, v, 543 ; Rom. rem., i, 345 ; sch., ii, 400
Hurst Castle (Bradley), iv, 202
Hurst Castle (Hordle), v, 111, 289, 290, 325, 331, 350, 363
Hurst Copse (Amport), iv, 337
Hurst Farm (Winchfield), iv, 109

Hurst Meadows (Kingsclere), iv, 267

Hurteleye, Hurtleghe, see Hartley

Husband, Azariah, iii, 508

Husbourne, see Hurstbourne

Huscarle, Alex., iv, 579; Rog., iv, 579

Huse, Husee, Husey, see Hussey

Husington, see Bossington

Hussborn, see Hurstbourne

Husselegh, Will., prior of Southwick, ii, 168

Hussey [Heuse, Hoese, Huse, Husee, Husey] (de la), Agnes, ii, 504; iv, 282; Alex., iv, 373; Alice, iv, 532; Ann, iv, 370 n; Cecily, iv, 547, 550; Christine, ii, 504; Constance, iv, 283; Edm., iv, 373, 376; (Sir) Hen., iii, 90, 106; iv, 282, 283, 284, 547, 549, 550, 555; v, 243; Hubert, iv, 347; Isabel, iv, 373, 407; Jas., iv, 373, 477; Jane, iv, 628; John, ii, 167, 168; iv, 34, 373, 407, 528 651 n; v, 200 n; Jos., iv, 605; Kath., iv, 282, 283; Mark, iv, 282; Mary, iv, 605; Matth., iv, 547; Maud, iv, 547; Naphtali, iv, 628; Nich., ii, 504; iii, 117; iv, 283; Pet., iv, 34; Rich., iv, 528 n; Rob., iv, 528 n; Rog., iii, 149, 150; iv, 407, 418, 532; Thos., iii, 305, 334, 340, 349; iv, 74, 209, 213, 302, 513; Walt., ii, 503; (Sir) Will., ii, 503, 504; iv, 361; fam., iv, 478

Hussey-Montagu, Edw., iv, 651; Isabel, iv, 651

Husseys, man. (Froyle), ii, 503, 504

Hustingshute, see Hardingshute

Hutchins, John, iv, 507; Martha, ii, 482

Hutchinson, Thos., iii, 99, 344

Hutleston, see Nettlestone

Huton, see Hutton

Hutt, Capt. G. W., v, 190, 192; Sir Will., v, 192

Huttoft, Hen., ii, 144, 175; iii, 491; iv, 504, 505; v, 99

Hutton [Hoton, Huton], Anne, iv, 210; Rev. H. F., iv, 449; Jane, iv, 139; John, ii, 321; iii, 291; iv, 608, 626, 636; Rich., iv, 210; Sir Tim., ii, 321

Huver, Huvre, see Iford

Hwarnepol (Heckfield), iv, 45

Hwherewelle, see Wherwell

Hwitancyrice, see Whitchurch

Hwlton, see Hulton

Hybesle, see Ibsley

Hyde (Broughton), iv, 496

Hyde, la (Charford), iv, 561

Hyde, the, (Crondall), iv, 6

Hyde (Fordingbridge), iv, 568; ch., iv, 576

Hyde, la, (I. of W.), v, 191 n

Hyde, man. (S. Damerham), iv, 536, 589

Hyde (de, de la), Ad., ii, 110, 111; Alex., ii, 115; iv, 541; Amphyllis, ii, 477, 513; iii, 413; iv, 22; Arth., iii, 97, 125; iv, 619, 621; Bridg., iv, 424; Edw., v, 88, 93, Elias, iv, 589; Hen., iii, 12; v, 93; Jas., iv, 541; Joan, iv, 477; (Sir) John, ii, 111, 382; iv, 408, 589; v, 208; Kath., iv, 477; (Sir) Lawr., ii, 477, 513; iii, 97, 125, 413; iv, 22, 541, 542, 587 n, 619, 621; Marg., iii, 96; (Sir) Nich., iii, 83, 96, 98, 99, 100; v, 191 n; Pistor, iv, 477; (Sir) Rich., iv, 56, 208, 424; Rob., ii, 477, 513; iv, 22; v, 191 n; Rog., iv, 477; Thos., ii, 73, 309, 366; v, 193, 194,

Hyde (cont.)
207; fam., iv, 253; arms, ii, 477; see also Hide

Hyde Abbey (Winchester), i, 321, 397; ii, 5, 9, 11, 12, 16, 19, 49, 59, 60, 61, 104, 116-22, 227, 231, 240, 474, 480, 481, 490, 514, 517; iii, 8, 38, 142, 269, 390, 392, 479, 481; iv, 123, 183, 184, 186, 195, 208, 243, 244, 260, 261, 265, 268, 334, 335, 336, 346, 400, 411 n, 413, 419, 420, 425, 432, 444, 447, 448, 550; v, 2 n, 20, 35, 36, 69, 303, 304, 417, 418, 466; abbots of, ii, 121; iv, 218; Thos. Bramley, ii, 122; v, 484; Grimbald, ii, 5, 116, 121; Rewalan, ii, 117, 121, 474

Hyde Cross (S. Damerham), iv, 589

Hyde Farm (Broughton), iv, 496

Hyde Farm (Mottisfont), iv, 507

Hyde Farm (S. Damerham), iv, 589

Hyde House (Bramley), iv, 141

Hydene (Linkenholt), iv, 324

Hydithetone (St. Helens), v, 190

Hydrozoa, i, 93

Hyetoune (Wolverton), iv, 270

Hyford (Longstock), iv, 450

Hyghhamysfield (Basingstoke), iv, 146

Hyldborne, see Headbourne Worthy

Hylhend (Sherborne St. John), iv, 158

Hyll, Hylles, see Hill and Hills

Hylle Pat Asshe (Eling), iv, 547

Hyllond (Liss), iv, 84

Hylton, Ld., iii, 111, 116, 118; fam., arms, iii, 116; see also Hilton

Hylton-Jolliffe, Will. S., iii, 113, 116, 118; Col., iii, 118; see also Jolliffe

Hymenoptera, i, 114, 120

Hymerford, John de, iv, 588

Hynbury, man., ii, 159

Hyndman, —, iv, 591

Hyne, John le, iii, 392, 396

Hynxton, man., ii, 114

Hythe (Fawley), ii, 181; iii, 292; iv, 655

Hyther (Ashmansworth), iv, 274

Ibbotson, Fred., iv, 558; Vaudrey, iv, 558

Ibsden (Itchen Stoke), iv, 193

Ibsley, ii, 172, 187; iv, 559, 560, 579-80, 604, 629; adv., iv, 580; char., iv, 580; ch., iv, 580; man., iv, 579; Nonconf., iv, 580; pop., v, 445; sch., ii, 400

Ibthorpe (Hurstbourne Tarrant), iv, 319; man., iv, 321

Ibthorpe Common, iv, 321

Ibworth Farm (Hannington), iv, 229

Icene, see Itchen Abbas

Icenhilde Weg, see Icknield Way

Ichneumon flies, i, 114

Ichylbridge, see Eastbridge

Ichyn, see Itchen Abbas

Ickleton (Cambs.), i, 302

Icknield Way, i, 326

Icthe, Joan, ii, 132; iv, 467

Ictis, i, 325

Idlecombe (Carisbrooke), v, 198 n, 221, 222

Idrop, see Ibthorpe

Idsworth, iii, 102, 103; v, 527; ch., iii, 109; man., ii, 86; iii, 106; pop., v, 444; Rom. rem., i, 310; sch., ii, 400

Iford (Holdenhurst), v, 82, 83, 109, 133

Ilchester, earls of: Hen. E. Fox-Strangways, iv, 543; Steph. Fox, iv, 537, 543

Ilchester [Tocliffe, Toclive], Rich. of, bp. of Winchester, ii, 102, 194, 197; iii, 53, 59; v, 55, 56, 168, 217

Iles (Heckfield), iv, 45

Ilesham (Christchurch), v, 85

Iles Meade (Heckfield), iv, 45

Ilgeramus, see Ingram

Illeston, Thos., iii, 255

Illingworth, John, iv, 175; Mich., iv, 175; Ralph, iv, 175; (Sir) Rich., iii, 383; iv, 175; Rob., iii, 383; Will., iii, 383; iv, 175

Ilman, fam., v, 184 n

Ilond Close (Ecchinswell), iv, 250

Ilsbiddenemode (Calbourne), v, 218

Imber (Wilts.), iv, 488

Imber, Eliz., v, 75, 80; John, ii, 322

Imberd, Rich., v, 466

Imbesete, see Empshott

Implements and weapons: A.-S., i, 388, 390, 396; Bronze age, i, 260, 261; Jutish, i, 387; Neolithic, i, 258; Palaeolithic, i, 34, 35, 254; v, 110, 124; Rom., i, 303, 338, 341

Impshott, see Empshott

Impstone (Pamber), iv, 433

Incent, John, ii, 197, 208

Independents, iv, 115, 486

Indewycombe, Will., v, 221 n

Industries, v, 451-91

Ine [Ini], king, ii, 414; iii, 42, 348; iv, 551; v, 158, 165, 206

Ingaldesthorp, see Ingoldsthorpe

Inge, Fromond, iv, 431; Iseult, iv, 431; Joan, iv, 431; John, iv, 435; Marg., iv, 431; Rog., iv, 121; Will., iv, 431

Ingelramus, see Ingram

Ingham (de), Aubree, iv, 521, 522; Joan, iv, 521; v, 99; John, iv, 481, 521, 533; Oliver, iv, 347, 481, 521, 522, 533; v, 98

Inglefield, Fran., v, 487; Moses, v, 487

Inglesham, ii, 140, 141, 143, 145

Inglesham, Hen., ii, 39, 149; Rob., ii, 226

Inglis, Sir Rob., ii, 354, 355

Ingoldsthorpe [Ingaldesthorp], Sir Edm., iv, 34, 526; Isabel, iv, 34; Joan, Lady, iv, 526; Marg., iv, 34; Thos., iv, 34

Ingpen, fam., see Inkepenne

Ingram [Ilgeramus, Ingelramus], iv, 341, 342; the monk, iv, 595

Ingram, Will., iv, 82

Ingulf, fam., iv, 354

Ingulph, prior of St. Swithun's, ii, 115

Ingworth, Rich., bp. of Dover, ii, 56, 57, 190, 191

Inhams, Great (Binsted), ii, 484

Inholmes (Elvetham), iv, 74

Inhurst, man. (Baughurst), iv, 276, 415, 435

Inhurst (Baughurst) tithing, iv, 275, 277

Ini, see Ine

Inkepenne [Ingpen, Inkepen, Inkpen, Inkpenn] (de), Adrian, iii, 312; Alice, iv, 420; Eliz., iii, 312; Fran., iii, 312; Hen., iv, 495; Isabel [Isabella], iii, 298; iv, 407; v, 481; John, iii, 298, 312, 376, 429; iv, 407, 420, 495, 528; Marg., iii, 298, 312; Margery, iv, 407; Rich., iii, 298, 312, 376; iv, 407, 528 n; Rob., iii, 298, 312, 376; iv, 407, 420, 495, 528; v, 494;

Inkepenne (*cont.*)
Rog., ii, 123 ; v, 5, 76, 481 ; Thos., iv, 407, 528 *n* ; Will., iii, 312, 376 ; —, v, 326 ; fam., iv, 406 *n*, 533 ; arms, iii, 312, 376
Inkpen (Berks.), ii, 137, 181, 186 ; iv, 406 *n*
Ink Pin Lane (Longparish), iv, 406
Inne [Inn], bailiwick (New Forest), ii, 427, 450
Innocent II, ii, 221
Innocent III, ii, 140, 143 ; iv, 288, 301, 525
Innocent IV, ii, 109, 146, 164 ; iv, 242, 539 *n*
Innocent VI, ii, 174
Innocent VIII, ii, 179
Inscriptions, ii, 3 ; v, 107 ; Early Christian, ii, 233 ; Rom., i, 276, 279, 280, 281, 282, 283, 284, 287, 291, 297, 300, 323, 335, 336, 337
Insects, i, 109
Insula, de, *see* Lisle
Inwood, Geo., ii, 478
Ipley [Ippeley, Ippley] (Fawley), ii, 145 ; iv, 615
Ireis, Thos. de, iii, 383
Ireland [Irlond], Alice, iv, 85 ; Betty, v, 115 ; John, iv, 85 ; Will., v, 115
Iremonger, Delicia, iv, 412 ; Joshua, iv, 412, 413 ; Rev. Lascelles, iv, 405 ; Rev. Thos. L., iv, 414 ; Will. H., iv, 403, 405, 412, 414
Iremuth, *see* Yarmouth
Ireton (Irton), Alex., iv, 339 ; Geo., iv, 339 ; Joan, iv, 339 ; Rich., iv, 339 ; Gen., ii, 327
Irischwebbe, Christina la, v, 481
Irishland, *see* Arneys
Irlond, *see* Ireland
Iron age, i, 261
Iron and Ironworks, v, 463
Ironmonger's Land (Basing), iv, 127
Iron Paddock Copse (Selborne), iii, 5
Irton, *see* Ireton
Isaac, abbot of Titchfield, ii, 181, 186
Isabel, queen (w. of Edw. II), ii, 23 ; iii, 506 ; iv, 89, 90, 130, 150, 214, 347, 545, 608, 631 ; v, 91
Isabel, queen (w. of King John), ii, 18 ; iv, 270
Isabel, d. of Edw. III, iv, 198 ; v, 184, 222, 241 *n*
Isenhurst, *see* Inhurst
Iseult, abbess of Tarrant, iii, 106
Isington (Binsted), ii, 483, 504
Isle (Greywell), iv, 76
Isle, del, *see* Lisle
Isles, Nicholas, bp. of the, ii, 153
Islia, prioress of Wintney, ii, 149, 151
Islip [Yslape], Rich. de, v, 11 ; Sim., archbp. of Canterbury, ii, 36
Ismongre, Will. le, v, 35
Isvangers (Steventon), iv, 171
Isynghurst (Froyle), ii, 501
Isyngton, *see* Isington
Itchel, man. (Crondall), iv, 1, 7 ; mills, iv, 8
Itchel, de, Rob., iv, 7 ; Walkelin, iv, 7
Itchel Bridge (Crondall), iv, 9
Itchen, riv., i, 395 ; ii, 85, 88, 160, 189, 223 ; iii, 297, 339, 350, 478, 481 ; iv, 183, 191, 192, 193, 195, 426, 430 ; v, 1, 306, 360, 409, 452, 559, 560, 561, 562, 563 ; navigation, v, 451 ; watercress cultivation, v, 455

Itchen Abbas, iv, 188, 191-2 ; adv., iv, 192 ; char., iv, 192 ; ch., iv, 191 ; man., ii, 126 ; iv, 191 ; pop., v, 447 ; Rom. rem., i, 307 ; iv, 191
Itchen Common, iv, 192
Itchen Stoke, ii, 25, 100, 126, 131 ; iii, 42 ; iv, 188, 192-5 ; v, 562 ; advs., iv, 194 ; ch., iv, 194 ; mans., iv, 193, 194 ; mills, iv, 194 ; pop., v, 447
Itchenswell, Itchingswell, Itchinswen, *see* Ecchinswell
Ivare, iv, 559
Ive, *see* Ives
Ivel [Jewel], Rob., v, 191 ; Thos., v, 164 *n*, 191
Iveley Farm (Cove), v, 542
Iver, *see* Iford
Ives [Ive, Ivez] (de), Andr., iv, 635 ; v, 305 ; Anne, v, 112 *n* ; Arabella, v, 112 ; Edw., v, 112, 113 ; Edw. O., v, 112 *n* ; Hugh, iv, 550, 635 ; John, iv, 636 ; v, 114 ; J. Rob., iv, 70 ; Maud, iv, 635 ; Will., ii, 287, 366 ; iv, 635, 636 *n*
Ivetott (Newnham), iv, 156
Ivez, *see* Ives
Ivimey, Jos., iv, 607
Ivory Lodge, *see* Eyeworth
Ivrey, Rog. de, iii, 457
Ivychurch Priory (Wilts.), iv, 524
Iwardby, Joan, iv, 444 ; John, iv, 443, 444 ; Kath., iv, 443 ; Nich., iv, 443
Iwerste, *see* Ewhurst
Iweschot, *see* Ewshott
Iwnest, *see* Inhurst
Iwode (Basingstoke), ii, 209 ; iv, 105, 128, 129, 130 *n*
Ixnesford (Kingsclere), iv, 250
Izard, fam., iv, 658

Jack Higgs' land (Baughurst), iv, 277
Jackman [Jakeman], Rich., v, 213 ; (Rev.) Will., iv, 169 ; v, 155 *n*
Jackson, Cordelia, iv, 550 ; Geo., iv, 550 ; John, v, 173 ; Lawr., iv, 218
Jacob [Jacobs], Ad., ii, 255 ; Giles, iv, 453 ; Joan, iv, 258 *n* ; Will., iv, 258 *n* ; fam., v, 163
Jacomin, —, iii, 535
Jago, John, iv, 219
Jakeman, *see* Jackman
James I, ii, 85, 87, 248, 428, 447, 460, 474, 519 ; iii, 84, 109, 114, 205 ; iv, 6, 19, 33, 36, 64, 84, 85, 132, 133, 136, 138, 180, 198, 208, 252, 317, 318, 320, 321, 345, 397 *n*, 427, 430, 433, 444, 449, 452, 454, 472 *n*, 495, 497, 512 *n*, 516 *n*, 539, 540, 541, 583, 611, 632, 641, 651 ; v, 108, 212, 229, 243, 257, 278, 285, 286, 378
James II, ii, 339 ; iii, 177 ; iv, 266, 345, 444 *n*, 483 ; v, 257, 354, 385
James, prior of St. Fromond, ii, 226
James, Andr., iii, 502 ; v, 254 ; Arth., v, 198 ; Rev. Edw., ii, 482 ; (Rev.) John, ii, 380, 381, 385 ; iii, 528 ; iv, 32 ; v, 241 *n* ; Rich., ii, 70 ; v, 198 ; Thos., v, 256, 287 *n*, 461 ; T., v, 537 ; Will., v, 198, 523, 524 ; Dr., v, 256
James & Rosewall, white lead makers, v, 461
Janaway, Thos., ii, 482, 495
Janckenes Welle (Bentley), iv, 27
Jane (Seymour), queen, iv, 427 ; v, 233 *n*

Jardine [Jardyns], Edw., iv, 213 ; John, iv, 213 ; Sir Rob., v, 550
Jarman, Thos., v, 107
Jarvis, *see* Gervis
Jason, Sir Geo., v, 96 ; (Sir) Rob., v, 97, 113
Jay, *see* Jeay
Jeanes [Jeynes], John, v, 126 ; Thos., ii, 145
Jeay [Jay], Frances, iv, 112 ; Steph., iv, 502 ; Thos., iv, 502
Jefferey, Sarah, iv, 649 ; *see also* Jeffreys
Jeffreys, Geo., Ld., ii, 97 ; iii, 181
Jeffreys [Jefferies, Jefferyes, Jeffries], Arth. F., ii, 470 ; iv, 70 ; Eliz., iv, 61, 62 ; Capt. G. D., iv, 70 ; Jas., iv, 494, 497 ; Jeffery, iv, 62 ; John, iii, 205 ; iv, 635, 637 ; Marg., iii, 12 ; Will., iv, 212 ; v, 166 ; *see also* Jefferey
Jenens, *see* Jennings
Jenkin Place (Bentley), iv, 27
Jenkins, (Sir) Hen., iii, 282, 467 ; Sir Leoline, iii, 511 ; Will., iv, 628
Jenkinson, Chas., v, 100
Jenkyns, Rev. Hen., iii, 286 ; —, Lady, iii, 286
Jennens, *see* Jennings
Jenner, Arth., iv, 534 ; Sir Will., iii, 278
Jennings [Jenens, Jennens, Jenyns], Chas., iii, 484 ; Geo., iv, 507 ; John, iv, 9, 91 ; Rich., iii, 178
Jephson, Anne, ii, 492 ; Frances, iv, 69 ; (Sir) John, ii, 487, 502 ; iii, 367 ; Mary, ii, 505 ; (Sir) Will., ii, 487, 492, 502, 505 ; fam., ii, 504 ; arms, ii, 501
Jerett, Levi, iv, 499
Jermy, Eliz., iv, 278 ; Fran., iv, 278
Jerome, Lt.-Col. Hen. J. W., iv, 2 ; —, v, 18
Jervis [Jervys], John, iii, 88 ; v, 394 ; *see also* Gervis
Jervoise, A. T. E., v, 519 ; Ellis, v, 517 ; Frances, iv, 112, 283 ; Rev. Fran. E., iv, 83 ; Fran. H. T., iii, 367, 368, 369, 387 ; iv, 83, 175, 176 ; v, 557, 558 ; Fran. J. E., iii, 362, 367, 368, 369, 387 ; Fran. M. E., iii, 367 ; v, 519 ; Geo. P., iii, 367, 370, 375, 387 ; Capt. H., v, 527 ; Sir Jervoise C., v, 527 ; J. C., v, 527 ; Lucy, Lady, iii, 367 ; iv, 210, 283 ; Mary, iv, 283 ; Mary P. E., iii, 367 ; Rich., iv, 283 ; Sir S., v, 525 ; (Sir) Thos., iii, 125, 367 ; iv, 112, 172, 210, 283, 301, 365, 485, 642 ; v, 340 ; Tristram H., iii, 367 ; iv, 175 ; *see also* Gervis and Jervis
Jervys, *see* Jervis
Jesson, Thos., v, 100
Jewel, *see* Ivel
Jews, iv, 4 ; v, 32, 47, 309 *n*, 311
Jeynes, *see* Jeanes
Jeysaunt, John, iv, 279 ; Steph., iv, 279
Joan, queen, ii, 221 ; iii, 506 ; iv, 91 ; v, 223, 317
Joan, princess of Wales, ii, 475, 476 ; iv, 130, 347
Joan (d. of Hen. II), v, 306
Jobson, Eliz., iii, 213 ; iv, 166, 172, 203 ; John, iv, 166, 172, 203
Jocelin, bp. of Bath and Wells, iv, 72, **73**, 626 ; de Louvaine, v, 48
Jochys (Priors Dean), iv, 436
John, king, ii, 13, 140, 164, 169, 172, 194, 203, 207, 253, 416, 422, 474, 479 ; iii, 65, 113, 137, 152, 176, 186, 315 ; iv, 47, 68, 72, 77,

John (*cont.*)
88, 90, 94, 108, 110, 129, 150, 184, 189, 196, 198, 200, 206, 213, 226 *n*, 246, 252, 253, 270, 314, 315, 318, 319, 323, 329, 333, 345, 346, 347, 350, 360, 373, 376, 392, 397, 400, 416, 417, 423, 431, 434, 436, 440, 471, 472, 473, 475, 477, 486, 487, 493, 498, 503, 524, 527, 531, 547, 553, 558, 563, 597, 607, 650; v, 88, 241, 243, 288, 289 *n*, 307, 360, 361, 415, 416, 417

John XXII, pope, ii, 25, 195, 197; iii, 8

John, iv, 561; v, 183, 455; abbot of Netley, ii, 149; bp. of Ardfert, ii, 223; iv, **179**; bp. of Cyrene, ii, 45; parson of Enham, iv, 379; prior of St. Swithun's, ii, 115; prior of Selbourne, ii, 176, 179; the serjeant, iv, 293; **vicar** of Christchurch, iv, 620

John, Lewis, iv, 501

John of Gaunt's Deer Park (King's Somborne), iv, 469, 470, 472

Johnson, Benj., iii, 180; Chris., ii, 282, 283, 287, 293, 302, 309, 310, 312, 313, 314, 330, 366; Eliz., iv, 336; Geo., v, 73; Hen., iv, 602; Hen. G., iii, 342, 343; Herb., iv, 440, 441, 473, 476; John, iv, 336; v, 19; Rich., ii, 83; iv, 167; Rob., iv, 353; Sam., iv, 3; S. H. J., iv, 409; —, iv, 409

Johnston, Geo., iv, 9; John A., iv, 9; John L., iv, 5, 9, 13

Johnstone, Sir Fred., v, 547, 548, 553, 554

Joichel, John, ii, 253

Jolliffe [Jolif, Joliffe], Eliz., iii, 168; Grace, v, 143; Jas., v, 282; John, iii, 112, 116; J., v, 277; Thos., iii, 168; v, 214; Rev. Thos. R., iii, 120; Tovey, v, 143; (Sir) Will., ii, 393; iii, 70, 71, 112, 328; Dr. W. J., v, 279; fam., arms, iii, 116; *see also* Hylton-Jolliffe

Jonas, Eliz., iii, 249; Thos., iii, 247

Jones, Anne, iv, 622 *n*; Caroline, iii, 200, 201; Chas., iii, 109; Clara, iv, 522; Dav., iv, 616; Edw., iv, 502; Eliz., iv, 200; Geo. F., v, 242; Hen., iv, 622 *n*; Inigo, v, 347 *n*; Mary, iii, 488; Rev. Morgan, iii, 314; Rev. Reg., iv, 200; Rob., iii, 447; Thos. J., v, 125; Will., iv, 266, 324, 614; Col., v, 341; —, Lady, iv, 244

Jordan, the draper, v, 479

Jordan, Dorothy, v, 179; Jane, v, 123; Nich., v, 285; Rich., iv, 259, 374; Thos. M., iv, 259; Will., v, 123

Josep, Gilb., ii, 135

Joseph, iv, 211

Joy, Rich., ii, 84

Joyce, Eleanor, iv, 363; F. A., v, 173, 200

Joyes (Sherborne St. John), iv, 158

Joyes Ende (Eling), iv, 547

Judicales, John, ii, 255

Judith, ctss., v, 300

Julian, prior of Christchurch, ii, 160

Juliana [Julia], abbess of Romsey, ii, 132; d. of Geoff., count de Perche, iv, 77; prioress of Wintney, ii, 149, 151; w. of Alan, iv, 366

Julilushborow (Romsey), iv, 452

Julyans Will (Romsey), iv, 452

Jumièges, Rob. de, ii, 9; v, 298

Jumièges Abbey (France), ii, 20, 106; iii, 130, 133; v, 469

Juniper, Will., v, 125; Winifred, v, 125 *n*

Juniper Hill (Chilton Candover), iv, 186

Juran, v, 282

Jurdew, Thos., iii, 241

Justin, iv, 18; v, 112

Justyce [Justice], Mary, ii, 125; Steph., iii, 184-5

Jutes, i, 374-91; ii, 3, 415; v, 294, 359; antiquities, i, 379, 386, 387

Jvare, *see* Eyeworth

Kacchefrensh, de, Alice, iii, 374; John, iii, 374

Kadebiry, *see* Cadbury

Kanc', Walt. de, *see* Kent, Walt. de

Kandavor, Kandever, Kandevera, *see* Preston Candover

Katherine (of Aragon), queen, ii, 53, 188; iv, 72, 163, 165, 348, 427

Katherine (of Braganza), queen, iv, 240, 500 *n*, 516 *n*, 541; v, 353

Katherine (Howard), queen, iii, 376, 456; iv, 259, 423, 597, 598, 646

Katherine (Parr), queen, iv, 587, 591

Katherine (of Valois), queen, v, 368

Kaumes, Ralph, iv, 475 *n*

Kay, G., v, 541; Will., iv, 19

Keane [Keen, Keene, Kene] (de), Greg., v, 95; John, v, 213; Maud, v, 95; Nich., iv, 46 *n*; Rich., v, 144, 212 *n*; Rob., v, 86; Col., v, 352

Keate, Edw., iii, 308; Rev. John, iv, 42, 43, 44, 45; Rev. John C., iv, 42, 44

Keats, Edw., iv, 194; John, v, 13, 195, 256

Keble, John, ii, 100; iii, 421, 443; v, 134; fam., arms, iii, 421

Keble College (Oxf.), iv, 576

Keblewhite [Kybulwhite], John, iv, 134; —, v, 461

Keck, Fran., iii, 483; Jane, iii, 464

Kedell, riv., iv, 570

Keele, Edw., iv, 511 *n*

Keen, Keene, *see* Keane

Keightley, Thos., iii, 98, 99

Keileway, Keilway, *see* Kellaway

Keisnetum (Normandy), v, 191

Keith, Ld., iii, 149

Kekewich, Rob., v, 280, 284; Will., v, 225

Kelk, Sir John, iv, 393, 513, 514; Sir John W., iv, 393, 394, 513, 514

Kellaway [Keileway, Keilway, Keylway(e), Keylwey, Keylwey], Ambrose, iv, 583; Anne, iv, 330, 647; Edw., iv, 583; Fran., iv, 330, 583; Joan, iv, 330, 583; John, iv, 330, 583; Mary, iv, 647; Rob., iv, 455 *n*, 597 *n*; Sybil, iv, 446 *n*; Thos., iv, 330, 583; (Sir) Will., ii, 67; iv, 330, 446 *n*, 583, 584, 647, 649; fam., iv, 572

Kelleseye, *see* Kelsey

Kelly, Rev. Arth., iv, 174; E. F., iv, 316; F., v, 570; Geo., iii, 167; Pet., v, 539; Sarah, iii, 167

Kelsale, Rog., iii, 496

Kelsey [Kelleseye], Edw., iv, 492; Hen., iv, 492; Rob., ii, 170

Kembeshete, *see* Kempshott

Kembridge, Pet., iii, 294

Kemer, Rich., iv, 604

Kemes, John, v, 207; Marg., v, 207

Kemeton, *see* Kimpton

Kemish, Anne, iv, 354, 355; Rich., iv, 354, 355, 357

Kemmis, Col. Will., v, 116

Kempe [Kemp], Agnes, v, 247 *n*; Amy, v, 212; Ant., iv, 656; v, 273; Chas., iv, 287; Frances, iii, 421; iv, 618; John, iv, 616, 618; v, 147, 247 *n*; Mary, v, 211; Nich., iv, 367; Thos., iv, 46, 618; v, 200, 211; Toby, v, 168 *n*

Kempenfelt, Adm., v, 395

Kempshott, iii, 355, 357; iv, 113, 114, 179, 180, 181, 396 *n*; adv., iv, 181; man., iv, 179, 180

Kemp-Welch, John, v, 127

Ken, Thos., ii, 95, 339; v, 57, 211; *see also* Kenne

Kendall [Kendal, Kendale] (de), Agnes, iv, 630; Aubrey, iv, 630; Beatrice, iv, 102; Edm., iii, 9, 10, 31, 68; iv, 450, 618, 630; (Sir) Edw., iv, 102; v, 243; Eliz., (Lady), iv, 102; Felicia, iv, 630; Joan, iv, 142; John, iv, 102, 142; Marg., iv, 102, 450, 630; Rob., iv, 102, 106; Thos., iv, 102

Kendall, Little (Sherfield), iv, 104

Kendefer, iv, 183 *n*

Kendle, G. R., v, 561

Kene, *see* Keane

Kenet, Kenett, *see* Kennett

Kenne (de, le), Joan, iv, 276, 434, 435, 458; John, iv, 458, 492, 508; Marg., iv, 458, 492; Saer, iv, 434 *n*; Thos., iv, 458, 523; Will., iv, 276, 434; *see also* Ken

Kennedy, Jas. W. J., iv, 409; Miss, iv, 2; —, v, 576

Kennerly, man. (Godshill), v, 173

Kennerly, Little, (Godshill), v, 173

Kennerly, John de, v, 173

Kennett [Kenet, Kenett], Fanny, iii, 240; Hen., iii, 240; John, iii, 170; Mary A., iii, 120; Pet. le, iv, 512; Wyllyam, ii, 57; —, v, 518

Kent, ctsses. of, iv, 198; Alice, iv, 608; Eliz., iv, 130, 347; Joan, iii, 143; v, 91; Lucy, iv, 130; Marg., ii, 191; iii, 143; iv, 347; dchss. of, v, 401; earls of, ii, 488, 512; iv, 151, 644; Edm., ii, 191, 474, 475, 476, 477; iii, 130, 131, 142, 347; iv, 392, 512 *n*, 526; Edm. of Holand, ii, 475; iv, 130; Hubert de Burgh, iii, 223; iv, 88, 198, 392; v, 91; John, ii, 475, 476; iii, 143; iv, 130, 347, 392; Thos. de Holand, ii, 143, 475, 476; iii, 187, 499; iv, 130, 347, 348, 608, 627, 631

Kent [Kanc'] (de, of), Agnes, iii, 458; Eliza, iv, 399; Giles, v, 264; Hester, *see* Chetwynd, vsctss.; John, ii, 223, 275; iii, 241, 458; iv, 399, 426, 430, 468; Kath., iv, 413; Nich., ii, 492; Rich., ii, 176, 179; iv, 266, 413; Sam., v, 80; Sim., iv, 430; Sophia, ii, 492; Thos., ii, 167, 168; iv, 46 *n*; Walt., v, 568; Dr., v, 78; Mrs., iv, 221; fam., iv, 396, 397

Kenteliscombe (S. Damerham), iv, 588

Kentish, Jas., iv, 218; Thos., iv, 218

Kent's Alley House (Headbourne Worthy), iv, 426

Kenulf, *see* Cynwulf

Kenyon, Edw., ii, 83

Keppel, Aug., vsct., v, 394, 399

Kerby, Mary, iii, 281; *see also* Kirby

Kerchil, John de, v, 473

Kern [Kerne], man. (Brading), ii, 180; v, 163, 291
Kerne, tithing (E. Medine), v, 138
Kernet (de), Hen., iv, 424, 425; Hugh, iv, 424; Isabel, iv, 424; John, iv, 424; Will., iv, 424
Kersey manufacture, v, 482, 484, 485, 486
Kersley, John, iii, 21; Olive, iii, 21
Kerspoule (Lyndhurst), iv, 631
Kerye, Rich., v, 484
Keswick [Kesewyk(e)], Hen., iii, 96, 193; iv, 548 n, 605; H., ii, 290
Ketel, iii, 269
Keton [Ketone] (de) (Sir), John, ii, 214, 262, 282; v, 40; Rob., ii, 150, 157
Kettyll, Margery, iv, 259
Kew, Alex., ii, 381; Rob., ii, 381
Kewen, Joan, iii, 456; Thos., iii, 456
Kewurthe, Jas. de, iv, 265
Key [Keye], John, iv, 96; Thos., iv, 396
Keyhaven (Milford), v, 115; man., v, 117, 120; salt works, v, 470
Keyhaven, tithing (Christchurch), v, 82
Keyhaven and Lelton, man. (Milford), v, 117, 120
Keylway(e), Keylwey, see Kellaway
Keynes [Caines], Isabel, iv, 326; Joan, iv, 326; John, iv, 326; v, 188; Thos., iv, 326
Keyneys Court, see Caines Court
Keyrewent, see Caerwent
Keys, Thos., v, 163, 187 n, 198 n
Keyt, Edm., ii, 301
Kidson, Capt., iii, 118
Kidwelly (Cardigan), ii, 173
Kidwelly [Kydwelly], Avice, iv, 276, 435; Eliz., iv, 316 n; Jane, iv, 316; Joan, iii, 367; iv, 199, 316; Margery, iv, 316 n; Mary, iv, 112; Mich., iv, 316; (Sir) Morgan, iv, 199, 206, 276, 434, 435; Pet., iii, 367; iv, 316
Kilback, —, ii, 97
Kildare, Will. Barnett, bp. of, ii, 51
Killigrew, Margery, iii, 43; Will., iii, 43
Kilmeston, iii, 302, 311, 312, 323-5; adv., iii, 325; char., iii, 325; ch., iii, 325; mans., iii, 323; pop., v, 447
Kilmeston Gymming, man. (Kilmeston), ii, 213; iii, 324
Kilmeston hunt, v, 513
Kilmeston Plunkenet, man. (Kilmeston), iii, 323; iv, 457 n
Kiln pond (Mortimer West End), iv, 56
Kilns, Roman, i, 306, 326, 328, 345
Kilpin, Chas. J., iv, 267
Kimberley, de, John, iv, 110 n; Rob., iv, 110
Kimbridge, man. (Mottisfont), iv, 506, 508
Kimbridge [Kingbrig] (de), Christine, iv, 508; Mich., iv, 508
Kimbridge Mill, v, 396
Kime, John, see Kyme, Sir Thos.
Kimmer Farm (Faccombe), iv, 314
Kimpton, iv, 22, 333, 366, 367, 369; iv, 372-6, 391; adv., iv, 376; char., iv, 376; ch., iv, 374; mans., iv, 372; pop., v, 438; Rom. rem., i, 295; iv, 372; sch., iv, 376
Kimpton Down, iv, 372
Kimpton Lodge, iv, 372
Kimpton Wood, iv, 372
Kinewald, see Cenwalh

King [Kinge, Kyng], Agnes, ii, 124; Anne, v, 172; Fanny, v, 204; Gregory, v, 496; Hen., iv, 447, 448; H., iii, 373; iv, 204, 205; Jas., iv, 232; John, v, 526, 538, 539; J. H., iii, 373; iv, 204; v, 140; Rich., iv, 643; v, 526 n; Thos. M., iv, 497; Will., iv, 335; v, 261; W., ii, 516; Miss, iii, 453; Mrs., v, 116; —, v, 546
King Arthur's round table (Winchester), v, 10
Kingates (Niton), v, 188
Kingberwes (S. Damerham), iv, 587 n
Kingbrig, see Kimbridge
Kingescamp, iv, 489, 490
Kingescamp, Will. de, iv, 490 n
Kingesland (King's Somborne), iv, 470
Kingeslandes (Stratfield Turgis), iv, 63
Kingesmel, see Kingsmill
King John's Hill (E. Worldham), see Lodge Hill
King John's Hill (Kingsclere), see Cottington Hill
King John's House (Southampton), v, 90
King's Acre (Stockbridge), iv, 483
King's Brook, v, 483
Kingsbury (de), Gerald, iii, 64; John, iv, 188, 237
Kingsclere, ii, 62, 102, 117, 381; iv, 113 n, 245, 249-67, 319, 332 n; v, 324, 331, 337, 426, 427, 544; advs., iv, 265; char., iv, 266; chs., iv, 261; cloth manufacture, v, 484; mans., ii, 213; iv, 246, 251-61, 267; mkt. and fairs, iv, 252; v, 417; mills, iv, 251, 252; Nonconf., iv, 266; pop., v, 442; racing stables, iv, 250; v, 546-53; Rom. coins, i, 345; schs., iv, 266
Kingsclere, hund., iv, 245, 273; v, 423
Kingsclere Downs, v, 546
Kingsclere Lordship, tithing (Kingsclere), iv, 245
Kingsclere Parsonage, tithing (Kingsclere), iv, 245
Kingsclere Woodlands, iv, 249, 250, 257, 266
King's College (Cambs), ii, 306; iv, 380, 381, 573, 576, 606, 612
Kingscote, —, v, 514
King's Enham, man. (Andover), iv, 345, 354, 377
King's Enham Heath, iv, 320, 321
King's Freshwater (Freshwater), v, 210, 240
Kingsgate (Winchester), v, 3, 4, 34
King's Hatherden, see Hatherden
King's horse-croft (Basing), iv, 123
King's House (Lyndhurst), ii, 436, 439, 440, 450; iv, 630, 633; v, 569
King's House (Winchester), v, 12
King's Hurstbourne, see Hurstbourne Tarrant
Kingsland, ii, 160
King's Langley (Herts), ii, 56
Kingsleaze (Kingsclere), iv, 214, 266
Kingsley, ii, 471, 480, 489, 490, 496, 514, 515-18; ch., ii, 516; mans., ii, 515; pop., v, 437; sch., ii, 518
Kingsley, Chas., ii, 100; iii, 350; iv, 32, 33, 40, 41, 616
Kingsley Heath, ii, 515
King's Longe Coppice (Hurstbourne Tarrant), iv, 319, 320
Kingsmede (Stockbridge), iv, 483
King's Mill (Alton), ii, 483

King's Mill, (Basingstoke), iv, 134, 135
King's Mill (Priors Barton), v, 482, 483
King's Mill (Winchester), v, 49
Kingsmill [Kingesmel, Kyngesmill], Alice, iv, 290, 296, 327; And., iv, 320; And. de P., iv, 254, 268; Anne J., iv, 254; Lady Bridg., iv, 263, 264; Cecily, iii, 214, 241; Constance, iv, 254, 264, 278, 290, 294, 327; Dav., iv, 379; Eliz. (Lady), iv, 254, 290; Ellen, iv, 122; Frances, iv, 254, 327; (Sir) Geo., iv, 278, 327; (Sir) Hen., iv, 252, 254, 263, 327, 332; Hugh de, iv, 134; (Sir) John, ii, 67, 136, 369; iii, 214, 241; iv, 62, 254, 257, 264, 268, 286, 332, 410, 411; v, 326; Marg., iv, 290 n; Morpheta, ii, 61, 136, 137; v, 180; Penelope, iv, 327; Rachel, iv, 61, 62; Rebecca, iv, 264, 267, 327; (Sir) Rich., iii, 258, 358; iv, 122, 240, 278, 285, 286, 290, 327, 374; Sir Rob., iv, 254, 327; (Sir) Will., ii, 60, 115, 378; iv, 212, 225, 252, 254, 263, 264 n, 268, 327, 332, 374; Will. H., iv, 254; —, v, 329; fam., iv, 313; arms, iii, 266
King's Quay (Whippingham), v, 200
King's Somborne, ii, 63, 163, 172; iv, 108, 400, 438, 439, 444, 449, 469-82, 483, 484, 487, 561 n; v, 324, 331; advs., ii, 20; iv, 480; char., iv, 480; chs., iv, 470, 478-80; deanery, ii, 21, 62, 96, 101; fishery, iv, 472; man. house, iv, 470; mans., iv, 470; mills, iv, 472; Nonconf., iv, 480; pk., iv, 469, 470, 472; pop., v, 445; sch., iv, 470; town fields, iv, 469
King's Somborne, hund., iv, 438
Kingston (I. of W.), v, 209, 210, 249-51, 279, 281, 284; adv., v, 251; ch., v, 250; man., v, 249; pop., v, 449; sch., ii, 407
Kingston (Portsea), ii, 164; iii, 191, 194; ch., iii, 196
Kingston (Ringwood), iv, 606
Kingston, North, (Ringwood), iv, 606
Kingston [Kyngeston, Kyngestone] (de), Alice (Lady), iii, 59, 269; iv, 159, 193, 194; Eleanor, iv, 388, 617; v, 204 n, 249; Jas., v, 249; (Sir) John, iii, 59, 269, 461; iv, 159, 388, 617; v, 163, 213, 243, 249; Jordan, iv, 173, 198, 213, 231, 249, 251; Margery, v, 249; Mary, iv, 159, 388, 617; v, 204 n; Maud, v, 249; Nich., iii, 269; iv, 159; Rich., iv, 610; Susan, iv, 159; (Sir) Thos., iii, 59, 269; iv, 159; Will., v, 173, 249; fam., v, 184
Kingston Deverill, man. (Wilts), ii, 146, 148, 149
Kingston-upon-Hull, Evelyn Pierrepont, dk. of, iv, 494, 497 n, 522; earls of, Rob. Pierrepont, iv, 494, 522; Will. Pierrepont, iv, 494, 522
Kingswell, Edw., iv, 83, 103; Rich., iv, 85; Thos., v, 243; Sir Will., iv, 83, 103; —, iv, 166
King's Worthy, i, 321; ii, 73; iii, 389; iv, 415, 416, 430-33; v, 539; adv., iv, 432; char., iv, 433; ch., iv, 432; mans., iv, 430; mill, iv, 432; Nonconf., iv, 433; pop., v, 448

Kingsworthy Court (King's Worthy), iv, 430
Kingsworthy House (King's Worthy), iv, 430
Kingsyate, ii, 69
Kington, Great, Little (Dorset), iv, 82
Kington Nunnery (Wilts), iv, 302
Kinytheton, see Knighton
Kipling, Thos., v, 214
Kipping [Cuppyng] (de), Ela, ii, 487; John, ii, 487; Nich., iv, 225, 226
Kippings, man. (Church Oakley), iv, 225, 226
Kirby, Christine, iv, 431; John, iv, 431, 537; Rich., iv, 537; Rob., iii, 251; Will., iv, 431; see also Kerby
Kiriel, Nich. de, v, 23
Kirkby [Kirkeby] (de), Andr., v, 251; Anne, iv, 457 n; v, 251; Christine, iv, 457 n; Gerard, iv, 457; John, iii, 241; iv, 457, 458; v, 76; Marg., iii, 241; Rob., iv, 457 n; Sarah, iii, 241; Thos., ii, 208; iii, 241; iv, 457, 458, 459; Will., iii, 241; iv, 457
Kirkham, Will. de, ii, 162
Kirkpatrick, Geo., v, 188; Jas., v, 187; John, v, 187; Jos., v, 187; Rich. T. G., v, 188
Kirkstall Abbey (Yorks), iv, 653
Kirkstead Abbey (Lincs), v, 476
Kirton, Marg., v, 93; Steph., v, 93, 94 n
Kisby, Anne, iv, 253; Rob., iv, 253
Kitbridge, v, 264
Kitchin, Geo. W., dean of Winchester, ii, 115, 245, 256
Kite Hill (Binstead), v, 151
Kittescroft (Eversley), iv, 41
Knap [Knappe] (Colemore), iv, 423
Knaplock, Rob., ii, 273, 368, 389
Knapp (Christchurch), v, 81, 97, 98; mill, v, 94, 98
Knapton, John Vescy, Ld., iv, 54 n
Knapton, Alban, iv, 627, 628; Albinas, iii, 206; Cecilia (Cecily), iv, 647; Mary, iv, 647; Ralph, iv, 342; Rich., iv, 627; Rob., iv, 627, 628, 647; Will., iv, 627, 628, 647
Knatchbull, H. E., v, 576; Rev. W., iv, 337
Knight [Knyght], Aaron, iv, 625; Andr., iii, 263; iv, 486; Anne, iii, 225; iv, 486, 493; v, 155; Bulstrode, iv, 172; Chris., ii, 497; Constance, ii, 492; Denise, iv, 203; Edw., ii, 497, 501; iii, 21, 53; iv, 103, 172, 424; v, 517, 518; Eliz., ii, 210, 478, 500; iv, 172, 625; Ellis, iv, 291, 425; E., iv, 4, 65; Hen., iii, 348; iv, 13, 40, 49, 71, 79, 80, 97, 107, 112, 136, 158, 170, 174, 217, 230, 234, 264, 281, 291, 303, 403; v, 72, 79; Jane, iv, 259; Joan, iii, 263; v, 243 n; John, ii, 474, 483, 498, 500, 501; iii, 125, 241, 273, 487; iv, 259, 279, 486; v, 164, 243 n; Sir Julius, ii, 448; Matth., iv, 486; Mich., v, 155, 164; Montagu, ii, 483, 496, 497, 501, 514; iii, 20; iv, 172, 173; v, 519; Mylan, iv, 625; Nich., ii, 478, 497; Priscilla, iv, 70; (Sir) Rich., ii, 492, 493, 497, 500; iii, 21, 487; iv, 75, 189, 486; v, 164, 169; Rob., iv, 492, 493; iv, 189, 316; Sam., ii, 489; iv, 29, 181, 275, 331, 485; Steph., ii, 478; (Sir) Thos., ii,

Knight (cont.)
497, 514; iii, 20, 70, 263; iv, 172, 424, 486, 493, 494; v, 168, 277 n; Ursula, iv, 486; Will., ii, 29, 294, 501; iii, 21, 125, 503; iv, 20, 172, 203, 479, 486, 589; —, iii, 536; iv, 17, 183; v, 166, 465; fam., v, 182; arms, ii, 478, 498
Knighton, man. (Newchurch), v, 142, 182
Knighton, tithing (E Medine), v, 138
Knight's Bridge (Kingsclere), iv, 250
Knightsbridge, Rob. of, iv, 408
Knightsbridge House (Kingsclere), iv, 250
Knight's Enham, iv, 333, 346, 354, 356, 377-9, 381; adv., iv, 379; char., iv, 379; ch., iv, 378; man., iv, 377; pop., v, 438
Knights Hospitallers, see St. John of Jerusalem, knights of
Knights lands (Hurstbourne Tarrant), iv, 324
Knights Templars, see Templars
Knokyn, John de, iv, 253
Knoll Down (Rockbourne), iv, 581, 587 n
Knolle (Whitchurch), iv, 300
Knolles Coppice (Hurstbourne Tarrant), iv, 321
Knollys [Knolle, Knolles] (de), Sir Fran., iv, 60, 261; Hen., iii, 434; v, 172, 227, 228; John, iv, 179; Rob., iii, 435, 436; iv, 363; Thos., iii, 62, 434; v, 228; T. W., ii, 350; fam., arms, iii, 435; see also Knowles
Knott, see Nott
Knottingle, John, v, 130 n
Knottingslee (Sopley), v, 128
Knowl [Knowle] (Kingsclere), iv, 255 n, 256, 257, 296, 332 n
Knowles [Cnolle, Knovill, Knoville, Knowell, Knowl] (de, de la), Amice, iii, 46; Avis, iii, 535; Bevis, iii, 255; iv, 206, 396; Chas. J., iv, 325; Eleanor, iv, 369 n; Gilb., ii, 170; Rob., ii, 203, 205; —, ii, 385; v, 392; see also Knollys
Knowl Hill (Kingsclere), iv, 257
Knowls Farm (Kingsclere), iv, 257
Knox, Lt. Col. R., v, 519
Knulle, Great, (Long Sutton), iv, 18
Knyght, see Knight
Knyght Bridge (Longparish), iv, 408
Knyght Chambre, le, (Penton Mewsey), iv, 382 n
Knyghteton, see Knighton
Knyppel, Will., v, 483
Knyvet [Knyvett], Sir Ant., iii, 186, 187; Edm., iv, 361; Joan, iv, 645; Will., iv, 645
Krockere, see Crocker
Krompe, Joan, ii, 135
Kudelinton, John de, iv, 396
Kurne, see Kern
Kybbell, Geo., iv, 342; John, iv, 342
Kybulwhite, see Keblewhite
Kydwelly, see Kidwelly
Kyllavon, Hen., v, 285
Kyllere, Rich. le, iv, 349
Kymbridge (Timsbury), iv, 486
Kyme [Kime, Kymbe], Cecily, Lady, v, 147; Sir Thos., v, 147
Kymer, Gilb., iv, 576
Kymmere, see Kimmer Farm
Kympston, see Kilmeston
Kynegils, see Cynegils
Kyneleye, see Kennerly
Kyng, see King

Kyngbrigg, man. (Mottisfont), see Kimbridge
Kyngesbarghe (S. Damerham), iv, 586
Kyngesham, Alice, iv, 342; Rob., iv, 342
Kyngeslese, see Kingsleaze
Kyngesmill, see Kingsmill
Kyngeston, Kyngestone, see Kingston
Kynnesman, R., ii, 507
Kynzteton, see Knighton
Kyppynges (Liss), iv, 84
Kyrkebyesmede (Overton), iv, 211
Kytebrigge (Carisbrooke), v, 222

Labaanc, Oidelard, iv, 256 n; Rich., iv, 256, 296
Lace industry, v, 254, 457
Lacertilia, i, 205
Lacey, F. E., v, 575; John, v, 29; see also Lacy
Lachemere (Pamber), iv, 433
Lachenietahalla (Winchester), v, 1
Lacherne, see Kern
Laci, Lacie, see Lacy
Lackham, man. (Wilts), iv, 53
Lacock Nunnery (Wilts), v, 238, 259, 279, 280
Lacombe, Thos., v, 165
Lacton, ii, 146
Lacy [Laci, Lacie] (de), Alice, iv, 560; Anne, ii, 125; Cath., iii, 145; C., iv, 5; Geo., iii, 325; Hen., iii, 145, 325; iv, 536, 560; Marg., iv, 536, 560; Walt., iv, 624; Will., iii, 324, 325; see also Lacey
Ladde, Amice, abbess of Wherwell, ii, 137
Lade, Benedict de la, v, 130 n
Laden, Thos., v, 460
Ladene, see Priors Dean
Ladle Hill (Litchfield), iv, 267
Ladoke, Will., ii, 171
Ladycroft (Barton Stacey), iv, 417
Lady Cross Lodge (Brockenhurst), iv, 626
Lady Houses (Stockbridge), iv, 483
Ladylonge (Hurstbourne Tarrant), iv, 321
Lady's Lake (Winchester), v, 19 n
Laffrenshemore, see Frenchmoor
Lafham, man., ii, 207
Laghton, ii, 147
Laigle [Aquila], de, Gilb., iv, 77; Juliana, iv, 77, 99
Laing, S., v, 113
Lainston, iii, 401, 444; man., iii, 444; pop., v, 447
Lake, Arth., ii, 197; Chris., iv, 614
Lakinges, Nich. de, ii, 154
Lamb, Caroline E., iv, 250, 267; Chas., v, 277; v, 85; Geo., iv, 219, 244; Ralph, ii, 202
Lambden, John, iv, 302 n
Lambert [Lambard, Lambart], Constance, iv, 208, 283; Edm., iv, 335 n, 507; Edw., iv, 507; Jane, iii, 54; Magdalen, iv, 610; Rich., iv, 208, 283; Rob., iv, 208; Sarah, iv, 335, 353, 507; (Sir) Thos., iii, 431; iv, 203, 208, 283; Will., iv, 36; Dr., v, 137
Lamboldesholde (Tunworth), iv, 174
Lamboll (Sherfield), iv, 104
Lambourne's Hill, Rom. rem., iv, 366
Lambyn, Steph., iii, 172
Lame, the, (Bradley), iv, 202
Lame, Rich., v, 485 n
Lammere, man., see Lomer

Lamore (Arreton), v, 142
Lamott, John, v, 261
Lamplew, Rich., v, 173
Lampole (Overton), iv, 211 n
Lamport, Hen., iv, 127; Rob., ii, 482
Lampultes (Freshwater), v, 240
Lamputte, la, (Liss), iv, 84
Lamy, Greg. de, v, 485, 485 n
Lancaster, duchy of, iv, 108, 366, 538
Lancaster, Avelina, ctss. of, iii, 171; iv, 213; Maud, ctss. of, iv, 109; Blanche, dchss. of, ii, 43, 509; iv, 471; dks. of: iv, 89, 367; v, 365, 366; Hen., ii, 509; iv, 366, 470, 476, 499; John of Gaunt, ii, 45, 509; iv, 469, 470, 471; v, 367; earls of: Edm., iv, 213; v, 362; Hen., ii, 173, 174, 509; iii, 104; iv, 109, 471, 473, 504, 538
Lancaster, Sir Jas., ii, 376; iv, 139, 140, 266; John of, see Bedford, duke of; Maud, ii, 509; Will., iv, 623
Lancelevy (Sherfield Loddon), iv, 101, 104
Lancelevy [Lanceleue, Lancelevee, Launcelevee, Launcelevy] (de), Alice, iv, 258, 259; Joan, iii, 52, 263; John, iv, 257, 259; v, 135; Rog., iii, 52, 204, 263
Lanch, ii, 493
Land, —, v, 523
Landa, Rich. de, iii, 194
Landford, man., iv, 540, 541
Landford Wood, iv, 541
Landguard [Landguard, North], man. (Brading), v, 163, 214
Landguard, Great, man. (Brading), v, 164
Landon, Rog., iv, 25, 112, 174, 425, 430; Miss, v, 285
Landport (Portsmouth), ii, 102; iii, 193
Lane (atte), Arth. B., iv, 496; Edw., iv, 568; Egidia, iv, 568; John, ii, 161; iii, 483; Susan, iii, 483; Thos., ii, 87; Will., v, 5
Lane End (Bembridge), v, 157
Laner, Hugh, ii, 367
Laney, Rev. Benj., iii, 93
Langberewe, John de, v, 235 n
Langbridge, man. (Newchurch), v, 140, 177, 181
Langbrook, Will., iv, 392
Langeberghe (S. Damerham), iv, 587 n
Langebrigge, see Langbridge
Langelond (Whitchurch), iv, 300
Langelonde (Penton Mewsey), iv, 381
Langemede, la, (Hordle), v, 111
Langepoule (Overton), iv, 211
Langerige, fam., see Langrish
Langerisse, Langeryssh, man., see Langrish
Langethornesforlong (Kimpton), iv, 372
Langford, ii, 140, 143, 145
Langford [Longford] (de), Agnes, iv, 266; Anne, v, 237; Aubrey, v, 129 n; Denise, v, 251; Edm., v, 251; Edw., v, 237; Eliz., v, 251, 253; Gilb., iv, 519; Isabel, v, 237 n; Joan (Lady), iv, 342, 519, 524; v, 237; John, iii, 262; v, 224, 225, 237; Maud, iv, 519; Rich., v, 237; Rob., v, 237; Rog., iv, 519, 610; v, 129, 237; (Sir) Thos., iii, 262; v, 237; Walt., iv, 342, 476, 487, 519, 524, 610; v, 129; Sir Will., v, 237
Langhome (Stratfieldsaye), iv, 57

Langhorn, John, iii, 483; Steph., iii, 483; Will., iii, 483
Langland, Will., ii, 473
Langley, man. (Eling), ii, 169, 172; iv, 553, 554
Langley [South Langley], man. (Fawley), iii, 275, 294; iv, 553, 615
Langley [Longley], (de, of), Edm., see York, dk. of; Jane C., iii, 439; John, iv, 550; Marg., iv, 569; Rich., iv, 550; Thos., iv, 380, 569
Langley Meade (Romsey), iv, 452, 453
Langlois, Benj., iv, 201
Langred, see Landguard
Langrish [Langrishe, Langrissh, Langryshe], iii, 63, 64-5; man., iii, 69
Langrish [Langerige, Languish], Browne, iii, 112; John, iii, 69, 70; Mary, iv, 443; Nich., ii, 179; iii, 6, 70; Rob., iii, 69; Thos., iii, 69; Will., iii, 70
Langrish House (East Meon), iii, 65
Langrude, John de, iii, 466
Langstone [Langston] (Havant), iii, 122, 129; mill, iii, 122
Langstone Harbour, iii, 122, 129; v, 359, 402; fisheries, v, 468; oyster dredging, v, 468
Langton (de), Sim., v, 308; Steph., archbp. of Canterbury, iv, 88; v, 308, 309; Thos., bp. of Winchester, ii, 48; v, 54; Walt., bp. of Coventry and Lichfield, iii, 457; fam., arms., v, 54
Languish, see Langrish
Lanham Down, Rom. rem., i, 306
Lankester & Sons, v, 461
Lannoy-Hunter, (Lt.-Col.), Hen., iv, 57, 62, 104
Lansdowne, mqss. of, iii, 500
Lanthony Abbey (Glouc.), iv, 417, 422
Lanyngton Cops (Eling), iv, 547
Larchestoke, see Laverstoke
Lardners (Upper Clatford), iv, 360
Larke, Thos., iv, 330
Larode, ii, 471
Larugmedes (Rotherwick), iv, 99
Larymore, Neville, iii, 320
Lascelles, Gerald, iv, 545; see also Lassell
Lasham, iii, 356; iv, 66, 67, 81-3, 202; adv., iv, 83; char., iv, 83; ch., iv, 83; man., iv, 81; pop., v, 439
Lasham, Ellen, v, 79
Laspaund, v, 147
Lasseham, see Lasham
Lassell, Miss., v, 84; see also Lascelles
Latches, see Longlathes
Latch Farm (Christchurch), v, 85
Latchingdon (Essex), iv, 304
Latchmore (Bramley), iv, 433
Latchmore Green, Rom. rem., i, 345
Latelais [Latelays], Harison, iii, 131; Jonah [Jonas], iii, 131, 242
La Terriere, Capt. Bulmer de S., iii, 437; Col. Fenwick B. de S., iv, 631
Latham [Lathum], John, iv, 453; Rowland, ii, 185, 186
Lathbury, John, ii, 444; Rich., ii, 180
Lathum, see Latham
Latimer [Latymer] (le), Joan, iv, 577; John, iv, 82; Rob., iv, 82
Latinarius, Hugh, v, 113
Latin Gate (Faccombe), iv, 315
Latton, Will., iv, 190
Latymer, see Latimer

Laud, Will., archbp. of Canterbury, ii, 88, 89, 95, 323, 500; iv, 36; v, 248
Laudimor, John de, iii, 386, 388
Launcel, Margery, iii, 46; Walt., ii, 177; iii, 46
Launcelevee, Launcelevy, see Lancelevy
Launcelyn, Sim., ii, 188; Thos., ii, 188
Laundrey Meade (Elvetham), iv, 74
Laune, Thos., v, 65
Laurence Wotton, see Wootton St. Lawrence
Lauriton, Geoff. de, iii, 415
Lauton, Thos., iv, 151
Lavender [Lavendere] (la), John, ii, 120; Lucy, iv, 598
Laverstoke, ii, 117; iv, 197, 208-10, 216, 282, 283, 284, 300; v, 490; adv., iv, 210; ch., iv, 208, 209; man., iv, 208; mill, iv, 209; v, 489, 490; pk., iv, 208, 282; pop., v, 442
Laverstoke, John de, v, 456
Laverstoke-cum-Freefolk, iv, 210
Laverstoke House (Laverstoke), iv, 208, 209
Lavington (Wilts.), ii, 227
Lavington [Lavyngton], Cecilia de, abbess of Wherwell, ii, 40, 137; iv, 201; John, iv, 296 n; Thos., iii, 257; v, 482
Lavinia, w. of Sygar, iv, 501
Lavrochestoche, see Laverstoke
La Warr, fam., see De la Warr
Lawder, John, prior of Southwick, ii, 167, 168
Lawerd, Agnes, iv, 25; Will., iv, 25
Lawes, Rev. Jas. T., v, 78
Lawes' exhibition (Winchester), v, 78
Lawnes, the, (Carisbrooke), v, 229
Lawrence, abbot of St. Vigor, ii, 227
Lawrence, John, v, 112; Will., v, 3 n, 5, 11
Lawson, Harriet, iii, 215; Sir John, v, 382
Laybrooke, man. (Ringwood), iv, 610
Laybrooke, de, Eustasia, iv, 610; Will., iv, 610
Layfield, (Rev.) Chas., iii, 93, 405; v, 78
Laylands Fields [Laylandes Furlong] (Faccombe), iv, 314
Laystede (Calbourne), v, 218
Layton, Joan, iv, 330; Roland, iv, 330; Dr., ii, 167, 168; see also Leighton
Lazenby (Yorks.), v, 271
Leach, see Leech
Lea Green (Hordle), v, 110
Leah, John de, ii, 29
Leake, see Leeke
Lebrun, Fremund, iii, 412
Leche, see Leech
Leches (Sherborne St. John), iv, 158
Leckford, ii, 117; iv, 438, 446-49, 458, 489; adv., iv, 449; char., iv, 449; ch., iv, 448; mans., iv, 413, 446, 481; New Farm, iv, 446, 447; Nonconf., iv, 449; pop., v, 439
Leckford [Lekforde], de, Alice, iv, 447 n; Emma, iv, 340; Isabel, ii, 129; Maud, iv, 358 n; Rich., iv, 447; Rog., iv, 340, 358 n; Will., iv, 447
Leckford Abbess, man. (Leckford), ii, 122, 126; iv, 446

Leckford Abbotts, man. (Leckford), ii, 121 ; iv, 447
Leckford Riches [Leckford Richards], man. (Leckford), iv, 447
Leconfield, Ld., v, 526
Le Court [Lee Court] (Greatham), ii, 506, 507
Leder, Frances, v, 192 ; Oliver, v, 192
Ledessete, *see* Ludshott
Ledmere, *see* Ludmore
Lee (Brading), v, 164
Lee (Romsey), iv, 452, 460, 468
Lee (Titchfield), *see* **Lee-on-the-Solent**
Lee, Lady Marg., v, 274 *n*
Lee (a, de la), Anne, ii, 478 ; iv, 102 ; Benj., v, 286 ; Chas., iii, 53 ; Dorothy, iv, 143, 180 ; Edw., ii, 69 ; Edw. A., ii, 491 ; Eliz., iv, 102 ; Ellen, iv, 102 ; Gilb., v, 377 ; Godf. B., ii, 366 ; Harriet, iii, 27 ; Hen., ii, 347, 366 ; Hen. P., iv, 143 ; H., iii, 467 ; Jane, iv, 102 ; Joan, iv, 103 ; John, iv, 102, 180 ; v, 164 *n* ; Rev. J. M., iii, 467 ; Lucy, v, 180 *n* ; Mary [Marie], iii, 53 ; iv, 455 ; Maud, iv, 102 ; Phil., iv, 197 ; Rich., iii, 396 ; iv, 332, 393 ; Rob., iii, 184 ; iv, 102 ; Steph., iii, 53 ; Thos., ii, 124 ; iii, 398 ; Will., ii, 478 ; iv, 102 ; Dr., ii, 302 ; *see also* Legh, Leigh, and Ley
Leech [Leach, Leche], Isaac, v, 455 ; John, ii, 296 ; iv, 8 *n*, 529 ; Dr., v, 538
Lee Court, *see* **Le Court**
Leeds, Thos. Osborne, dk. of, iii, 508
Lee Farm (Brading), v, 164
Leefe [Leffe], John, ii, 197 ; Pet., iii, 390
Lee House (Romsey), iv, 460
Leekblade, —, v, 536
Leeke [Leake], Sam., iii, 193 ; T., iv, 477 *n*
Lee Markes, man. (Titchfield), iii, 228
Lee-on-the-Solent, iii, 221 ; man., iii, 228
Leeson, Dr., v, 155, 156
Lefevre [le Faver], Maj. C. S., v, 356 ; Helena, iv, 46 ; John, iv, 46 ; v, 474 ; —, ii, 354 ; *see also* Shaw-Lefevre
Leffe, *see* Leefe
Lefroy, Ant., iv, 5 ; Benj., iv, 201 ; Chas., iv, 5 ; Chas. E., iv, 13, 14 ; Chas. J. M., iv, 6, 8, 14, 19 ; Isaac P. G., iv, 201 ; Janet, iv, 13 ; Rev. John H. G., iv, 8, 201 ; Pet. G., iv, 201 ; fam., iv, 198
Lefsi, iii, 145 ; iv, 18
Legard, Rob., v, 109
Legay, Isaac, iv, 537 ; Pet., iv, 537
Legford, *see* Leckford
Legg, Bethia, v, 281 ; Eliz., v, 281 ; R., v, 176 ; Will., v, 281 ; *see also* Legge
Leggatt, John, iii, 532
Legge, Rev. Aug. G., ii, 488 ; iii, 45, 89, 90 ; iv, 27 ; Frances C., iv, 232 ; Geo., v, 386 ; Hen., iii, 53, 89 ; Hen. B., ii, 519 ; iii, 12 ; Honora, iii, 45, 50, 323, 460, 461 ; Mary, iii, 143 ; —, iv, 347 ; Will., ii, 488 ; iv, 232 ; fam. arms, iii, 89 ; *see also* Legg
Legh (de, de la), Eliz., ii, 125 ; Joan, abbess of Nunnaminster, ii, 49, 124, 126 ; Marg., ii, 124 ; Mary, ii, 125 ; Maud, v, 123 ; Rob., prior of Christchurch, ii, 156 ; Thos., ii, **124, 125, 136,**

Legh (*cont.*)
151, 196 ; v, 113, 123 ; Will., v, 47 ; Col., v, 562 ; *see also* Lee, Leigh, *and* Ley
Legonier, *see* Ligonier
Leicester, Eleanor, ctss. of, iv, 53, 88, 89, 90, 360, 607 ; earls of : Rob. Dudley, ii, 81 ; iv, 356 ; **Sim. de Montfort,** *see* **Montford, Sim. de** ; Rob. Fitz Parnel, iv, 607
Leicester, Geo., iii, 19 ; Rich. of, iii, 506
Leigh [Lyegh] (de la), Agnes, v, 171, 176 ; Amelia, v, 280 ; Anne, v, 171, 176, 180 *n*, 229, 280, 283 ; Barnabas, v, 229, 230, 280, 283 ; Barnabas E., v, 219 ; Caroline, v, 291 ; Edw., v, 180, 280, 283 ; Eliz. (Lady), v, 280, 283, 292 ; Hen., iv, 199 ; Holmes, v, 148 ; Joan, v, 280 ; (Sir) John, ii, 479, 503, 505 ; iii, 43, 328, 330, 456 ; iv, 185 *n*, 259 ; v, 141, 171, 175, 176, 177, 180 *n*, 182 *n*, 229, 230 *n*, 252, 278, 280, 283, 284 ; Marg., ii, 505 ; v, 557 ; Marian, ii, 479 ; Mary, v, 280 ; Phil., iii, 328 ; iv, 549 ; Thos., ii, 479, 503 ; iii, 328 ; iv, 549 ; v, 280 ; fam., arms, ii, 503 ; iii, 328 ; *see also* Lee, Legh, *and* Ley
Leighehelme (Longstock), iv, 449
Leigh Park (Havant), iii, 122
Leigh Park beagles, v, 542
Leighton, Chas., iv, 36 ; Eliz., iv, 36 *n* ; Sir Thos., v, 332 ; *see also* Layton
Leith (de), John, iv, 618 ; Mary C. J., v, 237, 279, 280, 282 ; Gen. Rob. W. D., v, 280, 284
Lekforde, *see* Leckford
Lekhull (de), John, iv, 569 ; Kath., iv, 569 ; Will., iv, 569
Lemmereystone, *see* Limerstone
Lempriere, E., iv, 9 *n* ; Phil. R., iv, 9
Lende, Alice, iii, 373 ; iv, 214 ; Thos., iii, 373 ; iv, 214
Lendecumbe (Burghclere), iv, 277
Lenimcode, v, 210, 273
Lennard [Leonard], John, v, 135 ; Rich., iv, 352 ; Will., iv, 497 *n*
Lennox, Ludovic, dk. of, v, 24
Lens, Hugh de, abbot of Hyde, ii, 117
Lentune, *see* Lymington
Leofric, v, 296, 298
Leonard, *see* Lennard
Leonards (Beaulieu), iv, 651
Leonn, Will. le, v, 242
Leopold, king of the Belgians, v, 566
Lepe (Exbury), i, 325, 380 ; iii, 290, 291
Lepe House (Exbury), iii, 290
Lepene, *see* Pan
Leper's Grove (Yateley), iv, 21
Lepidoptera, i, 130
Le Roy-Lewis, Col., iii, 69, 71
Lesborne, ii, 471
Lescelond, *see* Lessland
Lescrope, *see* Scrope
Lesham, *see* Lasham
Leslie, Lewis, ii, 482
Lesse, John, iv, 149
Lessland, man. (Godshill), v, 162, 173
Lesteorde, iv, 549
Lester, Thos., iv, 272
Lester & Pack, bellfounders, iv, 86, 97, 136, 355, 497 ; v, 74
Lestock [le Stock], Rob., ii, 203, 205 ; Adm., v, 389
Lestrange, *see* Strange

Lestred, *see* Lesteorde
Letcombe, John, ii, **122**
Letelie, *see* Netley
Leteshelve, *see* Litchfield
Lethbridge, Chas., iv, 103
Lettele, *see* Netley
Letton (Milford), v, 117, 120
Letts, Thos., v, 236
Leutherius, bp. of Winchester, ii, 2
Levechild, Will., iii, 88, 97
Levedilonde (Carisbrooke), v, 222
Levegarestun, *see* Landguard
Leventhorpe, Dorothy, iv, 248 ; John, iv, 89 ; Thos., iv, 248
Leverley, man., ii, 163
Levers & Crooks Freehold (Ashe), iv, 198
Leversuch, Rich., v, 27
Leveson, Christine, Lady, iv, 271 *n* ; Sir John, iv, 271 *n* ; (Sir) Rich., iv, 271, 352
Leving, v, 212
Levington, Jas., v, 95 *n*
Levintun, *see* Limerstone
Levotelane (Sherborne St. John), iv, 158
Lewen [Lewyn], Edw., v, 99 ; Geo., v, 112 *n* ; Maud, v, 130 *n* ; Rob., v, 112 *n*, 113 ; (Sir) Will., v, 112, 130 *n* ; —, v, 467
Leweo, *see* Weyhill
Lewer, *see* Ewer
Lewes, *see* Lewis
Lewin, iv, 7, 22, 258, 290
Lewis [Lewes], Anna M., iii, 259 ; Eliz., iii, 150 ; Joan, iv, 571 ; John D., iii, 69 ; Marg., iv, 571, 580 ; Percival, iv, 571, 580, 605 ; Rich., iv, 571 ; Thos., iii, 259, 263, 264 ; (Sir) Will., ii, 197 ; iii, 67, 101 ; v, 65 ; —, iv, 447 ; fam., arms, iii, 259
Lewisham, Geo., vsct., iv, 232
Lewkenor, Anne, iv, 103, 172 ; Cath. [Kath.], iv, 413, 557 ; v, 247 ; Sir Chris., iv, 172 *n* ; Eleanor, iv, 82 ; (Sir) John, iv, 103, 172 ; Philippa, Lady, iv, 501 ; Rich., iv, 172 *n* ; (Sir) Rog., iii, 126 ; iv, 82, 413, 501, 557 ; Thos., iii, 126 ; iv, 82 ; v, 247
Lewston [Leyston] (de), John, iv, 315, 316 *n* ; Nichola, iv, 382 ; Philippa, iv, 315, 563 ; Rog., iv, 382 ; Thos., iv, 315, 563 ; Will., iv, 315, 563
Lewyn, *see* Lewen *and* Lewin
Lexford, John of, iv, 192
Ley, Sir Jas., iv, 393 ; Jane, iv, 393 ; Matth., iv, 65 ; *see also* Lee, Legh *and* Leigh
Leyborne [Leybourne, Leyburn] (de), Eleanor, iv, 254 ; Hen., iv, 110, 523 ; Idonea, iv, 81, 82 ; Isabel, iv, 81 ; Julia, iv, 110 ; Rog., iv, 254 ; Thos., iv, 110 ; Sir Will., v, 362
Leybrooke Common (Ringwood), iv, 606
Ley Down (Sutton Warblington), iv, 18
Leyforlang (Longstock), iv, 449
Leygh, *see* Lee
Leygrave, de, Alice, ii, 122 ; Juliana, ii, 122
Leylie (Burghclere), iv, 277
Leys, *see* Liss
Leyston, *see* Lewston
Leysyure, Eliz., iv, 60 ; Sir Steph., iv, 60
Libertyes (Milton), v, 124
Lichelad, Walt. de, iii, 93
Lichens, i, 75
Lichette (Dors.), ii, 163
Lichfeld, John ii, 125, 197

Lichfield, bps. of, iv, 230; Walt. de Langton, iii, 457
Lichfield, Will. Tucker, dean of, ii, 315, 319
Lickpit [Lichepit], man. (Basing), ii, 117; iv, 113 n, 123; man.-house, iv, 123
Lickpits (Basing), iv, 123
Liddell, J., iv, 106
Liddesulde, Lidescelve, Lideshull, see Litchfield
Lidesette, see Ludshott
Lidmer, see Ludmore
Lidshott, see Ludshott
Lidulse, Lieuselva, see Litchfield
Lige, la, see Lee-on-the-Solent
Ligginham Mede (Eling), iv, 547
Ligh, Sir John, ii, 367
Light, Eliz., iii, 295; Jos., v, 487
Lightfoot, John, iv, 101; Will B., ii, 384, 385
Ligonier [Legonier], Mary, ctss., iv, 154, 204
Likehorne, Thos., ii, 87
Lillebane, John de, iii, 494, 495
Lillymill (Bramley), iv, 141
Lillymill Farm (Bramley), iv, 141
Lillywhite, —, iv, 27
Lily [Lyly], John, iv, 628; Will., iv, 88
Limborne, man. (Havant), iii, 124
Limbrey, Hen., iv, 121, 240; John, iii, 384, 386; iv, 121 n; Magdalen, iv, 121
Lime-burning industry, v, 454
Limerstone (Brighstone), v, 163, 211, 214, 219; man., v, 200, 209, 212, 215
Limerstone, Ralph de, v, 212
Limesey [Limesi, Limosia] (de, of), Ad., iii, 59, 61; Hen., iii, 59; v, 125; John, v, 125; Lucy, v, 124; Rich., iii, 59, 505; Rob., ii, 160, 194, 196; Rog., iii, 59
Lincbrey, Hen., iii, 361
Linchehore, see Linkenholt
Linch Hill (Whitchurch), iv, 300
Lincoln, bps. of, v, 302; John de Buckingham, iv, 627; Phil., Repingdon, ii, 42; Hugh Wells, ii, 21
Lincoln, ctsses. of :—Hawise, v, 94; Marg. de Laci, iv, 560; earls of, ii, 492; v, 207; Hen. de Laci, iv, 560; John de la Pole, iv, 130, 348 n
Lincoln, Alvred de, iv, 588
Linden, Jas., v, 461 n
Lindsay, Montague, earl of, v, 340 n, 350 n
Lindsay, John, iii, 376
Linford (Fordingbridge), iv, 559
Linguire (de), Alice, iv, 568; Aubrey, v, 100; Hugh, iv, 568; Phil., iv, 568
Lingwede, Lingwood, see Ningwood
Linkenholt [Linkeholth], iv, 318, 324-5; adv., iv, 325; ch., iv, 325; man., iv, 324; v, 410, 411; pop., v, 438; sch., iv, 324
Linlee, de, Eleanor, iv, 141; Will., iv, 141
Lintott [Lintot], Mary, iii, 241; Thos., iii, 241; —, v, 487
Linwood, iv, 563, 579 n, 604, 615, 629-30; man., iv, 629
Linwood, East, iv, 630
Linwood (de), Nich., iv, 8; Pet., iv, 579, 629
Linwood Bog, riv., iv, 579
Linwood Walk, West, (New Forest), ii, 427
Linzee, Edw., iii, 180

Liphook (Bramshott), ii, 491, 495, 496; v, 428, 453
Lippen Wood, Little, (West Meon), i, 309
Lipscomb, Rob., iii, 377
Lipscombe (Eversley), iv, 33
Lire Abbey (France), iv, 360, 365; v, 148, 150, 155, 171, 176, 186, 189, 201, 206 n, 230, 231 n, 234, 241, 242, 245
Liscelande, see Lessland
Lisle [Lysley], Jane Dudley, Lady, see Northumberland, dchss. of; John Dudley, Ld., see Northumberland, dk. of; vscts., ii, 125; Arth., iii, 228, 229, 261, 392; iv, 651; v, 247; Edw. Grey, v, 247; John, iv, 564
Lisle [Insula, Isle] (de, del), Agnes, iv, 388, 389; v, 243; Alice, ii, 97; iv, 563, 564; Amice, v, 165; Anne, iv, 617; Ant., iii, 527; iv, 313, 342; v, 142 n, 205; Sir Arth. P. V., iv, 541; Bald., iii, 169; iv, 222 n; v, 202, 204, 219 n, 246; Barth., iv, 146, 353, 377, 379, 619; v, 172, 201, 204, 312; Beconshaw, iv, 565 n; Brian, v, 251; Bridg., v, 205; Cath., iii, 415; Chas., iv, 564, 580; Chas. C., iv, 563; Edw., iv, 313, 564; v, 205; Edw. H., iv, 564, 565; Eleanor, iv, 388, 617; v, 204 n; Eliz., iii, 169; iv, 141 n, 353, 373, 388, 390, 619; v, 162, 165, 172, 204, 247; Fran., iv, 159; Geoff., iii, 169; v, 145, 160, 197 n, 202, 204, 241, 243, 246, 251, 280; Geo., v, 204; Gerald, iv, 141 n; Godf., prior of Andwell, ii, 225; Hen., v, 165, 191, 201 n; Hugh, v, 246; Isabel, iv, 388; v, 191, 243; Jane, v, 243; Joan, iii 169; v, 247, 273; (Sir) John, iv, 16, 97, 180, 197, 231; iii, 21, 169, 404, 415, 484; iv, 21 n, 313, 353, 373, 374, 377, 388, 390, 515 n, 563, 564, 565, 617, 619, 623; v, 112, 142, 143, 145, 150, 155, 160, 160 n, 162, 163, 172, 173, 174, 182, 191, 191 n, 195, 198, 201, 204, 216, 221 n, 231, 243, 246, 247, 252 n, 273, 274, 280, 282, 284, 312, 363; Lancelot, iv, 313, 388; v, 204; Lawr., v, 247; Leonard, v, 247; Marg., iv, 373, 388, 389; Mary (Lady), iii, 269; iv, 159, 373 n, 388, 564, 619; v, 172, 182, 204, 205, 280; Maud, v, 168, 202, 246; Muriel, v, 168; Nichola, iv, 353, 515 n; (Sir) Nich., iii, 484; iv, 313, 342, 388, 617; v, 204; Oliver, v, 172, 237; Rob., iv, 642; v, 145 n; (Sir) Thos., ii, 190, 191; iv, 159, 313, 388, 390, 617, 619; v, 142, 142 n, 148, 149, 150, 204, 205, 247, 280; Walt., ii, 177, 179; v, 147, 155, 168, 174, 188, 191, 192, 202, 204, 243, 246, 284; (Sir) Will., ii, 391, 479; iv, 313, 564; v, 142 n, 168, 172, 188, 191, 201, 204, 205, 246; fam., iv, 391; v, 177, 184; arms, iii, 484; see also Estur, Lyle and Lysle
Lisle Court (Boldre), iv, 616
Lisle Court farm (Boldre), iv, 619
Liss, ii, 122; iii, 82, 116; iv, 71, 84-6, 110; adv., iv, 86; chs., iv, 85, 97; Lower Green, iv, 84; mans., iv, 84; mills, iv, 85; Nonconf., iv, 86; pop., v, 444; schs., iv, 86; Upper Green, iv, 84
Liss, hund., iv, 66

Liss, East, iv, 84
Liss, West, iv, 84
Liss Abbas [Abbess], man. (Liss) ii, 126; iii, 245, 246; iv, 66, 67, 84
Liss Place (Liss), ii, 507; iv, 84
Liss Turney [Listurmey], man. (Liss), iv, 66, 67, 84, 93
Lister [Lyster], Eliz., ii, 513; iv, 28; (Sir) Mich., ii, 513; iv, 28, 296, 507, 541 n; Sir Ralph, ii, 516; (Sir) Rich., ii, 131, 149, 478, 479, 486, 504, 513; iii, 43, 227, 228, 328, 330, 392, 530, 531, 533; iv, 388 n, 446, 447, 449, 454 n, 459, 488, 499, 502, 507, 541
Lister-Kay, Ellis C., iv, 607
Litchfield, iv, 245, 246, 249, 250, 255, 267-70, 327 n, 331, 332 n, 550; adv., iv, 270; ch., iv, 269; man., iv, 267; pop., v, 442; sch., iv, 269
Litchfield, South, (Ashe), iv, 198, 200
Litchfield Grange, man. (Ashe), iv, 198, 200
Litesland, see Lessland
Little, Anna V., iii, 200; Eliz., iv, 271; Thos., iv, 271
Littledown (Woodcott), iv, 331
Littledown Common (Bournemouth), v, 134
Littledown House (Holdenhurst), v, 133
Littlehales, Mary, v, 80
Little Somborne House (Little Somborne), iv, 480
Little Testwood Farm (Eling), iv, 546, 550
Little Testwood House (Eling), iv, 546, 550
Littleton, ii, 111; iii, 401, 422-3; adv., iii, 423; ch., iii, 423; man., ii, 114; iii, 422; pop., v, 447; sch., ii, 401
Littleton, man. (Kimpton), iv, 324, 368, 373-4, 527 n; v, 410, 411, 412
Littleton, Maud de, ii, 134, 137; see also Lyttelton
Littleton Copse (Kimpton), iv, 372, 374
Littleton Farm (Kimpton), iv, 372
Littleton Five-acres (Corhampton), Rom. rem., i, 309
Littletown [Littleton] (Newchurch), v, 182
Litton [Lytton], Alex., ii, 381, 385; Rob., iv, 224; Sir Will., iv, 587, 589
Liverworts, i, 75
Livescelve, Liveschella, see Litchfield
Lizards, i, 205
Llewellin & James, bellmakers, iv, 17
Llewellyn, G. C. B., v, 575, 576
Lloyd, Hen., ii, 315; Hugh, ii, 366; Joan, v, 280; Maj. J. H. G., iv, 547; L., v, 271; Rich. B., v, 280; Will., bp., ii, 339
Loader [Loder], Geo., v, 518; Thos., v, 483
Loates, Sam., v, 554
Lobb [Lobbe], Eliz., iv, 161 n; Rich., iii, 438; Thos., iv, 161 n
Lock [Locke, Lok, Lokke], John, ii, 486; iii, 120; iv, 483; P., v, 391; Rich., ii, 488; iii, 10; v, 482; Rob., ii, 488; iv, 393, 513 n; Thos., ii, 486; Will., ii, 486
Lock Burn, v, 69
Lockerley, iv, 489, 498, 499, 500-2, 515, 517; adv., iv, 502; char., iv, 502; ch., iv, 502, 509 n; mans., ii, 163; iv, 472 n, 500;

Lockerley (*cont.*)
mkt. and fairs, iv, 501 ; mills, iv, 500 ; Nonconf., iv, 502 ; pop., v, 446
Lockerley End, sch., ii, 401
Lockerley Green (Lockerley), iv, 500
Lockerley Hall (East Tytherley), iv, 515
Lockerley Water Farm (Lockerley), iv, 502
Lockhart, Jas., iv, 511, 541 ; John I., iv, 510, 511 ; Maria, iv, 511 ; Sarah, iv, 541
Locking, Will., ii, 64
Lockinge, East, (Berks.), iv, 229 n
Lockman, A. C., ii, 488 ; Eliz., ii, 488 ; John, ii, 197
Lock's Farm (Bishop's Waltham), i, 309
Locks Green (Calbourne), v, 218, 221
Lockton, Cath., iii, 293 ; Eliz., iii, 293 ; Harriet, iii, 293 ; John, iii, 293 ; Phil., iii, 293 ; Sophia, iii, 293
Lockyers (Christchurch), v, 97 n
Lockyn, Thos., v, 460
Locusts [Locustodea], i, 111
Loddon, riv., iv, 32, 42, 57, 60, 63, 64, 99, 103, 104, 106, 115, 117, 119, 128, 129, 134, 140, 141 n, 147, 149, 151, 154, 156 ; v, 409, 452, 560, 564
Loddon, Little, riv., *see* Bow, brook
Lode, Ivo de la, ii, 516 ; John atte, ii, 516
Lode farm [Kingsley], ii, 515
Lode Place, man. [Kingsley], ii, 516
Loder, *see* Loader
Lodeschylve, *see* Litchfield
Lodge (Hurstbourne Tarrant), iv, 321
Lodge [Loges], de, Geoff., v, 212 ; Hawise, v, 212 ; Mary, iv, 110 ; Walt., ii, 158
Lodge Bottom (King's Somborne), iv, 470
Lodge Hill, ii, 518
Lodsworth, man. (Suss.), iii, 78
Loewis, iv, 512
Loges, *see* Lodge
Logeshale, *see* Lopshill
Loggan [Loggon], Sam., ii, 82, 385 ; iv, 65
Logge, the (Overton), iv, 213
Logging, Johanna, ii, 502
Loggon, *see* Loggan
Lok, *see* Lock
Loker, Barbara, iii, 383 ; Eleanor, iii, 383 ; John, iii, 383 ; Rog., iii, 383
Lokerle Boteler, *see* Lockerley
Lokke, *see* Lock
Lomer [Lomere] (Corhampton), ii, 117, 121, 186 ; iii, 249
Lomer, de, Elias, iii, 249 ; Geoff., iii, 249, 253 ; John, iii, 249 ; Rob., iii, 249
Lomer Turville, man. (Corhampton), iii, 250
London, v, 229, 364, 369, 376, 377, 379, 471
London, bps. of, ii, 19 ; v, 308, 309 ; Fulk Basset, iv, 150 ; Rich. Bentworth, iv, 68 ; Hen. Compton, ii, 96 ; Rich. FitzNeal, v, 307 ; Thos. Kemp, iv, 46 ; Rob. Lowth, iv, 218 ; Cuth. Tunstall, iv, 165 ; Will. Warham, *see* Canterbury, archbp. of
London, (de, of), Andr., ii, 19, 115 ; Edw., ii, 120 ; John, ii, 122, 172 ;

London (*cont.*)
iii, 514 ; iv, 89 ; v, 454 ; Rich., ii, 171 ; Rob., iv, 445 ; Thos., ii, 139 ; Dr., ii, 57, 159, 302, 303
London, Little, (Newport), v, 253
London, Little, (Pamber), iv, 433, 435
London, Little, (Smannell), iv, 345 ; char., iv, 379
London Minstead (Minstead), iv, 635
Lone Farm (Worting), iv, 243
Long [Longe], Abigail, iii, 70 ; Alice, iii, 335 ; iv, 418 ; v, 78 ; Cath. T., iv, 93, 94 ; Ellen, v, 98 ; Geo., iii, 372, 373 ; Hen., iv, 418 n ; v, 114 ; John, iii, 251, 358 ; iv, 418, 639, 647 ; v, 98, 157 ; Marg., iii, 358 ; iv, 418 ; Mary, iii, 70 ; Nath., iii, 70 ; Rob., iii, 358 ; iv, 418, 419 ; v, 45, 114 ; Rog. le, ii, 201 ; Thos., iv, 418 n, 647 ; v, 114 n ; (Sir) Walt., iii, 251, 293, 313, 325 ; iv, 554, 647 ; v, 518, 528 ; Walt. J., iii, 253 ; v, 526, 527 ; Walt. V., v, 530 ; Will., iii, 332 ; fam., arms, iii, 251, 293, 325 ; iv, 418
Long Bridge (Upper Clatford), iv, 359
Longbridge Croft (Newtown), v, 265, 268
Longchamp, Hen. de, iii, 378, 381 ; Will., v, 307
Longcroft, Chas. J., iii, 125 ; fam., arms, iii, 126
Longden, Hen., iv, 586, 601
Longdown (Colbury), iv, 558
Longe, *see* Long
Longebrugge, *see* Langbridge
Longespee [Longespeye, Longspee], Ela, (Lady), ii, 176 ; iv, 150, 152 ; Emeline, ii, 123 ; Steph., iv, 522 ; Will. (de), iii, 506 ; iv, 150 n, 346, 347, 351, 540, 560 ; v, 37
Longford, Edw. M. Pakenham, earl of, iv, 54 ; Thos. Pakenham, earl of, iv, 54
Longford, fam., *see* Langford
Longford Home of Rest (Newchurch), v, 182
Longford Institute (Newchurch), v, 182
Longlands (Arreton), v, 140
Longlathes (Christchurch), v, 85
Longley, fam., *see* Langley
Longley Farm, iv, 98
Longman Eliz. A., iv, 299 ; Fran. P., iv, 447 ; G. H., v, 575 ; Hannah, iv, 299 ; John, iv, 299 ; Rob., iv, 299 ; Thos., iv, 15, 299 ; Will., iv, 299, 447 ; Mrs., iv, 288 ; —, iv, 49 ; v, 540
Longmead, North, (Kingsley), ii, 515
Longmoor (Greatham), iii, 506 ; v, 444 n
Longmoor (Hursley), ii, 491
Longparish, ii, 132 ; iv, 400, 406-9, 411, 417 ; v, 560 ; adv., iv, 409 ; char., iv, 409 ; ch., iv, 408, 422 ; ind., v, 454, 455 ; man. house, iv, 406 ; mans., ii, 133, 137 ; iv, 406 ; mill, v, 481 ; Nonconf., iv, 409 ; pop., v, 439 ; sch., ii, 401
Longparish House (Longparish), iv, 406
Long Pasture (Upton), iv, 330 n
Long's Bridge (E. Wellow), iv, 535
Long's jam factory (Whitchurch), iv, 300
Longspee, *see* Longespee
Longspiers [Longsperys], man. (Soberton), iii, 262

Longstock [Long Stoke], ii, 122, 172 ; iv, 411, 438, 449-51, 484, 489, 497, 538 ; adv., ii, 21 ; iv, 451 ; char., iv, 451 ; ch., iv, 451 ; man., iv, 473, 449, 480, 487, 503 ; Nonconf., iv, 451 ; peat ind., v, 454 ; Peat Spade inn, v, 454 ; pop., v, 439 ; Rom. rem., i, 313, 345 ; sch., ii, 401
Longstock Angling Club, v, 560
Longstock Harrington [Longstock Harangod], man. (Longstock), iv, 450
Longstock House (Longstock), iv, 449
Longstock with Millstreet, man. (Longstock), iv, 449, 451
Longstreet, man. (Wilts.), ii, 114
Long Sutton, *see* Sutton, Long
Long Sutton House (Long Sutton), iv, 18, 19
Long Towe (Pamber), iv, 433
Longueville, Grey, iv, 476
Longwood Farm (Owslebury), iii, 334
Longwood House (Owslebury), iii, 334
Lonsdale, Ld., v, 554
Looke (King's Somborne), iv, 470
Loomer, *see* Lomer
Loperwood, man. (Eling), iv, 546
Lophobranchii, ii, 200
Lopshill [Loppeshale, Lopsale, Lopushale] (S. Damerham), iv, 587 n, 589
Lopshill Common (S. Damerham), iv, 586
Lopwood Grove (Bentley), iv, 27
Lord, John, v, 214 ; Rob., iv, 526 ; Thos., v, 574
Lord's Wood (Upton), iv, 330 n
Lorimer, Agnes, iii, 250 ; John, iii, 250 ; Rog., iii, 250
Losinga, Herb., bp. of Norwich, ii, 117 ; Rob., abbot of Newminster, ii, 117, 121
Louccumbe, *see* Bowcombe
Lougham, tithing (Dors.), v, 133
Louis VIII, king of France, iv, 88 ; v, 310
Louis Napoleon, prince imperial, iv, 15
Loundres, Joan, iv, 279 ; Thos., iv, 279
Louvaine, (de), Eleanor, iv, 473 ; Isabel, iv, 473 ; John, iv, 473 ; Marg., iv, 473
Love, Dulcibella, iv, 13 ; Edw., iv, 474 n ; Harriet B. D., v, 291, 292 ; Hen. O., v, 291, 292 ; John, ii, 507, 508 ; iii, 76 ; iv, 241 ; Nich., ii, 323, 325, 327, 337, 366 ; iii, 458 ; iv, 6, 13, 92, 253, 254 ; v, 19 ; Rob., iii, 76, 112, 240 ; Susannah, ii, 507 ; Will., prior of Barton, ii, 180, 181 ; —, v, 453
Lovecombe, *see* Luccombe
Loveday, Rog., iii, 91
Lovedean, man. (Catherington), iii, 99
Lovedean [Loveden], Ant., iii, 99, 344 ; Isabel, iii, 99, 344 ; John, iv, 383 ; Sebastian, iii, 99, 344 ; Thos., iii, 99, 344 ; Walt., iv, 383
Lovel, John, Ld,, iv, 377, 378 ; Maud, Lady, iv, 377
Lovel, John, iv, 378 n, 379 ; v, 483 ; Mary, iv, 205 ; Sir Ralph, iv, 378 ; Will., iv, 338 n
Lovell, Agatha, iv, 64 ; Constance, iv, 283 ; F., v, 569, 570 ; Hen., iv, 283 ; Isabel, Lady, iv, 526 ; Joan, iv, 64 ; Maud, abbess of Romsey,

Lovell (cont.)
ii, 129, 132 ; Rich., iv, 64 ; (Sir)
Thos., iii, 150 ; iv, 526, 647 ;
Will., v, 161
Loverez [Loveratz, Loveray, Love-
raz, Luvers] (de), Alice, iii, 192,
414 ; iv, 457 ; Annora, iv, 171 ;
Geoff., iv, 171 ; John, iv, 522 ;
Rich., iv, 522, 523 ; Steph., iv,
522, 523 ; Sybil, iv, 342 ; Walt., iv,
522 ; Will., iv, 522
Lovibond, Edw., v, 200 ; John, v,
200, 280 ; Thos., v, 200, 213
Lovinge, Edw., v, 198 ; Thos., v,
181
Lovington, ii, 114
Low, W. M., v, 550
Lowe, Edw., iv, 22 ; Ellen, iii, 414 ;
iv, 22 ; Jas., iii, 408 ; John, iii,
414 ; iv, 22 ; Laur., iii, 414 ; iv,
22 ; Lucy, iii, 414 ; iv, 22 ; Rob.,
ii, 358 ; Stanley, v, 529
Lower Link (St. Mary Bourne),
Rom. rem., i, 304, 346 ; iv, 295
**Lower Pitham Copse (Stratfield
Turgis), iv, 63**
Lowes, Fred. J., iii, 207
Lowmede (Timsbury), iv, 486
Lowmer, see Lomer
Lowsley farm (Bramshott), ii, 491
Lowstedys (Calbourne), v, 218
Lowth, A., v, 576 ; Rob., bp. of
London, iv, 218
Lozinge, Will., ii, 228
Luard, Alice, iv, 518 ; Rob., iv,
518
Lucas, Ld., iv, 607
Lucas, Hen., v, 5 ; John, v, 483
Luccombe, man. (Bonchurch), ii,
138, 139 ; v, 155
Luce Hays (Sopley), v, 130
Lucelond, see Lessland
**Luckton, tithing (Westover), v,
133**
Lucy, abbess of Nunnaminster, ii,
126 ; prioress of Wintney, ii, 149,
151
Lucy, (de), Alice, Lady, iv, 286 ;
Anne, iv, 34, 41 ; Sir Berkeley,
iii, 58, 477 ; iv, 190, 290, 316,
318 ; Constance, iii, 346 ; iv, 190,
278, 290, 294 ; Eliz., v, 285 ; (Sir)
Geoff., iii, 107, 168 ; Godf., see
Winchester, bps. of ; Mary, iv,
290, 316 ; Maud, iv, 495 ; Phil.,
iii, 15, 524 ; (Sir) Rich., iii, 346,
498 ; iv, 278, 290, 294, 316, 317 ;
v, 285 ; Spencer, iv, 278 ; Steph.,
iii, 5 ; (Sir) Thos., iv, 190, 278,
286, 290 ; v, 285 ; (Sir) Will., iv,
34, 41, 294, 317, 495 ; fam., iv,
196
Luddeshelve, see Litchfield
Lude, la, (Rotherwick), iv, 99
Ludeshote, see Ludshott
Ludeshul, Ludeshulff, see Litchfield
Ludgershall (Wilts.), iv, 372, 373
Ludlow [Ludlowe], Anne, iv, 348 ;
Dorothy, iv, 610 ; (Sir) Edm., iii,
486 ; iv, 220, 320, 435 ; Sir Edw.,
iii, 294 ; Eliz., iv, 610 ; Geo., iii,
485 ; iv, 220 ; (Sir) Hen., iv, 220,
320 ; Joan, iv, 220 ; John, iii,
214, 241, 294 ; iv, 610 ; v, 327 n ;
Lettice, Lady, iv, 220 ; Nath., iv,
320, 321 ; Rich., iii, 214 ; (Sir)
Thos., iv, 282, 610 ; Will., iii, 214,
241, 485 ; iv, 220, 610 ; Col., v,
345 ; fam., iv, 219, 435 ; arms,
iii, 294 ; iv, 220
Ludmore [Ludmere], man. (Catherington), iii, 99
Ludshed Meade (Crondall), iv, 6
Ludshelf, see Litchfield

Ludshott [Ludshute], man. (Bram-
shott), ii, 471, 491, 492-3, 495
Lues, Will. le, v, 29
Luffa, Ralph, bp. of Chichester, v,
462
Luffield Priory (Lincs.), ii, 174
Luffwyk, John, iii, 96
Luke, iv, 352 ; prior of Southwick,
ii, 164, 168
Luke, Geo., iv, 412 ; Joan, iv, 570
Luke's Bridge (Maplederwell), iv,
149
Lukin, Maj.-Gen., iv, 231
Lumley, Joan, Lady, iii, 130 ; iv,
572 ; John, Ld., iv, 572
Lumley, Rich., iii, 419
Lunn, Florence de, v, 26
Lupton, Chas. R., iv, 15 ; Rog., ii,
306
Lush, Rob., iv, 266
Lushborow, Magna and Parva,
(Romsey), iv, 452
Lushington, Miss, ii, 518
Lussher, Mary, ii, 510 ; Nich., ii,
510
Lutershall [Lusteshall, Lutgares-
hall] (de), Cecilia, iii, 448 ; John,
iii, 448 ; Rich., ii, 195, 197 ;
Will., iv, 243
Lutine, le, (Bentley), iv, 27
Lutman, Mary, iv, 8 n ; Sam., iv,
8 n
Luttrell, Mary, v, 94 ; Tregonwell,
v, 94
Luvers, see Loverez
Luvre, see Iford
Luyt, Thos., iv, 605
Lwynespuynde (Faccombe), iv, 314
Ly, see Lee-on-the-Solent
Lyall, Mrs., v, 78
Lyatesland (Newtown), iv, 294
Lycknoll, see Linkenholt
Lyde, riv., iv, 99, 151, 156, 157,
176 ; v, 560, 564
Lyde Mill (Newnham), iv, 151, 157
Lydeshelf, see Litchfield
Lydezorde, John, ii, 150
Lye, see Lee-on-the-Solent
Lyegh, see Leigh
Lyes, see Lys
Lyffordes Cross (S. Damerham), iv,
586
Lyford, Mary, iv, 108
Lykehaye (Christchurch), v, 85
Lyle, W. J., v, 174 ; see also Lisle
and Lysle
Lyllyngdown Common (Sherborne
St. John), iv, 158
Lyly, see Lily
Lymbergh, Tidemann de, iv, 395
Lymborn, Ant., v, 31 n
Lymington, i, 381 ; ii, 63, 97, 139,
145, 154 ; iv, 622, 639-49 ; v, 82,
109, 119, 286, 311, 331, 356, 362,
363, 364, 409, 423, 431, 434, 450 ;
adv., iv, 648 ; char., iv, 649 ; ch.,
iv, 647, 648 ; coins, i, 345 ; inds.,
iv, 639, 644 ; v, 451, 460, 469,
470, 472 ; mans., ii, 159 ; iv,
644-7 ; mkts. and fairs, iv, 643 ;
v, 417 ; mills, iv, 639 ; Nonconf.,
iv, 649 ; pop., v, 450 ; Rom.
Caths., iv, 649 ; sch., ii, 387, 394,
401 ; iv, 649
Lymington, New, man. (Lymington), iv, 640
Lymington, Old, man. (Lymington), iv, 640
Lymington, riv., i, 6, 244 ; iv, 616,
626, 639 ; v, 409
Lymington, Cath., Lady, iii, 12 ;
Lds., ii, 382 ; iv, 288 ; v, 225,
226 ; John, vsct., see Portsmouth, earl of
Lymmer Feald (Long Sutton), iv, 18

Lymmers, man. (Kingsclere), iv,
260
Lymore (Milford), v, 116
Lyn (Arreton), v, 140
Lynch, la, (Overton), iv, 213
Lynch, John, ii, 197 ; Sam., iv, 610 ;
Will., iii, 535
Lynchford (Farnborough), iv, 15
Lyncoholt, see Linkenholt
Lyndhurst, ii, 102, 420, 450 ; iv,
544, 545, 553, 571, 604, 611,
615, 617, 619, 621, 624, 626,
630-3, 636, 650 ; v, 109, 356, 455,
569 ; advs., iv, 633 ; char., iv,
633 ; chs., iv, 633 ; fairs, iv, 633 ;
inds., v, 455, 470 ; man., iv, 540,
631 ; Nonconf., iv, 633 ; pk., iv,
633 ; pop., v, 446 ; racing, v,
543 ; Rom. Caths., iv, 633 ; sch.,
ii, 401
Lyndhurst, John S. Copley, Ld.,
iv, 631
Lyndhurst (de), Herb., iv, 631 ;
Rich., iv, 631 ; Will., iii, 32 ; iv,
631
Lyne, Eliz., v, 97 ; John, iv, 613 ;
Jos., v, 97 ; Rich., ii, 387 ; iv,
611, 613, 614 ; Thos., iv, 613,
614 ; v, 109
Lyne-Stivens, Bertram H., iv, 525,
528
Lynford (Longparish), iv, 406
Lynne, Walt., iv, 549
Lyntesford, Rich. de, ii, 195, 197
Lynton, Rich., ii, 163
Lyon, Ezekiel, iv, 169
Lyons, Edm., Ld., v, 85
Lyons (de), H. F., v, 541 ; Joan,
iv, 319 ; John, iv, 319, 330
Lyrypyn, Thos., v, 16
**Lys [Lyes], (de), Florence, iii, 241 ;
Phil., ii, 350 ; Rich., iii, 241 ;
Waleran, v, 91 n**
Lysewy, Joan, iv, 498 ; Rog., iv, 498
Lyshe, see Liss
Lysle, Chas., v, 119 n ; Thos., iv,
458 ; see also Lisle and Lyle
Lysley, see Lisle
Lyss, see Liss
Lyster, see Lister
Lyte, Hen. F., iv, 639
Lytlewerke, Agatha, iv, 435 ; Pet.,
iv, 435
Lyttelton, Arth. T., bp. of South-
ampton, iii, 112 ; see also Little-
ton
Lytton, see Litton
Lywood, L., v, 540 ; —, iv, 447 ;
fam., iv, 363

Mabel, abbess of Wherwell, ii, 137
Maberly, Jas., iii, 24 ; J. J., iii, 23 ;
Mary, iv, 276 ; Steph., iv, 276 ;
—, iv, 276
Mablyns (Long Sutton), iv, 18
Macartey, —, v, 354
Macclesfield, earl of, iv, 397 n
M'Creagh, Frances E., ii, 459 ; Sir
Mich., iii, 459
M'Creagh-Thornhill, Eva H. E., iii,
459 ; Maj. Mich., iii, 459 ; Mich.
C., iii, 459
Macdonald, Sir Arch., ii, 493 ; Sir
Arch. J., ii, 491 ; Sir A. K., iii,
8 ; G., iv, 140 ; fam., arms, ii, 493
McDonald, Alexander, & Co., v, 458
MacDonnell [McDonell], H. C., v,
576 ; Randal, iv, 36
MacGregor, John, v, 134
Macham, Thos., iii, 298 ; v, 172 ;
fam., iv, 514
Machelebruchet, la, (Sherborne St.
John), iv, 158

Machell, John, v, 96 ; Thos., v, 96
Machon, Edith, ii, 162 ; John, ii, 162 ; Margery, ii, 162
Maci, Hugh, iv, 568
McIntyre, John, iv, 98
Mackcliffe (Christchurch), v, 85
Mackerel [Mackarel, Mackerell, Makerel] (Sir) Ralph, v, 163, 198, 212, 217, 291 ; Rich., iii, 368 ; Thos., iii, 7, 15 ; Will., v, 117, 212, 215, 217, 291
Macket, Will., v, 168
Mackreth (Sir), Rob., iv, 201, 247, 248
Maclachlan, Mrs. A. N. C., iii, 30
Macnaghten, Stewart, iii, 489
Macnamara, Rev. Thos. B., v, 271
MacNeill, Will., v, 125
Macpherson, Capt., v, 162, 206, 274, 281
Madden, Sir F., ii, 140
Madge, Rev. F. T., ii, 256
Madhurst, John de, iii, 318
Maegla, v, 293
Maerdune, see Merdon
Magdalen College (Oxf.)., ii, 47, 55, 175, 179, 373, 483, 520 ; iii, 5, 6, 16, 46, 57, 62, 117, 442 ; iv, 121, 127, 135, 136, 138, 179, 222, 239, 344, 346, 354, 387, 476 ; arms, iii, 442
Magdalen Hill (Winchester), v, 309, 337, 426
Magdalen Hill Farm (Winchester), v, 77
Magdalen's Croft, see Longbridge Croft
Magewick, Geo., iv, 70 ; Rob., iv, 70
Maggotes Corner (Romsey), iv, 452
Maghe, Phil., prior of Andover, ii, 221
Magnay, Miss, v, 116
Maguire, —, v, 261 n
Mahon, Grace C. P., v, 193
Maiden Bradley (Wilts), iv, 570, 586
Maiden Down (Thruxton), iv, 387
Maiden Meade (Kingsclere), iv, 250, 261 n
Maidenwell, man. (Lincs), ii, 376 ; iv, 139
Maidstone (de), Nich., ii, 195 ; Rob., ii, 194, 195, 197 ; iv, 468
Maihiweston, man., see Pauncefoot Hill
Mailleshangre, see Malshanger
Maine [Mayn, Mayne], Sir Ant., iv, 409 ; Cuth., iv, 259 ; Eliz., iv, 259 ; Rev. John T., iii, 38, 39 ; Rich., iv, 392 ; Thos., iv, 392
Mainsborough, hund., iv, 182 ; v, 324, 328 n, 331
Mainsbridge, hund., iii, 401, 462 ; iv, 245, 550 n ; v, 324, 331
Mainsbridge, man., see Swaythling and Townhill
Mainsbridge (de), John, iii, 483 ; Thos., iii, 483 ; iv, 460
Mainstone, man., see Pauncefoot Hill
Mainwaring, Sir Hen., v, 521 ; Phil., v, 227 ; Capt., v, 521 ; see also Manwaring
Maitland, Geo. G., iv, 484 ; Marg. C., Lady, iv, 109
Major, Ann, iii, 528 ; John, ii, 510 ; iii, 486, 535 ; v, 514, 525, 533, 536 ; Rich., ii, 510 ; iii, 419, 486
Makeleshulle, see Muccleshill
Makerel, see Mackerel
Mal, see Malf
Malacopterygii, i, 201
Malan, César J. S., v, 134
Malday, Joan, v, 188, 237

Malden, Col., v, 176
Maldoit, see Mauduit
Maldon, ii, 31
Malduith, see Mauduit
Maleshanger, see Malshanger
Malet, Sir Alex., ii, 356 ; Rich., v, 163, 164, 166 ; Will., v, 166 ; see also Mallett
Malf [Mal], Godric, iv, 550, 609, 635 ; v, 114
Malherbe, Nich., iii, 442
Mallards (Christchurch), v, 85
Malle, Rich. le, iii, 368
Mallett [Mallet], J., v, 461 ; Rob., ii, 485 ; see also Malet
Mallings, see Malyns
Malmains, Nich., iii, 193
Malmesbury, Corisande E., ctss. of, v, 103 ; earls of, ii, 466 ; v, 88, 104, 108 ; Edw. J. Harris, v, 559 n ; Jas. Harris, ii, 349 ; iii, 437 ; iv, 656 ; v, 87, 95, 97, 98, 108 ; Jas. E. Harris, iv, 611 ; v, 86, 95, 97, 98, 108, 224, 559
Malmesbury, Will. of, iv, 407
Malmesbury Park (Bournemouth), v, 135
Malory, Dorothy, iv, 159 ; Kath., iv, 159 ; Marg., iv, 159 ; Margery, iv, 159 ; Steph., iv, 366, 374
Maloxdene (S. Damerham), iv, 589
Malshanger [Malsanger Yereley], man. (Church Oakley), ii, 470 ; iv, 223, 224, 229, 240, 327 n, 579
Malshanger House (Church Oakley), iv, 224
Malterson, John, v, 200 n
Malthouse Piddle (Greywell), iv, 76
Malting and brewing, v, 472
Maltravers, Will., Ld., see Arundel, earl of
Maltravers, Eliz., v, 160 ; John, ii, 142 ; iv, 150, 440, 474 ; v, 160, 227, 228
Malveisin, Will., iv, 319
Malwood Ridge (Bramshaw), ii, 446; iv, 623
Malwyn [Malwayn, Malweyn], Joan, iv, 455 ; John, iii, 406 ; iv, 455, 523 ; v, 200, 201 ; Will., iv, 455
Malyns [Mallings] (de), Alice, iv, 562 ; John, iv, 527 n, 562 ; Ralph, ii, 222
Mammals, i, 239
Man, see Mann
Manby, Hugh de, iv, 643
Mancer, Reg. le, v, 45
Manchester, dchsses. of : Eliz., iv, 563 ; Dodington Montagu, iv, 601 ; dks. : Chas. Montagu, iv, 601 ; Geo. Montagu, iv, 563, 601 ; Hen. Montagu, earl of, iv, 254, 471 n ; v, 344
Mancole Copse (Bentworth), v, 457
Mandeville, Ld., see Manchester, earl of
Mandeville [Mandevile, Maundeville] (de), Anne, Lady, v, 242 ; Arnulf, iv, 480, 481 ; Geoff., iii, 86, 107, 168 ; iv, 72 ; v, 202 n ; Hugh, v, 155 ; Sir John, v, 242 ; Rog., iii, 168 ; v, 181 ; Will., iii, 107, 168
Manere, John, ii, 157, 158
Manestoke, see Meonstoke
Manewood (Winchfield), iv, 109
Manfield, see Mansfield
Mangin, Sam. H., v, 111
Mangles, Frank, iv, 101
Manhouse, Thos., ii, 113
Manley, Col., v, 453
Mann [Man], Eliz., v, 200 ; Eustace, v, 200 ; Sir Horace, v, 574 ; John, iii, 207 ; v, 146, 151, 200, 201, 264, 271 ; Noah, v, 574

Manne, see Manno
Manners, Lady Eveline, v, 127
Manners (de), Alice, iv, 199 ; Eleanor (Lady), iv, 261, 526 ; John, iv, 198, 199 ; (Sir) Rob., iv, 198, 199, 200, 526 ; Rog., iv, 628 ; Thos., iv, 348, 526, 532, 628, 647
Manning, Edw., iv, 266 n ; Hen., v, 95 n ; Jas. L., v, 229 ; Rich., ii, 478 ; —, v, 547
Manningham, Thos., bp. of Chichester, ii, 337 ; iii, 427
Manno [Manne], iv, 417, 499
Mannock, Eliz., Lady, iv, 222 ; Frances, Lady, iv, 221 ; Sir Fran., iv, 221 ; Sir Will., iv, 221
Manor Court (S. Damerham), iv, 586
Manor Farm (Bentworth), iv, 68
Manor Farm (North Waltham), iv, 221
Manor House (Greatham), v, 519
Manory, Thos., iv, 64
Manredes (Yateley), iv, 21
Mansbridge, hund., i, 379 ; ii, 421
Mansbridge, man., ii, 147
Mansfield [Manfield], Hen., iii, 443 ; v, 315 ; Rich., F., v, 125 ; fam., v, 100
Manson, Mrs., v, 111
Mansynton, Giles de, iii, 418
Mant, Rich., ii, 353, 390 ; Sarah, v, 78
Mantel, Walt., iv, 196
Mantesberg, hund., see Bountisborough
Manton (Wilts), i, 298
Mant's charity, v, 78
Manvers, Chas. Pierrepont, ear of, iv, 383 n
Manwaring, John, iv, 28 ; see also Mainwaring
Manydon, Thos., ii, 114
Manydown, house (Wootton St. Lawrence), iv, 240
Manydown, man. (Wootton St Lawrence), ii, 114 ; iv, 239-40, 258, 275, 276 ; v, 411, 420
Manzy, Jas., ii, 145
Maonstoke, see Meonstoke
Mapedrewell, Mapelth, see Maplederwell
Mapes, Walt., ii, 418, 419
Maple, Sir J., v, 550
Maplederwell, ii, 224 ; iv, 113, 114, 149-52, 156, 157, 176 ; adv., iv, 152 ; chalk quarries, v, 454 ; char., iv, 152 ; ch., iv, 152 ; man., iv, 149 ; mills, iv, 151 ; Nonconf., iv, 149 ; pop., v, 439 ; sch., ii, 401 ; watercress beds, v, 455
Maplederwell Common, iv, 149
Mapledurham, man. (Buriton), iii, 86 ; iv, 85, 361
Mapledurham, West, man. (Buriton), iii, 88
Mapledurham Rectory, man. (Buriton), iii, 91
Mapledurwell, see Maplederwell
Mapleham (Brockenhurst), iv, 627
Maplers (Elvetham), iv, 74
Mapleton, John, iv, 98
Mapuldurwell, see Maplederwell
Mar, John, earl of, iv, 67, 90
Mar, Hen. de, iv, 494
March, Eleanor, ctss. of, iv, 130, 347 ; earls of, iv, 342 ; Edm. Mortimer, ii, 475, 476 ; iv, 130, 341, 342 n, 347, 426, 427, 430 ; v, 368 ; Rog. Mortimer, ii, 475 ; iii, 227 ; iv, 360, 361 n, 426, 427, 430, 612 ; Ld., ii, 347

March [Marche], (de la, le), Ad., iii, 530; Dav., v, 212; Joan, iii, 530; John, v, 165, 285; Lewis, v, 212; Mary, v, 212; Steph., v, 212, 262, 285; Walt., ii, 161; *see also* Marsh

Marchant [Markaunt], le, Ann., iii, 344; Hen., iii, 88, 89; iv, 396; Joan, iii, 88, 97; John, iii, 344; v, 125; (Sir) Rob., iii, 88, 97, 98; iv, 396; Thos., iii, 344; v, 125; Miss, v, 163; *see also* Mercator

Marchwood, iv, 546; ch., iv, 558; man., iv, 553; pk., iv, 547; sch., ii, 401

Marconi, Guglielmo, iv, 480

Marday, Thos., iv, 646

Marden, Geo., iv, 535; Rich., iv, 453, 535, 536, 549

Mardon (Hursley), *see* Merdon

Mareis, *see* Marsh

Mareland (Bentley), iv, 27

Marescal, Mareschal, *see* Marshall

Marett, Frances C., iii, 432

Mareys, *see* Marsh

Margaret, queen (w. of Edw. I), ii, 474; iii, 506; iv, 67, 89, 90, 130; iv, 347, 545, 597, 608, 611, 631, 633; v, 91, 243, 272 *n*

Margaret, queen (w. of Hen. VI), ii, 144; iii, 507; iv, 67, 89, 91; v, 263, 319 *n*, 320

Margaret of Savoy, v, 322

Margarine manufacture, v, 455

Margery, the cordwainer, v, 86

Margesson, M., iii, 84

Marine zoology, i, 89

Marisco, *see* Marsh

Maritime history, v, 359-408

Mark, ch., iv, 74

Mark, v, 270

Mark, fam., *see* Marke

Markaunt, *see* Marchant

Marke [Mark], John, iv, 363; v, 185 *n*; Rog., v, 164 *n*, 305; *see also* Markes

Marke Field (Romsey), iv, 452

Markes, ii, 182

Markes [Marks], Edm., iii, 228; Jas., iii, 435; Rich., iii, 69; Rog., iii, 228; Walt., v, 94; Will., iii, 228; *see also* Marke & Merks

Markets and fairs, ii, 474, 477, 508; iii, 6, 42, 67, 104, 116, 123, 136, 146, 159, 163, 166, 171, 176, 182, 183, 206, 211, 224, 233, 239, 256, 278, 279, 352, 390, 465, 466, 519; iv, 21, 34, 46, 47, 73, 79, 92, 129, 133, 140, 211, 212, 252, 278, 292, 300, 301, 346, 350, 351, 358, 388, 392, 396-8, 400, 411, 417, 452, 453, 483, 484, 493, 494, 501, 506, 535, 536, 546, 567, 609, 633, 643, 652; v, 36, 87, 88, 126, 218, 260, 409, 415, 416, 417, 426, 428, 432, 435

Markham, Sir Griffith, v, 335

Markland, Abra., ii, 196, 197; v, 65; Cath., v, 65

Marks, *see* Markes

Marland (Romsey), iv, 452

Marlborough (Wilts.), ii, 161; Rom. rem., i, 298

Marlborough, Jane Ley, ctss. of, iv, 393; Jas. Ley, earl of, iv, 393

Marlborough [Marlynburgh, Merleberge], Alvred de, iv, 147, 512; Rich., ii, 115; Will. (of), ii, 174, 175; v, 481

Marles Copse (Pamber), iv, 433

Marleys, Rob., ii, 174

Marliere, la, (Penton Mewsey), iv, 381

Marlow, Pet., ii, 113; —, v, 557

Marlynburgh, *see* Marlborough

Marmesfeld, Hen., iii, 498

Marmion [Marmyon], Joan, iii, 435; Pet., iii, 435; Pet. J., iii, 435; Phil., iii, 330, 340 *n*; Rob., iii, 435

Marny, de, Joan, iii, 218; Sir Rob., iii, 218; Will., iii, 218

Marprelate tracts, ii, 79, 80

Marriner [Maryner], Dorothy, iii, 164, 204; John, iii, 164, 204; Pet., iii, 164, 204

Marriott [Meriet, Merriott], John, iii, 360; iv, 77; Mary, iv, 77; Nich., iii, 361

Marrow Meade (Elvetham), iv, 74

Marschall (Sherfield), iv, 104

Marschall, fam., *see* Marshall

Marsden, Will., ii, 80, 81

Marsh, man. (Bucks.), iv, 395

Marsh, the, (Hartley Wespall), iv, 42

Marsh (Kingsclere), iv, 267

Marsh (Kingsley), ii, 516

Marsh [Mareis, Mareys, Marisco, Marshco, Marshe, Mersh, Mersshe] (de, atte), Camina, ii, 151; Chas., iv, 622 *n*; Edm., iii, 90, 118, 259; iv, 473, 474; Eliz., iv, 259; Florence, iii, 250, 251; Hereward, iii, 104; John, iv, 497; v, 42, 168; Jordan, ii, 181; Judith, iv, 335 *n*; Laurence, ii, 250; Lucy, iii, 169; Marg., iii, 250, 251, 528; Mary, iii, 118; Nich., iv, 473; Pet., ii, 516; Rainetta, iii, 104; Rob., v, 94; Steph., v, 264; Thos., iii, 250, 251; iv, 116; Will., iii, 169; v, 293; *see also* March

Marshall [Marescal, Mareschal(l), Marschall, Marshal], Agatha, iii, 48; iv, 605; Anselm, iv, 52, 474; Constance, ii, 494, 518, 519; iv, 605; Edm., iii, 48; Eliz., ii, 506; Geoff., iii, 370; Geo., ii, 327; Gervaise, iv, 607, 609; Gilb., iv, 77, 360, 607; Greg., v, 89 *n*; Hen., iv, 406; Joan, iv, 52; John, ii, 73, 494, 518, 519; iii, 48, 145; iv, 52, 605, 610; v, 91 *n*, 231; Kath., iv, 605; Maud, iv, 52, 474, 605; Mich., iv, 605; Ralph, iii, 6, 30; iv, 102, 605; Rich., ii, 482; iv, 150, 360, 607, 609; Thos., ii, 518; iv, 605; v, 47, 231, 479 *n*; Walt., ii, 94, 228, 229, 494; iv, 605; Will., ii, 422, 506; iv, 90, 360, 474, 607; v, 109, 231; W. R., v, 554; fam., iv, 458

Marshco, *see* Marsh

Marsh Court, man. (King's Somborne), iv, 472 *n*, 473

Marsh Court, man. (Stockbridge), iv, 477, 483, 486 *n*

Marshcourt, riv., iv, 483

Marsh Court Farm (King's Somborne), iv, 480

Marshe, *see* Marsh

Marsh Farm (Kingsley), ii, 516

Marsh Grove (Hartley Wespall), iv, 42

Marsh House (Bentley), iv, 27; v, 519

Marsh Place (Kingsley), *see* Marsh

Marshton (Arreton), v, 142

Marson, Fred B., iv, 44

Martel, Rog., ii, 154

Martelli, Anne, iv, 169; Fran., iv, 169; Isabella, iv, 169

Marten, fam., *see* Martin

Martin, riv., v, 559, 587, 592-4; v, 215; adv., iv, 594; char., iv, 594; ch., iv, 592; mans., iv,

Martin (*cont.*) 592; Nonconf., iv, 594; sch., ii, 401

Martin, East, (Martin), iv, 592

Martin, West, (Martin), iv, 592, 594

Martin [Marten, Martyn], (de), Benj., iii, 241; Chas. W., v, 262; Chris., ii, 497; David, ii, 214; Denny, v, 262; Eliz., ii, 151; iv, 172; Frances, v, 262; Isabel, iv, 592; Jas., iv, 226; Joan, iv, 35; John, v, 119, 166 *n*; Malachi, iv, 594; Marg., iv, 582, 588; Mich., ii, 497; iv, 172 *n*; Phil., v, 198, 262; (Sir) Rich., ii, 497; iii, 384; iv, 54; Rob., iv, 582, 583, 588; Thos., iii, 240; Thomasina, iv, 54; (Sir) Will. F., iii, 58, 384; iv, 592; Col., iv, 299; fam., v, 141

Martin Down, iv, 592

Martineau, John, iv, 44

Martins (Stratfield Turgis), *see* Nedes

Martre, (la, le), Isabel, v, 145; John, iii, 327; v, 145, 166; Juliane, v, 145 *n*; Reg., v, 145 *n*; Will., v, 145, 147

Martyn, *see* Martin

Martyngle, *see* Mattingley

Martyn Rent (Faccombe), iv, 316

Martyr, Pet., ii, 70, 71

Martyr Worthy, ii, 63; iii, 302, 325-7; iv, 432; v, 80; adv., iii, 327; char., iii, 327; ch., iii, 326; man., iii, 326; pop., v, 448; sch., ii, 401

Marvell, man. (Carisbrooke), v, 231

Marvell Farm (Newport), v, 231, 535

Marvin's Down (Wootton St. Lawrence), iv, 240 *n*

Marvylde, *see* Marvell

Marvyn, —, iv, 321; *see also* Mervyn

Marwell, man. (Owslebury), ii, 23, 37, 66, 212; iii, 333

Marwell, de, Alex., v, 481 *n*; Florence, v, 481 *n*; Will., v, 476

Marwell College (Owslebury), ii, 62, 105, 211; iii, 332

Marwelles (Church Oakley), iv, 224

Marwell Hall (Owslebury), iii, 332

Marwell Manor Farm (Owslebury), iii, 332

Marwell Park (Owslebury), ii, 211; iii, 334; palace, iii, 332, 335

Marwell Woodlock, man., *see* Marwell

Marwen's Meade (Long Sutton), iv, 18

Mary, princess (d. of Edw. I), v, 159, 219, 241 *n*, 265

Mary (of Cambridge), princess, *see* Teck, dchss. of

Mary, queen, ii, 70, 308, 369, 371, 379, 476, 478; iii, 43, 45, 130, 285; iv, 266, 427, 435, 454, 601, 608, 646; v, 94, 219, 245, 376

Mary, queen of Scots, iv, 636

Mary, abbess of Romsey, ii, 126, 132; abbess of Wherwell, ii, 137

Maryle, John, ii, 317

Marylebone, man., v, 274

Maryner, *see* Marriner

Maryuleyn, Isabel, ii, 130

Mascal [Mascall], John, iii, 512, 528; Marg., iii, 528

Maslyn, Rich., ii, 284

Mason, Anne, iii, 193; Ant., iv, 80; Eliz., Lady, iv, 80; Hannah, iii, 193; (Sir) John, ii, 115, 369, 375, 378, 385; iii, 204; iv, 80, 110, 488; J. R., v, 576; Sir Rich., v, 290; (Sir) Rob., iii, 193, 204

Mason (cont.)
iv, 8, 213 ; v, 5 ; Sam., iii, 295 ;
iv, 549 ; Thos., iv, 97 ; —, v,
554
Massam, Rich., iii, 117
Massaw, Agnes, ii, 124
Masseworth, (de), John, iii, 225,
226, 229 ; Will., iii, 226, 229
Massey [Massie] Amb., iv, 356 ;
Thos. H., iii, 22 ; Col., iv, 351
Masters, Will., iv, 595
Mastre, Baltesor de, v, 486
Matcham's Plantation (Christ-
church), v, 85
Materfast (Long Sutton), iv, 18
Matingeleghe, see Mattingley
Matson (Glouc.), iv, 145, 146 n
Matteom, Rob. de, iv, 369
Mattesdon, see Mattresdone
Matthew, Dominican prior, ii, 190,
191 ; prior of Southwick, ii, 168
Matthew, Alice, iv, 382 n ; Amb.,
iii, 383 ; And., iii, 383 ; Brian,
iii, 384 ; Jas., iii, 383 ; Jane, iii,
384 ; Joan, iii, 383 ; John, iv,
266, 382 n ; Will., v, 460 n
Matthews, Geo., iii, 118 ; Rev. H.,
iv, 71 ; Rich., iii, 118, 249 ; Sir
S., iv, 71 ; —, v, 542
Mattingley (Heckfield), iv, 31, 33,
45, 48, 49, 79, 226 n, 228 ; chap.,
iv, 50 ; man., iv, 47 ; mill., iv,
47 ; pop., v, 443 ; sch., ii, 401
Mattingley, (de), Pet., iv, 47 ;
Steph., iv, 47
Mattingley Clappers Bridge (Heck-
field), iv, 47
Mattingley Lodge (Heckfield), iv,
45
Mattockesford (Botley), ii, 137 ;
iii, 467
Mattresdone [Mattesdon], Phil. de,
iv, 146 ; see also Cliddesden
Mattyng, Will., v, 484
Maturin, Rev. B., v, 290
Maud, empress, iv, 346 ; v, 302, 360
Maud, princess (d. of Will. I), iv,
146
Maud, queen (w. of William I), ii,
9 ; iv, 208, 385
Maud, queen (w. of Hen. I), ii, 10,
126 ; iv, 346
Maud, queen (w. of Stephen), v, 303
Maud, abbess of Romsey, ii, 132 ;
abbess of Wherwell, ii, 132, 133,
137 ; d. of Alured, iv, 211 ; d. of
Sygar, iv, 501
Maude, John, iv, 340
Mauditt Hatch (Hartley Mauditt),
ii, 508
Mauduit [Maldoit, Malduith, Mau-
dit], (de), Agnes, iv, 205, 206 ;
Beatrice, iv, 533 ; Eleanor, iv,
369 n ; Hen., iii, 152 ; John, iv,
206 n, 369 ; Juliana, iv, 369 ;
Maud, iv, 206, 369 ; Rob., iii,
158 ; iv, 102, 103, 205 ; Thos.,
iv, 102, 103, 205, 206, 369, 533 ;
Warin, iv, 102, 369 ; Will., ii,
492, 508, 509 ; iii, 146, 158, 163,
218, 372 ; iv, 102, 103, 366, 369
Mauger, iv, 301
Mauleon, Savary [Saveric] de, iii,
86 ; v, 223, 310
Maulin, Little, (Ecchinswell), iv,
250
Maundeville, see Mandeville
Maunsel [Mauncel, Maunsell, Mayl-
meslle], (Sir) John, iii, 254 ; iv,
493, 494 ; Marg., iii, 533 ; Rich.,
iv, 524 ; Will., iii, 520, 533
Maupas, Hen., iii, 214, 241
Maupol, Pet. de, ii, 168
Maure, see Moore and More
Maurice, —, v, 532 ; see also Morris

Maury, Rich., ii, 154, 160
Mawardyn, Rich., iii, 496
Mawller, John, iv, 622 n
Mawme, Little, (Kingsclere), iv,
250
Mawne, John, iv, 301
Maxey, John, bp., ii, 182, 185, 186
Maxwell, Hen., iv, 8, 14
May, Felicia, iv, 354 ; Hugh, iv,
36 n ; Sir Humph., ii, 502, 503 ;
Jas., ii, 502, 503 ; (Col.) John,
iv, 139 ; v, 540 ; Joseph, iv, 578 ;
Rich., iii, 498 n ; Rob., ii, 367,
387 ; iv, 87, 98, 354 ; Thos., iv,
172 ; Walt., ii, 163, 164 ; Lt.-Col.,
iv, 128 ; Mrs., iv, 250
Maybury, Dr., iii, 300
Maydeford, John, iii, 396
Maydenhatch, Thos. de, iv, 533
Maydenhith, John, ii, 158
Mayden's Chambre (Winchester),
v, 6
Maydenwell, man. (Lincs.), see
Maidenwell
Mayes, man., see King's Enham
Mayhew, Frances, iv, 110, 112 ;
John, v, 184 ; Nich., iv, 110, 112 ;
Walt., iii, 375
Mayhneston, man., see Pauncefoot
Hill
Maylmeslle, see Maunsel
Maylsanger, see Malshanger
Mayn, Mayne, see Maine
Maynard, John, iv, 409 ; Rev.
Rob. F., iii, 101
Mayo, Eliz., iv, 458 ; Rev. Will.,
iv, 458
Mayor, Dorothy, ii, 94 ; Jos., iii,
328
May's Wood (Andover), iv, 346
Mayweston, man., see Pauncefoot
Hill
Mead, —, v, 576
Meade Myll Pilinge (Romsey), iv,
455
Meadow, Will., ii, 197
Meadows, Chas., iv, 383 n ; Evelyn,
iv, 383 ; Sir Phil., iii, 445 ; iv,
383, 384 ; Sir Sydney, iv, 383 ;
Will. H., iv, 383
Meansborough, hund., i, 379
Mearman, Mrs. Geo., v, 145
Mears [Meares, Meyres], And., iii,
513 ; G., ii, 489 ; iv, 184, 234 ;
Thos., iv, 40, 62, 74, 126, 137,
379, 390, 410, 422, 488 ; v, 65,
123, 185, 277 ; see also Meere
Mears, C. & G., bell-founders, iv,
264
Mears & Stainbank, bell-founders,
iv, 44, 86, 107, 264, 272, 294, 328,
344, 534 ; v, 150
Measeplotts (Kingsclere), iv, 266 n
Measures, —, v, 116
Meaton, Edw., iv, 276 ; Fawler, iv,
276
Mede, la, (Church Oakley), iv, 224
Mede, Val. atte, iii, 98, 145 ; iv, 259
Medfurling (Linkenholt), iv, 324 n
Medina, riv., ii, 415 ; v, 197, 227,
253, 268, 269, 270 ; oyster beds,
v, 468
Medina River Oyster Co., v, 468
Medine, East, hund., v, 138, 210,
448 ; bailiffs of, iv, 548
Medine, West., hund., v, 138, 209,
448
Medine le Hatte, v, 210
Medine le Pitt, v, 210
Medscherde, la, (Wherwell), iv, 411
Medsted, ii, 483, 496 ; iii, 302, 303,
327-9, 349 ; adv., iii, 329 ; char.,
iii, 329 ; ch., iii, 329 ; man., iii,
328 ; pop., v, 437 ; sch., ii, 401
Medsted Court (Medsted), iii, 328

Medusae, i, 94
Meere, John, iii, 120 ; see also
Mears
Meershegge (S. Damerham), iv,
586
Mees, Lawr., de, iii, 512
Meetkerke, Adolphus, iii, 384
Meggott, Rich., ii, 115
Meggs, Chris., v, 73 ; Eliz., v, 73
Meinertzhagen, Dan., iv, 509
Meinfelin, iv, 366, 368
Melbury, de, Joan, iv, 580 ; John,
iv, 580 ; Rog., iv, 579, 580 ; v,
130 ; Will., iv, 579, 580 ; v, 130
Melchet Court (Melchet Park), iv,
542 ; v, 558
Melchet Park, ii, 169, 173 ; iv, 489,
510, 540-2, 543
Melcombe Regis (Dors.), ii, 32 ;
v, 419
Meleford, Melleford, see Milford
Meller, Young, iii, 168
Mellesley, see Munsley
Melneford, see Milford
Melton, de, Cecily, iv, 69, 251 ;
Dorothy, iv, 246, 251 ; Eleanor,
iv, 251 ; Hen., iv, 69, 251 ; (Sir)
John, ii, 198, 262, 282, 366 ; iv,
69, 246, 251, 261 ; (Sir) Will.,
iv, 68, 69, 251
Membury, Sim., ii, 198, 263 ; v, 16
Memelne, mill (Niton), v, 188
Mendip, Anne, Lady, iv, 552 ; v,
274 ; Welbore Ellis, Ld., iv, 552 ;
v, 274
Menestoche, Menestoke, see Meonstoke
Mengeham, Mary, v, 482
Mengham (Hayling Isl.), iii, 129
Meon, riv., i, 54, 66, 67, 378, 379, 380,
391 ; ii, 3 ; iii, 64, 217, 220, 228,
233, 257, 268, 284, 285, 319, 342 ;
iv, 288 ; v, 409, 465, 560, 564
Meon, East, i, 378 ; ii, 9, 26, 38,
59, 241, 243, 244, 247 ; iii,
63, 64-75 ; iv, 416 ; v, 294, 324,
328 n, 331, 342, 454, 524 ; adv.,
ii, 20, 21 ; iii, 75 ; chaps., iii, 74 ;
char., iii, 75 ; chs., iii, 72 ; ind.,
v, 484 ; mans., iii, 65 ; pk., iii,
67 ; pop., v, 444 ; sch., ii, 398
Meon, East, hund., iii, 63
Meon, West, i, 378 ; ii, 101 ; iii, 245,
302, 303, 342-5 ; v, 342, 574 ;
adv., iii, 344 ; char., iii, 345 ;
ch., iii, 344 ; mans., ii, 61, 114 ;
iii, 343 ; pop., v, 440 ; Rom.
rem., i, 309 ; sch., ii, 406
Meonstoke, i, 378 ; ii, 68, 223 ;
iii, 245, 246, 254-7 ; v, 293,
294, 324, 328 n, 331 ; adv., iii,
257 ; char., iii, 257 ; ch., iii, 256 ;
man., iii, 254 ; pop., v, 440 ;
sch., ii, 401
Meonstoke, hund., iii, 245
Meonstoke, Maud de, v, 480 n
Meonstoke Ferrand, man. (Meon-
stoke), ii, 261, 288 ; iii, 255
Meonstoke Perrers, man. (Meonstoke), ii, 261, 288 ; iii, 254
Meonstoke Tour, man. (Meon-
stoke), iii, 256
Meonstoke Waleraund, man., see
Meonstoke Perrers
Meon Valley, i, 377, 378, 394, 473
Meonwara, i, 377, 379, 380, 391 ;
ii, 3 ; v, 294
Meratune, see Merdon
Mercator, Rob., iii, 88 ; see also
Marchant
Mercer [Merciarius], (le, the), Chris.,
iii, 313 ; Pet., v, 22, 34, 477
Merceron, F. A., iv, 326 ; Fran. H.,
iv, 327, 328, 376 ; Hen., iv, 376
Merciarius, see Mercer

Mercier, Paul, iii, 536 ; v, 486
Merdon [Merden] (Hursley), iii, 401 ; man., ii, 12 ; iii, 418
Merdon Castle (Hursley), iii, 418
Mere, (de, of), John, ii, 147 ; v, 92 n
Mereborne (S. Damerham), iv, 587 n
Meredith, Rich., iii, 314
Meredune, Meretune, see Merdon
Merelond, see Mareland
Merestone, see Merston
Merewell [Mereville, Merwell], de, Hen. ; see Winchester, Woodlock, bp. of ; Nich., ii, 110
Merick, Maur., iv, 622 n
Meriet, see Marriott
Merifeld, see Merryfield
Merks [Merke], Rich., ii, 212 ; Thos., bp. of Carlisle, ii, 37, 44, 45 ; see also Markes
Merlaw, John, prior of St. Swithun's, ii, 115
Merlay, Rog. de, iii, 149, 150
Merleberge, see Marlborough
Merlynputtes (S. Damerham), iv, 586
Merman, iii, 145
Merre, la, see Mareland
Merrie Hill (Ecchinswell), iv, 250
Merrill, John, iii, 445
Merriott, see Marriott
Merris, John, v, 283
Merritown (Christchurch), v, 85 ; man., v, 98
Merritt, —, ii, 385
Merry, —, v, 554
Merryfield, man. (W. Tisted), iii, 61
Merry Gardens (Brading), v, 177
Merrygrove Coppice (Broughton), iv, 493
Merryman, Capt., v, 350
Merscourt, see Marsh Court
Mersey, Will. de, iv, 396
Mersh, see Marsh
Mershcopemed (Bentley), iv, 27
Mershegate (Eling), iv, 547
Mershton, see Merston
Mersshe, see Marsh
Merston (Arreton), v, 140 ; man., v, 145
Merston, West, man. (Arreton), v, 146
Merston, (de), Hen., iii, 241 ; Rob., v, 145 n
Merston Pagham, see Pagham, man.
Merton, de, Isabel, iv, 589 ; Rich., iv, 64 ; Walt., bp., ii, 105, 208, 209 ; iv, 130, 134, 138, 148 ; Will., iv, 589
Merton College (Oxf.), ii, 209, 268 ; iv, 131, 138
Merton Priory (Surr.), ii, 108 ; iii, 58 ; iv, 42, 43, 45, 46, 47, 50, 51, 107, 114 ; priors:—Rich., iv, 51 ; Thos. de Kent, iv, 46 n ; Walt., iv, 43
Mertwey (Linkenholt), iv, 324 n
Mervyn, Anne, ii, 492 ; Sir Edm., ii, 479, 492 ; iii, 117 ; Eliz., ii, 479, 492 ; Hen., ii, 479, 492 ; iii, 117 ; Sir Jas., iv, 370, 371 ; John, iii, 262 ; fam. arms, ii, 492 ; iii, 117 ; see also Marvyn
Merwell, see Merewell
Merwenna, abbess of Romsey, ii, 126, 132
Merwey (Andover), iv, 346
Meservis, Will., v, 127
Messer, —, v, 458
Messetone, see Marshton
Mestowe, hund., ii, 135 ; iv, 401
Mesy, see Meysey

Metcalfe [Metcalf], Eliz., ii, 520 ; Humph., iii, 29, 90 ; iv, 423 ; Jerome, ii, 87 ; Sam., ii, 520
Methodists, ii, 490 ; iii, 56, 80, 93, 120, 139, 142, 148, 151, 244, 257, 267, 273, 281, 287, 296, 319, 332, 371, 390, 394, 400, 424, 534 ; iv, 4, 14, 18, 26, 51, 98, 108, 115, 145, 221, 222, 229, 230, 242, 266, 274, 277, 299, 304, 324, 331, 356, 359, 399, 405, 409, 411, 422, 435, 449, 451, 468, 480, 486, 539, 558, 576, 591, 595, 601 ; v, 127, 136, 169, 177, 186, 193, 197, 201, 204, 215, 235, 264, 271, 277
Mettingham, John de, ii, 203
Meux [Mewis], Alice, v, 173, 175, 250 ; Anne, v, 250 ; Barth., v, 250 ; Eliz., (Lady), ii, 493 ; v, 250, 271 ; Jane, v, 192, 250 ; Joan, v, 147 ; (Sir) John, v, 147, 161, 188, 250 ; Lewis, v, 173, 184, 250 ; Mabel, Lady, v, 250 ; Rich., v, 250, 251 ; Thos., v, 173, 250 ; (Sir) Will., ii, 392, 493 ; iv, 271 ; v, 146, 147 n, 148, 162, 173, 250 ; fam., v, 182, 249 ; see also Mew and Mews
Meux-Worsley, see Worsley
Mew, Frank, v, 250, 542 ; see also Meux and Mews
Mewce, Mewes, see Méws
Mewesbridge (Calbourne), v, 218
Mewis, see Meux
Mews [Mewce, Mewes], Ellis, iv, 259, 374, 471 ; Frances, iv, 259, 471 ; John, ii, 69 ; v, 268 ; Lydia, Lady, iii, 449 ; v, 93 ; (Sir) Pet., ii, 95, 96, 97 ; iii, 264 ; v, 54, 87 n, 93 ; see also Meux and Mew
Mewshay (Winchester), v, 2
Mexborough, earl of, iv, 250
Meyler, Rich., iii, 457 ; iv, 427 ; v, 355 n, 536
Meynell, Joel de, iv, 607
Meyres, see Mears
Meyrick, Ellen K., iv, 26 ; Sir Geo., v, 88, 100, 570, 573 ; Jane, iv, 258 ; John F., iv, 258 ; W., v, 576
Meyrick Park (Bournemouth), v, 134
Meyrick's annuity and scholarships, v, 137
Meysey [Mesy], de, Eve, iv 382 ; John, iv, 389 ; Rich., iv, 381 ; Rob., iii, 415 ; iv, 381, 382
Meysey Hampton (Glouc.), iv, 381 n
Michael, prior of Ellingham, ii, 230
Michel, see Michell
Michelborne, Alice, iii, 98 ; Joan, iv, 437 ; Lawr., iii, 98 ; Thos., iii, 98
Micheldever, ii, 21, 23, 99, 101, 116, 117, 118, 119 ; iii, 389, 390-4, 399 ; iv, 187, 195 ; v, 308, 324, 328 n, 331, 557, 558 ; adv., iii, 393 ; char., iii, 394 ; ch., iii, 393 ; mans., ii, 121 ; iii, 390 ; iv, 432 ; Nonconf., iii, 394 ; pop., v, 448 ; Rom. rem., i, 307, 391 ; iii, 390 ; schs., ii, 401
Micheldever, hund., iii, 389 ; iv, 415, 438
Micheldever, riv., iv, 417 ; v, 562 ; watercress cultivation, v, 455
Micheldever, (de), Agnes, iii, 392 ; Geoff., iii, 392 ; Phil., iii, 392, 396 ; Rich., iii, 392 ; Rob., iii, 392 ; Sim., iii, 392 ; Thos., v, 476 ; Thomasine, iii, 392 ; Will., iii, 392
Michell [Michel], Eliz., iv, 326 ; Hen., v, 155 ; Rich., iv, 326 ; Rob., ii, 211 ; v, 94 ; see also Mitchell

Michelmersh [Michelmares, Michelmarsh], ii, 25, 172 ; iii, 401, 423-7 ; iv, 489 ; adv., iii, 426 ; char., iii, 427 ; ch., iii, 426 ; man., iii, 424 ; iv, 508 ; pop., v, 446 ; schs., ii, 401
Michelton, see Roake
Middeltune, see Longparish
Middenbury, i, 345
Middle (N. Stoneham), iii, 479
Middle Bridge (Romsey), iv, 452
Middle Chine (Bournemouth), v, 134
Middle Coppice (Damerham), iv, 587
Middle Copse (Maplederwell), iv, 149
Middlecot, tithing, iv, 337
Middlemarch [Middlemarsh], Thos., v, 162, 192 ; Will., v, 144, 212 n
Middlemore, Hen., iv, 225
Middleneye, Ralph de, ii, 156
Middleton (Brading), see Milton
Middleton, (Droxford), see Midlington
Middleton, tithing (Freshwater), v, 240
Middleton (Longparish), iv, 406
Middleton [Midleton, Mydlington] (de), Sir Chas., v, 400 ; Geo., iv, 647 ; Gilb., ii, 150 ; Sir Hugh, v, 157 ; H. B., iv, 484 ; Jas. E., iii, 437 ; John, v, 330 ; Marg., ii, 128 ; Nath., iii, 484 ; Rich., ii, 146, 149 ; Thos., iii, 175, 503 ; Will., iii, 515 ; iv, 484 ; —, v, 384
Middleton Hall (Longparish), iv, 406
Middlewood (Liss), iv, 84
Midgham (Fordingbridge), iv, 567 ; mans., iv, 572
Midgham, de, Avice, iv, 572 ; Hawise, iv, 572 ; Maud, iv, 376 n ; Will., iv, 376 n
Midlemawme, the, (Ecchinswell), iv, 250
Midleton, see Middleton
Midlington, (Droxford), iii, 275, 286
Mienstock, see Meonstoke
Miggeham, see Midgham
Mikeltone, John, ii, 212
Milborowe (Shipton Bellinger), iv, 513
Milbourne [Mylbourne], Eliz., iv, 327 ; Rich., iv, 327, 609 ; Sim., iv, 327, 609 ; Sir Thos., iii, 414 ; iv, 609
Milbride (Romsey), iv, 452
Milbrook, see Millbrook
Mildecombe, (de), Marg., iii, 204, 262 ; Walt., iii, 204, 262
Mildehale, Constantine de, iii, 62
Mildeston (Wilts), ii, 137
Mildmay, Anne, iii, 333, 334 ; Carew, iii, 333, 334 ; iv, 471 ; Carew H., v, 212 ; Dorothy, v, 212 ; Fran. B. St. J., iii, 340 ; Sir Hen., ii, 327, 328 ; iii, 333, 334 ; iv, 62 ; v, 355 n ; Sir Hen. B. P. St. J., iv, 472 ; Sir Hen. P. St. J., iv, 72, 73, 80, 81, 90, 91, 92, 93, 98, 112, 374, 471 ; v, 212, 252, 355 ; Hugh, v, 515 ; Humph. F. St. J., iii, 340 ; Jane, iv, 471 ; v, 5, 212 ; Paulet St. J., iv, 471, 472 ; Lady St. J., iv, 112 ; fam., iv, 73, 74, 444 ; arms, iii, 333 ; see also St. John
Mildmay House (Winchester), v, 5
Miles-Bailey, G. M., iv, 446, 447, 448
Milestones, Roman, i, 336, 337
Milford, ii, 139, 154 ; iv, 603, 604 ; v, 81, 82, 110, 114, 115-24, 291,

Milford (*cont.*)
318 ; adv., ii, 21 ; v, 123 ; ch., v, 120 ; ind., v, 116, 470 ; man., ii, 159 ; v, 116 ; mills, v, 117, 120 ; Nonconf., v, 124 ; pop., v, 442 ; sch., ii, 401
Milford Baddesley, man. (Milford), v, 117, 120, 212
Milford Barnes, man. (Milford), v, 117, 123
Milford Lake (Highclere), iv, 285
Milford Montagu, man. (Milford), v, 116
Milford-on-Sea, *see* Milford
Military organisation, v, 356-8
Militia, v, 355, 356
Mill [Mille, Myll(e)], Alex., iv, 637 ; Alice, iv, 637 ; Cath., iv, 413, 537 ; Cecily, iv, 557 ; Sir Chas., iii, 435, 437 ; iv, 553 ; Dowsabella, v, 230 ; Edm., iii, 135 ; Geo., iii, 434 ; iv, 553, 554 *n*, 611, 622 ; v, 127, 130, 143, 150, 151, 152, 177, 230, 289 ; (Sir) John, ii, 139 ; iii, 120, 428, 432, 433, 434, 436 ; iv, 413, 450, 552, 553, 557, 611, 617, 618, 619, 628 ; v, 111, 113, 130, 143, 151, 152, 230, 275, 326, 517, 528, 539 *n* ; (Sir) Lewkenor [Lewknor], iv, 413, 552, 557 ; Marg., Lady, iv, 460 ; Mary, (Lady), iii, 485 ; iv, 617, 618, 619, 628 ; Nath., iii, 298, 535 ; v, 80 ; (Sir) Rich., iii, 435, 436, 438 ; iv, 434, 460, 554, 617, 618, 619, 622, 628 ; v, 143, 150, 151, 230, 275 ; Rog., iv, 637 ; Thos., iii, 434 ; iv, 413, 622 ; Will. atte, iv, 407 ; fam., arms, iii, 435 ; *see also* Barker-Mill and Mills
Millard, Jas. E., ii, 369 ; iv, 137
Millbrook, ii, 71, 108 ; iii, 401, 427-32 ; v, 419 ; adv., iii, 431 ; char., iii, 432 ; ch., iii, 431 ; man., ii, 61, 114 ; iii, 428 ; pop., v, 447 ; sch., ii, 401
Mill Court (Binsted), ii, 486
Millcourt Gooshatche (Froyle), ii, 504
Mille, *see* Mill
Milleford, *see* Milford
Miller [Millers, Milyr], Sir C. H., ii, 506 ; Sir C. J. H., ii, 501, 513 ; Edm., iii, 112 ; Eliz., (Lady), ii, 478, 493 ; iv, 442, 529 ; v, 234, 250 ; Esther, iv, 529 ; Herb. the, iv, 211 ; Hester, iv, 529 ; Humph., iii, 230 ; (Sir) Jas., v, 547, 550 ; Jane, v, 250 ; (Sir) John, ii, 493 ; iii, 283 ; iv, 106, 529 ; v, 100, 171, 229, 230, 250 ; Mark, v, 243, 274 ; Mary, v, 243, 274 ; Rich., iv, 103 ; Sarah, ii, 478 ; (Sir) Thos., ii, 493, 502 ; iii, 54 ; v, 171, 172, 229, 242, 274, 517 ; —, ii, 311 ; fam., arms, ii, 493
Miller's farm (Fordingbridge), iv, 568
Milles, *see* Mills
Milleward, Walt., iv, 213
Millhamby (Amport), iv, 339
Millhams (Christchurch), v, 85
Millingate, Anne, iii, 370 ; John, iii, 358, 360, 370
Millipedes, i, 163
Millman, Mrs., iv, 359
Mill Marsh (Brading), v, 156
Millmore (Greywell), iv, 76
Mill Piece (Bentworth), iv, 68
Mill-pond, stream, v, 563
Mill Rife (Hayling), v, 469
Mills [Milles, Mylles], Cecil, iv, 609 ; Isaac, iv, 286 ; Jas., iii, 114 ; Jane, v, 215 ; (Sir) John, ii, 380 ;

Mills (*cont.*)
iv, 289 *n*, 609 ; v, 573 ; John D., iv, 609 ; v, 84 ; Rob., iii, 80, 530 ; iv, 173, 198, 201 ; Thos., iii, 200 ; Will., iv, 609 ; Mrs., v, 84 ; —, iv, 171 ; *see also* Mill
Mills, ii, 137, 223, 224, 491, 506 ; iii, 6, 23, 24, 51, 52, 67, 78, 86, 96, 102, 113, 122, 129, 134, 144, 151, 159, 172, 210, 221, 224, 226, 239, 249, 264, 271, 279, 288, 294, 295, 298, 305, 308, 310, 312, 316, 318, 320, 325, 331, 334, 340, 344, 390, 404, 414, 433, 438, 465, 479, 482 ; iv, 9, 16, 34, 40, 43, 47, 64, 68, 72, 73, 85, 87, 94, 106, 111, 115, 121, 128, 134, 149, 151, 154, 157, 167, 178, 191, 193, 194, 209, 213, 216, 248, 251, 252, 253, 256, 257, 282, 286, 289, 290, 300, 317, 330, 335, 339, 341, 342, 351, 353, 354, 364, 378, 380, 389, 396, 402, 403, 406, 407, 410, 412, 427, 432, 448, 451, 453, 455, 457, 458, 470, 476, 481, 484, 491, 493, 494, 496, 498, 507, 513, 517, 527, 532, 543, 546, 555, 564, 565, 568, 569, 570, 571, 578, 580, 590, 598, 609, 611, 618, 620, 627, 638, 650, 652 ; v, 48, 49, 97, 98, 100, 115, 117, 120, 124, 126, 130, 139, 144, 145, 175, 188, 200, 220, 238, 241, 242, 248, 250, 256, 268, 272, 410
Milner, Ralph, ii, 83
Milroy, Rev. And. W., iv, 158
Milton, man. (Brading), v, 160, 161, 182
Milton (Christchurch), ii, 152 ; v, 81, 83 *n*, 124-7, 318 ; adv., v, 127 ; char., v, 109 ; ch., v, 126 ; mans., v, 124 ; mkt., v, 126 ; mills, v, 124, 126 ; Nonconf., v, 127 ; pop., v, 442 ; sch., ii, 401
Milton, New, (Christchurch), v, 124
Milton (Portsmouth), iii, 140, 141, 194 ; man., iii, 195
Milton [Multon] (de), Rich., ii, 203, 205 ; Rog., ii, 157, 158 ; Walt., v, 118 ; Will., ii, 187, 188 ; iv, 190
Milton Abbey (Dors.), v, 90
Milyr, *see* Miller
Minchin, Clarinda, iii, 259 ; Falkner J., iii, 259 ; Humph., iii, 259, 263
Mincingfield, tithing (Bishop Waltham), iii, 275
Mindisherne (Beaulieu), iv, 650
Minley (Yateley), iv, 1, 2, 20, 31, 32 ; adv., iv, 26 ; ch., iv, 25 ; man., iv, 21, 23 ; prehist. rem., i, 258
Minley Grange (Minley), iv, 21
Minnett, Fran. A., iv, 623
Minns, Rev. G. W., ii, 236 ; iii, 222, 223, 297, 480
Minstead, ii, 25 ; iv, 489, 544, 550, 555, 609, 615, 629, 632, 635-8 ; v, 109, 305 ; adv., iv, 638 ; char., iv, 638 ; ch., iv, 638 ; man., ii, 464 ; iv, 543, 635 ; v, 568 ; mill, iv, 638 ; pop., v, 442 *n*, 446 ; sch., ii, 401
Minstead (de), Andr., iv, 635 ; Christina, iv, 636 ; Isabel, iv, 636 ; John, iv, 636 ; Thos., iv, 636 ; Will., iv, 635
Minster Field (Abbotts Ann), Rom. rem., i, 300
Minster House (Winchester), v, 13
Miocene age, i, 22, 26
Mionstoke, *see* Meonstoke
Mirabel [Mirables], man., ii, 182, 186

Mirefeld, *see* Merryfield
Misholt Copse (Steventon), iv, 171
Misleden (Stockbridge), iv, 483
Missenden, de, Bern., iv, 443 ; Sir Edm., iv, 443 ; Isabel, iv, 443 ; Juliana, Lady, iv, 443 ; Kath., iv, 443 ; Thos., iv, 226, 443
Missing, Jas., iv, 646 ; John, v, 113 ; Thos., iv, 646
Mitcheldever, *see* Micheldever
Mitchell, Mrs., v, 265 ; *see also* Michell
Mitchelmarsh, *see* Michelmersh
Mitcomb Regis, ii, 148
Mitford, Hen. R., iii, 291 ; John, iv, 622 *n* ; Mary R., iii, 350 ; iv, 218 ; Will., iii, 291, 295 ; iv, 622 *n* ; Col., v, 466 *n*, 501
Mitley, Pet., v, 34
Mitton, Fran., iv, 352 ; Hen., iv, 352 ; John, iv, 352
Miz Maze (Breamore), iv, 596
Moberd, And., v, 305
Moberly, Geo., ii, 359, 360, 366 ; v, 211
Mockbeggar (Ibsley), iv, 579, 580
Moderstone, *see* Mottistone
Modesfunte, *see* Mottisfont
Modristan, *see* Mottistone
Mody, *see* Moody
Moels, de, Isabel, iv, 531, 564 ; John, iv, 531, 564 ; Maud, iv, 531, 564 ; Muriel, iv, 531 ; Nich., iv, 531, 562, 564 ; Rog., iv, 531, 564
Moene, *see* Meon
Moenestoke, *see* Meonstoke
Moens, W. J. C., iv, 623 ; Mrs., iv, 616
Mohun, de, Eliz., iv, 77 ; Isabel, iv, 77 ; Joan, iv, 77 ; (Sir) John, iv, 77 ; Lucy, iv, 174 ; Mary, iv, 77 ; Maud, iv, 77 ; Philppa, iv, 77 ; Reg., iii, 229 ; iv, 77, 174 ; Will., iv, 77 ; v, 48
Moires, Anne, iv, 532 ; Fran., iv, 532
Mokylshyll, *see* Muccleshill
Moldesleyhill, Moleslee, Mollesleghe, Mollesleyhill, *see* Munsley
Moleuxe, Hugh, iv, 590 ; Thos., iv, 590
Moleyns [Molcynes, Molines, Molyns] (de), Ad., ii, 287 ; v, 319, 369 ; Anne, iii, 361 ; iv, 105 ; Ant., v, 98 ; Sir Barentine, iv, 106 ; v, 98 ; Bridg., iv, 105 ; Eliz., v, 105 ; Geo., v, 98 ; John, iii, 224, 241 ; Marg., iii, 69 ; Mary, iii, 361 ; (Sir) Mich., iv, 105, 106 ; v, 98 ; Phil., iii, 224, 241 ; Rich., iv, 573 ; v, 98 ; Thos., v, 113 ; Will., iii, 361 ; iv, 105 ; v, 98
Molineux, *see* Molyneux
Molloy, Capt., v, 396
Molluscs, i, 103
Molton, Rog. de, iii, 97
Molyneux, vsct., v, 349
Molyneux [Molineux], Edm., iv, 107 ; Sir Rob., ii, 47
Molyns, *see* Moleyns
Mompesson, Anne, iv, 271 ; Thos., iv, 447
Monachus, *see* Monck
Monasteriis, *see* Mouster
Monceux, Ingram, iv, 104, 475 ; John, iv, 475 ; Marg., iv, 475 ; Maud, iv, 475 ; Waleran, iv, 104, 475 ; Will., iv, 475, 506
Moncheney, de, Denise, iv, 52 ; Joan, iv, 52 ; John, iv, 52 ; Warine, iv, 52 ; Sir Will., iv, 52
Monck [Monachus, Monk, Moyne, Munck] (la, le), Alice, v, 570 ; Eliz., iv, 268 ; v, 129 ; Geoff.,

Monck (cont.)
iv, 431 ; Geo., iii, 178 ; iv, 346 ;
v, 382 ; (Sir) Hen., iv, 268 ; v,
96, 128, 129 ; Joan, iv, 268, 570 ;
v, 96, 129 ; John, iii, 187 ; iv,
268, 570 ; v, 129 ; Marg., iv, 570 ;
Margery, iii, 466 ; Nich., ii, 190,
191 ; Ralph [Ralf], iv, 268, 431 ;
Rich., iv, 570 ; Rob., iv, 268 ;
Thos., iii, 466 ; Walt., iv, 382 ;
Will., iv, 268, 431 ; v, 129
Monckton Meade (Romsey), iv, 452
Monday [Mondaie], Eliz., iv, 336 ;
Rich., iv, 336 ; Thos., iii, 178
Money, Walt., iv, 275
Moneyburst (Longstock), iv, 449
Money-Coutts, Hugh, iv, 84
Monk, see Monck
Monkestone, see Monxton
Monkhouse, John, ii, 496
Monks' Bay (Bonchurch), v, 155
Monksfrith (King's Somborne), iv,
470
Monk Sherborne, ii, 205 ; iv, 113,
114, 165, 167, 170, 223, 231-8 ;
adv., iv, 238 ; char., iv, 238 ; chs.,
iv, 231, 233, 435 ; common lands,
iv, 231 ; mans., iv, 231, 233 ;
pop., v, 439
Monk Sherborne Priory, ii, 41, 106,
204, 205, 226-9, 495 ; iv, 117, 127,
142, 145, 148, 159, 169, 176, 226,
228, 231, 232, 240, 242, 434, 435
Monk Sherborne Wood (Monk
Sherborne), iv, 231
Monkwood (Ropley), iii, 55
Monmouth, Rob. Carey, earl of, v,
377 ; fam., iv, 245 n
Monmouth, (de, of), Cecily, iv, 521 ;
John, iv, 278, 521 ; v, 98 ;
Withenoe, iv, 278
Monnox, Geo., iii, 98
Monro, Rev. Horace G., iv, 57, 63
Monson, vsct., iv, 105 ; Eliz.,
vctss., iv, 105 ; Lady Eliz., iv,
105
Montacute, fam., see Montagu
Montacute Priory (Somers.), iii,
271
Montagu [Montague], Eliz., dchss.
of, iv, 651 ; Mary, dchss. of, iv,
651 ; dks. of : Geo. Montagu,
iv, 651 ; John Montagu, iv, 650,
651 ; v, 224 ; Ralph Montagu,
iv, 651 ; Jane M., Lady, iv,
654 ; Lds., ii, 464, 469, 500, 513 ;
Hen., iv, 219 ; Hen. J., iv, 652,
654, 655 ; John W. E., iv, 652 ;
Isabel, mchnss. of, iv, 34 ; v, 118 ;
John Nevill, mqss. of, iv, 34 ; v,
118 ; Ant. Browne, vsct., ii, 513,
514, 516 ; iii, 442 ; iv, 34, 196,
200 ; Magdalen, vctss., iv, 200
Montagu [Montacute, Montague,
Montcuyt, Mountague] (de),
Anne, iv, 172 n ; Chas., iv, 601 ;
Dodington, iv, 601 ; Edw., v,
385 ; Eleanor, iv, 608 ; Eliz., iv,
77, 652 ; Hen., iv, 254 n, 471 n ;
v, 344 ; Geo., iv, 563, 601 ; Jas.,
bp., ii, 85, 87 ; (Sir) John, iii,
135, 410, 459 ; iv, 608 ; v, 117 n,
118, 393 ; Kath., iv, 608 ; Marg.,
iii, 135, 410 ; Sim., iv, 82 ; (Sir)
Thos., ii, 155, 475 ; iii, 135, 410 ;
iv, 130, 347, 545, 608, 632 ; v,
117 n, 118, 277 ; (Sir) Will., ii,
156, 157 ; iv, 77, 172 n, 261,
265, 427, 508, 516, 579, 608, 612,
619 ; v, 92, 114, 117, 118, 211,
219, 220, 222, 225, 241 n, 253,
277, 314 ; —, ii, 385 ; fam., arms,
iii, 135, 410, 442, 481
Montagu-Douglas-Scott, Walt. F.,
iv, 652

Montagu-Stuart-Wortley, E. J., v,
84, 108
Monte, see Mount
Monteagle [Mounteagle], Lds., iv,
21 ; Will. Stanley, iii, 45
Monteagle, Mary, iii, 45
Montebourg Abbey, v, 171, 174,
181, 202
Mont Fichet [Munfichet], de, Agnes,
iv, 142 n, 165 n ; John, iv, 165 n ;
Maud, iii, 362
Montfort, Sim. de, ii, 19, 176, 473,
519 ; iii, 103, 104, 254 ; iv, 88,
89, 198, 458, 475, 645 ; v, 32,
310, 362 ; fam., iv, 493
Montgomerie, Mrs., iv, 546
Montgomery (de), Sir Basil, iv,
458 ; Eliz., iii, 105 ; Fulk, iii,
254 ; iv, 493, 494, 495 ; Hugh,
iii, 103, 134 ; iv, 645 ; (Sir) John,
iii, 95, 105, 149 ; Rob., see
Shrewsbury, Earl of ; Rog., see
Shrewsbury, earl of ; Rose, iii,
149 ; Sir Thos., iii, 105
Monthermer (de), Edw., iii, 135,
410 ; iv, 515 ; Isabel, iii, 456 ; iv,
515 ; Joan, iii, 135 ; Marg., iii,
135, 410 ; Ralph [Ralf], iii, 135,
247, 410, 456 ; iv, 457, 515 ; Thos.,
iii, 135, 410 ; iv, 515 ; fam.,
arms, iii, 247, 410
Montibus, Eubold de, iii, 441
Montresor, Col., v, 569
Mont St. Michel, abbey of (France),
iv, 126, 138
Montserrel, Rich. de, iii, 478
Monxton, iv, 333, 379-80, 385 ;
adv., iv, 380 ; ch., iv, 380 ;
man., iv, 342, 343, 379 ; mills, iv,
380 ; pop., v, 438
Monxton Oakcuts (Monxton), iv,
379
Moody [Mody], Arabella L., iii,
244 ; Hen., iii, 201 ; Isaac, iii,
124, 193 ; John, iii, 124, 193 ;
iv, 371 ; v, 87 ; John S., v, 526 n,
537 ; Will., ii, 350 ; iv, 477 ;
Mrs., iv, 558
Mookells (Ecchinswell), iv, 250
Moor (Arreton), v, 140, 142
Moor Abbas, see More Abbess
Moor Closes, man. (Bramshaw), iv,
623
Moorcote (Eversley), iv, 32
Moor Court (Romsey), iv, 452, 456
Moordown (Bournemouth), v, 134,
135
Moore [Maure, Mora, Moure, Mours],
(atte), Agnes, iv, 202 ; Alice, iv,
94, 435 ; Ant., iv, 94 ; Cecily, iv,
434 ; Edw., v, 163 ; Eliz., iii, 127 ;
Eustace, ii, 337 ; Sir F., v, 543 ;
Garrett, v, 546 ; Hen., iv, 434,
435 ; Ingram, iv, 434, 435 ; Jane,
v, 163 ; John, iii, 181 ; iv, 299,
434, 435 ; v, 99 ; Marg., iv, 630 ;
Mary, iv, 522 ; Mary S., v, 170 ;
Rich., iv, 40, 94, 434 ; Rob., iv,
434 ; Thos., ii, 501 ; (Sir) Will.,
ii, 79 ; iii, 97, 250 ; iv, 630 ; W.
H., iv, 525 ; Mrs., v, 265 ; —, v,
12 ; fam., iv, 233 ; see also More
Moorecourt, man ii, 114
Moore Place (Eversley), see Brams-
hill, Great, man
Moore Place Farm (Eversley), iv,
40, 41
Moor Malwyn, see More Malwyn
Moors, riv., iv, 606 ; v, 85, 97, 109
Moortown (Ringwood), iv, 606
Mora, see Moore and More
Moralls, man. (Portchester), iii, 159
Morant [Moraunt, Morrant], Edw.,
iv, 618 ; Edw. J. H. E., iv, 609,
618, 626, 627, 628, 629 ; Geo.,

Morant (cont.)
iv, 16 ; Hay, v, 569 ; John, iv,
336, 606, 608, 613, 618 ; v, 459,
572 ; Jordan, iv, 334 ; Capt.
Will., v, 572 ; —, ii, 464, 634 ;
Mrs., iv, 606
Morant's Hall (Winchester), v,
459 n
Mordaunt, Eliz., Lady, iv, 370 ;
John, Ld., iv, 370 ; Lewis, Ld.,
iv, 370 ; John, vsct., v, 265 n
Mordaunt, Miss, iv, 210
More, man. (Ambersham), iii, 78
More [Maure, Mora] (atte, de, de
la), Ad., iii, 136 ; Alice, iv, 214,
215 n ; Amice, iv, 485 ; Anne, iv,
453 ; Ant., iv, 101, 104 n, 214,
215 n ; Beat., iv, 219 ; Christine,
ii, 130 ; iv, 219, 220 ; Dowsabel,
iv, 453 ; (Sir) Edw., ii, 295, 301,
366 ; iv, 87, 97, 98 ; Eleanor, iv,
260 ; Gwen, iv, 144 ; Hen., iii,
485 ; iv, 166 n, 220 ; Joan, iv, 16,
220, 624 ; v, 96 ; John, ii, 228,
503 ; iii, 43, 464, 465, 468, 485 ;
iv, 104, 219, 453, 454, 488 ; v,
96 ; Kath., iii, 375 ; Mary, iv,
97 ; Nich., iii, 485 ; iv, 220 ;
Payn, iv, 493 ; Ralph, v, 191 ;
Rich., ii, 171, 211 ; iii, 373, 374,
388 ; iv, 99, 104, 215 n, 219 ; v,
484 ; Rob., iv, 624 ; v, 96 ; Thos.,
ii, 211 ; iv, 9, 43 n, 101, 104 n ;
Walt., ii, 212 ; Will., iv, 219, 220,
276 ; v, 483 ; —, iv, 260 ; fam.,
arms, iii, 465 ; see also Moore
More Abbess, man. (Romsey), ii,
131 ; iv, 455
Morecourt, ii, 114
Morell, Mrs., v, 484
More Malwyn, man. (Romsey), ii,
131 ; iv, 455
Moremeade (Weyhill), iv, 395
Morenses (Hartley Wespall), iv, 42
Morestead, iii, 111 ; iii, 302, 329-30 ;
v, 429, 544 ; adv., iii, 330 ; ch.,
iii, 330 ; man., ii, 114 ; iii, 330 ;
pop., v, 448
Morestead Down, iii, 329
Morestead House (Morestead), iii,
329
Moreton, Aug. J. F., v, 170 ;
Ralph, v, 553 ; Rich., iv, 5 ; see
also Morton
Moretownesway (Calbourne), v, 218
Moreville [Morville] (de), Ellen, v,
182 ; Eudo, iv, 515 ; John [Ivo],
v, 182 ; Maud, iv, 515
Morewell (de), Joan, iv, 367 ; John,
iv, 366, 367 ; Rog., iv, 366
Morflett, Eliz., iv, 21, 25 ; Rob., iv,
25
Morgan, Ant., iv, 571, 573 ; v, 241,
282 ; Chris., iv, 388 n, 617 ; Hen.,
ii, 337 ; Isabel, ii, 129 ; Joan, iv,
388 n, 617 ; John, iii, 318 ; Kath.,
iv, 571, 573 ; v, 241 ; Morris, v,
147 ; Rich., iii, 487 ; Sir Thos.,
ii, 337 ; Will., iii, 71, 109 ; —,
v, 518
Morgaston Wood (Sherborne St.
John), iv, 158 n, 160
Morhala, man., see Murrell
Morhale [Morhala] (de), Arth., iv,
93 ; Emma, iv, 93 ; Gunilda, iv,
93 ; Pet., iv, 93 ; Steph., iv, 93
Morin, John, v, 190, 164 ; Rich.,
iv, 377 ; Rob., v, 190 ; Will., v,
190
Morison, Cath. W., iv, 442 ; see also
Morrison
Morley, Anne, Lady, iv, 172 ; Eliz.,
iii, 48 ; Fran., iii, 285 ; Geo., bp.,
ii, 93, 94, 95, 337, 380, 389 ; iii,
206, 278, 527 ; iv, 419 n ; v, 14,

Morley (cont.)
58, 271 ; Hen., v, 222 ; Col. Herb.,
v, 341 ; Jas., iv, 180 ; John, iii,
97 ; Rob., v, 285 ; Sarah, iv, 253 ;
Thos., iii, 264 ; Sir Will., iv, 172 ;
Col., v, 344
Morley's Cross (Christchurch), v, 85
Mornington, Cath. P. T. L. Welles-
ley, ctss. of, iv, 100 ; earls of :
Rich. Wellesley, iv, 100 ; Will.
P. T. L. Wellesley, iv, 93, 100
Moro, dk. de, v, 176
Morosini, Filippo, v, 370
Morrall, man., see Murrell
Morrant, see Morant
Morrell, Rob., iv, 374
Morris [Morres, Morrice, Morrys,
Morys], Anne, iii, 71 ; iv, 105,
225, 226, 258 ; Fran., iii, 71 ; iv,
225, 226, 258 ; v, 177, 277 n ;
John, ii, 263, 273, 290, 365 ; iv,
605 ; —, v, 16 ; see also Maurice
Morrison, (Sir) Chas., iv, 595 ;
Rich., iv, 595 ; Miss, iv, 616,
620 ; see also Morison
Morrys, see Morris
Morse, Rog., v, 486
Mortain, ct. of, iv, 438
Mortaine, Alice, v, 161 ; John, v,
161
Mortelhunte, see Mottisfont
Morthing, ii, 147
Mortimer [Mortemer], (de), Andr.,
ii, 315 ; Anne, ii, 475 ; Edm., ii,
475, 476 ; iii, 227, 372 ; iv, 130,
341, 342 n, 347, 426, 427, 430 ;
v, 368 ; Eleanor, ii, 475, 476 ;
iv, 427 ; Eliz., ii, 475 ; Hugh, iii,
364 ; iv, 256, 296, 426, 458 n ;
Joan, iv, 427 ; Joyce, iii, 364,
365 ; Marg., iv, 427 ; Maud, iv,
360 ; Percy, iv, 198, 200 ;
Philippe, ii, 475 ; Ralph [Ral,
Ralf], ii, 420 ; iii, 9, 372, 429,
441, 463, 466, 467, 504 ; iv, 52,
256, 257, 296, 341, 342, 419, 426,
438, 458 ; v, 112 ; Rob., iii, 227,
364, 365, 366 ; Rog., ii, 143, 475 ;
iii, 9, 227, 372 ; iv, 189, 196 n,
256, 360, 361 n, 362, 418, 419,
426, 427, 430, 458 n, 612, 631 ;
v, 33 ; fam., arms, iii, 227, 463
Mortimer West End, iv, 31, 56-7 ;
adv., iv, 57 ; ch., iv, 56 ; man.,
iv, 56 ; Nonconf., iv, 56 ; pop.,
v, 440 ; sch., ii, 401
Morton (Brading), v, 156 ; man.,
v, 164 ; Rom. rem., i, 313 ; v,
156, 164
Morton, (de), Sir Geo., iv, 62 ; John,
ii, 48, 179 ; iv, 225, 336 ; Nich.,
ii, 16 ; Rachel, iv, 61, 62 ; Thos.,
ii, 115 ; see also Moreton
Morton Common (Brading), v, 156
Morville, see Moreville
Morwell, la, (Kingsclere), iv, 265
Morye Copice (W. Wellow), iv, 535
Morys, see Morris
Mosaics, Roman, i, 268, 278, 288,
296, 300, 305, 306, 307, 308, 311,
314, 315, 316, 368, 372
Moseclyre, Moseclyve, see Muscliff
Mosedene (Overton), iv, 211
Moss [Mosse], Hen., ii, 518 ; Fran.,
iv, 471 ; v, 94 ; J. S., iii, 300 ; v,
541
Mosses, i, 71
Mostyn, Capt. Savage, v, 390 ; Sir
Thos., v, 533
Mote-thing Hill (Kingsclere), iv,
246 n
Mothe, Will. iv, 221
Moths, i, 134
Motor-car industry, v, 461
Motteston, see Mottistone

Mottisfont, ii, 172 ; iii, 423 ; iv,
479 n, 489, 493, 497, 499, 500,
502, 503-10, 518, 637 ; adv., iv,
492, 509, 524 ; A.S. rem., i, 397 ;
ch., iv, 508 ; mans., iii, 392, 495,
503, 506 ; mkt. and fairs, iv,
506 ; Nonconf., iv, 510 ; pop., v,
446 ; sch., ii, 401
Mottisfont, John, iii, 392
Mottisfont Priory, ii, 20, 49, 55,
104, 172-5 ; iv, 163, 354, 359, 363,
442, 449, 451, 473, 476, 478, 480,
482, 484, 487, 492, 495, 499,
503-6, 507, 527, 538, 540, 553,
558
Mottisfont Treasury, man. (Mottisfont), iv, 506, 509
Mottistone, ii, 26 ; v, 209, 210, 211,
215, 219, 251-3, 284, 535 ; adv.,
v, 252 ; char., v, 253 ; ch., v,
252 ; man., v, 251 ; pop., v, 449
Mottlesfourde (Lyndhurst), iv, 631
Motys (Froyle), ii, 501
Moulshay Farm (Sherfield), iv, 104
Moulton-Barrett, Octavius, v, 220
Moundenard, John de, iv, 459
Moundsmere, man. (Preston Cand-
over), ii, 168, 311 ; iii, 375
Moundsmere Farm (Preston Cand-
over), iii, 372
Mount, the, (King's Worthy), iv,
430
Mount, man. (Mottisfont), iv, 507
Mount [Monte], (de), Alan, iv, 33 n ;
Alured, iv, 501 ; Christine, iv,
258 ; Frances D., iv, 258 ; Harry,
iv, 258 ; Jane, iv, 258 ; John, iv,
320 ; Will., iv, 258
Mountague, see Montagu
Mounteagle, see Monteagle
Mount Edgcumbe, Geo. Edgcumbe,
earl of, iv, 361 ; v, 180, 181, 184,
192, 244 ; see also Edgcumbe
Mount Farm (Mottisfont), iv, 507
Mountgomeries (Crondall), iv, 13 n
Mount Grace Priory (Yorks.), ii, 231
Mount Hyde (Mottisfont), see
Mount, man.
Mountjoy (Carisbrooke), i, 377
Mountjoy, Laura, Lady, ii, 486,
503 ; Lds., ii, 479 ; Walt., iv,
597 ; Will., ii, 486, 503 ; iv, 28 ;
Will. Stewart, vsct., iv, 54 ;
Anne Stewart, vsctss., iv, 54
Mount la Hyde (Mottisfont), see
Mount, man.
Mount Pleasant (Tadley), iv, 219
Mount Pleasant (Wherwell), iv, 411
Mount Royal (Lyndhurst), iv, 630
Mount-Temple, Will. F. Cowper,
Ld., iii, 437 ; iv, 452, 454, 468 ;
v, 562
Moure, see Moore and More
Mourhayes (E. Wellow), iv, 535
Mourn, Will., iii, 267
Mours, see Moore and More
Mourton, see Morton
Mousehoale (Ecchinswell), iv, 250
Mouster [Monasteriis], (de), Pet., ii,
41 ; Will., ii, 223
Mowbray, de, John, iii, 386, 387 ;
Olive, iii, 386 ; Rob., v, 300 n
Mowle, John, iii, 427
Mowles (Ecchinswell), iv, 250
Mowne, John, v, 192
Mowshold (Ashmansworth), iv, 274
Moyles Court (Ellingham), iv, 563,
565, 565 n
Moyne, see Monck
Muccleshill [Muccleshell], (Holden-
hurst), v, 82, 133
Muchelmarays, Muchelmaries, see
Michelmersh
Muckson (Romsey), iv, 455
Mucscroft (Longstock), iv, 449

Mude, riv., v, 84
Mudeford (Christchurch), v, 84
Mudmore (Fordingbridge), iv, 568
Muggeridge, —, v, 163
Muggeshyll, see Muccleshill
Muggleston (Brighstone), v, 213
Mugliston, Rev. J., iv, 192
Mukeleshull, see Muccleshill
Mulchet, see Melchet Park
Mulcock, Hen. J., iii, 58, 329 ; v,
517
Mulcwellcroft (Hartley Mauditt),
ii, 508
Muleford, see Milford
Muleward, Rog., ii, 198
Mulford, see Milford
Mulholland, Will., iv, 319
Mulkeshull, see Muccleshill
Mulle, la, see Mill Court (Binsted)
Mulleford, see Milford
Mullemede (Eversley), iv, 33
Mullens, Tim. L., iv, 157 ; see also
Mullins
Mullesford, see Milford
Mulleweye, la, (Breamore), iv, 598
Mullins, fam., v, 538 ; see also
Mullens
Mullion (Cornw.), ii, 173
Mulneford, see Milford
Mulsho, de, Joan, iv, 338 n ; John,
iv, 338 n
Multon, see Milton
Mulwelyssh (Sherborne St. John),
iv, 158
Munck, see Monck
Munday-on-the-Hill, see Compton
(King's Somborne)
Munde, Marg., iv, 167 ; Thos., iv,
167
Mundy, And., iii, 438 ; John, iv,
353 ; Mary, iv, 324 ; Rob., iv,
324 ; Will., v, 482
Munestagne, see Monxton
Munestoke, Munestokes, see Meon-
stoke
Munfichet, see Mont Fichet
Munns, Alf., v, 527
Munsley [Munnesleigh, Munsley
Hill], man. (Godshill), v, 175
Muntferaunt, Imbert de, iv, 21 n
Murdac, iv, 339 n
Murdac, Rich., iv, 340
Murding (Christchurch), v, 97, 98
Murding, Hugh de, v, 98
Murford, Pet., iii, 499 ; v, 342
Murray, Geo. D., iii, 224 ; Jas. A.,
iii, 224 ; Julia, iii, 224
Murrell, man. (Odiham), iv, 93
Murrell, tithing (Odiham), iv, 67
Murrell Green (Odiham), iv, 93
Mursele, Walt. de, iii, 111
Musard, Alice, iv, 477 ; Isabel, ii,
161 ; iv, 477 ; Will., ii, 161 ; iv,
477
Muschamp [Muschampe], Denny,
iv, 54 n ; Eliz., iv, 54 n ; Mary,
iv, 54 n ; —, v, 142 n
Muscliff [Museclyve], man. (Bourne-
mouth), v, 135
Muscliff, tithing (Westover), v, 82,
133
Mushulle (Kimpton), iv, 372
Muspratt, Thos., iv, 529 ; v, 27
Mustwood (Wherwell), iv, 401
Muxemede [Muxene], le, (Romsey),
iv, 457, 459
Mychelmers, see Michelmersh
Mydlington, see Middleton
Mylbourne, see Milbourne
Myll, Mylle, see Mill
Mylles, see Mills
Mylle Wey, le, (Sutton Warbling-
ton), iv, 18
My Lord's Pond (Hayling), v,
469

Mynne, Anne, iv, 103, 172 ; Eliz., iv, 172 ; Geo., iv, 103, 172 ; John, iv, 569
Mynstrelstrete (S. Damerham), iv, 586
Myriapoda, i, 163

Nairne, Ld., v, 574
Naish, man. (Milton), v, 126
Naish Farm (Christchurch), v, 95 n
Nancole Copse (Bentworth), iv, 68
Naper, see Napper
Napier, Diana, iv, 46 ; Gerard, iii, 419 ; Sir Nath., iii, 307, 419 ; iv, 46 ; fam., arms, iii, 419 ; see also Napper
Naples, Berard of, prior of Andover, ii, 219, 220, 221
Napoleon III, iv, 15
Napper [Naper], Rich., le, ii, 220 ; —, v, 517 ; see also Napier
Narbrough, Sir John, v, 381
Nares, Jas., iv, 32 ; Sir John, iv, 32, 40 ; Mary, iv, 40
Nash [Nasshe], (atte), John, v, 274, 482
Nashes farm (Boldre), iv, 619
Nashlin Feild (Eversley), iv, 33
Nason, Hen., v, 518, 527, 529
Nasshe, see Nash
Natanlea, i, 384, 385
Natanleag, see Netley
Natanleod, v, 293
Nately Eastrop, see Up Nately
Nately Scures, ii, 73 ; iv, 113, 114, 153-5, 176, 178 ; adv., iv, 155 ; char., iv, 155 ; ch., iv, 153, 154 ; man., iv, 153 ; mill., iv, 154 ; pop., v, 439
Nathan, Jacob, iii, 201
Natteleges Estrope, see Up Nately
Naval Academy, see Royal Naval College (Portsmouth)
Naylor, Chas., ii, 115
Neacroft (Bransgore), v, 108 n
Nea Heath (Harbridge), iv, 604
Neale [Neal, Neile], Agnes, iii, 270 ; Eliz., iii, 101 ; Sir Fran., iii, 171 ; iv, 335 ; Grace, Lady, iv, 620 ; Sir Harry B., iv, 616, 620 ; v, 85 ; John, ii, 495 ; v, 524 ; Julia S., v, 245 ; Rich., bp. of York, ii, 89 ; Rob., iv, 620 ; Thos., iii, 67, 101, 270, 343 n ; iv, 484 ; Walt., iv, 335 ; Will., iii, 67, 71, 270 ; fam., arms, iii, 272
Neatham (Holybourne), ii, 490, 512, 513 ; v, 546 ; grange, ii, 512, 514 ; mkt., v, 409 ; mills, ii, 512 ; pop., v, 437
Neatham, hund., ii, 471 ; iii, 3
Neceswude (Eling), iv, 547
Nedes (Stratfield Turgis), iv, 63
Needles (Freshwater), v, 88, 240, 286 ; lighthouse, v, 394
Neeton, see Niton
Neile, see Neale
Nelson, Horatio, vsct., v, 400
Nemo, Nich., iv, 395, 396
Neolithic Age, i, 256
Nervett, see Neyrnoit
Neteham, see Neatham
Netherblackden Coppice (Hurstbourne Tarrant), iv, 319, 321
Nether Court, man. (Silchester), iv, 53
Netherdonningle (Odiham), iv, 97
Netherparte, le, (Baughurst), iv, 275
Nether Stowey (Somers.), iv, 42
Netherthrowayes (Hurstbourne Tarrant), iv, 321
Netherton (Faccombe), iv, 314, 317

Netherton Hall (Faccombe), iv, 314
Netherway, John, v, 119 ; Sybil, v, 119 ; Will., v, 119
Nether Wallop, Netherwellup, see Wallop, Nether
Netley, iii, 462, 472, 476 ; iv, 548, 549 ; v, 293, 331, 462 ; adv., iii, 478 ; ch., iii, 478 ; coins, i, 345 ; iii, 472 ; grange, ii, 147 ; hosp., iii, 472 ; man., iii, 477 ; v, 418
Netley, Old, iii, 472
Netley Abbey, ii, 11, 39, 56, 104, 142, 146-9 ; iii, 462, 472-6, 477, 483, 488 ; iv, 535, 539, 549, 555, 628
Netley Castle (Netley), iii, 472, 473, 477 ; iv, 320 ; v, 351
Netley Hill, iii, 283
Netley Marsh, iv, 546 ; ch., iv, 558 ; sch., ii, 401
Nettlecombe, man. (Whitwell), v, 203
Nettlecombe, tithing (E. Medine), v, 138
Nettlestone (St. Helens), v, 190 ; man., v, 165, 191
Neuman, see Newman
Neuroptera, i, 112
Neuton, see Niton
Neverd, Will., v, 523
Nevill, Lds. : v, 314 ; Ralph, iv, 348 n
Nevill [Neville, Nevyle, Newtown], Alan (de), iv, 540 ; Alice, iii, 135 ; iv, 348, 608, 612 ; v, 117 ; Anne, ii, 143 ; iv, 151 ; v, 320 ; Beatrice, iv, 254 ; Cecily, iv, 329, 330 ; Edith, iv, 348 n ; Sir Edw., iv, 441 ; Eliz., (Lady), iv, 130, 329, 347, 348 ; Frances, v, 172 ; Geo., iii, 195 ; iv, 151, 185, 441 ; v, 118 ; Gilb., iv, 329 ; (Sir) Hen., iv, 130 n, 348, 441 ; v, 172 ; Hugh, iv, 347, 360 ; Isabel (Lady), iii, 195 ; iv, 151 n, 521, 524 ; Joan, iv, 351, 352, 521 ; (Sir) John, ii, 475 ; iii, 195 ; iv, 34, 130, 329, 347, 348, 579, 629 ; v, 118 ; Lucy, iv, 34 ; Muriel, v, 165, 191 ; Nich., iv, 323 ; Philippa, iv, 254 ; Ralph, ii, 17 ; iv, 323, 347, 348 n ; Rich., iii, 135, 410, 507 ; iv, 151, 156, 157, 348, 608, 612 ; v, 320, 369, 370 ; Thos., ii, 17, 111, 115 ; v, 370 ; Walt., v, 191 ; (Sir) Will., iv, 254, 351, 392, 521 ; v, 165 ; fam., arms, iii, 135, 411
Newark Priory (Surr.), iii, 347 ; iv, 512, 514 ; Rich., prior of, ii, 179
New Barn Down (Hurstbourne Priors), iv, 288 ; Rom. rem., i, 304, 345
New Barn Farm (Hurstbourne Priors), iv, 288
Newbolt [Newebolte], Chas., v, 73 ; Frideswide, v, 73 ; Matilda H., v, 79, 80
Newbridge (Copythorn), iv, 546
Newbridge (Shalfleet), v, 272
Newburgh, Ld., see Barrett of Newburgh, Ld.
Newburgh, Rob. de, iv, 590 ; Thos. de, iv, 150 n
Newbury (Berks), ii, 137
Newbury, Rich., ii, 216
Newbury Race Co., v, 553 n
Newcastle, shipping, v, 377
Newcastle, dk. of, iv, 591
Newchurch, ii, 139, 145, 230 ; v, 138, 177-187 ; adv., v, 186 ; char., v, 187 ; chs., v, 184 ; Holy Well Spring, v, 182 ; man., v, 179 ; Nonconf., v, 186 ; pop., v, 448 ; rector of, ii, 26 ; sch., ii, 407
Newchurch, Geoff. of, abbot, ii, 139

New College (Oxf.), ii, 261, 262, 263, 264, 265, 266, 267, 268, 269, 276, 291, 293, 294, 306, 360, 389, 392 ; iv, 50, 51, 180
Newcome, Capt. Geo., iv, 3 ; Harriet S., iv, 5 ; Maj. Hen. G., iv, 3 ; Pet., iv, 535 ; Sybilla C., iv, 2, 3
Newcourt Parva, man., ii, 186
Newdigate, Mary, v, 233 ; Sir Rich., v, 233
Neweboulte, see Newbolt
Neweham, see Newnham
Newe House, le, (Winchester), v, 6, 7
Neweman, see Newman
Newemylle Brygge (Liss), iv, 84
Newenham, Will. de, ii, 220
Newenham monastery (Devon), ii, 142
Newent (Glouc.), glass manuf., v, 491
Neweton Emessore, v, 219
New Forest, i, 381, 385, 394 ; ii, 140, 409-70 ; iv, 531, 544, 545, 548, 549, 550, 553, 563, 568, 571 n, 572, 573, 578 n, 579, 595, 603, 604, 607, 609, 611, 641, 642, 650, 652, 655 ; v, 300, 308, 324, 337, 356, 370, 409, 431, 556 ; peat, v, 454 ; ponies, v, 505, 506 ; potteries, i, 326-8, 345 ; prehist. rem., ii, 260 ; quarries, v, 463 ; sport, v, 565-74
New Forest, hund., ii, 152 ; iv, 559, 615-38 ; v, 81, 331 ; pop., v, 442 ; workhouse, iv, 546
New Forest hunt, v, 572
Newfound (Wootton St. Lawrence), iv, 239, 242
Newhall (Essex), iv, 36
Newhouse, man., ii, 114
Newland (Newtown), iv, 292
Newland, man. (Southwick), see Newlands
Newland, Ann, iii, 18 ; Bingham, v, 525 ; Geo., iv, 19 ; Jane, iv, 19 ; John, iii, 18 ; Rich. B., iii, 124 ; Rob., iv, 391 ; Thos., iii, 381 ; —, v, 197
Newlands (Beaulieu), iv, 650
Newlands (Odiham), iv, 92
Newlands, man. (Southwick), ii, 168, 182, 186 ; iii, 163
Newlands (Whitchurch), iv, 300
Newlands Farm (Odiham), iv, 92
Newlands Farm (Southwick), iii, 162
Newlyn, Eliz., iv, 436 ; Hen., iii, 6 ; John, iv, 436 ; Pet., iii, 251 ; Phil., iv, 436 ; Rich., iv, 436 ; —, v, 4 9, 564
Newman [Neuman, Neweman] (le), Ant., v, 31 ; John, iv, 266 ; v, 482 ; Rich., v, 202 ; Thos., v, 202 ; Will., iv, 60, 131, 500 ; v, 202, 203 n ; —, v, 469, 576
Newmangen, Rob., iv, 536
Newmans Ryding (Hurstbourne Tarrant), iv, 321
New Minster (Winchester), see Hyde Abbey
Newnham, iv, 87, 113, 114, 149, 150, 151, 152, 153, 156-8 ; adv., ii, 226 ; iv, 158 ; char., iv, 158 ; ch., iv, 157 ; man., iv, 156 ; Manor Farm, iv, 156 ; mills, iv, 157 ; pop., v, 439 ; sch., ii, 401 ; iv, 156
Newnham, man. (Binstead), v, 151
Newnham Farm (Binstead), v, 152
Newnham Green, iv, 156
Newplace Priory, see Newark Priory
Newport, ii, 63, 91, 98, 139, 180, 455 ; v, 209, 221, 227, 230, 231,

Newport (*cont.*)
234, 235, 253-65, 268, 272, 278, 284, 287, 288, 311, 315, 339, 347, 409, 426, 428 ; adv., v, 263 ; chant., ii, 62 ; v, 263 ; chap., ii, 69, 231 ; v, 256, 264 ; char., v, 264 ; cheese cross, v, 253 ; chs., v, 262 ; grammar school, ii, 387, 391 ; v, 227, 254 ; house of industry, v, 432, 433, 488 ; inds., v, 451, 457, 466, 491 ; leper hosp., v, 418 ; man., v, 261 ; mkts. and fairs, v, 253, 260 ; mills, v, 256 ; Nonconf., v, 264 ; old houses, v, 254 ; pop., v, 449 ; printing, v, 461 ; Rom. Caths., v, 264 ; Rom. rem., i, 317, 348 ; sch., ii, 407 ; treaty, v, 261, 350
Newport, Mountjoy Blount, earl of, v, 256
Newport, Eliz., iii, 259 ; John, ii, 206 ; iii, 258, 263 ; iv, 93 ; v, 318, 319 ; Rich., ii, 213, 214 ; iii, 258 ; iv, 93
Newsam, Jas., iv, 388 *n*
Newthorpe (Yorks.), iv, 497
Newtimber (Warblington), tithing, iii, 128, 136
Newtimber, Will. de, iii, 136
Newton, South, man. (Wilts.), iv, 540
Newton, Francis, ii, 115 ; Sir Isaac, iii, 420 ; iv, 288, 289 ; Thos. de, ii, 161, 163
Newton Bury, man. (Eling), iv, 552
Newton Park (Boldre), iv, 616
Newton Regis, *see* Niton
Newton Stacey (Barton Stacey), iv, 415, 416, 417 ; chap., iv, 422
Newton Tony (Wilts.), iv, 540
Newton Valence, ii, 471 ; iii, 24-30, 402 ; iv, 549 ; v, 430 ; adv., iii, 29 ; char., iii, 30 ; chs., iii, 28 ; man., iii, 3, 17, 26 ; iv, 388, 513 ; pop., v, 438 ; sch., ii, 401
Newtown (Basingstoke), i, 305
New Town (Ibsley), iv, 579, 615
Newtown (I. of W.), v, 209, 225, 265-8, 311, 315, 355, 426, 472 ; adv., v, 268 ; char., v, 268 ; ch., ii, 230, 231 ; v, 267 ; iron, v, 464 ; mkts. and fairs, v, 265, 267 ; Nonconf., v, 268 ; oysters, v, 468
Newtown (Newbury), iv, 273, 277, 292-4 ; adv., iv, 294 ; char., iv, 294 ; ch., iv, 292, 294 ; mkts., iv, 292 ; pop., v, 442 ; sch., ii, 401 ; iv, 292
Newtown (Soberton), iii, 258
New Town (Tadley), iv, 219
Newtown, John de, *see* Nevill
Newtown House (Newtown), iv, 292
Newtown River, i, 385 ; v, 227, 272 ; oyster beds, v, 468
Newts, i, 207
Neylond, John, v, 119
Neyrnoit [Nervett], Alice, v, 119 ; Hen., v, 119 ; John, v, 118, 119, 124
Nhottele, *see* Nutley
Nibeslei, *see* Ibsley
Niccolle, *see* Nicoll
Niccols, *see* Nicholls
Nichol, Letitia M., v, 235 ; *see also* Nicholle and Nicoll
Nicholas IV, ii, 21, 118, 133, 165
Nicholas, v, 16, 19, 46 ; bp. of the Isles, ii, 153 ; of Ely, ii, 19 ; iv, 576, 607 ; v, 56, 217, 479 ; the fuller, v, 479 *n* ; prior of Andwell, ii, 225 ; prior of St. Denis, ii, 163
Nicholas, Edw., iii, 27, 208, 406, 414 ; Jane, Lady, iv, 406 ; John,

Nicholas (*cont.*)
ii, 338, 339, 340, 366 ; iii, 27 ; Mary, ii, 502 ; Matth., iv, 208, 209, 414, 493 ; Rob. B., iii, 27 ; Will., iii, 27
Nicholle [Nichole, Nicholl], (de), Alvred, iv, 588 ; Sir Chas. G., iv, 232 ; Frances C., iv, 232 ; Will., iii, 483 ; *see also* Nichol and Nicoll
Nicholls [Niccols, Nichols], Ant., iv, 112 ; Eliz., iv, 112 ; John, iv, 458 ; Marg., iv, 458 ; Will., iv, 624
Nicholson, Will., iii, 70, 76, 77, 111, 336 ; iv, 84 ; Mrs., iv, 437
Nicoll [Niccolle, Nycoll], Alice, iii, 528 ; Annys, iii, 528 ; Basil, v, 181 ; Chris., iv, 539 ; Hen., iv, 402 ; John, v, 557, 558, 558 *n* ; Sam., v, 572 ; Will., iii, 528 ; Col., v, 529 ; *see also* Nichol and Nicholle
Nietham, *see* Neatham
Nigel, iv, 619 ; v, 95, 101, 114, 125, 126, 141, 143, 164, 173, 274
Nightingale, Florence, iv, 458, 535 ; Frances, iv, 458 ; Mary, iv, 536 ; Will. E., iv, 536 ; Will. E. S., iv, 458 ; Will. S. S., iv, 536
Nimpha, Bern. de, ii, 164
Nimrod, *see* Apperly, — [Nimrod]
Ningwood (Shalfleet), v, 164 *n*, 210, 272 ; man., ii, 152, 159 ; v, 273
Ninham, Will., v, 166 *n*
Nith (King's Somborne), iv, 470
Nitheravene, Will. de, ii, 160
Niton, ii, 63 ; v, 138, 149 *n*, 184, 187-9, 211, 235, 244 ; adv., v, 189 ; brick manuf., v, 466 ; char., v, 189 ; ch., v, 188 ; mans., v, 187 ; Nonconf., v, 189 ; pop., v, 448 ; sch., ii, 407
Noakes, S. S. A., iv, 365
Noar, man. (Newton Valence), iii, 27
Noar Hill, iii, 4, 24, 26
Noble Poverty, almshouse of, *see* St. Cross, hospital of
Nochesland (Burghclere), iv, 277
Noclei, *see* Nutley
Noctuæ, i, 141
Node Close (Ryde), v, 178
Node Hill (Newport), v, 256, 264, 265
Noel [Nowell], Edw., iii, 224, 46) ; iv, 450 ; Eliz., iii, 224, 466 ; iv, 450 ; Sir John, iv, 477 ; Maria, iii, 484 ; Mary, Lady, iv, 477 ; Matth., iv, 366 ; Rachel, Lady, iv, 450 ; Rich., ii, 166, 168 ; iv, 259 ; Will., iv, 366 ; Wriothesley, B., iv, 450
Noht, Walt., v, 126
Noke Down (Deane), iv, 205
No Man's Land (Morestead), iii, 329 ; pop., v, 448
Nonehampton, *see* Northington
Noneton [Nonyngton] (de), Baldric, v, 188 ; Margery, v, 188
Nonhampton, *see* Northington
Nonnewade (Christchurch), v, 85
Nonoelle, *see* Nunwell
Norbury, Joan, iii, 105 ; Sir John, iii, 95, 105
Norcott, Mrs., v, 30
Nordley, man., ii, 146, 148
Norensis, Rob., v, 304 *n*
Norewyz, Noreys, *see* Norris
Norfolk, shipping, v, 377
Norfolk, ctsses. of : Alina Bigod, iv, 150 ; Maud le Bigod, iv, 52, 474 ; dks. of : Bern. Edw. Howard, iii, 130 ; John Howard, iv, 361, 624 ; Philip Howard, iii, 130 ; Thos. Howard, iii, 130 ;

Norfolk (*cont.*)
earls of : iv, 53 ; Hugh le Bigod, iv, 52, 474 ; Rog. le Bigod, iv, 52, 150, 399, 474 ; Thos., iv, 52
Norhamptone, *see* Northington
Norlandes (Eversley), iv, 33
Norley (Baddesley), iv, 616
Norley Copse (Kingsclere), iv, 250
Norman, iv, 443
Norman [Normand], Agnes, iv, 341, 362, 392 ; Giles, iii, 429 ; iv, 340, 341, 362, 367, 392, 522 ; Joan, iii, 429 ; iv, 340, 341 ; Marg., iv, 392 ; Rog., iii, 429 ; iv, 339, 340, 341, 342, 358, 362, 363, 366, 367, 368, 392, 393, 394, 522, 523 ; v, 312 ; Will., ii, 163 ; fam., iv, 364
Norman Court, man. (West Tytherley), iv, 226, 496, 519, 520, 521, 522-3
Norman Court Farm (Upper Clatford), iv, 359, 363
Normand, *see* Norman
Normandy Hill, ii, 474, 478
Norman House (Christchurch), v, 89-90
Norman's Court, man. (Upper Clatford), iv, 362
Normanton, earls of, iv, 565, 567, 579, 605 ; v, 559 ; Hen. J. Agar, iv, 564 ; Sidney J. Agar, iv, 580, 602, 604, 606 ; Welbore E. Agar, iv, 606
Norreys, Norrice, *see* Norris
Norrington, *see* Northington
Norris [Noreys, Norewyz, Norreys, Norrice, Norrys], (le, de), Agnes, v, 281 ; Anne, iii, 139 ; Cecily, v, 281 ; Geo., iii, 240 ; Gilb., ii, 180, 181 ; Hen., iv, 208, 283 ; Isabel, Lady, iv, 34 ; v, 118 ; Jem, v, 527 ; (Sir) John, v, 332 *n*, 333, 389, 481 *n* ; Laur., v, 281 ; Lionel, iii, 333 ; Randolph, iii, 87 ; Rich., v, 198 ; Rob., v, 243 ; Thos., v, 144, 176, 281 ; Ursula, iv, 208, 283 ; Walt., v, 281, 285 *n* ; (Sir) Will., iii, 195 ; iv, 34, 142, 281 ; Rev. Will. B., iii, 139
Norris Castle (Whippingham), v, 198
Norsworthy, G., iii, 440
North, Rog., Ld., iv, 367
North, Alienor, ii, 125 ; Anne, iv, 572 ; Brownlow, ii, 99 ; iii, 111 ; Dorothy, Lady, iv, 367 ; Fran., ii, 99, 197, 339 ; Isabel, iv, 572 ; (Sir) John, iv, 367, 572 ; Nich., v, 16 ; Rich., iv, 572 ; Will., iv, 572 ; —, v, 516
Northale, man. (Arreton), v, 143
Northam (Redbridge hund.), iv, 544
Northam (Southampton), iii, 491, 494 ; v, 396 ; ind., v, 455, 461 ; man., ii, 160, 163 ; Rom. rem., i, 332-4 ; shipbuilding, v, 398, 403
Northampstead, ii, 159
Northampstead, par., *see* Northington
Northampton, earls of, iv, 290, 334 ; v, 364 ; Chas. Compton, iv, 290 ; Geo. Compton, iv, 316 ; Mary Florence, mchnss. of, iv, 511
Northanger (Eling), iv, 550 *n*
Northavon, man. (Sopley), v, 129
Northaye, Ad. de, ii, 211
Northbrook (Basingstoke), iv, 131
Northbrook (Micheldever), iii, 390
Northbrook, earls of, ii, 466 ; iii, 391 ; iv, 432, 433 ; v, 557, 558
Northbudbrygge, *see* Budbridge
Northcote, man. (Devon), ii, 172
North Court (Shorwell), v, 279, 282 ; man. house, v, 278
Northcroft (Odiham), iv, 93

North Danes (Milford), v, 116
Northdoune (Eastrop), iv, 148
North Down (Hurstbourne Tarrant), iv, 321
Northemore (Romsey), iv, 452
North End (N. Stoneham), iii, 479
North End farm (Harbridge), iv, 604
Northentone, see Hinton, North
Northerwood House (Lyndhurst), iv, 316
Northesk, earls of, iii, 330, 334
North Farm (Faccombe), iv, 314
North Field (Gatcombe), v, 249
Northgarston (Romsey), iv, 452
Northington, ii, 116, 119, 121; iii, 389, 394-7; iv, 183, 184 n, 196; adv., iii, 397; char., iii, 397; ch., iii, 397; coins, i, 346; mans., iii, 395; pop., v, 448; sch., ii, 402
Northington, man. (Christchurch), see Hinton, North
Northington (Overton), iv, 197, 211
Northington, Jane, ctss. of, iv, 154; earls of, iv, 78; Rob., iv, 154, 204
Northington [Nonhampton, Norhamptone], (de, of), Hen., ii, 119; iii, 395, 396; Rob., iv, 152
Northinton (Freshwater), see Norton
Northlands (Winchester), iv, 484
Northlegh (Boldre), iv, 618
Northleigh, Will., iv, 259
Northlode, Alice, ii, 129; Cecily, iv, 588; John, iv, 588, 589; Maud, iv, 588; Thos., iv, 588
Northney (Hayling Island), iii, 129
Northocle, see Oakley, North
Northro, Will. de, iv, 53
Northumberland, Eliz. Percy, ctss. of, iv, 651; Jane Dudley, dchss. of, ii, 167; iii, 11; dks. of, v, 329; John, ii, 167; iv, 587, 591; v, 374; earls of, ii, 44; Algernon Percy, v, 345; Joceline Percy, iv, 651
Northwautham, see Waltham, North
Northwode, see Norwode
Northwood (I. of W.), ii, 231; v, 209, 210, 221, 234, 243, 268-71; advs., v, 271; chars., v, 271; chs., v, 270; grange, ii, 230; mans., v, 269; Nonconf., v, 271; pop., v, 449; Rom. Cath., v, 271; sch., ii, 407
Northwood (Hayling Isl.), see Hayling, North
Northwood Park (Northwood), v, 250, 268
Nortle, see Norley Copse
Norton (Freshwater), v, 210, 240
Norton (Selborne), ii, 116, 177, 471; iii, 8, 16
Norton, man. (Wonston), see Norton St. Valery
Norton, (de), Agnes, iii, 387; Ann, iii, 34; Ant., iii, 99, 344; Chas., iv, 537; Sir Danl., iii, 163; Eliz., ii, 87, 506; iii, 34, 240, 264, 370, 456; iv, 16, 46; Felicia, iv, 630; Geo., iii, 387; Hen., iii, 42; Honor, iii, 163; (Sir) Jas., ii, 16, 176; iii, 7, 9, 31, 370; iv, 630 n; Joan, Lady, iv, 247, 248; (Sir) John, ii, 67, 139; iii, 8, 18, 31; iv, 15, 16, 247, 248, 424, 425, 630; v, 326 n, 327 n; Marg., iii, 9; iv, 424, 630 n; Ralph, iii, 10; (Sir) Rich., ii, 506; iii, 8, 19, 28, 31, 34, 99, 107, 145, 163, 165, 240, 264, 304, 324, 344, 387, 388, 430, 459; iv, 15, 16, 85, 424, 630; v, 335, 336, 340; (Sir) Rob., iii, 195; iv, 102; Thos., iii, 9; iv, 46, 536, 537, 539, 630; Will., ii, 58, 160, 167, 168, 273; iv, 540;

Norton (cont.)
Col., v, 341, 343; fam., arms, iii, 370
Norton Farm (Selborne), iii, 5
Norton Farm (Wonston), iii, 455, 458; v, 541
Norton Green (Freshwater), v, 245
Norton St. Valery [Norton St. Wallery, Norton Vallery], man. (Wonston), ii, 213; iii, 402, 457; iv, 415
Nortwold, John de, ii, 109
Norwich, bps. of, iv, 77; v, 366; Herb. Losinga, ii, 117
Norwode [Northwode], Eliz., iv, 247; Joan, iv, 247, 248; John, iv, 247
Notehangre, see Ecchinswell
Nothing Hill (Kingsclere), iv, 246
Notle (Beaulieu), iv, 650, 651
Notscilling, Godf. de, iii, 435
Nott [Knott], Gen. Hen., iii, 453; John, iv, 657; Walt., iv, 656, 657; Dr., v, 79; —, v, 166
Nottele, see Nutley
Notteleston, see Nettlestone
Nottingham, Kath., ctss. of, iv, 646; earls of:—Chas., iv, 646; Thos., ii, 162
Nova Villa, see New Town
Nova Villa de Sandelford, see Newtown (Newbury)
Novus Burgus de Clere, see Newtown (Newbury)
Nowell, see Noel
Nowes, John, iv, 460, 469
Noyes [Noyse], Cath., iv, 389; Harry, iv, 389; Rob., iv, 353, 397; Valentine, ii, 84
Nubbelaye, John de, ii, 213, 214
Nuclega, see Nutley
Nugée, F. T., iii, 170, 172
Nugent, A. J. F., iv, 5; J. O'R., v, 542; Rob., iv, 388 n
Nugi, Geoff., iv, 378; Joan, iv, 378; John, iv, 378; Will., iv, 378
Nuller, Thos., iii, 327
Nuneaton Priory (Warws.), iii, 110, 111; Sybil, prioress of, iii, 111
Nunewille, see Nunwell
Nunez, A. F., v, 524
Nunn, Hen., v, 535; —, v, 205, 254
Nunnaminster (Winchester), ii, 5, 7, 12, 49, 55, 60, 61, 62, 104, 116, 122-6, 188, 502, 504, 505; iv, 84, 191, 353 n, 446, 449, 451, 486; v, 2, 38, 48, 303, 472, 474; Agnes, abbess of, ii, 126; v, 475, 476; wool-trade, v, 475
Nunwell [Nunnewell], man. (Brading), v, 163 n, 164, 191, 262; woods, iii, 470
Nupert, John, iv, 484
Nursery Field (King's Worthy), iv, 430
Nursling, ii, 4, 25, 108; iii, 401, 433-9; iv, 544, 552; v, 275; adv., iii, 439; char., iii, 439; ch., iii, 438; mans., ii, 61, 114; iii, 433, 450; pop., v, 446; Rom. rem., i, 311, 325, 346; sch., ii, 402
Nursling Beaufo, man. (Nursling), iii, 435
Nursling Prior, man. (Nursling), ii, 61, 114; iii, 433; iv, 553
Nutbane (Weyhill), iv, 395, 396
Nutbeames (Stratfieldsaye), iv, 57
Nutcrofts (Long Sutton), iv, 18
Nutelegha, Nutes, see Nutley
Nutescheolva, see Litchfield Grange
Nuthampton, see Northington
Nuthanger, see Ecchinswell
Nuthaven, John de, iv, 579
Nuthilve, see Litchfield Grange

Nutley [Nutle, Nutleghe, Nutleye], ii, 16, 168; iii, 355, 356, 369-71; adv., iii, 371; ch., iii, 371; man., iii, 370; pop., v, 440
Nutley [Nhottele], Jas., iv, 301; John, v, 27 n, 39
Nutshalling, see Nursling
Nutshelf, see Litchfield Grange
Nutshelling, see Nursling
Nutson, Thos., iii, 496
Nuttele, see Nutley
Nutteleston, see Nettlestone
Nutting, Rev. G. H., iv, 107
Nuvelesse (Wolverton), iv, 270
Nycoll, see Nicoll
Nykkes (Newnham), iv, 156
Nyncknoll, see Linkenholt
Nyren, John, iii, 239; v, 574; Rich., iii, 239; v, 574
Nyteshull, see Litchfield Grange
Nyton, see Niton
Nywenham, see Newnham
Nywenton, ii, 110

Oades, Jas., iii, 376; John, iii, 361; see also Ode
Oakcuts Wood (Upper Clatford), iv, 360
Oake, man. (Broughton), iv, 494, 495
Oake [Hoke, Oke, Quercu] (atte, de), Ad., iv, 495; Hen., v, 110; John, iv, 495, 590; v, 29; Nich., iv, 495; Rich., iv, 495
Oakes, Edm. H. A., iv, 326
Oakfield (Arreton), v, 140
Oakfield (St. Helens), v, 190
Oakhanger (Selborne), iii, 3, 4, 5, 16; man., ii, 176, 177, 471, 494; iii, 10; iv, 549
Oakhanger, [Acangre] de, Gilb., iii, 11; Jas., ii, 176; iii, 11; Will., iii, 11
Oakland, (atte, de), Eleanor, iv, 64; John, iv, 63, 64, 141; Rich., iv, 64, 141
Oaklands (E. Tytherley), iv, 516
Oaklands (Stratfield Turgis), iv, 64, 141 n
Oakley (Mottisfont), ii, 465; iv, 507, 544
Oakley, East, (Wootton St. Lawrence), iv, 239, 240, 242
Oakley, North, man. (Kingsclere), iv, 247, 248, 257, 259, 270; chap., iv, 265
Oakley, North, tithing (Kingsclere), iv, 245, 266 n
Oakley [Hockley, Ockley, Ocle], (de), Barth., iv, 47, 226 n, 228; Emma, iv, 47; Hugh, iv, 47; Humph., iii, 387; Jas., iv, 47; John, ii, 474; Nich., iv, 225, 443; Rose, iv, 47 n, 226, 226 n, 228; Steph., iv, 226 n
Oakley Enclosure (New Forest), i, 326
Oakley Farm (Mottisfont), iv, 503, 507
Oakley Hall (Deane), iv, 201, 205, 206, 207, 226
Oakley Manor (Church Oakley), iv, 224
Oakley oak, ii, 465; iv, 503
Oaks, the, (Blackwater), iv, 21
Oakwood, iii, 3; brick making, v, 466
Ober Water, i, 244
O'Bryen, Mary, iii, 215
Ochangra, see Oakhanger
Ochere, see Ogber
Ockley, see Oakley
Ocknell Clump (New Forest), ii, 454

Ocle, Oclye, see Oakley
Ocling, see Church Oakley
Ocsen, ii, 479
Oda, see Odo
Odber [Odbeare], Parkinson, v, 97 ; Rob., v, 97, 125 ; —, v, 467
Oddingsel, Rowland de, v, 3, 45
Ode, Christian name, see Odo
Ode, Joan, v, 483 ; Rich., v, 483 ; see also Oades
Odecote, see Woodcott
Odehams (W. Wellow), iv, 535
Odeknolle, see Odiknolle
Odeman, v, 173 n
Odetone, Odetune, see Wootton
Odiham, ii, 41, 101, 204, 251 ; iv, 18, 62, 66, 67, 68, 71, 72, 76, 77, 79, 87-98, 101, 104, 105, 108, 109, 110, 153 ; v, 308, 311, 324, 328 n, 331, 336, 409, 423, 429, 434, 435, 544 ; adv., ii, 21 ; iv, 97 ; castle, ii, 14 ; iii, 68 ; iv, 81, 88, 94 ; v, 463 ; chalk quarries, v, 454 ; char., iv, 98 ; ch., iv, 94 ; commons, iv. 88 ; fairs, iv, 92 ; v, 435 ; George Hotel, iv, 87 ; ind., v, 484, 488 ; man., iv, 84, 86, 90 ; mills, iv, 87, 94 ; Nonconf., iv, 98 ; park, iv, 90 ; pop., v. 444 ; racing, v, 543 ; Rom rem., i, 346 ; schs., ii, 367, 387, 402 ; iv. 87, 98 ; stud, iv, 90
Odiham, hund., iv, 66
Odiham, Will. de, ii, 27, 118, 121
Odiknolle, man., ii, 156, 159
Odo [Oda, Ode], v, 164 ; of Bayeux, ii, 484 ; iv, 549, 623 ; v, 97, 224 n, 300 ; of Winchester, ii, 496 ; iii, 357, 457 ; iv, 146, 438, 655 ; v, 172.
Odyam, see Odiham
Odyer, John, v, 265
Offley, Frances, iv, 359
Ogams, ii, 234
Ogber [Ogbeare] (Christchurch), v, 85, 95 n
Ogbourne Priory (Wilts), iv, 337, 338, 342, 380, 385, 386, 396
Ogden, Rev. Abra., iv, 230
Ogdens [Ogden] (Fordingbridge), ii, 173 ; iv, 568
Oglander (de), Alice, v, 164 n, 165 ; Anne, v, 159 n ; Charity, v, 191 ; Elias, v, 191 ; Eliz. S., v, 168 ; Geo., iii, 139 ; v, 150, 163, 165, 166, 168, 181 n, 191, 192 ; (Sir) Hen., v, 164, 165, 168, 169, 181 n, 190 n, 191, 231 n, 262 ; Herb., v, 164 n ; (Sir) John, v, 24, 138, 140, 143, 152, 157, 160, 161, 165, 168, 176 n, 178, 183, 189 n, 191, 210, 211, 215, 224 n, 229 n, 231, 237, 250, 261, 263, 347 ; John H., ii, 470 ; v, 156, 160, 161, 163, 164, 165, 183, 190 n, 191, 192 ; John H. G., v, 165 ; Louisa, Lady, v, 169 ; Mary, v, 211 ; Oliver, v, 159 n, 168 ; Pet., ii, 152, 160 ; v, 164 n ; Reg., v, 164, 165 ; Rob., v, 164, 165 ; Roberta, v, 164, 165 ; Rog., v, 164 ; Susannah, v, 191 ; Thos., v, 165, 192 ; (Sir) Will., iii, 387, 388 ; iv, 92, 549, 554 ; v, 119, 159 n, 161, 164, 165, 166, 168, 169, 183, 191, 192 ; fam., v, 238
Ogle, Ld., v, 12, 343
Ogle, Sir Chaloner, iii, 326 ; iv, 432 ; v, 389 ; Sir Chas., iii, 326 ; iv, 432 ; Newton, dean of Winchester, ii, 115 ; Sir Will., ii, 326, 329 ; iii, 449 ; v, 344 ; fam., arms, iii, 326
Ogrum, Jane, iv, 476
Oidelard, iii, 372 ; iv, 256, 257
Oirant, v, 160 n

Okanger (Kingsley), ii, 515
Oke, see Oake
Okeborne, prior of, ii, 41
Okeden, Hen., iv, 605 ; John, iv, 316, 563, 604, 605 ; Maud, iv, 315, 316, 563 ; Phil., iv, 563, 605 n ; Sybil, iv, 604 ; (Sir) Will., iv, 315, 316, 563, 605, 610, 630
Okestreete (Lockerley), iv, 500
Okhangre (Selborne), see Oakhanger
Okinbrig, John de, iv, 508
Okle, see Oakley
Olaf, king of Norway, ii, 7 ; iv, 346 ; v, 296
Old, see Olde
Old Barge, riv., v, 563
Oldberie Piece (Steventon), iv, 171
Oldbury (Hartley Wespall), iv, 42
Oldcastle, Sir John, ii, 46
Old Castle Hill (Southampton), v, 315
Old Close Park (Alice Holt forest), ii, 490
Oldcourt (Faccombe), iv, 314
Olde [Old], Alice, iv, 611 ; Hen., iv, 611 ; Rob., v, 213
Olde Hall (Liss), iv, 84
Oldelond, la, iv, 589
Oldes, man. (Ringwood), iv, 611
Oldfishbourne, man., ii, 168
Oldham, Eliz., iv, 428 ; Hugh, iv, 218, 428
Old Hop Garden (Itchel), iv, 6
Olding, Eliz., iv, 549 ; Will., iv, 549
Old Lodge (Nether Wallop), iv, 525
Oldmede, le, (Odiham), iv, 88
Old Minster (Winchester), see St. Swithun's Priory
Old Orchard (Faccombe), iv, 314
Old Winchester Hill, i, 380 ; Rom. rem., i, 346
Olferton, see Wolverton
Oligocene age, i, 21
Olive, Gregory, v, 109
Oliver [Olyver], Anne, iv, 354, 355 ; Eliz., iv, 14 ; Marg., iv, 537 ; Oliver, iv, 486 ; Rev. Rob B., v, 203 ; Sam., iv, 537 ; Thos., iv, 354 ; Will., ii, 211, 229
Oliver Cromwell's Battery (Winchester), v, 346 n
Oliver's Battery (Abbotstone), iv, 193
Oliver's Battery (Basing), iv, 115
Oliver's Dell (Basing), iv, 115
Olne, Ralph de, v, 165
Olward, iii, 269
Olyver, see Oliver
Olyves, Alice, v, 191
O'Neill, Dan., v, 345
Onley, Clemence, iii, 78 ; John, iii, 78, 300 ; Thos., iii, 300
Onslow [Onslowe], Aug., v, 517 ; Rosa A., iii, 58 ; Will., iii, 43 ; Col., v, 516
Oodie Furlong (Longstock), iv, 449
Ophidia, i, 205
Opie, Barbara, iii, 383, 384 ; Nich., iii, 384 ; Rich., iii, 383, 384
Opnatelegh, see Up Nately
Oppethebutten (Kimpton), iv, 372
Optune, see Upton
Ora, see Ower
Oram, Will., v, 30 n
Oram's Arbor (Winchester), v, 21
Orbell, Jos., v, 518
Orchards, acreage, v, 508, 509
Orchin, J., v, 527
Ordd, Jas., ii, 382, 385
Orde-Powlett, Jean iv, 46, 117, 191 n, 251 ; Thos., iv, 46, 117, 122, 191, 251 ; v, 204, 224, 225, 251 ; Will., iv, 46, 157 ; Will. H., iv, 249 ; Will. P., iv, 122, 191, 193 ; Will. T., iv, 251

Ordie, see Headbourne Worthy and King's Worthy
Ordwald, iii, 403
Orell, Alice, iv, 116 ; John, iv, 116, 159
Orenet, see Chernet
Orestull, Rich. de, ii, 154
Orford, earl of, iv, 248
Orleans, dk. of, v, 85
Orlee (Abbotts Ann), iv, 334 n
Orloff, count, v, 393
Orlton, Ad., see Winchester, bp. of
Orman, Maj. Chas. E., iv, 21
Ormeresfelt, see Dogmersfield
Ormesby, Edw., iv, 25
Ormonde, ctsses. of : Eleanor, v, 128 ; Lora, ii, 516 ; iv, 194 ; dk. of, iv, 345 ; earls of, iv, 194 ; Jas., v, 128 ; Thos., v, 128
Ornaments, A.S., i, 382, 383, 388, 389, 397 ; Danish, i, 397 ; Goidelic, i, 261 ; Jutish, i, 387 ; Rom., i, 278, 283, 284, 297, 306, 311, 343, 345, 346, 349 ; Teutonic, i, 395
Orr, Sam., iv, 625, 626 n
Orsmelin, iii, 196
Orthoptera, i, 109
Ortingshote, see Hardingshute
Orton, Will., iii, 231
Orvilliers, — d', v, 394
Orweye, Thos. de, v, 89 n, 113
Osbaldeston, —, v, 515, 524
Osbern, bp. of Exeter, iii, 20 ; the falconer, iv, 572
Osbert, abbot of Hyde, ii, 117 ; the linendraper, v, 22, 477
Osborne, man. (Whippingham), v, 198, 199
Osborne [Osborn], Anne, iv, 94 ; Sir Danvers, iv, 472 ; Eliz., Lady, iv, 472 ; Rev. E. C., iii, 467 ; John, iv, 94, 472, 514 n, 541, 620 ; J., ii, 516 ; Pet., iv, 93 ; Ralph, iv, 620 ; Thos., iii. 508 ; Will., iv, 568 ; Maj., iv, 542 ; fam., arms, iii, 508
Osborne Cottage (Whippingham), v, 198
Osborne House (Romsey), iv, 460
Osborne House (Whippingham), ii, 291 ; v, 199
Osburga, i, 375
Osegodesstret (Bramley), iv, 141
Oselbury, see Owslebury
Osey, Will., iii, 499
Osfevre, le, John, v, 45 ; Maud, v, 45 ; Nich., v, 34
Osgar, iv, 401
Osgood, Laur. H., iv, 327 ; Rebecca, iv, 327
Osgot, v, 167
Oskrewell, see Coskeville
Oslac, i, 375
Osman's Lands (Kingsclere), iv, 266, 267
Osmod, ii, 474
Osmondley, see Ossemsley
Osmund, iv, 381, 449, 506
Osric, v, 295
Ossemsley [Ossolie] (Milton), v, 81, 126
Ossulston, Ld., ii, 346
Ossumburna, see Somborne, Upper
Ostagslane (Sherborne St. John), iv, 158
Ostagyscrofte (Sherborne St. John), iv, 158
Ostariophysi, i, 200
Ostaven, iv, 609
Ostre, Rich. atte, iv, 170
Ostrey Woods (Romsey), iv, 452
Oswald, ii, 2
Oswald, Mordaunt & Co., v, 458
Osward, John, iv, 362 n
Othen, Everard de, v, 174 n

Other, iv, 224, 227
Otho, papal legate, ii, 118, 142
Otoiche (Bremore), iv, 536 n, 598
Otterbourne, ii, 96, 290; iii, 440-4; iv, 502; adv., iii, 443; char., iii, 443; chs., iii, 443; man., ii, 317; iii, 441; pop., v, 447; quarry, v, 454; Rom. rem., i, 346; sch., ii, 402
Otterbourne Common, iii, 441
Otterhunter, Rog. le, v, 48
Otterwood (Beaulieu), iv, 544, 650, 651, 652, 654
Ottery St. Mary (Devon), ch., ii, 268, 288
Otto, iv, 340
Otway, Thos., ii, 337
Ou, fam., see Ow
Ouchterlony, Sir Jas., iii, 353, 499
Ouges-doune (Gatcombe), v, 246
Ouldestokecherytie, see Stoke Charity
Ouldstoke, see Stoke Charity
Oure Lady Mersshe (Breamore), iv, 596
Oures, Walt., ii, 212
Our Ladye Lake (Winchester), v, 31 n
Ouse, John de, iv, 643
Ousqueto, John de, ii, 41
Oustbourn, see Osborne
Outing, Nich., v, 172
Outwick (Breamore), iv, 596, 598
Over, Will., v, 77
Overbremer (Breamore), iv, 597
Over Burgate, see Burgate, Over
Overbury House (Winchester), v, 7
Over Court, man. (Silchester), iv, 53
Overdroveweys Copse (Hurstbourne Tarrant), iv, 319
Overelden, see Eldon, Upper
Overman, Thos., v, 229
Overton, ii, 40, 114; iv, 200, 210-19, 221; v, 311, 423, 441 n, 523; advs., iv, 217; char., iv, 218; ch., iv, 210, 216; ind., v, 455, 457, 475, 484, 488, 490; mans., iv, 197, 202, 212, 294; mkt. and fairs, iv, 211, 212; v, 417, 435; mills, iv, 213; v, 490; pop., v, 442; Rom. rem., i, 346; sch., ii, 402
Overton, hund., iv, 197; v, 324, 328 n, 331
Overton (de), Geoff., iv, 202; Isabel, iv, 498, 520, 610; Joan, iii, 218, 279; Mich., iv, 458, 520; Ralph, v, 144; Thos., iii, 43, 218, 225, 226, 229, 279, 328; iv, 458, 520, 524, 610; Will., iii, 42, 43, 229, 279, 328, 333, 334; iv, 458, 498, 520, 522, 524, 610
Overy, Julian, ii, 137
Oviatt [Oviet], Edw., iv, 551; Esther, iv, 558; Hen., iv, 551; John, iv, 551; Rich., iii, 415; Thos., iv, 551; Will., iv, 551
Ovingefort, v, 143
Ovington, ii, 122; iii, 302, 312, 331-2; iv, 188; adv., iii, 331; char., iii, 331; ch., iii, 331; man., ii, 114; iii, 331; pop., v, 448
Ow [Ou] de, Osborne, iv, 27, 28; Will., iv, 52, 205, 227, 440, 443, 469, 474
Owen, Sir Dav., iii, 387; Hen., iii, 387; John, iii, 387; Mary, iii, 387; Rob., iv, 519; Thos., ii, 78; W., iv, 586
Ower (Eling), iv, 546, 551, 589
Ower, Lower, Upper, (Hurstbourne Priors), iv, 288
Owers, man., ii, 121

Owlesbury, see Owslebury
Owles Hole (Aldershot), iv, 3
Owre-at-Owrebridge (Romsey), iv, 452
Owslebury, i, 324; ii, 66, 84, 211; iii, 302, 332-5; v, 77, 528; adv., iii, 335; char., iii, 335; ch., iii, 335; man., iii, 333; pop., v, 448; sch., ii, 402
Owton, —, v, 540
Oxeheye, see Oxeye
Oxenbourn, tithing (E. Meon), iii, 64
Oxenbourn Down, iii, 64, 85
Oxenbridge, man., ii, 114
Oxenbridge, Edw., iv, 290 n, 295; Godard, iv, 291; (Sir) Rob., iv, 288, 289, 290 n, 291, 295, 296, 316; Will., iv, 295; fam., iv, 409
Oxeneford, Eyas de, iii, 155
Oxeney [Oxene] (Kingsley), ii, 515, 516
Oxeye (Lymington), iv, 646; v, 470
Oxford, bp. of, iv, 518
Oxford, Eliz., ctss. of, ii, 478; earls of: Aubrey de Vere, ii, 440; iv, 632, 636; Rob. de Vere, ii, 147; iii, 483, 487
Oxford University, ii, 146; v, 249
Oxlease (Romsey), iv, 452
Oxney, riv., see Slea
Oxsen, John, iv, 64
Oyley, d', Chris., v, 274; Sarah, v, 274
Oysell, John, iii, 214; Nich., iii, 214
Oyster industry, v, 265, 468

Pace [Paice], Eliz., iii, 293; John, iii, 485; Rich., iv, 506; Thos., iii, 293, 294; iv, 413; v, 114 n
Pack & Chapman, bellfounders, iv, 557; v, 65
Packham House (Fordingbridge), iv, 568
Pacy, Thos., ii, 67; v, 327 n
Paddon, Capt. Geo., v, 388; John E. iii, 216; Jos., iii, 215; Mary A., iii, 216; Rob., iii, 83, 96, 98, 105, 125
Padnell (Blendworth), iii, 84
Padwick [Padwicke], Will., iii, 99, 130, 134, 168; —, v, 544, 546, 555
Padworth (Berks), ii, 227; man., iv, 160
Page [Paye], Geo., v, 517; Greg., iii, 114; Harry, v, 367; Joan, iii, 337; iv, 180 n; John, iv, 83; Jonas, v, 32; Jos., iv, 140; Walt., v, 163; (Rev.) Will., iii, 337; iv, 180 n, 229
Pageham, see Ap Adam and Pagham
Pagen, iv, 616
Paget [Pagett], Barbara, iii, 431; Dulcebella, iv, 557; Jas., iii, 431, 436
Pagglesham [Pagelham], John, iii, 68; Will., iii, 114
Pagham, man. (Arreton), v, 146
Pagham [Pageham] (de), Agnes, iv, 8 n; Alice, ii, 512; iv, 8; John, iii, 150, 227; iv, 8, 536 n; v, 146; Laur., ii, 512; iii, 150, 168; iv, 8, 28; Mary, v, 146; Parnel, iv, 28; Phil., iii, 150; iv, 8, 28; Will., iii, 150, 226; iv, 8 n; v, 146; see also Ap Adam
Pagles Green (Hartley Mauditt), ii, 508
Pagnell, see Paynel
Paice, see Pace

Pain [Paine], Chas., v, 541; C. E., v, 541; H. G., iii, 136; John, v, 558; Mary E., iii, 394; see also Payne
Painholt Wood (King's Somborne), iv, 470
Painshill (Lockerley), iv, 500, 502
Painshill Farm (Lockerley), iv, 502
Pairok, Maud de, iii, 406
Pak, Rich., v, 213
Pakenham, Constance, v, 247; (Sir) Edm., ii, 479, 492, 495; iii, 169; v, 247, 248; Edw. M., iv, 54; Eliz., ii, 492; Hugh, iv, 42, 43; Joan, iv, 42, 44; Sir John, ii, 479, 492; iii, 169; iv, 42, 44; v, 247; Kath., ii, 492; Marg., ii, 492; iii, 169; v, 247; Thos., iv, 54; fam., arms, ii, 495
Palace Gate Farm (Odiham), iv, 91
Palace House (Beaulieu), iv, 650
Palæolithic man, i, 34, 253
Palavicino, Sir Horatio, v, 377
Paley, Fred. A., v, 134
Palk, Col. Edw. A., iv, 546, 550
Pallance Gate (Northwood), v, 268
Palliser, Sir Hugh, v, 394
Palmer [Palmarius, Paumer] (le), Alice, iii, 536; Anne, v, 172; Chas., v, 208 n; Eliz., v, 208 n; Eust., iv, 104; Frances, iii, 90, 98; iv, 255; Jas., iv, 601; Jas. N., iv, 601; John, iv, 154, 215, 255, 424, 604; v, 76, 459; Kath., iii, 299; Mary, iv, 154; Owen, v, 23; Rev. Rich,, v, 168; Rob., iv, 123; Roundell, ii, 357, 358, 521; iii, 8, 10, 15, 16; v, 5; Thos., v, 494; Will., iv, 176
Palmers [Binsted], ii, 484
Palmer's Ford (Christchurch), v, 85
Palmer's Hill (Burghclere), iv, 277
Palmerston, vscts., iv, 452, 468, 469, 554; Hen., iv, 412 n, 454; Hen. J., iii, 437; iv, 454, 455, 456, 459, 460; v, 256
Palmes, Anne (Lady), iv, 104; Brian, iv, 69; v, 118; (Sir) Fran. iv, 51, 69, 71, 104, 107, 212, 276; v, 118; (Sir) Guy, iv, 69, 276; v, 118; John, v, 118; Mary, iv, 107
Palshyd, Rich., iii, 178
Palton (de), Eliz. (Lady), iv, 526, 628; Giles, iv, 551; Joan, Lady, iv, 551; Sir John, iv, 551; Rob., iv, 554; (Sir) Will., iv, 526, 551, 628
Paltons (Copythorne), see Paultons
Pamber, ii, 376; iv, 34, 35, 113, 167, 231, 233, 236, 238, 276, 415, 416, 433-5; adv., iv, 435; char., iv, 234, 435; ch., iv, 435; man., iv, 433; Nonconf., iv, 435; pop., v, 439
Pamber Common, iv, 433
Pamber End (Pamber), iv, 433
Pamber Farm (Pamber), iv, 433
Pamber Forest, i, 384; ii, 189, 227; iv, 45, 47, 60, 122, 139, 141, 159, 160, 166, 214, 251, 433, 434, 435
Pamber Priory, see Monk Sherborne Priory
Pamplyn, Rob., iv, 641
Pan, man. (Whippingham), v, 200
Pancevolt [Pancevot], man. (Headbourne Worthy), see Worthy Pauncefoot
Pancevolt, fam., see Pauncefoot
Pancraslane (Liss), iv, 84
Paneter, Rich. le, ii, 206
Panford, Edw., iii, 361
Pann, John, see Paul, John

Pantesfoote, man. (Headbourne Worthy), see Worthy Pauncefoot
Panton, Thos., iii, 136
Papald, iv, 501, 517
Paper-making, v, 489-90
Papillon, H. P., iv, 84
Paramur, Will., v, 470
Parchemyner, Walt. le, v, 34
Parco, see Park
Parell, John, v, 119
Parfite, Rob., v, 263
Pargiter, Sam., iv, 455
Parham, Walt. de, iv, 468
Paria [Paricia], Maud, ii, 132
Paris [Parys], Alex., v, 125 ; Alice, ii, 137 ; Rob., v, 142 ; Thos., ii, 57
Park, man. (Brading), v, 165, 191
Park, tithing, W. Medine, v, 210
Park [Parco], (atte, de), Christine, iv, 407 ; C. J., iii, 130 ; Joan, iii, 485 ; v, 228 ; John, iv, 406, 407, 408 ; J. C., iii, 130 ; Lucy, v, 228 ; Thos., v, 228 ; Walt. v, 142 ; Will., iii, 96 ; v, 142 ; see also Parkes
Park Copse (Kingsclere), iv, 253
Park Corner (Heckfield), iv, 44
Park Corner (Itchel), iv, 6
Parker, (le, the), Aline, iv, 7 n ; Denise, iv, 7 n ; Geo., iii, 167, 240, 316 ; Hugh, iv, 90, 94 ; Sir Hyde, v, 399 ; Isabel, iv, 572 ; Joan, iv, 9 ; John, iv, 7 n, 572, 573 ; Mary D., v, 264 ; Rob., iv, 88, 90, 94 ; Thos., ii, 167 ; iv, 570 n, 572 ; Will., iii, 376 ; iv, 94
Parkers (Newnham), iv, 156
Parkers, man. (Odiham), iv, 94
Parkes, Will., iv, 17 ; see also Park
Park Farm (Godshill), v, 171
Parkhous, Will., ii, 258
Park House (Shipton Bellinger), pop., v, 438
Park House racing stables (Kingsclere), iv, 250 ; v, 546-53
Parkhurst (Carisbrooke), v, 222, 270, 431
Parkhurst, Mich., iv, 218 ; Rich., iv, 172, 414
Parkhurst Forest, i, 385 ; ii, 415, 435, 441, 455, 462 ; v, 221, 264, 383
Parkinson, Bridg., iii, 535 ; Capt., iii, 499
Park Prewett, farm (Sherborne St. John), iv, 158, 160
Parkridge Wood (Romsey), iv, 452
Parkstone, Upper (Dors.), v, 134
Park Stream, iv, 469, 472
Park Water, iv, 540
Parlesham (Eling), iv, 547
Parley, tithing (Westover), v, 133
Parley, East, (Christchurch), v, 85 ; adv., v, 108 ; chap., v, 108 ; man., v, 100 ; Nonconf., v, 109
Parley Green (Christchurch), v, 85
Parliamentary representation, v, 311, 355
Parmenter, Gilb., iv, 211
Parr [Parre], Constance, iv, 370 ; (Sir) John, ii, 480 ; iv, 370 ; Tom, v, 554
Parres, Rev. John, iv, 56
Parry, Thos., iv, 22
Parson, Hen. B., iv, 154 ; see also Parsons
Parsonage Croft (Faccombe), iv, 318
Parsonage Farm (Long Sutton), iv, 18
Parsonage Farm (Newchurch), v, 177

Parsonage Green (Stratfield Turgis), iv, 63
Parsonage Piece (Steventon), iv, 171
Parsonage Tithing (Kingsclere), iv, 261
Parsons, Hen., iii, 283 ; H., v, 398 ; see also Parson
Parsons & Sons, motor-car makers, v, 461
Partington [Portington], Anne, v, 97, 113 ; John, v, 208 n ; Thos., v, 113
Partridge, Edw., iv, 617 n
Parvis, Nich., iv, 41
Parvus, Alvric, iv, 627 ; Hugh, iv, 626
Parys, see Paris
Pasbrigg, Edw., iv, 388 n
Pasbures land (Kingsclere), iv, 261 n
Paslew [Passelewe], Aveline, v, 233 ; Brian, v, 251 ; John, v, 216 n, 251, 275 ; Rich., v, 230 ; Rob., v, 32, 129 ; Sarah, v, 251 ; Will., v, 251, 275
Pasley, Col., v, 396
Pasquier, Jas., ii, 223, 224, 225
Passebroc, man. (Titchfield), see Posbrook
Passeflamberd, Walt. de, iii, 375
Passelewe, see Paslew
Passfield (Bramshott), ii, 491
Pastrow, hund., iv, 308 ; v, 324, 331
Pastury, le, (Romsey), iv, 452
Paten, Joan, ii, 130
Pathurst, John, iii, 39
Patmore, Coventry, iv, 639
Patney, man. (Wilts.), ii, 114
Patney, Will., ii, 284
Patrick [Patricke, Patrycke], Joan, v, 181 ; Lawr., iii, 114 ; Symkyn, iii, 507 ; Walt., iv, 617
Patricksford (Eversley), iv, 33
Patterson, Will. J., iii, 202
Paul [Pann, Paull], Ann, iii, 207 ; John, iv, 421 ; Thos., iii, 207
Paulet [Paulett, Polet, Powlett], Ladies : Anne, iv, 433, 456, 495, 578 ; Eleanor, iv, 166 ; Eliz., ii, 76 ; Kath., iv, 393 ; Lds. : ii, 338 ; Chas., iv, 320, 323, 335 ; Chideock, ii, 76, 487, 516 ; iii, 270 n, 379 ; iv, 67, 90, 91, 549 ; Edw., iv, 334, 335 ; Fran., iv, 433 ; Hen., iv, 335, 339 ; Thos., iv, 456, 578 ; v, 330 ; see also Poulett
Paulet, Agnes, iv, 393 ; Alicia [Alice], iii, 293 ; iv, 126 ; Anne [Ann] (Lady), iv, 73, 104, 210, 283, 339 n, 433 ; Aug. J. H. B., iv, 344, 385, 637 ; Barbara, iv, 13 ; Chas., iv, 46, 107, 115, 116, 117, 122, 123, 127, 139, 191 n, 192, 193, 250, 251, 321, 323, 409, 433 n, 545, 632 ; v, 224 ; Constance, iv, 116, 123, 141, 193, 370 ; Dulcebella, iv, 557 ; Edw., iv, 409 ; Eleanor, iii, 9, 213 ; iv, 125 ; Eliz., iii, 32, 367 ; iv, 13, 125, 126, 456, 494, 527, 624 ; Frances, iv, 323 ; Fran., iii, 370 ; iv, 183, 339 ; (Sir) Geo., ii, 124, 138, 151, 304, 369 ; iii, 293, 467 ; iv, 6, 13, 339, 389, 494 n, 526, 550 ; (Sir) Hampden, iv, 104, 345 n, 494, 495, 526, 527, 624 ; Harry, ii, 382 ; iv, 46, 117, 191 n, 251, 339, 409 ; v, 224 ; Sir Hen., iv, 196, 409, 529, 550 ; Hen. W. M., iv, 339 ; Hercules, iii, 54 ; Honora, iv, 433 ; Jane, iv, 320, 433 n ; Jean Mary, iv, 46, 117 ; (Sir) John, ii, 56, 124, 138, 151, 215, 519 ; iii, 9, 367, 477, 483 ; iv, 36, 73,

Paulet (cont.)
115, 116, 119, 122, 123, 124, 126, 135, 141, 174, 179, 183, 193, 208, 210, 271, 283, 315, 334, 335, 337, 433, 434 ; v, 79 ; Kath., iv, 208, 283 ; Lucy, iv, 210, 283, 409 ; Magdalen, iv, 323 ; Norton, iii, 18, 32, 370 ; iv, 339, 550 ; (Sir) Rich., ii, 125, 151, 304 ; iii, 367, 368 ; iv, 179, 210, 283, 557, 624, 637 ; Thos., iii, 477 ; iv, 598 ; Thos. N., iv, 339 n ; (Sir) Will., ii, 136, 148, 151, 445 ; iii, 9, 250, 251, 270, 277, 281, 285, 293, 301, 362, 368, 436, 477, 483, 484, 488 ; iv, 13, 36, 46, 64, 80, 107, 108, 116, 117, 120, 123, 124, 125, 126, 130, 132, 135, 153, 157, 179, 183, 189, 191, 192, 193, 196, 210, 243, 244, 246, 251, 255, 261, 265, 266, 320, 334, 335, 336, 339, 348, 359, 393, 397, 409, 433, 434, 460, 525, 526, 528, 539, 549, 550, 552, 554, 555, 557, 598 ; v, 8, 223 ; Capt., v, 333 ; fam., iv, 128, 276, 320, 344, 611, 642 ; arms, iii, 270, 477 ; see also Orde-Powlett and Poulett
Paulin, Joan, v, 231 ; John, v, 231
Paulsgrove chalk quarries, v, 454
Paulsgrove Grove (Portsmouth), v, 455
Paultons (Copythorne), iv, 546, 552
Paumer, see Palmer
Pauncefoot, Pauncefote, man. (Headbourne Worthy), see Worthy Pauncefoot
Pauncefoot [Pancevolt], Bern., ii, 421 ; iii, 425, 504 ; iv, 428, 468, 469, 480 ; Eliz., iv, 428 ; Humph., iv, 428, 480 ; John, iv, 456 ; Lemuel, iv, 428, 456, 480 ; Maud, iv, 456 ; Pet., iv, 456 ; Rich., iv, 456 ; Rob., iv, 428 ; Thos., iv, 476, 480 ; Walt., iv, 456, 495
Pauncefoot Court (King's Somborne), iv, 476
Pauncefoot Hill, man. (Romsey), iv, 452, 456
Paunsford, man. (Headbourne Worthy), see Worthy Pauncefoot
Pauperism, v, 432, 433, 435
Pavar, Will., v, 485 n
Pavely [Pavilly] (de), John, ii, 187 ; v, 187 ; Reg., iv, 85 ; Rob., v, 187
Pavements, Roman, i, 286, 287, 288, 294, 296, 300, 304, 306, 309, 310, 363, 368 ; iv, 5, 60
Pavilion court (Winchester), iv, 282 n ; v, 38, 39, 48
Pavilly, see Pavely
Pavy, Rich., v, 220 n, 251
Pawmer's Bridge (Christchurch), v, 85
Paye, see Page
Payfrere, Sir Fulk, iv, 110
Paygnel, see Paynel
Payn, v, 39
Payne [Payn], (de), Alice, iii, 425, 450 ; iv, 506 ; And., iii, 425 ; iv, 450, 476 ; Joan, iv, 330, 459, 570, 583, 588 ; John, ii, 190, 191 ; iv, 502 ; Maud, iv, 547 n ; Phil., v, 200 ; Ralph, iv, 476 ; (Sir) Rob., ii, 119, 459 ; iv, 139, 419, 422, 502 ; Rog., iv, 502 ; Sim., v, 230 ; Thos., iv, 483, 528 ; iv, 330, 459, 506, 570, 583, 588 ; Tom, v, 535 ; Will., iii, 459 ; iv, 547 n ; v, 200 ; see also Pain
Payne-Gallwey, Ralph, v, 559
Paynel [Pagnell, Paygnell, Paynell, Peynel] (de), Beatrice, ii, 150 ; Eve, ii, 521 ; Godheld, iv, 116 ; Hawise, iv, 174 ; John, ii, 521 ;

Paynel (*cont.*)
iii, 11 ; Thos., ii, 492, 521 ; iii, 11, 158 ; iv, 193, 226 ; Will., ii, 521 ; iii, 11, 17 ; iv, 174
Paynes Farm (King's Somborne), see Pauncefoot Court
Paynshill, ii, 159
Paytevyn, see Petevyn
Paythforlang (Carisbrooke), v, 222
Payton, see Peyton
Peace, Will., v, 486
Peachey, (Sir) Bulstrode, ii, 513 ; iv, 172 ; Edw., iii, 293 ; Eliz., iv, 172 ; Erlysman, iii, 293 ; (Sir) John, ii, 513 ; iv, 374, 424 ; Lambert, iii, 207 ; Will., iii, 293
Peacock [Peacocke, Pecock], Gabriel, ii, 53, 54 ; Warren, v, 118 ; Capt., v, 535 ; fam., iv, 617 ;
Peak [Peak Tygall], man., (East Meon), iii, 71
Peak, tithing (East Meon), iii, 63, 245
Peake, Will., iv, 28 ; Lt.-Col., v, 341
Pealeaze, —, iv, 491
Pearce, Fran., iii, 131 ; Humph., v, 521 ; John, v, 470 ; Luke, iv, 324 ; Rob., iv, 550 ; v, 517, 539 ; Rob. C. S., iv, 546, 550 ; Stanley, v, 573 ; Zachary, ii, 115 ; see also Pearse
Peare, Will., v, 187 n
Pearse [Peers, Peres, Pers], Jas., ii, 375, 385 ; John, ii, 146 ; v, 329 ; Will., v, 539 ; Dr., ii, 214 ; see also Pearce
Pearson [Pereson], Thos., v, 212 ; —, ii, 205 ; see also Pierson
Pease [Pece, Pese], Edw., iv, 288 ; v, 177 ; Will., iv, 460
Peat Pitts (Longstock), v, 454
Pecche [Peche, Pechie, Pechy], (de), Barth., iii, 362 ; iv, 88, 129, 142, 159, 165 ; Eliz., iv, 142 n ; Herb., iii, 362 ; iv, 142, 165, 231 n ; Joan, iii, 362 ; iv, 142 ; (Sir) John, iii, 362 ; iv, 142, 165, 166, 231 n ; Lambert, v, 249 ; Thos., ii, 119, 121
Pece, see Pease
Pecham, see Peckham
Peche, Pechie, Pechy, see Pecche
Peckham [Pecham] (de), Sir Harry, v, 329 ; John, ii, 164, 165, 173 ; Maud, ii, 126 ; Thos., iii, 131
Pecock, see Peacock
Pedwardyn, (de), Alice, iii, 378 ; Sir Rob., iii, 379 ; (Sir) Rog., iii, 378, 379 ; Sir Walt., iii, 379
Peel, Edm., v, 155 ; Sir Rob., iv, 516
Peel Common (Fareham), v, 542
Peers, see Pearse
Peeter, Hen., iv, 214 ; Kath., iv, 214
Peirson, see Pierson
Peisford (Lymington), iv, 639
Pelagus, Sim., iv, 323
Pelecypoda, i, 103
Pelegrini, Raymond, ii, 195, 197
Pelham (Newton Valence), iii, 24
Pelham, Chas. A., v, 161 n, 174, 178 ; Henrietta, v, 176 n ; Sir John, ii, 492 ; v, 247 ; Kath., Lady, ii, 492 ; v, 247 ; fam., v, 203
Pell, Will., iv, 301
Pellerin, Auguste, v, 455
Pelleue, Rich., ii, 229, 230
Pember, Pembere, par., see Pamber
Pember, Edw. H., iv, 616 ; G. H., v, 522
Pemberton, see Pemerton
Pembre, see Pamber
Pembridge [Pembrugg], de, Amice, iv, 569 ; Hawise, iv, 569 ; Hen.,

Pembridge (*cont.*)
iv, 569 ; (Sir) Rich., iv, 545, 569, 626, 631
Pembroke, ctsses. of : Eleanor, iv, 53, 88, 89, 90, 360, 607 ; Gervaise, iv, 607, 609 ; Marg., iv, 278 ; earls of : iv, 198, 338, 365, 532 n, 533 n, 545 ; v, 338, 344 ; Anselm, iv, 52, 360, 474 ; Aymer, ii, 24 ; iii, 11, 17, 23, 26, 227, 239 ; iv, 53, 387, 513 ; v, 98 ; Gilb., iv, 77, 360, 607 ; Hen., iv, 587 n ; John, iii, 227 ; iv, 52 ; Phil., v, 224 ; Rich., iv, 52, 150, 360, 607, 609 ; Thos., iv, 278 ; Will., ii, 128, 129, 422 ; iii, 3, 23, 26, 29, 135, 217, 356, 455 ; iv, 333, 360, 387, 389, 474, 544, 587 n, 591, 607, 632
Pemerton [Pemberton], Geo., iii, 408, 417, 536 ; iv, 139, 356 ; v, 77
Pendilton, Rich., iv, 40
Penebere, see Pamber
Penerley (Beaulieu), iv, 650
Penfold, Eliz. P., iii, 131
Penford, Eliz., iii, 467
Pengelly, Sir Thos., iv, 476
Penigtone (Milford), see Pennington
Penintone, par., see Weyhill
Penintune (Milford), see Pennington
Penleaze, fam., v, 84
Penley, Great, (Froyle), ii, 501
Penn [Penne], (de la), Agatha, iv, 60 ; John, iv, 58, 605 ; (Sir) Will., iv, 605 ; v, 381, 382, 383
Penna, man., see Pan
Pennant, Thos., ii, 452
Penne, la, (Harbridge), iv, 605
Penne, fam., see Penn
Pennegaford, iv, 587 n
Pennethorne, Anne, v, 274 ; John, v, 274 ; Rose, v, 274
Penningford (S. Damerham), iv, 586
Pennington (Milford), iv, 603 ; v, 82, 116, 470, 472 ; chant., v, 123 ; ch., v, 123 ; man., v, 118
Pennington [Ponyngton], (de), Ann, iv, 373 ; Isaac, iv, 373 ; John, v, 481
Pennington Narvett, man. (Milford), v, 119, 119 n
Pennyplott (Eversley), iv, 33
Penros, Joan, iv, 420 ; John, iv, 420
Penruddock, Chas., iv, 578 ; Edw., iii, 458 ; iv, 578, 595 ; Eliz., iv, 578 ; (Sir) Geo., iv, 578, 595 ; (Sir) John, iv, 578, 595 ; Rob., iv, 578 ; Thos., iv, 578
Penton, —, v, 5
Penton Grafton, see Weyhill
Penton Lodge (Penton Mewsey), iv, 381
Penton Mewsey, iv, 333, 352, 381-4, 395 ; adv., iv, 384 ; char., iv, 384 ; ch., iv, 383 ; man., iv, 381 ; pop., v, 438 ; sch., ii, 402 ; iv, 384
Pentridge (Dors.), iv, 587
Penwood (Highclere), iv, 285 ; v, 559
Peny, Joan, iii, 429 ; iv, 392, 522 n ; John, iv, 392 ; Rob., iii, 429 ; iv, 341, 392, 393, 522 n
Penyngton Meysy, see Penton Mewsey
Penyston, Fran., iv, 3
Penyton (Dors.), ii, 159
Pepercherchesfeld (Lockerley), iv, 500
Peperlond (Sherborne St. John), iv, 158, 165
Peperstiche Feald (Crondall), iv, 6
Peperwhyt [Pepwhyt], Eliz., iv, 142, 143 ; John, iv, 641 ; Thos., iv, 142, 143

Pepirlond, see Peperlond
Pepyn, John, ii, 231
Pepys, Sam., iii, 178
Percehay [Perchehaie], Lavinia, iii, 392 ; Rob., iv, 266 n
Percesoces, i, 199
Perceval [Percival], Chas. G., iii, 78 ; Charlotte, v, 213 ; Jos., v, 78 ; Sir Phil., iv, 613 n ; Rob., v, 213
Percey, see Percy
Perchard, John, ii, 54
Perche, Geoff., count of, iv, 77
Perchehaie, see Percehay
Perchet, man. (Romsey), see Spurshot
Percival, see Perceval
Percy [Percey, Perci], (de), Alan, iii, 239 ; Algernon, v, 345 ; Eliz., iv, 651 ; Ellen, ii, 137 ; Geoff., iii, 254 ; iv, 493 ; Hen., iv, 571 ; Hugh, v, 186 ; Jas., ii, 507 ; Joan, iv, 440, 481 ; Joceline, iv, 651 ; Nich., iv, 150 ; (Sir) Thos., iv, 151, 571 ; v, 366 ; Will., iii, 237, 239, 254 ; iv, 440, 449, 477, 481, 493, 646 ; v, 114 n ; fam., v, 48 n
Perers, see Perrers
Peres, see Pearse
Pereson, see Pearson
Pergent, see Peryent
Periam (Kimpton), iv, 372
Perient, see Peryent
Perin, see Perrin
Perkins, Anne, iii, 167, 240 ; Edm., v, 100 ; Fran., iii, 167, 240, 289, 373, 375 ; Sir Fred., iii, 277 ; Hen., iii, 167, 240 ; Jacob, v, 100 ; Jas. F., v, 100 ; Marg., iii, 167, 240 ; Rich., iii, 240 ; Thos., iii, 167, 240 ; fam., arms, iii, 167
Perkinson, Rich., iii, 84
Perman, Juliana, v, 192 ; Rich., v, 192
Pern, Alf., iii, 467
Perné, Jan, v, 491
Perocke (Milton), v, 124
Perot, see Perrott
Perrers [Perers], (de), Alice, iii, 255 ; Bern., v, 33
Perreton (Arreton), v, 140, 148
Perreton, Old, (Arreton), v, 148
Perrin [Perin], Chris., iii, 241, 306 ; Eliz., iii, 241 ; Hen., ii, 387 ; iii, 241, 305, 353
Perrott [Perot], (de), Alice, ii, 316 ; iv, 199 ; Beatrice, iv, 543 ; Isabel, iv, 542 ; Ralph, iii, 290 ; iv, 543 ; Reg., iii, 290 ; iv, 542, 543 ; Thos. F., v, 184 ; T., v, 144 ; Will., ii, 316 ; iv, 199
Perry, Jas., v, 151
Perryam, Will., ii, 485
Perryland, man. (Bentley), see Pury
Pers, see Pearse
Pershore, abbot of, v, 3
Pershore, Rob., v, 39
Pershute, (de), John, iv, 492 ; v, 273 ; Marg., v, 273 ; Maud, iv, 555 ; Nich., iv, 457, 492, 507, 555, 618 ; Pet., iv, 457, 507 ; Rich., iv, 456, 457, 499, 506, 507 ; Will., iv, 457, 555
Persse, H. S., v, 546, 554
Pertone, Godf., v, 305
Peryent [Pergent, Perient], Joan, iv, 449 ; (Sir) John, iv, 449, 484, 623
Peryton, see Perreton
Pescod, John, iii, 12, 27, 29 ; Judith, iv, 444 ; Nich., iii, 12, 29, 293 ; Rich., iii, 12, 27 ; iv, 444 ; Thos., iii, 12, 27, 29
Pese, see Pease

Peshale, Rich. de, iii, 387
Peskett, —, v, 527
Pestour, see Baker
Petefyne, see Petevyn
Peter, king of Castile, ii, 475
Peter [Piers], iv, 219; v, 2; archbp. of Rouen, iv, 68; bp. of Corbavia, ii, 16, 29, 123, 213; the mercer, v, 477; of Portsmouth, v, 50; prior of Christchurch, ii, 154; of York, ii, 139
Peterborough, Eliz., ctss. of, v, 265 n
Peterfeud, see Petersfield
Peters, E. E., v, 146; J. C., v, 148; Sam., v, 146, 148
Petersfield, ii, 101, 102; iii, 82, 111-21; iv, 361; v, 311, 346, 355, 356, 423, 426, 428, 431, 434; adv., iii, 120; char., iii, 120; ch., iii, 118; inds., v, 454, 461, 475, 482, 484; man., iii, 116; mkt. and fairs, v, 416, 417; pop., v, 444; sch., ii, 402
Petersfield, (de, of), John, iii, 253; Rog., ii, 148; iv, 85, 549
Peterson, Joachim, v, 172; Rob., iv, 651
Peterworth, see Pittleworth
Petevyn [Paytevyn, Petefyne], Phil., iv, 184; Rich., ii, 48; Rob., iv, 592; Rog., iv, 592; see also Poitou
Petre, Lady, iv, 88
Petre, Hen., v, 535; Will., iv, 189
Petrefeld, Petresfeld, see Petersfield
Pett, Anne, iv, 259, 260, 374; Eliz., iv, 260, 374; John, iv, 259, 374; Pet., v, 381; Phineas, iv, 260, 374; —, v, 378
Petteham, see Putham
Pettry Court, see Potrey Court
Petty [Pettye], (Sir) Will., iii, 248; iv, 453, 467; v, 484; —, ii, 337; fam., v, 487
Petty's Brook (Sherfield), iv, 103
Peverell [Peverel], (de), Agnes, iii, 468, 483; v, 129; (Sir) Andr., iii, 486; iv, 282, 283; Barton, iii, 486; Dionisia, iv, 588; Edith, v, 125; Geoff., iii, 256; (Sir) Hen., iii, 468; iv, 383; v, 118, 124, 125, 129; Hugh, iv, 588; Joan, iv, 588; John, iv, 383, 551 n; Kath., iv, 282; v, 118; Margery, iv, 551 n, 588; Rich., iv, 382; (Sir) Thos., iii, 468, 486; iv, 314, 315, 383, 563, 588; v, 118, 125; Will., iii, 413, 468; iv, 383; v, 129
Peveseye, John de, ii, 214
Pevrel, v, 147
Pewcrege, Rich., v, 484
Pewkes, the, (Rotherwick), iv, 99
Pewsey, man. (Wilts.), ii, 121
Pewter vessels, i, 297, 298
Pexall [Pexsall], Anne, iv, 166, 203; Barbara, iv, 166; Edith, iii, 213; iv, 166, 168, 169, 203; Eleanor, Lady, iv, 166, 203; Eliz., iv, 166; John, iv, 169; Margery, ii, 502; iv, 166; Ralph, iii, 213; iv, 166, 168, 169, 203; (Sir) Rich., ii, 72, 474, 502; iii, 53, 213, 229; iv, 142, 166, 169, 173, 203; fam., arms, ii, 474
Peynel, see Paynel
Peyntour, John, v, 87; Will., v, 87
Peyton [Payton] (de), Eleanor, iv, 53; Sir John, iv, 53; v, 471; admiral, v, 396
Phelipps [Phelips], Charity, iii, 449, 451; iv, 441, 446, 447, 476, 481; Fran., v, 177; Sir Jas., iii, 449, 451; iv, 447; (Sir) Thos., iii, 449,

Phelipps (cont.)
451; iv, 441, 446, 447; fam., arms, iii, 449
Phelps, Rich., ii, 515; iv, 29; —, iv, 592
Philibert, de, John, iv, 121; Phil., iv, 360
Philip IV, of France, v, 362
Philip II, of Spain, v, 376
Philip, abbot of Quarr, ii, 139
Philippa, queen, ii, 43, 203, 485; iii, 506; iv, 89, 379, 501, 515, 516, 545, 627, 631, 633
Phillater, Edw., v, 469
Phillips [Philip, Philippes, Philips, Phillip, Phillipps], Anne, iii, 120; Avis, iv, 49; Awsten, iv, 133; Fran., v, 141 n; Hen., iv, 49; John, iv, 48; v, 316; John Rouse, iii, 54; Lionel, iv, 94, 99, 100; Maria, iv, 313; Prudence, iv, 49; Rich., ii, 301; Susan M., v, 120; Will., ii, 315; iv, 558, 634; Rev. W. J. G., iv, 558
Phillpotts, J. S., ii, 365
Philp, Rich., iv, 33 n; Thos., iv, 33 n
Philpot [Philpott, Philpotte, Phyllpot, Phylpot], Agnes, iv, 388, 389; Anne, iv, 617; Eliz., ii, 125; iii, 484; iv, 390; (Sir) Geo., iii, 407, 421, 484; iv, 339, 353, 388, 390, 617; v, 182; (Sir) Hen., iii, 486; iv, 388, 617; Jas., v, 461; (Sir) John, ii, 72; iii, 289, 407, 421; iv, 339, 351, 363, 380, 388, 617; v, 119, 182; Mary, iv, 353; (Sir) Pet., ii, 72, 125; iii, 407, 486; Thos., iii, 407; iv, 388, 617; v, 182; Will., iv, 597; fam., v, 280 n; arms, iii, 289, 407, 484
Phipps, Rev. Jas., iv, 76
Phitelet, iv, 561 n
Phœnix Green (Hartley Wintney), iv, 79
Phyllpot, Phylpot, see Philpot
Phytophaga, i, 118
Piccadilly Hill (Monk Sherborne), iv, 231
Picheford, Geoff. de, iv, 215
Pickard [Pycarde], Denise, iv, 7 n; John, iv, 498; Rob., iv, 7 n
Picked Post (Fordingbridge), iv, 559
Pickelswade (Christchurch), v, 97 n
Pickering, Ant., iv, 93; Bridg., iv, 93; Constance, iv, 93 n; Leonard, iv, 370; Nath., iv, 94; Miss, iv, 370
Picket Close (Ryde), v, 178
Picket Post (Ringwood), iv, 607
Pickett, J., v, 458
Pickford Hill (Kimpton), iv, 372
Picot, iv, 561 n, 570
Picquigny, Vidame of, iii, 166
Piddle, Little, man., ii, 156
Piddleton, man., ii, 156
Pidele, de, Margery, v, 188; Rob., v, 188
Pidford (Arreton), v, 140, 247 n, 248
Pie, see Pye
Pierrepont, Eliz., iv, 494, 522; Evelyn, iv, 494, 497 n, 522; Hen., iv, 509; Rob., iv, 494, 522; Will., iv, 494, 522
Piers, see Peter
Pierson [Peirson], John, iii, 235, 334, 443; see also Pearson
Pigeon, John, iii, 409; Petronilla, ii, 151; Will., iv, 266
Pigott, Baron, iv, 104
Pigott [Pigot], Rev. Botry, iii, 363; Rich., iii, 395; Mrs., iv, 103 n
Pigs, v, 501, 506; price of, v, 494, 495

Pikadoles Copyce (Hurstbourne Tarrant), iv, 319, 320
Pike, Anne, iv, 196; Chas., v, 518; Geo., iv, 196; Will., iii, 200; v, 155, 172, 182; —, v, 229; fam., v, 173; see also Pyke
Pikedelonde-juxta-Dounam (Kimpton), iv, 372
Pike's Hill (Lyndhurst), iv, 631
Pikestaff, Sim., v, 29
Pilcot (Dogmersfield), iv, 72, 73, 109; man., iv, 73; mill., iv, 72, 73
Pile, Lucy, iv, 62; Rich., iv, 226; Thos., iv, 22; see also Pyle
Pilersehacche (Odiham), iv, 88
Pilesdone, de, Emma, iv, 8; Ivo, iv, 8; John, iv, 8
Pilfold, Rich., iii, 207
Pilgrim's Copse (Ashe), iv, 198
Pilgrim's Copse (Micheldever), v, 418
Pilgrim's Farm (Burghclere), iv, 277
Pilgrim's Palace (East Tisted), v, 418
Pilgrims' Place (East Tisted), v, 418
Pilkington, Chas., ii, 356
Pillcroft (Hartley Mauditt), ii, 508
Pillebridge (Aldershot), iv, 3
Pilley, man. (Boldre), iv, 615, 618; v, 81
Pilley (de), Rich., iv, 618; Rog., iv, 618, 621
Pillhill, brook, iv, 334, 335, 359, 360, 379, 380, 387
Pilot Hill (Faccombe), iv, 314
Pimperne, man. (Dors.), ii, 169, 172
Pimperne, Thos. de, ii, 170, 172
Pince, John, ii, 167
Pincerna, see Butler
Pinchey, Thos., ii, 87
Pincke [Pyncke], Eliz., iv, 180; Hen., iv, 82, 180, 181; John, iv, 82, 222; Rich., iv, 243; Rob., iv, 180; Thos., iv, 180; Walt., iv, 180, 222; Will., iv, 180 n, 181, 222; see also Pinke
Pindar [Pynder], Geo., iv, 16; Thos., iii, 270
Ping, Jonathan, v, 5
Pinhoe, man. (Devon.), iii, 20
Pinhorn, John, v, 274
Pinke [Pink, Pynke], (Sir) John, iii, 40, 58, 353, 394; v, 79; Rog., ii, 315, 327; Thos., ii, 482; see also Pincke
Pinkerton, John, v, 452 n
Pinkney, Walt. of, v, 303
Pinnock, Rev. Jas., iv, 83; John, bp. ii, 202; —, v, 461
Pinth, John, iii, 306
Pipson, le, (Yateley), iv, 21
Pirifist, Pet. de, iv, 247
Pirishute, see Spurshot
Pisa, Al. of, ii, 193
Pistar, see Baker
Pistell, Sarah, iii, 241; Will., iii, 241
Pistes, de, Rog., iv, 422, 499; Walt., iv, 422
Pistor, see Baker
Pitchorn (Kingsclere), iv, 267
Pit-dwellings, i, 260, 262, 263
Pithouse (Sopley), v, 128, 130 n
Pitman, see Pittman
Pit's Enclosure (New Forest), i, 326
Pitt (Hursley), iii, 401, 417, 421; v, 530
Pitt [Pitte, Pytt], Anne, iv, 62, 101; Chris., iv, 61, 62; Dionysia, iv, 61; Edith, iv, 61, 62; Edw., iv, 59, 60, 61, 62, 64, 141; Elia, ii, 124; Eliz., iv, 61, 62; Frances, iv, 62; Fran., iv, 61,

Pitt (*cont.*)
62 ; Geo., iii, 39, 414 ; iv, 22, 46, 51, 57, 59, 60, 61, 62, 63, 65, 101, 216, 485 ; Hen., iii, 298 ; Jane, iv, 61, 62 ; John, iv, 61, 62, 614 ; Kath., iv, 61, 62 ; Lora, iv, 62 ; Lucy, iv, 22, 62 ; Mary, iv, 62 ; Nich., iv, 62 ; Rachel, iv, 61, 62 ; Rob., iv, 336 ; v, 93 ; Sam., iv, 62 ; Thos., iv, 62, 335, 336 ; (Sir) Will., ii, 99 ; iii, 96 ; iv, 43, 59, 61, 62, 64 ; Will. A., iv, 46 ; —, v. 458 ; fam., v, 139 ; arms, iii, 414 ; *see also* Pittis & Pitts
Pitter, John, iii, 411 ; Rob., iii, 411, 413 ; fam., v, 558
Pittes, *see* Pitts
Pitt Grounds (Kingsclere), iv, 266 *n*
Pittis, John, v, 264 ; Rich., iii, 294 ; R. R., v, 143 ; —, v, 189, 536 ; *see also* Pitt & Pitts
Pittleworth, man. (Bossington), iv, 492, 508, 509
Pittleworth Farm (Bossington), iv, 491
Pittman [Pitman], Edm., ii, 379 ; iv, 94 ; Hugh, iv, 385 ; John, iv, 386 ; fam., iv, 387
Pitt Place (Mottistone), v, 251
Pitts [Pittes], Geo. F., iii, 469 ; Hen., ii, 77 ; John, ii, 315 ; Mrs., ii, 80 ; *see also* Pitt & Pittis
Pitts Deep (Boldre), iv, 616 ; v, 466
Place, man. (Nether Wallop), *see* Wallop Buckland, Nether
Place Farm (Nether Wallop), iv, 527
Place House (Liss), iv, 85 *n*
Place House (Titchfield), iii, 220
Place House Farm (Liss), iv, 85 *n*
Place Meade (Leckford), iv, 446
Placy, John, v, 484 ; Rob., v, 484
Plague, ii, 32-6, 264 ; v, 419, 426
Plainbairn Copse (Selborne), iii, 5
Plaitford, iv, 489, 537, 542-3 ; adv., iv, 543 ; ch., iv, 543 ; man., iv, 540, 541, 542 ; racing, v, 543 ; sch., ii, 402
Plaitford Common, iv, 542, 543
Plaitford Green (Plaitford), iv, 542
Plaitford Wood, iv, 542
Plaiz, Hugh de, iii, 196
Plantagenet, Arth., *see* Lisle, vsct. ; Bryget, ii, 125 ; Eliz., v, 247
Plash, le, (Stockbridge), iv, 483
Plassetts (Upper Clatford), iv, 360
Plasshet, le, (Godshill), v, 173
Plastow Green (Kingsclere), iv, 266
Platt, T. P., ii, 493, 495
Player, Eliz. L., v, 180 ; Geo., v, 180, 186 ; Hen., v, 178, 181 ; Thos., v, 178, 186 ; fam., v, 177
Playfoote, John, iii, 178 ; Rich., iii, 193
Playstowe (Carisbrooke), v, 222
Playstowes (Broughton), iv, 493
Plegmund, archbp. of Canterbury, ii, 5
Pleistocene age, i, 253, 254, 255-6 ; mammal rem., i, 41, 42
Pleseys [Plessey], (Sir) John (de), iv, 45 *n*, 596 *n*
Plestor (Selborne), iii, 4
Pleyford, *see* Plaitford
Pleyinghulle (Lyndhurst), iv, 631
Pleystowe, la, (Selborne), iii, 7
Pliocene age, i, 22, 26-30
Plokenet, *see* Plunkenet
Plott House (Ecchinswell), iv, 250
Plough-shares, v, 500
Plowden, Dorothy, iv, 248 ; (Sir) Edm., iii, 164, 167, 204 ; iv, 83, 248 *n*, 444 ; Fran., iii, 164 ; iv, 444 ; (Rev.), Jas., iv, 83, 248, 444 ; Jas. C., iv, 248 ; Jonathan,

Plowden (*cont.*)
iv, 153 *n* ; Mabel, iii, 164, 204 ; Thos., iv, 83, 444 ; Will. H. C., iv, 247, 248
Plugenet, *see* Plunkenet
Plumber, le, Christine, iv 620 ; Ralph, iv, 620
Plumley Heath (Harbridge), iv, 604
Plummer, Rev. J. T., ii, 511
Plunkenet [Plokenet, Plugenet] (de), Ad., iii, 35 ; (Sir) Alan, iv, 207 ; iii, 32, 255, 323 ; iv, 82, 150, 152, 206, 328, 369, 493, 547, 610, 631 ; Joan, ii, 207 ; iii, 323 ; iv, 328, 493 ; Sybil, iii, 255 ; iv, 328 ; fam., arms, iii, 324
Plymouth, shipping, v, 362, 364, 377, 379, 382, 386, 387
Plymouth Brethren, iv, 86, 108, 139, 497, 576, 633 ; v, 109, 245, 291
Poblyngesperke (Bramley), iv, 141
Pococke [Pocock], Ellen, ii, 69 ; Sir Geo., v, 100 ; John, v, 287 *n* ; Rob., ii, 385 ; T., iv, 272 ; —, v, 392
Podenhale, de, Joan, iv, 148 ; (Sir), John, iv, 148, 318
Podmore, E. B., v, 523 ; Rob. B., v, 541
Podney, Little, (Christchurch), v, 85
Podney Magna (Christchurch), v, 85
Poer, *see* Poore
Point Gate (Portsmouth), v, 461 *n*
Poirson, Nich., v, 382
Poitou, Rog. of, iv, 314 ; *see also* Petevyn
Pokesdown (Bournemouth), v, 83, 109, 133, 134, 135
Pokesole, tithing (Fareham), iii, 209
Pokon House (Longstock), iv, 449
Poland Farm (Odiham), iv, 93, 94
Poland Mill (Odiham), iv, 87, 92, 93
Polayn, *see* Poleyn
Poldon, Will. de, v, 279
Pole, Lady Marg., iii, 105, 135, 411 ; iv, 608 ; v, 92, 219
Pole, (atte, de la), Abra., v, 520 ; Alice, ii, 519, 521 ; iii, 370 ; iv, 395 ; Arth., v, 247 ; Aubree, iv, 521, 522 ; Cath., (Lady) iv, 395, 454 *n*, 608 ; Sir Chas., iv, 256, 271, 272, 276 ; Constance, Lady, v, 247, 249 *n* ; Edm., ii, 519, 522 ; iv, 399 ; Eleanor, iv, 260 ; Eliz., iv, 34 ; (Sir) Geoff., ii, 125 ; v, 247, 249 *n*, 324 ; Jane, iv, 454 *n* ; John, ii, 283, 366 ; iii, 9, 415 ; iv, 130, 224, 296 *n*, 318 *n*, 579 ; Marg., iv, 34 ; Mary, ii, 125 ; iv, 260 ; Maud, iv, 224, 579 ; Mich., iv, 395 ; Millicent, Lady, iv, 272 ; Sir Pet., iv, 248, 271, 272 ; v, 520 ; Reg. [Raynolde], ii, 58, 72, 159, 162, 373 ; (Rev.) Rich., iii, 415 ; iv, 130, 248, 272, 296 *n* ; Rob., iv, 521 ; Sir Thos., iv, 395, 399 ; Sir Walt., iv, 34 ; (Sir) Will., ii, 519, 521 ; iv, 395, 396, 399, 454 *n*, 545 ; Gen., v, 520 ; fam., iv, 202, 248 ; arms, ii, 519
Polelond (Kingsclere), iv, 250
Polemtune, *see* Polhampton
Polet, *see* Paulet and Poulett
Poleyn [Polayn], Amice, iv, 508 ; Aubrey, iv, 458 ; John, iv, 508, 657 ; v, 482 ; Marg., iv, 508 *n*, 657 ; Matth., iv, 458, 508 ; Thos., iv, 508 ; *see also* Pollen
Polhampton, man. (Overton), ii, 108 ; iv, 197, 213-15, 218 ; chap., iv, 218 ; ch., iv, 218 ; cider manufacture, v, 475
Polhampton, Rich. de, iv, 214

Polhampton Farm (Overton), iv, 210
Political history, v, 293-358
Pollack (S. Stoneham), iii, 481, 484
Pollard, John, ii, 193 ; Lt.-Col. W. C., iv, 546, 551
Pollard's End Copse [Pollardescrofte, Pollardyscroft] (Sherborne St. John), iv, 158, 167
Pollen, Edw., iv, 383 ; Hester, iv, 473 ; (Sir) John, iv, 354, 357, 374, 383, 473 ; v, 532 ; Sir John W., iv, 473 ; Louisa, Lady, iv, 367 ; Sir Rich. H., iv, 357, 367, 374 ; Susannah, iii, 432 ; *see also* Poleyn
Polling, man. (Odiham), iv, 92, 94
Pollins (Mottisfont), iv, 508
Polmont [Polymond], John, iii, 498, 499
Polstin, Rog., iii, 225
Polton, Kath., ii, 135
Polymond, John, *see* Polmont
Polymond Tower (Southampton), *see* St. Denys' Tower
Polyzoa, i, 97
Pomariis, John de, ii, 220, 221
Poncyn, John, prior, ii, 231
Pondethed More (Yateley), iv, 21
Ponet, John, *see* Winchester, bps. of
Ponsales (Christchurch), v, 85
Ponsholt, *see* Punsholt
Pont Audener, Hen. of, iii, 506
Pontchardun, *see* Punchardon
Pont de l'Arche [Ponte Arche], de, Maud, ii, 160 ; Ralph, iv, 387 *n* ; Rob., iii, 23, 26, 29, 372, 375, 377 ; iv, 387, 513 ; v, 304 ; Will., ii, 160 ; iii, 23, 26, 375, 377 ; iv, 387 ; v, 21, 302
Pontesdowne (Sydmonton), iv, 250, 254
Pontoise, John of, *see* Winchester, bps. of
Ponyngton, *see* Pennington
Poole [Pool, Poule], Constance, v, 219 ; Esther, iv, 26 ; Sir Geoff., v, 219 ; Jane, iv, 604 ; John, ii, 185 ; iv, 604 ; Nich., iii, 310 ; Thos., iv, 604 ; Will., iv, 518
Pooley [Pullie], Alice, iv, 318 ; Fran., iv, 318 ; John, ii, 290
Poolhampton Farm, *see* Polhampton Farm
Poore [Poer, Poor, Pore], (le), Agnes, ii, 222 ; Aline, iv, 427 ; Edm., v, 69 ; Eliz., iv, 296 ; Geoff., iv, 296 ; Herb., ii, 226 ; iii, 59, 60 ; John, iv, 447 ; Rich., ii, 226 ; iii, 59 ; iv, 314, 380 ; Rob., iv, 296 ; Maj. R. M., v, 575 ; Will., iii, 207, fam., iv, 354
Poors (Upper Clatford), iv, 361
Poors Common, v, 84
Poorsland (Basing), iv, 115
Pope, John, iv, 639 ; v, 144, 151 ; Rich., iv, 363 ; Rog., ii, 181
Popham, ii, 116, 117, 121, 272 ; iii, 356, 389, 397-9 ; iv, 256, 264 ; v, 462 ; adv., iii, 398 ; char., iii, 399 ; ch., iii, 397 ; iv, 222 ; man., iii, 397 ; iv, 186 *n* ; pop., v, 440 ; Rom. rem., i, 306, 321, 346 ; sch., ii, 402
Popham, (de, of), Agnes, iv, 165 ; Alex., iv, 389 ; Alice, ii, 484 ; Edw., iv, 165 ; Eliz., ii, 484 ; iii, 358 ; iv, 418, 522 ; v, 280 ; Sir Fran., iv, 389 ; Gilb., ii, 484 ; iii, 21, 398 ; Grace, v, 160, 280 ; Helena, Lady, iv, 389 ; Hen., ii, 484 ; iii, 21, 398 ; iv, 521, 588, 646 ; v, 228 ; (Sir) John, ii, 272, 484, 485 ; iii, 358, 398 ; iv, 186 *n*, 522, 562, 646 ; v, 151, 160, 195,

Popham (*cont.*)
199, 206, 228 *n*, 280 ; Marg., iv, 418, 647 ; Margery, ii, 484 ; Mary, v, 195, 206 ; Maud, iv, 418 ; Phil., iii, 358 ; iv, 418 ; Rob. [Rog.], ii, 121, 170, 484, 488 ; iii, 21, 241, 398 ; v, 312 ; Sarah, v, 280 *n* ; Sibil, iv, 588 ; v, 228 ; Steph., ii, 484 ; iii, 21, 398 ; iv, 522 ; v, 228 *n*, 270 ; fam., iv, 524 ; v, 155, 173, 182, 281 ; arms, iii, 369
Popham Beacons, iv, 198
Popham Down Copse (Woodmancott), iv, 186
Popinjay, Rich., iii, 178 ; v, 225
Population returns, v, 435-50
Porcher, —, ii, 356
Porchester, par., *see* Portchester
Porchester, Ld., *see* Carnarvon, **earl of**
Porchester, Edw. of, ii, 155
Porchfield (Newtown), v, 265, 268
Pordale, Rich., v, 485 *n*
Pore, *see* Poore
Porifera, i, 92
Porsey, *see* Portsea
Port, v, 293, 294
Port, de, le, Ad., ii, 3, 187, 223, 226, 240, 496 ; iii, 271, 414 ; iv, 50, 116, 146, 150, 152, 158, 159, 176, 184, 189, 231, 238, 344, 373, 435 ; v, 304 ; Alice, v, 220 *n* ; Emma, iii, 239 ; Hawise [Hadwise], ii, 226 ; iii, 192 ; Hen., ii, 216, 226 ; iii, 192, 271, 386 ; iv, 115, 145, 153, 159, 231, 238, 240, 242, 373 ; Hub., iv, 149 ; Hugh, ii, 226, 484, 492, 496 ; iii, 8, 9, 68, 123, 142, 145, 171, 192, 227, 229, 234, 246, 269, 358, 360, 366, 372, 383, 392, 397, 414, 425, 458 ; iv, 35 *n*, 39, 45, 63, 74, 115, 117, 121, 123, 127, 141, 145, 150, 158, 160, 174, 179, 184, 188, 195, 208 *n*, 225, 227, 228, 231, 240, 247, 255, 256, 257, 267, 268, 337, 339, 341, 342, 358, 372, 373, 396, 419, 420, 457 *n*, 502, 510, 513, 525, 532, 547, 549, 559, 561, 564, 579, 584, 618, 625 ; v, 97, 100, 124, 129, 130, 135 ; Joan, iii, 96 ; John, ii, 226, 496 ; iii, 192, 239, 386 ; iv, 45, 46, 47, 116, 117, 127, 148, 153, 160, 232, 255 *n*, 269, 332 *n*, 337, 338, 510, 579 ; v, 220 *n*, 304 ; Mabel, ii, 226 ; iv, 116 ; Maud, iv, 116 ; Phil., iv, 338 ; Rog., ii, 223, 224 ; iv, 150, 151, 176, 178 ; Sibyl, ii, 226 ; Thos., iv, 337, 338, 513 ; Will., ii, 496 ; iii, 96, 269 ; fam., iv, 340 *n* ; arms, iii, 192
Portal, (de), Lieut.-Col. Bertram P., iv, 211 ; Charlotte, Lady, iv, 209 ; Sir Gerald, iv, 209 ; Harry, iv, 208, 209 ; Hen., iii, 480 ; iv, 209, 213, 282 ; v, 489, 490 ; Jean F., v, 489 ; John, iv, 200, 209, 216 ; v, 490, 538 *n* ; Jos., iv, 198, 200, 209, 213, 283, 320 ; v, 490 ; Melville, iv, 200, 209, 210, 216, 282 ; Col. Rob., iv, 198, 200 ; (Sir) Will., iv, 200, 208, 213 ; v, 490 ; Sir Will. W., iv, 210, 213, 215, 216, 225, 229, 283, 285 ; Sir Wyndham S., ii, 470 ; iv, 140, 209, 225, 283 ; v, 490 ; W., v, 521 ; —, v, 537
Portbury [Portbyri], man. (Somers.), ii, 169, 172 ; iv, 645
Portchester, ii, 32, 76, 96, 164, 181, 186 ; iii, 140, 151-61 ; iv, 346 ; v, 85 *n*, 307, 319 *n*, 328 *n*, 360, 365, 368, 400 ; adv., ii, 20,

Portchester (*cont.*)
21 ; iii, 161 ; char., iii, 161 ; ch., ii, 241, 247 ; iii, 159 ; man., iii, 158 ; pop., v, 441 ; Rom. rem., i, 324, 326, 328-30, 346 ; iii, 154 ; v, 359 ; sch., ii, 402
Portchester, Edw. of, ii, 155
Portchester Castle, ii, 166, 328-30 ; iii, 151-58 ; iv, 373 ; v, 462, 463
Portchester Forest, ii, 189 ; iii, 158
Porter (le), John, iii, 146 ; v, 546 ; Rich., v, 50 ; Mrs., iv, 547 ; —, v, 197
Portesmutha, *see* Portsmouth
Porteus, Beilby, ii, 197 ; v, 65
Portewey (Overton), iv, 211
Portfield (Christchurch), v, 83, 85, 86
Portington, *see* Partington
Portland, isle of, (Dors.), iii, 87
Portland, Frances Weston, ctss. of, iv, 470 ; v, 339 ; Eliz. Bentinck, dchss. of, iii, 466 ; iv, 450 ; dks. of, ii, 181 ; iv, 250, 640 *n* ; v, 547, 551, 553, 555 ; Hen. Bentinck, iii, 279 ; iv, 450 ; Will. Bentinck, iii, 466 ; Will. H. Cavendish, iv, 450 ; earls of :— Jerome Weston, iv, 470 ; v, 224, 225, 337, 338 ; Rich. Weston, v, 54, 157, 224
Portland Cement Manufacturers, v, 268
Portlande, Thos., ii, 157, 158
Portlandis, Ralph de, *see* Revelendus
Portman, vsct., v, 134
Portman, Sir Hen., iv, 456 ; Sir Hugh, iv, 456 ; Sir John, iii, 106 ; iv, 456 ; Sir Will., iv, 456
Porton (Wilts.), ii, 159 ; iv, 406 *n*
Porton, de, Geoff., iv, 501, 519, 524 ; Rob., iv, 519, 524
Port-reeves Meadow (Overton), iv, 212
Portrenemede [Portrevenmede], (Christchurch), v, 85, 87 *n*
Portsdown, hund., iii, 140 ; v, 324, 328 *n*, 356
Portsdown Hill, iii, 172 ; v, 455
Portsea, ii, 73, 101, 102, 168, 486 ; iii, 130, 140, 141, 172, 191 ; v, 400, 412 *n*, 425, 430, 434, 455 ; adv., ii, 21, 291 ; iii, 197 ; char., iii, 201 ; ch., iii, 197 ; man., ii, 182, 186 ; iii, 192 ; pop., v, 450 ; printing, v, 461 ; racing, v, 543 ; salt ind., v, 470
Portsea, (de, of), Ad., iii, 192 ; Adeliza, iii, 414 ; And., iii, 192, 194, 414 ; iv, 457 ; Bald., ii, 226 ; iii, 192, 414 ; Rich., iii, 192, 414 ; iv, 457
Portsea harriers, v, 536
Portsmouth, ii, 93, 98, 102, 139, 154, 165, 168, 203, 207, 291, 386 ; iii, 140, 172-202 ; v, 259, 293, 306, 311, 312, 318, 319, 324, 328 *n*, 329, 335, 338, 349, 353, 356, 359-408, 409, 423, 426, 427, 428, 430, 431, 432, 433, 450, 546, 576 ; char., iii, 200 ; chs., iii, 191, 197 ; dockyard, iii, 173 ; v, 370, 372, 380, 385, 387, 391, 398, 402-8, 458 ; God's House, *see* that title ; ind., v, 451, 461, 468, 469, 474 ; mkts. and fairs, iii, 182, 183 ; v, 416 ; Nonconf., iii, 199 ; pop., v, 450 ; racing, v, 543 ; Rom. Caths., iii, 199 ; schs., ii, 387, 390, 391, 402, 403
Portsmouth, Louise, dchss. of, iii, 184 ; earls of : iv, 287, 288, 289, 290, 296, 371, 434, 534, 611 ; v, 554 ; Isaac N. Wallop, iv, 532 ;

Portsmouth (*cont.*)
John Wallop, iii, 361 ; iv, 146, 289, 409 ; v, 224, 289 ; Newton Fellowes, iv, 289 ; v, 521 ; Newton Wallop, iv, 146, 147, 409
Portsmouth, (de, of), Edm., iv, 139 ; Nich., ii, 208 ; Piers, v, 50
Portsmouth and Arundel Canal, v, 452
Portswood, iii, 481, 487, 491 ; v, 454 ; priory, *see* St. Denis, priory of, (Southampton)
Portus Adurni, i, 330
Port Way, iv, 299
Posbrook [Posbroke, Postbrook], man. (Titchfield), ii, 186 ; iii, 228
Posingeworth, John de, iv, 450
Potbottom Farm (Laverstoke), iv, 222
Potbridge, iv, 109
Potenalesland (Heckfield), iv, 45
Potenger [Pottinger, Potynger], John, ii, 259, 325, 331, 366 ; v, 30 ; Rich., iv, 19
Poteria, de, Jas., iv, 531 ; John, iv, 531 *n* ; Matt., iv, 530, 531, 532 ; v, 304 *n*
Pothecary, Frank, iv, 525, 527 ; Walt., iv, 527 ; —, iii, 437
Potier, Claude, v, 491
Potrey Court (Over Wallop), iv, 532
Potte, la, (Odiham), iv, 93, 94
Potter's Fore, Little, (Itchel), iv, 6
Pottery, v, 454, 490 ; A.S., i, 396 ; Brythonic, i, 262 ; Jutish, i, 387 ; Rom., i, 268, 275, 284, 288, 289, 290, 294, 295, 297, 300, 302, 303, 304, 305, 306, 307, 309, 310, 311, 312, 313, 315, 316, 317, 318, 326, 327, 328, 334, 341, 345, 347, 348, 349, 370
Pottery Common (Grately), iv, 371
Pottery Drove (Over Wallop), iv, 530
Pottery Farm (East Wellow), iv, 535
Pottery Field (Over Wallop), iv, 530
Pottinger, *see* Potenger
Potts, Rog., v, 143
Potynger, *see* Potenger
Poukelond (Bentley), iv, 27
Poukelond (Longstock), iv, 449
Poule, *see* Poole
Poulett, Will. Hen., earl, v, 527 ; Ann, Lady, v, 168 ; John, Ld., v, 168
Poulett, W. P., v, 507, 513, 514, 523 ; *see also* Orde-Powlett & Paulet
Poulner (Ringwood), iv, 606, 612, 613, 632
Poulner, North, (Ringwood), iv, 606
Poulter, J., ii, 357
Poultons (Overton), iv, 215
Poultry, price of, v, 495, 496
Pounde (Hurstbourne Tarrant), iv, 321
Pounde [Pound, Pownde], Ant., iii, 54, 124, 131, 150, 242 ; v, 174, 237 *n* ; Eliz., ii, 516 ; iii, 149, 163 ; iv, 194 ; Ellen, v, 237 *n* ; Hen., iii, 149 ; Honor [Honora], iii, 131 ; v, 174 ; (Sir) John, ii, 516 ; iii, 124, 150, 242 ; iv, 194 ; v, 174 ; Kath., v, 174 ; Mary, v, 174 ; Mercy, iii, 124 ; Rich., iii, 54, 124, 242 ; v, 174 ; Thos., iii, 124, 149, 150 ; v, 237 ; Will., iii, 54, 124, 149, 163, 242 ; v, 174, 326 ; fam., arms, iii, 53
Poundesolte, man., *see* Punsholt
Pounds [Poundes], John, iii, 202 ; Thos., ii, 86
Pounteslondes (Christchurch), v, 85
Poussant, John, ii, 222
Poveray, Ad., v, 48

Powderham (Crondall), i, 346
Powell [Ap Hoel, Powel], Capt.
  Buckworth, v, 569; Emma, v,
  213; Harcourt, v, 213; Maj.
  Hen. L., v, 84; Hen. M., v, 573,
  574; John, iv, 611; John H., v,
  213; Joshua, iv, 658; Lewis, v,
  92 n; Mary A., v, 213; Thos., v,
  213; Will. M., iv, 631; —, ii, 339
Power, John, iv, 450; Thos., iv, 289
Powerscourt, Rich. Wingfield, Ld.,
  iii, 161
Powes, Emma, ii, 130
Powleslane (Newport), v, 262
Powlett, see Paulet and Poulett
Powling Meade (Odiham), iv, 88
Pownall, Capt. Philemon, v, 391
Pownde, see Pound
Powney, Maj. Cecil du P., iii, 334;
  Rev. Hen., iv, 369, 384, 530
Powys, Eleanor, Lady, iv, 427, 430;
  Lds.: Edw. Charlton, ii, 475;
  iv, 347, 348, 427, 430; Edw.
  Grey, ii, 475; John Grey, ii, 475,
  476; iv, 347, 348
Poyly (de), Annora, v, 262; Hen.,
  v, 262; John, v, 262; Jordan,
  v, 262; Will., v, 262
Poynet, John, see Winchester, bps.
  of
Poynings [Poyninges] (de), Sir
  Adrian, iv, 97; Alice, iv, 116,
  159, 193, 194; Constance, iii,
  9; iv, 116, 193; Eleanor, iv, 159;
  Sir Hugh, iv, 116, 159; Isabel, ii,
  496; iii, 9, 59, 239, 269; iv, 116,
  141, 159, 193, 337, 372, 433;
  v, 98; Joan, iv, 496; iv, 116, 141,
  193, 194; Sir Luke, ii, 496; iii,
  239, 269; iv, 116, 141, 159, 193,
  337, 372, 433; Mary, iv, 97;
  Philippa, iii, 227; (Sir) Thos., ii,
  228, 496; iii, 227, 263, 269; iv,
  97, 116, 141, 159, 193, 337, 388,
  433; fam., arms, ii, 497; iii, 263
Poynter, John, iv, 443; v, 484
Poyntz (de), Fran., iv, 604; Jane,
  iv, 604; Sir John, iv, 604; v,
  118; Sir Nich., iv, 456; Will. S.,
  iii, 78; —, v, 514
Poyntz-Sanderson, Mrs., iii, 144
Praeres, Rob. de, v, 304 n
Prallingworth, iii, 209, 217
Pranell, Agnes, iii, 327; —, iii, 327
Pratellis, de, see Priaulx
Pratt [Prat], Hen., ii, 486; John,
  iv, 643; v, 29, 460; Rich., iii, 344
Pratt's Down (Hurstbourne Priors),
  iv, 288
Preaux, see Priaulx
Preishawe, man., see Preshaw
Premslond, see Princelet
Prentis, Geo., iv, 256
Presbyterians, ii, 515; iii, 199,
  534; iv, 4, 98, 266, 558, 594, 613;
  v, 109, 132, 136
Preselande, see Presland
Preshaw, man. (Corhampton), ii,
  121; iii, 251
Preshaw House (Corhampton), iii,
  251
Presland [Preselande], Rog. de, ii,
  127, 161
Press, John, v, 521
Presshawe, man., see Preshaw
Prestall, Isabel, iii, 387; John, iii,
  387
Prestcote, John, iv, 338 n
Preste Candevere, see Preston Can-
  dover
Prestetone, see Preston
Presthawe, see Preshaw
Prestlond (Romsey), iv, 452
Preston, man. (St. Helens), v, 188,
  191, 212

Preston, Ld., iv, 345
Preston, (de), Alice, ii, 150; Anne,
  v, 127; Caleb, v, 127; Chris., iv,
  278; Ivo, v, 164 n; John, v, 161;
  Juliana, v, 161; Kath., iv, 278;
  Mary, iv, 105; Silvester, v,
  211 n; Will., ii, 177
Preston Candover, ii, 187; iii, 355,
  356, 371-7; iv, 66; adv., iii,
  377; char., iii, 377; ch., iii, 376;
  man., ii, 164, 168; iii, 372;
  pop., v, 440; Rom. rem., i, 306,
  344; sch., ii, 403
Preston Vavasour [Preston Trub-
  ville, Preston Vavesor, Preston
  Vavisor] (St. Helens), v, 192
Prestyngton, see Preston
Pretyman, Geo., see Tomline
Prevetmede (Bramley), iv, 141
Previtteschernaker (Sherborne St.
  John), iv, 158
Preymead, le, (Crondall), iv, 6
Priaulx [Pratellis, Preaux], (de),
  Ingram, iv, 443; John, v, 123;
  Pet., ii, 474; v, 290, 453, 486;
  Will., ii, 474, 479
Price, Georgina, v, 158; Godf., iii,
  84, 109, 111; O. T., v, 570;
  Rob., iv, 484; Uvedale, iv, 484;
  Will., ii, 387; Mrs., v, 542
Prickett, Will., ii, 91
Priddle, Little, (Whitchurch), iv,
  300
Priddle, Hen. C., v, 170, 189
Pride, Thos., iii, 178
Prideaux, Nich., iii, 431, 469;
  Rog., iii, 469;
Prideaux-Brune, (Rev.) Chas., iii,
  219; v, 108; Chas. G., iii, 219;
  Rev. Edw. S., iii, 219
Priestlands (Romsey), iv, 468
Priest Wood (Tunworth), iv, 174
Prince, Hen., v, 48 n; Sam., iv,
  107, 175
Princelet, man. (Newchurch), v, 184
Prince of Wales's harriers, v, 535,
  539
Printing, v, 461
Prior, Aubrey, iv, 460 n; Christine,
  iii, 373; iv, 214; Edw., iv, 249;
  Emma, iv, 548; Ingilram [Ingel-
  ram], iii, 373; iv, 214; Jemima
  F. S., iii, 432; John, iii, 373;
  iv, 214, 215, 500 n, 548; Rob.,
  iv, 460 n
Prior's Acre (New Forest), ii, 450,
  451
Prior's Barton, man. (Winchester),
  v, 19
Prior's Barton House (Winchester),
  v, 19
Priorscourt, see Longstock with
  Millstreet
Priors Dean, iii, 63; iv, 415, 423,
  436-7; adv., iv, 437; chap., iv,
  437; mans., ii, 164; iv, 436; pop.,
  v, 444
Prior's Downe (Long Sutton), iv,
  18
Prior's Freshwater (Freshwater),
  v, 240, 242
Prior's Lodging (Christchurch), v,
  95
Prior's Withie (Christchurch), v, 85
Priorswood, ii, 177
Priory, tithing (Andover), iv, 346
Priory (Odiham), iv, 87
Priory (St. Helens), v, 190
Priory Farm (Andwell), iv, 176
Priory Manor (Stratfieldsaye), iv,
  61
Pritchard [Pritchare], Geo., iii,
  101; John, ii, 31; iii, 101
Privett [Privet], iii, 63, 302, 303,
  336; v, 295 n; adv., iii, 336;

Privett (cont.)
  ch., iii, 336; v, 463; man., iii,
  336; pop., v, 444; sch., ii, 403
Prospect (Monxton), iv, 379
Prosperous (Hurstbourne Tarrant),
  iv, 319
Prosteton, see Preston
Prouesdell (Laverstoke), iv, 208
Prujean, John, iii, 487
Prullethorne (Abbotts Ann), iv,
  334 n
Prury, man., see Pury
Pryfetesflod, see Privett
Prymesflode, see Princelet
Prynnees Mead (W. Wellow), iv,
  535
Pryors Meade (Whitchurch), iv, 300
Pryvate, Pryvet, see Privett
Pseudo-Bombyces, i, 141
Pterophori, i, 153
Puckaster Cove (Niton), i, 318,
  325; v, 187
Pucknall [Puckinhall] (Hursley),
  iii, 401, 421
Puckpool, man. (St. Helens), v,
  192
Puckpool [Cokepole], (de, of), John,
  v, 192, 192 n; Sim., v, 192 n;
  Thos., v, 192 n
Pudding House Farm (Headbourne
  Worthy), iv, 426
Puddle, ii, 131
Puddletown, man., ii, 159
Puddletrenthide, man., ii, 121
Pudsey, —, v, 373
Puingiant, Rich., iii, 477
Pukenhale, see Pucknall
Pulchra Quercu, Will. de, ii, 225
Puller, Thos., v, 43
Pullie, see Pooley
Pulteney, John, iv, 646; v, 123;
  John G. B., iv, 646; Keppel, iv,
  616, 646, 647; v, 119, 123
Pulto, John de, iv, 618
Punchard, Rob. de, iii, 415
Punchardon [Pontchardun, Pun-
  chardoun], (de), Alice, iv, 605;
  Anne, iv, 315, 316, 563; Bart.,
  iv, 315, 318, 563 n; Eliz., iv,
  563; Florence, iv, 315 n, 316,
  563 n; Giles, iv, 315 n, 316;
  Hawis, iv, 605; Hen., iv,
  315 n, 316; John, iv, 315, 579;
  v, 238 n; Margery, iv, 563 n;
  Maud, iv, 224, 315, 563, 579,
  605; Oliver, iv, 314, 315, 316,
  317, 318, 326, 563 n, 605; v,
  305; Philippa, iv, 315, 563;
  Rich., iv, 315, 563, 566; Rob.,
  iv, 315, 552, 563, 605; Sybil, iv,
  579; Walt., iv, 315, 316; Will.,
  iv, 563, 605; fam., iv, 604 n
Punchardons, see Faccombe Punchardon
Punda, Ralph de, iii, 239
Punkerton's Woode (Faccombe),
  iv, 317
Punsholt [Punsalls, Punsholes, Pun-
  sold], man. (W. Meon), iii, 344
Pupeholemeade (Liss), iv, 84
Puppellebere (Priors Dean), iv, 436
Purbeck, Sarah, iii, 536
Purbrook (Farlington), iii, 148;
  adv., iii, 151; ch., iii, 151
Purcell, Thos., iv, 433, 434
Purchas, Thos., ii, 187; Will., iv,
  247
Purchier, Will., ii, 375
Purde, Joyce, ii, 486; Will., ii, 486
Purdue, John, v, 95; Will., iv, 344,
  376
Purefoy, Capt. Rich. P., iii, 370,
  375; fam., arms, iii, 375
Purewell (Christchurch), v, 109
Purkiss, —, v, 457 n

Purschite, man. (Romsey), see Spurshot
Purtockes (Vernhams Dean), iv, 329
Purvis, A. B., iv, 595 ; Sir John B., iv, 595 ; John C., iv, 595 ; Mrs., iv, 595 n
Pury, man. (Bentley), iv, 9, 28
Pury, John, ii, 113 ; Will., iv, 601
Pushall, Charlotte, v, 148 ; Rob , v, 148
Puteleorde, see Pittleworth
Putham, man. (Heckfield), iv, 46, 47
Putnam, see Puttenham
Putt [Putte], (de la), Rich., ii, 177 ; iii, 46 ; v, 198 ; Thos., ii, 339
Putte, man. (Hambledon), iii, 242
Puttenham [Putnam], Alice, iv, 105; Anne, iv, 105, 225 ; Geo., iv, 105 ; Hen., iii, 262 ; iv, 105, 232 ; Marg., iv, 105 ; Mary, iv, 225, 232 ; Rich., iv, 105, 142, 232 ; v, 135 ; Rob., iv, 105 ; v, 327 n ; Will., iv, 105, 232
Puttoc, Elfric, ii, 114
Putton [Puttoun], (de), Jas., iv, 523 ; John, iii, 415 ; iv, 523 ; Will., ii, 193 ; iv, 506, 523
Pycarde, see Pickard
Pychehornes (Kingsclere), iv, 250
Pyckerett (Milton), v, 124
Pydeford, see Pidford
Pye [Pie], Ant., iv, 110 ; Marg., iv, 97 ; (Sir) Thos., iv, 97 ; v, 393, 394
Pyel, see Pyle
Pyke [Pyk], Aubrey, iv, 548 ; (Rev.) John, iv, 394 n, 548 ; see also Pike
Pykmerscrofte (Faccombe), iv, 314
Pykydnede (King's Somborne), iv, 470
Pylcote, see Pilcot
Pyle [Pyel], (de), Edw., iv, 371, 534 ; Eleanor, iv, 532 ; Hen., iv, 532 ; Jane, iv, 427 ; John, iv, 532 ; Marg., iv, 532 ; Thos., v, 191 n ; Warin, ii, 231 ; Will., ii, 301 ; Dr., v, 79 ; see also Pile
Pyle Farm (Chale), v, 148 n
Pylewell Park (Boldre), iv, 616
Pyncke, see Pincke
Pyncroft (Farley Chamberlayne), iv, 443
Pynder, see Pindar
Pyngbrygge, Edw., ii, 259, 260
Pynke, see Pinke
Pynkemere (Faccombe), iv, 314
Pynmour, le, (Sherborne St. John), iv, 158, 167
Pynson, R., ii, 294
Pyntun, Ad., v, 305
Pyot's Hill (Basing), iv, 115, 123 n
Pypering, John, iii, 498
Pypulbere, see Puppellebere
Pyralides, i, 144
Pyrrye, Will., iv, 597
Pytt, see Pitt
Pytte House (Christchurch), v, 130
Pytteney, Rich. de, iv, 590

Quabbe, see Quob
Quakers, see Friends, Society of
Quarley, iv, 198, 333, 338, 344, 369, 380, 385-7 ; adv., iv, 386 ; ch., iv, 385 ; man., iv, 342, 385 ; pop., v, 438 ; sch., ii, 403
Quarley, Thos. de, iv, 338, 339
Quarley Hill, iv, 385
Quarr Abbey, i, 348 ; ii, 11, 37, 56, 104, 137-9 ; iv, 619, 620, 646, 654 ; v, 91 n, 141, 142, 143, 147, 148,

Quarr Abbey (cont.)
150, 151, 152-4, 155, 159, 181, 182 n, 184, 198, 213, 215, 230, 243, 256, 259, 261, 274, 275, 312, 418, 462, 469, 470 ; mill, v, 94, 135 ; quarries, v, 462 ; tanneries, v, 455 ; wool trade, v, 476
Quarr House estate (Binstead), v, 152
Quarrying, v, 462-3
Quay Gate (Yarmouth), v, 286
Quedementune, see Corhampton
Queenes tenement, le, (Penton Mewsey), iv, 381
Queen's Bower [Queen Bower] (Newchurch), v, 162 n, 184
Queen's Camel (Somers.), see Camel
Queen's College (Oxf.), ii, 203, 204, 228, 386, 495, 496 ; iii, 55, 386, 412 ; iv, 142, 145, 158, 228, 231, 238, 354, 377, 378, 379, 399, 435 ; v, 123, 230, 234, 263, 270, 271 ; arms, iii, 527
Queen's Coppice (Melchet Park), iv, 540
Queen's Court man., see Tytherley, East, man.
Queen's Pavilion (Aldershot), iv, 2
Queenwood College (W. Tytherley), iv, 519 ; v, 446 n
Queenwood Farm (East Tytherley), iv, 515
Quercu, see Oake
Querle, Will., v, 242 n
Queynte, see Quintin
Quickthorne, —, v, 182
Quidhampton (Overton), ii, 162 ; iv, 197, 200, 210, 282 n ; chap., iv, 218 ; man., ii, 163 ; iv, 215 ; mills, iv, 216
Quidhampton, fam., see Quydhampton
Quidington, man., see Marvell
Quin, Rich. G., iii, 469
Quinci [Quincy], (de), Marg., iv, 607 ; Maud, ii, 149 ; Seyer, iv, 607
Quintan's Plantation (Steventon), iv, 171 n
Quintin [Queynte, Quyntyn], (de, le), Hugh, iv, 507, 616, 618 ; John, iv, 507 ; Rich., iv, 476, 507 n ; Will., ii, 154, 155, 160 ; v, 109
Quob (Titchfield), iii, 229
Quob Copse (Titchfield), iii, 229
Quob Farm (Titchfield), iii, 229
Quor, Rich., v, 183
Quydhampton [Quidhampton], Eliz. iii, 48 ; Iseult, iii, 48 ; John, iii, 48
Quyntyn, see Quintin
Qwharley, see Quarley

Race Close (West Wellow), iv, 535
Racing, v, 543
Rackhams Meadow (Christchurch), ii, 159 ; v, 85, 95 n
Radcliff, ii, 159
Radcliffe, A. N., iv, 586 ; Rev. C. D., iii, 224 ; Delmé, v, 526 n ; Eliz., iii, 224 ; Col. Emilius C., iii, 224 ; —, iv, 430 ; fam., arms, iii, 224 ; see also Radclyffe and Ratcliffe
Radclyffe, Chas. J., iv, 325 ; (Sir) Hen., iii 150, 189 ; v, 174, 177, 331 ; Honora, iii, 150 ; iv, 174 ; Rob., iii, 150 ; v, 174 ; fam., arms, iii, 131 ; see also Radcliffe and Ratcliffe
Radford, Arth., iv, 561 n ; Eliz., iv, 561 n ; Matilda, iii, 214, 241 ; Thos., iii, 214, 241

Radstock, Ld., iii, 297
Radyng, de, John, iii, 89 ; Marg., iii, 89 ; Maud, iii, 89 ; Will., iii, 89 ; see also Reading
Ragged Appleshaw (Weyhill), iv, 395
Ragge Park Wood (Upton), iv, 330
Ragget [Raggot], John, ii, 444 ; Rich., iv, 98
Raggs, the, (Andover), iv, 321
Railways, v, 434
Rainald [Reginald], iv, 512 ; v, 159, 273 n, 455 ; bp. of Ross, ii, 153 ; prior of Christchurch, ii, 153, 160
Rainer, see Reiner
Raleigh, (de), Sir Edw., v, 238 ; Geo., v, 181, 238 ; Hen., v, 238 ; Joan, v, 200, 238 ; John, v, 238, 238 n ; Mabel, v, 238 ; Sim., v, 201, 238 ; Thos., v, 146 n, 182, 200, 238, 238 n ; Sir Walt., iv, 345 ; v, 334 ; Will., v, 182, 238 ; see also Winchester, bps. of ; —, v, 374
Ralph [Ralf, Raoul], iv, 145, 339, 341, 342, 351 ; iv, 579 ; v, 129 ; dean of Twyneham, ii, 152, 160 ; prior of Andwell, ii, 222, 225 ; prior of Christchurch, ii, 153, 160 ; prior of St. Cross, ii, 222 ; rector of Dibden, iv, 658 ; reeve of Newtown, iv, 293 ; of Waterville, v, 304 n
Ramehill Field (Overton), iv, 211
Rammesdelle, see Ramsdell
Rammesholte (Kingsclere), iv, 250
Ramridge, man. (Weyhill), iv, 394, 395, 397 ; Rom. rem., i, 297 ; iv, 395
Ramridge House (Weyhill), iv, 394, 395
Ramsay, see Ramsey
Ramsbury, Edm., de, ii, 156, 160
Ramsdean (East Meon), iii, 65
Ramsdell [Ramsdale] (Wootton St. Lawrence), iv, 219, 239 ; ch., iv, 242 ; sch., iv, 247
Ramsey [Ramsay], Edw., v, 175, 180, 184 ; Jas., ii, 272 ; John, v, 180 ; Rob., v, 180
Ramsholte (Deane), iv, 205
Ranckhams, see Rackham's Meadow
Rande, Ralph, iii, 35 ; Rob., iv, 622 n
Randell, Chas., iv, 26 ; John C., iv, 21, 26 ; Rich., v, 115
Randolph [Randolf, Randulf], Rev. Chas., iv, 373 ; Chas. F., iv, 373 ; Joan, iv, 199, 226 ; v, 118 ; John, ii, 128 ; iii, 158 ; iv, 199, 226 ; v, 118 ; Mary A., iv, 373 ; Will., iv, 366, 374
Ranelagh, Selina, Lady, iv, 522 ; Arth., Ld., iv, 522
Ranley (Milford), v, 116
Rannulf, iv, 560
Ransom [Ransome], John, v, 458 ; Mrs., iv, 139
Rante, Rog., iv, 365
Ranville [Raunville], de, Lucy, iii, 414, 457 ; Marg., iv, 457 ; Rich., iii, 414 ; iv, 457 ; Will., iii, 241
Raoul, see Ralph
Rascalls, see Rastalls
Rashleigh, Jonathan, iii, 159, 227, 234, 235 ; Phil., iii, 159, 234
Rashley, Chas., iv, 623
Rastall [Restall], John, iii, 80 ; iv, 225, 226 ; Nich., iv, 225, 226 ; Rose, iv, 226, 228 ; Walt., iv, 226, 228
Rastalls [Rastawells] (Church Oakley), iv, 226

Rat (Arreton), v, 140
Ratcliffe, Rev. Thos., v, 177 ; see also Radcliffe and Radclyffe
Rath rise (Carisbrooke), v, 229 n
Rat Island, see Burrow Island
Rattlesden, de, Eleanor, v, 162 ; Sir John, v, 162
Raudon (Carisbrooke), v, 230
Raumpenz, Hugh de, iv, 373
Raunville, see Ranville
Ravelin, iv, 254
Ravenesholme, John de, iv, 28 n
Ravenhill (Overton), iv, 211
Ravensbeake (Beaulieu), iv, 650
Ravens Cot Farm (Pamber), iv, 433
Ravenscroft, —, iv, 170
Rawden, Col., v, 341
Rawlins, G., v, 522 ; —, iv, 458 n
Rawlinson, Eleanor, iv, 363 ; John, iv, 363
Rawstorne, H. F., iii, 210, 214
Ray, Rob., iv, 81, 98
Raydon, grange, ii, 147
Raymond, prior, ii, 194
Raymond, Eliz., Lady, iv, 271 ; (Sir) Jemmett, iv, 271, 272
Raynbird & Co., v, 459
Raynolds, see Reynolds
Rayny, de, John, iii, 229 ; Will., iii, 229
Raynysford, Jane, ii, 125
Reachmore (Bramshaw), iv, 623
Read [Reade, Rede, Reed], Alex., iv, 527 ; Alice, iv, 318 ; Andr., iv, 316, 318, 325, 363, 507 ; Anne, iv, 318 ; Barth., iv, 338, 339 ; Cecily, ii, 130 ; Edw., iv, 136, 317 ; v, 99 ; Eliz., iv, 278, 338 ; Fran., iv, 316, 317 ; Geo., iv, 317 ; Hen., iv, 316, 317, 318, 424 ; Innocent, iv, 278, 327, 531 ; John, ii, 293, 365, 366 ; iv, 327, 339, 384, 399, 516, 518 ; Marg., iv, 527 ; Moses, v, 339 ; Nich., iv, 327, 527, 531, 532 ; (Sir) Rich., ii, 290 ; iv, 316, 324, 327, 530, 531, 534 ; Rob., iv, 301, 316, 318, 325 ; v, 483 ; Thos., iv, 327 ; Will., iv, 339 ; see also Reid
Reading, abbot of, iv, 595
Reading [Redyng], John, ii, 364 ; v, 27 ; Will., iv, 349 ; see also Radyng
Readinges (Kingsclere), iv, 250
Reading University College, v, 511
Rea Transport Co., v, 458
Rebert, Will., v, 213
Rebez, John de, v, 11
Rechesburna, see Rockbourne
Redan Hill (Aldershot), iv, 4
Redbridge (Millbrook), i, 380 ; iii, 430 ; v, 39, 362, 429 n, 458
Redbridge, hund., iv, 544 ; v, 324, 331
Redburgh, Adam de, iv, 548
Redcliff (Yaverland), v, 206
Reddysdale, Lucy, iv, 16 ; Rich., iv, 16
Rede, see Read
Rede Engge (Heckfield), iv, 45
Redenham, man. (Fyfield), iv, 358, 367 ; chap., iv, 368 ; Rom. rem., i, 294
Redenham, de, Joan, iv, 367 ; Rog., iv, 367 ; Thos., iv, 367
Redenham House (Fyfield), iv, 366, 387
Redfields (Crookham), iv, 5
Redhill (Medstead), ii, 483
Reding (King's Somborne), iv, 470
Redlands (E. Wellow), iv, 535
Redman, Rich., bp. of St. Asaph, ii, 185
Redmead (Arreton), v, 142 n
Redmond, —, iv, 398

Redrice House (Upper Clatford), iv, 359
Redstreat Meade, le, (Crondall), iv, 6
Redvers, de, Adeliza, ii, 154 ; v, 164 n ; Agnes, iv, 226 ; Bald., ii, 137, 152, 153, 154, 168, 203, 230 ; iv, 597, 598, 620, 622, 640, 641, 643, 645, 648 ; v, 83, 86, 87, 90, 91, 94, 95, 96, 112, 114, 115, 123, 128, 132, 141, 152, 188, 213, 220, 232, 241, 279, 286, 303 ; Gerold, iv, 226 ; Hawise, ii, 154, 155 ; Hugh, ii, 168 ; iv, 553, 597, 598, 601 ; Joan, iv, 645 n ; John, v, 91 ; Mary, iv, 645 n ; Rich., ii, 152, 153, 154, 231 ; iv, 620, 622, 645 ; v, 86, 88, 90, 91, 94, 96, 98, 100, 114, 115, 123, 132, 135, 136, 141, 151, 164 n, 171, 174, 180, 184, 188, 222, 224, 227, 234, 241, 242, 256, 260, 263, 273, 284, 285, 288, 469 ; Will., ii, 137, 154, 203, 230 ; iv, 553, 640, 645 n ; v, 87, 91, 94, 114, 125, 172, 183, 188, 224, 230, 234, 243, 245, 263, 270, 271, 274, 291, 470 ; fam., v, 305 ; see also Rivers
Redway, man. (Arreton), v, 148
Redyng, see Reading
Reed, see Read
Reedes, le, (Heckfield), iv, 45
Reedes (Whitchurch), iv, 300
Reeve [Reve, Reyve], Anne, iv, 495 ; Chas., iv, 568 ; Joan, iv, 621 ; John, iv, 621 ; Rob., iii, 178 ; Rog., ii, 373 ; v, 42 ; Thos., iv, 623 ; v, 132, 155, 177
Reeves, Geo., iii, 427 ; Will., v, 524 ; —, iv, 348 ; see also Ryves
Regge (Eling), iv, 547
Regill, Rob., iv, 289
Reginald, see Rainald
Reid, Andr., iii, 144 ; see also Read
Reigate, Hen. de, iv, 527
Reignolds, Eliz., iv, 147 ; see also Reynolds
Reiner [Rainer], ii, 254, 255 ; the dyer, v, 277
Religious houses, ii, 104
Remi, iv, 443
Remington, Eleanor [Elinor], Lady, iv, 143, 166 ; Sir Rob., iv, 143, 166
Renawd, John, iii, 526, 528
Rende, Hen., v, 29, 42
Renigh, Rob., v, 373
Renne, Joan, iv, 166 n
Renneger [Reneger, Renniger], John, iv, 216, 494, 497 ; Marg., iv, 215 ; Mich., iii, 412 ; iv, 215, 216, 226, 493 ; Rob., iv, 493, 494, 497
Rennell, Thos., ii, 115 ; v, 78
Rennett, Chas., iii, 343
Renniger, see Renneger
Rents, v, 502, 504, 505, 510
Repingdon, Phil., bp. of Lincoln, ii, 42
Repling, Ad. of, iii, 400
Reptiles, i, 43, 204
Reresby, Eliz., Lady, iv, 105 ; Sir Geo., iv, 105 ; Mary, iv, 105 ; Tamworth, iv, 105
Resel, Will., iv, 93
Restall, see Rastall
Restwold, Rich., iv, 395 n
Ret, Alwin, iv, 519
Retheresfield, see Rotherfield
Retherwyke, see Rotherwick
Reve, see Reeve
Revel, Will., iv, 49
Revelendus [Ralph de Portlandis], iv, 47, 226 n
Revenore, see Rowner

Rew, man. (Godshill), v, 173, 464
Rewalan [Rivallonus], abbot of Newminster, ii, 117, 121, 474 ; iv, 47
Rewe, see Rew
Rewfield (Godshill), v, 173 n
Rey, Sampson le, v, 466 n
Reynardson, Edw. B., iv, 549 ; Sam., iv, 476 ; Sarah, iv, 476 ; Vere H., iv, 549 ; Vere H. B., iv, 546
Reynold, see Reynolds
Reynoldham (Mottisfont), iv, 503
Reynolds [Raynolds, Reynold], (de), Cath., iii, 535 ; Chas., iv, 632 n ; Eliz., iv, 200 ; Joane, ii, 501 ; John, ii, 315 ; John H., v, 256 ; Rev. Joshua, iii, 451 ; Sir J. R., iv, 453 ; Priscilla, iv, 75 ; Rich., iii, 184 ; (Sir) Rob., ii, 197 ; iii, 199, 277, 312 ; iv, 75, 76, 200 ; Thos., v, 114 ; Walt., ii, 150 ; Will., v, 117 ; see also Reignolds
Reyson, John, iv, 570 ; Rich., iv, 570
Reyve, see Reeve
Rhinefield (Brockenhurst), iv, 626
Rhodes, Jos., iii, 458 ; Rich., iii, 458
Ricardo, Mortimer, v, 110 ; Mrs., v, 84
Rice [Ricz, Rys], Ant., v, 174 ; Chas., iv, 649 ; John, v, 172, 173 ; Thos., v, 172, 180
Rich [Riche], (la, le), Alex., v, 476 ; Alice, iv, 382, 384 ; Gerv., ii, 202 ; Marg., iii, 367 ; Pet., iv, 107 ; Rog., ii, 203, 205 ; Thos., iv, 382, 384 ; Will., iii, 367
Richard I, ii, 160, 203 ; iii, 46, 173, 174, 176, 182, 487 ; iv, 148, 150, 195, 200, 222, 251, 256, 303, 319, 329, 395, 423, 472, 474, 483, 558, 595 ; v, 270, 306, 360, 415
Richard II, ii, 119, 135, 148, 162, 166, 204, 206, 216, 222, 231, 232, 267, 305, 425, 475 ; iv, 133, 147, 231, 244, 263, 334, 369, 395, 560, 598 ; v, 222, 257, 266, 267, 273
Richard III, ii, 143 ; iv, 185, 199, 206, 348 n, 516, 528, 624 ; v, 320
Richard, king of the Romans, see Cornwall, earl of
Richard, v, 28, 191 ; abbot of Hales-owen, ii, 184 ; abbot of Titch-field, ii, 181, 186 ; bishop's ser-jeant, iv, 211 ; canon of Nor-wich, ii, 123 ; the clerk, iv, 374 ; the dyer, v, 477 ; earl, iv, 563 ; v, 291 ; of Ilchester, ii, 13 ; the merchant, iv, 293 ; parson of St. Lawrence, v, 194 n ; prior of Andwell, ii, 225 ; prior of Barton, ii, 181 ; prior of Christchurch, ii, 170 ; prior of Merton, iv, 51 ; prior of Newplace, ii, 179 ; prior of Selborne, ii, 176, 179 ; le tapener, v, 481 n ; vicar of St. Helen's, v, 193 n
Richards, Anne, v, 208 ; Rev. C., v, 239 ; (Sir) Edw., ii, 485 ; iii, 420 ; v, 157, 191, 206 n, 207, 208 ; Eliz., v, 208 ; E. T., iii, 151 ; Rev. Geo., ii, 392 ; v, 264 ; German, v, 156, 194, 207, 208 ; Hen., iii, 247 ; (Sir) John, iii, 101, 111, 241 ; v, 164, 208 n ; John M., v, 182 ; Maria, iii, 241 ; Rich., iii, 249 ; iv, 523 ; Walt., iv, 94 ; Will., iii, 247 ; Lady, v, 156 n ; —, v, 501, 524
Richardson, Maj. Ivan, iv, 21 ; J. M., v, 546 ; S. W., ii, 386
Riche, la, par., see Ryde
Riche, fam., see Rich

Richemund, *see* Richmond
Richer, iv, 77, 490 *n*; archd. of Winchester, iv, 19; the clerk, iv, 419
Richmond, Marg. Beaufort, ctss. of, iii, 143, 411; iv, 130, 348; v, 92; dks. of, v, 350 *n*, 571; Jas., v, 95 *n*; Edm. Tudor, earl of, iv, 348
Richmond [Richemund] (de), Ad., iv, 213; Anne, iv, 374; John, iv, 374; Legh, ii, 100; v, 206; Thos., iv, 374
Richo, Bart., ii, 220
Ricketts, Geo. W., iii, 334
Rickman, Kath., iv, 554; Rebecca, v, 113, 177; Rob., v, 117; Thos., v, 113, 117; Will., v, 112, 113, 117, 554
Ricz, *see* Rice
Ridding, Rev. Chas. H., iv, 357; Geo., ii, 364, 366; v, 16; Lady Laura, iii, 453; W., v, 576
Riddings Farm (Kingsclere), iv, 250 *n*, 261
Riddlesden, John, iii, 184; Steph., iii, 205
Ride, *see* Ryde
Ridel, Geoff., v, 21
Ridge (Eling), iv, 549
Ridge (Romsey), iv, 452, 468
Ridge [Ridg], Eliz., iii, 184; Geo., iii, 325; Humph., iii, 70; John, iii, 70; (Sir) Thos., ii, 486; iii, 70; iv, 611; v, 513; —, v, 513
Ridges, —, v, 474
Ridgeway, ii, 88
Ridgeway Copse (Laverstoke), iv, 208
Ridgeways (Hurstbourne Tarrant), iv, 321
Ridley, A. W., v, 575; Thos., iii, 334
Ridley Wood (New Forest), ii, 446
Ridout, Chas. E., iv, 631
Ridoutt, —, iii, 184
Rigg [Rigge, Riggs, Rygg], Amb., ii, 93; Edw., v, 27; Marg., iii, 212; Ralph, iii, 212; Rog., iii, 211; Tomysyn, iv, 25; Will, iv, 25
Rigge, la, (King's Somborne), iv, 470
Rigge (Longparish), iv, 406
Rihullemersche (Liss), iv, 84
Rimecuda, iv, 607 *n*
Rincveda, *see* Ringwood
Rinel, John de, iv, 380
Ring, John, iii, 101, 201, 244
Ringbourne [Ringborne, Ryngebourne], Agnes, iv, 419; v, 100, 275; Edith, ii, 317; Kath., iv, 419; Rob., iv, 84, 419 *n*; v, 100; Will., iv, 84, 407, 418, 419; v, 100, 242, 243 *n*, 275
Ringbournes, man. (Barton Stacey), iv, 418
Ringstones (W. Wellow), iv, 535
Ringwood, i, 322, 346; ii, 38, 71, 143, 229, 419; iv, 601, 603, 606-14; v, 109, 564; adv., iv, 612; assessment, v, 423; bridge, v, 429 *n*; char., iv, 613; ch., iv, 611; ind., iv, 606; v, 433, 457, 474, 475, 488; man., ii, 207; iv, 603, 607; v, 219; mkts. and fairs, iv, 609; v, 417, 426; mills, iv, 609; Nonconf., iv, 613; pop., v, 445; schs., ii, 387, 394, 403; iv, 613; volunteers, iv, 356
Ringwood, hund., ii, 420; iv, 603; v, 324, 331
Ringwood, Ant., iv, 510; Chas., iv, 510, 511, 571; Eliz., iv, 510, 511 *n*; Hen., iv, 510, 511, 571; Isab., iv, 510, 511; Jane, iv,

Ringwood (*cont.*)
637; Joan, iv, 510, 571, 605 *n*; John, iv, 510, 511, 571, 637; v, 327; Thos., iv, 510, 571
Riperiis, *see* Rivers
Ripley (Sopley), ii, 159, 421; v, 81, 127, 130
Ripon [Rippon], Will., ii, 138, 139; v, 141
Rippenden, Chris., v, 111
Rippia, Steph. de, ii, 228
Rippon, *see* Ripon
Risely Common (Heckfield), iv, 45
Rishton, ii, 156
Ristone, Hugh de, iv, 618
Rithe, *see* Rythe
Rivallis [Ryeval], Pet. de, ii, 172, 514; v, 32
Rivallonus, *see* Rewalan
Riven, man. (Suss.), v, 77
Rivere, *see* Rivers
River Hill farm (Binsted), ii, 485
Rivers, earls: Ant., v, 219, 223, 225, 285, 290, 320; John, iv, 62; Geo. Pitt, Ld., iv, 22, 46, 51, 57, 59, 60, 61, 62, 63, 216
Rivers [Riperiis, Rivere, Ryvere], (de, de la), Christian, iv, 570 *n*; Dulcibella, iv, 13; Edm., iv, 570 *n*; Sir Geo., iii, 298; Jane, Lady, iv, 61, 62; Joan, iv, 569; v, 116; (Sir) John, ii, 173; iii, 483, 487; iv, 13, 96, 559, 560, 568, 569, 570, 571, 572, 576; v, 147, 165, 174; Juliane, iv, 636; Marcellus, ii, 485; Marg., iii, 487; Margery, iv, 560, 564, 569, 571, 572, 582; Maud, iv, 569; Maurice, v, 207 *n*; Lieut.-Gen. Pitt, iv, 592; Rich., iii, 487; iv, 498, 501, 564, 569 *n*, 582, 589; Thos., v, 116, 117; Will., iv, 498, 537, 636; *see also* Redvers
Riversdown (Warnford), iii, 269
Rivett, Fran., iv, 259, 471, 472
Margery, iv, 259 *n*, 471; —, iv, 470
Rivil, Jonathan, iv, 624
Roach, Reg., v, 147 *n*; W., v, 147; Capt., v, 112
Roads, v, 429, 431, 433, 451, 501; British, i, 262; Roman, i, 270, 294, 309, 318, 319, 320, 321, 322, 326, 358, 378
Roake, man. (Broughton), iv, 495
Robbins, Jas., v, 461; *see also* Robins
Roberd, *see* Roberts
Robert, ii, 206; v, 98, 172, 212, 218; abbot of Netley, ii, 146, 149; abbot of Quarr, ii, 139; the chaplain, v, 86, 205 *n*; dk. of Normandy, iii, 186; iv, 645; v, 300, 301, 360; of Jumièges, v, 298; the priest, v, 270 *n*; prior of Andwell, ii, 225; prior of Breamore, ii, 169, 172; prior of St. Swithun's, ii, 115
Roberts [Roberd], Rev. Ad., iv, 380; Alice, ii, 177; Chas., v, 518; Dorcas, iv, 412 *n*; Edw., v, 150 *n*; Sir Gabriel, iv, 412 *n*; Jasper, v, 110; John, v, 150 *n*; Rich., iii, 101; W., v, 144; Dr. v, 192; Mrs., iv, 140; —, v, 454; fam., v, 147
Robertson, Rev. E., v, 253; Will. T., iv, 1
Robin Hood's Barrow (Bournemouth), v, 134
Robins, Thos., iv, 617, 619; *see also* Robbins
Robinson [Robynson], Chris., ii, 388; Hugh, ii, 315, 331, 366; John, iv, 551 *n*; J. E., iii, 334;

Robinson (*cont.*)
Admiral Mark, iii, 250; Nath., ii, 91, 94; iii, 529, 533; Rich., iv, 75 *n*; Will., v, 235; W. T., v, 554; Mrs., v, 116
Robson, C., v, 575
Robstead, man., ii, 172
Roby, Arth., ii, 191
Robynnet, John, v, 465 *n*
Robynson, *see* Robinson
Robys, Thos., prior of St. Denis, ii, 164
Roche, *see* Roches
Rochebrok (Calbourne), v, 220 *n*
Roche Court (Fareham), iii, 210; iv, 167
Roches [Roche, Rupibus] (de, de la, des), Alice, iii, 256; iv, 172, 202; Beatrice, iv, 253 *n*; Edw., iii, 68; Emma, iii, 229; iv, 202, 289; Geoff., iii, 212, 362, 363; iv, 171, 202; (Sir) Hugh, iii, 229, 263, 363; iv, 172, 202, 539; Joan iii, 52; iv, 173, 202; (Sir) John, iii, 52, 212, 263, 362, 449; iv, 172, 202, 420 *n*; v, 312; Lucy, iii, 212; iv, 172; Martin, iii, 212, 449; iv, 171, 172, 202; v, 305; Mary, iii, 212; iv, 172, 202; Pet., *see* Winchester, bp. of; Will., iv, 420; fam., arms, iii, 52, 212, 263
Rochester, bps. of:—John Fisher, ii, 53; John Hilsey, ii, 54, 190; Walt. de Merton, ii, 105, 208, 209; iv, 130, 134, 138, 148; John Warner, v, 180
Rockbourne [Rockburne], ii, 169, 172; iv, 559, 581-6, 594; v, 414 *n*; adv., iv, 586; char., iv, 586; ch., iv, 581, 584; man., iv, 560, 572, 582, 596; v, 419; pks., iv, 584; pop., v, 445; sch., ii, 403
Rockbourne Down, iv, 581
Rock Close (Longstock), iv, 449
Rockclose (Romsey), iv, 452
Rocke Downe (Broughton), iv, 493
Rocken End (Niton), v, 187
Rockford [Rockford Moyles] (Ellingham), ii, 229; iv, 562, 563, 604; v, 100; chap., iv, 564, 567; man., iv, 564
Rockford Common (Ellingham), iv, 563
Rockford Moyles, tithing (Fordingbridge), iv, 560
Rockhampton, Phil. of, v, 114
Rockstead (Rockbourne), iv, 584
Roclee, *see* Rookley
Rodbrige, *see* Redbridge
Rode, man. (Godshill), *see* Roud
Rode, la, ii, 177
Rodeberge, *see* Rowborough
Rodedic, hund., iv, 603, 615; v, 81
Rodeneye, *see* Rodney
Rodentia, i, 245
Rodeswode Mill (St. Mary Bourne), iv, 295
Rodney, Lds., v, 516; Geo. B. Rodney, iii, 304; iv, 190; v, 399
Rodney [Rodeneye] (de), Jane, iii, 306; Rich., iv, 361, 604; —, v, 499
Roe, Jos. S., iii, 432; Mrs., iv, 83
Roeshott Common (Christchurch), v, 83
Roffa, Alice de, ii, 128
Roffey, Jas., v, 529
Rogate-Bohunt, man., ii, 494
Rogedon (Carisbrooke), v, 222
Roger, ii, 196, 506; iv, 218, 531 *n*, 548, 587, 589; v, 161, 191, 242, 243 *n*; abbot of Quarr, ii, 139; bp. of Bath and Wells, iv, 73 *n*; bp. of Salisbury, iv, 97; v, 302;

Roger (*cont.*)
of Dunstaple, v, 46 ; the dyer, v, 477 ; the fuller, v, 479 *n* ; prior of Christchurch, ii, 160 ; prior of St. Swithun's, ii, 115
Rogers [Roger], Anne, iv, 283,473 *n*, 567, 617 *n*, 656 ; (Sir) Edw., iii, 99 ; iv, 373, 389 ; v, 191 ; Eliz., iv, 35, 283 ; (Sir) Geo., iii, 99 ; iv, 373 ; Geo. V., iii, 342 ; Hen., iv, 368, 369, 389, 391, 657 ; Joan, iii, 99 ; (Sir) John, iii, 88, 97, 98, 414, 415, 416 ; iv, 283, 301, 338, 373, 388, 397, 399, 457, 473, 656, 657 ; v, 112, 164 *n* ; Marg., iv, 373, 388, 389 ; Margery, iv, 617 ; v, 280 ; Mary, iii, 99 ; Mary A., iii, 342 ; Thos., iv, 35, 649 ; Will., v, 160 ; fam., iv, 473 ; v, 280 *n* ; arms, iii, 414
Roghedowne (Hannington), iv, 229
Roghforlang (Longstock), iv, 449
Roke, man. (Romsey), iv, 460
Roke Farm (Odiham), iv, 98
Rokeland, Nich., ii, 203, 205
Rokeley, *see* Rookley
Rokes, man., *see* Sackville's Court, man.
Rokes, Alice, iv, 363 ; Margery, iv, 363 ; Thos., iv, 363
Rokeseya, Rokkeseye, *see* Rockstead
Rolfe, Hugh, iii, 318 ; Will., iii, 318 ; —, ii, 354 ; *see also* Rolph
Rolle, Lds. :—Hen., iv, 516 ; John, iv, 516
Rolle, Denys, iv, 515 ; Sir Fran., iv, 500 *n*, 516 *n* ; Sarah, iii, 376 ; iv, 502, 518 ; fam., iv, 516
Rolleston (Staffs.), sch., ii, 295
Rolleston, Geo., v, 200 ; Matth., v 200 ; Sam., v, 200 ; Will. V., v, 200
Rollse, Anne, iv, 9 ; Ant., iv, 9
Rollstone Farm (Fawley), iii, 293
Rolph, Maj., v, 350 ; *see also* Rolfe
Roman, Christian, v, 264
Roman Catholics, ii, 495 ; iii, 207, 215, 534 ; iv, 4, 14, 15, 18, 51, 138, 576, 633, 649 ; v, 109, 136, 186, 197, 222, 264, 271
Romano-British Hampshire, ii, 265
Roman remains, i, 269, 274, 278, 280-4, 286-92, 295-318, 328-49, 350-72 ; iii, 76, 129, 151, 154, 277, 339, 343 ; iv, 51, 56, 57, 60, 101, 129, 185, 186, 191, 274, 288, 295, 346, 366, 372, 387, 395, 402, 417, 440, 493, 500, 519, 546, 568, 050, 655 ; v, 156, 465 *n*
Rombrigg, man. (Eling), *see* Rumbridge
Romsey, i, 330, 346 ; ii, 63, 71, 96, 101, 102, 126, 127, 163, 290 ; iv, 438, 439, 452-69, 656 ; v, 39, 77, 324, 340, 418, 428, 430, 434 ; adv., iv, 468 ; assessment, iv, 380, 423 ; chant., iv, 468 ; char., iv, 468 ; ch., iv, 445, 460, 488 *n* ; ind., v, 451, 454, 459, 461, 474, 482, 484, 487, 490 ; iv, 453, 455 *n* ; leper hosp., iv, 460 ; mans., iv, 453 ; mkt. and fairs, iv, 417, 435, 452, 453 ; mills, iv, 455 ; Nonconf., iv, 468 ; sch., ii, 403 ; iv, 468, 469 ; volunteers, v, 356
Romsey, (de), Alice, (Lady), iv, 459, 583, 588 ; Anne, iv, 568, 569 ; Eleanor, iv, 330, 537 ; Eliz., iv, 569 ; Joan, iv, 330, 459, 583, 588 ; John, ii, 181, 182, 184, 186 ; iv, 330, 340, 341, 459, 513 *n*, 550, 554, 568 ; Marg., iv, 583 ; Mary, iv, 330, 459 *n*, 583 ;

Romsey (*cont.*)
Maud, iv, 459, 496, 554 ; Nich., ii, 128 ; Radigund, iv, 569 ; Rich., ii, 120, 122 ; iv, 459, 568 ; (Sir) Thos., ii, 281, 282, 283, 366 ; iv, 330, 459, 570, 583, 588 ; (Sir) Walt., iv, 330, 341, 459, 507, 513 *n*, 537, 554, 582 *n*, 583, 588 ; Will., iv, 550, 554, 568, 569 ; fam., iv, 553, 592
Romsey Abbey, ii, 8, 10, 49, 60, 104, 108, 126-32, 238, 240, 241, 248 ; iii, 436 ; iv, 195, 254, 439, 447, 453, 454, 455, 459, 460-8, 488, 508, 540, 549, 553, 554, 555, 556, 620, 635, 657 ; v, 270, 313, 469 ; wool trade, v, 476
Romsey Extra (Romsey), iv, 452 ; man., iv, 454 ; pop., v, 445
Romsey Horseys, man. (Romsey), iv, 459, 499, 507, 554, 588
Romsey Infra (Romsey), iv, 452 ; man., iv, 453, 455 ; pop., 445 *n*, 446
Romyn, (des), Alice, iv, 172, 202 ; Hen., iii, 106, 136 ; iv, 172, 202 ; v, 142, 247 *n* ; Joan, iii, 106 ; v, 247 *n* ; John, iii, 106, 107 ; Rich., iv, 110
Ronedonne, Joan de, ii, 127
Ronseldespathe (Barton Stacey), iv, 417
Roo, Rob., iv, 472
Rookcliffe (Milford), v, 116
Rooke, Sir Geo., v, 385, 386, 388 ; Giles, iv, 580
Rookes, Edw., iii, 117, 328
Rooke's Farm (Rotherwick), iv, 99
Rookley (Arreton), ii, 180 ; v, 138, 139, 140, 147, 235, 239
Rookley [Roucle, Roukele], (de), Ad., v, 147 ; Geoff., iii, 124, 167 ; iv, 147, 216, 273 *n*, 500 ; Isabel, iii, 124 ; iv, 500 ; v, 147, 162 *n* ; Jas., v, 231 ; Joan, v, 200, 216, 217 ; John, v, 144, 146, 147, 160, 161, 162, 174, 200, 208 *n*, 216, 217, 252, 275 ; Rob., v, 147
Rooksbury Park (Wickham), v, 558 *n*
Rooksdown Lane (Worting), iv, 243
Roos, Ld., *see* Ros, Ld.
Roos [Roose], (de, of), Ann, (Lady), iii, 388 ; Beatrice, iv, 569 *n* ; Eustacia, iii, 486 ; Hannibal, iv, 523 ; Phil., iv, 294 ; Sir Rob., iii, 388 *n* ; Will., iii, 486 ; *see also* Ros, Ross, Rouse
Ropley [Ropeleia, Ropeley, Roppele, Roppeleghe], ii, 288, 496 ; iii, 37, 55-8 ; v, 517, 519 ; adv., iii, 57 ; char., iii, 57 ; ch., iii, 57 ; gold torque, i, 346 ; man., iii, 56 ; pop., v, 438 ; sch., ii, 403
Ropley, —, v, 165 *n*
Ropley Manor [Cottage] (Ropley), iii, 55 ; v, 518
Roque, Dav., iii, 536
Rorke, Pet., iii, 487
Ros, Philippa, Lady, iv, 348, 526 ; Edm., Ld., iv, 526 ; Thos., Ld., iv, 348, 526
Ros, Eleanor, iv, 348 ; Marg., iv, 370 ; *see also* Roos, Ross, Rouse
Rose, prioress of Wintney, ii, 149, 151 ; wife of Revelendus, iv, 47
Rose, Amb., iv, 604 ; Eliz., iv, 604 ; (Sir) Geo., ii, 351 ; iv, 631 ; v, 84, 86, 88, 107 ; (Sir) Geo. H., v, 86, 87 ; Sir Geo. P., v, 86 ; John, iv, 604 ; v, 484 ; Margery, v, 216 *n* ; Rog., v, 216 *n* ; Will. S., v, 85 ; Maj., v, 356 *n* ; fam., v 89
Rose Hill, *see* Hildon House
Roselingesaker (Hordle), v, 111

Roses, i, 70
Rositer, Hen., iv, 549
Ross, Reg., bp. of, ii, 153
Ross [Rosse], Alex., iii, 535 ; iv, 40 ; v, 222 ; Eliz., v, 192 ; Geo., v, 192 ; Jas. T. C., v, 193 ; Will., iii, 432, 489 ; v, 110 ; Mrs., iv, 525 ; —, iv, 656 ; *see also* Roos, Ros, Rouse
Roswyk in Pengareg, ii, 173
Rother, riv., i, 67 ; ii, 506, 508 ; iii, 17, 23 ; iv, 84, 85
Rothercombe (East Meon), iii, 70
Rotherfield, man. (East Tisted), iii, 32 ; iv, 631
Rotherfield, Ad., iii, 32 ; Eliz., iv, 16 ; Isabel, iii, 32 ; John, iii, 32 ; Sir Will., iv, 16
Rotherfield Park (East Tisted), iii, 3, 30
Rotherley Coppice (Headbourne Worthy), iv, 430
Rotherwick, iv, 66, 67, 97, 99-101, 152 ; adv., iv, 101 ; char., iv, 101 ; ch., iv, 100, 104 *n* ; man., iv, 99 ; pop., v, 444 ; sch., ii, 403 ; iv, 101
Rothschild, Leopold de, v, 554, 555
Rotirburgh, *see* Rowborough
Rotrou, archbp. of Rouen, iv, 71
Rotsey, Ant., iii, 97
Rouceby, John, ii, 267
Roucestre, (de), Alice, ii, 478 ; Elias, ii, 478
Roucle, *see* Rookley
Roucombesdene (Linkenholt), iv, 324
Roud, man. (Godshill), v, 138, 173
Rouen (France), St. Mary's ch., iv, 246, 250, 251, 260
Rouen, archbps. of :—Geoff., iv, 68, 70 ; Pet., iv, 68 ; Rotrou, iv, 71
Roughbarowe, *see* Rowborough
Rough Burghfield (Stratfieldsaye), iv, 57
Rough Grove (Aldershot), iv, 3
Roughner, *see* Rowner
Roughrigge, v, 230
Roukeley, *see* Rookley
Round Ash (Tangley), iv, 326
Round Mead (Basingstoke), iv, 139
Round Park (Heckfield), iv, 45
Rouse [Rous, Rowse], (de), Anne, ii, 130 ; Ant., iii, 114 ; Barbara, ii, 492 ; John, iv, 644 ; v, 117 ; Joyce, ii, 130, 131, 132 ; Maud [Matilda], ii, 49, 135, 137 ; Thos., iii, 415 ; *see also* Roos, Ros, Ross
Rout, Geo., iii, 71 ; Jas., iii, 71 ; Mary, iii, 71 ; Rich., iii, 71 ; Will., iii, 71
Routh, R. A., iv, 368
Rouwenore, *see* Rowner
Rowborough, man. (Brading), v, 165
Rowborough, man. (Carisbrooke), ii, 139 ; v, 230, 234 ; man. house, v, 221
Rowcliffe, —, iv, 27
Rowde, *see* Roud
Rowdon, (Rev.) John, iv, 432
Rowe, John, v, 117
Rowell, John, iv, 164
Rowe Meadow (Basingstoke), *see* Round Mead
Rowenor, *see* Rowner
Roweste (Redbridge hund.), iv, 544
Rowland, the moneychanger, v, 3
Rowlands Castle (Chalton), iii, 102, 134 ; v, 431 ; brick manuf., v, 466 ; Rom. rem., i, 310, 346
Rowledge (Binsted), ii, 490
Rowley, Maj. W. C., iv, 409

Rowner, iii, 217, 218-19 ; iv, 568, 572 ; v, 100 ; adv., iii, 219 ; ch., iii, 219 ; man., iii, 218 ; pop., v, 441

Rownhams (North Baddesley), ii, 187 ; iii, 463 ; iv, 189 ; sch., ii, 403

Rownhams House (North Baddesley), iii, 463

Rowridge (Carisbrooke), v, 231

Rows, the, salt works, v, 470

Rowse, see Rouse

Roy, Will. G., iv, 547

Royal Boscombe and West Hants Hospital (Boscombe), v, 134, 137

Royal Clarence Victualling Yard (Gosport), v, 388

Royal Hants County Hospital (Winchester), v, 21, 78, 249

Royal National Sanatorium (Bournemouth), v, 134

Royal Naval College (Portsmouth), v, 400

Royal Naval College (Whippingham), v, 197

Royal Oak (Winchester), v, 78

Royal Victoria Hospital (Bournemouth), v, 134, 137

Royal Victoria Hospital (Netley), iii, 472

Roydon, man. (Brockenhurst), ii, 148 ; iv, 628 ; brick manufacture, v, 466

Rudborne [Rudborn], Rob., ii, 111, 115 ; iv, 239 ; Thos., iv, 413

Rudbrugstrete (Eling), iv, 547

Rudde [Rude], (atte, de la), Geoff., ii, 205 ; Marg., iii, 53, 448 ; Rich., iii, 53, 448

Rude, la, (Lasham), iv, 81

Rude (Odiham), iv, 88

Rudlodge Ford (E. Wellow), iv, 535

Rudston, John, iv, 69

Rudyerd, Benj., iv, 94, 110, 112 ; Bridg., iv, 112 ; Frances, iv, 110, 112 ; Jas., iv, 110, 112 ; John, iv, 110 ; Lawr., iv, 110, 112 ; Mary, iv, 110, 112

Ruenore, see Rowner

Ruffin, Eliz., v, 140 ; Sarah, v, 140 n, 264 ; Will., v, 140, 150

Rufus [Ruffus], Alice, iv, 326 n ; Hugh, iv, 326 n ; Walt., iii, 196

Rufus stone, iv, 635 ; v, 568

Rugenhore, see Rowner

Rugg [Rugge], (de, de la), Rev. Lewis, iv, 250 ; Rich., iv, 100 n ; Walt., iv, 100 n

Rugge (Romsey), iv, 452

Ruggeditch, see Rodedic

Rughedon, Will. de, iv, 88

Ruif, Rich., v, 479 n

Rumbold, Chas., iv, 205 ; C., v, 537 ; Geo., iv, 358 ; Jas., iv, 243, 244 ; —, iii, 373 ; iv, 204, 248 n

Rumboll, Thos., iv, 358 n

Rumbridge [Rumbrigg] (Eling), iv, 546, 553 ; man., iv, 548 ; salt ind., v, 470

Run, the, (Christchurch), v, 83

Runcorne, Thos., iii, 421

Runnygear, John, ii, 373

Rupibus, Pet. de, see Winchester, bps. of

Rurygge (Carisbrooke), v, 230

Rus Will. le, iv, 579, 629

Ruscombe (Berks.), iv, 607 n

Rushford Common (Christchurch), v, 83

Rushington, man. (Eling), see Rumbridge

Rushmer Down (Hurstbourne Tarrant), iv, 321

Rushmere, tithing (Hambledon), iii, 238, 242

Rushmere, Will., iii, 146

Rushmoore (Baughurst), iv, 275

Rushworth, Cath., v, 242 ; Edw., v, 242, 244

Russell, Lds. :—iv, 301 ; John, v, 355 ; Will., iii, 391 ; iv, 432

Russell [Russel], Barth., v, 275 ; Alice, v, 206 ; A. G., v, 522 ; Eleanor, v, 183, 206, 275 ; Eliz., iv, 209, 497 ; Fran., iii, 391 ; iv, 139 ; Geoff., iii, 262 ; Gert., iii, 391 ; Isabel, v, 207 ; Joan, v, 164, 207 n ; John, iii, 262, 391 ; iv, 432 ; v, 200 n ; Rev. J. G., ii, 391 ; Kath., v, 206 ; Marg., v, 207 ; Martha, iii, 262 ; Sir Maurice, v, 164, 206 ; Rachel, iii, 391 ; (Sir) Ralph, ii, 114 ; iii, 26, 262 ; iv, 342 ; v, 183, 206 ; Rich., iv, 218 ; v, 174, 181 ; Rob., v, 163 ; (Sir) Theobald [Pet.], v, 183, 206, 275, 277, 313, 364 ; Thos., v, 183, 207 n ; Will., ii, 173 ; iv, 134 ; v, 156, 161, 164, 165, 174, 181, 183, 191, 193, 198, 203, 206, 213, 242, 275 ; Will. J., iv, 606 ; —, v, 474, 513, 536 ; Wriothesley, iii, 391 ; fam., v, 147 ; arms, iii, 391

Russells (Eversley), iv, 33

Russell's Coppice (East Tytherly), iv, 497

Russhelese, le, (Sherborne St. John), iv, 158

Russheton, v, 135 n

Russington, de, Joan, iv, 617 ; Walt., iv, 617

Rustiton, Laur. de, iv, 361, 604

Rutherfield, see Rotherfield

Rutherford, Aaron, iv, 389

Rutherwyk, see Rotherwick

Rutland, earls of :—iv, 151, 494 n ; Rog., iii, 318 ; Thos., iv, 348, 526, 532, 628, 647

Rutteleston, Ruttleston, man., see Nettlestone

Rutty, Arth. F., ii, 384, 385

Ruyecroft (Highclere), iv, 285

Rya, Maud de, iv, 93

Ryal, John, ii, 163

Ryal Heath (Sandown), v, 166

Rycher, fam., iv, 45 n

Rychers (Heckfield), 45

Rycroft, Sir Nelson, iii, 358 ; iv, 180 ; Sir Rich., iii, 358 ; iv, 180 ; v, 521, 523

Ryde, v, 138 n, 177-9, 253 n, 259, 260, 269 n, 312, 364, 401, 402, 433 ; brick making, v, 466 ; chs., v, 178, 186 ; man., v, 180 ; Nonconf., v, 186 ; Rom. Caths., v, 186 ; Rom. rem., i, 348 ; sch., ii, 407

Ryde, Lower, v, 178 n

Ryde, Upper, v, 178 n

Rydeforde, la, (Arreton), v, 142

Ryde House (Ryde), v, 181

Ryder, Jas., iii, 487

Rye, la, (Newchurch), see Ryde

Rye [La Rye], man (Odiham), iv, 93

Rye, de la, Denise, iv, 93 ; Rob., iv, 93, 94 n

Ryedemede, see Redmead

Rye Farms (Odiham), iv, 94

Ryes, de, Eudo, iv, 198 ; Hubert, iv, 198

Ryeval, see Rivallis

Rygg, see Rigg

Rygges (Farley Chamberlayne), iv, 443

Rykmansforde (Elvetham), iv, 74

Rylands, John, v, 182 ; Mrs., v, 182

Ryman, Humph., iii, 279 ; iv, 520, 524 n ; Joan, iv, 520, 524 n ; John, iii, 279 ; iv, 520 ; Rich., iv, 520 ; Will., iii, 225 ; iv, 520 n

Rymer's pond (Faccombe), iv, 317

Rynefield Lodge (New Forest), v, 568

Ryngebourne, see Ringbourne

Ryplinges (Itchen Stoke), iv, 193

Ryprose, Eliz., ii, 131, 132

Rys, see Rice

Ryse (Eling), iv, 556

Rythe, le, par., see Ryde

Rythe [Rithe], atte, Christine, v, 281 ; Geo., iii, 9, 117 ; iv, 85 ; Isabel, iii, 9 ; Jas., iii, 9 ; John, ii, 301 ; v, 281 ; Marg., iii, 396 ; Marlion, iii, 9 ; Rich., iv, 157 ; Rob. iv, 85 ; Will., iii, 395, 396

Rytherwyke, see Rotherwick

Ryvere, see Rivers

Ryves [Ryve], Christian, iv, 20, 21 ; Edm., iv, 420 ; Geo., ii, 319 ; Hen., v, 230 ; John, iv, 21, 419, 420 ; Sir Rich., iv, 21, 25, 26 ; Rob., v, 24, 114 ; Rog., v, 42 ; see also Reeve and Reeves

Sabina, prioress of Wintney, ii, 149, 151

Sackville, (de), Anne, Lady, iv, 363 ; Barth., iv, 360, 363 ; Cecilia, iii, 72, 346 ; Clarice [Clarissa], iv, 353, 362 ; v, 201 ; John, iv, 363 ; Margery, iv, 363 ; (Sir) Thos., iii, 72, 346 ; iv, 362, 363 ; fam., iv, 361

Sackville Court Farm (Upper Clatford), iv, 359, 364

Sackville's Court, man. (Upper Clatford), iv, 363

Sacy [Sausay, Stacey], de, Agnes, iv, 417, 418 ; Aimery, iv, 416, 417, 418, 434 ; Isabel, iv, 417, 418 ; Lettice, iv, 491 n ; Pet., iv, 434 ; Rogo, iv, 416, 417, 434, 477 ; see also Stacy

Sadelerscroft (Bramley), iv, 141

Sadleir, Rich. V., iii, 536

Sadler, Agnes, v, 31 ; John, v, 461 ; Ralph, iv, 444 ; Will., v, 31, 539

Sadlier, Mary, iii, 325

Saer, iv, 141 n

Saer [Sare], (de), Isabel, iv, 358 n ; Pet., v, 45 ; Rich., iv, 358 n

Safe, Will., iv, 357

Saffron Walden (Essex), sch., ii, 296

Sage, Ralph le, iv, 380

Sagio, see Saye

Saindon (Godshill), v, 174

St. Albans, Aubrey, dk. of, iv, 110, 111

St. Amand, Rich. Beauchamp, Ld., iv, 185

St. Amand, Sir Aumary [Almaric], iii, 324, 334, 416 ; iv, 360, 510 n, 572 ; Eleanor, iii, 416 ; iv, 510 n

St. Anastasius by Wyke (Winchester), ii, 264

St. Andrew's Castle (Hamble), v, 331, 465

St. Asaph, bps. of : Will. Lloyd, ii, 339 ; Rich. Redman, ii, 185 ; Thos. V. Short, iv, 430

St. Barbe, Anna, iv, 454 ; Edw., iv, 452, 454 ; Frances, iv, 454 ; Hen., iv, 454 ; Honora, iv, 389 ; (Sir) John, iv, 367, 389, 454, 469 ; —, v, 472, 538

St. Blumund, Isumbert de, iv, 247

St. Boniface Down (Ventnor), v, 179

St. Brice's day massacre, ii, 8

St. Catherine's Down (Chale), ii, 180 ; v, 235

St. Catherine's Hill (Christchurch), i, 381 ; v, 85

St. Catherine's Hill (Winchester), i, 384 ; iii, 339

St. Catherine's Point, lighthouse, v, 394, 401
St. Chad's Well (Bedhampton), iii, 142
St. Clare (St. Helens), v, 190, 192
St. Clare, Alice, ii, 485; Humph., ii, 485; John, ii, 485, 486; Phil., ii, 485; Rob., ii, 485; see also Sinclair
St. Coperthwait, —, iv, 228
St. Cross, hospital of, (Winchester), ii, 12, 20, 37, 46, 55, 62, 63, 105, 193-7, 211; iii, 281, 284, 290, 301; iv, 4, 14, 20, 26, 222, 265, 277, 284, 285, 290, 291, 300, 303, 304, 576; v, 1, 19, 39, 48, 59, 77, 417
St. Cross, priory of, (Newport), ii, 106, 224, 225; v, 262
St. Cross Farm (Newport), v, 262
St. Davids, bps. of, ii, 164; Will. Lucy, iv, 294; David Martin, ii, 214
St. Denis, priory of, (Southampton), ii, 12, 20, 49, 104, 160-4, 206, 254; iii, 492, 495 n, 525; iv, 474, 477, 498, 499, 501, 518, 524; v, 169
St. Denys (Southampton), i, 332; iii, 526
St. Denys Tower (Southampton), iii, 502
St. Edmund Hall (Oxf.), v, 249
St. Edmund's College (Salisbury), ii, 306
St. Elizabeth's College (Winchester), ii, 49, 105, 212-14, 224, 268, 273, 303, 304; iii, 421; iv, 255, 256, 261, 402; v, 14
Ste. Mère Eglise, Will. de, iii, 179
St. Ethelwold's cup, ii, 7, 112
St. Florent, abbey of, (France), iv, 355, 356
St. Fromond, James, prior of, ii, 226
St. George's Down (Arreton), v, 140
St. Giles' fair, ii, 10, 473; iv, 282 n; v, 36-41, 415, 428
St. Giles' Hill [Down], v, 24, 36, 38, 300
St. Helens, ii, 26; v, 138, 189-93, 313, 325, 327, 364, 371, 374, 376, 386, 389, 390, 394, 395, 396, 397; adv., v, 193; char., v, 193; ch., v, 192; mans., v, 190; Nonconf., v, 193; Old House, v, 192; pop., v, 448; Rom. Caths., v, 190; sch., ii, 408; v, 193; spring, v, 189
St. Helen's Priory (I. of W.), ii, 106, 215-16; v, 168, 190, 193 n
St. Hilary, Pet. de, iv, 568
St. Hubert's Cross (Winchester), see Bub's Cross
St. Ives (Ringwood), iv, 606
St. John, Lds., iv, 108 n, 143, 166, 433; v, 325, 326; Edm., v, 100; Hugh, v, 100; John, iv, 578, 606, 617, 632; v, 100; Thos. (de) Poynings, ii, 228; iv, 337, 388; Will. Paulet, see Winchester, marquess of
St. John (de) Alice, iv, 116, 159; Amadeus, iv, 257; Amb., iv, 606; Barbara, iii, 458; Chas., iv, 632; Chas. E. H., iv, 93; Edm., ii, 496; iii, 59, 239, 269, 362; iv, 35 n, 116, 141, 159, 179, 193, 372, 396 n, 433, 561, 579 n; v, 98, 130; (Sir) Edw., ii, 519, 521; iii, 366; iv, 159, 247, 258, 259, 268, 270, 271, 532; v, 521; Eleanor, iv, 193, 251; Eliz., iii, 239; iv, 116, 141, 193, 268, 396 n, 444, 561, 579 n; (Rev.) Ellis, iv, 112, 259, 374, 533, 536,

St. John (cont.)
539; Eve [Eva], ii, 521; iii, 11; iv, 268; Frances, iv, 259, 374, 471; Godeheld, iv, 116; Goodyer, iv, 509; Hen., iii, 458; iv, 112, 444, 445; Hen. E., iv, 216; Sir Hen. P., iv, 216, 259, 471; Hugh, ii, 486, 496; iii, 9, 23, 362; iv, 35, 116, 141 n, 337, 341, 373, 433; Isabel, ii, 496; iii, 250; iv, 116, 159, 179, 193, 372, 433, 579 n; Jane, iv, 471; v, 5, 212; Joan, iv, 247, 257, 271; (Sir) John, ii, 220, 221, 227, 497; iii, 9, 59, 229, 239, 253, 356, 362, 366, 458; iv, 35, 89, 116, 121, 123, 134, 141 n, 142, 153, 158, 159, 175, 179, 193, 225, 247, 251, 255 n, 257, 332 n, 338, 341, 343, 373, 374, 433, 444, 445, 579; v, 327 n, 539, 540; Mabel, iv, 116; Marg., ii, 496; iv, 116, 159, 433, 561, 579 n; v, 100; Margery, iv, 259 n, 471; Martha, iv, 73; Mary, iv, 445; Oliver, iv, 259 n, 374, 444, 471; Rev. Oliver D'O., iv, 509; (Rev., Sir) Paulet, iv, 73, 74, 80, 91, 94, 259, 374, 443, 471, 509; Sir P., v, 545; Rich., iv, 247, 564; (Sir) Rob., ii, 497, 500; iii, 68, 145, 229, 239, 253, 350, 476; iv, 45 n, 116, 117, 121, 141, 142, 159, 184, 193, 195, 225, 226, 247, 255, 269, 337, 338, 341, 373, 457, 510, 513, 532 n, 562, 564, 579, 584; v, 97, 100; Rog., ii, 496; iv, 116, 247, 257; Rev. St. Andrew, iv, 606; Susan, iv, 445; Ursula, iii, 458; Will., ii, 226, 492, 496, 498; iii, 271, 366, 458; iv, 116, 159, 165, 193, 231, 374, 444, 445, 484 n; —, v, 327; fam., iv, 39, 63, 135, 256, 359, 420, 502; v, 305; arms, ii, 496; iii, 239; see also Mildmay
St. John Baptist's Hospital (Portsmouth), see God's House
St. John Baptist's Hospital (Winchester), ii, 105, 200-202; iii, 293; iv, 389, 481 n; v, 5, 41, 418
St. John-Mildmay, see Mildmay
St. John of Jerusalem, knights of, ii, 105, 187-8; iii, 8, 463, 465; iv, 190, 247, 269, 284, 332, 333, 396, 562; v, 100, 117, 189, 190, 196, 212, 418, 494; arms, iii, 463; iv, 562
St. John's College (Camb.), ii, 382, 383; v, 217, 245
St. John's College (Oxf.), ii, 360; iv, 449
St. John's Cross (Abbotts Ann), iv, 334
St. John's Hospital (Andover), iv, 356; v, 418
St. John's Hospital (Basingstoke), ii, 208-10; iv, 134, 138; v, 418
St. John's Hospital (Fordingbridge), ii, 105, 211, 229; iv, 576; v, 418
St. John's House [St. John's Rooms] (Winchester), v, 2, 39
St. John's Oakfield (St. Helens), v, 190
St. Julian's hospital (Southampton), see God's House
St. Katharine Coleman (Lond.), iv, 200
St. Katharine's Hospital (Lond.), iv, 385, 386
St. Kenett's brook, v, 31
St. Keverne (Cornw.), ii, 141, 143
St. Lawrence, ii, 73; v, 138, 193-5, 388; adv., v, 194; char., v, 195;

St. Lawrence (cont.)
ch., v, 194; man., v, 203; pop., v, 448; sch., ii, 408
St. Lawrence, of, Rob., iii, 505; Sim., iii, 512; Will., iii, 511
St. Lawrence Hall (St. Lawrence), v, 193
St. Leger (de), Anne, Lady, v, 128; Eliz., Lady, iv, 45; Sir Geo., v, 128; (Sir) Thos., iv, 43, 45, 58 n
St. Leonard, hermitage of, (Strat-fieldsaye), iv, 57-8, 61
St. Leonards (Sherfield-upon-Loddon), iv, 104
St. Leonard's Grange (Beaulieu), iv, 654
St. Leonard's House (Rishton), ii, 156
St. Manefeo [St. Manifeo, St. Manufeuto, Sancto Manufeodo], de, Ad., iv, 45, 46, 156, 555; Alice, iv, 338; Cecily, iv, 434; Hen., iv, 45; John, iv, 45, 50 n, 156, 338, 339; Rob., iv, 45, 46, 47, 50, 60, 156, 226, 227; Thos., iv, 45, 50, 156, 338; Walt., iv, 434
St. Manuel, Ad. de, iv, 174
St. Manufeuto, see St. Manefeo
St. Martin (de, of), Amphyllis, v, 228; Eleanor, v, 228; Erenburgia, iv, 189; Hugh, iii, 227; iv, 19, 189, 196; Ingram, iv, 196; Joan, iii, 459; iv, 521, 588; v, 228, 279; John, v, 228; Jordan, iv, 521; Lawr., iv, 521, 588; v, 228, 229; Reg., iv, 521, 588; v, 228, 230; Sybil, iv, 521, 588; v, 228; Will., iv, 19, 189, 352, 521; v, 228, 270; fam., iv, 524
St. Martin's Abbey (France), iii, 131
St. Mary and St. Nicholas College (Camb.), see King's College
St. Mary Bourne, ii, 241, 244, 247; iv, 273, 288, 289, 295-9; v, 429; adv., iv, 299; v, 77; char., iv, 299; ch., iv, 288, 296; mans., iv, 295; Nonconf., iv, 299; pop., v, 441; prehist. rem., i, 258; Rom. rem., i, 304, 346; iv, 295; Rom. rd., i, 320, 321; iv, 295; sch., ii, 403; iv, 295, 299; watercress cultivation, v, 455
St. Mary de la Pré, abbey of, (Northants), iv, 366, 368
St. Mary de Pré, abbey of, (Leic.), iv, 535 n
St. Mary Extra, iii, 274, 275, 297-9; adv., iii, 299; char., iii, 299; chs., iii, 298; pop., v, 446; sch., ii, 403
St. Mary Magdalen's Hospital (Southampton), ii, 105, 205-6
St. Mary Magdalen's Hospital (Winchester), ii, 13, 47, 93, 105, 197-200, 293; v, 7, 77, 418
St. Mary of Lire, abbey of, (France), iii, 529; v, 470
St. Mary Overy, priory of, (Lond.), iv, 387
St. Mary's Abbey (Winchester), see Nunnaminster
St. Mary's College (Winchester), see Winchester College
St. Mary Vallemont, abbey of, (France), iv, 57, 58, 62
St. Maur, see Seymour
St. Neots (Hunts.), ii, 6
St. Nicholas (Carisbrooke), v, 234, 253, 268, 272, 274, 279; pop., v, 449
St. Nicholas, hospital of, (Portsmouth), see God's House
St. Olave's (Hart St., Lond.), iv, 200

St. Omer, de, Alice, iv, 624 ; Eliz., iv, 624 ; Marg., iv, 624 ; (Sir) Thos., iv, 624 ; Will., iv, 624

St. Owen, de, Gilb., iii, 247 ; Joan, iii, 247

St. Paul, John de, ii, 128

St. Paul's (Lond.), Matth. Nicholas, dean of, iv, 208, 209, 414, 493

St. Pawle, Guido, earl of, see St. Pol, Guy, count of

St. Peter's Abbey (Gloucester), ii, 108, 324, 325 ; iv, 367, 368, 373, 527 ; John de Felda, abbot of, iv, 373

St. Peter's Abbey (Winchester), see Hyde Abbey

St. Philbert, de, Hugh, iv, 211, 362 ; (Sir) John, ii, 496 ; iii, 239 ; iv, 116, 159, 362, 433, 561 ; v, 100 ; Marg., ii, 496 ; iii, 239 ; iv, 116, 159, 433, 561 ; v, 100 ; Rog., iv, 362 ; Thos., iv, 362 ; Will., iv, 362 ; fam., iv, 361 ; arms, ii, 496 ; iii, 239

St. Pierre, Iseult, iv, 431

St. Pier-sur-Dire, Rob. of, ii, 231

St. Pol, Guy, count of, ii, 198 ; Waleran, count of, iv, 316, 367

St. Quintin, de, Hugh, iii, 294 ; iv, 553, 564, 625 ; John, iv, 360, 361, 588 ; Walt., ii, 229 ; iv, 564, 567

St. Remy, Rob. de, iii, 89

St. Sauveur-le-Vicomte, abbey of, (France), ii, 229 ; iv, 563, 564, 567

St. Stephen's (Westminster), iv, 110, 111

St. Swithun's Priory (Winchester), ii, 17, 20, 27, 44, 48, 60, 61, 108-15 ; iii, 130, 145, 203, 307, 315, 317, 320, 321, 329, 343, 423, 424 ; iv, 1, 3, 6, 8, 13, 14, 18, 19, 170, 193, 194, 215, 229, 239, 240, 242, 258 n, 273, 288, 289, 290, 296, 300, 301, 304, 419, 426, 469, 470 n, 474, 491, 512, 656 ; v, 2, 23, 39, 151, 165, 206, 211, 215, 216, 307, 410, 417, 419, 420, 423, 466, 468

St. Valery [Walery], de, Bern., iv, 655 ; Guy, iii, 457 ; Hen., iii, 457 ; (Sir) John, iv, 369, 407 n ; Reynold, iv, 655, 656 ; Rich., iii, 457 ; Rog., ii, 121 ; Thos., iii, 457 ; fam., iv, 657 ; arms, iii, 457

St. Victor-en-Caux (France), iv, 419

St. Vigor of Cerisy, abbey of, (France), iv, 145, 152, 153, 158, 231 ; Lawrence, abbot of, ii, 227

St. Vincent, Ld., v, 400

St. Walery, see St. Valery

Salbury, Will., ii, 146

Salcot, John, ii, 120, 122

Sale, Ralph de la, iv, 68

Salebourne, see Selborne

Salemonville, de, Thos., iv, 302 ; Will., iv, 302

Salesbourne, see Selborne

Salesbury, see Salisbury

Salewike, de, Nich., iv, 146 ; Will., iv, 146

Salide, v, 126

Salidus, abbot of Hyde, see Selid

Salisbury, bps. of : ii, 164 ; iv, 71, 324, 589 ; v, 120, 126 ; Joscelin de Bohun, iv, 58, 97 ; Thos. Burgess, ii, 354 ; iv, 23, 88 ; John Capon, ii, 388 ; John Davenant, iv, 568 ; John Fisher, v, 218 ; Edw. Gheast, v, 587 ; Alex. Hyde, ii, 115 ; iv, 541 ; Geo. Moberley, ii, 359 , 360, 366 ; v, 211 ; Herb. le Poor, ii, 226 ; iii, 59, 60 ; Rich. le Poor, see

Salisbury (cont.)
Durham, bps. of, ; Roger, iv, 97 ; v, 302 ; John Thomas, iv, 61 ; Walt. de la Wyle, iv, 591 ; Rob. Wyville, v, 313

Salisbury, ctsses. of, ii, 58 ; iv, 619 ; v, 151 ; Alice, iv, 348, 608, 612 ; v, 117 ; Ann, iii, 508 ; Charlotte, v, 103 ; Ela, iv, 536 n, 560 ; Eleanor, iv, 130, 347, 348, 608 ; Eliz., iv, 77 ; Kath., ii, 157 ; iv, 608 ; Marg., iii, 105, 135, 411 ; iv, 608 ; v, 92, 103, 109, 219, 324 ; earls of :—ii, 492 ; iv, 151, 334, 373, 409, 428, 430, 536, 568 ; v, 99 n, 118, 124, 228, 366 ; Edw. iv, 560 ; John Montagu, iii, 410 ; iv, 608 ; Rich. Nevill, iii, 410 ; iv, 348, 608, 612 ; Rob. Cecil, iv, 334, 396, 397, 427, 430, 587, 589, 590, 591 ; Thos. (de) Montagu [Montacute], ii, 475 ; iii, 410 ; iv, 130, 347, 545, 608, 632 ; v, 117 n, 118, 277 ; Will. Cecil, iv, 427 n, 589 ; Will. de Longespée, iii, 506 ; iv, 150 n, 346, 347, 351, 540, 560 ; v, 37 ; Will. (de) Montagu [Montacute], ii, 156, 157 ; iv, 77, 261, 265, 508, 579, 608, 619 ; v, 92, 114, 117, 118, 222, 225, 253, 277, 314

Salisbury [Salesbury], Edw. of, ii, 492 ; v, 90 n ; Hugh, iii, 181 ; John, ii, 56, 185, 186, 253 ; Margery, v, 231 ; Rog. of, earl, v, 95 ; Will., ii, 120

Salisbury and Southampton Canal, v, 452

Salisbury-Avon Canal, v, 452

Salisbury cathedral, iv, 71, 323, 499, 623, 626 ; chancellor of, iv, 79, 86, 97 ; dean and chapter, iv, 379, 537, 626

Salmon, Alice, iii, 411 ; Edm., iv, 419 n ; John, iv, 419 ; v, 483 ; Thos., iii, 411 ; iv, 416, 418, 419 ; Will., ii, 502

Salt, v, 451, 469-72

Saltarn, Harry L., iv, 634

Salter, Benj., v, 168 ; John, iii, 114

Saltern Close, Great, (Boldre), iv, 619

Salterns, Great, (Portsmouth), pop., v, 441

Saltlond (Carisbrooke), v, 230

Saltmarsh (Christchurch), v, 83, 95 n

Saltmarsh, Anne, iv, 105 ; Phil., iv, 105 ; Will., iii, 361 ; iv, 105

Salvag, see Savage

Salvation Army, iv, 139, 299, 304, 613, 649 ; v, 169, 186, 245, 264

Salvervilla [Saververilla], (de), Gilb., iv, 257 ; Manasseh, iv, 257 ; Maud, iv, 257 ; Rob., iv, 257 ; Will., iv, 257

Salvo, John de, v, 485 n

Salynglond, see Saltlond

Samar, Rich., ii, 444

Samber, Will., iv, 620

Samborne, par., see Somborne

Samborne [Samborn, Sambourne, Somborne], (de), Eliz., iv, 617 n ; Jas., iv, 357 ; John, iv, 617 ; v, 172 ; Julius, iv, 351 ; Rob., ii, 181 ; Will., ii, 110

Samford [Sampforde], Hugh, v, 117 ; Rich., v, 458

Samfords (Kingsley), ii, 515

Sampson, Alan, iv, 456 ; Alex., iv, 456 ; Edw., v, 201 ; Eliz., ii, 129 ; Hugh, iii, 512 ; John, iii, 224 ; Rich., iv, 456 ; Thos., ii, 128 ; Walt., iv, 456 ; Will., iii, 52

Samsoneswode (Wootton St. Lawrence), iv, 239

Sancta Cruse, Alan de, ii, 196

Sancta Maria, Pet. de, ii, 197

Sancto Austolo, Phil. de, iv, 340, 341

Sancto Manufeodo, see St. Manefeo

Sandale, John, see Winchester, bps. of

Sande, man., see Sandown

Sandelford de Knoll (Kingsclere), iv, 257

Sanders, Eliz., ii, 77 ; John, iv, 112 ; Nich., ii, 77, 80 ; —, v, 150 ; see also Saunders

Sanderville [Sandervill], de, Manser, iv, 171 ; Phil., iv,, 171, 174

Sandes, see Sandys

Sandford, man. (Godshill), ii, 231 ; v, 174, 175

Sandford, man. (Kingsclere), iv, 252, 256, 327 n

Sandford (Kingsley), ii, 515

Sandford (Ringwood), iv, 607

Sandford [Sandleford, Sanford], (de), Ad., v, 2 ; Humph., iii, 167, 240 ; Joan, iii, 168 ; Rich., iii, 150, 168 ; Rob., iv, 7 ; Thos., iii, 149, 150, 168 ; iv, 257

Sandford Priory, see Sandleford

Sandham, man., see Sandown

Sandhill, man. (Fordingbridge), iv, 571, 573 ; v, 98

Sandhill Heath (Fordingbridge), iv, 567

Sandhills (Highcliff), v, 84

Sandhurst (Carisbrooke), v, 229 n

Sandleford, fam., see Sandford

Sandleford Priory (Berks.), iv, 257, 276 n, 292

Sandle Heath (Fordingbridge), iv, 567, 576, 577

Sandon, John de, ii, 155

Sandown, v, 138 n, 156, 157, 253 n, 327 ; adv., v, 169 ; brick-making, v, 465 ; char., v, 170 ; chs., v, 168 ; man., v, 165 ; Nonconf., v, 169

Sandown, tithing (E. Medine), v, 138

Sandown Castle, v, 157, 351

Sandpits (Hartley Wespall), iv, 42

Sandputte, la, (Kingsley), ii, 515

Sands, see Sandys

Sandwich, earls of : Edw. Montagu, v, 385 ; John Montagu, v, 393

Sandwich, de, Julia, iv, 110 ; (Sir) Ralph., iii, 166 ; iv, 89, 110

Sandy Balls (Fordingbridge), iv, 601, 606

Sandy Bay (I. of W.), v, 328

Sandys [Sandes, Sands], Ladies : Anne, iii, 250, 253 ; Eliz., iv, 161, 363, 450 n ; Joan, iv, 160, 317, 362, 378, 450 n ; Margery, iv, 175 ; iv, 137, 359, 553 ; Mary, iv, 354 ; Sybil, iv, 353, 362 ; Lds. : ii, 382 ; iv, 341 ; v, 571 ; Edwin, iv, 450 ; Hen., iv, 487, 507 ; Thos , ii, 516 ; iii, 124, 361 ; iv, 159, 161, 450 n, 487 ; Will., ii, 174, 175, 215, 369, 370 ; iii, 18, 96, 124 ; iv, 128, 137, 138, 160, 161, 163, 170, 317, 354, 359, 362, 363, 442, 450 n, 451, 452 n, 473, 476, 478, 480, 484, 487, 495, 503, 504, 506, 507, 527, 553, 558, 610

Sandys [Sandes, Sands, Sondes], Agnes, iii, 372 ; iv, 610 ; Edith, iv, 348 n ; Sir Edwin, iv, 161 ; (Col.) Hen., iv, 161, 163, 183, 450 ; Joan, iii, 96, 361 ; iv, 160 ; Sir John, ii, 478 ; iii, 96, 361, 499 ; iv, 160, 317, 362, 378, 450 n ; Mary, iii, 124 ; Reg., iv,

Sandys (cont.)
102 ; Sir Rich., iv, 541 ; Sybil,
iv, 358 ; (Sir) Thos., iii, 334, 361 ;
iv, 341, 353, 358, 359, 362, 450 n,
610 ; (Sir) Walt., iii, 361, 372,
447 ; iv, 160, 341, 353, 358, 362,
367, 378, 450 n, 484 n, 487, 506,
610 ; v, 6 n ; (Sir) Will., ii, 174,
519 ; iii, 18, 124, 334, 361, 429 ;
iv, 160, 252, 353, 354, 358, 359,
362, 378, 450 n, 509, 608 ; —, v,
328 ; fam., iv, 363, 364, 368, 442 ;
arms, iii, 124, 334
Sandys Manor (Andover), iv, 353
Sanford, see Sandford
Sansaver, Hugh, iv, 377 ; (Sir)
Ralph, iv, 377
Sanztere, John, iii, 57, 57 n
Saolf, see Saulf
Saolt, v, 116
Sappley Mede (Overton), iv, 211
Saravia, Adrian, ii, 528 ; Chris., iii,
528
Sardene, de, Hen., iii, 406 ; Nichola,
iii, 406
Sare, see Saer
Sareson, see Sarson
Sarisbury (Titchfield), iii, 221, 222 ;
sch., ii, 404
Sarisbury Green, v, 455
Sarson, man. (Amport), iv, 337,
340, 341-2, 380 n ; mills, iv, 342
Sarson, tithing (Amport), iv, 337
Sarson Wood (Amport), iv, 337
Sartoris, Chas., iii, 271 ; E. J., iii,
233
Sarum, Old, i, 322 ; castle, iv, 117
Sarweton, see Swarraton
Satchell, tithing (Hound), iii, 472
Sauberton, see Soberton
Saulf [Saolf], iv, 255, 515, 617 ; v,
100, 114
Saumerez, Sir Jas., v, 399 ; see also
Somery
Saumo, Lambert de, iv, 508
Sauncere, Julia, iii, 330 ; John, iii,
330
Saunders [Saundres], And., iv, 554 ;
Arch. C., iv, 546, 554 ; Cecil R.,
iv, 554 ; Sir Chas., v, 390, 391,
392 ; Fran., iv, 244 ; John, iv,
554 ; Nich., iii, 449 ; S. E., v,
198, 458 ; Thos., iv, 3 ; Thos. W.,
v, 134 ; Will., iv, 244 ; v, 65 ;
Mrs., v, 132 ; see also Sanders
Saunderson, Rev. Randall, iv, 397
Sausay, see Sacy
Sauser, Rob. le, v, 227
Sauveur, count, v, 524
Savage [Salvag], (la, le), Alina, iv,
302 ; Dan., ii, 91 ; Edw., iv, 143,
166, 203 ; Elinor, iv, 143, 172,
203 ; Jane, iv, 433 ; Joan, iii,
373 ; iv, 214 ; Sir John, iv, 143,
166, 172, 203, 204, 302 ; Lucy,
iv, 302 ; Maud, iv, 302 ; Rich.,
iii, 373 ; iv, 214 ; Rog., iv, 302 ;
(Sir) Thos., iii, 419, 434, 436,
485 ; iv, 342, 380 n ; Thomasine,
iv, 302 ; (Rev.) Will., iv, 217,
258, 302 ; v, 137 ; fam., iv, 341 ;
arms, iii, 485
Savageston, Saveiston, see Sarson
Saveleia, see Shelveley
Savervilla, see Salvervilla
Savigny, abbey of, v, 94
Savile [Savil], Sir John, v, 223 n ;
Capt., v, 345
Savoner, Rob., iv, 292
Savord, v, 167
Savour, Joshua, iii, 178
Sawbridge, Capt. E. H., ii, 501
Sawin, v, 155, 173, 290, 582
Sawyer, Capt. Herb., v, 391 ; Rich.,
ii, 48 ; Sir Rob., iv, 278, 285,

Sawyer (cont.)
286, 397 ; —, v, 514, 528, 536 ;
fam., v, 453 n ; see also Sayer
Saxi, iv, 278, 360, 387
Saxon, John, iv, 256
Saye [Sagio, Say], (de), Alice, iv,
58, 62 ; Emma, iv, 58 ; Evelyn G.,
v, 84 ; Giles, iii, 531 ; Isabel, iv,
58, 60 ; John, iv, 176 n ; Reg.,
v, 477 ; Rob., iv, 58, 142 ; Sybil,
iv, 58 ; Sir Thos., iv, 58, 60 ; (Sir)
Will., ii, 285 ; iii, 107 ; iv, 58, 60
Saye and Sele, Lds., ii, 262, 317 ;
Jas. Fiennes, iv, 199 ; Will.
Fiennes, iii, 442 ; iv, 206, 279,
545, 632
Sayer, Thos., iii, 461 ; see also
Sawyer
Sayers, —, iv, 15
Scaldeford, man. (Brading), see
Scotlesford
Scaldeforde (Twyford), see Shaw-
ford
Scale, E. M., iii, 201, 202
Scaleby, Sim. de, ii, 17
Scales, Will., iv, 319
Scarlett, —, v, 532
Scarsdale, Ld., iv, 348
Scathlok, Steph., v, 484
Scaudedene, see Shalden
Scaudeflete, Scealden fleot, see
Shalfleet
Scece, see Shute
Sceva, iv, 495 n
Schaldeford, see Shawford
Schalston, see Chalton
Scharpe Croft (Andover), iv, 346
Scherleg, see Shirley
Scherpe, see Sharp
Schilwareton, see Cholderton
Schirefelde, see Sherfield
Schirlega, see Shirley
Schlenting, see Shanklin
Schoedde, Sir J., iv, 634
Schools, ii, 251
Schorde, la, see Sherde
Schorham, Will. de, v, 459
Schortefrende, Will., iv, 588
Schorwell, see Shorwell
Schroeder, Isabel, iv, 5, 27, 30
Schusche, Alan de, iv, 268
Schyde, see Shide
Schyreburne, see Sherborne St. John
Schyte, man. (Petersfield), see Sheet
Sclater, Eliz., iii, 384 ; Magdalen,
iii, 384 ; iv, 121 ; Penelope, iii,
384 ; P. L., iv, 87 ; Rich., iii,
384 ; Thos., iii, 384 ; fam., iv,
240
Sclater-Booth, Geo. L., iv, 121
Sclaters (Basingstoke), iv, 139
Sclive (Christchurch), v, 95
Scordich, Nich. de, iv, 589
Scosfleot (Calbourne), v, 220 n
Scot, Maj.-Gen. Pat. G., iv, 17 ;
Rev. Rob. F., iv, 17 ; Dr. Will.,
iv, 17 ; see also Escote and Scott
Scotchells Brook (Brading), v, 166
Scotland (Godshill), v, 170
Scotland [Eschotland], Jordan, iii,
372, 375 ; Thos., v, 515, 537,
540 ; Will., iii, 372, 375, 377
Scotlesford, man. (Brading), v, 166
Scotney, (de), Aubrey, iv, 491 ;
Imbert, iv, 491 ; Joan, iv, 491 ;
John, iv, 491, 506 ; Mabel, iii,
455, 491 ; Pet., iii, 455 ; iv, 491 ;
Sarah, iv, 491 ; Walt., iii, 455 ;
iv, 491 ; fam., arms, iii, 455
Scots (Kingsley), ii, 515
Scott, Ld. Hen., ii, 458
Scott, Arch. E., iii, 17, 32 ; iv, 423,
424 ; Cecilia, v, 169, 264 ; Rev.
Chas., iii, 408 ; Eliz., iv, 652 ;
Geo. A. J., iv, 423 ; Sir Gilb.,

Scott (cont.)
iv, 286 ; Hen., iv, 652 ; Jas., iv,
424 ; Jas. W., iii, 28 ; iv, 424 ;
v, 517 ; John, ii, 163 ; v, 200 n ;
Sir Walt., v, 85 ; Will., iv, 215 n ;
Miss, v, 264 ; Mrs., iv, 474 ; see
also Escote and Scot
Scotteford, man., see Scotlesford
Scottescombe (Brading), v, 166
Scottesford, man., see Scotlesford
Scottes Place (Sopley), v, 130
Scott's Hill Common [Scottes Com-
mon] (Christchurch), v, 83, 85
Screeche, Ellen, iii, 283 ; John, iii,
283
Scrivener, John, iii, 434
Scrope [Scroope], Eliz., Lady, v,
118 ; Isabel, Lady, v, 207 n ;
Lds. :—Hen., iii, 153 ; v, 108, 318,
368 ; Thos., v, 118
Scrope [Lescrope, Scroope, Scrop],
(de, le), Geoff., v, 290 ; Hen., ii,
128 ; Nich., ii, 78 ; Sir Will.,
iii, 214, 241
Scullard [Skullard], Agnes, iv, 361 ;
Brocas, iv, 361 ; Geo., iv, 361 ;
Jane, iv, 361 ; John, ii, 494 ; iii,
293 ; iv, 361
Sculpture, Norman, ii, 241 ; Saxon,
ii, 238
Scures [Escures], (de), Beatrice, iv,
232 ; Eva [Eve], iii, 234 ; iv,
373 ; Jas., iv, 153, 232 ; (Sir)
John, ii, 31, 272, 485 ; iii, 69, 171,
234 ; iv, 153, 232, 373, 521 ; v,
11 n ; Matth., iv, 172, 234 ; iv,
153, 232 ; Rich., iv, 232 ; Rog.,
ii, 181 ; iii, 148, 151, 234, 293,
400 ; iv, 114 n, 153, 232, 373 ;
Sybil, iv, 153, 232, 521 ; Will.,
iii, 148
Scures Hill (Nately Scures), iv,
153, 176
Scuteshangre (Odiham), iv, 88
Seaford (Suss.), shipping, v, 362
Seager [Seagar, Segar], Edw., iv,
96 ; Hen., iii, 179, 180 ; Will., v,
109
Sea Grove (St. Helens), v, 190
Seal (Brading), v, 159
Sealands (Yateley), iv, 21
Seale (Surrey), iv, 29
Seale, Pet., iii, 535
Seals, i, 5
Searchfield, man. (Charford), iv,
562
Seare, Rev Chas. J. G., iv, 205
Searle, Anne, iii, 361 ; Geo., iv,
96 ; Gilb., iv, 148, 149 ; Pet., iv,
149 ; Rich., iii, 535 ; Rob., iii,
361 ; Thos., iii, 68 ; Will., iv, 148 ;
see also Serle
Seaton, John Colborne, Ld., iv, 631
Seaview (St. Helens), v, 190
Seawell, A. E., iv, 27 ; v, 556 ; see
also Sewell
Seaxnatune, East, see Exton
Sebastian, L., iv, 365
Sebright, Tom, v, 524
Seccheford, see Searchfield
Sechingworth, see Segenworth
Sedbergh (Yorks.), sch., ii, 306
Sedenhams (Christchurch), v, 85
Sedgrave, Rich., ii, 301, 302
Sedgwick, Obadiah, iv, 274
Seede, John, v, 130
Seely, (Sir) Chas., v, 147, 211, 216,
217, 228, 231, 242, 244, 246,
248, 251, 252
Seericke, Arth., v, 132
Segar, see Seager
Segenworth, man. (Titchfield), iii,
217, 220, 229
Segontium, i, 273
Segrave, Steph. de, iv, 88

Segrim's mill (Winchester), v, 49
Segwyn, Raymond, iv, 347
Seifrid, iv, 215, 282
Seindon (King's Somborne), iv, 470
Seintlowe [Seyntlowe], (de), Christine, iv, 224, 579 ; Nich., iv, 224, 579
Seintlyngges, see Shanklin
Sekkyls (Kingsley), ii, 515
Selborne, ii, 47, 452, 471, 506 ; iii, 3, 4-16 ; v, 324, 328 n, 331, 518 ; adv., iii, 15 ; char., iii, 16 ; ch., iii, 13 ; coprolite ind., v, 453 ; grange, iii, 6 ; mans., ii, 176 ; iii, 5 ; mkts. and fairs, ii, 6 ; v, 417 ; pop., v, 438 ; quarries, v, 463 ; Rom. Brit. rem., i, 340, 346 ; sch., ii, 404
Selborne, hund., iii, 3-35 ; v, 418 n
Selborne, earls of, ii, 467 ; Roundell Palmer, ii, 357, 358, 521 ; iii, 8, 10, 15, 16 ; v, 5
Selborne Common, iii, 5
Selborne Hill, iii, 5
Selborne Makerel, man. (Selborne), iii, 7
Selborne Priory, ii, 55, 104, 175-80, 371, 515, 520 ; iii, 5 ; iv, 121, 126, 138, 149 ; tannery, v, 455
Selby, Thos., ii, 158
Seldene, see Shalden
Sele Priory (Suss.), ii, 220
Selid [Salidus], abbot of Hyde, ii, 117, 121 ; iii, 391
Selins, v, 145 n
Sellecroft (Yateley), iv, 21
Selsey, diocese of, ii, 101
Selve, Odet de, v, 328 n
Selyman, Rob., v, 129, 172
Selymbria, Will., bp. of, ii, 45
Seman, Rich., iii, 53 ; v, 126
Semelye, Anastasia, iv, 512 ; Thos., iv, 513 n
Semer, see Seymour
Sench [Senche], Clarissa, iv, 302 ; John, iv, 302 ; Martin, iv, 216, 301, 302
Sencliz, see Shanklin
Sendale, John, see Winchester, bps. of
Sendy, Agnes, iv, 316 ; Anne, iv, 315, 316, 563 ; Arth., iv, 316, 317 ; Lawr., iii, 535 ; Thos., iv, 315, 316, 563 ; Will., iii, 535 ; iv, 316
Sengette Boddene (Wootton St. Lawrence), iv, 239
Sentlyngges, see Shanklin
Septon, see Shipton Bellinger
Sereweton, see Swarraton
Serge manufacture, v, 485
Serle, Alex., iv, 96 ; Alice [Alicia], ii, 137 ; v, 150 ; Charlotte M., iii, 468 ; Eliz., iv, 557 ; Fran., iii, 279, 310 ; Gilb., iii, 387, 468 ; iv, 92, 458, 459, 549, 554, 557 ; Jas., iii, 489 ; John, ii, 391 ; iii, 279, 483 ; v, 166, 264 ; Nich., v, 150 ; Pet., iii, 387, 468, 469 ; Susanna, iv, 557 ; Thos., v, 233 ; Wentworth, iii, 387 ; Will., ii, 478 ; v, 149, 150 ; fam., v, 282 ; see also Searle
Serlo, iv, 231, 587
Servington, Dav., iv, 588 ; Edith, iv, 588 ; Edw., iv, 588 ; Nich., iv, 588 ; Oliver, iv, 588 ; Walt., iv, 588 ; fam., iv, 589
Sessions, Dorothy, iii, 80
Setley, West, ii, 148
Setteville, Will. de, iii, 228
Seuewic, see Southwick
Seutecome (Brighstone), v, 212
Sevenhampton [Sevenhamton], (de, of), Rog., iv, 637 ; (Sir) Walt., ii, 255 ; iv, 293 ; v, 40

Sevenstrete (S. Damerham), iv, 587 n
Severyngton, de, Isabel, iii, 89 ; Nich., iii, 89
Sevier [Sevior], John, iv, 496 ; v, 77
Sewale, see Sewell
Seward, see Siward
Sewell [Sewale, Suell] (de), Eliz. M., v, 155 ; Isabel, iv, 392, 562 ; Jas. E., ii, 365 ; John, iv, 392, 562 ; Thos., ii, 139 ; Will., ii, 361 ; Rev. W. D., v, 234 ; see also Seawell
Sewer, see Siward
Sexey, Hugh, iii, 247
Sextie, —, v, 553
Seymour, Ld. Hen., v, 198 ; Rich., Ld., iv, 551 ; Thos., Ld., ii, 131, 188 ; iii, 8, 463, 465 ; iv, 189, 193, 454, 597 ; Ld. Will., iii, 17
Seymour [St. Maur, Semer], Agnes, iv, 354 ; Anne, ii, 125 ; (Sir) Edw., ii, 55, 125, 149 ; iii, 333, 477 ; iv, 75, 80, 85, 93, 110, 111, 225, 289, 455, 497, 506, 509, 608 ; v, 92, 327 n ; Eve, iv, 382 ; Frances, iii, 477 ; Sir Hen., ii, 66, 67, 75, 76, 212 ; iii, 8, 332, 333, 335, 340, 341 ; iv, 646 ; v, 95, 96, 97 ; Isabel, iv, 75, 354 ; Jane, queen, see Jane (Seymour) ; Joan, iv, 354, 610 ; (Sir) John, iii, 8, 340 ; iv, 75, 84, 85, 354 ; v, 97 ; Marg., ii, 131 ; Margery, iv, 354 ; Maud, iv, 75, 84 ; Nich., iv, 382 ; Rob., iv, 541 n ; Susan, v, 97 ; Thos., iv, 383, 610 ; Will., iii, 477 ; iv, 75 ; Mrs., iii, 233 ; fam., iv, 381 ; arms, iii, 333, 477
Seymour's Place [Farm] (Andover), iv, 354
Seyncler, Seyntcler, see Sinclair
Seyntebeide, Maud de, iv, 382
Seyntlowe, see Seintlowe
Seysiniaco, Gerard de, ii, 25
Shabdowne (King's Somborne), iv, 470
Shadsdon, see Shoddesden
Shafte, Joane, v, 72 ; Marg., ii, 124
Shafterlond (Liss), iv, 84
Shaftesbury, Emily, ctss. of, iv, 454 n ; Ant., earl of, ii, 338 ; iv, 454 n, 583, 589, 594
Shaftesbury, Ethelgiva, abbess of, iv, 183 n, 251 ; John of, iv, 405
Shalbourn (Wilts.), ii, 122
Shalcombe, man. (Shalfleet), ii, 138, 139 ; v, 234, 274
Shalcombe Down, i, 386
Shalcombe Farm (Shalfleet), v, 272
Shaldeford, see Shawford
Shalden, iv, 66, 67, 101-3 ; v, 79 ; adv., iv, 103 ; ch., iv, 103 ; pop., v, 437 ; Rom. rem., i, 346 ; iv, 101 ; sch., ii, 404
Shalden Green (Shalden), iv, 101
Shalden Lodge (Shalden), iv, 101
Shalfleet, ii, 21, 26, 180, 241, 248 ; v, 209, 210, 215, 218, 265 n, 272-8 ; adv., v, 277 ; char., v, 277 ; ch., v, 275 ; man., ii, 159 ; v, 220, 272 ; mill, v, 272 ; Nonconf., v, 277 ; pop., v, 449 ; Rom. rem., i, 348 ; sch., ii, 408
Shalfleet Wood (Shalfleet), v, 275
Shalford, see Shawford
Shallett, Rich., v, 346 n
Shalloon manufacture, v, 487
Shallows, the, (Boldre), iv, 616
Shamblehatche (Crondall), iv, 6
Shamblehurst (S. Stoneham), ii, 126, 148 ; iii, 481, 487
Shambler, Will., v, 143
Shameles (E. Wellow), iv, 535

Shamelhurst, see Shamblehurst
Shamlord [Shamblers, Shamblord, West Shamlord], man. (Whippingham], v, 197 n, 198, 269, 270, 364
Shamlord, East, (Whippingham), v, 198
Shanklin, v, 138, 195-7 ; advs., v, 197 ; char., v, 197 ; chs., v, 195 ; man., v, 195 ; Nonconf., v, 197 ; pop., v, 448 ; Rom. Cath., v, 197 ; Rom. coins, i, 349
Shanklin, East, v, 195
Shapley Heath (Winchfield), iv, 109
Shard, —, v, 525
Shareshull, Will. de, ii, 220
Sharland (Hursley), iii, 421
Sharnesfield, Nich., iii, 187
Sharp [Scherpe, Sharpe], Aubrey, v, 45 ; Geo., v, 528 ; Hen., v, 45 ; John, ii, 180 ; iii, 6 ; v, 525, 525 n ; Marg., iii, 463 ; Risdon D., v, 110 ; Sam., iv, 453 ; Thos., iii, 463 ; fam., v, 487
Sharpricks [Sharprix], man. (Boldre), iv, 619 ; v, 82, 112, 113
Sharrow, Martha, iv, 422
Shave (Minstead), iv, 638
Shaw (Berks.), ii, 226, 227, 290
Shaw, Thos., iv, 145 ; Toby, iii, 84
Shawfleet, see Shalfleet
Shawford (Twyford), iii, 339 ; v, 563 ; coins, i, 346 ; mill, iii, 339, 340 ; v, 475
Shawford House (Twyford), iii, 339 ; iv, 471
Shaw-Lefevre, Chas., iv, 44, 46, 47, 430, 611 ; v, 5, 224 ; Emma L., iv, 47
Shear Down Farm (Harrington), iv, 229
Shearer, Alex., v, 180 ; Augusta, v, 180 ; Bettesworth P., v, 180
Sheat (Brighstone), see Shute
Sheat (Gatcombe), ii, 138 ; v, 209, 237, 248
Sheat House (Gatcombe), v, 246
Shedden, Beatrice, v, 201 ; —, v, 535
Sheddon, —, v, 118, 572
Shedfield (Droxford), ii, 213 ; iii, 275, 285, 287 ; sch., ii, 404
Sheen Priory (Surrey), ii, 107, 219, 231 ; iv, 365 ; v, 176, 189, 229, 242, 245
Sheet (Brighstone), see Shute
Sheet (Petersfield), iii, 113, 323 ; man., iii, 116 ; mill, iii, 113 ; pop., v, 444
Sheet (Whippingham), see Shide
Sheep, v, 501, 503-8 ; price of, v, 494, 495, 496, 497, 503
Sheep Down (Hurstbourne Tarrant), iv, 319
Sheephouse Field (Overton), iv, 211
Sheep's Down (Swarraton), iv, 195
Sheep Sutton, see Sutton, Long
Sheerness (Kent), v, 386, 387
Sheffield, Nich., ii, 375, 385
Sheford, John de, ii, 165
Sheires, Geo., ii, 519
Sheldon, Anastasia, iii, 72 ; iv, 511 ; Edw., iii, 72, 326 ; iv, 511, 527 ; Will., iv, 511
Shelford, Eliz., iv, 144
Shelley, Eliz., ii, 55, 60, 61, 124, 125, 126 ; Hen., ii, 76, 87 ; iii, 88, 90 ; (Sir) John, iii, 308 ; (Sir) John, C. E., iv, 191 ; Juliana, Lady, iv, 443 ; Mary W., v, 134 ; Percy B., v, 107 ; (Sir) Thos., ii, 76 ; iii, 88 ; iv, 443 ; Sir Will., iii, 88 ; fam., arms, iii, 88
Shelly Common (Eling), iv, 546, 555
Shelveley, man. (Eling), iv, 507, 555

Shelvetey, de, Alured, iv, 555; Thos., iv, 555
Shelvestrode, Rog., iii, 11, 17
Shenton, —, v, 488 n
Sheppard [Shepherd, Shepperd], Sam., iv, 351; Sophia, iv, 127, 140, 344, 369, 376, 387, 391; (Rev.) Thos., iv, 127, 140, 344, 386, 391; v, 269; Will., ii, 175; iii, 201
Shepparde Piddle (Greywell), iv, 76
Sheppard's Lane (Longparish), iv, 406
Sheppark (Barton Stacey), iv, 417
Shepton [Sheptone], (de), Joan, iv, 523; John, ii, 213, 214; iv, 523; Thos., ii, 129
Shepwricht, John le, v, 458
Sher, riv., see Wey
Sherborne, West, see Monk Sherborne
Sherborne, Lds.:—Edw. L. Dutton, iii, 425; Jas. H. L. Dutton, iii, 425; John Dutton, ii, 477, 516, 518, 519; iii, 53, 425; iv, 486
Sherborne [Shirborne, Shyrebourn], (de), John, iv, 16; Mary, ii, 519; Rob., ii, 158, 167, 197, 294; v, 66; Thos., ii, 115; Will., iv, 392
Sherborne Coudray, man., see Vyne, the
Sherborne St. John [Sherborne Decani], ii, 226, 381; iv, 113, 114, 142, 158-70, 231, 234, 247; v, 427, 435; adv., iv, 170; chalk quarries, v, 454; char., iv, 170; ch., iv, 167; fish pond, iv, 159; mans., iv, 158; v, 414 n, 419; mills, iv, 146, 159; pop., v, 439; Rom. rem., i, 346; sch., ii, 404
Sherbrooke, Rob. Lowe, vsct., ii, 358
Sherde (Brighstone), v, 213
Shere (Surr.), ii, 146, 147; iv, 539
Sherfield [Shirfelde], Marg., iv, 527; Rich., iv, 527; Rog., iv, 527; Steph., iv, 176
Sherfield Court (Sherfield-upon-Loddon), iv, 104, 105
Sherfield-English, ii, 73; iv, 489, 510-11; adv., iv, 511; ch., iv, 511; man., iv, 502, 510, 541; mill, iv, 510; pop., v, 446; sch., ii, 404
Sherfield Hall [Sherfield Hill Park] (Sherfield-upon-Loddon), iv, 104
Sherfield Hill, iv, 103
Sherfield-upon-Loddon, iv, 44, 63, 66, 67, 103-9, 113; adv., iv, 107; bridge, iv, 103, 106; char., iv, 108; ch., iv, 106; man., iv, 104, 475; mills, iv, 106; Nonconf., iv, 108; pk., iv, 106; pop., v, 439; sch., ii, 404; iv, 108
Sherfield Warren (Sherfield English), iv, 510
Sheridan, (Rev.) Edw., iii, 201; iv, 577
Sherley, see Shirley
Sherman, Thos., iv, 204
Shernecombe, Rob. de, iii, 340
Sherrard, Ellen, iii, 460; Rob., iii, 460
Sherrington, Will., iii, 264
Sherwin, Will., ii, 210; —, iv, 15
Sherwood, Walt., iv, 627
Shete (Gatcombe), see Sheat
Shete (Petersfield), see Sheet
Shete (Whippingham), see Shide
Shete Farm (Ropley), iii, 57
Shett, see Sheet
Shevelegh, de, Pet., iii, 361; Sarah, iii, 361
Sheynclyng, see Shanklin

Shide (Whippingham), ii, 230; v, 200, 210, 228, 230, 235, 263; mill, v, 139
Shide Bridge (Arreton), v, 140
Shide Down, v, 210, 234
Shields, Rev. B. J., iv, 149
Shifford, West, (Berks.), ii, 227
Shikehorn, Will., v, 44
Shilton (Oxon), ii, 140, 141, 143, 145
Shilton Warren (Chilton Candover), iv, 185
Shipbuilding, v, 269, 370, 372, 373, 376, 380, 385, 386, 387, 391, 398, 403, 458
Shipley, Jonathan, ii, 115; iii, 339, 405; Mrs., iii, 339
Shipman, Rog., v, 80
Shipman's Bottom (Faccombe), iv, 314
Shipping returns, v, 364, 374, 375, 377, 379, 380
Shipton [Shupton], (de), Gilb., iii, 293; Joan, iv, 492; John, iv, 492
Shipton Bellinger, iv, 333, 383, 391, 393, 489, 512-14; adv., ii, 21; iv, 514; ch., iv, 513; mans., ii, 114; iv, 512; pop., v, 438; sch., ii, 404
Shipton Mayne (Gloucs.), ii, 126
Shirborne, see Sherborne
Shirdoune (Hannington), iv, 229
Shirebourne Decani, see Sherborne St. John
Shirefeld, see Sherfield
Shirefunte (S. Damerham), iv, 586
Shirfelde, see Sherfield
Shirlen's Copse [Shirland Crofte] (Newnham), iv, 156, 157
Shirley (Millbrook), ii, 162, 163; iii, 402, 427; iv, 520, 522; ch., iii, 431; man., ii, 193; iii, 429
Shirley (Sopley), v, 127, 128
Shirley, hund., ii, 421; v, 81
Shirley [Scherleg, Sherley, Surlie] (de), Isabel, iii, 429; Jack, v, 517, 533, 534; Jas., v, 533, 534; Jane, ii, 125; John, iii, 429; iv, 514; Nich., iii, 429, 494, 495; Rog., iii, 429; Sim., iii, 429
Shirlock, see Shurlock
Shirnham, Juliana, ii, 129
Shirrell Heath, iii, 285
Shite, man. (Petersfield), see Sheet
Shittelhams (Romsey), iv, 452
Shoare, Eliz., iii, 488
Shobley (Ellingham), iv, 559, 563
Shoddesden, man. (Kimpton), iv, 373 n, 374, 376 n
Shoddesden, Great, (Kimpton), iv, 372; Rom. rem., i, 295, 346
Shoddesden, Little, (Kimpton), iv, 372
Shoddesden, West, (Kimpton), iv, 366, 374
Shoemakers, trade regulations, v, 456
Shoflet (Whippingham), v, 183
Shoflet Creek (Whippingham), v, 200
Sholing, ii, 147, 148; iii, 297; v, 427; brick-making, v, 465; ch., iii, 299; prehist. rem., i, 260; Rom. coins, i, 346
Shonne, John, iv, 341, 392; Julia, iv, 392
Shooting, v, 556-60, 565-8
Shopton, see Chewton
Shorefield Copse (Milford), v, 116
Shoreham (Suss.), v, 362
Shorewell, ii, 26
Shorey, Geo. P., iv, 614
Shorling, see Sharland

Shorston, Rob. de, v, 480 n
Short, Hugh, v, 117 n; Thos. V., iv, 430
Shortelond (Breamore), iv, 598
Shortheath Common, iii, 4
Shorthose, W., v, 140
Short Lane (Penton Mewsey), iv, 381
Shortled Furlong (Faccombe), iv, 314
Shortrigg (Rowborough), v, 230
Shortstiche (Romsey), iv, 452
Shorwell, v, 209, 211, 234, 249, 278-84; adv., v, 284; char., v, 284; ch., v, 282; Nonconf., v, 284; pop., v, 449; sch., ii, 408
Shorwell, North, man., see North Court (Shorwell)
Shorwell, North, tithing (W. Medine), v, 210
Shorwell, South, man., see West Court (Shorwell)
Shorwell, South, tithing (W. Medine), v, 210
Shorwell [Schorwell] (de), Joan, v, 279; Rob., iv, 490 n; v, 231, 279; Will., iv, 490 n; v, 241, 279
Shory, Thos., iv, 468
Shotesbroke, Amice, ii, 521; Rob., iii, 416; iv, 283
Shothanger Copse (Monk Sherborne), iv, 231
Shottere, John, iv, 537
Shotteshale, ii, 147, 148
Shreton, ii, 163
Shrewsbury, Frances, ctss. of, v, 93; earls of, v, 354; Geo., iii, 105; iv, 636; Hugh de Montgomery, iii, 103, 134; iv, 645; John, v, 93; Rob. de Montgomery [de Belesme], iii, 94, 103, 134, 145; iv, 645; v, 301; Rog. de Montgomery, iii, 103, 131, 134, 136, 145; iv, 314, 381, 549, 616, 619, 620, 625, 644; v, 101, 114, 125, 126, 129
Shrimpton, Marg., iv, 200; Mich., iv, 200; Will., iv, 301
Shroner, Rom. rem., i, 346
Shrubb (Shalden), iv, 101
Shrubb, C. P., v, 532; John L., iv, 616; John P., iv, 622
Shrub Copse (Selborne), iii, 5
Shuckburgh, Abigail, iv, 209; Cath., Lady, iv, 200, 363; Sir Chas., iv, 200, 363; Sir John, iv, 200, 209; v, 490; Sir Stewkley, iv, 209
Shuldeleye, Will. de, iv, 340
Shulvele, see Shelveley
Shupton, fam., see Shipton
Shupton Berenger, see Shipton Bellinger
Shurlock [Shirlock], Sarah, iii, 325; Will., ii, 127
Shute (Brighstone), ii, 137, 138; v, 209, 213
Shute, fam., see Chute
Shuttleworth, P. N., ii, 359
Shyde Down, see Shide Down
Shyrebourn, see Sherborne
Shyrefeud, Shyrefeld, Shyrfeld, see Sherfield-English and Sherfield-upon-Loddon
Shyrefeld Werblynton, see Sherfield-upon-Loddon
Sibbertoft, man. (Northants), iv, 506
Sibil, v, 231
Sibley, Eliz., iii, 345
Sida, Side, see Shide
Sidemontaine, see Sydmonton
Sidenham, see Sydenham
Sidford, man. (Eling), see Langley
Sidley Wood (Ashmansworth), iv, 274

INDEX

Sidmanton, Sidmonton, *see* Sydmonton

Sidmouth, Henry Addington, vsct., ii, 354

Sidnam, *see* Sydenham

Sidney, Frances, iii, 318 ; Sir Hen. iii, 318, 424 ; Sir Phil., iii, 318, 424 ; Sir Rob., iii, 424, 425 ; Sir Will., iii, 318, 424 ; fam., arms, iii, 424

Sidown Hill (Highclere), iv, 285

Sidown Warren (Woodcott), iv, 331

Siffride, Joan, iv, 378 ; John, iv, 378 ; Nich., iv, 378 ; Will., iv, 378

Sifrewast [Syfrewast] (de), Agnes, iv, 282 ; Ann, iv, 282 ; Godf., iv, 215 ; Hen., iv, 282 ; Hugh, iv, 180 ; Isabel, iv, 282 ; John, iii, 361 ; iv, 215, 216, 358 ; Maud, iii, 367, 368 ; Nich., iii, 367 ; iv, 282 ; Philippa, iv, 282 ; Ralph, iv, 215 ; Rich., iii, 360, 363, 367, 368 ; iv, 215 ; Rob., iv, 215, 282 ; Rog., iii, 360, 362, 367 ; iv, 180, 215, 216, 282 ; Will., iv, 215, 282 ; fam., arms, iv, 180, 215

Sigayn, Christian, v, 46 ; Rob., v, 46

Sigeberht [Sigebryht], i, 393 ; iii, 504 ; v, 295

Siggesford (Eling), iv, 547

Siginworth, *see* Segenworth

Silchester, ii, 102 ; iv, 31, 51-6, 435 ; adv., iv, 56 ; char., iv, 56 ; ch., iv, 54 ; man., iv, 52 ; man.-house, iv, 51 ; Ogam stone, i, 279 ; ii, 234-6 ; pop., v, 440 ; Rom. town, i, 262, 268, 269, 270, 271-84, 293, 305, 306, 319, 320, 321, 322, 346, 350-72, 384, 392 ; iv, 51 ; v, 463 *n* ; sch., ii, 404

Silchester Brook, iv, 52, 219

Silchester Common, iv, 51, 433 *n*

Silchester Hall (Silchester), iv, 52

Silchester House (Silchester), iv, 51

Silk industry, v, 451, 487, 488

Silk Meadow (Stratfield Turgis), iv, 63

Silk Mill Cottages (Overton), iv, 212

Silkstead [Silksted] (Compton and Hursley), ii, 87, 114, 320 ; iii, 401, 406, 417

Silkstead [Sylkestede], Thos., ii, 48, 49, 113, 114, 115 ; iii, 422

Silley, John, iv, 589

Silver, Thos., ii, 353 ; Thos. B., iii, 127

Silver Hill (Winchester), v, 6

Silvester, the chaplain, v, 11 *n*

Silvester [Sylvester], Edm., v, 46 ; Edw., iii, 184, 270 ; Harriet, iii, 54 ; John, iii, 54, 76 ; iv, 436 ; Will., v, 483

Simeon, Christian name, *see* Simon

Simeon [Symeon], Benedicta, v, 281 ; Sir Edm. C., v, 219, 273 ; Eliz., iv, 329 ; Geoff., ii, 294 ; Joan, iii, 116 ; v, 281 ; (Sir) John, v, 211, 252, 254, 281, 535 ; Sir John S. B., v, 219 ; Louisa E., Lady, v, 219 ; Sir Rich., v, 228 ; Sir Rich. G., v, 219, 267 ; Sim., iv, 329 ; Steph., iii, 116 ; v, 281

Simmonds, Blackall, v, 539 ; Mary, iv, 26 ; *see also* Symonds

Simon, bp. of Achonry, ii, 37, 180, 232 ; mayor of Winchester, v, 34 ; parson of Crondall, iv, 15, 17 ; prior of Barton, ii, 181 ; prior of St. Swithun's, ii, 114 ; of Puckpool, v, 192 *n* ; the treasurer, iv, 211

Simonetti, Asselinus, ii, 220

Simpson, *see* Sympson

Simson, Edm. C., iv, 538 ; Si Rich., v, 267 ; *see also* Sympson

Sinah Common (Hayling), iii, 130

Sinar Lake (Hayling), v, 469

Sinclair [Seynclar, Seyntcler], Ad., ii, 177 ; iii, 15 ; D. P. v, 194 ; John, iii, 298 ; *see also* St. Clare

Sincock, Capt. Rob., v, 385

Sindhurst (Farnborough), iv, 15

Sindhurst Moor (Farnborough), iv, 15

Singer, Washington, iv, 494, 498, 519, 521, 522, 523

Singleton, John, iv, 275

Sinocacre (Barton Stacey), iv, 417

Sire, Will. le, v, 480 *n*

Sireborne, *see* Monk Sherborne

Sired, iii, 123

Sirefelle, *see* Sherfield English

Sirlei, *see* Shirley

Sirr, Jos. D'A., iii, 330 ; iv, 607

Sisters Gardens (Romsey), iv, 452

Sithe, *see* Sheet

Sivell, Thos., v, 154

Siward, iv, 57 ; v, 113 ; earl, v, 298

Siward [Seward, Sewer, Syward], Eliz., v, 624 ; Joan, iv, 624 ; (Sir) John, ii, 282 ; iv, 624 ; v, 39, 96, 108 ; Julia, v, 96 ; Ralph, iv, 302 ; Rich., iv, 360, 361, 363

Skalgrove (Crondall), iv, 6

Skegnes, Frances, iv, 476

Skelton, Capt. Chas., v, 385 ; Joan, Lady, iv, 160, 317 ; Sir Thos., iv, 317, 362 ; T. A., iii, 487

Skelyng, Joan, iv, 130

Skervill Court, *see* Sherfield Court

Sketle, Thos., ii, 167

Skevington, Thos., ii, 144, 146 ; iii, 515

Skeyers Farm (Wootton St. Lawrence), iv, 239

Skidmore (Escudemore), John, iv, 459 ; Walt., iv, 459

Skidmore Farm (Romsey), iv, 452, 459

Skikelthorp, Will., v, 69

Skilling [Skillyng, Skylling], Alice, iii, 415 ; Anne, iv, 296 *n* ; Edw., iii, 324 ; iv, 470 ; Eliz., iv, 374 ; Jane, iii, 324 ; John, ii, 506 ; iii, 445, 446, 456 ; iv, 374, 477 ; Marg., iii, 324 ; Mary, iii, 324 ; Mich., ii, 215 ; iii, 415, 445 ; iv, 296 *n* ; Rebecca, iv, 296 *n* ; Rich., ii, 445 ; Swithun, iii, 324 ; Will., iii, 324, 415, 458 ; iv, 296, 446, 477 ; fam., iv, 483 ; arms, iii, 324, 445

Skinner [Skynner, Skynnere], (le), Barbara, iii, 384 ; Hen., iv, 488 ; Seman, v, 34, 40 ; Susanna, iii, 69 ; Thos., iii, 384 ; v, 484 ; Will., iii, 69 ; v, 485 *n*

Skinner's Grove, iv, 466

Skirvington, Thos., v, 324

Skotland (Godshill), v, 170 *n*

Skullard, *see* Scullard

Skulle, Will., iv, 262, 374

Skylling, *see* Skilling

Skynnere, *see* Skinner

Slacham (Fordingbridge hund.), iv, 559

Slackstead [Slackestede], man. (Farley Chamberlayne), ii, 116, 121 ; iv, 444, 550

Slackstead, tithing (Farley Chamberlayne), iv, 443

Slade [Sladd], John, ii, 78, 79 ; iii, 373 ; iv, 281 ; Judith, iv, 281 ; Maria, iv, 281

Slade, la, (Laverstoke), iv, 208

Slade Farm (Priors Dean), iv, 436

Slader, Frances, iii, 241 ; Will., iii, 241

Slades (Up Nately), iv, 176

Sladishevede (S. Damerham), iv, 587 *n*

Slastede, *see* Slackstead

Slater Ball Syndicate, v, 155

Slatwoods (Cowes), v, 198

Slaughter Close (Basing), iv, 115

Slea [Slee], riv., ii, 515, 518

Sleaford [Slayford] Bridge (Kingsley), ii, 515

Sleddale, Alan de, v, 195 *n*

Slegh, John, ii, 228, 519 ; v, 285

Sloane, Will., iii, 483

Sloane-Stanley, Fran., iv, 393, 513, 514 ; Rev. Geo., iv, 393 ; Hans, iv, 552 ; Laura M., iv, 393 ; Rog. C. H., iii, 293, 294 ; iv, 546, 552 ; v, 274 ; Will., iv, 552 ; Will. H., iv, 552 ; *see also* Stanley

Slocomb (Carisbrooke), v, 222

Sloden Coppice (New Forest), ii, 448

Sloman, Rev. Chas., iv, 558

Sloper, Rob., iv, 107

Sly, Hen., iv, 168

Smale, Joana, iii, 525 ; Thos., iii, 525

Smalebroo, *see* Smallbrook

Smaleherepathe (Penton Mewsey); iv, 381

Small, Geo., iv, 213 ; John, v, 574

Smallbrook, man. (Newchurch), v, 183

Smallbrook, man. (Wilts.), iv, 42

Smallbrook [Smalebroo], de, Hugh, v, 183 ; Will., v, 183

Smannell, iv, 345, 379 ; adv., iv, 356 ; char., iv, 358 ; ch., iv, 355 ; Nonconf., iv, 356

Smark, Will., iv, 501

Smart, Geoff., v, 480 *n*

Smedemor, Will., v, 109

Smerat, Steph. v, 456

Smetheburgh (Kingsclere), iv, 250

Smirke, Sir Edw., v, 479

Smith (the), Alf., v, 183 ; Anastasia, iv, 432, 511 ; Anne, iii, 204 ; Barth., iii, 72, 241 ; iv, 431, 511 ; v, 80 ; Benet, v, 47 ; Betty, v, 143 ; Caleb, v, 127 ; Clement, ii, 293, 366 ; v, 474 ; Cobb, iv, 548 ; Courtenay, ii. 351 ; C. R., ii, 236 ; Edm., iii, 325 ; Eliz., iv, 214, 432 ; v, 127 ; Eustace, iv, 631 ; Frances, iv, 432 ; Geo., iv, 604 ; Grace, v, 270 ; G. D., v, 553 ; Hen., iv, 98, 214, 356, 451, 497, 604, 630 ; v, 79 ; Hen. L., iv, 511 ; Herb., iv, 548 ; Jas., iv, 431, 511 ; v, 200 *n* ; Jane, iii, 240 ; Jasper, iv, 604 ; Joe, v, 530 ; John, iv, 139, 152, 314, 358, 511, 604 ; v, 200 *n*, 235 ; Sir John S., ii, 478 ; Joshua, iv, 551 *n* ; Julian, iv, 98 ; Kath., iii, 251 ; Mary [Maria], iv, 511, 536 ; v, 127 ; Matilda, iv, 393 ; Millicent S., iv, 441 ; Nich., iv, 604 ; Rich., ii, 88 ; iii, 297, 299 ; v, 271 ; Rob., iii, 310 ; v, 188 ; Rog., v, 463 ; Sam., iv, 536 ; v, 270 ; Steph., v, 192, 227 ; Sybil, iv, 604 ; Sydney, ii, 351 ; Thos., iii, 149 ; iv, 5, 250 *n*, 267, 393 ; v, 270, 390, 525, 527 ; Thos. A., iii, 457 ; iv, 391, 393 ; v, 514, 525 *n*, 528, 531, 533, 537 ; T., v, 516 ; V. C, v, 576 ; Will., ii, 387, 391 ; iii, 12, 202, 240, 457 ; iv, 589 ; v, 463 ; Will. H., ii, 458 ; Will. S., iv, 536 ; Mrs., iv, 535 ; —, iv, 266 ; v, 147, 465, 536 ; *see also* Smyth and Smythe

Smithborowe (Wolverton), iv, 270, 271

Smith-Dampier, Jane M., iii, 341, 408
Smithers, Steph., v, 538, 540
Smith's charity, v, 79
Smuggling, v, 401, 431
Smyth, Anne, iv, 457; Rev. Geo. W., iv, 368; Joan, iii, 391; (Sir) John, iii, 393, 483; v, 340; Thos., ii, 212; iv, 457; Will., ii, 181; fam., v, 458; see also Smith and Smythe
Smythborough, see Smithborowe
Smythe, Andr., iv, 21, 25; Chas., iv, 481; Eliz., iv, 21; Hen., iv, 266; Louisa, iv, 481; Walt., iii, 334, 443, 487; iv, 481; Will., v, 266; see also Smith and Smyth
Smythes Place, le, (Bramley), iv, 141
Snakes, i, 204
Snape, la, ii, 180
Snell [Snel], Joan, iv, 224, 579; Nich., iv, 591; Rich., iv, 587, 589, 590; Thos., iv, 224, 579
Sneyd, Rev. W., v, 185
Snoddington, man. (Shipton Bellinger), iv, 513; chap., iv, 514
Snook [Snoke], Hen., iii, 144; Thos., ii, 157
Snow [Snowe], Thos., iii, 30; Will., v, 460
Soaper, John, iii, 165, 170; see also Soper
Soartin, v, 148, 206
Soberton [Sobertona], i, 378; ii, 184; iii, 245, 246, 257-68; adv., iii, 267; char., iii, 267; chs., iii, 264; mans., iii, 258; Nonconf., iii, 267; pop., v, 440; sch., ii, 404
Soberton (de, of), Hen., iv, 219; v, 304 n; John, ii, 168
Soberton Down (Soberton), v, 545
Soche, Godwin, v, 3
Social and economic history, v, 409
Soet [Soete], v, 209, 248
Soflet (Whippingham), v, 183
Softley, Rich., iii, 123
Sokyngworth, see Segenworth
Solar, see Soler
Sole, le (Long Sutton), iv, 18
Soler [Solar, Solere] (atte), Hen., iv, 589; John, iv, 482; Will., ii, 229; iv, 590
Solers [Soleres], de, Hen., iv, 592; Rich, iv, 314, 315; Will., iv, 563, 566, 567
Somborne, Kings, see King's Somborne
Somborne, Little, ii, 172, 201; iii, 401; iv, 428 n, 438, 480-2; v, 514; adv., iv, 482; ch., iv, 482; mans., iv, 440, 480; pop., v, 447; sch., ii, 400
Somborne, Upper, man. (King's Somborne), ii, 114; iv, 438, 440, 443, 474; chap., iv, 480; Manor Farm, iv, 474
Somborne, fam., see Samborne
Somer, Hen., iv, 282; Hugh, iv, 214; Kath., iv, 282; Steph., iv, 214; Will., iv, 214
Somercote, ii, 376
Somerford, man. (Christchurch), ii, 159; v, 88, 94-5, 109; fishery, v, 95 n, 467; grange, ii, 159; v, 84, 109; mill, v, 95
Somerford Grange (Highcliff), v, 84, 95
Somerley, man. (Harbridge), iv, 579, 580, 603, 604, 605, 610; v, 559
Somer's (Hartley Wintney), iv, 79
Somers, fam., see Summers

Somerset, Marg. de Holand, ctss. of, ii, 475; iv, 130, 347; dks. of, ii, 63, 64; Edm. Beaufort, v, 223, 320; Edw. Seymour, iv, 75, 80, 85, 93, 110, 111, 225, 289, 455, 497, 506, 509, 608; v, 92, 327 n; Hen. Beaufort, v, 223; John Beaufort, iv, 475; iii, 143; iv, 130, 347, 540; John Seymour, iv, 75; Will. Seymour, iii, 477; iv, 75
Somerset, (de), Aimery, iii, 425; Alice, ii, 151; Denise, iii, 425; Edw., iii, 84, 105; Hen., iii, 105, 109; (Sir) John, ii, 163; iii, 105; v, 93 n; Mary, Lady, v, 93 n; Will., iii, 105
Somersets (St. Mary Bourne), iv, 295
Somershill, iv, 114
Somersmede (Timsbury), iv, 486
Somers-Smith, Rob. V, iv, 586
Somerville, Kenelm, v, 215
Somery, (de), Hen., v, 305; John, iii, 377; Nichola, iii, 95; Rog., iii, 95; see also Saumerez
Sondes, see Sandys
Sondrehulla (Calbourne), v, 218
Sonnebury (Froyle), ii, 501
Son of Abraham, Benedict, v, 33
Son of Ace, see Son of Azo
Son of Aethehun, Tata, v, 112
Son of Aiulf, Edm., iv, 542
Son of Alan, John, iv, 366; see also Fitz Alan
Son of Aldelin, Will., v, 304; see also Fitz Aldelin
Son of Amisius, Rog., iv, 45 n
Son of Azo [Ace], Benedict, iii, 512; Geoff., iii, 505
Son of Azor, Gozelin, v, 167, 173, 183, 195, 200, 213, 231, 272, 274, 280; Will., v, 141, 142 n, 145 n, 147, 155, 155 n, 158, 160, 161, 162, 163, 165, 167, 173, 181, 183, 200, 206, 212, 213, 234, 241, 242, 251, 274
Son of Baderon, Gilb., iv, 278; Will., iv, 245 n, 278, 339
Son of Baldri [Baldric], Hugh, iii, 378; iv, 57, 191, 225
Son of Baldwin, Rich., v, 213
Son of Brixi [Brisei], Alsi, iv, 525; v, 284
Son of Croc, Rainald, v, 243 n
Son of Elias [Elyas], Walt., v, 49; Will., iv, 592; see also Fitz Ellis
Son of Folcher, Rog., iii, 505
Son of Geoffrey, John, iv, 607; see also Fitz Geoffrey
Son of Gerold [Gerald], Rob., ii, 420; iii, 455; iv, 227, 391, 392, 393, 394, 491, 513, 568; see also Fitz Gerald
Son of Godfrey, Pet., iii, 383
Son of Hamon, Alan, iv, 366; Will., iv, 366, 368; see also Fitz Hamon
Son of Henry, John, iv, 360; v, 163 n; see also Fitzhenry
Son of Herbert, Herb., iv, 548; Matth., iii, 134, 195; v, 181; see also Fitzherbert
Son of Hubert, Eudo, iv, 198
Son of Hugh, see Fitz Hugh
Son of Ivez, Will., v, 305
Son of John, Geoff., iv, 561; John, v, 128; Matth., iii, 409, 410; v, 183; Rob., iv, 77 n; v, 128; Thos., v, 117; see also Fitz John
Son of Luke, Mich., iv, 352
Son of Madoc, Rob., iii, 386
Son of Mark, Rog., v, 270
Son of Martin, Nich., iv, 592; Rob., iv, 592 n; see also Fitz Martin

Son of Manne, Will., iv, 417
Son of Matthew, Herb., iii, 135; John, iii, 135; Pet., iii, 137, 195
Son of Meinfelin, Hamon, iv, 366, 368
Son of Milo, Rog., iii, 505
Son of Murdac, Rob., iv, 339 n, 340
Son of Nigel, Ralph, v, 164
Son of Odo, Steph., v, 164
Son of Osgar, Alf., iv, 401
Son of Osmund, Hugh, iv, 449
Son of Other, see Fitz Other
Son of Otto, Hugh, iv, 340
Son of Peter, Godf., v, 304 n; Herb., iii, 486; John, iii, 487; Reg., iv, 219; v, 2, 3; see also Fitz Peter
Son of Ralf, Geoff., iv, 352; Turstin, iii, 26, 29
Son of Reginald, John, iv, 219; Pet., v, 273; see also Fitz Reginald
Son of Remi, Herb., iv, 443
Son of Richard, Rich., v, 191; Rog., v, 305
Son of Robert, Rich., iv, 148; Will., iv, 171 n; see also Fitz Robert
Son of Roger, Rich., v, 191; Walt., iv, 499; Will., v, 304 n; see also Fitz Roger
Son of Rolf, see Son of Ralf
Son of Saer, John, iv, 141 n
Son of Saulf, Alwi, iv, 515
Son of Seifrid, Ralph [Ralf], iv, 215, 282
Son of Stur, Will., iv, 438; v, 128, 142 n, 143, 145, 146, 151, 159, 160, 162, 172, 191, 198, 200, 202, 219, 228 n, 236, 237, 246, 281, 282
Son of Thomas, see Fitz Thomas
Son of Thurstan [Turstin], Rich., ii, 484; iii, 21, 498; iv, 437; Will., iii, 21
Son of Torber [Turber], Alwi, iv, 519, 559 n, 572, 577, 582
Son of Ulf, see Fitz Ulf
Son of Walter, Svelfus, iii, 487; Will., iv, 592 n; v, 118; see also Fitz Walter
Son of William, Reg., v, 165; see also Fitz William
Soper, Amy, iii, 370; Frances, iii, 371; Patience, iii, 370, 373; Rich., iv, 258; Rob., ii, 392; v, 482; Will., ii, 443; iii, 370, 371, 373; v, 367, 368, 482 n; see also Soaper
Soperton, see Soberton
Sophia, princess, v, 269
Sopley, ii, 21, 68; v, 81, 82, 89 n, 127-32; adv., v, 132; chap., v, 127; ch., v, 127, 130; common, v, 127, 128; mans., v, 128; mills, v, 127, 130; Nonconf., v, 127; pop., v, 445; sch., ii, 404
Sorbiodunum, see Sarum, Old
Sorell, Eliz., iii, 496
Soresdene, see Sarson
Sorewell, de, Rob., v, 284; Will., v, 280
Sotesdene, see Shoddesden
Sotherington, see Temple Sotherington
Sotingor (Wherwell), iv, 411
Sottone Bishop, see Bishop's Sutton
Sotwell (Berks.), ii, 227
Sotwell, Marg., iv, 290 n, 296; Margery, iv, 354; Thos., iv, 354; Will., iv, 290 n, 351, 354
Sotwell's Farm, see Seymour's Place
Souberbielle, Edw., iv, 633
South [Southe], Clement, v, 484; Edw., iv, 371; Margery, iv, 83; Pet., iv, 25; Rich., iv, 371;

INDEX

South (*cont.*)
Rob., iv, 97 ; Sam., iv, 371 ; Thos., iii, 125 ; iv, 83, 491, 628
Southale, man. (Arreton), v, 143, 237
Southam, Rob., v, 97, 113
Southampton, i, 381, 384 ; ii, 5, 7, 8, 15, 17, 23, 32, 35, 36, 53, 54, 60, 62, 74, 75, 81, 91, 92, 93, 95, 96, 98, 101, 102, 105, 137, 142, 144, 145, 146, 148, 154, 160, 162, 163, 165, 177, 180, 181, 189, 203, 205, 223, 251, 290, 385, 386, 421 ; iii, 490-537 ; iv, 642 ; v, 295, 306, 311, 312, 316, 317, 319 *n*, 323 *n*, 331, 341, 359-408, 415-18, 420, 423, 426, 427, 428, 430, 431, 433, 434, 462 ; assessment, v, 324 ; Audit House, iii, 535 ; cattle show, v, 504 ; char., iii, 535 ; chs., i, 395 ; ii, 230, 241, 244 ; iii, 524-34 ; cricket, v, 575-6 ; dock and quays, iii, 504, 523 ; v, 361, 363, 367, 371, 393 ; fee-farm, iii, 506, 507 ; Franciscan friary, ii, 193 ; God's House, *see* that title ; leper hosp., v, 418 ; pier, iii, 524 ; v, 401 ; pop., v, 450 ; racing, v, 543, 546 ; Rom. rem., i, 347, 395, 396 ; St. Denis, priory of, *see* that title ; St. Julian's Hospital, *see* God's House (Southampton) ; schs., ii, 273, 368, 387, 388-90, 393, 404, 405 ; iii, 535 ; ship building, iii, 521 ; v, 367, 387, 391, 398 ; trade and ind., iii, 520 ; v, 451, 454, 456-7, 460, 461, 465-9, 473-4, 476, 48., 484-6, 489-71 ; volunteers, v, 356 ; Walloon settlement, ii, 75
Southampton, Arthur T. Lyttelton, bp. of, iii, 112
Southampton, Joan Wriothesley, ctss. of, iv, 651 *n* ; earls of, ii, 76 ; iv, 72, 545, 650 *n* ; v, 187 *n*, 197 *n*, 326, 330, 335 ; Hen. Wriothesley, iii, 20, 39, 168, 171, 192, 220, 224, 225, 231, 232, 253, 259, 343, 365, 389, 391, 394, 466, 479 ; iv, 8, 9, 72, 192 *n*, 388, 450, 454, 632, 651 ; v, 140, 224, 227 ; Thos. Wriothesley, ii, 58, 59, 121, 139, 145, 186, 213, 303, 450 ; iii, 20, 39, 135, 145, 146, 159, 192, 211, 212, 215, 220, 224, 225, 226, 227, 228, 230, 231, 242, 248, 253, 259, 261, 262, 283, 293, 343, 344, 365, 391, 392, 393, 400, 421, 458, 466, 479, 480, 481 ; iv, 8, 72, 110, 111, 192 *n*, 255, 283, 289, 324, 331, 358, 413, 432, 447, 450, 486, 493, 494, 502, 525, 608, 632, 650, 651 ; v, 92 *n*, 93, 96, 108, 132, 142, 143, 176, 275 ; Will. Fitz-william, ii, 144, 490, 513 ; iii, 18, 90, 105, 117, 135, 442 ; iv, 34, 85, 196, 200, 278 ; v, 269 *n*, 325
Southampton, de, of, Dorothy, ii, 163 ; Gervaise, iv, 547, 558 ; Rog., iv, 558 ; Will., ii, 190, 191
Southampton Castle, iii, 497-500
Southampton Common, iii, 494
Southampton Water, i, 378 ; iii, 490, 519 ; v, 359 ; prehist. rem., i, 256, 257
Southavon, man. (Sopley), v, 130
Southayes (Milton), v, 124
Southbourne (Bournemouth), v, 83, 133, 134, 155
Southcheveton, *see* Chewton, man.
Southcotes (Itchen Stoke), iv, 192
Southcott [Southcot], Rob., v, 119 ; Will., v, 156
Southdown, ii, 159

Southdown (Hurstbourne Tarrant), iv, 321
South Downs (Chilton Candover), iv, 185
Southe, *see* South
Southend (Soberton), iii, 258
Southerton, —, v, 575
Southese, man., ii, 121
Southey, Cath., iv, 616 ; Rob., iv, 616 ; v, 85
Southford (Whitwell), v, 203
South Garden, *see* Sutt Garden
Southgate (Winchester), v, 34
South Hants Cricket Club, v, 574
Southington (Overton), iv, 197, 213
Southington (Selborne), *see* Temple Sotherington
Southington House (Overton), iv, 211
Southley Copse (Overton), iv, 211
Southley Wood (Overton), iv, 211
Southmede (Breamore), iv, 598 *n*
Southover, Diamanda, iv, 495 ; John, iv, 495, 528
Southrope, man. (Herriard), iii, 368 ; iv, 66, 160
Southsea (Portsmouth), iii, 196 ; v, 402, 433
Southwade St. Lawrence, man. (St. Lawrence), v, 193
Southwanborow, Southwarghe-borgh, Southwargheburn, *see* Warnborough, South
Southwark (Surr.), ii, 146
Southwarmeborne, *see* Warn-borough, South
Southwathe (St. Lawrence), v, 194
Southwelbergh, ii, 156
Southwell, Geo. Ridding, bp. of, ii, 364, 366 ; v, 16
Southwell, Eliz., iv, 28 ; Geo., v, 522 ; John, iv, 486 ; Sir Rich., iv, 28 ; Rob., ii, 125 ; Ursula, iv, 486
Southwick [Southwike], ii, 63, 69, 93, 139, 164, 166, 167 ; iii, 140, 161-5 ; iv, 264 ; v, 307, 319 *n*, 418 ; adv., iii, 164 ; char., iii, 164 ; ch., iii, 164 ; fair, v, 417, man., ii, 168 ; iii, 162 ; pop., v, 441 ; Rom. rem., i, 347 ; sch., ii, 405
Southwick Priory, ii, 20, 49, 58, 59, 61, 104, 164-8, 311 ; iii, 161, 162, 193, 377 ; iv, 103, 146, 194, 258, 259, 423, 424, 436 ; v, 419 ; arms, iii, 375, 456 ; Guy, prior of, ii, 168 ; iv, 232 *n* ; Rich. Nowell, prior of, ii, 166, 168 ; iv, 259
Southwood, *see* Hayling, South
Southworth, John, iv, 8 ; Mary, iv, 8
Soutton (Brighstone), *see* Sutton
Sowley (Beaulieu), iv, 650 ; iron mills, v, 464
Sowley House (Beaulieu), v, 564
Sowley Pond (Beaulieu), v, 564, 568
Sowy, Nich. de, iv, 142 *n*
Spaigne, Hugh de, iii, 361
Span, man. (Godshill), ii, 180 ; v, 174
Spanish Green (Stratfield Turgis), iv, 63
Sparkes [Sparks], John, iii, 325 ; Rich., iii, 325 ; Will., iv, 213
Sparkford (Compton), ii, 114 ; iii, 401 ; v, 47 ; mill, v, 49
Sparkford, Edw. of, v, 481
Sparry, Rob., v, 117
Sparsholt [Sparshall], ii, 21, 73 ; iii, 401, 444-7 ; iv, 477, 486 *n* ; adv., iii, 447 ; char., iii, 447 ; chs., iii, 446 ; man., ii, 114 ; iii, 444 ; pop., v, 447 ; Rom. rem., i, 312, 347 ; sch., ii, 405
Sparsholt (Romsey), *see* Spurshot

Sparsholt [Spersholte, Spershute, Spurshot], (de), Hen., ii, 182, 186 ; Sir Nich., ii, 16 ; Phil., ii, 503 ; iii, 445 ; Rich., iii, 445 ; Will., ii, 503 ; iii, 324, 445
Spartali, Mich., v, 146, 174
Spaund, la, *see* Span
Spaycock, Jas., iii, 207
Speake, *see* Speke
Spearywell (Broughton), iv, 503 ; Nonconf., iv, 510
Speed [Spede], Elmer, v, 290 ; Harriet, iv, 558 ; John, iii, 54 ; iv, 558 ; Rev. John M., iv, 558 ; Rich., ii, 165 ; Sam., ii, 346
Speen (Berks.), i, 272, 319, 320
Speke [Speake], Dorothy, Lady, iv, 106 ; Eliz., Lady, iv, 106 ; (Sir) Geo., iv, 105, 121 ; Hen., iv, 327 ; Sir Hugh, iv, 106 ; Joan, iv, 326 ; (Sir) John, iv, 327 ; v, 188 ; Mary, iv, 121 ; Rich., iv, 327 ; Sim., iv, 327 ; Thos., iv, 327 ; Will., iv, 326
Spence, John, iv, 397
Spencer, earl, v, 178
Spencer [Spenser], Nich., v, 143 ; Will., v, 470
Speresholt, *see* Sparsholt
Sperlyng [Sperling], (de), And., iv, 395 *n* ; v, 117 *n* ; John, v, 231
Spersholte, Spershute, *see* Sparsholt
Spert, Thos., v, 373
Spice Mead (Crondall), iv, 6
Spicer, (le), Hen., v, 367 ; John, iv, 458 ; v, 95, 107, 142 ; Rebecca, v, 142 ; Rich., v, 367 ; Sir Sam., v, 142 ; Rev. Will. W., iv, 192
Spicer, H. and W. R., paper makers, ii, 483 ; iv, 71 ; v, 490
Spicker, John, v, 94, 95
Spiders, i, 165
Spier [Spyre], Jas., iv, 168 ; Jane, iv, 168 ; Rich., iv, 132 ; Susannah, iv, 217
Spigurnel, Kath., Lady, iv, 427 ; Sir Ralph, iv, 427 ; Thos., iv, 427
Spileman [Spillman], Cath., iv, 627 ; Christine, iv, 536 ; Isabel, v, 116 *n* ; Maud, iv, 627 ; Pet., iv, 627 ; v, 116 *n* ; Rob., v, 305 ; Will., iv, 627, 628 ; v, 116 ; fam., v, 117
Spiller, John, iv, 476
Spinae, *see* Speen
Spine [Spyny], (de), Maud, ii, 123, 124, 126 ; Will., ii, 165
Spinks, Sarah, iii, 432, 536
Spinney, Ad., iv, 373, 376 ; Denise, iv, 373 ; Hugh, iv, 366, 373 *n*, 376 *n* ; Isabel, iv, 373 ; John, iv, 366 ; Margery, iv, 373
Spircok [Spircock], Edm., iv, 338 *n*, 528 ; Hugh, iv, 362 ; John, iv, 362 ; Julia, iv, 528 ; Marg., iv, 373 ; Thos., iv, 362
Spiring, Geoff., ii, 192
Spirygs, Nich., v, 17
Spithead, i, 386 ; mutiny, iii, 186 ; v, 397 ; naval reviews, v, 404
Splette, la, (Long Sutton), iv, 18
Splotlonde (Hannington), iv, 229
Spolicombe (Froyle), ii, 501
Spolt, le, (Bentley), iv, 27
Sponges, i, 92
Sport, v, 513-76
Sprack, fam., v, 203
Spragg, John, v, 34
Sprai [Esprai], (de), Geoff., iv, 39 ; Herb., iv, 39
Sprake, John, iv, 570 ; Oscar, v, 236 ; Will., iv, 570
Springbourne (Bournemouth), v, 134, 135 ; sch., ii, 405
Springfield (Stockbridge), v, 554

Springham, Rich., ii, 516 ; iii, 12
Springvale (St. Helens), v, 190
Spring Wood (Hackwood Park), iv, 114
Sprot, E. M., iv, 27 ; v, 575, 576
Spurshot (Romsey), iv, 452, 456, 555
Spurshot, Great, (Romsey), iv, 457
Spurshot, Little, (Romsey), iv, 457
Spurshot, fam., see Sparsholt
Spye Bush Plantation (Swarraton), iv, 195
Spynile [Spynell], Ant., v, 485 n ; Bald., v, 483 n
Spyny, see Spine
Spyre, see Spier
Spyttel in Spyttelstrete (Romsey Infra), iv, 460
Spyttelstrete (Romsey), iv, 452
Square Burghfield (Stratfieldsaye), iv, 57
Squerell, Eleanor, ii, 151
Squire, John, v, 291 ; Jos., v, 245, 291
Squires, —, v, 517, 526, 527 n
Stac, Rob., v, 168 n
Stacy [Stacey], (de), John, ii, 208 ; iv, 92 ; v, 29 ; see also Sacy
Stafford, Marg., ctss. of, iv, 361, 458, 576 ; earls of, iv, 381, 458 ; Ralph, iii, 247 ; iv, 361, 576 ; Thos., iv, 361 ; Will., iv, 361
Stafford, Anne, v, 237 ; Constance, iv, 370 ; Dumfraville, v, 160 n ; Edw., iii, 116 ; iv, 361, 370 ; Eliz., v, 160 ; Hen., iii, 116 ; iv, 361, 576 ; (Sir) Humph., iii, 113 ; iv, 370 ; v, 160 ; John, ii, 286 ; iv, 370 ; Marg., iv, 370 ; Will., v, 237 ; fam., arms, iii, 247
Staines (Midd.), iv, 41
Stake, Alan, iii, 149 ; Ellen, iii, 149 ; Nich., iii, 214 ; Will., iii, 149
Stakelhurst, man., see Staplehurst
Stakes, man. (Farlington), iii, 150
Stakes Hill (Farlington), iii, 148, 150
Stallard, G. and A., paper makers, v, 490
Stallingforlonge (Kimpton), iv, 372
Stamford [Stanford], (de), John, ii, 162, 163 ; Ralf, iv, 242 ; Rich., ii, 163 ; Will., ii, 213 ; iii, 457
Stamford and Warrington, earl of, v, 547, 548, 554
Stamford fair (Lincs.), v, 38 n
Stamforlang (Longstock), iv, 449
Stampe [Stempe], Giles, iv, 325 ; Lydia, iv, 325 ; Thos., ii, 309 ; 366 ; iii, 23
Stampit, Adeline of, ii, 154
Stamshaw (Portsea), iii, 191, 193
Stamshaw clay, v, 453
Stanbridge, John, ii, 271
Stanbridge Earls, man. (Romsey), iv, 457, 458
Stanbridge Hall (Romsey), iv, 452, 458
Stanbridge Ranvilles, man. (Romsey), iv, 438, 457
Stanbrigge Comitis, Stanbrigge Erles, see Stanbridge Earls
Stanbroke, Phil., ii, 166, 167, 168
Stanchester Field (Chilton Candover), iv, 183 n ; Rom. rem., i, 306 ; iv, 185
Standbridge, see Stanbridge
Standen, East, man. (Arreton), v, 146
Standen, East, tithing (E. Medine), v, 138
Standen, Great East, (Arreton), v, 147
Standen, Little East, (Arreton), v, 147

Standen, West, man. (Arreton), v, 147
Standen, West, tithing (E. Medine), v, 138
Standen Elms (Arreton), v, 147
Standhurste (St. Mary Bourne), iv, 296
Standish, Arth., ii, 449 ; Thos., v, 200 ; Will., iii, 117 ; W. C., v, 529, 570, 573 ; W. P., iii, 332 ; v, 528, 556
Standon (Hursley), iii, 401, 417, 421
Stane, (de la), John B., iv, 103, 106 ; Pet., iii, 17 ; see also Stone
Staneberie, see Stenbury
Stanesby, see Stansby
Stanfigg (Newtown), iv, 292
Stanfit, ii, 169
Stanford, see Stamford
Stanham, see Stoneham
Stanhope [Stonhupe], (de la), Hen., iii, 361 ; Hen. S., iv, 198 ; Will., iii, 361
Stanley, Edw., ii, 322, 323, 366 ; Geo., iv, 552 ; v, 115 ; Hans, iv, 552 ; v, 182, 224, 274 ; Hen., iv, 550 ; Joan, iv, 77 n ; (Sir) Will., ii, 476 ; iii, 45, 293, 294 ; iv, 552 ; v, 212 ; see also Sloane-Stanley
Stanley's Common (Hordle), v, 110
Stanpit (Christchurch), ii, 152 ; v, 81, 100
Stanpit Field (Christchurch), v, 83
Stansby [Stanesby], Eliz., iii, 392 ; John, iii, 392 ; iv, 521 ; Rich., iii, 393 ; Rob., iii, 392 ; Will., iii, 392 ; iv, 521 ; v, 514, 518
Stanstead College (Chalton), iii, 103, 110
Stanstede, Rich., ii, 212, 272
Stanswood, man. (Fawley), ii, 181 ; iii, 294
Stanton, (de), Emma, iv, 191 ; Rog., v, 89 n, 128 ; —, ii, 391 ; see also Staunton
Stanton Drew, ii, 169
Stantons (Kingsclere), iv, 266
Stantor, Joan, iv, 512 ; Pet., iv, 512, 513 n
Stanwell, man. (Midd.), ii, 479, 492, 493 ; iv, 224
Stapelbrugge, Steph. de, ii, 27, 155
Stapeldon, see Stapleton
Stapele, la, (Wherwell), iv, 411
Stapellis, fam., see Stapely
Stapely [Stapeleg], man. (Odiham), iv, 92, 93 n
Stapely, tithing (Odiham), iv, 67, 88
Stapely [Stapellis], de, Ad., iv, 92 ; v, 305 ; John, iv, 92
Stapely Down Farm (Odiham), iv, 92
Staple Cross [Staple] (Christchurch), v, 85
Stapledon, see Stapleton
Stapleford (Wilts.), ii, 163
Stapleham (S. Damerham), iv, 589
Staple House (Winchester), v, 2
Staplehurst [Staplers], man. (Arreton), ii, 139 ; v, 148
Stapleton [Stapeldon, Stapledon], (de), Eliz., iv, 521 ; Joan, iv, 521 ; (Sir) Miles, iv, 521 ; v, 99 ; Nich., iv, 93 ; Rich., iii, 415 ; v, 188 ; Thos., iii, 308 ; Walt., bp. of Exeter ii, 31 ; iii, 22, 415
Staplewood Hill Eling, iv, 546
Stappell, see Stapely
Stappelweie (Lasham), iv, 81
Starch manufacture, v, 457
Stares, Clewer, iv, 646 ; G. H., iii, 300 ; Hen., iii, 205 ; Jas., iii, 205 ; John, iv, 56, 365 ; J. C., iii, 300 ; —, v, 465, 536

Stargroves (East Woodhay), iv, 306
Star Hill House (Elvetham), iv, 74
Starie, Elias, iii, 487
Starkey, Will., iii, 45
Starling, Noah, iv, 266
Starnes, C., v, 535
Staunden (King's Somborne), iv, 470
Staundenwode, Staunedenewode, see Standen
Staunton, Sir Geo. T., iii, 123 ; see also Stanton
Stavely, Ant., ii, 120
Staverton, Anne, iv, 34 ; Deodatus, iv, 34, 41 ; Edith, iv, 34 n ; Fran., iv, 34 ; Rich., iv, 34, 41 ; Thos., iv, 34
Stawell, Abigail, Lady, iv, 43, 44 ; Mary, Lady, ii, 477, 519 ; iii, 425 ; Lds., ii, 453 ; iii, 87, 143 ; v, 357, 513 ; Edw., iii, 322 ; Hen., ii, 477, 509, 516, 519 ; iii, 425 ; John, iv, 549 ; Ralph, iv, 43
Stawell [Stowell], Edw., iii, 39 ; Hen., iii, 322 ; Mary, ii, 516, 519 ; iii, 322 ; Will., ii, 195, 196, 197
Staytont, Geo. H., iv, 74
Steadcroft (Eversley), iv, 33
Steans Farm (Arreton), v, 150
Stedam (Suss.), ii, 490
Steele, Anne, iv, 493, 496 ; Eliz., iv, 496 ; Hen., iv, 497 ; Rich., ii, 391 ; iv, 356, 484 ; Will., iv, 496, 497, 628
Steep [Steepe], iii, 63, 77-81 ; adv., iii, 80 ; char., iii, 80 ; ch., iii, 79 ; man., iii, 78 ; pop., v, 444 ; sch., ii, 405 ; watercress, v, 455
Steep harriers, v, 537
Steephill (Newchurch), v, 182
Steephill Castle (Newchurch), v, 182
Steeple Ashton (Wilts.), ii, 126, 131
Steeplechasing, v, 545
Steeple Court [Steeple] (Droxford), iii, 286
Steeple Langford (Wilts.), v, 99
Stelhard, John, ii, 149
Stella, Hen. de, v, 268 n
Stempe, see Stampe
Stenbury, man. (Godshill), v, 174
Stenbury, tithing (East Medine), v, 138
Stenesnoc, iv, 45
Stenning, Rev. Geo. C., iv, 218
Stent, John, ii, 483, 501
Stent & Sons, paper makers, v, 490
Stenybury, la, see Stenbury
Stepe, John, ii, 178, 179
Stepellavynton, Jas. de, ii, 211
Stephen, king, ii, 12, 108, 160, 216, 421, 513 ; iii, 42 ; iv, 71, 86, 97, 102 n, 196, 324, 373, 626 ; v, 100, 302, 360
Stephen, 232 ; abbot of Tiron, ii, 225
Stephens, Anabella, iv, 167 n ; Eliz., v, 233 ; Capt. Fred., iv, 68 ; Hen., v, 233 ; Hen. C., iv, 337 ; (Rev.) John, iv, 254 ; v, 192 ; Juliana, v, 192 ; Mary, (Lady), v, 228, 233 ; (Sir) Rich., iii, 270 ; iv, 167 n ; v, 99, 125 ; Thos., ii, 58 ; (Sir) Will., v, 228, 233 ; Will. R. W., ii, 115 ; see also Stevens
Stephen's Castle Down (Bishop's Waltham), iii, 276
Stephenson, Geo. R., v, 269 ; see also Stevenson
Stephen's Wood (Sutton Warblington), iv, 18
Stephyns (Elvetham), iv, 74
Stepington, see Steventon
Steptoe, John, iii, 535

Sterling, John, v, 155 ; *see also* Stirling

Sternhold, Judith, iv, 444 ; Philippa, iv, 444 ; Thos., iii, 418 ; iv, 444

Sterre, iv, 502

Stertemede (Bramley), iv, 141

Stevenbir, *see* Stenbury

Stevenbury, man. (Preston Candover), iii, 373

Stevens [Stevyns], John, iv, 274, 501 ; J., v, 458 ; Rob., ii, 301 ; Thos., ii, 144, 145, 146, 148, 149 ; v, 126 ; Will., v, 99 n ; W. G., v, 554 ; *see also* Stephens

Stevenson, Rob. L., v, 134 ; *see also* Stephenson

Steventon, ii, 63 ; iv, 19, 113, 114, 166, 171-4, 197, 200 ; adv., iv, 174 ; char., iv, 174 ; ch., iv, 173 ; man., iv, 171 ; manor house, ii, 238 ; iv, 171, 173 ; pop., v, 442 ; sch., ii, 405 ; iv, 174

Steventon, Rob. de, iv, 171 n

Stevyns, *see* Stevens

Steward, Edm., ii, 65, 72, 115, 190 ; —, v, 544 ; *see also* Stewart & Stuart

Steward Land (Romsey), iv, 452

Stewards (Kingsley), ii, 515

Stewart, Alex., v, 280 ; Anne, iv, 54 ; Rev. Edw., iii, 447 ; Eliz., v, 280 ; Sir Herb., v, 17 ; Will., iv, 54 ; Major, v, 345 ; *see also* Steward & Stuart

Stewkley [Stewkeley, Stukeley], Cath., iv, 200, 209, 363 ; Eliz., iii, 322 ; Sir Hugh, iii, 250, 251, 322, 425 ; iv, 200, 209, 363 ; John, iii, 250, 253 ; iv, 151, 156, 157 ; Sir Thos., iii, 321, 322, 425 ; iv, 156, 351 ; Will., iii, 250 ; fam., iv, 336 ; arms, iii, 425

Steyland, Sim. de, iv, 607

Stibbert, Giles, v, 119, 120 ; Sophronia, v, 119, 120

Stichesfled (Carisbrooke), v, 222

Stick Eggs (Faccombe), iv, 316

Stickland, John, v, 73 ; Mabel, v, 73

Stickworth Hall [Stickworth Grove House] (Arreton), v, 140

Stiepe, *see* Steep

Stiffs Green (Stratfield Turgis), iv, 63

Stigand, v, 22 ; archbp. of Canterbury, ii, 9 ; iii, 65, 444 ; iv, 419 ; v, 51

Stile House (Arreton), v, 139

Stiles, Sir John, iii, 533

Stilla, Alwin, iii, 409

Stillingfleet, Edw., iv, 613 ; v, 95 n

Stirling, Susannah, v, 163 ; (Sir) W. G., v, 163 ; *see also* Sterling

Stivelton, *see* Steventon

Stoakes, *see* Stokes

Stobington, *see* Stubbington

Stoche, Stoches, *see* Bishopstoke, Itchen Stoke and Longstock

Stock (Burghclere), iv, 277

Stock, Rob. le, *see* Lestock

Stockbridge, ii, 102, 172 ; iv, 438, 451, 453, 472 n, 473, 477, 483-6, 489 ; v, 311, 318, 344, 355, 356, 416, 423, 434 ; adv., iv, 485 ; bridge, ii, 47 ; iv, 483 ; v, 429 n ; char., iv, 486 ; chs., iv, 485 ; fishing, iv, 483 ; v, 560, 561 ; ind., v, 459 ; man., iv, 484 ; mkt. and fairs, iv, 483, 484 ; mills, iv, 484 ; Nonconf., iv, 486 ; pop., v, 439 ; racing, iv, 483, 525 ; v, 543, 544 ; sch., ii, 405

Stockbridge Down (Stockbridge), iv, 483

Stockbridge Union beagles, v, 538

Stocker, Matth., iv, 139 ; Rob., iii, 361, 363

Stockes, *see* Stoke Charity

Stocketon, man., ii, 114

Stockheath Common (Havant), iii, 123

Stocking trade, v, 488

Stockman [Stokeman], John, iii, 67 ; iv, 591, 601 ; v, 123 ; Will., iii, 241 ; v, 117

Stockmead (Christchurch), v, 86

Stodham Farm (Liss), iv, 85 n

Stodham House (Liss), iv, 84

Stok, fam., *see* Stokes

Stokbriggeslond (Sherborne St. John), iv, 158

Stoke, par., (Fawley hund.), *see* Bishopstoke

Stoke (Hayling Isl.), iii, 129

Stoke, East, (Hayling Isl.), ii, 218 ; iii, 129 ; common, iii, 129 ; man., iii, 131

Stoke, West, (Hayling Isl.), iii, 129

Stoke, tithing (St. Mary Bourne), iv, 273 n, 288, 295

Stoke, fam., *see* Stokes

Stoke Charity, iii, 401, 447-51 ; iv, 441, 447 ; v, 343 ; adv., iii, 451 ; ch., iii, 449 ; man., iii, 448 ; pop., v, 447 ; sch., ii, 405

Stoke Common (Bishopstoke), iii, 309

Stoke House (Stoke), iv, 295

Stokeman, *see* Stockman

Stoke Park (Bishopstoke), iii, 309

Stokes [Estok, Stoakes, Stok, Stoke, Stokys, Stoock], (de, of), Ad., ii, 16 ; Alan, ii, 196 ; Anne, iv, 296 n ; Hannah, iii, 201 ; John, iv, 296 n, 352 ; v, 23, 37, 381, 451 ; Juliana, v, 37 ; Marg., v, 241 ; Nich., iv, 643 ; Philippa, ii, 127, 132 ; iv, 352 ; Rob., ii, 172 ; Rog., ii, 205 ; Thos., v, 241 ; Wallis, v, 305 ; Will., iv, 352, 353 ; v, 39

Stokes Bay, v, 333, 379

Stokys, *see* Stokes

Stomdene (Kimpton), iv, 372

Stonard, Joan, iv, 167 ; Lawrence, iv, 167

Stone (Arreton), v, 140

Stone, man. (Fawley), i, 380, 381 ; iii, 295 ; iv, 544, 549

Stone, (de la), Cath., iv, 256 ; Eliz., iv, 259 ; Frances, iv, 255 ; Hen., iii, 90 ; iv, 255 ; Mary, iv, 256 ; Percy, v, 229 n ; Pet., iii, 17 ; Phil., iv, 431 ; Will., iii, 90 ; iv, 255 ; Will. H., iii, 123, 127 ; —, v, 270, 576 ; *see also* Stane

Stone Cross (Yarmouth), v, 286

Stoneham, North, ii, 73, 117, 465 ; iii, 462, 478-81 ; v, 294, 559 ; adv., iii, 481 ; char., iii, 481 ; ch., iii, 480 ; man., ii, 121 ; iii, 479 ; iv, 453 ; mills, iii, 479 ; pk., iii, 478, 480 ; pop., v, 447 ; sch., ii, 402

Stoneham, South, ii, 108, 163 ; iii, 462, 481-9 ; adv., iii, 488 ; char., iii, 489 ; ch., iii, 488 ; man., iii, 482 ; paper mill, v, 489, 490 ; pop., v, 447, 450 ; sch., ii, 405 ; iii, 482

Stoneham [Stanham, Stonham], de, Greg., iii, 482 ; Nich., iii, 483 ; Rob., ii, 161, 163 ; Thos., iii, 483

Stonehanger Copse (Abbotts Ann), iv, 334

Stonehouse, Eliz., iv, 290 ; Sir John, iii, 125

Stoner, fam., *see* Stonor

Stoner Hill (Petersfield), iii, 111

Stoney Fairocke (Hurstbourne Tarrant), iv, 321

Stonham, *see* Stoneham

Stonhupe, *see* Stanhope

Stonkton, John, ii, 113

Stonor [Stoner, Stonore], (de), Alice, iv, 382, 512 ; Anne, iv, 383 ; Edm., iv, 199, 382 ; Eliz., Lady, iv, 383 ; Sir Fran., iv, 383 ; Sir Gilb., iv, 382 ; Joan, Lady, iv, 382 n, 383 ; (Sir) John, iii, 436 ; iv, 150, 199, 227, 382, 383 ; Marg., Lady, iv, 382 ; Sir Ralph, iv, 382 ; Rich., iv, 382 ; (Sir) Thos., iii, 436 ; iv, 382, 383 ; (Sir) Walt., iv, 102, 383 ; Sir Will., iii, 435, 436 ; iv, 383 ; fam., iv, 352

Stony Cross (Minstead), iv, 635

Stony Cross (S. Damerham), iv, 586

Stonyffrythe (Romsey), iv, 452

Stonyham (Stratfield Turgis), iv, 63

Stoock, *see* Stokes

Stopford, Sir Rob., v, 403 ; Walt. G., iv, 198

Stopham [Stopeham], (de), Brian, iv, 268 ; Eva, iv, 268 ; Isabel, iv, 268 ; John, v, 215 ; Ralph, iv, 268, 269 ; Rog., iv, 353 n

Storer, Jude, iii. 196

Storey, Jas., iv, 294 ; John, iv, 277

Storke, Alice, v, 96

Stotescumbe, Joan, iv, 492 ; Rog., iv, 492

Stoteville, de, Alice, iv, 58, 62 ; John, iv, 58, 225 ; Leonia, iv, 58 ; Rob., iv, 58 ; Will., iv, 57, 58, 62 ; fam., iv, 226

Stoughton, Bridg., iv, 437 ; Nich., iv, 437

Stour, riv., i, 376, 381 ; v, 133, 409, 559, 564 ; fishery, v, 466

Stour, Stoure, fam., *see* Stower

Stoureswathe, *see* Southwathe

Stourfield (Bournemouth), v, 135

Stourton, Kath., Lady, iv, 99 n, 537 ; Lds. :—Chas. P., iv, 617 ; John, iv, 579, 580

Stourton, (de), Charlotte, iv, 617 ; Christina, iv, 577 n ; Edw., iv, 580 ; Eliz., iv, 268, 580 ; v, 129 ; Fran., iv, 580 ; (Sir) John, iv, 93, 94, 268, 577 n ; Jos., iv, 617 ; Julia, iv, 93, 94, 577 n ; Walt., iv, 94, 577 n ; (Sir) Will., iv, 268, 579, 580 ; v, 129

Stowe, Thos., iii, 110

Stowell, *see* Stawell

Stower [Stour, Stoure], Eliz., v, 162 n, 174 ; Hen., v, 160, 166 ; John, v, 142 n, 143, 160, 162, 162 n, 166, 166 n, 216 ; Will., v, 174

Stracey, Jas., v, 522

Strachan, Jas., v, 280 ; Jane, Lady, v, 95 ; Sir John, v, 95 ; Mary, v, 280

Stradelyng, Joan, v, 207 n ; Sir John, v, 207 n

Stradfelle, *see* Stratfieldsaye and Stratfield Mortimer

Stradwick, Edm., iv, 374

Stralkyng, Joan, ii, 47

Strange, Ld., iv, 99 ; v, 544

Strange [L'Estrange, Lestrange], (la, le), Alice, iv, 560 ; Ankarette, iii, 104 ; Ebulo, iv, 560 ; Capt. Edw., v, 111, 112 ; Eleanor, iii, 104 ; Fulk, iii, 104 ; Hamon, iii, 104 ; Isabel, iii, 104 ; Joan, Lady, iv, 77 n, 521 ; v, 99 ; (Sir) John, iii, 104 ; iv, 77 ; Maud, Lady, iv, 77 ; Sir Rich., iv, 77 ; Rob., iii, 104 ; Rog., iv, 521 ; v, 99 ; Mrs., iii, 109 ; fam., arms, iii, 104

Stranghill, Will., v, 166 n
Strangways, Eleanor, v, 160 ; (Sir) Giles, v, 160, 169 ; John, ii, 485 ; fam., arms, ii, 485
Stratfield (Greywell), iv, 76
Stratfield, de, Edith, iv, 342 ; Hen., iv, 340, 342, 343 ; Rich., iv, 342, 343 ; Thos., iv, 501
Stratfield Mortimer, ii, 466 ; iv, 31, 56-7, 167 ; adv., iv, 57 ; ch., iv, 56 ; man., ii, 420 ; iv, 56, 60, 341 ; Nonconf., iv, 57 ; pop., v, 440
Stratfieldsaye, i, 320 ; ii, 466 ; iv, 31, 57-63, 108, 141, 167, 216 ; v, 463, 505, 557, 558 ; adv., iv, 62 ; ch., iv, 57, 61 ; hermitage, iv, 57-8, 61 ; mans., iv, 46, 57, 142 ; mills, iv, 60 ; Nonconf., iv, 62 ; pk., i, 320 ; iv, 44, 57, 60, 63 ; pop., v, 440 ; sch., ii, 405
Stratfieldsaye House (Stratfieldsaye), iv, 57, 59
Stratfield Stoteville, man. (Stratfieldsaye), iv, 57
Stratfield Turgis, ii, 382, 383 ; iv, 31, 42, 44, 57, 63-5, 114 n ; v, 463 ; adv., iv, 64, 65 ; char., iv, 65 ; ch., iv, 65 ; man., iv, 63 ; mill, iv, 64 ; pop., v, 440
Stratford (Christchurch), v, 85, 95 n
Stratford, Joan, ii, 129 ; John, archbp., ii, 16, 28, 29, 30, 102, 111, 118, 155, 161, 170, 195, 229 ; iii, 261, 461 ; iv, 42, 146, 153, 176 n, 302, 325, 493 ; v, 215, 235, 277
Strathememers (King's Somborne), iv, 470
Stratton, East, i, 321 ; ii, 99 ; iii, 389, 399-400 ; v, 557 ; adv., iii, 400 ; brick-making, v, 466 ; ch., iii, 400 ; man., ii, 121 ; iii, 399 ; pop., v, 448 ; sch., ii, 398
Stratton, West, (Micheldever), ii, 116, 117, 121, 223, 466 ; iii, 391
Stratton [Stretton], de, Ad., v, 91 ; Nich., ii, 17, 190, 191 ; Rich., iii, 392, 394 ; Steph., iii, 392, 394 ; Walt., iii, 392 ; Will., iii, 229, 392 ; iv, 111 ; fam., ii, 317
Stratton Farm (Kingsclere), iv, 266
Strattons (Kingsclere), iv, 250
Straw, prices of, v, 496
Strawberry cultivation, v, 455, 511
Straw-plaiting, v, 457
Streatley (Berks), i, 272
Streatwells, Mary, iv, 219 ; Thos., iv, 219
Streech, John, v, 483
Street (Christchurch), v, 82, 94
Street, le, par. (King's Somborne hund.), see Stockbridge
Street, Jas., v, 277 ; Thos., iv, 579 ; v, 114 ; Will., iv, 594
Street Meadow (Romsey), iv, 452, 460, 468
Strete [Streta] (Newchurch), v, 181
Strete (Redbridge hund.), iv, 544
Stretemede (Timsbury), iv, 486
Stretfeld Magna, see Stratfieldsaye
Stretfeld Turgeys, see Stratfield Turgis
Stretmede (Romsey), see Street Meadow
Stretton, fam., see Stratton
Strickland, Walt., iv, 183, 193
Strigul Castle (Monms.), iv, 52
Stringer, Hen., ii, 327 ; Jane, iv, 172 n ; Steph., iv, 172 n
Stroclynchesacre (Faccombe), iv, 314
Strode, le, (Bramley), iv, 141
Strode (Romsey), iv, 452

Strode, (de), Andr., iv, 258 n ; Eliz., iv, 472 ; Nich., ii, 119, 122 ; Will., iv, 472
Strokyngeslond (Kingsclere), iv, 250
Stronghill, John, iv, 536
Strother, Barbara, iv, 371, 384 ; Geo., iv, 371 ; Joshua, iv, 371, 384
Stroud (Langrish), ii, 152 ; iii, 65 brick-making, iii, 65 ; v, 465 n
Strowde Poole (Yateley), iv, 21
Stuart, Arabella, iv, 75 ; Gen. Chas., v, 110 ; John, v, 84, 85 ; Nich., ii, 511 ; iii, 9 ; Sir Sim., ii, 509, 516 ; iii, 9 ; Sir Sim. H., iii, 9 ; fam., arms, ii, 509 ; see also Steward and Stewart
Stuart de Rothesay, Chas. Stuart, Ld., v, 84
Stubbes, see Stubbs
Stubbington (Portsmouth), ii, 168 ; iii, 193
Stubbington, man. (Titchfield), ii, 181 ; iii, 217, 221, 229
Stubbington, Thos., v, 460
Stubbington Farm (Portsmouth), iii, 193
Stubbington House (Titchfield), iii, 221
Stubbington Lodge (Portsmouth), iii, 193
Stubbs [Stubbes], Chris., iii, 99, 344
Stubyngton, see Steventon
Stubynton, man., see Stubbington
Stuckton (Fordingbridge), iv, 576
Stuf, i, 375 ; v, 222, 293
Stukeley, see Stewkley
Stul, John, v, 459
Stulbinton, see Stubbington
Stumpe, Isabel, Lady, iv, 185, 296 ; Sir Jas., iv, 185, 296
Stuppe, Stupe, see Steep
Stur, iv, 438 ; v, 142 n, 143, 145, 146, 151, 159, 160, 162, 171, 191, 198, 200, 202, 236, 237, 246, 281, 282
Sturgys, Johanne, ii, 125
Sturminster (Dors.), ii, 163
Sturminster, Nich. de, prior of Christchurch, ii, 160
Sturminster Marshall (Dors.), iv, 655
Sturmore (Leckford), iv, 446
Sturmy [Esturmy], Agnes, iv, 75, 84 ; Geoff., iv, 75, 84 ; Hen., iii, 163 ; iv, 75, 84, 85, 92 ; v, 305 ; Laurencia, iv, 84 n ; Marg., iii, 163 ; iv, 75 n ; Maud, iv, 75, 84 ; Rich., iii, 403 ; iv, 75 n, 548 ; (Sir) Will., iii, 163 ; iv, 39, 75, 75 n, 84 ; fam., iv, 93
Sturt, (Sir) Ant., iv, 46 ; Diana, iv, 46 ; Humph., iv, 46
Sturtlemead (Binsted), ii, 484
Sturtons, man. (Odiham), iv, 94
Sturt Pond (Milford), v, 115
Sturun, John, iv, 293
Stutbins (Bradley), iv, 202
Stuteville, see Stratfieldsaye
Style (Romsey), iv, 452
Styles (Greywell), iv, 76
Styles [Styele], (de la), John, v, 231 ; Joshua H., iv, 325 ; Lydia, iv, 325 ; Mary, iv, 325 ; Rob., iv, 325 ; Will., v, 231
Stympe, Dr., ii, 72
Stynt, Nich., iv, 43 n ; Will., iv, 99 n, 243
Styntesford, Kath., v, 96
Styward, Nich., ii, 509, 510
Stywards (Kingsley), ii, 515
Suantune, see Swampton
Suarting, iv, 616
Subberton, Subertune, see Soberton
Sudberie, iii, 355

Sudgarston Copp, see Suggeaston Copse
Sudtone, Sudtune, see Bishop's Sutton and Sutton, Long
Sudynton, see Temple Sotherington
Suein, see Sweyn
Suell, see Sewell
Sueter, —, v, 574
Suffield, Will., v, 486
Suffolk, shipping returns, v, 377
Suffolk, Alice de la Pole, dchss. of, ii, 519 ; iii, 370 ; iv, 395 ; dks. of, ii, 144 ; v, 245, 332 ; Edm. de la Pole, ii, 519, 522 ; iv, 399 ; earls of :—Mich. de la Pole, iv, 395 ; Will. de la Pole, ii, 519, 521 ; iv, 395, 396, 399, 545
Sugar, Hugh, ii, 290 ; v, 17
Sugden, Edw. B., iii, 457 ; Rev. Fran., iii, 457
Suggeaston Copse (Woodcott), iv, 331, 332
Suggenwerch, Sugion, see Segenworth
Sulhamstead (Berks.), ii, 227
Sulivan, Sir Barth., v, 134
Sullivan, Arabella J., iv, 16, 22 ; Sir Fran. W., iv, 22 ; Rev. Fred., iv, 16, 22 ; Capt., v, 528
Sullons (Arreton), v, 145
Sumburn Album, Sumburn Regis, see King's Somborne
Summers [Somers], Alf., v, 518, 519 ; Anne, iv, 573 ; Edwin, v, 529 ; Geo., v, 529 ; John, iv, 573 ; Mary M., v, 170 ; Will., v, 517, 529
Summers & Payne, shipbuilders, v, 458
Sumner, Chas. R., ii, 99, 100, 361 ; iv, 29 ; G. H., iv, 17
Sumner's (Basing), iv, 127
Sundials, Saxon, ii, 238, 240, 241
Sunworth, man. (Buriton), iii, 91
Sunworth, (de), Ralph, iii, 91 ; Thos., iii, 91 ; Will., iii, 91
Supporton, see Soberton
Surian, Antonio, v, 322
Surlande (Burghclere), iv, 277
Surlie, see Shirley
Surrey, archd. of, iv, 29, 30
Surrey, Joan, ctss. of, iv, 560 n ; earls of, v, 373 ; John de Warenne, ii, 146, 505 ; iv, 418, 560, 561 ; v, 313
Susa, see Cusia
Sussebury, John, ii, 172
Sussex, Honora, ctss. of, iii, 150, 242 ; v, 174 ; earls of, iii, 153 ; v, 332, 333, 378 ; Hen., iii, 131, 242 ; iv, 476 ; v, 174 ; Hugh, iii, 95 ; John de Warenne, see Surrey, earls of ; Rob., iii, 131, 242 ; Will., iii, 95
Sustern Spital (Winchester), ii, 264 ; v, 14, 417
Sutdone (Highclere), iv, 285
Suthamton, see Southington
Suthcodibear Poyly, see Codibear
Suthetudeworth, see Tidworth, South
Suthhulle (Whitchurch), iv, 300
Suthill, John, ii, 118, 121
Suthwade St. Lawrence, see St. Lawrence
Suthwarborne, Suthwarneburne, Suthwermborowe, see Warnborough, South
Suthwyk, see Southwick
Sutt Garden (Romsey), iv, 452, 453
Sutton (Brighstone), iv, 212
Sutton, man. (Wonston), iii, 455
Sutton, Long, ii, 73, 110, 501 ; iv, 1, 18-20, 171 ; adv., iv, 20 ; char., iv, 20 ; ch., iv, 19 ; man.,

Sutton (cont.)
ii, 114 ; iv, 18 ; v, 420 ; Manor
Farm, iv, 18 ; Nonconf., iv, 20 ;
pop., v, 443 ; sch., ii, 401
Sutton, (de), Ad., iii, 460 ; Alan,
iii, 460 ; iv, 474 ; Alice, iii, 456,
460 ; Anne, iv, 73 ; (Sir) Edm.,
ii, 475, 476 ; iii, 456 ; iv, 526 ;
Maj. Fran. R. H. S., iv, 381, 383,
384 ; Frank, v, 542 ; Geo., iv,
527 ; Hannah, iii, 101 ; Hugh, iv,
362 ; Isabel, ii, 134 ; Jas., iv,
527 ; John, iii, 460 ; iv, 474 ;
Joyce, Lady, iv, 526 ; Nich., iv,
73 ; Pet., iii, 460 ; (Sir) Rich.,
ii, 134 ; iii, 460 ; iv, 474 ; v, 524,
531 ; Rob., iii, 460 ; Thos., ii, 22 ;
iii, 460 ; iv, 299 ; Unity, iv, 527 ;
Will., ii, 17 ; iii, 101, 396 ; iv,
382 n ; fam., arms, ii, 476
Sutton Common, iii, 41
Sutton episcopi, see Bishop's Sutton
Sutton Scotney (Wonston), ii, 213 ;
iii, 402, 453 ; iv, 415 ; v, 538 ;
man., ii, 168 ; iii, 456
Sutton Warblington (Long Sutton),
iv, 18 ; man., iv, 19
Sutwarneburn, see Warnborough,
South
Suwic, see Southwick
Swaddon, Will., v, 77
Swaine [Swain, Swayne, Swein],
Alice, iv, 380 ; Arth., iii, 96, 100,
101, 105, 125 ; iv, 342, 353, 363,
380 ; v, 117, 123 ; Edw., iii, 125 ;
iv, 342, 353, 363 ; Geoff., v, 162 n ;
Joan, ii, 151 ; Margery, v, 162 n ;
Mary, iv, 344 ; Rob., iii, 125 ; iv,
342, 344, 363 ; Rog., iii, 511 ;
Thos., iv, 62, 276
Swainstone, hund., v, 209
Swainstone, man. (Calbourne), v,
212, 218-19, 220, 265, 273, 285,
411, 413 n, 420
Swallick Wood [Swalowykeswood]
(Cliddesden), iv, 145
Swallowfield (Berks), iv, 35, 57, 108
Swallowtone, see Swarraton
Swalshottes More (Yateley), iv, 21
Swampton (St. Mary Bourne), iv,
245, 273, 295, 299 ; commons, iv,
295 ; man., iv, 256, 296
Swampton Green (St Mary Bourne),
iv, 295
Swandrop, see Swanthorpe
Swaneland (King's Somborne), iv,
470
Swanewych, Ralph de, iii, 124
Swanley, Capt., Rich., v, 111, 380
Swanmore (Droxford), iii, 275, 285,
287 ; anc. pottery, i, 349 ; sch.,
ii, 405
Swann, John, iii, 235
Swanthorpe [Swanrope] (Crondall),
iv, 5, 9
Swanton, man., see Swampton
Swanton, Fran., v, 78, 79
Swanwick (Titchfield), iii, 221, 222 ;
man., ii, 181, 186 ; iii, 217, 230 ;
iv, 651 n
Swanwick, Lower, (Titchfield), iii,
221, 222
Swapes, le, (Bramley), iv, 141
Swarraton, ii, 116, 187 ; iii, 42, 389,
394 ; iv, 188, 189, 195-6 ; adv.,
iv, 196 ; char., iv, 196 ; ch., iv,
196 ; mans., iv, 195 ; pop., v, 448
Swartelinghide, ii, 159
Swarton, see Swarraton
Sway (Boldre), iv, 616, 623 ; v, 81,
82 ; man., ii, 126, 131, 139, 159 ;
iv, 619 ; v, 89 ; mill, iv, 620 ;
sch., ii, 405
Sway, North, v, 114
Sway House (Boldre), iv, 616

Swayne, fam., see Swaine
Swayne's Mill (Kingsclere), iv, 257
Swaythling (S. Stoneham), iii, 462,
481 ; man., iii, 484
Swaythling, Ld., iii, 481, 483, 484 ;
v, 563
Sweatfords Water, iv, 581
Sweetapple, Thos., iv, 212
Swein, fam., see Swaine
Swef [Swoef], Rob., iv, 381
Swete, Joan, iv, 583 ; Thos., iv, 583
Swey, see Sway
Sweyn, king of Denmark, ii, 7-8 ;
v, 296
Sweyn [Suein], iv, 72
Swift, riv., iv, 319
Swift, Anne, iv, 354 ; Eliz., iv, 354 ;
Hen., iv, 354
Swinburne, Algernon C., v, 155 ;
C., iv, 210 ; Sir Edw., v, 282 ;
Emelia, Lady, v, 282
Swindell, F. C., v, 530
Swindon, ii, 126, 168
Swineshead (Calbourne), v, 218 n
Swinford, Cath., ii, 45 ; J. S., iv, 140
Swins'ys (Beaulieu), iv, 650
Swinton, Rev. John, v, 187
Swithun, St., ii, 4, 5, 6, 252 ; iv,
27 ; v, 418
Swoef, see Swef
Swyltenham, John de, ii, 134
Swynebrok, de, Edm., iv, 142 ;
John, iv, 142
Swynesflode, see Winslade
Swyngles Marsh (Yateley), iv, 21
Sydeforde, John, ii, 157
Sydelyng, (de), Agnes, iv, 646 ;
Amflesia, iv, 646 ; Emmote, iv,
646 ; Margery, iv, 646 ; Walt.,
iv, 646
Sydemanton, de, John, ii, 182, 188
Sydenham [Sidenham, Sidnam],
Chas., iv, 61, 62 ; Edith, iv, 62 ;
(Sir) Edw., iii, 194 ; iv, 62, 454 n ;
v, 471 ; Humph., iv, 454 ; Jane,
iv, 454 n ; Joan, iv, 326 ; Rich., iv,
326 ; Rog., iv, 216 ; Thos., iv,
326 ; Col. Will., v, 224, 351
Sydenham's Tangley, man. (Tang-
ley), iv, 326
Sydmonton, ii, 126, 128, 131 ; iv,
245, 246, 249, 250 ; v, 557 ;
chap., iv, 265, 266, 267 ; ch., iv,
264 ; man., iv, 254, 268 ; pop., v,
442 ; sch., ii, 405
Sydmonton Court (Sydmonton), iv,
250
Sydyngton, see Temple Sothering-
ton
Syeriward, Laur., iv, 409
Syeta, see Shute
Syfrewast, see Sifrewast
Sygar, iv, 501
Sygar's Moor (Lockerley), iv, 501
Sykes, Sir Tatton, v, 527
Sylkchester, see Silchester
Sylkestede, see Silkstead
Sylvester, see Silvester
Sym, Hen., iv, 455 n ; Parnel, iv,
455 n
Symeon, fam., see Simeon
Symes (Kingsley), ii, 515
Symes, Dr., iii, 437 ; —, v, 532
Symonds [Symons], Pet., ii, 388 ;
v, 13, 77 ; (Sir) Will., iii, 415 ;
v, 77, 403 ; —, iv, 248 ; see also
Simmonds
Symone hostilers (Penton Mewsey),
iv, 381
Symons, see Symonds
Sympson [Simpson], John, ii, 186 ;
iv, 522 ; Launcelot, iii, 117 ;
Thos., iv, 169, 170, 220, 221, 234,
238, 242, 276, 277, 435 ; Will.,
iii, 122 ; see also Simson

Symynggesplace (Faccombe), iv,
314
Synaguy [Syneguy], de, Edm., v,
92 ; Will., iv, 18, 19, 92
Synehurst, see Sindhurst
Syngyngland (Barton Stacey), iv,
417
Syward, see Siward.

Tachburn (Farley Chamberlayne),
iv, 444 n
Tachbury, de, Nich., iv, 550 ;
Rose, iv, 550
Taddiford Farm[Tadeford](Hordle),
v, 111
Tadebridge (Hordle), v, 111
Tadley, iv, 197, 219-21, 228, 233,
239 ; adv., iv, 221 ; chap., iv,
217 ; char., iv, 221 ; ch., iv,
220 ; mans., iv, 219 ; Nonconf.,
iv, 221 ; pop., v, 442 ; sch., ii,
406
Tadley Common, iv, 219
Tadley Place (Tadley), iv, 220
Tadley Place Farm (Tadley), iv, 219
Taillard, Alice, iii, 78, 300 ; Nich.,
iii, 78, 300 ; Rob., iii, 78 ; Thos.,
iii, 78
Taillour, Taillur, Tailour, see Taylor
Taisson [Tesson], Rob., iv, 564 ;
Walt., iv, 564
Talayate (S. Damerham), iv, 587 n
Talbot, Geoff., iii, 226 ; (Sir) Gilb.,
iii, 105 ; iv, 53 ; Joan, iv, 338 ;
Lawr., iii, 226 ; Mary, iii, 143;
Nich., iv, 64 ; Rich., iv, 53;
Thos., ii, 158, 160 ; v, 107 ; Will.
iii, 117, 143
Talbot woods (Bournemouth), v
134
Talemache, fam., see Tollemache
Tallemache (Wherwell), iv, 413
Tallman, Will., iii, 12
Talmage, Pet., iv, 358 n
Tame, see Thame
Tamworth [Tomworthe], Bridg.,
iv, 105 ; Cath., iv, 105 ; Colby,
iv, 105 ; Dorothy, iv, 105 ;
Eliz., iv, 105 ; Hen., iv, 49 ; John,
iv, 105
Tangelegh, Tangelie, see Tangley
Tangier (Church Oakley), iv, 224
Tangier Lodge (Wootton St. Law-
rence), iv, 240 n
Tangier Park (Wootton St. Law-
rence), iv, 240
Tangley, iv, 198, 225, 315, 317,
326-8, 332, 333, 376, 609 ; adv.,
iv, 328 ; chap., iv, 328 ; char.,
iv, 328 ; ch., iv, 328 ; mans., iv,
326, 520 ; Nonconf., iv, 326 ;
pop., v, 438 ; sch., ii, 405 ; iv,
326
Tangley Holt (Tangley), iv, 326
Tanhouse Garden (Selborne), v, 455
Tankard, F., v, 242
Tanke [Tank], Eliz., iii, 279 ;
Marg., iii, 300 ; Rob., iii, 279 ;
Will., iii, 279 ; fam., arms, iii,
279
Tankerville, Joan Grey, ctss. of, ii,
475 ; iv, 347, 348 ; earls, v, 574 ;
Hen. Grey, ii, 475, 476 ; John
Grey, ii, 475, 476 ; iv, 347, 348 ;
Rich. Grey, ii, 475, 476
Tankley, see Tangley
Tanley (Itchel), iv, 6
Tanner [Tannere], (la, le), John,
ii, 211 ; Margery, iv, 507 ; Pet.,
iv, 507 ; Rob, iv, 619 ; Thos., iv,
109
Tanners brook, iii, 468
Tanning industry, v, 451, 455

Tapener, le, Aylwin, v, 48 ; Rich., v, 481 n

Tappesham (Romsey), iv, 452, 453

Tapps, Sir Geo. I, v, 86, 93, 94, 95, 96

Tapps-Gervis, Sir Geo. W., v, 134

Tapps-Gervis-Meyrick, Sir Geo. A. E., v, 84, 93, 94, 95, 96, 109, 136 ; Sir Geo. E. M., v, 93 ; see also Gervis

Tarant, see Tarrant

Tarbutt, Percy, iii, 457 ; P. C., iv, 419

Tarleton, Rob., v, 31

Tarrant [Tarant, Tarente], (de), Geo., iv, 361 ; John, iv, 365, 425, 511 n ; Nich., ii, 110, 115 ; Rob. T., iv, 425

Tarrant Keynes, de, Hen., ii, 169 ; Hugh, ii, 169 ; Joan, ii, 169 ; Thos., ii, 169

Tarrant Nunnery (Dors.), iv, 319 ; Iseult, abbess of, iii, 106

Tartase, John de Aese, vicomte de, iii, 104

Tarver, Anne, v, 205 ; Jos., v, 205

Tary, Will., ii, 171

Tasker & Sons, ironfounders, iv, 326, 360

Tassam, Thos., iv, 562

Tatchbury, man. (Eling), ii, 116, 117 ; iv, 548, 550, 554 ; manor house, iv, 546

Tatchbury Mount (Eling), iv, 546

Tate, Carr, v, 192 ; Eliz., iv, 78 ; Sir Will., iv, 36 ; Zouche, iv, 78, 80 ; —, v, 544

Tauke [Tauk, Tawke], Edm., iv, 134 ; Eliz., iv, 459, 520 ; Ellen, ii, 130 ; Joan, iii, 225 ; iv, 134, 520 ; John, iv, 134, 459 n ; v, 247 ; Maud, iv, 134 ; Rich., v, 249 n ; Rob., iv, 134 n, 459, 498, 520 n ; Thos., iii, 258 ; iv, 134 n, 498, 520 n, 524, 610 ; v, 247 ; Will., iv, 134, 520, 524 n, 594 ; fam., arms, iv, 134

Taulkes, man. (Basingstoke), iv, 134, 520

Taunton, archd. of, v, 458 n ; bp. of, ii, 56

Taunton, Frances, iv, 441 ; Lydia, iv, 441 ; Rich., ii, 387, 394 ; iii, 527, 529, 535 ; iv, 399 ; Sarah B., iv, 441 ; Will., ii, 19, 115 ; v, 148 ; Will. L. T. P., iv, 441 ; Miss., iv, 440

Taverner [Tavenere], Edw., ii, 211 ; John, ii, 427, 446, 447 ; Maud, v, 482 ; Rog., ii, 427, 446, 447

Taw, Chas., iv, 573 ; Thos., iv, 573

Tawke, see Tauke

Tawyer, Thos., iv, 477 n

Tawyerescroft (Kingsclere), iv, 250

Taylor [Taillour, Taillur, Tailour, Tayleur, Taylour], (le), Ad., iv, 484 ; Alice, v, 173 ; Anne, v, 247 n ; Sir Chas., v, 538 ; (Rev.) Chris., ii, 511 ; iv, 564 ; Constance, v, 73 ; C. W., iii, 151 ; Donnithorne, v, 521 ; Edw. H., iv, 564 ; v, 120 ; Eliz., iii, 247 ; iv, 204 ; Giles, ii, 485 ; Jas. B., iv, 103, 104, 106 ; (Rev.) John, iii, 170, 172 ; iv, 51, 550 ; v, 19, 173, 184, 247 n, 382, 515 ; Mary, iv, 564 ; Matth., v, 191 n ; Pet., iii, 149 ; Phil., v, 73 ; Rebecca, iv, 56 ; Sam., v, 516, 526 n ; Thos., ii, 81 ; iii, 247, 363 ; iv, 203, 204 ; Walt., iv, 458 ; Will., iii, 150 ; v, 484, 517 ; W., iv, 56, 397 ; W. P., iv, 316 ; —, bellfounder, iv, 25, 238, 264, 286

Teaselies (Binsted), ii, 484

Teate, Capt. Matth., iii, 169

Teck, pr. Adolphus of, v, 551 ; Mary, dchss. of, iv, 14

Tedorde, see Tidworth

Tedworth hunt, v, 531

Teed, Rob., v, 529

Tegdown Copse (Brown Candover), iv, 183 n

Teggatt Brokelisford (Ringwood), iv, 609

Teleosteans, i, 197

Tellere, Thos., ii, 212

Temerdyng (Lockerley), iv, 500

Temmes [Temes], Joan, iii, 485 ; iv, 220 ; John, v, 280 ; Rob., iii, 485 ; iv, 220 ; Thos., v, 280

Templars, Knights, ii, 105 ; iii, 7, 10 ; v, 117, 163

Temple, Cowper, ii, 458 ; Hen., iv, 412 n ; Pet., iii, 398 ; Rich., iii, 39, 307 ; iv, 536 ; fam., arms, iii, 437

Templecombe, ii, 187

Temple Hanger (Selborne), iii, 5 ; Rom. rem., i, 341

Templemore, Ld., iii, 373 ; iv, 204

Temple Sotherington, man. (Selborne), iii, 3, 5, 7

Temton, Drew of, v, 99 n

Tenancy, conditions of, v, 506-7

Tennant, Steph., iv, 108, 109

Tennyson, Alfred, Ld., v, 241, 242

Teocreberie, see Tatchbury

Terell, see Tyrrell

Termassone, Arnoult, iv, 138

Territorial forces, v, 357

Terry [Thierry], Mich., iii, 360, 361 ; Rachel, v, 486 ; Rich., iv, 142 ; Steph., iii, 363, 371 ; iv, 20, 92 ; v, 514 ; Thos., iii, 363 ; Will., iv, 72 ; v, 486 n ; Capt., ii, 92 ; —, v, 517

Terstwood, Terstwude, see Testwood

Tesson, see Taisson

Test, riv., i, 331, 384 ; iii, 403, 413, 433 ; iv, 198, 208, 209, 210, 213, 282, 288, 295, 300, 402, 406, 407, 409, 411, 417, 446, 449, 452, 455, 457, 459, 469, 483, 486, 487, 498, 500, 503, 504, 546 ; v, 409, 490, 560, 561, 562

Test Mill (Romsey), iv, 455

Testwood, man. (Eling), ii, 148 ; iv, 547, 549, 552, 554, 635 ; fishery, iv, 556 ; mills, iv, 555, 556 ; v, 100 n

Testwood, Little, (Eling), iv, 550, 637

Testwood, (de), Cath., iv, 627 ; Eliz., iv, 549 ; Guy, iv, 635 ; John, iv, 549 ; Kath., iv, 549 ; Rich., iv, 549, 627 ; Sim., iv, 552 ; Will., iv, 549

Testwood House (Eling), iv, 546, 549

Tetbury (Gloucs.), ii, 137

Teutonicus, see Tyes

Tewkesbury Abbey (Glouc.), ii, 108, 142 ; iv, 587, 589

Textiles, v, 475-89

Teya, (de), Gilb., iii, 435 ; Maude, iii, 435

Thackham, Thos., ii, 392

Thaine [Thein] (le), Everard, v, 174 ; John, iv, 613

Thame [Tame], (de), Aegidia [Egidia], iii, 459 ; iv, 148 ; Philip, ii, 187 ; (Sir) Thos., iii, 459 ; iv, 148, 580 ; v, 456

Thatcher, Will., v, 144, 175, 184, 185

Thedden Grange [Thedden] (Alton), ii, 471, 479

Thein, see Thaine

Thekeston, Rich., iii, 395

Thele (Greatham), ii, 506, 507

Thele Bridge (Greatham), ii, 508

Thelwall, Sir Bevis, v, 157

Theobald, abbot of Tiron, ii, 224 ; archbp. of Canterbury, ii, 216 ; iii, 130 ; iv, 373

Theobald, —, v, 572

Thermyttes Tower, see Hermit's Tower

Therstwode, see Testwood

Theselies, see Teaselies

Thetford, John Salisbury, bp. of, ii, 56 ; John Sampson, bp. of, iii, 224

Thidden Farm, see Thedden Grange

Thierry, see Terry

Thingdon, ii, 207

Thiseldon with Burythorpp, man., ii, 121

Thistede, see Tisted

Thistle Barrow (Boscombe), v, 134

Thistleden, (de), Ad., v, 118 ; Isabel, v, 118 ; Hen., v, 114, 118, 124, 129 ; John, v, 118 n ; Tomasine, v, 118

Thistlethwayte, Alex., iii, 144, 147, 159, 161, 163, 164, 430 ; Fran., iii, 163 ; Mary, iii, 430 ; Rob., iii, 159, 163 ; iv, 494 ; Thos., iii, 161, 167, 168, 170, 172 ; iv, 494 ; —, v, 544 ; fam., iv, 498, 521, 523 ; arms, iii, 430

Thodeworth, see Tidworth

Thoe, iv, 205

Thoketon, see Tufton

Thomas, iv, 608 ; abbot of Hyde, ii, 118, 121 ; abbot of Netley, ii, 149 ; of Anvers, v, 45 ; archbp. of York, iv, 497, 506, 518, 524 ; bp. of Achaden, ii, 193 ; bp. of Annadown, ii, 129 ; of Brotherton, iv, 52 ; prior of Breamore, ii, 172 ; prior of Ellingham, ii, 229, 230 ; prior of Monk Sherborne, ii, 228 ; of Puckpool, v, 192 n

Thomas, Agnes, v, 483 ; Amy, iv, 502 ; Anna, ii, 49, 151 ; Christian, iv, 523 ; C., iv, 614 ; Rev. Geo. A., iii, 236 ; Hugh, v, 192 ; John, v, 79 ; John, bp., iv, 99 ; Rich., iii, 528 ; Walt., iv, 502 ; Will., iv, 523 ; Rev. W., v, 186

Thomerton, John de, v, 169

Thomes Yate (Winchester), v, 35

Thommesheyes (Dibden), iv, 655

Thompson [Thomson, Tomson], Eliz., iv, 241 ; Sir H., iii, 216 ; Marg. C., iii, 196 ; Rich., iv, 609 n ; (Sir) Will., vi, 241, 509 ; Col., v, 453 ; fam., v, 460

Thonewurth, see Tunworth

Thorleston, Ralph de, ii, 174, 175

Thorley, v, 209, 210, 284-5 ; adv., v, 285 ; ch., v, 285 ; man., v, 163, 272, 274, 284 ; pop., v, 449 ; sch., ii, 408

Thorn [Thorne], Rev. Will., v, 78 ; —, dn. of Chichester, v, 336

Thornburgh [Thornborough], Anne, iv, 374 ; Jane, iv, 448 ; (Sir) John, iv, 374, 447, 448 ; Rob., iv, 374, 375, 376 ; Will., iv, 374

Thorncombe, (de), Marg., iii, 406 ; Nich., iii, 406 ; Rob., iii, 406 ; v, 48 ; Thos., iii, 406 ; v, 39

Thornehull, see Thornhill

Thornenycombe (Vernhams Dean), iv, 329

Thorner, Jane, iv, 166 ; John, iv, 166, 167 ; Rob., iii, 534, 536

Thorness bay, v, 268

Thorney (Cambs.), ii, 6

Thorney Hill (Christchurch), v, 108 *n*

Thorngate, hund., iv, 489, 544, 615 ; v, 324, 331

Thorngate, Will., iii, 202, 208

Thorngate charities, iii, 208

Thornhill [Thornehull], Amb., iv, 487 *n* ; McCreagh, iv, 419

Thornhull (Bentley), iv, 506

Thornhurst, Mary, Lady, iv, 36 ; Sir Steph., iv, 36

Thorni, John de, ii, 182, 186

Thornie Howse (Crondall), iv, 6

Thorns-Anderwood, *see* Amberwood

Thornton, (de), Gilb., ii, 203 ; Hen., iv, 199

Thornycroft, John I., & Co., v, 458, 461

Thorold, Ant. W., ii, 100 ; Mrs., iv, 52

Thoroughgood, Thos., iv, 455

Thorp, Herb. B., iv, 176 ; Thos., iv, 177

Thorpe, (de), Ant., iii, 88 ; Barbara, iv, 447 ; Frances, iv, 537 ; Fran., iv, 446 ; Geo., iv, 446, 447, 449, 458, 502 ; Isabel, iv, 368 ; (Sir) John, iii, 499 ; iv, 99, 537 ; John H., iii, 289 ; Kath., iv, 99 ; Rich., iv, 499 ; Rob., iii, 187 ; Sybil, iv, 446 *n* ; Thos., ii, 224, 225 ; Will., ii, 479, 486, 503 ; 330 ; iv, 28, 446, 447, 485 ; v, 327 *n*

Thorpe's Copse (Stratfield Turgis), iv, 63

Thoyts, Rev. Fran. W., iv, 201 ; Mortimer, iv, 198, 201 ; v, 534

Threlkeld, Louisa, iii, 398 ; iv, 256, 487 ; Thos., iv, 256, 487 ; Will., iii, 398

Thresher, F. R., iv, 28

Throckmorton [Throgmorton, Throkmarton], Eliz., iv, 12 ; Sir Geo., iv, 12 ; John, v, 329 ; Sir Nich., ii, 188 ; iii, 463

Throkcleston, *see* Thruxton

Throop [Throupe], tithing (Westover), v, 82, 133

Througham (Beaulieu), iv, 655

Thruxton, iv, 333, 367, 368, 369, 387-91 ; adv., iv, 391 ; chap., iv, 391 ; char., iv, 391 ; ch., iv, 389 ; man., iv, 339, 353, 373, 387-9 ; mkt. and fairs, iv, 388 ; Nonconf., iv, 391 ; pop., v, 438 ; Rom. rem., i, 298, 302 ; iv, 387 ; sch., ii, 405 ; iv, 391

Thudden, John de, iii, 53

Thudeworth, *see* Tidworth

Thuinham, *see* Christchurch

Thulewe (S. Damerham), iv, 587 *n*

Thurburn [Thurberne], Rob., ii, 180, 290, 365 ; iii, 96 ; v, 16

Thurkcleston, *see* Thruxton

Thurley, Will., ii, 163

Thurlow, Edw., Ld., iv, 224, 225

Thurman, Edw., iv, 353

Thurmunds, man., ii, 114

Thurmyngley Wood (Hurstbourne Priors), iv, 288

Thursbrakedenelonde (Kimpton), iv, 372

Thursby, Geo., v, 570, 573 ; Sir John, v, 573

Thurstan [Thurstin], iii, 397 ; iv, 431 ; v, 23, 23 *n*

Thurston, Hen., iv, 629 ; Will., ii, 488

Thurstons (Binsted), ii, 488

Thurwall, Ellis, iv, 16 ; Joan, iv, 16

Thwerewelle, *see* Wherwell

Thyn, John, iv, 342 *n*

Thynden, John de, ii, 214

Tibeslei, *see* Ibsley

Ticefelle, *see* Titchfield

Ticelle, *see* Itchel

Tichborne [Ticceburnan], ii, 96 ; iii, 302, 312, 336-8 ; adv., iii, 338 ; ch., iii, 337 ; mans., iii, 337 ; man. oratory, ii, 22 ; pop., v, 447 ; sch., ii, 405

Tichborne [Ticheburne, Tychbourne, Tycheborne], (de), Agatha, iii, 344 ; Amice [Amicia], ii, 177 ; iii, 337 ; Amphyllis, ii, 477, 513 ; iii, 338 ; iv, 22, 180 *n* ; Anne, iii, 338 ; iv, 22, 279 ; (Sir) Benj., ii, 85 ; iii, 58, 312, 337, 338, 395, 396, 407 ; iv, 3, 180, 204, 279, 423, 437, 455 ; v, 12 ; Chideoke, ii, 84 ; Compton, iv, 423, 437 ; Edw., ii, 308 ; Eliz., ii, 125 ; iii, 396 ; iv, 423, 437 ; v, 483 ; Ellen, ii, 476, 477, 513 ; iii, 413 ; iv, 3, 22 ; Frances, iv, 447 ; Fran., iii, 337 ; iv, 3, 179, 180, 423 ; Geoff., v, 163, 214 ; (Sir) Hen., ii, 84 ; iii, 61, 324, 337 ; iv, 110, 423, 476 ; v, 129, 130, 132 ; Sir Hen. A. J. Doughty, iii, 61, 337 ; Sir Hen. J., iii, 337, 407 ; iv, 425, 447, 476, 486 ; v, 129, 212 ; Hen. M., iv, 511 *n* ; Jas., iv, 3 ; Jeremy, iv, 279 ; Joan, iv, 180 *n* ; (Sir) John, ii, 177 ; iii, 69, 312, 324, 337 ; iv, 179, 180 *n*, 181 ; v, 118, 212, 312 ; Sir Jos., v, 132 ; Sir Jos. H. B. Doughty, iv, 423 ; Lionel, iv, 511 ; Mabel, v, 212, 214 ; Marg., iii, 204 ; iv, 180 ; Martin, iv, 279 ; Mary, ii, 476, 477 ; iii, 396 ; iv, 3, 110, 447 ; Mich., iv, 511 ; M., ii, 137 ; Nich., ii, 84, 369 ; iii, 9, 61, 62, 324 ; iv, 179, 279, 572 ; v, 212, 215, 326, 327 ; Pet., ii, 76, 84, 125 ; iii, 161, 270 ; Sir Rich., ii, 476, 477, 493, 513 ; iii, 61, 337, 338, 419 ; iv, 3, 22, 204, 446, 476, 481, 486 ; v, 12, 33, 129, 130, 132, 335, 336 ; Rog., ii, 177 ; iii, 61, 62, 337, 338 ; iv, 179, 511 ; v, 212, 214 ; Susan, ii, 125 ; iii, 396 ; iv, 446, 476, 481, 486 ; v, 129, 130, 132 ; Thos., ii, 84, 124 ; v, 111 ; Walt., ii, 476, 477 ; iii, 61, 337, 344 ; iv, 3, 4, 204 ; White, iv, 3 ; Will., iv, 179 ; v, 212, 215 ; Mrs., ii, 76 ; fam., arms, ii, 476 ; iii, 61, 337, 407 ; iv, 3

Tichborne Down, v, 545

Ticheburne, *see* Tichborne

Tichefelde, *see* Titchfield

Tidbury Ring (Bullington), i, 344 ; iv, 402

Tidelingham, v, 142 *n*

Tidgrove (Kingsclere), iv, 245, 255 *n*, 257, 332 *n*

Tidpit (Martin), iv, 592, 594

Tidpit Common Down (Martin), iv, 592

Tidworth, South, iv, 333, 391-4, 489, 490 ; adv., iv, 394 ; ch., iv, 394 ; mans., iv, 391 ; mkt. and fairs, iv, 392 ; pop., v, 438 ; sch., ii, 405 ; iv, 394

Tidworth [Tudeworth], (de), John, iv, 528, 532 ; Juliane, iv, 533 ; Rich., iv, 528, 533, 628

Tidworth House (S. Tidworth), iv, 391

Tigelhangra, *see* Tegdown Copse

Tildesley [Tildesleghe], Hugh de, iii, 124 ; iv, 151

Tilehurst (Berks), ii, 290

Tilli, Hen. de, iv, 72

Tillingham's, Great, (Hartley Wintney), iv, 79

Tillington, Sir Rob., ii, 391

Tilney, *see* Tylney

Timsbury, iv, 438, 486-8 ; adv., iv, 488 ; char., iv, 488 ; ch., iv, 487 ; man., ii, 122, 126 ; iv, 454, 486 ; man. house, iv, 486 ; Nonconf., iv, 488 ; pop., v, 445 ; sch., ii, 405

Timson, Rev. E., v, 572 ; Hen., iv, 550 ; Maj., v, 570

Tincommius, i, 263 ; v, 293

Tindal [Tyndall], Gervase, v, 325 ; Nich., v, 218

Tineæ, i, 149

Tinker's Hill (Andover), i, 302

Tinmouth, John of, iv, 411 *n*

Tipper, Rich., v, 453 ; Will., iii, 19, 310, 483 ; iv, 94 *n*

Tippetts, —, v, 381

Tipping, Eliz., iv, 563, 567 ; Sir Thos., iv, 563, 567

Tiptoe (Hordle), v, 110

Tiptoft, (de), Agnes, iv, 526, 628 ; Edw., ii, 475 ; iv, 348, 526, 628 ; Eliz., ii, 475, 476, 492 : Joan, iv, 526 ; (Sir) John, ii, 475, 476 ; iii, 153 ; iv, 347, 348, 526, 628 ; v, 320 ; Joyce, ii, 475, 476 ; iv, 347, 348, 526 ; Sir Payne, iv, 628 ; Philippa, iv, 526 ; Rob., iii, 153 ; fam., arms, ii, 476

Tirenache, John, v, 109

Tiron Abbey (France), *see* Tyron Abbey

Tirrell, *see* Tyrrell

Tisac, Jan du, v, 491

Tisted, East, iii, 3, 30-5 ; adv., iii, 35 ; char., iii, 35 ; ch., iii, 34 ; man., iii, 7, 30 ; pop., v, 438 ; sch., ii, 398

Tisted, West, iii, 37, 58-62 ; adv., iii, 62 ; ch., iii, 61 ; man., iii, 59 ; pop., v, 438 ; Rom. rem., i, 347 ; sch., ii, 406

Tisted [Tystede], (de), Agnes, ii, 124 ; Alice, ii, 124 ; Hugh, iii, 60 ; Mary, ii, 130 ; Maud, iii, 48 ; Rich., iii, 60, 61 ; Rob., iii, 9, 59 ; Thos., iii, 48, 61, 99, 344 ; Will., ii, 290 ; iii, 48, 61, 99, 344

Titchenbridge (Yateley), iv, 21

Titchfield, ii, 69, 73 ; iii, 217, 220-33 ; v, 324, 331, 347, 418, 462 ; adv., iii, 232 ; char., iii, 232 ; chs., iii, 230 ; iron mill, v, 464 ; man., ii, 181, 186 ; iii, 223 ; mkt., v, 409 ; pop., v, 441 ; sch., ii, 405

Titchfield, hund., iii, 217 ; v, 328 *n*

Titchfield, riv., *see* Meon

Titchfield Abbey, ii, 39, 56, 105, 181-6 ; iii, 107, 168, 222, 248, 261, 293 ; v, 272, 319 *n*, 362, 368, 420, 421

Titchingham, man., ii, 138

Titegrave, Titegrove [Kingsclere], *see* Tidgrove

Titegrave (Redbridge hund.), iv, 544

Titt, Chas. P., iv, 534

Tobacco trade, v, 461

Tochiton, *see* Tuckington

Tocliffe, Rich., *see* Ilchester, Rich. of

Tocock, Rob., v, 533, 534 ; Thos., v, 533, 536

Todd, Geo., v, 31 ; Will., iii, 109, 353 ; —, v, 537

Toderick, Walt., ii, 87

Tokens, v, 428

Tokynton, *see* Tufton

Tol, the Dane, iv, 474

Tolderton, Rob., iii, 114

Toldervy, Rob., v, 486
Toll, Anne, iv, 94 ; Chas., iv, 94
Tollemache [Talemache, Tolemache], Bridg., iv, 154, 204 ; Christine, iv, 474 ; Hugh, iv, 440 ; John, iv, 474 ; Julia [Juliane], iv, 93, 94, 577 n ; Nich., iv, 413 n ; Rob., iv, 440, 474 ; (Sir) Will., iv, 93, 94, 474, 577 n
Tolouse, see Toulouse
Tomber, see Toomer
Tomkins, Anne, iv, 496 ; John C., v, 173, 174 ; Jos., iv, 497 ; Will. S., iv, 493, 496
Tomline [Pretyman], Geo., bp., ii, 99 ; iv, 646, 647 ; v, 119, 120 ; Will. E., iv, 646 ; v, 119, 123
Tomlins, Sam., ii, 95
Tomlinson, Rev. E. M., iii, 112
Toms, John, ii, 91 ; iii, 531
Tomson, see Thompson
Tomworthe, see Tamworth
Toneworth, see Tidworth
Toni, de, Marg., iv, 624 ; Parnel, iv, 624 ; Ralph, iv, 624
Tonnrig (Carisbrooke), v, 222
Tonstal (Christchurch), v, 89 n
Took, Thos. S., v, 84
Tooker, see Tucker and Whalley-Tooker
Tool manufacture, v, 457
Toomer [Tomber] (le), John, iv, 405 ; R., iii, 536
Toothill (Rownhams), iv, 452, 460
Topp, —, iv, 592
Torbay (Devon), v, 379
Torber, iv, 559 n, 572, 577, 582
Torcroft, ii, 147
Torigleage (Farley Chamberlayne), iv, 444 n
Torlei, see Thorley
Torleton juxta Coates, ii, 131
Tornamira, Pontius de, iii, 412
Torney [Tornay, Torneie] (de), Gilb., v, 305 ; Sim., iv, 377 ; Will., ii, 188 ; iv, 377
Torr, Rev. T. J., iii, 358
Torrington, Arth., earl of, v, 386 ; Geo. Byng, vsct., iii, 178 ; v, 388
Tortehulle (Odiham), iv, 88
Tortoises, i, 146
Tosier [Tosiear, Tozier], Clement, iv, 344, 530 ; v, 8, 150, 168, 248 ; Will., iv, 303, 497, 509, 523
Tostig [Tosti], earl, ii, 420 ; iv, 213, 607 ; v, 98, 113, 135, 164, 241, 242, 284, 299, 359
Totehill, Hugh, ii, 147
Toteshall (Alton), ii, 478
Totford, man. (Northington), iii, 396
Totford, de, John, iii, 396 ; Phil., iii, 396 ; Rob., iii, 396 ; Will., iii, 396
Tothill, man., v, 164, 206
Totington, man., ii, 137
Totintone, see Totton
Totland (Freshwater), v, 240, 288 ; adv., v, 245 ; ch., v, 245 ; sch., ii, 408
Totland Bay, v, 240
Totnall, Rich., v, 471
Tottenham, Rich., ii, 139
Totton (Eling), ii, 126, 146 ; iv, 546, 552, 555, 635 ; v, 413 ; inds., iv, 546 ; v, 469 ; man., ii, 148 ; iv, 547, 549
Touchett [Touchet, Tuchet], Anne, iv, 473 n, 657 ; Eliz., iv, 594 ; Geo., iv, 370, 371 ; Hen., iv, 473 n ; Jas., iv, 354, 552 ; John, iv, 473 n, 541 n, 657 ; John H., iii, 443 ; Marg., iv, 552 ; Mary, iii, 345 ; Rich., iv, 594
Touker, see Tucker

Toulouse [Tolouse], Hen., iv, 628 ; v, 275
Touncil Field (Hayling Isl), iii, 129
Tour, de la, Hen., iii, 256 ; Hugh, iii, 256 ; Thos., iii, 256 ; Will., iii, 256
Tovi, iv, 227, 491, 513 ; v, 151, 191
Tower Hill (Over Wallop), iv, 530
Towers, Rob., iv, 249
Towmanston (Farley Chamberlayne), iv, 443
Townesend (Martin), iv, 594
Townhill, man. (S. Stoneham), ii, 148 ; iii, 483
Townsend (Odiham), iv, 88
Townsend, G. B., v, 574 ; Sir Isaac, v, 57 ; Rich., iii, 414 ; iv, 258
Townshend, Chas., iv, 301 ; Thos., iv, 301
Townshend Manor House (Over Wallop), iv, 530
Towris, Rich., iii, 224
Toyd (Martin), iv, 592
Toyd's Farm (Martin), iv, 592
Tozande, Thos., iv, 318
Tozier, see Tosier
Tracey, Will., v, 374, 395
Tracy [Tracie] (de), Benedicta, v, 164 ; Joan, ii, 211 ; iv, 569, 576 n ; v, 159 ; John, iv, 569 ; v, 164 ; Thos., iii, 294 ; (Sir) Will., iv, 569 ; v, 159, 172 ; fam., v, 237
Tragett, Rev. T. H., iv, 538
Trandelmede (Bramley), iv, 141
Trappes, Ant., v, 200
Trattle, Mary, iii, 296
Trausantum, i, 331
Traveller's Rest (Whitchurch), iv, 300
Travers, Pet., ii, 157 ; Thos., iv, 183
Trayleman, John, v, 212
Tredcroft, Edw., v, 514, 518
Tredenham Lodge (Farnborough), iv, 15
Tredgo, Sim., iii, 464
Tredyngton, Thos., iii, 499 ; v, 316
Treeby, Alf., v, 84
Tregagle, Fran., iv, 541 ; Jane, iv, 541 ; John, iv, 541 ; Nath., iv, 541
Treget, Treigoz, see Tregoz
Tregonwell, Jane, v, 94 ; John, v, 94, 529 ; L. D. G., v, 134 ; fam., iv, 583 n
Tregoz [Treget, Treigoz, Tregos] (de), Clarice, iv, 512 ; Sir John, iv, 512 ; Rob., iv, 184, 278, 512, 514 ; Walt., iv, 278 ; Will., iv, 278
Trelawney, Jonathan, ii, 97, 98 ; v, 178, 193
Trembury, Sim., ii, 213
Trench, Helena, Lady, iii, 463 ; Rich. C., ii, 100 ; iv, 607
Trenchant, Alice, ii, 478 ; Edw., ii, 478 ; Will., ii, 478
Trenchants [Trenchauntes Place] (Alton), ii, 473, 478
Trenchard [Trinkard], Edm., v, 273 n ; Eleanor, v, 272 ; Sir Geo., iv, 620 ; v, 112 ; Giles, v, 273, 277 ; Hen., iv, 619 ; v, 89 n, 112, 113, 144, 161, 220, 272, 273, 275, 277 ; Joan, v, 273 ; (Sir) John, ii, 337 ; iv, 619 ; v, 112, 113, 144, 212, 270, 272, 273, 281 ; Marg., v, 273 ; Payn, v, 220, 272 ; Rich., v, 114 n, 192, 198, 270 ; Rob., v, 272 ; (Sir) Thos., iv, 527, 620 ; v, 113, 144, 192, 198 ; Waleran, v, 112, 285 ; (Sir) Will., v, 198, 270

Trenchardestapel (Over Wallop) iv, 527 n, 531
Trenchefan, Will., ii, 228, 229
Trendellond (Carisbrooke), v, 222
Trengof, Walt., ii, 181
Trente (de), Amice, iv, 403 ; John, iv, 403 ; Maud, iv, 403
Trentegeruns, Will., iii, 505
Tresham, Sir Thos., v, 329
Tresswell, John, iv, 516
Trethek, John, iv, 577
Trethorns (Swarraton), iv, 195 n
Trewe, fam., v, 460
Trewyn, Thos., ii, 230
Trgelhangra (Brown Candover), iv, 183 n
Tribe, John, iii, 68
Triggs, Greg., iii, 114
Trim, Mary, iii, 536
Trimmer, Rich., iii, 21 ; Rob., iv, 27
Trimnell, Chas., ii, 98 ; Will., ii, 115
Trinity College (Oxf.), iv, 112 n
Trinkard, see Trenchard
Tripacy, Hugh, ii, 192
Trisanton, riv., i, 331, 336
Tristre, land of (Lockerley), iv, 501
Triveri, Rich. de, ii, 109
Trobylfelde, see Turberville
Trojans cricket club (Southampton). v, 576
Troketon, v, 191 n
Trolles Ende (Heckfield), iv, 45
Trollope, Sir John, iv, 477 ; Susan [Susanna], iii, 484 ; iv, 477 ; Sir Thos., iv, 477
Tronchont's farm, see Trenchants
Trop, John, iii, 53
Troppe, tithing, see Throop
Trott, Cath., Lady, iv, 200, 209 ; Edm., iv, 209 ; Eliz., Lady, iv, 209 ; (Sir) John, iv, 200, 209, 363
Troublefield, see Preston Vavasour
Troubridge, Capt. Thos., v, 397
Troughear, Leonard, v, 219, 242, 288 ; Thos., v, 270
Trouin, Duguay, v, 385, 388
Trovylfeldys, see Preston Vavasour
Trowe, Margery, iv, 604 ; Thos., iv, 604
Trucketon, v, 191 n
Truckles (Brading), v, 191 n
True, Anne, iv, 244 ; Eliz., iv, 243 ; Jas., iv, 243, 244 ; Will., iv, 244
Truffle-hunting, v, 455
Trusbury, ii, 172
Trussell [Trussel], Edw., iv, 511 n ; Will., ii, 138
Trusset, Agnes, ii, 124
Trusty Servant, ii, 351 ; v, 17
Tubb, John, v, 529
Tuberville, see Turberville
Tuchet, see Touchett
Tucker [Tooker, Touker], Giles, v, 129 ; John, iii, 397 ; Reg., v, 482 ; Rich., v, 482 n ; Rob., v, 482 ; Will., ii, 315, 319 ; v, 482 n ; Capt., v, 336
Tuckford (Bournemouth), v, 134 n
Tuckington, see Tufton
Tuckton (Bournemouth), v, 134
Tuckton, tithing (Christchurch), 82
Tudeputte, see Tidpit
Tuderlegh, Tuderley, see Tytherley
Tudeworth, see Tidworth
Tudor, Edm., iv, 348
Tufton, iv, 273, 400, 402, 409-10 ; adv., iv, 410 ; chap., iv, 403 ; ch., iv, 410 ; man., ii, 133 ; iv, 409, 411 n, 412 n ; Manor Farm house, iv, 409 ; man.-house, iv, 409 ; pop., v, 441

Tufton, Christian, iv, 370 ; John, iv, 370
Tufton Goodworth, ii, 132
Tull, W. T., v, 140 ; Miss, v, 173
Tullwell Court (Glouc.), iv, 324
Tulse, Hen., v, 115 ; Kath., v, 100 ; Rog., v, 115, 117 n ; Will., iv, 620 ; v, 99, 100 ; fam., v, 96
Tumby, Mary, iv, 521 ; Steph., iv, 521
Tumuli, see Burials and burial urns
Tundry Hill (Dogmersfield), iv, 72
Tundry Pond (Dogmersfield), iv, 73
Tunicata, i, 101
Tunno, Edw. R., iii, 271
Tunstall, Cuth., bp. of London, iv, 165
Tunworth, ii, 382 ; iv, 113, 114, 174-6 ; adv., iv, 176 ; ch., iv, 174, 175 ; man., iv, 174 ; pop., v, 439 ; sch., ii, 405
Tunworth, Rich., ii, 261, 267
Tunwurda, see Tunworth
Turald, iv, 381
Turber, iv, 519
Turberville [Trobylfelde, Tuberville, Turbervil, Turbervyle] (de), Eleanor, iv, 542 ; Jas., ii, 309 ; Joan, v, 192 ; (Sir) John, iv, 542, 604 ; v, 192 ; Rich., v, 192
Turbury Common (Tadley), iv, 221
Turfields (Christchurch), v, 97 n
Turges, see Stratfield Turgis
Turgis, Hen., iv, 63, 114 n ; John, iv, 42, 63 ; Mary, iv, 537
Turgis Court (Stratfield Turgis), iv, 63, 64
Turgis Green (Stratfield Turgis), iv, 63
Turi, iii, 227
Turk [Turke, Turks], Beatrice, iv, 102 ; Sir Rob., iv, 102 ; —, ii, 266
Turkilleston, see Thruxton
Turle, Maj., v, 561
Turnebu, Aumary de, iv, 360
Turner [Turnour], Alice, ii, 177 ; Edw., v, 330 ; Fran., bp. of Ely, ii, 330, 339 ; Geo., v, 521 ; Jas., iii, 50 ; iv, 625 ; Rich., iii, 171 ; v, 519 ; Rog., ii, 91 ; Thos., iii, 395 ; v, 460 ; Will., ii, 177, 482 ; iii, 395 ; see also Turnor
Turnham, de, Edelina, iv, 254 ; Steph., iv, 254
Turnor, Miss, iv, 430 ; see also Turner
Turnynge Thorne (Faccombe), iv, 317
Turpin, Anne, iii, 487 ; Dick, iv, 15 ; Matth., iii, 487
Turpyton, Hugh de, ii, 479
Turstin, iii, 21, 414 ; iv, 18, 437
Turtles (Odiham), iv, 98
Turville [Turvill] (de), Dav., iii, 250, 251 ; Galiena, iv, 491 n ; Maurice, iii, 250 ; Pet., iii, 250 ; Will., iii, 250 ; iv, 35 ; fam., arms, iii, 251
Tutt, Edw., iii, 403 ; Rich., iv, 419 ; Thos., iii, 405
Tuttie, Thomasine, ii, 486, 487, 488 ; Will., ii, 486, 487, 488
Tweedmouth, Ld., iv, 287
Tweonea, Tweoxneham, see Christchurch
Twichens (Ecchinswell), iv, 250
Twillowe, John, ii, 37
Twinham, see Christchurch
Twisse [Twiste], Will., ii, 325, 389
Two Downs (Itchel), iv, 6
Twohide, see Toyd
Two Parting Coppice (Faccombe), iv, 314

Twychener, John, ii, 295, 296, 297, 298, 300, 366 ; Rich., ii, 296, 302, 366
Twychyn (Faccombe), iv, 314
Twyford, ii, 62, 86, 96, 211 ; iii, 42, 302, 339-41 ; v, 448 ; adv., ii, 20, 21 ; iii, 341 ; char., iii, 341 ; ch., iii, 341 ; man., ii, 66 ; iii, 340 ; v, 472 ; mill, v, 451 ; Rom. rem., i, 309, 347 ; sch., ii, 405
Twyford, Sam., v, 143 ; —, v, 524
Twyford Moors, Rom. rem., i, 310
Twyll Acre (Liss), iv, 84
Twynam [Tyneham], (de), Chas., iii, 489 ; Geo., iii, 310 ; v, 537 ; Hen., iii, 310 ; John, ii, 172 ; v, 507 ; —, v, 537
Twyne [Twynne], Anne, iv, 102 ; Edw., iv, 605 ; John, iii, 456, 457, 458, 459 ; Nich., iii, 458, 459 ; Oliver, ii, 510 ; Rich., iii, 456 ; Thos., ii, 479, 510 ; iii, 458 ; Will., iii, 458, 459 ; fam., arms, ii, 510
Twyneham, see Christchurch
Twynghoo, Edith, iv, 327 ; Edw., iv, 327
Twynlie (Ecchinswell), iv, 250
Twynne, see Twyne
Tyburn, man. (Midd.), v, 244
Tychbourn, Tycheborne, see Tichborne
Tydolneshide, Walt., ii, 155, 160
Tydresle, see Tytherley
Tyes [Teutonicus], Sir Hen., v, 273 ; Theodoric, iv, 436, 607 ; Waleran, iv, 360, 361, 363, 607 ; v, 223, 242, 246 n, 466
Tygall, Joan, iii, 71 ; Will., iii, 71 ; fam., arms, iii, 71
Tyghecroft (Pamber), iv, 433
Tyle Barn (Weston Patrick), iv, 108
Tylgale (Kingsley), ii, 515
Tylney, Dorothy, ctss., iii, 39 ; iv, 22, 100 ; earls :—John, iv, 22, 93, 100, 106 ; Rich., iii, 39 ; iv, 22, 100
Tylney [Tilney], Anne, iii, 39 ; v, 100 ; Eliz., iv, 112 ; Emma, iv, 93 ; Fred., iii, 39 ; iv, 22, 93, 99, 100, 101 ; v, 77 ; John, iii, 39 ; Rich., iv, 99, 101, 112 ; fam., iv, 223
Tylney Hall (Rotherwick), iv, 99
Tylney-Long, Cath., iv, 94, 100 ; Sir John, iv, 100
Tylney Park (Rotherwick), iv, 99
Tymberbury, see Timsbury
Tyndall, see Tindal
Tyneham, see Twynam
Tyrell's Ford (Sopley), v, 127
Tyrewache, Will., ii, 156
Tyron Abbey (France), iv, 176, 177 ; Steph., abbot of, ii, 225 ; Theobald, abbot of, ii, 224 ; Will., abbot of, ii, 221
Tyrrell [Terell, Tirrell, Tyrell], Adryan, ii, 125 ; Agnes, iv, 327 ; Constance, iv, 632 ; Eleanor, v, 130 n ; Sir Hen., v, 125 ; (Sir) Hugh, ii, 510 ; iv, 327, 431 ; v, 225, 315 ; Isabel, iii, 510 ; iv, 561 ; (Sir) John, iv, 326, 327 ; v, 125, 129 ; Margery, ii, 125 ; iv, 326 ; Olive, iii, 95 ; Rog., iii, 95, 114 ; (Sir) Thos., iii, 95, 468, 483 ; v, 118, 125 ; (Sir) Walt., ii, 421 ; v, 127, 300
Tyse, Phil., v, 117
Tyssen, Fran., iv, 433 ; Mary, iv, 433 ; Sam., iv, 9, 94 ; Sarah, iv, 9, 94
Tystede, see Tisted

Tytherley, East, ii, 162 ; iv, 489, 500, 506, 509 n, 515-18 ; v, 539 ; adv., ii, 163 ; iv, 518 ; char., iv, 518 ; ch., iv, 517 ; man., iv, 456, 457, 472 n, 494, 498, 501, 508, 515-17 ; man. house, iv, 516 ; mills, iv, 517 ; pk., iv, 515 ; pop., v, 446 ; sch., ii, 398
Tytherley, West, ii, 25 ; iv, 476, 487, 489, 509, 519-24, 582 ; advs., iv, 524 ; bailiwicks, iv, 523 ; char., iv, 524 ; ch., iv, 523 ; mans., iv, 342, 494, 498, 499, 507, 515 n, 519-23, 553, 573, 577 ; pop., v, 446 ; prehist. rem., iv, 519 ; sch., ii, 406
Tytherley, Philippa, iv, 444 ; Will., iv, 444
Tytlescombe, man., ii, 121

Ude, John, iii, 135 ; Matth., iii, 135
Udemancote, see Woodmancote
Uderle, West, see Tytherley, West
Uferantun, see Overton
Uggaton (Ugelton), man. (Brighstone), v, 212
Ulesfeld, see Ellisfield
Ulf, iv, 635
Ulfertona, see Wolverton
Ulgar, v, 116
Ulmar, iv, 596
Ulmis, de, Nich., prior of Carisbrooke, ii, 231 ; Odo, prior of Carisbrooke, ii, 231
Ulnod, iii, 68 ; iv, 492, 623 ; v, 164, 165, 173 n, 248
Ulstan, see Wulfstan
Ulster, Rich. de Burgh, earl of, iv, 81
Ultra Aquam, Pet. de, prior of Carisbrooke, ii, 231
Ulvetham, see Elvetham
Ulveva [Wulfgifu Betteslau], iii, 86 ; iv, 158, 208, 366, 377 n, 379, 604
Ulviet, ii, 421 ; iv, 550, 553, 572, 577 ; v, 130, 243
Ulvretune, see Wolverton
Ulvric, see Wulfric
Ulwarcombe, see Woolverton
Ulward, ii, 512 ; iii, 226, 263 ; iv, 7, 22
Ulwartone, see Wolverton
Ulwi, v, 95
Ulwin, iv, 443
Umfraville, Will. d', v, 160 n
Umfray, Joan, ii, 129 ; Rich., iii, 312
Umpton [Unton], Alex., v, 194 ; Anne, v, 194 n ; Edw., v, 193, 194 ; Thos., v, 193, 194, 207
Undercliff, man. (Newchurch), v, 182
Undercliff (St. Lawrence), v, 187, 193
Undermount (Bonchurch), v, 155
Underwood, John, ii, 209
Undor Wathe (St. Lawrence), v, 194
Ungulata, i, 5, 246 ; ii, 412
Unitarians, iii, 534 ; iv, 613 ; v, 136, 264
United Service Cricket Club (Portsmouth), v, 576
University College (Oxf.), iv, 430
University College (Reading), v, 511
Unlof, v, 141
Unton, see Umpton
Unwin [Unwyn], Joan, iv, 255 ; John, iii, 308 ; iv, 194, 425 ; Sim., iv, 194 ; Will., iv, 194, 225
Upchepyng, Nich., ii, 30
Upclatford, see Clatford, Upper

Upehulle, Agnes, iv, 598 ; Edm., iv, 598
Upelden, see Eldon, Upper
Up Green (Eversley), iv, 33
Upham, iii, 274, 275, 290, 299-301 ; adv., iii, 301 ; ch., iii, 300 ; man., iii, 300 ; pop., v, 440 ; Rom. rem., i, 309, 324 ; sch., ii, 405
Upham, Edw., iii, 300 ; Iseult, iii, 300
Upham beagles, v, 536
Uphusband, see Hurstbourne Tarrant
Upiate (S. Damerham), iv, 587 n
Up Nately [Upnatelegheseththrop], ii, 223, 224 ; iv, 113, 114, 149, 150, 151, 176-9 ; adv., iv, 179 ; ch., iv, 176, 178 ; man., iv, 176 ; mills, iv, 176, 178 ; pop., v, 439 ; sch., ii, 405
Uppelinch (Freshwater), v, 240
Upperblackden (Hurstbourne Tarrant), iv, 321
Upper Link (St. Mary Bourne), iv, 295
Upperthrowayes (Hurstbourne Tarrant), iv, 321
Upper Week Barn (Andover), Rom. rem., i, 304
Upping Copse (Goodworth Clatford), iv, 403
Uppinne (Abbotts Ann), iv, 335
Upsombourne Kaumes, man. (King's Somborne), iv, 474
Upton (Hurstbourne Tarrant and Vernhams Dean), ii, 137, 143 ; iv, 319, 324, 329 ; man., ii, 145 ; iv, 321, 330
Upton (Nursling), iii, 433
Upton [Uptone], (de), John, iii, 149 ; Kath., iii, 124 ; Maud, ii, 521 ; iii, 11 ; Nich., ii, 521 ; v, 319, 326 ; Rog., iii, 149 ; Will., iii, 124 ; iv, 501 ; fam., iv, 127
Upton Grey, ii, 226 ; iii, 355, 356, 382-6 ; iv, 108 ; adv., iii, 386 ; char., iii, 386 ; ch., iii, 384 ; man., iii, 383 ; iv, 156, 176 ; pop., v, 439 ; sch., ii, 406
Upwarneford, see Warnford
Upwellop, see Wallop, Over
Urchfont, man. (Wilts.), ii, 55, 122, 123, 125
Ure, see Ower
Urleston, see Earlstone
Urry, Anne, iv, 69 ; Dav., iv, 554 ; v, 242, 243, 245, 285 ; Eliz., iv, 69 ; v, 145 ; Isabel, v, 229 ; Joan, v, 230 ; John, v, 147 n, 242, 285, 290 ; Kath. [Cath.], iii, 415 ; iv, 554, 573 ; v, 241 ; Parnel, v, 142, 147, 216 n ; Rich., v, 216 n ; Rob., v, 142, 216 n, 229, 241, 243, 285 ; Roberta, v, 164 ; Thos., iii, 415 ; iv, 69, 573 ; v, 241, 242, 275, 285 ; Walt., v, 142 ; Will., iv, 69 ; v, 147, 150, 219, 229, 230, 285 n ; fam., v, 246, 248
Urry's Place (Carisbrooke), v, 229
Ursfelde, le, (Crondall), iv, 6
Usborne, Hen., iii, 478
Useflete, de, Nich., iii, 255 ; Thos., iii, 255
Ushott, see Ewshott
Uske, Ad., iii, 110
Uttoft, Bridg., iii, 436 ; John, iii, 436
Uvedale, Ant., ii, 84, 86 ; iii, 48, 70 ; iv, 492 ; Arth., iii, 98, 171, 234 ; iv, 153 ; Dorothy, iii, 171 ; iv, 153 ; Sir Edm., v, 289 ; Eliz., iii, 98, 227 ; iv, 35, 492, 523 ; Ellen, iv, 424 ; Frances, iv, 153 ; Hen., iii, 225, 228 ; John,

Uvedale (cont.)
ii, 224, 272, 277 ; iii, 171, 225, 227, 234 ; iv, 153, 232, 255 n, 492, 508, 523 ; Marg., iv, 424 ; Mary, iii, 225, 233, 234 ; Rich., v, 329 ; Rob., iii, 98, 227 ; iv, 492, 523 ; Sybil, iii, 234 ; iv, 153, 232 ; (Sir) Thos., iii, 48, 70, 225, 228, 234 ; iv, 35, 41, 153, 424, 492 ; Ursula, iii, 70, 334 ; (Sir) Will., ii, 84 ; iii, 153, 159, 171, 225, 233, 234, 235 ; iv, 64, 153, 232, 492 ; fam., arms, iii, 48, 234
Uverwallop, see Wallop, Over

Vache [Vaches], (de, de la), Eliz., iv, 45 n ; Hugh, iii, 52 ; Margery, iii, 52 ; Sir Phil., iv, 45, 46, 156
Vachell, Marg., iv, 146 ; Mary, iii, 90, 98, 118 ; Steph., ii, 86 ; iii, 90, 98, 118 ; Thos., iii, 90 ; Will., iii, 366 ; iv, 146
Vagrancy, v, 429
Vaillant, Pierre, v, 491
Vale Barn, ii, 292
Valence [Valentia], (de), Adamore, ii, 198 ; Andrew, ii, 84 ; Aymer [Aylmer], ii, 18, 24, 109 ; iii, 11, 17, 23, 26, 227, 239, 371 ; iv, 21 n, 242, 513 ; v, 98, 265 ; John, iii, 346 ; Maria, ii, 198 ; Nich., iii, 346 ; Will., ii, 17 ; iii, 3, 23, 26, 29, 135, 217, 356, 455 ; iv, 333, 389, 544
Valentine, prior of St. Swithun's, ii, 115 ; v, 34
Vale Parke (Crondall), iv, 6
Valery, Sir John de, iv, 206
Valeys, see Waleys
Valle, Walt. de, v, 33
Vallor, Ant., ii, 496
Valoignes, (de), John, iv, 146, 147 ; Marg., iv, 146 ; Nich., iv, 146
Valois, Rev. Phil., iii, 35
Val Osoul [Val Oseul], Thos. de, ii, 41, 231
Valpy, Rev. —, v, 73
Vanceyo, Denis, ii, 229
Vane, Sir Hen., iv, 301
Vaneham (Linkenholt), iv, 324
Vanne, John de, v, 173
Vanner [Vanur, Venour], (le), John, iii, 226 ; v, 237 n ; Reg., v, 148 n
Van Notten, Chas., iv, 271
Vanpidles (Kingsclere), iv, 261 n
Vanur, see Vanner
Vaughan, Dominic, v, 198 ; Edm., iv, 554, 555 ; Edw., iii, 189, 334 ; Geo., iii, 97 ; John, iii, 115 ; v, 198
Vaulandes (Heckfield), iv, 45
Vaus, Joan, iv, 214 ; John, iv, 98 ; Nich., iv, 93, 98, 214 n ; Rich., iv, 93, 214, 215 ; Rob., iv, 93, 214, 215 ; see also Vaux
Vaus & Crampton, engravers, v, 490
Vautort, John de, ii, 479
Vaux, Geo., (de), ii, 82 ; Gerard, iii, 480 ; v, 489 ; John, v, 489 ; Nich., ii, 369 ; —, v, 489 ; see also Vaus
Vavasour, (le), Maj. Ebenezer, iii, 201 ; John, v, 191 ; Rog., v, 191 ; Thos., v, 162, 191
Vectis, see Wight, Isle of
Veer, see Vere
Velmead, iv, 9 n
Velyne, Bridg., iv, 93 n
Venables, Barbara, iv, 491 ; Dorothy, iv, 355 ; John, iii, 43 ; Kath. [Cath.], iii, 48 ; iv, 61, 62 ;

Venables (cont.)
Nich., iii, 358 ; iv, 62, 355, 554 ; Philippa, iii, 326 ; Rich., iv, 355, 409, 468, 491 ; —, v, 383
Venoiz, see Venuz
Venour, see Vanner
Venta Belgarum, see Winchester
Ventnor, v, 138 n, 179, 240, 272, 433 ; chs., v, 186 ; Crab and Lobster inn, v, 179 ; man., v, 182 ; Rom. Cath., v, 179 ; Rom. rem., i, 349 ; sch., ii, 408 ; v, 179
Ventnor Farm Mead (Newchurch), v, 186
Venuz [Venoiz], (de), Amice, ii, 518 ; Constance, ii, 494 ; iii, 370 ; Geoff., ii, 518 ; iii, 17 ; iv, 195 ; Hugh, ii, 494 ; John, ii, 177, 493, 494, 518, 519, 520 ; iii, 17, 260, 370 ; Margery, ii, 518 ; Nich., ii, 494 ; iv, 571 ; Rich., ii, 518 ; Rob., ii, 518 ; iii, 17, 260 ; iv, 195 ; Sibyl, ii, 519 ; Thos., ii, 519 ; iii, 260 ; Will., ii, 518 ; iii, 17
Verder, Marg. de, ii, 127
Verderer's Hall (Lyndhurst), iv, 630
Verdun, Maud de, iii, 145
Vere [Veer], (de), Anne, iv, 370 ; Aubrey, ii, 440 ; iv, 632 ; Audrey, iv, 370 ; Constance, iv, 370 ; Denise, iv, 52 ; Eleanor, iv, 161, 216 n ; Eliz., iv, 370 ; Ethelreda, iv, 370 ; (Sir) Hen., iv, 370 ; v, 164 ; Isabel, Lady, iv, 370 ; John, v, 146 n, 161 ; Pet., v, 146 n, 161, 216 n ; Sir Rich., iv, 370 ; Rob., ii, 147 ; iii, 483, 487 ; Walt., v, 146, 148
Verica, i, 263 ; v, 293
Vernamesdeane, Vernansdeane, see Vernhams Dean
Verney, Frances, iv, 458 ; Ralph, ii, 338
Vernhamgreen (Vernhams Dean), iv, 330
Vernhams Bank (Vernhams Dean), iv, 329
Vernhams Dean, iv, 319, 324, 329-31, 341 ; adv., iv, 331 ; chap., iv, 331 ; char., iv, 331 ; ch., iv, 331 ; mans., iv, 321, 329, 330 ; Noncomf., iv, 331 ; pop., v, 438 ; sch., ii, 406 ; iv, 331
Vernhams Row (Vernhams Dean), iv, 329
Vernhams Street (Vernhams Dean), iv, 329
Vernham West, man. (Vernhams Dean), iv, 329
Vernislade (Carisbrooke), v, 222
Vernon, (de), Anne, iv, 348 ; Sir Chas., iv, 3 ; Eleanor, iv, 348 ; Geo., iv, 3, 19 ; (Sir) Hen., iii, 261 ; iv, 348, 358 ; Joan, iii, 124 ; Marg., v, 241 ; Mary, v, 91 ; Rich., v, 241 ; Thos., iv, 19, 348 ; Will., see Redvers, Will de
Verny Hill (Liss), iv, 84
Versona, Mich. de, iv, 424
Verwood, pottery manufacture, v, 491
Vesci, de, vscts, see De Vesci
Vescy, Sir John, iv, 54 ; Mary, Lady, iv, 54 ; Sir Thos., iv, 54
Vespasian, v, 293
Veyl, John (de, le), v, 86, 114
Vialls, Amos, iv, 622 n
Vicars hill (Boldre), iv, 616
Vickers, Col. T. E., iv, 486
Victoria, queen, v, 197, 198, 200, 201, 262, 566
Vidler, Jesse, iii, 399
Vidley Van (Milford), v, 116

Vienna [Vienne], (de), Ellen, iv, 498, 501 ; John, ii, 161 ; iv, 498, 501, 515
Vieville, baron of, v, 568 ; marquess of, v, 568
Views, the, (Fleet), iv, 5
Viliers, see Villiers
Villebois, Hen., v, 521 ; John T., v, 514, 515, 536 ; Thos. T., iv, 201 n ; —, v, 514
Villiers, Ld. Francis, v, 349
Villiers [Viliers], Sir Edw., iv, 185 ; Geo., v, 98, 335, 378, 379 ; Rog., iv, 492
Vilur, Godf. de, iv, 594
Vincent, warden of God's House, ii, 203, 205
Vincent, Hen. B., iv, 299 ; John, v, 481 n
Vindomis, i, 271, 319, 321
Vine hunt, v, 520
Vinels Copses (Amport), iv, 337
Vinitor, Ernald, v, 23
Vipont, Rob. de, iii, 223
Virsey, Rob., v, 263
Vitalis, the priest, iv, 323
Vivian, Sir Hussey, v, 572
Vivonia, de, Joan, iv, 258 n, 270 ; John, iv, 258, 270
Vobe, John, v, 263
Volunteer forces, v, 356
Vox, Steph. le, see Fox
Voxham (Bramley), iv, 141
Voyvell, see Wyvill
Vrynham, see Vernhams Dean
Vunithingi, Edw., iv, 626 ; Hugh, iv, 626
Vyne, The, (Sherborne St. John), iv, 122, 158, 159, 160-5, 167, 170, 341, 362, 378, 509, 610 ; chant., ii, 62 ; earthwork, i, 347
Vyneour, John le, ii, 165
Vyoun [Vyonn], John le, ii, 229, 230
Vytelhull (Gatcombe), v, 246, 247 n

Wace, Isabel, iv, 58 ; John, ii, 521 ; iv, 58 ; Marg., iv, 58
Wachedene (Sherborne St. John), iv, 158
Wackland, man. (Newchurch), v, 184
Wadchamp (Abbotts Ann), iv, 334 n
Waddington, John T., v, 78, 517
Waddon, man. (Dors.), ii, 148
Waddon chap. (Selborne), iii, 13
Waddune (Wherwell), iv, 411
Wade (Eling), iv, 552, 554
Wade (Havant), see Wade Court
Wade, (de, la), Cecil L., iv, 406 ; C., iii, 370, 375, 377 ; Hen., iii, 150, 158, 168 ; John, iii, 168 ; Juliane, iii, 124 ; v, 305 ; Mary, iii, 432
Wadebroke (Eversley), iv, 33
Wade Court (Havant), iii, 122, 124
Wade Hill Farm (Eling), iv, 554
Wade Park Farm (Eling), iv, 552
Wadham, Dorothy, ii, 485 ; Edw., ii, 485 ; Eliz., v, 229 n ; Florence, ii, 485 ; Jane, ii, 131 ; Joan, ii, 485 ; John, ii, 484, 485 ; v, 228, 229 n ; Kath., ii, 131 ; Laurence, ii, 485 ; Marg., ii, 485 ; v, 233 ; Sir Nich., ii, 131, 485 ; v, 223, 229 n, 233, 270 ; Will., iv, 142
Wagener's Wells, v, 464
Wager, commodore, v, 385, 388
Wages, rate of, v, 411, 413, 430, 432, 487 n, 494, 498, 502, 503, 504, 510
Waight, John, iii, 251 ; Martha, iv, 357
Wainfleet (Lincs.), sch., ii, 306

Waisel, man. (Wilts), see Washerne
Waite, see Wayte
Wake, Thos., Ld., ii, 475
Wake, Andr., iv, 326, 328 ; Charlotte, iv, 551 ; Eliz., iii, 459 ; iv, 326 ; Geo. A., iv, 551 ; Rev. Hen., iv, 534 ; Isabel, iv, 326 ; Joan, iv, 328 ; John, iv, 326, 327 ; Marg., ii, 475, 476 ; Margery, iv, 326 ; Ralph, iv, 326 ; Rich., iv, 551 ; Thos., iii, 459
Wakefield, Rob., iv, 91 ; Will. S., iv, 516
Wakelond, see Wackland
Wakemans (Kingsclere), iv, 250
Wakener's Wells, see Wagener's Wells
Wakeridge Warren (Kingsclere), iv, 266
Wakriges (Kingsclere), iv, 250, 261 n
Walaston, see Woollaston
Walberton, man., iv, 116
Walbridge Coppice (New Forest), ii, 444
Walde, par., see Wield
Walde, Rev. M. N., iv, 325 n
Walden, Rog., iii, 158
Walding (Romsey), iv, 452
Waldo, Mrs., iv, 140, 244
Waldon, ii, 146
Waldrich, Will., iv, 561
Wale, Rich., iv, 380
Walens, Hen., ii, 479
Waleran, the huntsman, iv, 341, 342, 351, 352, 438, 440, 480, 481, 498, 499, 521, 522, 536, 598 ; v, 98
Waleran [Walerand, Waleraund, Walerond, Walrand, Walraund], Alice, ii, 132 ; Aubree, iv, 521, 522 ; Cecily, iv, 521 ; Isabel, iv, 351, 521 ; John, iii, 255 ; iv, 481, 493, 533 ; Maud, ii, 132 ; iii, 255, 342, 547 n ; Nich., iv, 41 ; Phil., ii, 218 ; Rob., iii, 32, 35, 255 ; iv, 82, 342, 481, 493, 519, 524, 533, 547, 631 ; Thos., v, 114 ; Walt., iv, 352, 440, 499, 521, 524 ; Will., iv, 342, 547 n
Walesworth, see Walsworth
Waleton, Rob. de, iii, 104
Walewell (Breamore), iv, 598
Waleys [Valeys, Wayleys], (de, le) Agnes, iv, 630 ; Beatrice, iv, 260 ; John, iii, 415 ; iv, 630 ; Juliana, v, 197 n ; Rich., v, 197 n ; Walt., iii, 415 ; Will., ii, 228 ; iii, 260
Walford, John D., v, 78
Walhampton (Boldre), ii, 159 ; iv, 616, 620 ; v, 81, 82
Walkelin, bp. of Winchester, see Winchester, bps. of ; prior of Southwick, ii, 168
Walkelyn, Rich., v, 484
Walker, Dav. P., iv, 458 ; Edw., iv, 395 ; v, 340 ; Eliz., iii, 97 ; Harry, v, 574 ; Heneage, iv, 609 n ; Sir Hovenden, v, 388 ; John, iii, 149 ; iv, 598 ; v, 525 ; Rich., v, 285 n ; Maj. Rob., iv, 563 ; Tom, v, 574 ; Tyrwhitt, iv, 491 ; Wallace J., iv, 270 ; —, v, 570
Walker-Munro, Edw. L., iv, 626
Walkford (Milton), v, 124
Walkford Brook, v, 124
Walkford Common, v, 124
Walkington, de, Eleanor, iv, 543 n ; Will., iv, 543 n
Wall [Walle], Andr., ii, 492 ; iii, 204 ; Chas., iv, 498, 520 ; Chas. B., iv, 520, 522, 523 ; Geo. A. E., iii, 326 ; v, 527, 529, 539 ; Jos., iv, 28 ; Sam., iii, 326 ; iv, 432 ; Will., iv, 9, 28

Wallace, Rev. A., ii, 392 ; Col., v, 575
Wallbridge, Eliz., v, 150
Wallcott, Capt., v, 356
Walle, see Wall
Waller, Alice, iv, 656 ; v, 273 ; Charity, iv, 441, 446, 447, 476, 481 ; Hen., iv, 80 ; Joan, iii, 448 ; iv, 83 ; John, iii, 164, 448, 449, 451 ; iv, 80, 83, 433, 434, 447, 656 ; v, 129, 273 ; John A., iv, 260 ; Margery, iv, 83 ; Rich., iii, 448, 451 ; iv, 83, 656 ; v, 273 ; Rob., iv, 80 ; Susan, iv, 446, 476, 481, 486 ; Sir Will., iii, 396, 449 ; iv, 83, 254, 441, 446, 447, 455, 470, 475, 481, 482, 486, 656 ; v, 12, 88, 99, 100, 129, 130, 132, 273, 339, 340, 342
Walleston, see Woollaston
Wallingford (Berks), i, 271, 321 ; ii, 9, 227 ; iv, 656 ; v, 304 n ; prior of, ii, 495
Wallingford, Maud de, iv, 380
Wallington, riv., iii, 144
Wallis, A., iv, 140 ; John, iv, 336, 371, 390, 405, 530 ; W., iv, 589 ; Mrs., iv, 139, 589 ; —, v, 305
Walloons, ii, 75 ; iii, 528
Wallop, brook, iv, 493, 525, 530
Wallop, Middle, iv, 530, 534
Wallop, Nether [Lower], ii, 21, 71 ; iv, 327, 489, 497, 525-30, 532, 534 ; adv., iv, 530 ; char., iv, 530 ; ch., iv, 528 ; mans., iv, 525 ; Nonconf., iv, 530 ; pop., v, 439 ; sch., ii, 401
Wallop, Over [Upper], iv, 327, 337 n, 342, 343, 369, 489, 497, 499, 530-5 ; adv., iv, 534 ; char., iv, 534 ; ch., iv, 533 ; mans., iv, 531 ; Nonconf., iv, 534 ; pop., v, 439 ; sch., ii, 401
Wallop [Wallup, Wellop, Wollop] (de), Alice, iv, 409 ; Anne, iii, 365 ; iv, 210 ; Benedict, ii, 175 ; Dorothy, iv, 291 ; Eliz., iii, 448 ; iv, 83 ; Euphemia, iv, 532 ; Gerald [Girard], iv, 527 n, 532 ; (Sir) Hen., ii, 375, 378 ; iii, 225, 261, 365 ; iv, 105, 203, 204, 210, 253, 289, 358, 367, 409, 472 n, 516, 518, 532 ; Isaac N., iv, 532 ; (Sir) John, ii, 171, 172, 216, 382 ; iii, 168, 228, 261, 361, 364 n, 365, 366 ; iv, 72, 146, 258, 289, 291, 358, 368, 409, 532, 532 n ; v, 224, 289 ; Kath., iv, 518 ; Marg., iii, 261 ; iv, 146, 532 ; Matth., iii, 47, 376, 487 ; iv, 527 ; Newton, iv, 146, 147, 409 ; Oliver, iv, 72, 146, 358 ; Rich., iii, 261, 365, 448 ; iv, 83, 146, 528, 532, 534 ; v, 459 ; (Sir) Rob., iii, 261, 362, 365 ; iv, 116, 146, 253, 289, 301, 358, 409, 472, 516, 532 ; v, 117, 231 ; Steph., iii, 261 ; Thos., iii, 261, 264 ; iv, 146, 528, 532 ; Walt., ii, 175 ; Will., ii, 110, 182, 186 ; iii, 347, 535 ; iv, 393, 532 ; —, v, 453 ; fam., iv, 147, 290 n ; arms, ii, 489 ; iii, 261, 365
Wallop Buckland, Nether, man. (Nether Wallop), iv, 526, 532
Wallop Buckland, Over, man. (Over Wallop), iv, 494 n, 532
Wallop Fifehead, man. (Nether Wallop), iv, 525, 527
Wallop Heathmanstreet, man. (Nether Wallop), iv, 324, 525, 527
Wallop House (Nether Wallop), iv, 525
Wallop Moyles, man. (Over Wallop), iv, 525, 531, 534

Wallop Prioress, Over, (Over Wallop), iv, 533
Wallop's Manor (Soberton), iii, 261
Wallup, fam., *see* Wallop
Wally, John, v, 488 *n*
Walmore (Christchurch), v, 85, 97 *n*
Walnesbridge (Bournemouth), v, 135 *n*
Walpen [Walpan, Walpanne], man. (Chale), ii, 180; v, 170 *n*, 236, 238, 264
Walpole, Lt.-Col. Horace, iv, 44, 45, 47
Walpstreate, *see* Wopstrete
Walsh [Walysche], Walt., iv, 89, 90; Will., v, 473
Walsingham, Frances, v, 229; Sir Fran., ii, 480; v, 25, 171 *n*, 225, 229, 232, 233, 234, 377; Sir Thos., v, 30
Walsshcrofte, la, (Sherborne St. John), iv, 158
Walsworth, ii, 181, 186; iii, 140, 141
Walter, iv, 179, 247, 592 *n*; abbot of Quarr, ii, 139; bp. of Whitherne, ii, 153; the merchant, iv, 211; muleward of Kingsmill, iv, 134; prior of Merton, iv, 43; prior of St. Swithun's, ii, 115; the usher, iv, 431
Walter, Anne, v, 100; Eliz., v, 100; Godf., iv, 225; Hubert, v, 22; Phil., v, 100
Walters, A. V., iii, 281; —, v, 546
Walterville, Jordan de, iii, 258
Waltham, North, iv, 31, 197, 221-2; adv., iv, 222; chars., iv, 222; ch., iv, 222; man., iv, 221; Nonconf., iv, 221; pop., v, 440; Rom. rem., i, 306, 347
Waltham, South, *see* Bishop's Waltham
Waltham, Rich. of, iv, 211
Waltham Abbey (Essex), ii, 278; v, 284
Waltham Chase (Bishop's Waltham), iii, 278, 285
Waltham Marke (N. Waltham), iv, 221
Waltham Woolpit [Westputt], *see* Bishop's Waltham
Waltheof, earl, v, 300
Walton, Brian, iv, 25; Isaac, iii, 285; v, 57; Rev. Rich., v, 205
Walysche, *see* Walsh
Wamberge, Rob. de, ii, 15, 123
Wandisford, Mary, v, 288; Will., v, 288
Wandlesworth, de, Agnes, iii, 56; Thos., iii, 56; Will., iii, 56
Wanetyng, Will. de, iv, 343
Wanford, *see* Warnford
Wanklyn, Mrs. J. B, v, 136
Wansey, Thos., v, 111
Wanstead [Wanstede], man. (Southwick), ii, 168; iii, 164
Wanstead [Wanstede], (de, of), Geoff., iii, 146; Hen., v, 305; John, iii, 164
Wanstead Farm (Southwick), iii, 162
Wantage (Berks.), iv, 115
Warbeck, Perkin, ii, 143; v, 321
Warbelton, Warbleton, fam., *see* Warblington
Warberton, *see* Warburton
Warblington, ii, 21, 68, 76, 78, 86; iii, 128, 134-9; v, 450; adv., iii, 139; char., iii, 139; ch., iii, 137; man., ii, 114; iii, 68, 124, 134; Nonconf., iii, 139; pop., v, 441; sch., ii, 406; iii, 139; shipbuilding, v, 458

Warblington [Warbelton, Warbleton], (de), Hugh, iv, 141 *n*; Isabel, iv, 141 *n*; John, iii, 374; iv, 35, 64, 65, 105; Julia, iv, 105; Kath., iii, 374; iv, 35, 65, 105; Marg., iii, 262; iv, 65, 105, 232; Margery, iv, 105; Rob., iv, 142 *n*; Thos., iv, 19, 65, 104, 105; Will., iii, 262, 374; iv, 35, 104, 105, 107, 231, 475; fam., iv, 106
Warblington Hall (Long Sutton), iv, 18, 19
Warblinton, Warbliteton, *see* Warblington
Warborne, man. (Boldre), iv, 615, 621, 623
Warborne, par., *see* Warnborough, South
Warborne, John, iv, 621
Warbrook House (Eversley), iv, 32
Warbsdown (Surr.), iv, 140
Warburton [Warberton], Thos., iii, 457; Will., iii, 241; iv, 104; Will., bp. of Gloucester, ii, 486
Ward [Warde], man, ii, 182; v, 421
Ward [Warde], Chas. H., v, 110; Charlotte, v, 221; Edm. G., v, 146, 160, 240, 243, 250, 268, 270, 272; Geo., v, 146, 250; Geo. H., v, 268; H., v, 575; John, v, 523, 533, 570, 572; J. E., iv, 558; Sam., iii, 276; Thos., iv, 327; Will., ii, 215; v, 576; W. G., ii, 357; v, 269; Capt., v, 378; Maj., v, 530 *n*
Warder, Will., iv, 514
Wardington [Wardyngtone], Rich., de, ii, 26; iii, 75
Wardle, Thos., ii, 163
Wardroper, Rich., iv, 259
Wardyn, John, iv, 296 *n*
Wardyngtone, *see* Wardington
Ware, (de, la), John, ii, 178; Jordan, iv, 491 *n*; Rog., v, 132; *see also* De la Warr and Warre
Warefelde, John, iv, 382
Waregeburnæ Widonis, *see* Warnborough, South
Wareham (Stratfield Turgis), *see* Werham
Wareham, fam., *see* Warham
Wareham Farm, *see* Werham
Warelwast, Will., bp. of Exeter, iii, 20
Warenne, John de, ii, 146, 505; iv, 418, 560, 561; v, 313; Will., iii, 196; v, 301; *see also* Warren
Warener [Warennere, Warrener] (le), Agnes, iii, 372; Alice, ii, 129; Isabel, iii, 225, 226, 229; Joan, iii, 372; Thos., ii, 166; iii, 225, 226, 229, 250, 251, 372; T., ii, 274
Wares, Will., iv, 410
War Gate (Winchester), v, 18
Warham [Wareham] (de), Anne, iv, 203; Edw., iv, 355; Eliz., iv, 71, 373; iv, 226, 228, 258, 532; Geo., iv, 203; John, ii, 154; Mary, iv, 225; Nich., ii, 154, 160; Rob., iv, 228, 229 *n*; Thos., ii, 389; (Sir) Will., ii, 162, 163; iii, 373; iv, 226, 258, 294 *n*, 532; Will., archbp. of Canterbury, ii, 52, 294; iii, 71; iv, 165, 225, 227, 228, 229, 239, 249, 258; v, 18
Warine [Warin], ii, 203, 205; v, 28
Waring, Marg., iii, 298
Warishassefeld, ii, 186
Warmborough, *see* Warnborough
Warminster, man. (Wilts), iv, 369
Warnborne, *see* Warnborough, South

Warnborough, North, (Odiham), iv, 67, 87, 88, 93; v, 513; chap., ii, 367; iv, 97; man., iv, 93; mill, iv, 94
Warnborough, South, ii, 485, 515; iii, 355, 356, 378-82; iv, 67, 108; adv., iii, 381; chant., iii, 381; char., iii, 381; ch., iii, 379; man., iii, 378; pop., v, 443; sch., ii, 405
Warne, Jas., iv, 157; John, iii, 115
Warneburn, *see* Warnborough, South
Warneford (Abbotts Ann), iv, 334 *n*
Warner, Agnes, iv, 610; Ann, iv, 281; Avice, iv, 367; Chas., iii, 414; iv, 484; Eliz., iii, 467; Fred., iii, 414; Isabel, iv, 610; Jas., iii, 466; Joan, iv, 610; John, bp. of Rochester, v, 180; John, ii, 115, 158; iv, 25, 62, 74, 136, 201, 220, 242, 281, 367, 376, 414; J. C., iii, 466; Lee, v, 180; Rich., ii, 419; Sophia K., iii, 467; Thos., iii, 396; iv, 610; —, v, 469; fam., iii, 286
Warnford [Warnesford], i, 378, 380; ii, 25, 38, 117, 238, 240; iii, 245, 246, 268-73; v, 524; adv., iii, 272; ch., iii, 271; char., iii, 273; man., iii, 269; mills, iii, 271; Nonconf., iii, 273; pop., v, 440; sch., ii, 406; iii, 273
Warnford (de), Rich., ii, 86; Will., iii, 271
Warnford Park (Warnford), iii, 268
Warochesselle, *see* Wroxall
Warr, de la, fam., *see* De la Warr
Warre, Thos., iv, 571, 573; v, 471; *see also* Ware and De la Warr
Warren, the, (Eversley), iv, 34
Warren, the, (Micheldever), v, 557, 558 *n*
Warren, the, (Romsey), iv, 452
Warren [Warrin, Waryn], Alice, iv, 354; Gen. Sir Arth. F., iv, 243, 244; Edith, v, 96; Edm., iv, 624; Eliz., iii, 382; iv, 303; John, ii, 94; iv, 570; Sir J. B., v, 396; Mary A., iii, 381; Maud, iv, 570; Admiral Sir Pet., iii, 69; Sim., iv, 624; Susanna, iii, 69; Thos., iv, 354, 468; v, 96; Thos. A., iii, 382; Will., ii, 315; iv, 624; v, 326 *n*; *see also* Warenne
Warren Bottom Copse (Kingsclere), iv, 265
Warren Combe Hill (N. Waltham), iv, 221
Warrener, fam., *see* Warenner
Warreners Lodge (King's Somborne), iv, 470
Warren Hill (Christchurch), v, 84
Warren Hill (S. Tidworth), i, 381; iv, 391
Warrens (Bramshaw), iv, 624
Warrin, *see* Warren
Warror, *see* Werror
Warsash (Hook with Warsash), iii, 220, 222, 233; fishing, v, 469; salt ind., ii, 221; sch., ii, 400
Warsash House (Hook with Warsash), iii, 222
Warton, Jos., ii, 346, 347, 348, 349, 350, 351, 352, 353, 366; iv, 128, 176, 181; Thos., ii, 348; iv, 128, 181
Warwick (St. Mary Bourne), i, 304; iv, 295
Warwick, ctsses. of: Anne Nevill, ii, 143; iv, 151; v, 320; Isabel Beauchamp, iv, 151, 441; earls of, iv, 35, 624, 631; v, 338; Edw., iii, 411; iv, 608; Guy Beauchamp, iii, 520; Hen. Beau-

Warwick (cont.)
champ, iv, 151, 441; Rich.
Beauchamp, iv, 151, 441; Rich.
Nevill, iii, 410, 507; iv, 151, 156,
157; v, 320, 369, 370; Thos. de
Beauchamp, iv, 392 n, 627;
Thos. de Newburgh, iv, 150 n;
Will. de Beauchamp, ii, 509;
Will. Maudit, ii, 509
Warwick, Thos., iv, 557; Will., iv,
530
Waryn, see Warren
Warynswey (Faccombe), iv, 314
Wasey, Lionel T., iv, 250
Washdells, man. (Alton), see Tren-
chants
Washerne, man. (Wilts), iv, 540
Waspail, Joan, iv, 42; John, iv, 42;
Osbert, iv, 42; Will., iv, 42
Wasprai [Wasprai] (de), John, iv,
302; Phil., iv, 340, 359
Wasps, i, 114, 118
Wassche, la, (Highclere), iv, 285
Wasseling, John, iii, 406; Nich.,
iii, 406
Wastour, John, ii, 155
Watch House (Ryde), v, 178
Watchingwell, man. (Calbourne),
v, 163, 220, 227
Watchingwell, tithing (W. Medine),
v, 210
Watcombe (South Tidworth), iv,
393 n
Watercress cultivation, v, 455
Waterditch (Christchurch), v, 85,
108 n, 109
Waterford, Louisa, mchnss. of, v, 84
Watergarden (Leckford), iv, 446
Watergate Hanger, i, 310
Wateridge, John, iii, 371; Phil., iii
371
Waterlandes (W. Wellow), iv, 535
Waterloo [Waterlooville] (Farling-
ton), iii, 82, 141, 148; ch., iii,
151; pop., v, 441
Waterman, Edw., iv, 78; John, iv,
327; Penelope, iv, 327; Rebecca,
iv, 327; Rich., iv, 201 n
Waterman's (Kingston), iv, 613
Watermartens, man., see Taulkes
Water meadows, v, 506
Waters, John, iv, 122; Thos., iv,
594
Waterschete, Will. de, iv, 53
Waterswell Cross (Tangley), iv, 326
Waterton, Joan, iv, 573; Rob., iv,
571, 573
Waterworth, Rev. T., v, 168
Wateryng, Grace, iii, 193; John,
iii, 193
Watesford, de, Hen., iv, 302;
Joan, iv, 302; Pet., iv, 302
Watford, de, Hythe, iv, 130;
Will., iv, 130
Wathe, see St. Lawrence
Watson, Brook, iv, 154; John, bp.
of Winchester, ii, 76, 77, 78, 79,
115, 197, 480; iii, 65, 67; iv,
253; Sarah, iv, 623; —, iii, 499;
v, 335
Watteville, Rob. de, iii, 373, 377
Watton, Rob., iv, 330
Watts [Watt, Wattys], Anne, ii, 50;
Isaac, ii, 95; Isabel, iii,
216; John, iii, 184; v, 554;
Thos., ii, 50; iii, 398; v, 114;
—, iv, 22
Watyrdune (Abbotts Ann), iv,
334 n
Wauchan, Rob., iii, 383
Waugh, Will, iv, 250; v, 553
Wauton (de), Amisius, iv, 33;
Andr., iii, 96; Eliz., iii, 96;
Joan, iv, 213, 214 n; John, iv,
213; Will., iv, 33

Wavell [Wauville, Wavil] (de),
Dav., v, 147, 150; Fran., v, 214;
Gilb., v, 27; John, v, 117;
Rich., ii, 230; Thos., v, 214;
—, ii, 200
Waverley Abbey (Surr.), ii, 11,
490, 500, 512, 513, 514; iii,
442; iv, 195, 196, 198, 200, 215,
425
Wavil, see Wavell
Way, Dav., v, 214; John, v, 192;
Thos., v, 277; Will., v, 277;
—, v, 280
Wayleys, see Waleys
Wayne, Barbara A., iii, 379;
Emma, iii, 379; Thos. H., iii,
379; Thos. M., iii, 379; v, 517
Waynflete, Will., see Winchester,
bps. of
Wayte [Waite, Waytte] (le),
Agatha, iv, 64; Alex., v, 211;
Alice, v, 211; Amice, iv, 407;
Edw., iii, 167, 240, 264; Eliz.,
ii, 486; iii, 241; iv, 374; Hen.,
iii, 264, 298; iv, 403, 408, 410;
v, 211, 212; Honor, iii, 165, 166,
167, 170, 235, 240; Isabel, iii,
264; John, iii, 43, 226, 228, 229,
261, 328, 392; iv, 64; v, 65, 192,
211; Marg., iii, 229; iv, 418, 419,
432; Nich., iv, 407; Phil., iii,
264, 312; Rich., iii, 167; iv,
501; Rob., ii, 222; Sim., iii, 167,
240, 264; Steph., v, 211 n;
Thos., ii, 522; iii, 226, 228, 392
394; iv, 418, 419, 432; v, 211;
Will., iii, 96, 124, 150, 167, 229,
240, 241, 264, 283, 392, 394; iv,
374, 419; v, 48, 211, 212;
Mrs., iv, 431; —, v, 326; fam.,
arms, iii, 167, 229, 264
Waytes Court, man. (Brighstone),
v, 211
Wealagarstune, see Woodgarston
Wealden period, i, 13
Weapons, see Implements and
weapons
Weaver's Hill, iii, 5
Webb, Anne, iv, 374; Chas., iv,
139; Constance, iv, 425; Eliz.,
iv, 98; Helena M., iv, 98; Hugh,
iii, 70; (Sir) John, ii, 507; iv,
162, 163, 164, 165, 374, 476, 524,
572, 594; v, 129; Gen. John R.,
v, 224; John T., iv, 98; Kath., iv,
473; Rachel, iv, 473, 656; Rich.,
v, 98; Sarah, iv, 98; (Rev.) Thos.,
iv, 230, 301, 316, 374, 406 n;
(Sir) Will., iv, 425, 473, 594, 656,
657; v, 97
Webbe, Ambrose (le), ii, 379; v,
266; A. J., v, 19; Cath., iii,
415; Edw., ii, 379, 380, 385; iv,
266; H. R., v, 19, 576; John, iv,
294, 496; Rob., v, 480 n; Thos.,
iv, 496; v, 482; (Sir) Will., iii,
415; v, 132; fam., arms, iii, 415
Webber, Laura M., iv, 393; Matilda,
iv, 393; Rev., —, iv, 344
Webster, Sir Aug., iv, 492, 515;
Thos., v, 160
Wedmore (Somers.), iv, 74
Wedon, Ralph de, iv, 215 n
Wee, see Weyhill
Weeckes, see Weekes
Week, man. (Godshill), ii, 231; v,
138, 174; mill, v, 175
Week (St. Mary Bourne), iv, 185,
273 n, 288, 295; Rom. rem., i, 304
Week Common (Hartley Mauditt),
ii, 508
Weeke, par., ii, 99, 292; iii, 401,
451-3; v, 1; adv., iii, 452; char.,
iii, 452; ch., iii, 452; man., ii,
114; iii, 452; pop., v, 417

Weekes [Weeckes], Abra., iv, 441,
442; Ant., iv, 80; Eliz, iv, 80;
John, iv, 259; Rob., v, 189, 239
Weekes Row, see Wickes Row
Weeke Within, iii, 451
Weeke Without, iii, 451
Weggham, John de, v, 142
Wegull, John, ii, 212
Welbeck [Welbek], Frith, ii, 124;
John, v, 174
Welberewe (Pamber), iv, 433
Welch-Thornton, Alf., iii, 363;
Alf. B., iv, 167; Hen., iv, 167;
Hen. S., iv, 167
Weld, Clara, v, 93 n; Thos., iv, 617
Welde par., see Wield
Weleg, see Wheely
Welewe Gurnay, see Wellow, West
Welford, hund., iv, 400
Well (Long Sutton), iv, 18, 171;
man., iv, 19
Welle, iv, 598
Welleford, Geoff. de, ii, 194, 195,
197
Wellehigh, Welleigh, see Wheely
Welles, South, man. (Romsey), iv,
459
Welles [Welle] (atte, de), Alex.,
iii, 487; Cecily, iv, 616; Chas.,
iii, 487; iv, 481 n; Gilb., iii, 334,
442, 443, 487; iv, 481; Hen.,
iii, 334, 443, 487; iv, 481, 616,
618, 622; John, iii, 487; iv, 616;
v, 148; Marg., iii, 487; Phil., v,
484; Rob., iv, 253; Thos., iii,
334, 443, 487; iv, 481, 507, 521,
524 n, 616; Will., v, 163; fam.,
arms, iii, 442; see also Wells
Wellesborne, Sir John, ii, 304
Wellesley, Ld. Chas., iv, 59 n
Wellesley, Arth., see Wellington,
dks. of; Hen., see Wellington,
dks. of; Rich., iv, 100; Will.
P. T. L., iv, 93, 100
Wellesworthy (of), Clarissa, iv, 302;
Rog., iv, 302
Well House (Liss), iv, 84
Wellington, dks. of, iv, 56, 62, 64,
65, 105, 247, 250, 260, 270, 275,
276; v, 557; Arth. Wellesley, iv,
44, 54, 59, 60, 63, 141, 142, 248,
272; v, 256, 505, 521; Arth. C.
Wellesley, ii, 386; iv, 43, 59, 60,
61, 141, 143, 248, 272; Arth. R.
Wellesley, iv, 43, 44, 59, 61, 172,
173, 174; Hen. Wellesley, ii, 466;
iv, 59, 61
Wellop, see Wallop
Wellow (Shalfleet), v, 272; man.,
v, 274
Wellow, East, ii, 21, 146; iv, 489,
535-40, 554, 598; adv., iv, 539;
ch., iv, 538; grange, ii, 147;
ind., v, 453; man., ii, 148; iv,
535; mkts. & fairs, iv, 535, 536;
mills, iv, 536, 540; pop., v, 446;
sch., ii, 398
Wellow, West, i, 347; iv, 489 n,
535; adv., iv, 539; char., iv,
540; common, iv, 535; man.,
iv, 536; Nonconf., iv, 539; sch.,
ii, 398
Wellow Wood Common, iv, 535
Wells, (de), Cecily, iv, 459; Eliz.,
iii, 435; Fran., iv, 472; Gilb.,
ii, 78, 86; Hugh, ii, 21; Jas.,
iv, 207, 228; John, ii, 519;
iii, 19, 435; iv, 459; v, 574; P.,
iv, 530; Rob., iv, 13, 275, 281,
336, 376, 380, 408, 497, 534;
Thos., ii, 67; iv, 459; Winifred,
ii, 450; —, v, 547; see also
Welles
Wells, Roman, i, 279, 287, 305, 311,
358

Wellsworth, man. (Chalton), iii, 83, 107
Wellys, Thos., ii, 294
Welman, Rebecca, iv, 486
Welnetune, *see* Walhampton
Welstead [Welsted], John, iv, 326 ; Kath., iv, 92 ; Rob., iv, 92 ; Sim., iv, 326 ; Will., iv, 326
Welwa Ford (E. Wellow), iv, 535
Welynger [Wendling], Will. de, ii, 197
Wemering, *see* Wymering
Wenechetone, *see* Winston
Wenesi, iv, 372
Wenfleda iv, 411 *n*
Wengham, de, Alice, iv, 19 ; Annora, iv, 171, 174 ; Egelina, iv, 19, 171 ; Eliz., iv, 19 ; Geoff., iv, 19, 171 ; Hugh, iv, 18, 19, 174 ; Joan, iv, 19
Wenham, Rob., ii, 167
Wenlock, prior of, v, 168
Wenta, *see* Winchester
Wentworth, Hen., Ld., v, 215
Wentworth Lodge (Boscombe), v, 134
Weoleghe, *see* Wheely
Weralles, man. (Dors.), ii, 168
Wereburn, John de, iv, 618
Weremulle (Damerham), iv, 590
Wergeborne, *see* Warnborough, South
Wergs (Burghclere), iv, 277
Wergs (Heckfield), *see* Gilders
Werham (Stratfield Turgis), iv, 64
Wermeslade (Carisbrooke), v, 222
Werror, man. (Northwood), ii, 204, 205 ; v, 270 ; brick-making, v, 466
Werste, *see* Ewhurst
Wesley, John, ii, 98
Wesleyans, ii, 490, 506, 515, 521 ; iii, 120, 122, 200, 207, 215, 232, 235, 290, 296, 309, 534 ; iv, 4, 14, 18, 41, 76, 86, 98, 139, 242, 264, 291, 299, 304, 331, 391, 411, 433, 468, 480, 497, 530, 539, 576, 613, 649 ; v, 109, 136, 150, 154, 169, 177, 186, 189, 193, 197, 201, 239, 245, 264, 271, 277, 284, 291
Wessex, ii, 1-5 ; v, 293-8
West, Alice, ii, 158 ; iii, 11 ; v, 99, 101, 102, 126 *n* ; Chas., iii, 200 ; Eliz., iv, 199, 279 ; Fred R., v, 117 ; Rev. Hen. J., iv, 5 ; Joan, ii, 158 ; John, iv, 414 ; Kath., v, 85 *n*, 95 *n* ; Leonard, ii, 497 ; Lettice, iv, 220 ; Mary, iv, 97, 414 ; Sir Owen, iv, 97, 411, 414 ; Reg., iii, 11, 486 ; v, 99 ; Rich., iii, 11, 486 ; v, 99 ; Theresa, v, 117 ; (Sir) Thos., ii, 136, 158 ; iii, 8, 11, 12, 17, 23, 26, 29, 43, 295, 431, 438, 486 ; iv, 220, 335, 345 *n*, 402, 406, 412, 545, 549, 555, 577 *n*, 631 ; v, 99, 101, 102 ; Will., ii, 375 ; iv, 354, 412 ; v, 99 ; fam., iv, 624 ; fam., arms, ii, 497 ; iii, 295
Westaderle, *see* Tytherley, West
Westall, Thos., iv, 204
Westbourne (Bournemouth), v, 134, 135
Westbrook [Westbroke], man. (Berks), ii, 140, 145
Westbrook, man. (St Helens), v, 191, 192
Westbrook, ii, 147
Westbrook, Anne, iv, 131, 132 ; John, iv, 84 *n* ; Thos., v, 164
Westbrook House (Alton), ii, 477
Westbury [East Meon], ii, 26 ; iii, 63, 68, 245, 246
Westbury, Ld., iv, 122
Westbury, (de), John, ii, 113 ; iii, 68 ; Will., ii, 197

Westcarre [Westekarre, Westkarre], (de), Will., ii, 174, 175 ; iii, 533 ; v, 55
West Cliff (Bournemouth), v, 134, 135
Westcliff Hall (Dibden), iv, 655
Westcombe, Thos., iii, 313 ; iv, 356
Westcote, man. (Binsted), *see* Westcourt
Westcote [Westcott], (de), Alice, ii, 151, 512 ; iv, 8, 28 *n* ; Joan, iv, 425 *n* ; John, ii, 365, 512 ; iv, 7*n*, 8, 9, 28, 424 ; Marg., ii, 512 ; Margery, iv, 8, 9, 28 *n* ; Rich., ii, 218, 486, 489 ; iv, 425 ; Sybil, ii, 512 ; iv, 8 ; Thos., ii, 486 ; iv, 424, 425 ; —, v, 46
Westcourt, man. (Binsted), ii, 486, 488 ; mill, ii, 486
West Court (Shorwell), v, 172, 195, 280 ; man. house, v, 278
Westekarre, *see* Westcarre
West End (S. Stoneham), iii, 482 ; brickmaking, v, 465 ; char., iii, 489 ; ch., iii, 482 ;
West End Brook, iv, 56
West End Courte, *see* Western Court Farm
West End Green (Stratfieldsaye), iv, 57
Westercourte, *see* Western Court Farm
Western, —, ii, 350
Western Court Farm (Bishop's Sutton), iii, 43
Westfield House (Tufton), iv, 409
Westgate, Rob., ii, 115
West Hall (Southampton), ii, 203
Westhamstygh (Laverstoke), iv, 208
Westhay [Westhey] (St. Helens), v, 192
Westheath (Farnborough), pottery manufacture, v, 491
Westkarre, *see* Westcarre
Westlands (Kingsclere), iv, 266
Westley, man. (Sparsholt), iii, 445
Westley, ii, 173
West Medine le Pitte (Shide), v, 210
Westmere (Barton Stacey), iv, 417
Westminster, dks. of, v, 547, 548, 549, 551, 553, 554
Westminster Abbey, ii, 108, 486 ; iv, 33, 41 ; v, 108
Westmorland, Edith Nevill, ctss. of, iv, 348 *n* ; earls of, ii, 475 ; Hen. Nevill, iv, 130 *n*, 348 ; John Nevill, iv, 130 ; Ralph Nevill, iv, 347, 348 *n*
Westmyll Mead in Pylcote (Dogmersfield), iv, 72
Westney (Hayling Island), iii, 129
Westnowre (Calbourne), v, 218
Weston, man. (Buriton), iii, 89
Weston (Freshwater), v, 210, 240, 243 ; Rom. Cath., v, 245
Weston (St. Mary Extra), ii, 88 ; iii, 297 ; ch., iii, 299 ; mill, iii, 298 ; v, 458
Weston, man., ii, 137
Weston [Westone], (de), Christina, v, 162 ; Eleanor, iv, 473 ; v, 162 ; Eliz., ii, 494, 495 ; Frances, iv, 470 ; v, 339 ; Fran., iii, 247 ; Geoff., iv, 382 ; (Sir) Hen., iii, 114, 247 ; Isabel, iv, 473 ; v, 162 ; Jerome, iv, 470 ; v, 224, 225, 337, 338 ; Joan, iv, 255 ; (Sir) John, iii, 493, 494, 495 ; iv, 473 ; v, 160, 161, 162, 169, 182 ; Kath., v, 162 ; Marg., iii, 415 ; iv, 473 ; v, 162 ; Nich., iv, 247 ; Pet., v, 239 *n* ; Sir Rich., ii, 477, 513 ; iii, 114, 115, 247 ; v, 54, 157, 224 ; (Sir) Thos., ii, 166, 178, 179 ; iii,

Weston (*cont.*)
415, 473, 474 ; v, 162 ; Walt., v, 313 ; (Sir) Will., ii, 188 ; iii, 487 ; iv, 255 ; v, 162
Weston Bray Beife, Weston Brayboef, *see* Weston (Freshwater)
Weston Common, iv, 108
Weston Corbett, iii, 355, 356, 386-8 ; iv, 92, 108, 549, 554 ; adv., iii, 388 ; ch., iii, 387 ; man., iii, 386 ; iv, 108 *n* ; pop., v, 439
Weston Grove (St. Mary Extra), iii, 298
Weston Patrick, iii, 356, 386 ; iv, 66, 67, 97, 108-9 ; adv., iv, 109 ; ch., iv, 109 ; man., iv, 108 ; pop., v, 439 ; sch., ii, 406 ; woods, iv, 109
Westons (Soberton), iii, 256
Westover, liberty [hund.], v, 81, 82, 89, 91 *n*, 92, 133-7 ; man., v, 91, 92, 135
Westover, man. (Calbourne), v, 219 ; prehist. rem., i, 260
Westover (Milford), v, 116
Westover (Wherwell with Westover), iv, 411 ; man., iv, 412
Westover House (Calbourne), v, 218
Westower, *see* Westover
West Park (Rockbourne), iv, 582, 584, 586, 587
West Place (Milton), v, 124
Westport (Dors.), ii, 159
Westsetley (Brockenhurst), iv, 626
Westshirbourne, *see* Monk Sherborne
West Shore, *see* Southbourne
West Standen Farm (Arreton), v, 147
Westweare (Romsey), iv, 459
Westwode (Andover), iv, 346
Westwood (Linkenholt), iv, 324
Westwood (Portsmouth), ii, 207
Westwood (Sparsholt), Rom. rem., i, 312, 347
Westwood, man. (Wilts.), ii, 114
Wetham, ii, 126
Wetwang, Walt. de, ii, 195, 197
Wevill (Gosport), v, 388
Wexcombe, man., iv, 458
Wexcot, *see* Foxcott
Wey, riv., ii, 473, 491, 496, 511 ; iv, 158, 159 ; v, 409
Weyhill iv, 333, 350, 358, 366, 379, 381, 384, 394-99 ; v, 544 ; adv., iv, 399 ; char., iv, 399 ; ch., iv, 398 ; fairs, iv, 396-8 ; v, 428, 430, 435, 500, 504 ; mans., iv, 395 ; Nonconf., iv, 399 ; pop., v, 438 ; Rom. rem., i, 295, 297 ; iv, 395 ; sch., ii, 402 ; iv, 399
Weyhill Down, iv, 395
Weyhill House (Weyhill), iv, 395
Weymouth (Dors.), shipping, v, 364
Wez, Ralph de, iii, 57
Whale Island (Portsmouth), v, 405, 406
Whales, i, 250
Whalley-Tooker, Hyde S., iii, 94, 97, 99 ; v, 528, 541
Whapplode, Joan, iv, 185
Wharton, Dorothy, Lady, iv, 105 ; Phil., Ld., iv, 105, 106
Whatley, *see* Wheatley
Wheat [Wheate], Nich., v, 486 ; Sam., iv, 435
Wheatham Hill, iii, 111
Wheatland, Thos., iv, 499, 502 *n*
Wheatley (Binsted), i, 305 ; ii, 471, 483, 488
Wheatsheaf Common, ii, 491
Wheble, —, v, 534
Wheeler, Hen., ii, 486, 487, 488 ; iii, 10 ; John, iv, 604 ; Nich., ii,

Wheeler (*cont.*)
487, 489 ; Rob., iv, 649 ; v, 453 *n*,
459 *n*, 468 ; Will., v, 526 ; *see
also* Wheler
Wheelwright, Rob. the, iv, 507
Wheely (Warnford), iii, 271
Wheler, Sir Fran., v, 386 ; (Rev.
Sir) Geo., iv, 106, 126 ; Rev.
Granville, iv, 106 ; Martha, iv,
106 ; Sir Will., iv, 106 ; *see also*
Wheeler
Wheler's Court (Sherfield), iv, 103,
105
Whelpdale, And., iv, 74 ; Eliz., iv,
74
Wherwell [Wherwell with West-
over], iv, 400, 411-14 ; v, 302,
324, 331, 418, 423 ; adv., iv,
414 ; char., iv, 414 ; ch., iv, 413 ;
man., ii, 137 ; iv, 411 ; mkt.
and fairs, iv, 400, 411 ; mills, iv,
412 ; Nonconf., iv, 414 ; pop., v,
439 ; Rom. rem., i, 347 ; sch., ii,
406
Wherwell, hund., iv, 400
Wherwell Abbey, ii, 27, 40, 49, 60,
61, 62, 104, 108, 132-7 ; iii, 467 ;
iv, 335, 336, 400, 402, 403, 405,
406, 407, 408, 409, 410, 411, 412,
414, 534 ; v, 180, 181, 298, 303 ;
abbesses, ii, 137 ; v, 481 ;
Euphemia, ii, 132-3, 137 ; iv,
402, 412 ; Cecilia de Lavyngtone,
ii, 40, 137 ; iv, 401
Wherwell Harewood Wood, *see*
Harewood Forest.
Whetefield, le, (Highclere), iv, 285
Whetehamyslond (Liss), iv, 84
Whetelond (Dibden), iv, 655
Whetham (Liss), iv, 84 *n*
Whetham, Col., v, 353
Whicchurch, *see* Whitchurch
Whichbury, *see* Whitsbury
Whichcote, Chris., iv, 541 ; Sir
Fran., iv, 541 ; Jane, iv, 541 ;
Thos., iv, 541
Whidden, Jacob, v, 225
Whieldon, Arth. E., v, 521
Whilepill (Brockenhurst), iv, 626
Whippingham, ii, 139, 156, 180 ;
v, 138, 197-202, 206, 209, 253 ;
adv., v, 201 ; char., v, 201 ; ch.,
ii, 99, 230, 231 ; v, 201 ; mans.,
v, 198 ; mill., v, 197 ; Nonconf.,
v, 201 ; pop., v, 448 ; sch., ii, 408
Whire, la, (Wherwell), iv, 411
Whirsh, Hen., iv, 500 *n*
Whishaw, John, iv, 550
Whistlebury, *see* Whitsbury
Whistler, Geo., iv, 201 *n*
Whitaker, A. I., iii, 54 ; Fran., iv,
62 ; Jas., iv, 605 ; Jos., iii, 54 ;
J. I., iv, 617 ; Kath., v, 62 ;
Will. I., iv, 616, 623
Whitby, Anna M., v, 113, 117,
120 ; Capt., v, 117
Whitchurch, ii, 26, 71, 108, 234,
236, 260 ; iv, 197, 273, 274,
299-304 ; v, 311, 344, 355, 409,
431 ; adv., iv, 303 ; char., iv,
304 ; ch., iv, 284, 300, 302 ;
commons, iv, 300 ; farms, iv,
301 ; ind., iv, 300 ; v, 484, 488,
489 ; man., ii, 114 ; iv, 301 ;
mkts. & fairs, iv, 300, 301 ; v,
417 ; mills, iv, 300 ; v, 488, 489 ;
Nonconf., iv, 304 ; pop., v, 441 ;
sch., ii, 406 ; iv, 300
Whitchurch, hund., iv, 400
Whitchurch, de, John, iv, 496 ;
Reg., iv, 88
Whitchurch Parsonage, tithing
(Whitchurch), iv, 303
Whitcombe (Carisbrooke), v, 145,
221, 246, 248

Whitcombe, Jos. G., iii, 200
Whitditch (Eastrop), iv, 147, 148
White [Whyte, Wyght, Wyhte,
Wyte, Wytht], Agnes, ii, 477,
515 ; iii, 384 ; Alban, iv, 554 ;
Alice, iv, 565, 566 ; v, 119 ;
Anne, iii, 165 ; Bridg., iv, 263 ;
Capt. Chas., iv, 21 ; Edm., iii,
30 ; Edw., iii, 54, 124, 163 ; v,
28 ; Ellen, ii, 513 ; iv, 3, 22 ;
Frances, ii, 485 ; v, 127 ; Fran.,
iv, 122, 554 ; v, 195, 206 ; Rev.
Gilb., iii, 4, 16, 288 ; iv, 128 ;
Giles, iii, 98 ; v, 43 ; Grace E., v,
199 ; G., v, 398 ; Harry, v, 570 ;
(Rev.) Hen., ii, 516 ; iii, 98, 193 ;
iv, 3, 368, 554, 572 ; Hugh, iii,
361 ; Rev. Jas., v, 155, 156 ;
(Sir) John, ii, 57, 59, 168, 476,
478, 485, 487, 515 ; iii, 54, 124,
146, 159, 162 *n*, 165, 178, 204,
324, 413, 484 ; iv, 3, 263, 292,
457, 564, 565, 601, 624 *n* ; v, 16,
30, 119, 184, 199, 263, 264,
284, 461 ; John, bp., ii, 72, 73,
300, 301, 302, 308, 366 ; iii, 277 ;
iv, 278 ; v, 177, 234 ; John S.,
v, 198, 269 ; Josiah, ii, 327 ; J.,
ii, 290 ; Kath., iii, 165, 324 ; iv,
457, 571 ; Lynch, iii, 131 ; Marg.,
iii, 379 ; iv, 554 ; v, 119 ; Mary,
ii, 513 ; iii, 124 ; iv, 3, 4 ; v, 195,
206 ; Maur., ii, 128 ; Rebecca,
iii, 15 ; (Sir) Rich., ii, 478, 487,
516 ; iii, 204 ; iv, 217 ; v, 142 *n* ;
Rev. Rich. W., v, 195, 206, 274 ;
Rob., ii, 476, 485, 487, 513, 515 ;
iii, 193, 204, 294, 379, 413 ; iv,
3, 4, 22, 554, 564, 565, 571, 572,
580 ; v, 94, 109, 119 ; Rosa, v,
155 ; Saml., iv, 98 ; Steph., iii,
381 ; (Sir) Thos., ii, 67, 300, 309,
477, 478, 485, 487, 515, 516 ; iii,
179, 379, 381, 384, 535 ; iv, 13,
353, 554, 604 ; v, 77, 127, 458 ;
Ulward, iii, 130 ; Walt., v, 259 ;
Will., ii, 167 ; iii, 384 ; iv, 292,
459, 554, 565, 566 ; v, 119, 199,
243, 268, 456 ; Capt., v, 576 ;
Miss, iv, 27 ; v, 162, 206, 274,
281 ; —, ii, 485 ; v, 514, 528 ;
fam., arms, ii, 477 ; iii, 54,
379
White Bros., boat builders, v, 458
White Cliff Bay, v, 157
White Diche (Long Sutton), iv, 18
Whitear, Hen., iii, 241
Whitefield, man. (Brading), v,
146, 158, 159, 161, 192, 237
Whitefield [Whitefeld], de, Edw.,
v, 160 ; Will., iv, 150 ; v, 160
White Friars, *see* Carmelites
Whitehall (Ringwood), iv, 613, 614
Whitehart, Arth., iv, 522
Whitehayes (Christchurch), v, 84
Whitehead, Anne, iii, 448 ; iv, 523 ;
Augustine, iii, 429 ; iv, 148, 226 ;
Sir Beethom, v, 118 ; Christian,
iv, 523 ; Edw., v, 489 *n* ; Fran.,
iii, 153, 430 ; iv, 494 ; Geo., iii,
429 ; iv, 148 ; Gilb., iv, 521 ;
(Sir) Hen , iii, 163, 429, 430 ; iv,
148, 520 *n*, 523 ; v, 243 ; Sir Jas.
B., v, 116 ; John, ii, 492 ; iii, 429 ;
iv, 148, 498, 523 ; Julian, iii, 429 ;
Kath., iv, 83, 148 ; Maur. [Morris],
iii, 429, 448 ; iv, 148, 498, 523 ;
Philadelphia, iv, 414 ; (Sir) Rich.,
ii, 492, 493 ; iii, 163, 429, 430 ;
iv, 123, 148, 520, 523, 524 ; Rob.,
iv, 226 ; Sarah, iii, 163 ; fam.,
arms, iii, 429
Whitehill Close (Overton), iv, 211
Whitehorne, Alice, iii, 411 ; John,
iii, 411

White House (Minley), iv, 21
White House (Whippingham), v,
198 *n*
White lake (S. Damerham), iv,
587 *n*
Whiteley, Geo., iv, 476
White Lyon (Elvetham), iv, 74
Whitening industry, v, 454
Whiteparish (Wilts.), iv, 541, 542 ;
v, 454
White-Popham, Fran., v, 162,
195 ; Mrs., v, 162, 197
Whites, Lower, Upper, (Melchet
Park), v, 540
Whitewater, riv., iv, 44, 45, 47,
76, 87, 93, 156 ; v, 560, 564
Whiteway, Thos., iv, 354
Whitewell, *see* Whitwell
Whiteweyes, man., *see* Whitway
Whitewood, Jas., v, 172
Whitgift, Essay, v, 458
Whitherne, Walt., bp. of, ii, 153
Whitley Ridge (Brockenhurst), v,
491
Whitlocke (King's Somborne), iv,
470
Whitlok, Walt. de, v, 458
Whitmondeslye (Odiham), iv, 97
Whitmore, Geo., iv, 84, 85 ; Thos.,
iv, 84, 85 ; Will., ii, 474 ; v,
213
Whitsbury, ii, 169, 172 ; v, 559,
594-5 ; adv., iv, 595 ; char., iv,
595 ; ch., iv, 595 ; man., iv, 594 ;
Nonconf., iv, 595 ; sch., ii, 406
Whitway, man. (Burghclere), iv,
277, 279 ; brickmaking, v, 466
Whitway House (Burghclere), iv,
279
Whitwell, ii, 63 ; v, 138, 149 *n*,
202-4, 247, 248 ; adv., v, 203 ;
char., v, 204 ; ch., v, 203 ; mans.,
v, 202 ; Nonconf., v, 204 ; pop.,
v, 448 ; sch., ii, 408 ; v, 204
Whitwell, Hugh of, v, 117 ; Will.,
v, 117
Whood, —, iv, 355
Whorstede, *see* Horstede
Whyte, *see* White
Whyteland (Steventon), iv, 171
Whytenharpe (Romsey), iv, 452
Whyteye, Geoff., v, 148
Whythers (Farley Chamberlayne),
iv, 443
Whytherthull (Carisbrooke), v, 222
Whythygg, Will., iv, 382 *n*
Whytingstale, Alice, ii, 130
Whytun, Rob., iv, 495 ; Walt., iv,
495 *n*
Whytyngton [Whytyngtone] (de),
Christiane, ii, 124 ; Will., iii, 381
Wica, *see* Week
Wiccor, *see* Wyker (Portchester)
Wicham (Lasham), iv, 81
Wicheberia, *see* Whitsbury
Wicherley, Dan., iv, 301
Wichot, Will., ii, 38
Wick, hamlet (Binsted), *see* Wyck
Wick, man. (Binsted), *see* Wyke
Wick (Bournemouth), v, 134, 135
Wick (St. Mary Bourne), *see* Week
Wickart, John, ii, 115
Wickes Row (Upham), Rom. rem.,
i, 309
Wickett, —, v, 148
Wickham, i, 378 ; ii, 36, 186, 223,
272 ; iii, 217, 233-6 ; v, 328 *n* ;
advs., iii, 235 ; char., iii, 234 ;
ch., iii, 234 ; fair, v, 417 ; ind.,
v, 457 ; man., iii, 234 ; iv, 232 ;
pop., v, 441 ; sch., ii, 406
Wickham [Wikkam], Alice, ii, 50 ;
Chas., iii, 454 ; Edw., iv, 367 ;
Jas., v, 538 ; John, iii, 461 ;
Thos., iii, 390 ; iv, 367 ; Will., ii,

Wickham (cont.)
50 ; Winifred, iv, 367 ; —, iv, 473 ; v, 560 ; fam., arms, ii, 484
Widehaye, Barth., iii, 333, 337
Wide Meadow (Ellingham), iv, 567
Widemere, West, (S. Damerham), iv, 587 n
Widimead (Plaitford), iv, 542
Widley, iii, 140, 171-2 ; adv., iii, 172 ; char., iii, 172 ; ch., iii, 171 ; man., iii, 171 ; pop., v, 441
Widley, Geo., iv, 405
Widmore, Jas., iv, 267, 406, 409 ; (Rev.) Rich., iv, 356, 402, 406
Widowe's Garden (Long Sutton), iv, 18
Wield, iii, 302, 303, 345-7 ; iv, 188, 189 ; adv., iii, 347 ; char., iii, 347 ; ch., iii, 347 ; man., iii, 346 ; pop., v, 437 ; sch., ii, 406
Wield, Lower and Upper, iii, 345
Wig, see Wigge
Wigard [Wiggers] (Kingsclere), iv, 250
Wigge [Wig, Wygge], John, iii, 432 ; Rich., v, 26, 27 ; Will., ii, 315, 375
Wiggett, Anne R., iv, 161 ; G. H., iv, 170 ; Jas., iv, 161 ; Will., iv, 161 ; Will. L., iv, 161
Wight, Isle of, i, 253, 260 ; ii, 2, 3, 8, 33, 37, 60, 62, 69, 81, 91, 96, 98, 101, 106, 203, 230, 231, 386, 410, 415, 420 ; iv, 607, 619, 631 ; v, 138, 209, 222, 223, 293, 294, 299, 309, 311, 312, 318, 325, 327, 329, 336, 338, 347, 351, 502 ; A. S. rem., i, 387 ; hunting, v, 535, 543 ; inds., v, 453, 455, 458, 470, 475, 482 ; kings of, i, 380, 391 ; mineral products, v, 453 ; printing, v, 461 ; quarries, v, 462, 463 ; Rom. rem., i, 294, 313, 318, 325 ; Teutonic settlements, i, 374, 375, 377, 381, 383, 385, 390
Wightman, Will., ii, 478
Wigley, man. (Eling), iv, 489, 546, 552, 554
Wigmore, hon. of, iv, 340, 341, 342
Wigmore [Wygmore], Bald., iv, 491, 492 ; Eliz., iv, 491 ; John, iv, 491 ; Mary, iv, 260 ; Rich., v, 95 n ; Will., iii, 58 ; iv, 290
Wigthun, bp. of Winchester, ii, 4
Wihtgar, i, 275, 390 ; v, 222, 293, 294
Wihtgarasburh, see Carisbrooke
Wikkam, see Wickham
Wilberforce, Sam., ii, 100, 482 ; iv, 210 ; v, 211 ; Will., v, 211
Wilckes, see Wilkes
Wilcox, Edw., iii, 12
Wildbore, ii, 378
Wilde, —, v, 348 n
Wilder, Fran. B. S., v, 179 ; Capt., v, 527
Wilderness (Godshill), v, 170
Wilderness (Tadley), iv, 219
Wildfowl, v, 559
Wild Furlong (Hartley Wespall), iv, 42
Wildhern [Wildhearn] (Andover), iv, 324, 345, 356
Wilding, Thos., v, 540
Wildmoor [Wildmore] (Sherfield-upon-Loddon), iv, 67 n, 103, 104, 105 n ; 140, 156
Wilekin, fam., iv, 354
Wilford, Mary, iv, 370 ; Thos., iv, 370
Wilfrid, St., ii, 3, 240 ; v, 168
Wiliton, Ralph de, v, 91 n
Wilkes [Wilckes], John, iii, 250 ; v, 140, 157, 461 ; Thos., ii, 316 ; —, v, 350

Wilkins, Pet., iii, 211
Wilkinson, Hester, iv, 537 ; Will., iii, 354 ; iv, 537 ; v, 517
Willac, v, 81 n
Willenhall [Willinghale], Cath., iii, 90 ; iv, 256 ; Chris., iii, 90 ; iv, 256 ; John, v, 16
Willes, see Willis
Willesley Warren (Overton), iv, 213
Willhall, man. (Alton), ii, 471, 479
William I, ii, 9, 108, 216, 218, 219, 409, 415, 417, 418, 419, 420, 421, 474, 480, 492, 493, 496, 518 ; iii, 86, 130 ; iv, 33, 74, 91, 109, 129, 146, 191, 193, 208, 258, 261, 265, 270, 324, 330, 331, 346, 351, 355, 356, 373, 395, 399, 413, 503, 506 ; v, 140, 198, 222, 274, 299, 300, 359, 410, 418
William II, ii, 10, 219, 421 ; iv, 351, 356, 626, 635, 644 ; v, 51, 56, 57, 300, 568
William III, ii, 451, 452 ; iv, 249, 345, 452 ; v, 211, 213, 215, 267, 290, 385, 386
William, iii, 511 ; iv, 8, 27, 28, 231, 275, 290, 491 ; v, 37, 129, 165 ; abbot of Netley, ii, 147, 149 ; abbot of Quarr, ii, 139 ; abbot of Tiron, ii, 221 ; the archer, iv, 475 ; bp. of Angers, ii, 146 ; bp. of Selymbria, ii, 45 ; of Dover, v, 303 ; of Dunstaple, v, 44 ; of Edington, v, 63 ; the marshal, v, 308 ; prior of Monk Sherborne, ii, 226, 228 ; prior of Mottisfont, ii, 175
Williams, Anne M., iii, 200 ; Ascanius, iv, 617, 619 ; Brian, v, 112, 120 ; Chas., iii, 151 ; Daubeny, v, 158 ; Dav., ii, 357, 358, 366 ; E. A., iv, 139 ; F. V., v, 532 ; Geo., iv, 607 ; Giles, iii, 111 ; Isabel, iii, 375 ; (Sir) John, iii, 35, 101, 131 ; iv, 423, 619, 620 ; J., v, 461 ; Ludovic, v, 108 ; Nich., iii, 375 ; Peckham, iii, 131 ; Ralph, v, 460 ; Reg., iii, 375 ; Reg. F., v, 171, 174 ; Rob., v, 182 ; Rob. V. W., v, 171 ; Sally, v, 110 ; Thos., ii, 65 ; Will., iv, 351 ; v, 94 ; W. P., v, 529 ; Lady, iii, 79 ; —, iv, 325 ; v, 17
Williamsmore (Kingsclere), iv, 250
William's More (Yateley), iv, 21
Williamson, Edm. T., iii, 247 ; Hen., iii, 247 ; Hugh, iv, 388 n ; Isaac, ii, 383, 385 ; Stapleton, iii, 247 ; —, iv, 397
Willinghale, see Willenhall
Willinton, Ralph de, iv, 527
Willis [Willes, Wyllis], Caroline, iv, 384 ; Eleanor, iv, 637 ; Geo., ii, 69 ; Rev. G. A., v, 188 ; Sir Geo. H., v, 134 ; Hen., iv, 637 ; Jacob, v, 132 ; Jas., iv, 637 ; v, 94, 129 ; (Sir) John, iv, 506, 637 ; v, 97, 129 ; J., v, 532 ; (Sir) Rich., ii, 282, 310 ; iii, 363 ; v, 281, 340 ; Rich., bp. of Winchester, ii, 98 ; Thos., iv, 200 ; fam., arms, iii, 479
Will s-Fleming, John B., iv, 479 ; John E. A., iii, 469, 479 ; iv, 453, 488 ; v, 143, 151, 152 ; J., v, 541 ; Thos., iii, 479
Willoughby, (de), Lds. : Rich., iv, 176 n ; Will., iv, 584
Willoughby, Charlotte, iii, 69 ; Chris., iv, 510 ; (Sir) Fran., v, 381, 382, 383 ; Hugh, iii, 459 ; Isabel, iv, 510, 511 ; John, iv,

Willoughby (cont.)
522 ; Sir Rich., iii, 192 ; Sir Thos., v, 325 ; Will., iii, 192 ; v, 381 ; —, v, 46
Willoughby de Broke, Rob., Ld., iv, 520
Willshaw, Thos., v, 387
Willwelande (Kimpton), iv, 372
Wilmer, Rich., ii, 213 ; fam., v, 461
Wilmingham (Freshwater), v, 243
Wilmington Priory (Suss.), iv, 395
Wilmot, vscts. : Hen., v, 469 ; Chas., iv, 190, 196
Wilmot [Wilmott], Arabella J., iv, 16, 22 ; Arth., iii, 346 ; iv, 196 n ; Barbarina, iv, 22 ; Chas., iv, 190, 196 ; Edw., iii, 346, 421 ; iv, 196 ; Hen., iv, 16, 17 ; Joan, iii, 421 ; John, iii, 421 ; iv, 190, 196 ; Mary, iv, 283 ; Rich., iii, 201 ; Rob., iv, 16 ; Thos., iii, 421 ; Valentine H., iv, 16, 22 ; Will., iv, 283 ; —, iv, 284
Wilmot-Sitwell, —, iv, 27
Wilshere [Wilshire, Wilteshire] (de), Gilb., ii, 130 ; Will., iii, 21 ; v, 482
Wilson, Arth. C., ii, 384, 385 ; Clarence, iii, 433, 437 ; Courtenay F., iv, 551 ; Lady Frances E., iii, 459 ; Godf., iv, 385 ; Rev. R. F., iii, 463 ; Will., v, 42
Wilteneweie (S. Damerham), iv, 587 n
Wiltenysshbury, see Winklebury
Wiltes, Johanne de, v, 48 n
Wilteshire, see Wilshere
Wilton (Wilts), ii, 163, 172 ; iv, 497
Wilton Abbey (Wilts), iv, 540 ; v, 220 ; Alice, abbess of, v, 229
Wiltshire, ctsses. of : Constance Stafford, iv, 370 ; Marg. Stafford, iv, 370 ; earls of : ii, 338 ; Edw. Stafford, iv, 370 ; Jas. Butler, v, 319 ; John Stafford, iv, 370 ; Will. Paulet, see Winchester, mqsses. of
Wilverley Park (Lyndhurst), iv, 631
Wilverley Walk (New Forest), iv, 626
Wimbledon, de, Joan, iv, 373 n ; John, iv, 373
Wimborne (Dors.), iv, 576, 589, 614 ; v, 85
Wimborne [Wymborne], John, ii, 157, 158, 160 ; Thos., ii, 158
Wimbush [Wymbish], Barnes, iii, 347 ; Nich., iii, 214
Wimeringe, see Wymering
Wimperis, Edw. M., v, 134
Wina, bp. of Winchester, see Wini
Winall, John, v, 31
Winch, Thos., iv, 522
Winchecombe, see Wynchecombe
Winchelsey, Rob. archbp. of Canterbury, ii, 23
Winchester, i, 268, 272, 384, 391, 392 ; ii, 5-15, 17, 19, 28, 32-41, 47, 51, 56, 60, 62, 64, 65, 72, 73, 79, 80, 83, 85, 87, 88, 90, 92, 93, 95, 96, 98, 101, 104, 105, 109, 114, 122, 126, 132, 163, 168, 169, 172, 173, 187, 189, 198, 200, 201, 204, 223, 225, 252, 313, 409 ; iv, 129, 261, 426, 481 n ; v, 1-80, 294, 295, 297, 299, 300, 307, 310, 311, 323, 324, 328 n, 331, 334, 344, 346, 348, 351, 359, 373 ; v, 376, 380, 382, 393, 409, 414, 415, 417, 418, 419, 421, 423, 425, 428, 429, 430, 431, 433, 434, 463 ; advs., v, 75 ; aldermen, v, 29 ; almonry sch., ii, 259 ; ancient custom, v, 44 A.-S. rem. i, 396, 397 ; Austin

Winchester (*cont.*)

friary, ii, 192 ; Black Book of, v, 479 *n* ; Carmelite friary, ii, 193 ; cathedral, *see* Winchester Cathedral ; cathedral close, v, 12 ; chamberlains, v, 30 ; chant., v, 52 ; char., v, 76 ; chs., ii, 238, 240 ; v, 69 ; consuetudinary of, v, 479 ; coroners, v, 30 ; courts, iv, 282 *n* ; v, 33, 38, 47, 48 ; crosses, v, 6, 20 ; Dominican friary, ii, 189 ; fee farm, v, 22-24 ; fishing, v, 563 ; Franciscan friary, ii, 191 ; Godbiete liberty, v, 34 ; grammar sch., ii, 251-6 ; guilds, v, 41 ; hosp., iv, 81, 267 ; v, 429 ; house of correction, v, 424, 429 ; Hyde Abbey, *see* Hyde Abbey ; inds., v, 41-44, 451, 453, 454, 455, 456, 459, 460, 461, 467, 473, 475, 476, 477, 479, 481, 482, 483, 484, 488 ; Jews, v, 32 ; mkts. and fairs, v, 36-41, mayor, v, 26 ; mills, v, 49, 452, 479, 481 *n*, 488 *n* ; New College, *see* Winchester College ; Novices' Sch., ii, 257 ; Nunnaminster, *see* Nunnaminster ; plague, v, 49, 426 ; pop., v, 449, 450 ; prehist. rem., i, 260, 261, 262 ; racing, v, 543, 544, 545 ; Rom. rem., i, 285-93, 307, 328, 347 ; v, 1 ; Rom. rds., i, 309, 319, 321, 322, 324, 330 ; St. Bartholomew Hyde, par., v, 1, 69 ; St. Faith, par., v, 1, 76 ; St. Giles' fair, *see* that title ; St. Mary Kalendar, par., ii, 63 ; v, 73 ; St. Mary's Abbey, *see* Nunnaminster ; schs., ii, 388, 406 ; v, 13, 14, 79 ; serjeants, v, 30 ; soke, v, 19, 47, 427, 428 ; town clerk, v, 30 ; volunteers, v, 356 ; wards, v, 25

Winchester, Richer, archd. of, iv, 19

Winchester, bps. of, ii, 164, 361, 485, 503, 505, 514, ; iii, 21, 37, 41, 56, 57, 123, 237, 285, 303, 308, 309, 310, 313, 316, 317, 321, 322, 323, 324, 327, 330, 331, 337, 343, 344, 346, 353, 393, 403, 405, 408, 409, 426, 427, 431, 433, 455, 466, 482, 498 ; iv, 1, 2, 7, 8, 13, 15, 20, 28, 36, 86, 88 *n*, 97, 101, 109, 146, 185, 198, 213, 217, 230, 231, 243, 246, 275, 281, 282, 283, 289, 290, 292, 313, 323, 324, 331, 346, 356, 373, 379, 414, 468, 474, 534, 613, 649 ; v, 108, 115, 193 *n*, 209, 212, 223, 268, 275, 285, 304, 333, 369, 371, 409, 410, 411, 413, 419, 421, 466, 469, 480 *n* ; Ælfsige, iv, 6, 277, 334 ; Alhmund, iv, 27 ; Alwyn, ii, 8, 9, 216 ; iii, 65, 384, 422 ; v, 55, 56, 298 ; Launcelot Andrewes, ii, 87 ; Rigaud Asserio, ii, 16, 28, 190, 191, 192, 193, 195 ; iv, 399 ; v, 76, 277 ; Hen. Beaufort, ii, 45, 46, 111, 122, 196, 211, 258, 273, 279, 283, 286, 289, 290 ; iii, 452 ; iv, 14, 26, 159, 265, 304, 388, 524, 576 ; iv, 14, 26, 159, 265, 304, 388, 524, 576 ; v, 66 ; seal of, ii, 103 ; Bcornstan [Brinstan], ii, 6, 201 ; Thos. Bilson, ii, 83, 85, 314, 315, 316, 319, 366 ; iii, 89, 90 ; iv, 201, 317 ; v, 154 ; Hen. de Blois, ii, 11, 12, 105, 108 117, 126, 152, 154, 160, 169, 187, 193, 194, 211, 216, 226, 255 ; iii, 42, 43, 130, 215, 277, 281, 284, 301, 315, 335 ; iv, 19, 189, 222, 284, 303, 551, 586 ; v, 13, 14,

Winchester (*cont.*)

22, 56, 57, 59, 168, 302, 417 ; Brihtelm, iv, 193 ; Brithwold, ii, 114 ; Harold Browne, ii, 100 ; iv, 158 ; Pet. Courtenay, ii, 48 ; iv, 64 ; v, 56 ; Thos. Cowper, ii, 318 ; Walt. Curll, ii, 89, 90 ; iii, 259 ; iv, 254 ; Daniel, i, 375 ; ii, 2, 3, 4 ; Denewulf, ii, 116 ; iii, 277, 348 ; iv, 291 ; v, 1 ; Brian Duppa, ii, 93 ; Will. Edendon, ii, 31, 32, 34, 35, 36, 119, 162, 195, 197, 207, 213 ; iii, 29, 42, 255, 256, 260, 314, 415, 421 ; iv, 58, 63, 69, 147, 148, 179, 181, 374, 388, 392 *n*, 413, 459, 616 ; v, 11 *n*, 51, 58, 63 ; Nich. of Ely, ii, 19 ; iv, 211, 576, 607 ; v, 56, 217, 479 ; Ethelwold, ii, 6, 7, 51, 108, 114, 116, 122, 126 ; iv, 18, 240, 460 ; v, 6 ; Rich. Fox, ii, 50, 51, 113, 120, 163, 197, 202, 208, 215, 369, 370 ; iii, 42, 187, 333, 334 ; iv, 135, 165, 296, 425, 427, 512 ; v, 24, 51, 76, 322 ; Frithstan, ii, 6 ; iii, 11 ; iv, 202, 212, 219, 221 ; Steph. Gardiner, ii, 52, 53, 63, 64, 65, 70, 71, 291, 301 ; iii, 43 ; iv, 192, 248, 277, 430, 539 ; John Gervais, ii, 19 ; iv, 211, 293 *n* ; Will. Giffard, ii, 10, 11, 216, 221, 480 ; iv, 236 ; v, 239 ; Haedde, ii, 2, 101 ; Herefrith, ii, 4 ; Benj. Hoadly, ii, 98 ; iv, 61, 218 ; Rob. Horne, ii, 73, 74, 75, 76 ; iii, 351, 528 ; iv, 357, 429 ; Rich. of Ilchester [Tocliffe], ii, 102, 194, 197 ; iii, 53, 59 ; v, 55, 56, 168, 217 ; Thos. Langton, ii, 48 ; v, 54 ; Leutherius, ii, 2 ; Godf. de Lucy, ii, 13, 149, 160, 223, 230 ; iii, 15, 70, 304, 349, 350, 524 ; iv, 126, 170 ; v, 51, 55, 206, 234, 291, 306, 360, 451 ; Pet. Mews, ii, 95, 96, 97 ; v, 54 ; Jas. Montagu, ii, 85, 87 ; Geo. Morley, ii, 93, 94, 95, 337, 380, 389 ; iii, 206, 278, 527 ; iv, 419 *n* ; v, 14, 58, 271 ; Adam Orlton, ii, 30, 31, 119, 123, 124, 128, 134, 156, 162, 165, 171, 173, 177, 198 ; iii, 65, 461 ; iv, 45, 58, 60, 93, 99, 170, 179, 266, 268 *n*, 274, 413, 480, 518 ; v, 76 ; John of Pontoise, ii, 15, 19, 20, 22, 105, 109, 127, 134, 150, 176, 197, 206, 211, 212, 217, 229 ; iii, 101 ; iv, 58, 152, 222, 229, 239, 242, 254, 265, 273, 371 ; v, 38, 49, 56, 218 ; seal of, ii, 102 ; John Poynet, ii, 66, 67, 70 ; iii, 277, 281, 287, 333, 340, 341, 418, 484 ; iv, 277, 278, 294, 301, 514 *n*, 601 ; v, 123 ; Will. de Raleigh, ii, 17, 18, 23, 108, 203, 214, 371 ; iv, 293 ; v, 47, 50, 479 ; Pet. des Roches [Rupibus], ii, 14, 146, 155, 175, 181, 189, 203, 206, 211, 212, 223, 371 ; iii, 5, 6, 15, 59, 62, 107, 116, 158, 168, 191, 212, 217, 224, 230, 248, 261 ; iv, 6 *n*, 68, 121, 126, 133, 138, 150, 179, 179, 202, 211, 258, 278, 535 ; v, 47, 55, 479 ; seal of, ii, 102 ; John Sendale [Sandale], ii, 15, 23, 24, 25, 26, 27, 28, 118, 134, 155, 191, 192, 193, 216, 229 ; iii, 75 ; iv, 14, 152, 285, 399 ; v, 221, 277 ; Swithun, ii, 4, 5, 6, 252 ; iv, 27 ; v, 418 ; John Thomas, ii, 99 ; Ant. W. Thorold, ii, 100 ; Geo. Tomline [Pretyman], ii, 99 ; iv, 646, 647 ; v, 119, 120 ; Jonathan Trelawny, ii, 97, 98 ; v, 178, 193 ; Aylmer de Valence, ii, 18, 109 ; iv, 21 *n*, 242 ; v,

Winchester (*cont.*)

265 ; Walkelin, ii, 9, 10, 480 ; iii, 225 ; iv, 208 *n*, 211, 494, 625 ; v, 36, 51, 95, 151, 155, 462 ; John Watson, ii, 76, 77, 78, 79, 115, 197, 480 ; iii, 65, 67 ; iv, 253 ; Will. Waynflete, ii, 47, 48, 103, 119, 174, 179, 196, 208, 255, 284, 285, 286, 366, 486, 520 ; iii, 5, 46, 277, 442 ; iv, 35, 41, 42, 54, 64, 153, 170, 354, 381, 386, 476, 520, 524 *n* ; John White, ii, 72, 73, 300, 301, 302, 308, 366 ; iii, 277 ; iv, 278 ; v, 177, 234 ; Wigthun, ii, 4 ; Sam. Wilberforce, ii, 100, 482 ; iv, 210 ; v, 211 ; Rich. Willis, ii, 98 ; Wini [Wina], ii, 2 ; v, 56 ; Thos. Wolsey, *see* York, archbp. of ; Hen. Woodlock, ii, 23, 110, 111, 115, 118, 150, 154, 161, 165, 173, 211, 212, 220, 229, 231 ; iv, 33, 35, 41, 152, 266, 302, 318, 328, 332 *n*, 368, 399, 524, 622 ; v, 214, 235, 277 ; Will. of Wykeham, ii, 17, 36, 37, 38, 39, 40, 41, 42, 43, 44, 45, 102, 111, 119, 124, 128, 135, 162, 166, 171, 177, 178, 184, 185, 194, 198, 199, 201, 204, 208, 211, 213, 223, 224, 225, 226, 228, 254, 255, 258, 259, 261, 262, 265, 267, 268, 269, 276, 279, 305, 387, 522 ; iii, 40, 56, 71, 145, 233, 310, 372, 405, 441, 470, 478, 526 ; iv, 4, 9 45, 50, 74, 79, 90, 177, 199, 206, 212, 215, 218, 225, 239, 260, 279, 285, 328, 336, 386, 418, 461, 548, 555, 564 ; v, 11 *n*, 14, 16, 17, 18, 51, 58, 315, 462

Winchester, Consuetudinary of, v, 479

Winchester, diocese of, ii, 2, 3, 4

Winchester, Marg. de Quinci, ctss. of, iv, 607 ; Seyer de Quinci, earl of, iv, 607 ; mchnsses of : Agnes Paulet, iv, 393 ; Eliz. Paulet, iv, 125 ; Honora Paulet [Powlett], iv, 433 ; Jane Paulet, iv, 433 *n* ; Lucy Paulet, iv, 409 ; mqsses. of : iv, 26, 107, 109 *n*, 161, 191, 192 *n*, 193, 266 *n*, 320, 321, 337, 343, 495, 529, 578, 611, 632 ; v, 24, 42, 332, 339, 340, 347, 484 ; Aug. J. H. B. Paulet, iv, 344, 385, 637 ; Chas. Powlett, *see* Bolton, dk. of ; Geo. Paulet, iv, 339, 389 ; Harry Powlett, *see* Bolton, dk. of ; Hen. W. M. Paulet, iv, 339 ; John Paulet, ii, 519 ; iii, 483 ; iv, 36, 115, 116, 119, 122, 141, 174, 183, 271, 334, 335, 433, 434 ; Will. Paulet, ii, 130, 148, 151, 445 ; iii, 9, 250, 251, 277, 281, 285, 301, 362, 368, 477, 483, 484, 488 ; iv, 13, 36, 46, 64, 80, 107, 108, 116, 117, 120, 123, 124 *n*, 125, 126, 130, 132, 135, 153, 157, 179, 183, 189, 191, 192, 193, 196, 210, 243, 244, 246, 251, 255, 261, 265, 266, 320, 334, 335, 336, 339, 348, 359, 393, 397, 409, 433, 434, 460, 525, 526, 528, 539, 552 ; v, 223

Winchester [Winchestour], (de, of), Ad., v, 33 ; John, ii, 139, 179 ; Thos., ii, 163 ; Will., ii, 120, 182, 186 ; *see also* Winton

Winchester Castle, iv, 69, 160, 260, 320 *n*, 353 *n* ; v, 9-12, 242 *n*, 302, 310, 343, 352, 418, 462

Winchester Cathedral, i, 391 ; ii, 6, 8, 10, 104, 241, 247, 474, 480 ; iv, 194 *n*, 277, 278, 288, 377 *n* ; v, 50-59, 158, 198, 218, 297, 301, 418 ; d. & c., ii, 482, 514 ; iv, 3, 6, 9, 18, 19, 22, 218, 229, 239,

Winchester Cathedral (*cont.*)
242, 276, 289, 300, 301, 419, 422,
468, 474, 512, 513, 612; v, 95,
108; deans of, ii, 115; Geo. W.
Kitchin, ii, 115, 245, 256; Newton
Ogle, ii, 115; Thos. Rennell, ii,
115; v, 78; John Young, ii, 115;
iii, 320, 420
Winchester College, ii, 44, 47, 48,
49, 55, 191, 214, 221, 222, 223,
225, 251, 261-366, 387, 389,
522; iii, 56, 194, 197, 241, 256,
372, 470; iv, 6, 9, 50, 135, 150,
176, 177, 179, 186, 249, 313, 329,
330, 331, 355, 426, 430, 436,
547, 550, 554, 555; v, 14-19, 126,
146, 199, 238, 262, 495, 576;
arms, iii, 255, 376, 470; head
masters, ii, 366; pop., v, 449;
wardens, ii, 365
Winchester Field, iv, 146, 211
Winchester Street, tithing (Andover), iv, 346
Winchfield, ii, 71, 76; iv, 66, 67,
109-12; adv., iv, 112; ch., iv,
111; man., iv, 109; mill, iv, 111;
pop., v, 443; sch., ii, 406
Winchfield, Capt., v, 333
Winchfield House (Winchfield), iv,
109
Winchfield Lodge (Winchfield), iv,
87, 109
Winchilsea, Ld., v, 574
Winckworth, *see* Winkworth
Windebanke, Frances, iv, 318;
Sir Thos., iv, 318
Windemill (Farnborough), iv, 15
Windenaie, *see* Witnal
Windesores, fam., *see* Windsor
Windham, *see* Wyndham
Windlesham (Surr.), ii, 227
Windley Common, *see* Sutton Com-
mon
Windmill Down (Hambledon), v,
574
Windmill Farm (Priors Dean), iv,
436
Windmill Field (Bentworth), iv, 68
Windsor, St. George's Chapel, iv,
43, 44, 257, 459, 460
Windsor, Lds., ii, 487, 516; iv, 69;
Andr., ii, 476, 487, 504; iv, 69,
70, 353; Will., iv, 142
Windsor [Windesores, Wyndesore]
(de, of), Alice (Lady), ii, 486;
iii, 451; iv, 69, 105, 143; Andrews, iii,, 530 n, 536; iv, 468;
Anne, iv, 224, 374; Sir Ant., iii,
212; iv, 374; v, 326 n; Brian,
ii, 486; iv, 69, 143, 224 n; Edith,
ii, 492; Eliz., iv, 69; Geoff., iii,
448; v, 22; Geo., iv, 29, 30;
Hugh, iii, 448; Jas., ii, 486; iv,
69; John, iii, 258, 259, 261, 448;
v, 313; Marg., iv, 29, 258; (Sir)
Miles, ii, 479, 486, 487, 492, 493,
504, 507; iv, 69, 143, 224; Odin,
iv, 15; Rich., ii, 479, 486, 504;
iv, 69, 224; Thos., ii, 487, 504;
iii, 267; iv, 105, 142, 143; Will.,
ii, 179, 180, 479; iii, 255, 259;
iv, 142, 224; fam., ii, 488; arms,
ii, 487, 504
Winesflet, *see* Winchfield
Winesflot, *see* Winslade
Winesham, de, Ralph, iii, 60; Rog.,
iii, 60
Wine trade, v, 362, 367, 376, 415
Winford, Will., ii, 263; v, 16
Winford Farm (Newchurch), v,
184
Winfred, *see* Boniface, St.
Wingfield [Winxfeld, Wyngsfeld]
(de), Hen., iii, 42; (Sir) John,
iii, 161; iv, 7; Lewis, iii, 42;

Wingfield (*cont.*)
Marg., iv, 169; Sir Rich., ii, 67;
iii, 161; Tom, v, 534
Wingrove, F., v, 566, 567; H. F.,
v, 566, 567
Wini [Wina], bp. of Winchester, ii,
2; v, 56
Winklebury (Basingstoke), iv, 129
Winkton, man. (Christchurch), ii,
154; v, 98, 100 n, 108 n; chap.,
v, 108; mills, v, 100
Winkton, tithing (Christchurch),
v, 81, 82, 83
Winkton House (Christchurch), v,
84
Winkton Lewen, man. (Christ-
church), v, 100
Winkton Lodge (Christchurch), v,
84
Winkton Westbury, *see* Bock-
hampton
Winkworth [Winckworth], C., iv,
422; Hugh, iv, 367; Nich., iii,
298
Winlow, Will., iv, 613; v, 177
Winnall, iii, 302, 348; v, 1; adv.,
iii, 348; ch., iii, 348; man., ii,
114; iii, 348; pop., v, 448
Winnaston, man. (Wilts), ii, 114
Winsinton, Bald. de, iv, 531
Winslade, iv, 113, 114, 115, 174,
179-81; adv., iv, 181; char., iv,
181; ch., iv, 181; mans., iv, 179;
pop., v, 439
Winsome Field (Hurstbourne
Priors), iv, 288
Winsor, man. (Eling), iv, 547, 548,
555
Winston, man. (Newchurch), v,
183
Wintan ceastre, Winteceastre, *see*
Winchester
Winter [Wynter], Jos., v, 78; Rob.,
ii, 50; Thos., iii, 200; Will., iii,
180; v, 377; Will. P., iii, 202;
v, 170
Winterborne Stoke (Wilts), ii, 217,
219
Winterbourne, man. (Wilts), ii, 121
Winterbourne, Little, man. (Wilts),
iv, 342, 519
Winterbourne [Wynterburn] (de),
Alice, iv, 496; Emma, ii, 151;
John, iv, 496; Will., iv, 540
Winter Hill (Whitchurch), iv, 300
Wintershill (Upham), iii, 275, 289,
299, 300
Wintershill [Wintershull, Wyntereshall, Wyntereshull, Wyntershill,
Wyntershull, Wyntreshall, Wyn-
treshulle] (de), Agnes, iv, 255;
Alice, ii, 128, 132; iv, 255;
Amice, iv, 104, 105, 160; Beatrice, iii, 486; iv, 254, 265; Constance, ii, 137; Edm., iv, 255;
Isabel, ii, 134, 137; Joan, iv,
255; v, 147; John, iii, 346, 364,
486; iv, 104, 105, 106, 160, 255;
v, 147; Juliane, iv, 255; Thos.,
iii, 106, 486; iv, 255; Walt., iii,
486; iv, 255; (Sir) Will., iii, 346,
486; iv, 251 n, 254, 255; v, 142;
fam., v, 161
Winterslow (West Tytherley), iv,
519
Wintney Herriard Grange (Herriard), iii, 368
Wintney Priory, ii, 49, 104, 107,
149-51; iii, 362, 368, 447; iv,
79, 80, 81, 92 n, 170
Winton (Bournemouth), v, 83 n,
133, 134, 135
Winton [Wynton], (de), Andr., ii,
164, 168; Christine, abbess of
Nunnaminster, ii, 126; Hen., ii,

Winton (*cont.*)
175; Joan, iv, 352, 382; (Sir)
John, ii, 179; iii, 260, 441, 444;
iv, 382, 383; Nich., ii, 177, 179;
Pet., ii, 182, 186; Phil., ii, 165;
Rich., iii, 259, 441, 444; Sim.,
iii, 441; Thos., ii, 180; iii, 441;
iv, 352; v, 227 n, 237; Will., ii,
168; *see also* De Winton and
Winchester
Winxfeld, *see* Wingfield
Wipingeham, *see* Whippingham
Wirgg, the, (Stratfieldsaye), iv, 57
Wise [Wyse], Nich., v, 482 n;
Will., ii, 211; —, iv, 631; v, 527
Wiseman, Alice, iii, 105; Edm., iii,
105
Wishanger, man. (Headley), iii,
51, 53, 401
Wishanger Common, iii, 52
Wislac, iv, 616, 625, 628; v, 100,
130, 288
Wistric, iv, 572
Wit, Alwin, iv, 261
Witcharley, Dan., iv, 409
Witciree, *see* Whitchurch
Witeberge, man., iv, 594 n
Witehulle (Kimpton), iv, 372
Witgar, iii, 123
Wither, Alethea B., iv, 241; Chas.,
iv, 201, 207, 220, 226 n; Dorothy,
iv, 232, 243; Eliz., iv, 28, 207,
242; Geo., iii, 203, 239; iv, 28,
116 n, 201, 207, 221, 227, 228,
232, 253, 254, 423; Gilb., iv,
207, 226, 227, 228; Henrietta
M., iv, 201, 207, 226 n; Joan,
iv, 239, 241; John, iii, 39; iv,
239, 241, 242; Mary, iv, 232;
Paul, iii, 39; Rich., iii, 361; iv,
239, 516; Rob., iv, 239; Susan,
iv, 242; Thos., iv, 239; Will., iii,
39; iv, 223, 232, 239, 240, 241,
242, 243, 244; —, v, 12
Withers, Eliz., iii, 205; Geo., iii
205; Harry F., iv, 577; Hicks,
iv, 484; Jas., iii, 353
Withford, man., *see* Wyford
Withington, F. E., v, 546, 554
Witley (Surr.), iv, 77
Witnal (Whitchurch), ii, 108; iv,
300, 301
Witney (Wilts.), ii, 208; iv, 293;
v, 265
Witney, John de, v, 154
Witro, the falconer, v, 100
Wittenstall, Marg., v, 207
Witteville, *see* Wyvill
Wittier, Jas., ii, 379
Wittingley forest, iv, 251, 260
Witvil, *see* Wyvill
Wivelrod, man. (Bentworth), ii,
483; iv, 68, 70
Wixenford (Eversley), iv, 33
Wlfferton, *see* Wolverton
Wluithesmede (Kingsclere), iv, 250
Woburn, Will., ii, 146
Wocrofte (Stratfield Turgis), iv, 63
Wode, man. (Brading), v, 162
Wode (Whippingham), *see* Wood-
house
Wode, fam., *see* Wood
Wodehous (Whippingham), *see*
Woodhouse
Wodehouse, John, Ld., iv, 23
Wodehouse, Edm. R., iv, 21; Laura
S., iv, 23; *see also* Woodhouse
Wodelock, *see* Woodlock
Wodemede (Bramley), iv, 141
Wodemeye, la, (Andover), iv, 346
Wodemilne (Winchester), v, 451
Wodenham, John, ii, 157, 160
Wodensdyke (Linkenholt), iv, 324
Woder (Wodier), Barth. le, v, 481
Woderne, John, v, 484

Wodestock, *see* Woodstock

Wodesun, *see* Woodson

Woditon, *see* Wootton

Woking (Surr.), iv, 150

Woking, Aldershot and Basingstoke Canal, v, 452

Wolches (Liss), iv, 84

Wolfe, Gen. Jas., v, 357, 390; John, iii, 149

Wolgar, Will., iii, 123

Wolhayes (Christchurch), v, 84

Wollascot, Anne, iii, 240; Edw., iii, 240; Susan, iii, 167, 240; Thos., iii, 167, 240; Will., iii, 167, 240; iv, 106

Wolleseld, le, (Winchester), v, 11, 35

Wolleyshulle (Lyndhurst), iv, 631

Wollop, *see* Wallop

Wolmer forest, *see* Woolmer forest

Wolsey, Thos., ii, 51, 120; iv, 165, 212, 497, 506, 518, 524

Wolston (Southampton), ii, 88

Wolveleye (Calbourne), v, 218

Wolveridge, Ant. J., iv, 73; Frances, iv, 69; (Sir) Jas., iv, 69, 73, 92, 93 *n*; John, iv, 69

Wolverton, iv, 245, 246, 246 *n*, 247, 249, 270-72; adv., iv, 272; char., iv, 272; ch., iv, 272; man., ii, 466; iv, 60, 198, 224 *n*, 256, 257, 258, 265, 270, 276, 532; pop., v, 442; sch., ii, 406

Wolverton, man. (Brading), v, 161, 163, 164 *n*, 183

Wolverton, Ld., v, 569

Wolverton (de), John, v, 194, 231, 282; Nichola, v, 250; Ralph, v, 194, 231, 250, 282; Thos., iv, 366

Wolverton Common, iv, 270

Wolverton End (Kingsclere), iv, 266

Wolverton House (Wolverton), iv, 270

Wolverton Wood, iv, 270

Wolvesey (Winchester), ii, 37; v, 13, 47; pop., v, 450

Wolvesey Palace (Winchester), ii, 12, 13, 18, 97, 117, 198, 199, 212, 213, 293, 302, 319; v, 2, 13-14, 303 *n*

Wolveton, man. (Brading), *see* Wolverton

Womme, Thos., ii, 500

Wonston [Wonsington], ii, 73, 108, 197; iii, 401, 453-61; iv, 358, 402; adv., iii, 460; char., iii, 461; ch., iii, 460; man., ii, 114; iii, 455; pop., v, 447; sch., ii, 406

Wood [Wode] (atte), Ant., ii, 325; v, 17; Arth. H., v, 519; G. G., iii, 273; Hen., iii, 201; John, ii, 479; iii, 117; iv, 80, 103; v, 201 *n*, 235; John G., ii, 483; iv, 103; Jos., iv, 303; Rob., ii, 163, 164; Thos., iii, 487; iv, 80; v, 146; Thos. F., v, 147; Will., iv, 80; v, 484; Will. P., ii, 356; —, iii, 346; iv, 492; fam., arms, ii, 479

Woodborough (Wilts), iv, 594 *n*

Woodcastle, *see* Woodgarston

Woodcock, Edw., iv, 409; Rev. Ellorough, iv, 408; John, iv, 51

Woodcocks (Longstock), iv, 449

Woodcote, man. (Bramdean), ii, 83; iii, 47; Rom. rem., i, 307, 347

Woodcote (Fleet), iv, 5

Woodcote House (Bramdean), iii, 49

Woodcott [Woodcote], par., ii, 188; iv, 327 *n*, 331-2; adv., iv, 332; ch., iv, 332; farms, iv, 331; man., iv, 269, 331; pop., v, 442

Woodcott [Woodcote] (Fawley), ii, 181; iii, 275

Woodcott, de, Hen., iv, 255, 256, 269, 332; Philippa, iv, 255; Ruald, iv, 184, 255, 256, 257, 260, 269, 332; Sanchea, iv, 255, 269, 332

Wooder, Fran., iii, 124

Woodesend Coppice (Faccombe), iv, 314

Woodfidley, man. (Fordingbridge), iv, 573

Woodford [Wudfold], (de), Alan, iv, 550, 572; Ann, ii, 490; John, v, 285; Margery, iv, 572; Matth., iii, 405; Maud, iv, 550; (Rev.) Saml., ii, 486, 490; v, 51

Woodgarston (Monk Sherborne), iv, 114, 153, 223, 231, 281; man., iv, 232, 239 *n*

Wood-green, iv, 559, 568, 603, 629; pop., v, 445

Woodham, Edm., iv, 472; Thos., iv, 444; Thos. B., iv, 472; Rev Thos. F., iv, 444, 472; Rev. Will., iv, 472

Woodhay, East, iv, 273, 274, 275, 305-7, 316; adv., iv, 306; char., iv, 307; ch., iv, 306; mans., iv, 305; pop., v, 442; sch., ii, 399

Woodhouse (Andover), iv, 345, 353, 354; char., iv, 379

Woodhouse (Whippingham), v, 200

Woodhouse, Rev. E. J., iii, 58; Rich., iv, 256; Rob., iv, 440

Woodhouse Ashes (Blendworth), iii, 84

Woodhouse Farm (Woodlands), iv, 267

Woodhouse Lane (Blendworth), iii, 84

Woodifield, Eliz., iv, 634; Rob., iv, 634

Woodlands (Netley Marsh), iv, 546

Woodlands (West Meon), iii, 344

Woodlands Vale (St. Helens), v, 190, 192

Woodley (Romsey), iv, 452, 468

Woodley, Jack, v, 517

Woodlock [Wodelock], (de), Agnes, iii, 485; Eleanor, iv, 510; Hen., *see* Winchester, bps. of; Joan, iv, 477, 510; John, iii, 485; Marg., iii, 485; Marjory, iv, 420; Nich., iii, 324; iv, 510; Rob., iii, 485; Rog., iii, 425; iv, 420, 477, 510; Ursula, iv, 420; Walt., iii, 324; Will., iii, 333, 485; fam., arms, iii, 324

Woodman, John, v, 27

Woodmancott, ii, 116, 117; iv, 31, 182, 184, 186-7; adv., iv, 187; ch., iv, 187; man., ii, 121; iv, 186; pop., v, 442

Wood Mill (South Stoneham), v, 458, 563

Woodnut, Will., v, 266

Woodpitts (Hartley Wintney), iv, 80

Woodroffe [Woodrofe], Rev. Benj., iii, 366; Rich., ii, 378, 382; Will., iv, 444

Woodrow, Will., iii, 171

Woods, Hen., iii, 271, 320; P. H., iv, 277; Col. Will., iii, 271, 320

Woodside (Elvetham), iv, 74

Woodside (Lymington), salt works, v, 470

Woodside (Vernhams Dean), iv, 329

Woodson (Wodesun), John, ii, 113; Will., iv, 656

Woodstile Coppes (Abbotts Ann), iv, 334

Woodstock [Wodestock], de, (Sir) Jas., ii, 227; iv, 46 *n*; Joan, iv, 46 *n*

Woodville [Wydevil, Wydvil], (Sir) Ant., iii, 158; v, 219, 223, 225, 263, 285, 290, 320; Edw., iii, 158; v, 223; Eliz., v, 263; *see also* Elizabeth (w. of Edw. IV)

Woodward, Edw., iii, 171; iv, 172 *n*; Eliz., iv, 172; John, v, 140, 177; Will., iv, 172; W., v, 461; —, iv, 183

Woody Bay (Whitwell), v, 202

Woody Furlong (Longstock), *see* Oodie Furlong

Woodyer, Alice, iv, 258; Dorothy, iv, 258; Thos., iv, 258; —, iv, 210

Wool, Rich., iii, 341; *see also* Wooll

Woolbury Ring (Leckford), iv, 446, 480

Wooll, John, iv, 181; *see also* Wool

Woollaston [Walaston, Walleston], Chris., ii, 91, 482; Hannah, iii, 270; Jonathan, iii, 270; iv, 304; Rich., iii, 270; iv, 304

Woolley, ii, 137

Woolls, Maj. T. A., v, 356

Woolmer Forest, ii, 432, 434, 440, 441, 452, 453, 454, 483, 490, 491, 494, 506, 508, 515, 518, 519; iii, 3, 4, 5, 8, 10, 11, 16; iv, 84; Rom. rem., i, 306, 326, 340, 347; stone quarries, v, 463

Woolmer Lodge (Bramshott), ii, 491, 493; Rom. Cath., i, 495

Woolnough, J. B. W., iv, 137

Woolston (St. Mary Extra), iii, 275, 297; v, 387; inds., v, 453, 458; man., iii, 298; mill, iii, 298

Woolton Hill (East Woodhay), iv, 273, 305; char., iv, 307; ch., iv, 306

Wool trade, v, 416, 418, 422, 426, 451, 475, 476, 494

Woolverton [Great Wolverton], man. (Shorwell), v, 203, 281

Woolverton, Little, [Woolverton under Wathe] (Whitwell), v, 194, 203

Woolverton, fam., *see* Wolverton

Woolwich (Kent), shipping expenditure, v, 375, 383, 386, 387

Woor (Christchurch), v, 85

Wooton, Will., iv, 19

Wootton (I. of W.), ii, 73; v, 138, 197, 204-6, 221, 246; adv., v, 205; brick making, v, 466; chants., v, 206; chs., v 205; man., v, 204, 274, 280; pop., v, 448

Wootton (Milton), iv, 615; v, 81, 124

Wootton Bridge (Wootton), v, 204

Wootton Copse (Wootton, St. Lawrence), iv, 243

Wootton Creek, v, 140, 151; oyster beds, v, 468

Wootton St. Lawrence, ii, 73, 108; iv, 113, 223, 224, 229, 231, 232, 234, 239-42, 243, 244, 247, 258; adv., iv, 242; char., iv, 242; ch., iv, 228, 240; man., iv, 239-40; v, 419, 420; Nonconf., iv, 242; pop., v, 439; sch., ii, 406

Wopbury (Romsey), iv, 452

Wopstrete (Mottisfont), v, 503

Worcester, bps. of, ii, 19; v, 308, 309; Godf. Giffard, iv, 7, 9; Edw. Stillingfleet, iv, 613

Worcester, Rich. Edes, dean of, v, 256

Worcester, ctsses. of:—Eliz. Tiptoft, ii, 475, 476, 492; Isabel Beauchamp, iv, 151, 441; **earls**

Worcester (cont.)
of, ii, 485 ; Edw. Somerset, iii, 84, 105 ; Edw. de Tiptoft, iv, 348 ; Hen. Somerset, iii, 105 ; John Tiptoft, ii, 475 ; iii, 153 ; iv, 347, 526, 628 ; v, 320 ; Rich. Beauchamp, iv, 151, 441 ; Thos. Percy, iv, 151 ; Will. Somerset, iii, 105 ; mqsses. of :— Edw. Somerset, iii, 105 ; Hen. Somerset, iii, 105, 109
Worcester, (of) Thos., ii, 119, 122 ; Will., ii, 121
Wordia, see Martyr Worthy
Wordsworth, Chas., ii, 310, 360 ; Chris., ii, 330
Worgan, John, iv, 325 ; Mary, iv, 325
Workman, Will., ii, 383, 385
Worldham, East, ii, 177, 471, 483, 490, 494, 514, 515, 518-21 ; char., ii, 521 ; ch., ii, 520 ; man., ii, 518 ; pop., v, 437 ; sch., ii, 398, 521
Worldham, West, ii, 471, 508, 521-3 ; ch., ii, 522 ; man., ii, 521 ; pop , v, 437
Worlidge, John, v, 425, 475, 497
Wormenhall [Wormenhale], John de, ii, 171, 208
Wormley (Herts.), iv, 304
Worsley, Anne, ii, 368 ; v, 170, 171, 176, 194, 229 ; Barbara, iv, 605 ; Sir Bower, v, 180 ; Bridg., v, 239 ; Chas., v, 176, 252 n ; Dav., v, 248 ; (Sir) Edw., ii, 97 ; v, 188, 246, 248, 249, 250, 347 ; Edw. M., iv, 271 ; v, 248, 250 ; Edw. V., v, 250 n ; Eliz., iv, 271 ; v, 180, 248, 250 ; Rev. Fran., v, 239 ; Geo., v, 171 ; Giles, v, 180, 181 ; (Rev., Sir) Hen., iii, 407 ; iv, 185, 271 ; v, 170 n, 171, 176, 194, 235 ; (Sir) Jas., ii, 56, 124, 138, 148, 151, 159, 174, 485 ; iv, 619, 621 ; v., 148, 170 n, 171, 174, 176, 180, 192, 194, 223, 229, 250 ; Jane, iv, 248, 271 ; (Rev.) John, v, 140, 147 n, 160, 161, 162, 164, 171, 174, 180, 182, 192, 194, 199, 202, 237. 247, 248 ; Marg., v, 180 ; (Sir) Rich., ii, 67, 69, 304, 368, 391, 485 ; iv, 184 ; v, 123, 161, 162, 170, 171, 172, 173, 174, 176, 177, 180, 182, 201, 202, 223, 224, 237, 240, 247, 264, 287 n, 289, 393, 453 ; (Sir) Rob., iii, 39, 407 ; iv, 183, 184, 186, 271 n ; v, 163, 170, 171, 173 n, 176, 180, 181, 202 ; Thos., iv, 605 ; v, 140, 171, 174, 176 n, 180 n, 192, 198, 202, 220, 238, 247 n, 248, 273, 289 ; —, ii, 338 ; v, 142 ; fam., v, 203
Worsley-Holmes, Sir Hen., v, 126, 140, 288 ; Sir Leonard, v, 150 ; Rich. F., v, 150 ; fam., v, 145 n ; see also Holmes
Worth [Worthe], Agnes, iv, 628 ; Eliz., iv, 628 ; Hugh, v, 471 ; John, iv, 628 ; Marg., iv, 628 ;
Worthi Martre, see Martyr Worthy
Worthy, see Headbourne Worthy, King's Worthy and Martyr Worthy
Worthy Comitis, see Headbourne Worthy
Worthy Down, iv, 430 ; v, 545
Worthy Mortimer, see Headbourne Worthy
Worthy Pauncefoot, man. (Head-bourne Worthy), iv, 428
Worting, ii, 117 ; iv, 113, 223, 243-4 ; adv., iv, 244 ; char., iv, 244 ; ch., iv, 243, 244 ; man.,

Worting (cont.)
iv, 243 ; pop., v, 439 ; Rom. coins, i, 347 ; sch., ii, 406 ; tumuli, iv, 243
Worting [Wortyng], (de), Isabel, ii, 485 ; Maud, iv, 134 ; (Sir) Thos., ii, 485 ; iv, 134
Worting House (Worting), iv, 243, 244
Worting Town End (Basingstoke), iv, 139
Wothing, see Worting
Wotton, de, Ela, iv, 582 ; John, iv, 582 ; Rich., iii, 333, 417 ; Steph., ii, 197
Wraxton, Rich., ii, 174
Wren, (Sir) Chris., ii, 88 ; v, 18 ; Matth , ii, 88
Wrenford, Mary, iii, 168 ; Thos., iii, 168
Wright [Write], Anne, iv, 433 ; Dorothy, iv, 422 ; Eliz., iv, 422 ; Ellen, iv, 112 n ; Geo., iv, 444 ; Hen., iv, 220 ; v, 208 ; Jas., iv, 320 ; John, v, 208 ; (Sir) Martin, iii, 459 ; iv, 422 ; Mary, iv, 433 ; v, 208 ; (Rev., Sir) Nathan, iv, 433, 434 ; Nich., iii, 68 ; Powlett, iv, 433, 434 ; Rev. Rob., iv, 192 ; Thos., ii, 297 ; Will., ii, 78 ; iii, 29, 71, 459 ; iv, 444 ; v, 208 ; —, v, 66 ; fam., v, 165
Wrighton, Thos., ii, 120
Wright's lands (Heckfield), iv, 51
Wrightson, —, iv, 560
Wringmershe, ii, 137
Wriothesley, Eliz., iv, 651 ; Hen., see Southampton, earl of ; Jas., iii, 231 ; Joan, iv, 651 n ; Rachel, iv, 432 ; Thos., see Southampton, earl of ; —, v, 326 ; fam., arms, iii, 224, 343
Write, see Wright
Writher, John, v, 483
Wrockeshal, see Wroxall
Wroth, Agnes, iv, 526 ; Edw., iv, 92 ; Eliz., iv, 526 ; Sir John, iv, 526 ; Marg., iv, 526 ; Rich., iv, 92
Wrottesley, Sir Rich., ii, 347
Wroughton (Wilts.), ii, 114
Wroughton, Alice, iv, 290, 296 ; Geo., iv, 617, 618, 619, 621, 622 ; Sir Giles, iv, 393 ; Kath., iv, 393 ; Mary, iii, 434 ; iv, 617, 621, 622, 628 ; Thos., iii, 434 ; iv, 409, 617, 618, 619, 621, 622, 628 ; Will., iv 290
Wroxall [Wroxhale] (Newchurch), v, 138, 171, 179, 183 ; brick making, v, 466 ; Rom. rem., i, 349
Wroxall, North, (Newchurch), iv, 184
Wroxall, South, (Newchurch), iv, 184
Wroxhale, (de), Joan, iv, 588 ; Sir John, iv, 588 ; Maud, iv, 588
Wudecote, see Woodcote
Wudehull (Lasham), iv, 81
Wudemancote, see Woodmancote
Wudfold, see Woodford
Wulfgifu, see Ulveva
Wulfheard, v, 295
Wulfhere [Wulphere], i, 391 ; v, 294
Wulfic, prince, iii, 428, 430
Wulfric [Ulvric], iii, 269, 333 ; iv, 500, 570 ; v, 249 ; abbot of Newminster, ii, 121 ; the hunts-man, iv, 438
Wulfris, Kath., iii, 536
Wulfrith, iii, 317
Wulfsig, prior of St. Swithuns, ii, 114
Wulfstan [Ulstan], ii, 6 ; iv, 498, 513

Wulhaye, see Wheely
Wullafes, v, 220 n
Wulphere, see Wulfhere
Wurdia la Martre, see Martyr Worthy
Wuresbyrigels (Fyfield), iv, 366
Wurthye, see Headbourne Worthy
Wurting, see Worting
Wyard, Nich., ii, 479 ; iv, 492, 508
Wyatt [Wyeth, Wyett], Dan., iv, 98 ; Sir Hen., iii, 225 ; John, v, 134 ; Lewis, iv, 122 ; Rich., ii, 504 ; Sir Thos., iii, 225 ; Mrs., iv, 658 ; —, iv, 371
Wyavill, see Wyvill
Wybarne, Benj., iii, 486 ; John, iii, 443, 486 ; Kath., iii, 486
Wych, Rich., ii, 376
Wychard, Rob., bp. of Glasgow, iii, 153
Wychey (King's Somborne), iv 470
Wyck (Binsted), ii, 483 ; Rom. rem., i, 306
Wyck, man. (Binsted), see Wyke
Wydcombe [Wydecoumb], man. (Whitwell), ii, 231 ; v, 202
Wydele, Wydelig, see Widley
Wydeslade, John, iv, 374
Wydevil, see Woodville
Wydnecumbe, see Wydcombe
Wydvil, see Woodville
Wyer, fam., see Wyker
Wyeth, Wyett, see Wyatt
Wyfold, Annes, iv, 49 ; Em., iv, 49 ; Thos., iv, 49
Wyford, man. (Tadley), iv, 219, 220, 435
Wyford Farm (Tadley), iv, 219
Wygaunt, Ad., iii, 89
Wygeton, Gilb., ii, 205 ; v, 200 n
Wygge, see Wigge
Wyght, see White
Wygmore, see Wigmore
Wyhte, see White
Wyke, man. (Binsted), ii, 487
Wyke (St. Mary Bourne), see Week
Wyke, par., see Weeke
Wyke, ii, 137, 145
Wyke, fam., see Wykes
Wykeham, (de, of), Alice, iii, 441 ; Aubrey, v, 251 ; Eliz., iv, 279 ; Fiennes, v, 262 ; John, ii, 166, 316 ; Marg., iv, 199 ; Nich., ii, 124, 196, 208, 261, 262 ; Rich., ii, 208 ; Sibil, ii, 166 ; (Sir) Thos., ii, 317 ; iii, 441 ; iv, 199, 206, 279 ; Will., ii, 17, 36, 37, 38, 39, 40, 41, 42, 43, 44, 45, 102, 111, 119, 124, 128, 135, 162, 166, 171, 177, 178, 184, 185, 194, 198, 199, 201, 204, 208, 211, 213, 223, 224, 225, 226, 228, 254, 255, 258, 259, 261, 262, 265, 267, 268, 269, 276, 279, 305, 387, 522 ; iii, 40, 56, 71, 145, 233, 310, 372, 405, 441, 470, 478, 526 ; iv, 4, 9, 45, 50, 74, 79, 90, 177, 199, 206, 212, 215, 218, 225, 239, 260, 279, 285, 328, 336, 386, 418, 461, 548, 555, 564 ; v, 11 n, 14, 16, 17, 18, 51, 58, 76, 315, 462 ; fam., ii, 318 ; arms., iii, 441 ; v, 262
Wykehill (Froyle), ii, 501
Wykenesham by Thurmyngley Wood (Hurstbourne Priors), iv, 288
Wyker (Portchester), ii, 186 ; iii, 159
Wyker [Wyer], Agnes, v, 174 ; Thos., v, 174
Wykes [Wyke], Joan, iv, 330, 459, 583 ; John, iv, 583, 604 ; Marg., iv, 604 ; Rog., iv, 330, 459, 583 ; Thos., iv, 99

Wykfort, Sir Aumary, iii, 69
Wykham, par., *see* Wickham
Wyldemore, *see* Wildmoor
Wyldewater, le, (Eling), iv, 555
Wylds, the, (Liss), iv, 84
Wyle, *see* Wylie
Wylehall, *see* Winnall
Wylet, Sim., ii, 214
Wylhay, *see* Wheely
Wylie [Wyle, Wyly], (de, de la), Geo., iv, 158; Isabel, iv, 392; Nich., iv, 392; Walt., iv, 591
Wyllis, *see* Willis
Wyllow, *see* Wellow
Wyly, *see* Wylie
Wymanes (Andover), iv, 346
Wymanston, man., ii, 114
Wymarke [Wymarks], Edw., iii, 197, 388; iv, 285
Wymbish, *see* Wimbush
Wymble Hill (Crondall), iv, 6
Wymborne, *see* Wimborne
Wymering [Wymerynnge], ii, 21; iii, 140, 165-70; adv., iii, 170; char., iii, 170; ch., iii, 169; man., ii, 207; iii, 166; pop., v, 441
Wymond, Joan, v, 230; Rob., v, 230
Wynall, *see* Winnall
Wynard, *see* Wynnard
Wyncestre, *see* Winchester
Wynchecombe, [Winchecombe] (de), Bennett, v, 129; Tideman, ii, 143, 146
Wynchefend, Wynchingfeld, *see* Winchfield
Wyncleford, Geoff. de, iv, 342
Wyndesore, fam., *see* Windsor
Wyndessled, *see* Winslade
Wyndeyate (Carisbrooke), v, 222
Wyndham [Windham], Anne, iv, 23; Arundel, iii, 247; Sir Chas., iii, 420; Geo., iv, 537; v, 132, 524, 525, 528; Helyar W., iv, 23; Hen., iii, 247, 248, 249; Hen. P., iii, 247, 250; Hugh, iii, 318; (Sir) John, ii, 485; iv, 23; v, 132; Kath., iv, 40, 537; v, 132; Percy, v, 532; Thos., iv, 20, 23; (Sir) Wadham, iii, 248; iv, 33, 537; Will., iv, 40; v, 132; Mrs., iii, 422; —, ii, 338; v, 570, 572; fam., iv, 21; arms, iii, 247
Wyndham's Pond (Yateley), iv, 21
Wynerde (Hurstbourne Priors), iv, 288
Wynesflode, Will., v, 26
Wyneston, *see* Winston
Wynfred, John de, ii, 213, 214
Wyngsfeld, *see* Wingfield
Wynhale, Wynhall, *see* Winnall
Wynnard [Wynard], Eliz., iii, 456; iv, 374; John, iii, 456; iv, 374; Thos., iv, 374
Wynne, Cath., iv, 522; Elizeus, v, 180; Ellis, iv, 288, 289 *n*; John, ii, 171; iii, 273; Rich., iv, 522; Rich. B., iv, 522
Wynter, *see* Winter
Wynterburn, *see* Winterbourne
Wyntereshall, Wyntershull, Wyntershill, Wyntershull, *see* Wintershill
Wynton, *see* Winton
Wyntreshall, Wyntreshulle, *see* Wintershill
Wynwyk, John de, iv, 506
Wynyard, Capt. F. G., v, 575
Wynyatt, Eliz., v, 199; Nich., v, 199
Wyon, —, v, 452 *n*
Wyppingham, *see* Whippingham
Wyrley, Humph., iii, 484
Wyse, *see* Wise
Wyshame, Ellen de, iv, 498, 501
Wysseshete, *see* Ewshott
Wystard, Rich., iii, 496

Wyte, *see* White
Wytecumbe, *see* Wydcombe
Wytewell, *see* Whitwell
Wytheneye, de, Alice, iii, 57; Rich., iii, 57
Wytheye Wood (Sherborne St. John), iv, 158
Wytht, *see* White
Wyttenham, Jas. de, ii, 172
Wytton, Rob. de, iii, 434
Wyvill [Voyvell, Witteville, Witvil, Wyavill, Wyvyll], de, Anna, v, 160; Annora, v, 164, 181; Hugh, iv, 619; v, 159; John, v, 160, 162 *n*, 164, 181, 191 *n*; Jordan, v, 159 *n*; Maud, v, 159 *n*; Rich., v, 164; Rob., iv, 251; v, 159 *n*, 313; Rog., iii, 32; Steph., v, 183; Thos., v, 164; Will., v, 159 *n*

Yabyndon, *see* Avington
Yafford House (Shorwell), v, 278
Yalden, Marg., v, 77; Rich., iii, 29, 30; Will., iii, 114, 115
Yaldhurst (Milford), v, 81, 120
Yar, riv., i, 376, 385; v, 142, 143, 177, 182, 244, 286, 291
Yarborough, earls of, v, 157, 170, 171, 173, 174, 176 *n*, 177, 180, 182, 194, 202, 203; Henrietta A. M. C., ctss. of, v, 171
Yarborough, Rev. J. C., ii, 248
Yardesley, *see* Malshanger
Yardley, Barth., iv, 576 *n*; Rich., iv, 589
Yare, Will., iv, 4, 25
Yarmouth, v, 209, 219, 225, 240, 241, 242, 259, 269, 272, 286-92, 308, 311, 312, 314, 339, 355, 360, 364, 426, 428, 431, 449; adv., v, 290; castle, v, 289, 351; char., v, 291; ch., v, 290; gates, v, 286; hospital, v, 291; man., v, 285, 288, 289; mkts. & fairs, v, 286, 287; Nonconf., v, 291; sch., ii, 408
Yarranton, Andr., v, 88, 464
Yarrow Land (Stratfieldsaye), iv, 57
Yatcombe, *see* Gatcombe
Yate, Agnes, ii, 374; Eliz., iv, 290; Frances, iv, 221; Fran., iv, 290, 296; Geo., iv, 221, 222; Jas., iv, 522; John, iv, 221; Rich., ii, 374; Thos., ii, 374; iv, 290; *see also* Gate and Yates
Yateley, iv, 1, 2, 14, 20-6, 31, 32; adv., iv, 26; char., iv, 26; ch., iv, 23; common, iv, 20; mans., iv, 21; mill, iv, 22; Nonconf., iv, 26; Pest House, iv, 26; pop., v, 443; sch., ii, 406
Yately Hall (Yateley), iv, 21
Yately Heath Wood (Elvetham), iv, 74
Yates, Arth., v, 537 *n*, 540, 546; Fred., v, 540; Gen., iv, 516; v, 539; —, v, 537 *n*; *see also* Yate
Yaverland, ii, 100; v, 138, 206-8; adv., v, 208; chant., v, 208 *n*; ch., ii, 248; v, 208; fort, v, 206; man., v, 143, 193, 206-8, 242; pop., v, 448
Yavington House (Avington), iii, 308
Yaxley, Hen., iv, 441, 474
Yeates Feald (Yateley), iv, 21
Yeatley, *see* Yateley
Yeatman, H. F., v, 526, 538
Yeckley, Rich., ii, 125
Yedele, John, iv, 274 *n*
Yellebeon, Will., iv, 419
Yelman, fam., v, 184 *n*
Yeovil (Somers.), iv, 469
Yerdeley, *see* Malshanger

Yerlega, *see* Gerdeleigh
Yernemouth, *see* Yarmouth
Yestele, *see* Eastleigh
Yew Tree Farm (Kingsclere), iv, 257
Yhateleghe, *see* Yateley
Yhurst, *see* Ewhurst
Yng, Hugh, archbp. of Dublin, ii, 294
Ynggylbye, Johan, ii, 57
Ynmore, de, Joan, iv, 216; Rob., iv, 216
Yoells, tithing (Catherington), iii, 94
Yonge, [Yong], (le), Annora, v, 262; Ant., iii, 78; iv, 9; Charlotte, iii, 418, 440, 444; Jane, iv, 9; John, bp. of Gallipoli, ii, 294; Nich., v, 262; Phil., ii, 113; Thos., iii, 180; Will., iii, 78; W. J., iv, 586; Miss, iv, 586; fam., iii, 300; *see also* Young
York, iv, 139; cathedral, iv, 497, 506, 509 *n*, 518 *n*, 530, 534
York, archbps. of, iv, 492, 503; Aldred, iv, 506; Will. Fitz Herbert, iv, 524; Gerard, ii, 11; Walt. Giffard, iv, 7, 74; Will. de Melton, iv, 68, 246, 251; Rich. Neile, ii, 89; Thos., iv, 497, 506, 518, 524; Thos. Wolsey, ii, 51, 120; iv, 165, 212
York, dchsses. of, iv, 99; Cecily, iv, 427, 430; Isabel, ii, 475; Joan, ii, 475, 476; iv, 130, 347, 501, 516 *n*; Philippa, iv, 77; v, 162, 223, 241; dks. of: v, 223, 384, 572; Edm., ii, 44, 475, 476; iv, 130; Edw., ii, 475; iv, 77, 545, 631; Hen., iv, 632; Rich., ii, 204, 475, 476; iii, 227; iv, 341, 427; v, 223
York, Pet. of, ii, 139
Yorke, Phil., ii, 345
Young [Younge], Anne, iv, 210, 283; Arth., v, 430; Edw., ii, 348; iii, 300; Geo., v, 158, 180, 183, 192, 535; Georgiana, v, 158; G. H., v, 543; H. G., v, 147 *n*; John, ii, 115; iii, 320, 420; Kath., iv, 344; Nich., iv, 93; Sir Pet., ii, 197; (Sir) Rich., iv, 103; v, 248; Sam., iv, 625; Thos., iv, 363; (Sir) Will., iv, 210, 283, 554, 625; v, 205; fam., v, 152, 186; *see also* Yonge
Yoverlond, *see* Yaverland
Ypres, Will. of, iv, 483; v, 303
Yslape, *see* Islip
Ytene, i, 381
Ytinstoce, *see* Itchenstoke
Yuleshate, *see* Empshott
Yvo, abbot of Titchfield, ii, 182, 186
Ywode (Basingstoke), *see* Iwode

Zealand, Maud, dchss. of, iv, 471; Will., dk. of iv, 471
Zouche, Eliz., Lady, iv, 646; Joan, Lady, iv, 531; Lds., iv, 33 *n*, 41; Edw., iv, 36, 77, 80, 90, 91; John, iv, 531; Nich., iv, 646
Zouche, (de la), (Sir) Edw., iv, 36, 78, 80, 91; Eleanor, iv, 251, 561; Eliz., iv, 36 *n*, 77, 80, 431; Eudo, iv, 431; Isabel, iv, 562; (Sir) Jas., iv, 36, 77, 78, 80, 91, 98; Joan, iv, 431; John, iv, 251, 431, 561; Marg., iv, 431, 531; Mary, iv, 78, 80; Oliver, iv, 561, 562; Rich., iv, 499, 502; Rob., iii, 364, 366; Rog., iii, 86; Sophia, iv, 91; Thos., iv, 431; Will., iii, 364; iv, 431
Zyllebon, Walt., iv, 419 *n*
Zynlan [Zynzan], Rob., v, 85 *n*, 95 *n*

CORRIGENDA

Vol. I, page 444, line 21, *for* ' Roger Fitz Gerold ' *read* ' Robert Fitz Gerold.'

Vol. II, page 114a, line 32, *delete* Hursley ' Oxenbridge.'

,, ,, 146a, line 23, *after* ' William Woburn, 1429 ' *add* ' Richard Feckenham 1449 (Exch. K.R. Acct. bdle. 81, no. 20).'

,, ,, 149b, line 5, *after* ' William 1311 ' *add* ' William Deverel 1346 (Exch. K.R. Acct. bdle. 79, no. 14).'

,, ,, 149b, line 10, *after* ' Richard de Middleton, after 1396 ' *add* ' John Bray 1416 (Exch. K.R. Acct. bdle. 81, no. 10).'

,, ,, 197a, line 27, *for* ' Richard Hayward ' *read* ' Richard Harward.'

,, ,, 485b, line 11, Mr. C. Crump, M.A., suggests that the manor of Binsted St. Clare here dealt with is the Binsted which is coupled with Haliwell in the hundred of Waltham [*Feudal Aids*, ii, 335, 357) because in the grant of free warren to the Bishop of Winchester referred to on page 486 the manor is said to adjoin the Forest of Bere. In the parish of Droxford there are houses called Holywell House and St. Clair's Farm, which may indicate the sites of these manors.

,, ,, 501a, last line, *for* ' the house was entirely rebuilt in 1867 ' *read* ' the house was built in the 16th century and altered in 1867.'

,, ,, 505a, lines 14-15, *for* ' The nave and tower were rebuilt in brick in 1722 ' *read* ' The tower was rebuilt in brick in 1716 and the nave in 1812.'

,, ,, 505a, line 9 from below, *for* ' 11 inches ' *read* ' 21 inches.'

Vol. III, page 78a, line 5, *for* ' Sir Vincent Hardwick ' *read* ' Sir Vincent Hammick.'

,, ,, 78b, line 6 from below, *for* ' Charles George Perceval, seventh earl of Egmont ' *read* ' Augustus Arthur, eighth earl of Egmont.'

,, ,, 110b, line 24, *delete* ' past the New Inn.'

,, ,, 149b, line 24, *for* ' 1857 ' *read* ' 1837.'

,, ,, 150a, line 10 from below, *for* ' 1322 ' *read* ' 1422.'

,, ,, 150, note 44, *for* ' 88 ' *read* ' 38.'

,, ,, 150, note 46, *for* ' 260 ' *read* ' 26a.'

,, ,, 163a, lines 9-21, *for* ' Sir Daniel Norton died . . . his nephew Francis Thistlethwayte ' *read* ' Sir Daniel Norton died seised of the manor in 1636, leaving a son and heir Daniel. Daniel left a son Richard, who married Anne daughter of Sir William Earle.[17] Richard died 10 December 1732 [17a] without issue and the manor appears to have passed to his cousin Richard Whitehead, who died 25 December 1733, leaving all his estates to his nephew Francis Thistlethwayte.'

,, ,, 165a, line 34, *for* ' Anne, first wife of John White and widow of John Pound of Drayton ' *read* ' Anne, second wife of John White and widow of Anthony Pound of Drayton ' (from copy of inscription made in 1886 by Mr. Herbert F. Roe, R.N., when the brass was intact and gave the date of Anne's death as 1557).

,, ,, 222a, line 13, *for* ' Sarton ' *read* ' Garton.'

,, ,, 254b, line 17 from below, *for* ' 1231 ' *read* ' 1246.'

,, ,, 282b, line 31, *for* ' Sir Henry Jenkin's ' *read* ' Sir Henry Jenkyn's.'

,, ,, 286a, line 19 from below, *for* ' Lady Jenkyns ' *read* ' the trustees of the late Sir Henry Jenkyns and is let to Mr. F. J. Kingsley.'

,, ,, 287b, line 13 from below, *for* ' bishop of Winchester ' *read* ' rector of Droxford.'

,, ,, 289b, last line, *for* ' 1599 ' *read* ' 1560.'

,, ,, 290a, line 1, *for* ' 1728 ' *read* ' 1732.'

,, ,, 299a, line 4 from below, *for* ' Kinnard ' *read* ' Kennard.'

,, ,, 304b, line 9, *for* ' Mr. J. F. Christie ' *read* ' Mr. J. F. Christy.'

,, ,, 306a, line 33, *delete* ' undated.'

,, ,, 322b, line 22, *for* ' 1612 ' *read* ' 1642.'

,, ,, 333b, line 2 from below, *for* ' In 1786 ' *read* ' In 1790.'

,, ,, 341b, line 20, *for* ' From 1829 . . . to the living ' *read* ' In 1704 Henry Mildmay left the advowson to Emmanuel College, Cambridge, but the presentation remains with the Mildmay family.'

,, ,, 425b, lines 7-13, *for* ' passed to his son James Henry Legge Dutton, Lord Sherborne . . of his father in 1883,' *read* ' passed by will to his third son, Ralph Dutton, on whose death without male issue it went to his nephew Henry Dutton, who sold it in 1899 to Mr. George Whitely, now Lord Marchamley, from whom it passed to the present owner, Mr. Henessy.'

,, ,, 466a, lines 12-15, *delete* ' In the north . . . village.'

,, ,, 466a, line 28, *for* ' Botley ' *read* ' Netley ' and *delete* ' and in its grounds . . . years.'

,, ,, 466a, line 33, *for* ' is occupied ' *read* ' was lately occupied.'

,, ,, 466a, line 36, *for* ' Swaythling road opposite the vicarage ' *read* ' Southampton road near the rectory.'

,, ,, 466b, line 17 from below, *for* ' statue ' *read* ' picture.'

,, ,, 467b, lines 26-27, *for* ' and since 1903 . . . Rev. E. C. Osborne ' *read* ' the bishop of Winchester, to whom it has lately been transferred by Mrs. Morley Lee.'

,, ,, 467b, line 14 from below, *for* ' Henry Jenkins ' *read* ' Henry Jenkyns.'

,, ,, 467b, line 7 from below, *for* ' Sir Henry Jenkins ' *read* ' Sir Henry Jenkyns.'

Vol. IV, page 232b, line 3 from below, *for* ' whose younger son, Mr. Sydney Eggers Bates, at the present day resides at Woodgarston ' *read* ' whose younger brother, Mr. Sydney Eggers Bates, at the present day owns Woodgarston.'

,, ,, 240a, line 15, *for* ' grandson ' *read* ' son.'

,, ,, 291b, line 15 from below, *for* ' 802 ' *read* ' 902.'

,, plate facing page 466, *for* ' Hall ' *read* ' Wall.'

CORRIGENDA

Vol. IV, page 565a, line 19, *for* ' burning ' *read* ' beheaded.'

,, ,, 601b, lines 6-7, *for* ' There are three bells . . . tenor of 1637 ' *read* ' There are four bells, 1st to 3rd by John Wallis of Salisbury, dated respectively 1604, 1613 and 1591 ; 4th by John Danton of Salisbury, 1629.'

,, ,, 612a, lines 23-24, *for* ' St. George, St. Bartholomew, St. Christopher ' *read* ' St. Michael, St. John the Baptist.'

,, ,, 612a, lines 25-26, *for* ' St. Mary and St. John the Baptist ' *read* ' St. Barbara or St. Faith (probably the former, but the figure is much worn) and St. Margaret.'

,, ,, 655b, line 36, *for* ' Langdown House, the property and residence of Mrs. Benskin,' *read* ' Langdown House, the property and residence of Sir Robert H. Hobart, K.C.V.O., C.B.'

Vol. V, page 84b, line 13 from below, *for* ' Sandhills, the property and residence of Sir George Rose ' *read* ' Sandhills formerly the property and residence of Sir George Rose.'

,, ,, 127a, lines 29-30, *for* ' two bells marked 1593 W.I.I.R. R.W.R.M.' *read* ' two bells, the first dated 1599, the second uninscribed but ancient.'

,, ,, 174b, line 1, *for* ' a son Richard, on whose death without issue his share ' *read* ' a son Richard, who at his death in 1548 left a son, who only survived his father a few weeks, at whose death his share.'

,, ,, 238a, last line, *for* ' Aumale ' *read* ' Aumarle.'

,, ,, 268b, lines 34-5, *for* ' was built in 1837 on the site of a former residence called Belle View by Mr. George H. Ward, uncle to the present owner and,' *read* ' was built about 1790 on the site of a former residence called Belle View by George Ward, who died in 1829. His son George Henry Ward made some additions to the house in 1836 and was succeeded in 1849 by his nephew William George Ward, who died in 1882 and was father of the present owner. The House.'

,, ,, 273a, lines 24-6, *for* ' since he was holding the manor in 1328 ' *read* ' His son Henry was holding the manor in 1328.'

,, ,, 273, *add to note* 18, ' See suit as to the abduction of Henry, the heir of Henry Trenchard, a minor (De Banco R. Trin. 1 Edw, III, m. 55 d.).'

,, ,, 435, line 7, *for* ' 138, 910 ' *read* ' 156, 176.'

SUBSCRIBERS TO THE VICTORIA HISTORY OF HAMPSHIRE AND THE ISLE OF WIGHT

HIS MAJESTY THE KING
H.R.H. PRINCESS HENRY OF BATTENBERG

The Rt. Hon. The Lord Aberconway, K.C.
The Rt. Hon. The Lord Aberdare
W. M. Ackworth, Esq.
Mrs. Adair
A. P. Agar, Esq.
W. L. Ainslie, Esq.
Miss Aitchison
The Rt. Hon. The Viscount Alverstone, G.C.M.G.
Richard Andrews, Esq.
The Rt. Hon. The Lord Annaly, K.C.V.O.
His Grace The Duke of Argyll, K.G., K.T.
A. H. Arnold, Esq.
The Rt. Hon. Evelyn Ashley
P. J. Atkey, Esq., M.R.C.S., L.R.C.P., D.PH.
C. B. Balfour, Esq., J.P., D.L.
E. E. Ball, Esq.
Col. R. Barclay, C.B.
The Hon. Francis H. Baring
William Wycliffe Barlow, Esq.
J. C. Barnard, Esq.
Richard Barrow, Esq.
H. Frederick D. Bartlett, Esq.
E. Bashford, Esq.
Sydney Eggers Bates, Esq.
Miss Mary Bateson
P. B. Ironside Bax, Esq.
T. W. Baxendale, Esq., J.P., D.L.
The Rt. Hon. William W. B. Beach
G. Beck, Esq.
Richard Bell, Esq.
William Benham, Esq.
Julius Bertram, Esq.
Major H. Bethune
W. L. P. Bevan, Esq., M.D.
Rev. R. F. Bigg-Wither, M.A.
Henry F. Blackford, Esq.
J. H. Blizard, Esq.
The Rt. Hon. The Lord Bolton, F.S.A.
Miss Bonham-Carter
Samuel Bostock, Esq.
Rev. F. H. Bowden-Smith, M.A.
Alfred Bowker, Esq.
Percy May Bright, Esq.
C. Bryans, Esq.
Edward Buckell, Esq.
Wilfred Buckley, Esq.
Miss Burrell
Capt. T. D. Butler, C.V.O., M.V.O.

The Rt. Hon. The Lord Calthorpe
Christopher H. H. Candy, Esq.
J. A. Carlyon, Esq.
The Rt. Hon. The Earl of Carysfort, K.P.
Mrs. R. M. Caulfield
Charles Cave, Esq., J.P.
Sir Charles Cayzer, Bart., F.R.G.S.
Charles Cecil, Esq.
Major T. H. Chamberlain
B. E. C. Chambers, Esq.
F. E. Chapman, Esq.
Miss Chawner
Mrs. Hampden Chawner
R. H. Cholmondeley, Esq.
W. M. Christy, Esq.
George Churcher, Esq.
W. E. Churcher, Esq.
C. L. Chute, Esq.
E. H. Clark, Esq.
Mrs. Clarke
Col. Stephenson R. Clarke, C.B.
Major E. F. Clayton
Col. H. R. Clinton
Thomas Cochrane, Esq.
Richard Edward Coles, Esq.
Rev. C. H. Compton, M.A.
Henry F. Compton, Esq., J.P., D.L.
A. K. Cook, Esq.
Henry T. H. Cook, Esq.
G. A. Cooper, Esq.
J. E. Cooper-Dean, Esq.
Sir Eyre Coote
Col. Cornwallis-West
Miss Cory
Herbert V. M. Cotes, Esq.
Rev. E. I. L. Crawhall, M.A.
Lt.-Col. Richard Pearson Crozier
Laurence Currie, Esq.
William Curtis, Esq., M.R.C.S., L.S.A.
W. Dale, Esq., F.G.S., F.S.A.
The Hon. Hew Dalrymple
The Hon. Mr. Justice Darling
Lt.-Col. Dawson
The Rt. Hon. Mr. Justice Day
William Dean, Esq.
The Rt. Hon. The Earl of Derby, G.C.V.O.
William H. Deverell, Esq., D.L., J.P.
Rev. P. H. Ditchfield, M.A., F.S.A.

LIST OF SUBSCRIBERS

Henry Elliot Dixon, Esq., M.A.
W. B. Doubleday, Esq.
F. T. Douglas, Esq.
Capt. Cecil Drummond
J. W. Duncan, Esq.
W. M. East, Esq.
Rev. Ernest A. Edghill, M.A.
Cecil Edwards, Esq.
James Coster Edwards, Esq.
H. J. Elwes, Esq., F.R.S.
P. H. Emerson, Esq., M.B.
A. T. Everitt, Esq.
Rev. William L. W. Eyre
Sir William Farrer, F.R.G.S., F.S.A., F.G.S.
William Farrer, Esq., D.Litt.
Ven. Archdeacon Fearon, D.D.
G. J. Fenwick, Esq.
G. F. Ferrand, Esq.
Rev. A. Finch, M.A.
Henry Branson Firth, Esq.
J. H. Fisher, Esq.
The Rt. Hon. The Earl Fitz William, K.C.V.O., D.S.O.
J. Willis Fleming, Esq.
Thomas Alfred Flooks, Esq.
The Rt. Hon. The Lord Foley
R. Forrest, Esq.
Miss Fortescue
Rev. Charles Wilmer Foster, M.A., F.S.A.
Mrs. Franklyn
Samuel Frewer, Esq.
H. C. Gallup, Esq.
John Carpenter Garnier, Esq.
A. D. George, Esq.
Owen Gidden, Esq.
F. Giffard, Esq., R.N.
Owen Gilbert, Esq.
H. Glasspool, Esq.
Maurice G. Carr Glyn, Esq., J.P.
The Lady Adelaide Goff
O. E. D'Avigdor Goldsmid, Esq., D.L.
Sir Laurence Gomme, F.S.A.
J. F. Goodheart, Esq.
John Gordon, Esq., LL.D., K.C., M.P.
Herbert Goss, Esq., F.L.S., F.G.S.
Lt.-Gen. The Hon. Somerset Gough-Calthorpe
Her Grace The Duchess of Grafton
Sir Arthur Grant, Bart.
H. E. Gregory, Esq.
E. Hyla Greves, Esq., M.D.
F. L. Griffin, Esq., M.B.
E. L. Griffith, Esq.
The Hon. Richard C. Grosvenor
Montague Guest, Esq.
Bertram B. Hagen, Esq.
The Rt. Hon. The Viscount Hambleden
George Hampton, Esq.
Thomas James Hankinson, Esq., F.S.A., J.P.
Col. H. B. Hanna
J. R. Harding, Esq.
Bernard Harfield, Esq.
R. G. Hargreaves, Esq., J.P.

William Morton Harman, Esq., M.D., F.R.C.S.I.
Heath Harrison, Esq.
W. H. Harrison, Esq.
T. H. Harvey, Esq.
F. J. Haverfield, Esq., M.A., LL.D., F.S.A., Camden Professor of Ancient History
Mrs. J. H. Haynes
Hugh S. Heal, Esq.
Capt. Heathcote
C. G. Heathcote, Esq.
Arthur Conolly Gage Heygate, Esq.
Henry J. Hibberd, Esq.
Miss A. N. S. Hoare
Lady Hodgson
Stuart Hogg, Esq.
William Holding, Esq., D.C.L., J.P.
Frederick Gardnor Hopkins, Esq.
Col. Horace
F. W. Horey, Esq.
W. E. Horne, Esq., M.P.
J. A. Hosker, Esq., M.R.C.S.
T. A. Houghton, Esq.
Rev. C. H. B. Hudson, M.A.
E. Hudson, Esq.
F. J. Hughes, Esq.
R. P. Humphrey, Esq.
Mrs. S. H. Hurford
Jamieson B. Hurry, Esq., M.D.
E. Hutton, Esq.
Miss Ingham
Capt. H. E. W. Iremonger, R.N.
The Rt. Hon. The Viscount Iveagh, K.P., G.C.V.O., LL.D., F.R.S.
John Jeffreys, Esq.
Lady Jenkyns
The Dowager Lady Jenner
F. M. E. Jervoise, Esq., D.L., J.P.
Sir Harry Clarke Jervoise, Bart.
Rev. G. E. Jeans, M.A., F.S.A.
Harry Johnson, Esq.
Henry Johnson, Esq.
Rev. A. G. Joyce, B.A.
Rev. J. E. Kelsall, M.A.
James Martin Kennedy, Esq., M.D.
The Rt. Hon. The Lord Kenyon, K.C.V.O.
W. J. Kerr, Esq.
Nathaniel Kevan, Esq.
Mrs. Edward King
Charles T. King, Esq.
Ernest Powell King, Esq.
T. M. Kitchen, Esq.
Major E. F. Knight
Montague G. Knight, Esq., D.L., J.P
William John Knight, Esq., D.L., J.P.
Hugh Knowles, Esq.
Edmund Lamb, Esq., F.C.S., F.R.G.S.
Mrs. Lane
Harold Button Lankester, Esq.
Leonard W. Lankester, Esq.
The Hon. Gerald W. Lascelles, F.Z.S.
Henry Lashmore, Esq.
The Misses Lassell

W. F. Lawrence, Esq., J.P.
Graham Charles Lawson, Esq.
Arthur H. Lee, Esq., J.P.
W. C. Lefroy, Esq., M.A., F.S.A., J.P.
Rev. Augustus Q. Legge, M.A.
J. Hamilton Leigh, Esq.
Col. G. B. Lemprière
H. Le Roy Lewis, Esq.
Miss M. Liddell
C. A. Linzee, Esq.
Rev. H. G. Liveing, M.A.
His Excellency Sir Chih-Chen Lofêngluh, K.C.V.O.
Mrs. Long
W. H. Longbottom, Esq.
T. G. Longstaff, Esq., M.D.
Rev. Canon C. Lovett-Cameron, M.A.
Capt. Lulwyche
Rev. A. C. Maclachlan, M.A.
The Rt. Hon. The Earl of Malmesbury
James Malpas, Esq., M.R.C.S., L.R.C.P.
John Charles Mason, Esq.
Rev. Thomas Heywood Masters, M.A.
James J. May, Esq.
Edmund G. B. Meade-Waldo, Esq.
Robert Meikle, Esq.
D. Meinertzhagen, Esq.
Alfred M. Miller, Esq.
The Hon. Algernon H. Mills
Rev. G. W. Minns, LL.B., F.S.A.
Capt. Clayton Mitchell, R.N.
John Cornelius Moberley, Esq., M.A.
The Rt. Hon. The Lord Montagu of Beaulieu
Claud G. Montefiore, Esq., M.A.
Walter Morrison, Esq., J.P.
Mrs. A. Morrison
F. Moser, Esq.
L. W. Munro, Esq.
Miss E. Myers
W. H. Myers, Esq., J.P., D.C.
Rev. F. P. Napier
John Robert Nash, Esq.
Clement Buckley Newbold, Esq.
Henry Newbolt, Esq.
Miss J. W. M. Nicholson
W. G. Nicholson, Esq., M.P., J.P.
The Rt. Hon. The Earl of Normanton
The Rt. Hon. The Earl of Northbrook, G.C.S.I.
The Rt. Hon. The Lord Northcliffe
W. H. S. Northcote, Esq.
Admiral O'Calloghan, C.V.O., C.B.
Rev. R. W. Odell, M.A.
Fergus Menteith Ogilvie, Esq.
John H. Oglander, Esq., F.S.A.
A. W. Oke, Esq., B.A., LL.M., F.S.A.
Thomas A. Oliver, Esq.
F. Ord, Esq., M.R.C.S., L.R.C.P.
Miss Meta Orred
Peter A. Ouvry, Esq.
Alfred Palmer, Esq., J.P.
Alexander Paris, Esq.
Edwin Parsons, Esq.

Arthur William Pearce, Esq.
Francis W. Pember, Esq.
Mrs. Penton
E. K. Perkins, Esq.
Julian Perkins, Esq.
Rev. E. G. Phillimore, B.A.
F. S. Phillips, Esq.
George Phillips, Esq.
Sir Lionel Phillips, Bart., D.L.
H. R. Pink, Esq.
Mrs. Playfair
The Hon. Kenelm Pleydell-Bouverie
G. V. Poore, Esq.
Major E. R. Portal
Melville Portal, Esq.
Sir William Wyndham Portal, Bart., F.S.A.
His Grace The Duke of Portland, K.G., G.C.V.O.
Mrs. H. M. Powell
J. C. Powell, Esq.
Mrs. Helena Pratt
Rev. A. W. Pulteney, M.A.
Keppel Pulteney, Esq.
Arnold Pye-Smith, Esq., J.P.
The Rt. Hon. The Earl of Radnor, V.D.
Captain Ramsay
W. Ransom, Esq.
William Read, Esq.
The Lady Laura Ridding
Mrs. Rivett-Carnac
Thomas Godolphin Rooper, Esq.
Lady Roscoe
Mrs. Thomas Ross
J. Horace Round, Esq., M.A., LL.D.
Capt. A. H. Royds
F. W. Rummens, Esq.
J. A. Rutherford, Esq.
Charles Julius Ryland, Esq.
Mrs. Rylands
The Rt. Rev. H. E. Ryle, D.D., Dean of Westminster
Rev. G. Sampson, M.A.
Robert Scarlett, Esq.
Archibald E. Scott, Esq.
A. E. Seawell, Esq.
The Rt. Hon. The Earl of Selborne, K.G., G.C.M.G.
Frank Shalders, Esq.
Rev. Arnold M. Sharp
H. Sharpe, Esq.
Capt. Shawe-Storey
Capt. Sir John Courtown Shelley, Bart.
W. R. Sheldon, Esq., M.A.
The Rt. Hon. The Lord Sherborne
Mrs. E. Silver
J. Silvester, Esq.
William Barrow Simonds, Esq., D.L., J.P
Mrs. Eustace Smith
James Richard Smith, Esq., J.P.
William R. Smith, Esq., C.B.
H. H. Smith-Carington, Esq., J.P.
Percy Snelling, Esq.
Rev. Arthur B. Sole, M.A.

LIST OF SUBSCRIBERS

W. E. Soltau, Esq.
The Rt. Rev. The Lord Bishop of Southwark
John Tricks Spalding, Esq., J.P.
Gerald S. Spicer, Esq.
Mrs. Squarey
C. Sloane Stanley, Esq.
John Stares, Esq.
Rev. Walter Statham, B.A.
Rev. Canon Stenning, M.A.
Mrs. Stevenson
John Pakenham Stilwell, Esq.
Thomas Stopher, Esq., F.S.I.
F. G. Streeter, Esq.
The Hon. Frederick Strutt
Miss C. Stubington
Heywood Sumner, Esq.
Lady Sutton
The Dowager Lady Swaythling
W. M. Tapp, Esq., LL.D., F.S.A.
J. B. Taylor, Esq.
Mrs. Thomas
Mrs. B. T. L. Thomson
W. Steel Tomkins, Esq.
Gilbert A. Tonge, Esq., J.P.
Frederick Townsend, Esq., M.A., F.L.S.
Alfred Trapnell, Esq.
H. W. Trinder, Esq.
Percival Fox Tuckett, Esq.
John Turner-Turner, Esq., J.P.
Rev. Canon Arthur Sutton Valpy, M.A.
F. Crowther Smith Vivian, Esq.

George T. Vivian, Esq.
C. R. Wainwright, Esq.
T. W. Walford, Esq.
Horace Walker, Esq.
J. H. Wall, Esq.
F. Ward, Esq.
Mrs. Ward
W. T. Warren, Esq.
Lt.-Col. H. J. Watson
Harry Webb, Esq.
His Grace The Duke of Wellington, K.G.,
    G.C.V.O.
Rev. Lewis Westmacott, M.A.
William Ingram Whitaker, Esq.
Rev. Reginald A. R. White, M.A.
Sir Beethom Whitehead, K.C.M.G.
John L. Whitehead, Esq.
C. T. Whittington, Esq.
Edward Wilding, Esq.
J. W. Willis-Bund, Esq., M.A., LL.B., F.S.A.
F. E. Willmot, Esq.
Rev. Sumner Wilson, M.A.
G. Winch, Esq.
Rev. W. H. Windle-Cooper, M.A.
Lloyd Wollen, Esq.
Alexander Wood, Esq.
Mrs. C. C. Wood
H. Wood, Esq., M.A., J.P.
Mrs. A. Woodman
Grosvenor Woods, Esq., K.C.
Francis Young, Esq.

PUBLIC AND PRIVATE LIBRARIES

LONDON

Admiralty Library, Whitehall
The Athenæum Club
The Bath Club
Battersea Central Public Library
Bermondsey Public Library
Bishopsgate Institute
The Board of Agriculture
The British Museum
The Carlton Club
Chelsea Public Library
The Conservative Club
The Guildhall Library
Hammersmith Public Library
Hampstead Public Library
The House of Commons Library
The Incorporated Law Society
The Junior Carlton Club
The Junior Naval and Military Club
Kensington Public Library
King's College
Lincoln's Inn Library
The London Library
The National Liberal Club
The New University Club
The Reform Club

The Royal Societies' Club
Sion College
The Society of Antiquaries of London
The Surveyors' Institution, Westminster
Tottenham Central Library
The Travellers' Club
The United University Club
The Victoria and Albert Museum
Westminster Public Library
Westminster and Southland Training College
Dr. Williams' Library
Wimbledon Public Library
Zoological Society of London

THE PROVINCES

North Devon Athenæum, Barnstaple
Birmingham Corporation Reference Library
Bolton Central Reference Library
Bournemouth Free Library
Bradford Free Public Library
Brighton Public Library
Bristol Public Library
Cambridge Free Library
Cambridge University Library
Cardiff Free Public Library
Carisbrooke Museum Library

LIST OF SUBSCRIBERS

Cheltenham College
Croydon Public Library
Eton College
Gloucester Public Library
Gosport and Alverstoke Public Library
Hampshire County Council
Hove Free Public Library
Hull Public Library
Kingston-on-Thames Public Library
Leeds Library
Leeds Public Library
Leicester Free Public Library
Leicester Permanent Library
Leigh (Lancs.) Public Library
Liverpool Public Library
Chetham's Library, Manchester
Manchester Free Library
John Rylands Library, Manchester
Victoria University, Manchester
Gilstrap Free Library, Newark-on-Trent
Newcastle-on-Tyne Literary and Philosophical
    Society
Newcastle-on-Tyne Public Library
Northampton Public Library
Nottingham Free Library
Bodley's Library, Oxford
Christchurch, Oxford
Magdalen College, Oxford
New College, Oxford
Oxford City Public Library
Oxford Union Society
Bedales School (Staff Library), Petersfield
Portsmouth Public Library
Preston (Lancs.) Free Library
Reading Free Public Library
Reading University College (presented by The
    Lady Wantage)
Southampton Free Library
Winchester Cathedral Library
Winchester College Library
Winchester Free Library
Royal Library, Windsor Castle

SCOTLAND

Aberdeen University Library
The Advocates' Library, Edinburgh
Edinburgh Public Library
Edinburgh University Library
The Signet Library, Edinburgh
Glasgow University Library
Mitchell Library (Moir Collection), Glasgow
St. Andrews University Library

IRELAND

King's Inn Library, Dublin
The National Library of Ireland
Trinity College, Dublin

THE COLONIES

Adelaide Public Library, South Australia
New South Wales Public Library, Sydney
Victoria Public Library, Melbourne, Australia
Toronto Public Library, Canada
Toronto University Library, Canada
Victoria Public Library, British Columbia
The General Assembly Library, Wellington,
    New Zealand

AMERICA

Albany State Library
Boston (Mass.) Athenæum
Boston (Mass.) Public Library
Brookline (Mass.) Public Library
Cambridge (Mass.) Public Library
Chicago Public Library
Cincinnati Public Library
Columbia University Library, New York
Connecticut Historical Society
Cornell University Library, Ithaca
Forbes Library, Northampton, Mass.
Harvard University Library
Illinois University Library
Indiana State Library
Iowa State Library
Maine State Library
Massachusetts State Library
Michigan State Library
Newberry Library, Chicago
New Hampshire State Library
Newton (Mass.) Library
Grosvenor Public Library, New York
New York Historical Society
New York Public Library
New York State Library
Ohio State Library
Peabody Institute, Baltimore
Pennsylvania State Library
Philadelphia Free Library
Providence Free Library
The Library of Congress, Washington
Wisconsin State Historical Society
Worcester (Mass.) Free Public Library
Yale University Library

THE CONTINENT

Royal Library, Berlin
Royal Library, Copenhagen
Royal Public Library, Dresden
Royal University Library, Göttingen
Lille University Library
Royal Library, Münich
National Library, Paris
Imperial Public Library, St. Petersburg
Royal Library, Stockholm
Upsala University Library